Masters of the Field
The Fourth United States Cavalry in the Civil War

John L. Herberich

4880 Lower Valley Road • Atglen, PA 19310

Other Schiffer Books on Related Subjects:
Firestorm at Gettysburg, ISBN: 978-0-7643-0618-1
Their Horses Climbed Trees, ISBN: 978-0-7643-1391-2
Bluejackets, ISBN: 978-0-7643-3375-0

Copyright © 2015 by John L. Herberich

Library of Congress Control Number: 2015937036

All rights reserved. No part of this work may be reproduced or used in any form or by any means—graphic, electronic, or mechanical, including photocopying or information storage and retrieval systems—without written permission from the publisher.

The scanning, uploading, and distribution of this book or any part thereof via the Internet or via any other means without the permission of the publisher is illegal and punishable by law. Please purchase only authorized editions and do not participate in or encourage the electronic piracy of copyrighted materials.
"Schiffer," "Schiffer Publishing, Ltd. & Design," and the "Design of pen and inkwell" are registered trademarks of Schiffer Publishing, Ltd.

Designed by John P. Cheek
Cover design by Molly Shields
Type set in Minion Pro

ISBN: 978-0-7643-4891-4
Printed in China

Published by Schiffer Publishing, Ltd.
4880 Lower Valley Road
Atglen, PA 19310
Phone: (610) 593-1777; Fax: (610) 593-2002
E-mail: Info@schifferbooks.com

For our complete selection of fine books on this and related subjects, please visit our website at www.schifferbooks.com. You may also write for a free catalog.

This book may be purchased from the publisher. Please try your bookstore first.

We are always looking for people to write books on new and related subjects. If you have an idea for a book, please contact us at proposals@schifferbooks.com.

Schiffer Publishing's titles are available at special discounts for bulk purchases for sales promotions or premiums. Special editions, including personalized covers, corporate imprints, and excerpts can be created in large quantities for special needs. For more information, contact the publisher.

For my companion of over four decades, my loving wife Jane, for giving me the luxury, time, and patience necessary for the completion of this work. It would not have been possible otherwise.

Dedication

To the men of the 4th Regiment United States Cavalry and Colonel Robert H. G. Minty's Saber Brigade, for whom the term *glory* has specific meaning:

The selfless participation
in a just cause
or a
righteous ideal
that is greater than oneself

For those who made the ultimate sacrifice, may this work allow your names and deeds to linger a little longer in history's memory . . .

As I have relied so heavily on writings of those who were there, I do so once again, paraphrasing from the words of Brigadier General Robert Minty:

I have written this narrative with the single purpose and desire that history may do justice to you, the aggregate of noble men who formed . . . as gallant a body of officers and soldiers as ever mounted horse or drew sabers . . . in defense of their country or flag.
National Tribune, March 3, 1892; January 26, 1893.

Maps and Illustrations

The Cavalry Charge at Dug Springs	xvii
Frontier Forts - 1861	7
Missouri - 1861	34
The Western Theater 1861-62	49
Western Theater Railroads 1861-62	58
Middle Tennessee	65
Reeds Bridge, Chickamauga	118
The 4th United States Cavalry at Reed's Bridge	123
Atlanta Campaign: May 1 - May 23, 1863	163
Atlanta Campaign: May 24 - July 30, 1863	169
Kilpatrick's Raid, August 18-21, 1864	197
The Battle of Lovejoy's Station (Nash Farm)	207
City of Selma, Alabama and its Defenses	237

Contents

Preface x
Foreword xiii
Acknowledgments xiv
Prologue xv

1855 – 1860: Prelude to War

I. Organization and Operations Prior to the Civil War 1
    Prewar Enlistment and Training: Private James Larson 4
    Service on the Frontier 7
    Fort Leavenworth, Kansas Territory 7
    Fort Wise, Colorado Territory 8
    Oklahoma Indian Territory 10
    Expeditions Against the Kiowa and Comanche 10
    Fort Smith, Arkansas, New Year's Eve 1860 11

II. Surrendering the Frontier 12
    Texas Secedes 13
    Open Rebellion on the Frontier 13
    The Companies of the 1st United States Cavalry 14
    Lieutenant Colonel William H. Emory, 1st U.S. Cavalry 15
    The "Service School of the Plains" 18
    Twenty-Two Future Generals 19

III. The Federal Cavalry at the Beginning of the Civil War 19
    The Horse 21
    The Accoutrements 22
    The Evolution of Cavalry Organization and Tactics 22
    The Evolution of the 4th United States Cavalry 25
    The Awarding of Brevet Rank 26

1861: A Taste for Death

I. The War Begins 28

II. The Eastern Theater 29
    Companies A and E 29
    Private Charles E. Bates, Co. E 29
    Bull Run (First Manassas) 30
    The Enlistment of James H. Wiswell, Co. C 33

III. The Western Theater 34
    The State of Missouri 34
    General Nathaniel Lyon, United States Army 35
    Expedition from Springfield to Forsyth, Missouri 37
    The Early Volunteers 37
    The Battle at Wilson's Creek (Oak Hill) – August 10, 1861 38

Missing in Action 44
Springfield, Missouri—October 25 45
Saline County and Blackwater Creek (Shawnee Mound) 45

1862: Finding Form

I. The Western Theater 49
Forts Henry and Donelson, Tennessee 50
Nashville, Tennessee 54
New Madrid and Island No. 10 54

II. Pittsburg Landing (Shiloh) –April 6-7 55

III. Cavalry Division Army of the Mississippi 57
Brigadier General Gordon Granger, United States Volunteers 57
Corinth, Mississippi 59
Boonville, Mississippi 59

IV. Army of the Ohio – Major General Don Carlos Buell 60
Incident at Athens, Alabama 60
Huntsville, Alabama 60
The Battle of Perryville, Kentucky 61

V. Army of the Cumberland –Major General William S. Rosecrans 61
Cavalry Division, Army of the Cumberland 62
First Brigade, Second Cavalry Division 63
Companies L and M 63

1863: Stones River to Chattanooga

I. Middle Tennessee 66

II. Stones River Campaign–Murfreesboro, Tennessee 68
Rescuing McCook's Ammunition Train 70
New Year's Day 1863 71
Panic at Stewart's Creek 72

III. Cavalry Division, Army of the Cumberland: Rosecrans – Stanley – Minty 75
Colonel Robert H. G. Minty, United States Volunteers 75
First Brigade, Second Division 76
Expedition Against Wheeler's Cavalry 77
The Saber 78
Incident with Forrest's Battery: The Killing of Captain Freeman, C.S.A 81
Permanent Camp 82
Foraging 83
Foraging Expedition and Skirmish at Bradyville, Tennessee 84

IV. Riding with Sheridan 85
Expedition to Unionville 85
Thompson's Station 86
The Saber Brigade 88

V. The 4th Regiment United States Cavalry 89
    Companies A and E Return from the Eastern Theater 89
    Expedition to Liberty and Snow Hill 90
    Blacks in Service: Jackson Kelley, 4th United States Cavalry 91
    The 4th US Cavalry and Freeman's Battery at Franklin, Tennessee 92
    "Camp Minty" 95
    The Cavalry Raid 95
    Companies D and I: Expedition to Middleton 96
    Companies F and H Return from the Frontier 98
    Confronting Morgan's Cavalry at Bardstown, Kentucky 100
    Chicago Board of Trade Battery, Illinois Volunteers 103

VI. The Tullahoma (Middle Tennessee) Campaign 103
    Scout on Middleton and Eagleville Pikes 105
    Expedition To and Skirmish Near Lebanon 105
    Shelbyville, Tennessee 106
    The Charge at Guy's Gap 107
    The Battle at Shelbyville 108
    Aftermath 112
    Camp at Salem, Tennessee 112
    August 1863—Detached Duty 113
    Expedition to Sparta and Calfkiller Creek 114

VII. The Chattanooga Campaign 116
    September 18—Reed's Bridge 120
    The Stand at Reed's Bridge 121
    The Night of September 18–19 124

VIII. The Battle of Chickamauga Creek 124
    Saturday, September 19 124
    Sunday, September 20 125
    The Lost Patrol 126
    Retreat to Chattanooga 127

IX. The Siege of Chattanooga 130
    A Daring Escape 130
    Chasing Wheeler's Cavalry 131
    Maysville, Alabama 136
    Expedition to Whitesburg and Decatur 138
    The Battle of Chattanooga 139
    Huntsville, Alabama 140

X. Masters of the Field 142

1864: Through the Heart of the Confederacy

I. Grant-Sheridan-Sherman-Thomas: All the generals who were to win for the Union 147
    Major General George H. Thomas, U.S.A 147

II. Sherman's Meridian Campaign 149
    General Sooy Smith's Failed Expedition 149

  Ellis Bridge 151
  The 4th United States Cavalry at Okolona, Mississippi 152

III. Preparing for the Atlanta Campaign 157
  The Spencer Carbine 157
  Nashville, Tennessee 159
  The Court Martial of Colonel Robert H. G. Minty 159
  The Secret Mission of the Horse Marines 161
  The Death of Major General Jeb Stuart, C.S.A. 162

IV: The Atlanta Campaign–May 1864 162
  Rome, Georgia 165
  Infantry Duty 168
  Sherman's Cavalry 170
  Dallas, Georgia 171
  Big Shanty, Georgia 173
  Brice's Crossroads, Mississippi, June 10, 1864 175
  The Battle at Noonday Creek 175
  A Lonely End 178
  Kennesaw Mountain 180
  Roswell, Georgia 182
  Garrard's Raid to Covington 184
  Stoneman's Raid: The Battle at Flat Rock (Shoals) 188
  A Well-Deserved Leave 192

V. The Siege of Atlanta–August 1864 193
  Fighting in the Trenches 193

VI. Kilpatrick's Raid 197
  The Destruction of Jonesboro, Georgia 201
  Lovejoy's Station–Nash Farm 204
  A Question of Facts 214

VII. The Fall of Atlanta 214
  Chasing Hood–October 1864 215
  Disbanding the Saber Brigade 217
  Major General James H. Wilson, U.S.A. 217

VIII. The Franklin–Nashville Campaign 218
  The Defeat of Hood's Army 218
  Defending Nashville 218
  "The Little Regiment" 220
  The Election of 1864 220
  Under a New Command 222
  The Battle of Nashville 223
  The Battle of Nashville–Day Two 225
  The Battle at West Harpeth River 226

1865: The Beginning of the End

I. The Last Campaign 231

II. Wilson's Selma–Macon Campaign 236
    Selma, Alabama 237
    The Final Battle at Selma 239
    The Massacre at Goodwin's Farm 243

III. Up in Smoke 245
    Montgomery, Alabama 246
    Columbus, Georgia 247
    Macon, Georgia 247

IV. The Final Days 249

V. The Casualties 252

Epilogue 254

Appendix 255
    A. Staff Officers of the Fourth Regiment United States Cavalry 255
    B. "Twenty-two Future Generals" 256
    C. The Officers of the 4th United States Cavalry During the Civil War 257
    D. Enlisted Field Commissions by Date of Commission 257
    E. 4th U.S. Cavalry officers at Franklin, Tennessee, April 10, 1863 259
    F. Civil War Roster Fourth United States Cavalry 259
    G. 4th United States Cavalry Regulars on the Battle Monument at West Point 282

Endnotes 283

Bibliography 321
    Archival Documents & Collections 321
    Government Publications 321
    Published Sources 321
    Internet Sources 324

Index 327

Preface

When starting this journey through time and history, I was surprised to find how little information was available on the 4th Regiment United States Cavalry prior to and during the Civil War. Thus began the process of creating a timeline and tracking down all available information about the 4th Regulars. Once that started, I began to "meet" some of the officers and men of the 4th US Cavalry through their published works and personal letters.

Sergeant James Larson, Company H, rides with the 4th Cavalry from 1859 through 1865. Fortunately for us, he leaves a personal memoir published by his daughter in 1935, long after his death in 1921. A true professional soldier and a valued witness to the events, he tells his story in a very matter-of-fact way that gives unique and personal insight to the men who fought this awful war. Of particular interest is his enlistment and basic training, which occurred just six months after that of my great-grandfather, John Martin Herberich. They would have shared almost identical experiences. Larson's work is particularly useful filling in the huge gaps in information available for the prewar years, when the companies of the 4th US Cavalry were scattered at outposts throughout the far West. His company, along with Company F, are the last to rejoin the regiment in the Western Theater in August 1863. Sergeant Charles E. Bates, Company E, is a 14-year-old runaway who joins the cavalry in 1858. One can assume he is mature for his age. Not surprisingly, he is a bit of a free spirit with an entrepreneurial bent not totally suited for military life. However, he does reenlist as a veteran on December 18, 1862, serving three more years. He is reduced in rank on more than one occasion and shares with us his personal experience in the brig. He is also cited for "gallantry and soldier like conduct" by his regimental commander at Murfreesboro. Considering his education, he writes very interesting letters that reflect basic opinions and attitudes of his generation. A and E are the only two companies to serve in the Eastern Theater under generals McClellan and Burnside, and Bates's letters provide the most detailed account of that assignment. The squadron will rejoin their regiment in the Western Theater in March 1863.

Corporal James H. Wiswell (Company C) voluntarily enlists in the Regular Cavalry for a term of three years in April 1861, with three of his "chums" from Hyderville, Vermont. An educated young man in his early twenties, he is one of the more prolific letter writers, keeping his parents and sisters informed of his well-being and circumstances during his wartime experiences. His letters cover the remaining companies of the regiment from mid-1861 to April 1864. His penmanship and writing abilities eventually take him out of the saddle, as he serves with the Quartermaster Corps during his last years. He shares opinions of his military commanders, as well as his views of politics that are not always welcomed by his father, who seems sensitive to any criticisms of the Union Army or Federal government. James will take his discharge before the end of the war, finding a government position in the Quartermaster Department of the Army in April 1864.

Lieutenant Colonel William H. Emory, 1st (later renamed 4th) US Cavalry, is the senior regimental commander present in the Far West when the war begins and Union troops are forced to evacuate their western posts. A son of the South, his correspondence is important in helping to understand the deep personal and emotional struggle felt by those who, as military officers and Academy graduates, had sworn allegiance to the flag, and had to watch—almost helplessly—as everything they have dedicated their lives to—the bonds of loyalty, family, and friendship—are pulled apart. In May 1861, in a moment of despair, he submits his resignation, only to change his mind, be reinstated, and go on to serve his country with distinction as a major general, United States Army.

For a major part of the war, the 4th United States Cavalry was part of a cavalry brigade made up of three or more cavalry regiments. The 4th Regulars were the only Regular United States Army cavalry regiment in the Western Theater. All of the other cavalry regiments were volunteer regiments, often formed by the states, such as the 4th Michigan Volunteers and the 7th Pennsylvania Volunteers, who made up the brigade to which the 4th United States was attached. Several members of these regiments subsequently published regimental histories that contributed much to this history of the 4th United States Cavalry.

Captain Joseph G. Vale, 7th Pennsylvania Volunteer Cavalry, publishes his account of the war in his 1886 brigade history *Minty and the Cavalry*. Colonel Robert H. G. Minty commanded the Saber Brigade, which primarily consisted of three cavalry regiments: the 4th United States, Minty's own 4th Michigan Volunteers, and Vale's 7th Pennsylvania Volunteers. Until 1996, Vale's book contained the most information on the activities of the 4th Regulars for the eighteen months they were part of Minty's Brigade. Vale's stated hatred for the Confederacy tends to override his objectivity in some cases, although noted Civil War cavalry historian Stephen Z. Starr considers Vale "a generally reliable regimental historian."

Colonel William B. Sipes commanded the 7th Pennsylvania Cavalry during a portion of the war and wrote his regimental history in 1906. His focus was deservedly on his own regiment, often to the exclusion of and lack of credit to the other two regiments in Minty's Brigade. This is reflected in his title, *The Saber Regiment*.

Captain Henry Albert Potter, 4th Michigan Volunteers, is, along with James Wiswell, one of the most prolific letter writers and keen observers of events. He is a 22-year-old school teacher when he enlists as a sergeant in the 4th Michigan Volunteer Cavalry in July 1862, and is quickly promoted to 2nd lieutenant, and later captain of Company H. Michael P. Ruddy, a great-grandson of Henry Potter, collected and edited the letters and diaries of the Captain and generously made them available to researchers. Captain Potter provides a real and truly personal account of the war.

All quoted material—especially personal letters—are presented with their original grammar, punctuation, and spelling to the extent possible.

Two recently published works are essential to this history: Rand Bitter's *Minty and His Cavalry* (self-published in 2006) and David Evans's *Sherman's Horsemen: Union Cavalry Operations in the Atlanta Campaign* (published in 1996). Rand Bitter has produced the definitive study of Colonel Robert H. G. Minty and the activities of Minty's Saber Brigade. His exhaustive research brings to focus not only all of the materials regarding the colonel, but also the extensive correspondence of officers who served with Minty—most notably Major George W. Fish, 4th Michigan Regimental Surgeon and an avid writer and keen observer of events; and Major Robert Burns, who became Minty's assistant adjutant. Historian David Evans describes Burns as an active correspondent and "a reliable observer."

Of David Evans's work, noted Civil War historian Wily Sword writes that this book is "a model study of cavalry operations in the Western Theater." Another historian describes it as "undoubtedly the definitive account of Union cavalry operations in the Atlanta Campaign." Prior to Evans's work, there was a general lack of information available about the activities of the cavalry in the Western Theater in general and the 4th Regulars in particular. As Evans points out, generations of historians have focused on the great battles and leaders in the Eastern Theater, often to the exclusion of what was happening in the West. As one reviewer writes, Evans "provides the definitive account of this hitherto neglected aspect of the Civil War."

Donald C. Caughey, a retired Army cavalry officer, has taught military science at the College of William and Mary, Colorado School of Mines, and UC-Colorado Springs. In 2007, he began a blog site (regularcavalryincivilwar.wordpress.com) as a prelude to the 2013 publication of his book, *The 6th United States Cavalry in the Civil War*. A prolific writer, Caughey and his co-author, Jimmy J. Jones, are masters of research, making significant contributions to the early history of the United States Cavalry. They have been generous both in time—reviewing the early manuscripts—as well as making invaluable contributions to this project.

For those unfamiliar with Civil War history, the United States government undertook a massive project in the 1880s and 1890s to compile, edit, and organize all available military correspondence dealing with the Civil War. Known as *The War of the Rebellion: A Compilation of the Official Records of the Union and Confederate Armies* [also *Official Records*, or *ORs*], this work contains a number of firsthand accounts and reports of the activities of the 4th United States Cavalry.

Having completed my graduate work prior to the advent of computers, I was cautious about using Internet sources. However, it quickly became apparent that a whole new library of information was available, allowing access to resources that would otherwise not have been practical or possible to obtain that were extremely useful in filling in background information.

While the story of the 4th United States Cavalry is told against the great backdrop of the Civil War, the governing events are presented only as they directly affect the companies of the 4th Regiment, or as needed to move the timeline along. To that extent, it is limited to and totally dependent upon the research and writings of others. The extensive use of footnotes is an attempt to credit the works of those whose facts, words, sentences, and paragraphs are used intact. These references create a bibliography that can be referred to for further research.

The 1st and 2nd Regiments of United States Cavalry were created in March 1855. They joined three previously existing mounted regiments. In August 1861, these five regiments were reorganized, designated as Cavalry (rather than Mounted Regiments or Dragoons), and given the same uniforms and insignia—the crossed saber. They were also renumbered by seniority. The 1st and 2nd Cavalry, as the two newest, were renumbered the 4th and 5th Cavalry.

Finally, my interest in this project grew from a scrap of paper discovered among my grandmother's few remaining possessions. It contained the simple notation regarding her father-in-law, "1st Sgt. John M. Herberich, Company I, 4th US Cavalry." Prior to that accidental discovery, there had been no previous family awareness of our Civil War ancestor. When he retired from the Union Army in 1872 to live in San Antonio, Texas, there was, as with the Deep South, a strong bias of Civil War sentiment. That bias runs deep in many families, including my own.

Foreword

The United States Army had five mounted regiments at the outbreak of the Civil War. A sixth regiment of Regulars was formed in 1861. These six regiments provided the solid, professional nucleus for the large mounted forces that became so important to the Union victory in the Civil War. Four of the six Regular regiments—the 1st, 2nd, 5th, and 6th Cavalry—served with the Army of the Potomac for most of the war. These four regiments served as the heart of the Reserve Brigade, which was the heart of the Army of the Potomac's Cavalry Corps.

The 4th US Cavalry, by contrast, served in the Western Theater with the Army of the Cumberland. The 4th U.S. was an integral part of the Army of the Cumberland's finest mounted unit, Colonel Robert H. G. Minty's Saber Brigade.

These men left their mark on many a battlefield, but until the publication of John L. Herberich's *Masters of the Field: The Fourth United States Cavalry in the Civil War*, almost no good sources existed to document their exploits other than Sgt. James Larson's very rare 1932 memoir, *Sergeant Larson, 4th Cavalry*.

Interested in the exploits of his ancestor, Sergeant John M. Herberich, who served in the 4th US Cavalry during the Civil War, Herberich has mined the available primary source material and has done an excellent job of cobbling together the history of this overlooked and largely forgotten Regular cavalry regiment and of describing the important role that it played in the campaigns of the Army of the Cumberland. Herberich effectively documents the exploits of this regiment as it campaigned, describing engagements large and small in detail. At the end of the book, the reader comes away with an appreciation of the ordeals and travails faced by a United States Regular cavalryman at the time of the Civil War. He brings this forgotten unit back into the spotlight and focuses on the role of common soldiers like his great-grandfather, Sergeant Herberich. John Herberich has done an excellent job of commemorating the service of his ancestor and of the other men who followed the guidon of the Fourth United States Cavalry.

This book is an excellent addition to the bookshelf of anyone interested in the role of the cavalry in the Civil War, life in a Regular Army unit, and in the campaigns of the Army of the Cumberland.

Eric J. Wittenberg
Columbus, Ohio

Eric J. Wittenberg is a Civil War historian, author, and attorney. He has written more than a dozen books focusing on the cavalry in the Civil War and numerous articles in popular magazines. He was the winner of the 1998 Bachelder-Coddington Literary award and is active in battlefield preservations.

Acknowledgments

This book would not have been possible without the groundbreaking research of Rand K. Bitter, the biographer of Brigadier General Robert H. G. Minty. *Minty and His Cavalry* is in itself a library of information about the history of the cavalry in the Western Theater. An amateur historian on a quest much like my own, Rand gave me the inspiration and courage to tackle the daunting experience of writing this regimental history. As he wrote in his book in a personal note to me: "Long may the memory of their gallantry and deeds live on."

Since I first met cavalry historian Don Caughey through his blogsite in 2007, he has been extremely generous in sharing information and providing moral support. He also led me to my research assistant, Patty Millich.

Patty spent hundreds of hours researching and reviewing handwritten documents to track down all available information about the men who rode with the regiment during the war. This turned out to be a Herculean task to which she is well suited. Patty also helped track down obscure newspaper articles relating to the men of the 4th Cavalry and used her skills as an English major and teacher in the final editing process.

Vicki Carrico, a life long friend, helped from the beginning with the continual reviewing and editing process. She also used her computer skills to put the massive amount of information provided by Patty Millich into a manageable document that is now the definitive roster of the men of the 4th United States Cavalry during the Civil War.

Special gratitude goes to Beverly Lozoff for her meticulous review of the finished manuscript, finding everything the rest of us missed.

And finally, I owe much to my editor-in-house, my wife Jane, an English and French teacher who endured ten years of interruptions with my question, "Honey, can you read this?"

Michael P. Ruddy, the great-grandson of Captain Henry Albert Potter, 4th Michigan Volunteer Cavalry, represents a number of people I have met along the journey who have taken the time and interest to not only preserve the personal history of the Civil War as seen through the letters of the participants, but to make their stories available to researchers and the general public. These letters provide true insight into the hearts and minds of the men who fought America's Civil War.

Through my early research in Texas, where my great-grandfather retired in 1872 after serving with the 4th Cavalry to reestablish the system of forts on the frontier, I met Carolyn Christopher, a newly found second cousin and great-granddaughter of 1st Sgt. John M. Herberich, who introduced me to the family history in San Antonio, as well as the frontier forts of Texas. Carolyn also provided the keen eyes of an experienced English teacher in editing the final text for content and grammar.

Ted Savas, a publisher and a founding member of our South Bay Civil War Round Table, San Jose, California, was very generous with his time and advice. Another member, Hal Jespersen, created the beautiful maps which add so much detail to the story.

For her generous support and information, I would also like to thank Dr. Libra R. Hilde, Assistant Professor of History at San Jose State University—my alma mater, where it all began in the history department so many years ago.

Prologue

"Glory, disgrace and disaster . . ."[1]

The war that was to end in quick glory began in disgrace at Bull Run, a name that was to become a euphemism for a rout.[2] The awakened Federal government now had to prepare for a real war and desperately needed something to boost morale and unify the citizens to arms. That event was provided by companies of the 1st [later renamed 4th] United States Cavalry at a dusty water hole in Southwest Missouri on August 2, 1861.

Among the new technologies introduced in this first Industrial Age war were the use of railroads to move troops and supplies, the telegraph, and the print media. The growth of the rail network necessitated communication between the stations, which led to the birth and growth of the telegraph. The telegraph allowed the Civil War to become a national media event, and the country was about to have its first media star—the cavalry. As volunteer regiments were raised by various cities and states, it was common practice for the local newspaper to "embed" a reporter. Franc B. Wilkie, a correspondent for the Iowa *Dubuque Herald* and the *New York Times*, accompanied the First Iowa Regiment into Missouri on its "only campaign" of the war. Thomas W. Knox of the *New York Herald* "followed the Army of the West wherever it went" and published a book at the end of the war. Both reported on the events at Dug Springs, a watering stop about twenty-three miles southwest of Springfield, Missouri.[3]

It was August 1, and the temperature was over 100 degrees. Newly appointed Brigadier General Nathaniel Lyon was commanding his 6,000 member Army of Southwest Missouri that included four Companies (B, C, D, and I) of the 1st United States Cavalry. Captain David S. Stanley commanded the 250 officers and men. Companies B and I were detached for separate scouting activities around Greenfield, Missouri, and were not present at Dug Springs.[4]

Lyon received information that rebel forces, comprised of the Missouri State Militia and Texas secessionists, were advancing on Springfield in three columns and with superior numbers to his own. Determined to take offensive action to save the state for the Union, he moved his force south, down the Fayetteville Road, "to meet the largest and most advanced of the enemy forces." His command marched about ten miles the first day and resumed the march early on the morning of August 2.[5]

When Lyon called a halt at 9 a.m. near Dug Springs, nearly two-thirds of his ragtag volunteer army had fallen out of ranks as a result of the lack of water, preceded by weeks of poor rations.[6] Scores of men had dropped from exhaustion, with several dying from excessive heat and thirst.[7] When the main portion of the command came within sight of the spring, there was total chaos. It became impossible for the contingent of officers and men of the Regular Army to maintain any order or discipline over the volunteers. The area was quickly trampled into a muddy mire, until the pool "was more like earth than water."[8]

Once order was restored, Lyon sent out scouting parties and positioned Captain Frederick Steele's 2nd United States Infantry battalion to guard the southern end of the valley, while the balance of Lyon's command bivouacked around Dug Springs.[9] The only other camp in advance where water could be obtained was some four or five miles farther on, "where the rebel forces under Brigadier General James S. Rains were some 3,000 strong . . ."[10]

Within the hour, "a scouting party of the enemy's cavalry was discovered a hundred yards in advance on the road." Two companies of Steele's battalion "were deployed as skirmishers, one on either side of the road, to act as flankers through the bushes." A shell from the Union battery dispersed the rebels. "After advancing about a mile and a half, the enemy's cavalry, in considerable force, was discovered crossing and recrossing the road in front," and was then lost from view in a dense forest.[11] The terrain "was extremely broken up and covered with thick underbrush and scrub timber, thus not particularly conducive to deployment for a general attack."[12]

It was impossible to estimate the strength of the enemy. The company of mounted rifle recruits was deployed to skirmish through a cornfield, with Company B, Second Infantry, acting as a reserve. "Captain Stanley's troop of cavalry was a short distance in the rear, on the right of the road." They were ordered to hold their position. The rebels had two small fieldpieces on the slope of the hill on either side of the road, and for several hours were firing random shots with no effect.[13] Later that afternoon, the rebel advance, being mostly mounted, "became bold" and threatened Lyon's forces "from several points."[14]

Part of the rebel forces—a portion of the Missouri State Guard Cavalry—was led by Colonel James McQueen McIntosh, formerly captain, Company D, 1st United States Cavalry. Captain Stanley had served as 1st Lieutenant under McIntosh, who resigned his commission in May 1861 to fight for the South. In the days and years ahead, there would be a number of occasions when former comrades at arms in the 1st US Cavalry would meet on opposite sides of the battlefield.

At about 5 p.m., the line of Regular infantry skirmishers "was attacked on the left and front by a large body of cavalry, some 200 or more of whom were on foot and about the same number mounted." At the same time, the rebels were advancing along the road in column with two pieces of artillery. The Union infantry repulsed the first attack, but was soon overwhelmed and forced to retreat upon the reserve. Captain Steele came to their support with two companies of his battalion, advancing on the enemy and driving him rapidly back. At the same time, Captain Stanley's cavalry took position to prevent the Union flank from being turned.[15] What happened next is not clear.

According to General Lyon, his advance guard of infantry opened fire and, at the same time, "without orders from me, by a spontaneous emotion, the advance guard of my cavalry [the 1st U.S.] charged and drove back the rebels . . ."[16] Another contemporary version has Captain Stanley's troops "dashing upon [the enemy's] lines with the saber, cutting through them, routing them in disorder . . . capturing two hundred with their horses, arms, and equipments complete."[17] Even Captain Steele, in concluding his final report, states: "Captain Stanley's troop having gallantly charged and cut through his line . . . the enemy was now in complete rout. We fell back in good order upon a position chosen by General Lyon . . ."[18]

What appears to be closer to the truth is the eyewitness account of newly commissioned 2nd Lieutenant George B. Sanford, 1st Dragoons, when writing of his first combat experience. He describes "a very gallant charge . . . made by a part of 'C' troop 1st Cavalry" under newly commissioned 2nd Lieutenant Michael J. Kelly. Kelly was one of a number of new and inexperienced civilian appointments necessary to fill the vacancies left by the recent resignations. "He mistook the trumpet call to halt for the signal to charge and dashed into the enemy's lines completely routing them at that point," though nearly all of his own men were killed or wounded. Potential disaster was avoided when the rest of "C" troop under Captain Stanley and Sanford's 1st Dragoons (renamed the 1st Cavalry in August 1861) moved to the front in support "and the enemy fell back."[19]

It really didn't matter what actually happened; the media won the day. The press version of the battle, written by an unknown correspondent from the *Dubuque Herald*—quite possibly Franc Wilkie—appeared nationally in a *Harper's Weekly* article as follows:

> Captain Steele was still on the left, and a body of nearly eight hundred infantry, with a few mounted men, came forward on the enemy's right with the evident intention of engaging and surrounding the Captain's two companies. Company C of the First cavalry was in the rear (lately front), near Captain Steele and Lieutenant M. J. Kelly, with twenty men from his company, made a Balaklava charge right in the face of the bullets and bayonets of the whole rebel infantry. Four of the twenty were killed and six wounded, but they succeeded in breaking the infantry and putting them to flight. Four horses were wounded so badly that it was necessary to kill them — one receiving nine, and another eleven rifle balls. One of the men–Sergeant [Thomas W.] Sullivan–received three terrible, though not fatal wounds. As he was falling from his horse he waved his saber, and shouted "Hurrah for the old Stars and Stripes!" When brought to camp he seemed to forget his wounds in his joy at having struck a blow for the Union. One of the enemy's wounded inquired of Lieutenant Kelly, with great earnestness, "Are you cavalry men or devils!" The lieutenant replied that it was possible they might be a composition of both. "Well," said the man, "we can't stand such a charge as that. You can whip us all out if you've got a decent army of such soldiers."[20]

This August 24, 1861, article was accompanied by a glorious, full-page illustration of the battle captioned *Splendid Charge of the United States Cavalry at the Battle of Dug Springs, Missouri*.[21]

Captain Stanley's official losses were reported as four killed and six wounded—one mortally—out of a total of forty-two engaged. Sergeants Albert Coats and Thomas W. Sullivan were mentioned for their gallantry.[22] Both enlisted men would be commissioned 2nd Lieutenants within the next six months, with Coats transferring to the newly formed 6th Cavalry in 1861. Another enlisted man under Lieutenant Kelly, Corporal Elbridge Roys, received a commission to 2nd Lieutenant the following year for his conduct during the charge. With experience, 2nd Lieutenant Kelly would grow into a fine officer, but for the time being, he would not be given another command.

Of the first troopers in the 1st US Cavalry killed in the Civil War, Private John Austin Gibbons, age twenty-four, Company C, from Dubuque, was reported to be "the second Iowa soldier to be killed in action."[23] Also killed from Company C was Corporal Frederick Kline; correspondent Franc Wilkie reported his death: "Kline had his saber lifted over the head of a Secessionist who begged for quarter. Kline granted it, and was turning away, when the cowardly scoundrel shot him through the eye, killing him dead on the spot." The rebel was immediately cut to pieces by Union troopers.[24]

While there is no way to gauge the effect of the publicity created by the incident at Dug Springs in generating new enthusiasm for the Cavalry and helping to increase desperately needed enlistments, this was a disaster for Company C, 1st Cavalry. Not until one looks over the casualty lists of the injured is the scope of this tragedy apparent: four were killed during the charge and another was mortally wounded. Of the six men reported wounded, three suffered wounds so severe that they led to their discharge due to disability. Thus, the total number of men lost to Company C in this engagement was eight.[25] With the number of troopers involved in the charge reported from twenty to forty, and the total number of troopers in Company C at approximately fifty-five, this was a costly victory.[26]

Perhaps no other nation entered war as ill prepared as the Federal government of the United States in 1861, unless one includes the loosely formed Confederate States of America. What there was of a Federal Army was scattered over thousands of square miles of the frontier west of the Mississippi. At the outbreak of war, a majority of the best-trained officers resigned their commissions to fight for what they deeply believed to be their "state's rights." In the haste to rebuild the officer corps, untrained civilians filled vacant positions, very few with prior military training. The immediate call to arms on both sides resulted in untrained and "undisciplined mobs" of volunteers armed with little but their own knives, shotguns, and antique rifles. There were few supplies of any kind, much less an organized delivery system. It was into this maelstrom that the small Regular Army of the United States, numbering less than 18,000, was immediately drawn. If the trained and disciplined military were to survive, it would have to do everything asked of them, and more. At the beginning of the Civil War, there were only five mounted regiments; two of them designated as cavalry. This is the story of the Fourth Regiment United States Cavalry.

1855-1860: Prelude to War

He had followed the dear old flag . . . sprinkling it with his blood in many a combat. How can he fight against it? How he hopes and prays that his state will not go; that he will not be obliged to make the choice.[1]

I. Organization and Operations Prior to the Civil War

After the Revolutionary War, it was the general policy of the Federal government to finance and maintain as small an army as practical, and so it was that on the eve of the Civil War, with a population of approximately 31,500,000 citizens, the "effective strength" of the United States military was "somewhat over 14,000," of which less than 4,000 were cavalry, and they were "scattered in seventy-nine frontier outposts west of the Mississippi."[2]

During the 1800s, mounted regiments in the United States evolved from a need to patrol the vast areas of ever-expanding territories and to interact with Native American Indian tribes in the inevitable conflicts and dislocations of the nineteenth century. On March 3, 1855, two new cavalry regiments (the 1st and 2nd Cavalry) were constituted, not by an act expressly dealing with Army organization, but by an addition to an appropriations bill in the United States Congress. "The necessities of the country demanded it . . . [as] the annexation of Texas and the conquest of New Mexico and California had increased the area of the Republic nearly one third."[3] The Fourth Regiment United States Cavalry was originally organized on March 26, 1855, at Jefferson Barracks, Missouri, as the 1st Cavalry. The two new cavalry regiments were organized in the same manner as the three existing horse regiments, but General Orders prescribing their organization made them a distinct and separate arm. "Like their predecessors among the dragoons and mounted riflemen, the new outfits were composed of ten eighty-seven-man companies; unlike the older units, the two new cavalry regiments were armed with rifled carbines as well as with sabers and Navy Colt 36-caliber revolvers."[4] Thus, the five regiments of the Federal mounted force were made up of two regiments of dragoons, one regiment of mounted riflemen, and the two new regiments of cavalry.[5] "Dragoon" is a French term describing a horseman who was trained to fight both on foot and while mounted. The United States Regiment of Dragoons was formed in 1833 for patrolling the Great Plains regions. In 1836, a second regiment of dragoons was formed to fight the Seminoles in Florida. The Regiment of Mounted Riflemen was constituted at Jefferson Barracks for service in the New Mexico and Arizona Territories in 1846.

The cavalry regiments created in 1855 "proved popular enough to attract unusually promising young officers." As one historian has pointed out, the rosters of the new outfits read like a "Civil War roll of honor" for both the Confederacy and the Union.[6] Among the names: George B. McClellan, Robert E. Lee, and the famed Confederate cavalry leader James Ewell Brown (Jeb) Stuart.

Jefferson Davis, the future president of the Confederacy and then-Secretary of War in President Franklin Pierce's government, appointed Colonel Edwin Vose Sumner, a senior career officer of over thirty-six years, to command the new First Cavalry. In March 1861, Sumner would be promoted to brigadier general to take temporary command of the Department of Texas. In July 1862, he was promoted to major general, United States Volunteers. He died in March 1863. Lieutenant Colonel Robert E. Lee, 2nd Cavalry, was Lincoln's first choice to replace Sumner as the next commanding officer of the new 1st Cavalry.

Joseph E. Johnston, a Virginian and West Point graduate of 1827, was appointed lieutenant colonel for the new regiment. He would be named Quartermaster General of the United States Army in June 1860, only to resign in April 1861, to help organize the Confederate volunteers in Virginia. He would command the Confederate troops who won the first major battle of the war at Bull Run.[7] Johnston would be replaced by Lieutenant Colonel William J. Hardee, promoted from major, 2nd Cavalry. Hardee, Academy Class of '34 and a native son of Georgia, resigned in January 1861 to become one of the more successful Confederate generals, having "written the book" used by infantry on both sides and rising to the rank of lieutenant general, Confederate States of America.[8]

Jefferson Davis has been criticized for his tendencies to "appoint officers from among his southern favorites," which was to have serious consequences at the outbreak of the Civil War.[9] This may not be a fair criticism, as a majority of military officers, particularly cavalry, traditionally came from southern states at this time.[10] Of the 176 officers in the Army's five mounted regiments, 104 were Southerners, "and most of them stood by their native states, including four of the five colonels."[11]

The first major appointed to the new 1st Cavalry was Braxton Bragg. He declined the promotion and resigned from the Army on January 3, 1856, becoming a sugar planter in Louisiana. Remaining loyal to his state, he would become one of the leading generals of the South and would command the Army of Tennessee against former members of his cavalry regiment at Chickamauga and Chattanooga.[12] A second ajor—John Sedgwick from Connecticut, a West Point graduate Class of '37—joined the regiment in March 1855. He was considered an excellent officer and, with all the resignations—including that of Colonel Robert E. Lee—he would become the third colonel to command the Regiment on April 25, 1861.[13] The third major, William H. Emory, transferred from the 2nd Cavalry in May 1855. He would become lieutenant colonel of the Regiment in January 1861, when Hardee resigned. As temporary commander of Federal forces in the Oklahoma Indian Territories, he would successfully lead the remaining Union Army to the safety of Fort Leavenworth, Kansas, at the outbreak of the war. Emory would become brigadier general, United States Volunteers, rising to major general, USV.[14]

One of the first captains assigned to the newly formed regiment was George McClellan, Company D. During 1855-56, McClellan visited Europe with a commission of American officers and brought back a Prussian saddle that, with modifications, became the "McClellan Saddle," and was used by the cavalry until the horse cavalry was abandoned in 1942.[15] McClellan resigned his commission in 1857 to become a railroad executive, and in that capacity he met young attorney Abraham Lincoln. He would become President Lincoln's general-in-chief of the Union Armies and one of his greatest disappointments.

Of the ten captains commanding companies of the 1st United States Cavalry present for duty in January 1861, five would resign and join the Confederacy, two would become general officers in the United States Volunteers, and one, Captain Eugene Asa Carr, would become a brigadier general, United States Army. Captain Delos B. Sacket would become Inspector General, US Army. Four former captains of the 1st Cavalry would also join the Confederacy. Of the twenty junior officers present (1st and 2nd Lieutenants), nine would resign and join the Confederacy. The officers remaining with the First Cavalry at the beginning of the Civil War, as well as those who succeeded them, were rarely, if ever, in the field with the regiment. As will be shown, most were on "detached service" with newly formed United States Volunteer regiments and commands. There was a desperate need for men of military experience, and this burden fell heavily on active and retired members of the Regular Army, as described by Sergeant James Larson, 4th United States Cavalry:

> The volunteers were to be raised as quickly as they could be armed and equipped and mustered in and drilled and made into soldiers in the shortest time possible. To accomplish that the officers of the regular army, or as many as could be spared, were required at once to take command of volunteer organizations. The enlisted men of the old army were as badly needed to be divided by regiments among the new volunteers, divisions and corps as samples of true soldiery, which was very necessary in so hastily making soldiers out of such large number of men from civil life.[16]

The United States government was totally unprepared for what was about to happen. Lincoln initially relied on "volunteers" for his army, and it would take the first year of the war and the disastrous Union defeat at Bull Run in July 1861 before the enormity of the war would be realized. Even then, the majority of the Union army, and particularly the cavalry, would come from United States Volunteer regiments raised by the Northern states—over 227 cavalry regiments by the end of 1863.[17] In May 1861, the Lincoln administration ordered the creation of the 6th Cavalry Regiment and Congress to "set up a table of organization for the volunteer cavalry that was based on that of the newest Regular Regiment."[18] The six Federal cavalry regiments would suffer a shortage of men throughout the war, because the Federal government could not compete with the bounties paid by the states to entice new recruits for their volunteer regiments. This also reflected the tendency of the citizens of that time toward state rather than federal loyalty.

At the time of formation in 1855, a cavalry regiment originally had ten companies, designated "A" through "K." There was no "J" designation "because in the day of handwritten orders and correspondence, 'I' and 'J' were easily confused."[19] Each company was commanded by a captain, who was assisted by a 1st and 2nd lieutenant. Two companies constituted a squadron and two squadrons a battalion, which was commanded by a major. Originally, a company could have any number of privates up to seventy-two. In 1863, the number was increased—though rarely achieved—to one hundred. The size of a regiment could range from approximately 864 to a full complement of 1,200 men.

As the Civil War wore on, the six regiments of Federal Cavalry actually operated with a much smaller number of men due to recruiting difficulties, injury, illness, or loss of mount. Along with the creation of the 6th Cavalry Regiment by presidential proclamation in May 1861, the number of companies was increased from ten to twelve. Companies L and M of the 4th Regiment were organized in the field near Murfreesboro, Tennessee, in November 1862.[20]

In actual field service during the Civil War, officers above the rank of captain were rarely present with the regiment, and company rosters ranged between forty-five and fifty-five men. Two companies combined to form a squadron, and usually three were considered a battalion.[21] Because of the extreme shortage of officers created by defection to the Confederacy and the explosive growth of the volunteer regiments at the beginning of the Civil War, companies and squadrons were frequently led by junior officers (1st or 2nd lieutenants), most of whom were newly commissioned officers from the ranks of enlisted men within the regiment. During the battle at Franklin, Tennessee, in April 1863, five companies of the regiment were commanded by former enlisted men, three having received their field commissions to 2nd lieutenant just two months earlier.

In August 1861, these six mounted regiments were combined into one corps to be known as "Cavalry," and they were renumbered in order of their seniority. As the First Cavalry was the fourth-oldest mounted unit, it was redesignated as the Fourth Regiment United States Cavalry. It was not until after the Civil War that the federal cavalry was expanded with the Seventh through Tenth regiments.

From the beginning of the Civil War until April 1863, "there had been many changes in the organization of cavalry regiments; and to such an extent had it been carried by various acts of Congress, that it was . . . impossible to say what really was the legal organization of a horse regiment."[22] The issue was supposedly settled with General Order No. 110 from the War Department, Adjutant General's office, April 29, 1863:

> A Regiment of Cavalry would consist of Twelve Companies or Troops. One Colonel, 1 Lieutenant Colonel, 3 Majors, 1 Surgeon, 2 Assistant Surgeons, 1 Regimental Adjutant (a Lieutenant), 1 Regimental Quartermaster (Lt.), 1 Regimental Commissary (Lt.), 1 Chaplain, 1 Veterinary Surgeon, 1 Sergeant Major, 1 Quartermaster Sergeant, 1 Commissary Sergeant, 2 Hospital Stewards, 1 Saddler Sergeant.

There was also a regimental band. This was the organization on paper; as it turned out, it had little to do with the reality of the Civil War. A company of cavalry would have one captain, one first lieutenant, one second lieutenant, one first sergeant, one quartermaster sergeant, one commissary sergeant, five sergeants, eight corporals, two trumpeters, two farriers or blacksmiths, one saddler, one wagoner, and sixty to seventy-eight privates.[23] These orders were rarely, if ever, met, and the officers and men of the cavalry regiments and companies in the field were forced to deal with the daily practicality of war, rather than policy from Washington. There were any number of "Extra or Daily duties" assigned to the troops to keep the posts and the units functioning. Among them were clerk, hospital attendant, cook, baker, mail carrier, blacksmith, company tailor, saddler, teamster, quartermaster duties, caring for sick horses, and "health." The more literate of the enlisted men could also be on "detached service" from their companies at various posts as clerk at Regimental Headquarters, or assigned to the Regimental Quartermaster Corps. During the Civil War, the term "Troop" was occasionally substituted for company, but did not become the official term until 1880.[24] Each company had a guidon (company flag): "swallow-tail in design, the top half of which was red with the regimental number in white, the bottom half white, with the troop (company) letter in red."[25] The guidon came to represent those many long dead who had "laid down their lives" for the honor of their company. Every soldier "would unhesitatingly follow his guidon all the way to hell, or clobber any outsider who lived who would make the mistake of slandering anything or anyone belonging to his troop or regiment."[26] During the war, this would extend to the brigade and division battle flags as well. Many a soldier died carrying their flag into battle or fighting to keep it from being captured—the ultimate humiliation.

The troops received various types of carbines, including a Springfield that was muzzle-loading and the Merrill and Perry, both of which loaded at the breech. Their pistols were Army or Navy-patterned

Colt revolvers, their sabers the Prussian type used by dragoons. It is generally reported that although most cavalrymen favored sabers at the beginning of the war, their use declined in favor of the carbine and the pistol.[27] The Fourth Regiment United States Cavalry, the Seventh Pennsylvania Volunteer Cavalry, and the Fourth Michigan Volunteer Cavalry, as members of Brigadier General Robert H. G. Minty's famed Saber Brigade, would prove the exception. By 1862, the 4th US Cavalry was armed with the Model 1853 Sharps carbine (short-barreled rifle), the Model 1860 Colt Army revolver, and the U.S. Model 1860 light cavalry saber.[28]

"From every section and circumstance men enlisted in the mounted arm of the service."[29] The army had no literacy test or citizenship restriction required for enlistment.[30] Newly arrived immigrants and unemployed Irish and Germans "were lured by generous bounties."[31] By 1850, 60% of the enlistees were foreign born.[32] "The Irish had an irresistible affinity for horses and fighting," and they represented almost half of the "foreign" element in the frontier cavalry. Somewhat fewer—about 20%—were the Germans, invariably called "Dutchies." Aggressive fighting men, they were more precise-minded than the Irish, and from them came almost all the regimental sergeant majors and a large part of the first sergeants.[33]

The German noncoms never attempted to achieve popularity with the men or curry favor with the officers but were harshly rigid, tough-minded, and generally feared by the enlisted men. They knew the 'book' like no others, lived by it, and expected all others to do likewise.[34]

This would seem to describe John Martin Herberich, who would rise through the ranks from private to first sergeant of Company I. Born in Wurzburg, Bavaria, Germany, in 1840, he immigrated to the United States in 1853, arriving with his family at the Port of New Orleans. On his nineteenth birthday (December 19, 1859), he enlisted as a private in the 1st United States Cavalry at the recruiting office in St. Louis, Missouri. He listed his occupation as "cigar maker."[35] James Larson—a contemporary of Herberich's from 1859 to 1867—also rose to the rank of 1st sergeant, Company H, and became a major contributor to the history of the 4th Regiment with his autobiography written in the later years of his life. He, too, "knew the 'book'... lived by it, and expected all others to do likewise."

Prewar Enlistment and Training: Private James Larson

James Larson was born February 14, 1841, and raised on a farm in northern Wisconsin. At the age of nineteen, he decided he wanted to be a soldier and joined the 1st United States Cavalry at St. Louis, Missouri, in June 1860—six months after nineteen-year-old John Herberich had done the same. In his autobiography, Larson tells the story of his enlistment and training, which would have been almost identical to that of Private Herberich. The following description of their training will stand in stark contrast to the training of the volunteers and conscripts raised to stop the rebellion.

At the First Cavalry recruiting office in St. Louis, recruits were greeted by a handsome looking sergeant... wearing a short jacket of dark blue cloth and trousers of the same color. The trimmings were of bright yellow and looked splendid on the blue cloth. A broad yellow stripe ran down the outside of each trouser leg. On his jacket collar and cuffs were small stripes, also yellow, and on each arm just above the elbow were the tokens of his rank: three narrow stripes running across the sleeves in a parallel line about a quarter inch apart, in the shape of a triangle. He wore a cap with two sabers of shining metal crossed just above the vizard, and under them, also in polished metal, the number of his regiment and the letter of his company. He also wore his side arms, belt and saber.[36]

Lieutenant Albert V. Colburn, 1st US Cavalry, was on detached service as recruiting officer in St. Louis during this time: "This young lieutenant, in his fine well fitting uniform and shoulder straps, waist belt and saber, appeared a perfect picture of a soldier and gentleman."[37] After a cursory physical, enlistment papers were filled out for a term of five years. The new recruit then took the oath "to protect and defend against all enemies foreign and domestic," and with their signature, became a soldier in the 1st United States Cavalry.[38]

The recruits boarded rail cars for the short ride to Jefferson Barracks, Missouri, described as "a pleasant post perched on a beautiful bluff overlooking the Mississippi River" three miles south of St. Louis.[39] "There they received basic dismounted drill, were outfitted, then shipped to the frontier posts in groups varying from six to sixty as the demand indicated."[40] Upon their arrival at Jefferson Barracks, the new recruits were taken to their barracks, which would be home for the next two months. Sergeant Larson describes the room as:

> about seventy feet long and about thirty feet broad. The furniture consisted of single iron bedsteads placed in a line on each side of the room with the heads of the beds against the wall and a space of about two feet between the beds. Along the middle of the room stood two arms-racks and some tables and benches, and that completed the simple and plain furniture. It was a surprise, however to note the cleanness and airiness that existed. The floor and everything else was clean and white as if it were in the care of a good woman housekeeper; but of course, it was not. The men kept their room in order themselves. The bedding was all rolled up at the heads of the beds, and as I learned later, was kept there all day and no one was allowed to spread it or lie down on a bed in daytime.

Supper that first night consisted of "some loaves of bread and tin cups filled with black coffee."[41]

Beginning at dawn, "life would move to the rhythm of bugle and drum."[42] Under the tutelage of the drill sergeants, the recruit: "would learn discipline, hone his skills at drill, and experience the army's mysterious organization and chain of command. He would learn how to pitch and strike a tent, how to kindle a fire in the field, and how to make the best of his strange new outdoor life, picking up the old soldier's tricks for securing rude comfort."[43] "Greenhorns know no rest. They learned to *Dress Up. Keep Step. Wheel into Line.* Then the manual of arms: *Shoulder Arms! Right Face! Forward March! Right Wheel! Left Wheel! Halt! Order Arms!* Squad drill. Troop drill. Squadron drill. Regiment drill."[44]

Continuing with Larson's description:

> As soon as a recruit mastered the drill in a lower grade he was advanced to the next, and so on until he got up to the most advanced class, which was constantly increased, and was drilling in platoon and all different kinds of company formations at common time, quick and double time. . . . [T]here were no horses at the barracks, so we could not receive instructions in mounted drill at that place, and it was rumored in the post that as soon as we had completed the foot drill we should leave for the frontier, which was not far in those days.[45]

By the end of the first month of training:

> nearly all the recruits . . . were formed into one squad, about ninety in all. From that time on our drill became very interesting. We went through all movements as a regular company in all manners and forms and at all the different times in marching.
>
> Up to that time we had not received instructions in the manuals of arms, saber, carbine or revolver. We had not been issued any weapons or belts at all, nor did we get any instructions in guard duty.[46]

In his autobiography, Larson describes another level of his early military education, which served him well, and helps account for his rapid rise in rank:

> . . . The old hands who had served several enlistments were very talkative and fond of telling their experiences, in the evenings when we were together in our room, and any new recruit who cared to learn more than he was forced to, could gather much valuable information by listening to them. By listening closely, I learned a great deal about the important inside features of army life; the duties of a soldier, what he had a right to do under certain circumstances, and what he had no right to do. Those were details which our drillmasters never mentioned. In fact, they seemed to take it for granted that we would learn by experience–and we did, but it was costly experience for many careless fellows who had contented themselves with going only as far as they were pushed.[47]

> . . . I made friends with all the old-timers and former service men who were with our outfit, asked them all the questions I could think of, and received a great deal of valuable information.[48]

Private Larson was quick to learn the basic rule of survival in any military: know the rules. Having little formal education, he had difficulty reading and writing. Wanting to overcome this shortcoming, and with little else to read, he taught himself to read with the "Blue Book" (*Articles of War*) and *U. S. Cavalry Tactics*. "After I had made some progress in reading and getting to understand it, I became interested and continued to read and study military law and tactics whenever I had an opportunity."[49]

Drilling and marching became a little more complicated when the recruits were issued sabers and spurs:

> The saber was suspended from the waist belt by a hook attached to a ring on the scabbard, near the hilt, so that the long saber hung down beside the left leg. In marching the saber would frequently get between the legs of the wearer, or somebody else, causing him to stumble and throw the entire line out of step.[50]
>
> . . . The spurs gave us even more trouble for a while. A soldier, in marching, is not allowed to cast his eyes to the ground closer than thirty steps away, and therefore, we could not watch the spurs on the heels of the fellows in front of us. The result was that we were forever stepping on some other fellow's spurs, which invariably upset both the wearer and the 'stepper'. Consequently, our marching was weird and wonderful for a while after all our traps had been hung on us, but we soon got used to it. Before long, by simply looking at the shoulders of the men in front of us, we could march almost breast to back without stepping on anybody's spurs.[51]

By the end of July, the stay at Jefferson Barracks was getting monotonous with the constant foot drill: ". . . as there were no horses there. We were issued a short, old fashioned infantry gun – a muzzle loader with an iron ramrod known as a Jaeger which was pronounced 'Yoguer'. . . With this shooting stick, we received an infantry cartridge box full of cartridges and a small cap box also well filled. To this was added knapsack, haversack and canteen; a complete infantry outfit except bayonet on the Jaeger . . ."[52]

At the end of their training, the recruits were made ready for a march. A young lieutenant of artillery on his way to Leavenworth, Kansas, was to take command of the detachment, at least to Fort Leavenworth. They were formed into a temporary company; an old soldier appointed as first sergeant, four other old soldiers as duty sergeants, and eight others as corporals. The entire company numbered ninety men.[53]

> Early one morning in the beginning of August (6th or 7th) 1860, we got orders to pack up at once and by 8 A.M. we stood in line on the parade ground with the knapsacks strapped on our backs and a gray U.S. blanket, which contained our clothing, rolled tight and strapped on top; haversack and canteen hanging by the side; belt with cartridge box and cap box buckled around the waist and the Jaeger in hand, ready to march to the station and take cars for St. Louis.[54]

The artillery officer arrived and the recruits "wheeled by fours and marched to the [train] station where we boarded the cars . . ."[55]

> Arriving at St. Louis, we marched through the city to the levee and went aboard a steamer *Minnehaha*, which was lying ready with steam up, waiting for us. Very soon she cast loose, backed out from among the other boats, and paddled down the Mississippi to the mouth of the Missouri River and we were on our way to the wild Indians and buffaloes.[56]

Service on the Frontier

In August 1855, the newly formed 1st Cavalry was assigned to Fort Leavenworth, to "maintain law and order in the Kansas Territory between pro and anti-slavery factions and to protect the settlers from attacks by the Cheyenne Indians."[57] Among its other functions, the United States Army also provided protection for settlers' wagon trains and explored and surveyed the hostile Indian country. The national debate surrounding the 1856 election as to whether Kansas would come into the Union as a slave state or free "put the adjective 'bleeding' before the name Kansas for years."[58] When open warfare broke out between slavery and antislavery factions, "nearly all the 1st Cavalry and the 2nd Dragoons, together with some infantry companies, were sent there to keep the peace."[59] From the fall of 1857 until the summer of 1860, six companies of the 1st Cavalry were stationed at Fort Riley, Kansas Territory, under the command of Major John Sedgwick, the rest "maintaining small garrisons scattered throughout the state."[60] Kansas entered the union as a free state in January 1861.

Fort Leavenworth, Kansas Territory

After chugging up the Missouri River, the paddle-wheeler carrying James Larson and the company of new recruits reached "a miserable, dirty village ... [of] dilapidated business houses which fronted the steamboat landing." In front of a warehouse, a guard paced "stiffly back and forth ... his bayonet glistening in the sun."[61] A day later, Larson's company arrived at Fort Leavenworth, a "conglomeration of stone, brick, log, and frame buildings which resembled a country visage."[62] Within a couple of days "everything was in order" for the "big march" to Fort Riley, about 120 miles away, and "every mile of it was to be made on foot." They were accompanied by "three government wagons, each drawn by six big mules" that contained rations and tents. There was also an "ambulance" drawn by four mules. This was a covered wagon fitted with seats designed to carry passengers, or the sick and wounded. The march would take three to four days, during which time practical training continued for the recruits:

> ... We always left camp at sunrise and marched briskly and got in camp early in the afternoon. That gave the young artillery officer a chance to instruct us in pitching and striking tents. Everything in the army, at least in time of peace, must be done with regularity. Wagons must be properly parked and tents, in putting them up, must rise all at the same time and stand on a perfectly straight line. If they did not we had to take them down and do it over again.[63]

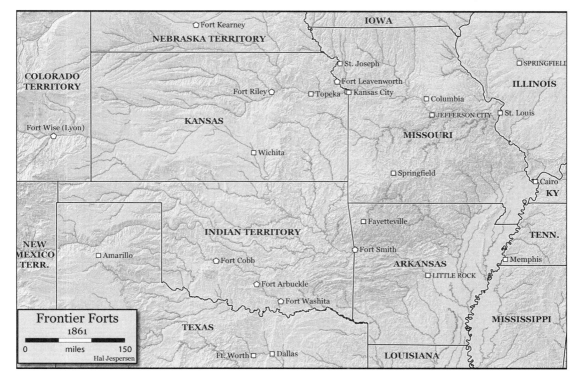

Frontier Forts 1861

It was August, and it was hot and dusty. The inexperienced recruits soon exhausted their water supply:[64]

> ... The water on which we expected to camp ... was nothing but a buffalo wallow ... a stagnant pool ... with very shallow water that was red with buffalo urine. In the hole lay several buffalo skulls and other bones, and near the hole lay a partly decomposed carcass of a buffalo, smelling very bad. No wood was available either, not even a twig or brush. The only way we could concoct our buffalo tea into coffee was by use of fuel made by the same animal called buffalo chips. There was plenty of that though, and it burned like charcoal, but the smoke smelled as bad as the water in the pool.[65]

Around August 10, the company arrived at Fort Riley, which was headquarters of the 1st Cavalry Regiment. Established on the north bank of the Kansas River in 1853, Fort Riley was one of a series of military posts created to protect travelers and commerce along the Oregon-California and Santa Fe Trails. During the summer of 1860, the headquarters was transferred farther west to the site of old Bent's Fort, Colorado Territory, near the headwaters of the Arkansas River. It would take almost a month to get ready for the march to Bent's Fort:

> In early September a government wagon train arrived from Leavenworth and with it Captain [Robert] Ransom [Co. H] and his wife ... The train had a large supply of commissary and quartermaster stores, which we had to escort on our way to the regiment.[66]
> ... It took some time to get ready for the march. Even small things for Mrs. Ransom, that were expected by mail, had to be waited for.[67]

Among the supplies was a shipment of the new Sharps breech-loading carbine, which was distributed among the new recruits. It was seven inches shorter and weighed only half as much as the Jaeger, and it could be loaded and fired very rapidly:

> All that was necessary was to spring the lever, insert a cartridge, close it, and put on a cap. It was the fastest firing gun in use in the army at that time and we carried it until, for gallant service in the Civil War, particularly at Okolona, Mississippi, we received the Spencer carbine [in February 1864].[68]

Continuing with Larson's account:

> At last everything was ready and orders issued ... and on the appointed day knapsacks were packed, blankets rolled and buckled on top, carried to the wagon, and we formed line, wheeled by fours and marched out of Fort Riley to begin the longest stretch of our march–630 miles.
> ... Included in the company was the 1st Cavalry band, which now had to join that part of the regiment camping on the Arkansas near Ben's [Bent's] Fort because it was now the headquarters of the regiment, with Major John Sedgwick in command.[69]

Fort Wise, Colorado Territory

It was during the first week of October 1860, when Private Larson and the wagon train "marched into the camp of the then 1st Cavalry, early in the morning."[70] The camp, made up of two rows of Sibley tents, was about a hundred yards from the Arkansas River, which was lined with "great cottonwood trees that stretched far up and down the river."[71] The Sibley tent was the most common of the army tents and was "patterned after the cone-shaped Indian tepees and was large enough for a dozen troopers."[72] "Some distance above the camp was the high bluff upon which stood the old Indian trading post named Bent's Fort."[73] As Larson recalled, their reception in camp was "quite cool and devoid of any demonstration." The recruits "rested in place," while it seemed the officers were "quarreling about the number of men each company was entitled to and the manner in which they ought to be drawn." Finally, "Sergeant [James] Carey [Co. F] came with a little box under his arm, followed by a lot of officers, and the work of distributing us among the companies began." There were four companies of the 1st Cavalry at headquarters: Cos. F, G, H, and K. Larson was drawn for Company H. His company commander was Captain Edward W. B. Newby, whose army experience began with the war with Mexico in 1847. He was one of the original captains appointed to the new regiment in 1855.[74] Larson continues:

> For about ten days we did no duty whatsoever except cleaning our things and drawing such clothing as we needed and other things to complete our uniform, such as the hat and black feather, cross sabers, letter of company and number of regiment, all of brass, which we polished to a shine and fastened in front on the hat. The feather was fastened on the right side of the hat, the brim on that side being turned up and fastened to the hat with the American eagle, also of brass. To complete the dress uniform we received a pair of brass epaulettes to be worn on the shoulders of the jacket. We also received the regular cavalry saber, revolver and spurs, but no horse, which we were informed would not be issued until we know how to take care of it.
> ... The rumor got afloat that the major was planning to establish a permanent post on a large level flat containing perhaps a section or more of land about a mile above Bent's Fort.[75]

Strangely enough, at about that same time, young Private Larson ran into an old friend from Wisconsin who was passing through the area. "He was driving a 'bull team' that had come from Kansas City and was on its way west. He brought news of the most terrible war between the North and South," that would be coming "in a short time." Larson was unsure how to respond, "because at that time there seemed to be no thought among the men in the army that a real war might be coming."

> Perhaps that was because we were so far out of the center of things and heard little news that was not already old. Whatever the reason, there had been no discussions of the possibility, and even such mention as I had heard made of the trouble between the North and South had been made in a joking manner, as a soldier is likely to refer to anything that he thinks is being done entirely by politicians and for nothing more than purely political purposes.[76]

> ... However, Major Sedgwick had planned to build Fort Wise and now, whether the government assisted or not, he with his characteristic stubbornness so often exhibited later when the storm finally broke, determined to build it anyhow."[77]

Shortly after Major Sedgwick's arrival, old Bent's Fort was leased to the U.S. military and used as a commissary warehouse. A new and more permanent fort was needed to maintain troops and military supplies and keep the peace. The Colorado gold rush had begun in the summer of 1860, with the inevitable massive influx of migrants that, in turn, created problems with the Indians. The Federal government authorized the creation of a new fort near the location of Bent's Fort. It was to be named Fort Wise, in honor of then-Virginia Governor Henry Wise. After the Civil War began, the name was changed to Fort Lyon to honor the memory of the first Union general to fall in battle, General Nathaniel Lyon. However, the War Department would not appropriate the funds "just then." "The expression 'just then' gave rise to considerable speculation among the officers, as well as the men."[78]

Companies F, G, H, and K built Fort Wise and remained there through May 1861.[79] First Lieutenants Eli Long and Jeb Stuart were among the officers present, both destined to become generals and commanders of cavalry units in their opposing armies. For the time being, however, their rivalry was in the competition to see whose company could build better and faster.[80] Between the four companies of the 1st Cavalry and two companies of the 10th Infantry posted at Fort Wise in 1860-61, six of the officers present, including John Sedgwick and Jeb Stuart, would die on the battlefields of the Civil War.[81]

December 1860 found the headquarters of the 1st Cavalry and Private Larson "snugly housed in very comfortable quarters" at Fort Wise:

> Everything now had the appearance of a regular military post ... men's quarters, officers' quarters, building for commissary and quartermaster stores and the large corral for the horses and mules. Even a tall flagstaff stood in the middle of the parade ground with the Stars and Stripes waving in the breeze from morning until night every day, and two pieces of field

artillery, which had been brought in by the mounted rifles, stood by the flagstaff.[82]

By this time "war talk had ceased to be mere rumors." As Larson writes: "South Carolina had really seceded from the Union [December 20, 1860]. The war rumors, which we far away on the frontiers had laughed at and joked about, had by that time reached maturity."[83]

Oklahoma Indian Territory

While Companies F, G, H, and K were building Fort Wise, the balance of the regiment (Companies A, B, C, D, E, and I) were disbursed among the various frontier forts. They were under the command of Major William H. Emory, who had arrived at Fort Arbuckle on October 12, 1858.[84] Fort Arbuckle, near present-day Davis, Oklahoma, was established in 1851 "in the unsettled Indian Territory to protect the Civilized Indians, Chickasaws and Choctaws, from the wild rampaging Kiowa and Comanche Indians. The Wichitas and Caddos tribes were also in the area." The fort also protected the wagon train emigrants heading for the gold fields of California "using the Dona Ana and California Trails between Fort Smith [Arkansas] and Santa Fe, New Mexico, which passed through the area." The post was used to resupply troops in the field and had a "good hospital where the seriously wounded were brought to recover." Unlike some of the other forts, Arbuckle had facilities for "family establishments" and a "pleasant social life."[85] There were two other forts in the Territory: Fort Cobb, in the Chickasaw Nation, near present-day Anadarko, Oklahoma; and Fort Washita, in southern Oklahoma Indian Territory, near Durant, Oklahoma. Fort Cobb was established in October 1859 by two companies of the 1st Cavalry and one company of the 1st Infantry under command of Major William Emory.[86] Fort Washita was established in 1841 by General Zachary Taylor—the future president—to "protect the peaceful Choctaw and Chickasaw Indians" who were "busy building schools and establishing law and order in southern Indian Territory." Their prosperity was "threatened by raiding Plains Indians and instability on the frontier." The fort served as a staging area for "forays west against raiding Plains tribes." A number of future Civil War leaders served there: Randolph March, George McClellan, and Braxton Bragg. It was also the first posting for newly arrived Private Herberich in February 1860, where he was assigned to Company I, commanded by Captain Eugene Carr. James B. McIntyre, 1st Lieutenant, Co. I, would command the regiment in the field longer than any other officer during the Civil War. Fort Washita would become the focal point for Federal forces in March 1861, when newly promoted Lieutenant Colonel Emory was ordered to establish his headquarters there. With the secession of Texas in February 1861, and the outbreak of hostilities, he was forced to abandon all three forts in April 1861, leading all of the Federal forces in the Oklahoma Indian Territory to the safety of Fort Leavenworth.[87]

Expeditions Against the Kiowa and Comanche

For the 1st Cavalry, the three years preceding the Civil War were marked by a "succession of marches, expeditions, and campaigns against the Indians."[88] The most notable of these engagements occurred with the Chocktaw Nation near Fort Arbuckle, Indian Territory, at Caddo Creek. There were other encounters near Pawnee Fork, Kansas; Blackwater Springs [near Bents Ford, Nebraska]; and at Cottonwood Creek, Kansas, in which six companies were engaged. "During the summer of 1860 the regiment took the field to make demonstrations against the Comanches and other hostiles..."[89] The records for this period are sketchy, and those available are often difficult to read. The following provides some insight into the activities of the 1st Cavalry during the year prior to the outbreak of the rebellion.

April 1860 Muster Rolls list all companies as "In the field." Companies C and I, which would have included newly arrived Private Herberich, had been "encamped near Fort Cobb" since April, "awaiting the departure" of the expeditions against the Indian tribes. Captain Thomas J. Wood, Co. C, was commanding the squadron. In May, Companies D and E were at Fort Cobb, while the rest remained in the field. On May 13, Companies A and B, posted at Fort Arbuckle, Oklahoma, Indian Territory, were "ordered to unite under the command of Capt. Samuel D. Sturgis in an expedition against the hostile Comanche and Kioway [sic] Indians."[90]

These six companies of the Regiment were to become part of the "Southern Column Comanche and Kiowa Expedition" led by Captain Sturgis.[91] It was comprised of 419 enlisted men and eleven officers, averaging out to about seventy men and two officers per company. During the first week of June, Sturgis's command left Fort Cobb, and by June

30 were "encamped on the Small Fork of the Cimmaron." From there they marched to the banks of the Grand Saline, having covered a total distance of 385 miles.[92]

By July 5, Companies C and I had joined with the command "near old Fort Atkinson on the Arkansas river." They marched toward Walnut Creek "on a scout against the Kiowa Indians," arriving on July 18. They continued to a point about seventy-five miles below Pawnee Fork, where they camped on July 28. From there they marched to Saline Creek, making camp on July 31 after having marched a total distance of "about 400 miles."[93]

Joined by Companies D and E from Fort Cobb on August 1, the six companies of the Regiment were "in camp on Grand Saline." From there they "pursued large bands of Kiowas and Comanches on the 3rd, 4th, and 5th . . . engaging and pursuing them until sunset." The command was now "encamped on Cottonwood Creek," having "marched 440 miles."[94] Captain William N. R. Beall, commanding the squadron of Companies A and B with "3 officers and 128 men," reported "having an engagement with the Kioway [sic] Indians on Beaver Creek near the Republican Fork, Kansas Territory, August 6th." Pvt. Michael Whelan, 1st Cav., Co. B, was reported "severely wounded."[95]

Meanwhile, the balance of the 1st Cavalry Regiment (Companies F, G, H, and K), commanded by Major Sedgwick, "left camp at Aubrey Crossing of the Arkansas River July 7th and encamped on Smokey Hill, July 31st," having marched 307 miles. "A detachment of these companies had an action with a party of Kiowa at Blackwater Spring 24 miles north of Bents Ford on the 11th of July and 2nd Lt. [George] Bayard and two privates were severely wounded."[96] On 1 August, Sedgwick's command "left camp on Smokey Hill . . . and encamped near Bents Ford, Kansas Territory" on August 29, having marched a distance of 355 miles.[97]

In his book on cavalry history published in 1865, Major Albert G. Brackett, USA, writes:

> Captain Samuel D. Sturgis, with six companies of the 1st Cavalry, had the most important Indian fight of the year at Solomon's Fork on the Arkansas River, where he defeated a large band of Camanches [sic]. This occurred on the 3d of September [1860]. The officers accompanied him, all of whom distinguished themselves, were . . . Captains [William N. R.] Beall, McIntosh, and Carr; and Lieutenants [Philip] Stockton, [Richard H.] Riddick, [John R.] Church, [Edward] Ingraham, [Lunsford L.] Lomax, [Oliver H.] Fish, and Andrew Jackson, jr.[98]

With the exceptions of Sturgis and Carr, all of the officers mentioned by Brackett would resign their commissions at the beginning of the war to fight for the Confederacy. Captain Wood would be promoted to lieutenant colonel, 1st Cavalry in May 1861, and in November would be promoted to colonel, commanding the 2nd [later 5th] US Cavalry.[99] George Dashiell Bayard—"one of the most promising" of the young officers—survived his wounds and would rise to the rank of brigadier general, United States Volunteers. He was mortally wounded at the Battle of Fredericksburg, Virginia, in December 1862.[100]

This arduous two-month experience "in the field," not to mention the distances covered, would provide invaluable practical training for the officers and men of the 1st Cavalry in the upcoming conflict, especially for the newest recruits.

In one of the peculiar ironies of history, it was on one of the earlier Indian expeditions in July 1857 that the life of the future Union Chief of Cavalry, Army of the Cumberland David S. Stanley was likely saved by famed Confederate Cavalry leader Jeb Stuart. As Stanley records in his memoirs, when his pistol misfired at a charging Indian:

> at that moment Stuart dashed his horse upon the indian, cut him on the head with his sabre, and laid him prostrate. But in the same instant, the cool old chief put the bullet he had intended for me into Stuart's breast. The indian was killed and for a time we thought Stuart was mortally wounded.[101]

Fort Smith, Arkansas, New Year's Eve 1860

Fort Smith, on the Arkansas River, was established in 1838, two years after Arkansas gained statehood. By the late 1850s, it had become the "Motherpost of the Southwest," supplying military posts farther to the west. It became a focal point of Civil War operations in the region, as both armies prized the facility and its location. When the fort was abandoned by Captain Sturgis on April 23, 1861, it would become the new headquarters for Texas Confederate Brigadier General Ben McCulloch.[102] Samuel Sturgis was one of the original captains assigned to the regiment in March 1855, transferring from the 2nd Dragoons. A West Point graduate (class of '42), he would be promoted to major May 1, 1861, and command several companies of the 1st US Cavalry in Missouri in 1861, under Brigadier General Nathaniel Lyon. Like many of the senior cavalry officers remaining with the Union, he would soon be on detached service from his regiment as a brigadier general of Volunteers, serving with distinction during the war.[103]

II. Surrendering the Frontier

Since the early 1800s, the army and its mounted forces had been helping protect settlers, travelers, and Indians along the frontier as it expanded ever westward. Since its creation in 1855, the 1st Cavalry had patrolled the frontier out of Fort Leavenworth, Kansas Territory; helped maintain and garrison the series of forts in the Oklahoma Indian Territory; and established new forts farther west. By 1861, they served in a 600-mile-wide arc from Fort Wise, in the southeast corner of Colorado, through the Oklahoma Indian Territory to Fort Smith on the Arkansas border, patrolling thousands of square miles of the western frontier. It was an incredibly hard and challenging life in hostile and dangerous territory that would demand much of the men who dedicated themselves to their flag and country. Performing the tasks asked of them by their government, they were only vaguely aware that the United States was coming apart. But that awareness was sudden and swift, as Texas joined the exodus of states seceding from the Union, unleashing pro-secession rebellion across the entire frontier. The growing hostility by those they had risked their lives to protect stunned the soldiers. The division of loyalties, once unspoken among the officers and men, was now in the open and a source of great sadness and anger to many. Their leadership and command structure was dissolving before their eyes. For the men who had committed their lives and loyalties to the rigid discipline of the military, it had to have had a demoralizing effect. With all this, they were suddenly faced with the reality that their position was untenable, and they would have to abandon not only the forts, but also the territories and people, including the Indians, that they had protected for so many years with so many sacrifices.

The events in the East leading up to secession absorbed most of the attention of Washington and the military command. Isolated from the "States" by distance and time, those in service on the frontier were totally unprepared for what was about to happen. The early months of 1861 found genial conversations turning into heated debates. Sides were slowly being taken as the unthinkable became more and more possible: the idea of open rebellion against the government and the possibility of the military firing on its citizens and soldiers firing on their own. "Was there really some foundation for the war rumors that sometimes appeared in the newspapers?" writes Sergeant Larson. "Was it possible that the North and South would ever go to war about the Negroes? It was not known that any of the officers believed it and, among the men, the idea was laughed at as a joke." However, as Larson continues, by the end of 1860, "war talk had ceased to be mere rumors. South Carolina had really seceded from the Union. The war rumors, which we far away on the frontiers had laughed at and joked about, had by that time reached maturity."[1] News from the States—sporadic at best—was brought by the occasional traveler or the infrequent monthly mail. In any case, for the military units disbursed among the outlying forts of the western frontier, the news arrived thirty days or more after the actual event and rumors were rampant. "All good fellowship and confidence in one another had disappeared."[2] "Some of the officers . . . at no little sacrifice, cast their lots with the seceded states, breaking close, tender and cherished ties of comradeship, and severing their connection with a service they revered and honored."[3]

Captain Jeb Stuart, who had volunteered in 1859 to serve as aide to Robert E. Lee in the attack on the abolitionist John Brown at Harper's Ferry, "declared that his interest was with the South, all that he possessed in the world was in the South, as well as his family and friends, and he could not fight against it."[4] According to Sergeant Larson, "he acted honorably. He made a plain statement to both officers and men of the position he was in and did not try to work on anybody else's mind or induce men to take his view of the matter," as some other officers had.[5] Stuart would rise to the rank of major general, Confederate States of America (CSA). He was mortally wounded leading his Confederate cavalry in battle at Yellow Tavern, May 11, 1864, "after he had emptied his pistol while firing at the Union cavalry."[6]

For the actions of others, there was bitterness and contempt. Larson recounts the actions of "another officer, a captain of infantry [at Fort Wise], whose name was pronounced nearly like Jeb's but spelled Steward, who was as guilty of treason as the historical Arnold."

> There he stood before us, wearing the uniform of an officer in the United States Army, calling the President a damn black abolitionist and other such names, and telling us how the South had been imposed on by the Northern or black republican states. ... [He] would not fight for a black republican President, and we need not do it either. He was going to leave in a day and would take as many of us along as wanted to go.[7]

Of the thirty-four officers who were with the 1st US Cavalry in January 1861, eighteen would resign their commissions by year's end. While most left to join the Confederacy, still others would take appointments in the United States Volunteers in hope of higher commissions and commands.

Texas Secedes

The Army in the West found itself responding to ever increasing threats. Southern sentiment ran high in Texas and the Western Territories, and it soon became apparent that the United States Army had a greater problem on its hands than the Indians. In most cases, there was no possibility of actually defending the forts in case of open hostilities. By spring, the army began moving and consolidating its surplus supplies and commissary stores—tempting targets for the pro-secessionists. Even the Indian Nations were taking sides; on 7 February, the Choctaw Nation—themselves slaveholders—declared its adherence to the Southern states. When Texas became the seventh state to secede from the Union on February 1, 1861, pro-Southern sentiment swept rapidly across the Western frontier, pushing out all Union representation in its wake. Brigadier and Brevet Major General David E. Twiggs, USA, commanded the Department of Texas at the outbreak of hostilities. A Georgian from a distinguished military family, he was one of the four highest ranking general officers of the line on the army roster, which included Major General Winfield Scott, who was nearing the end of his career. Headquartered at San Antonio and sympathetic to the Southern cause, Twiggs allowed himself to fall into negotiations with Southern sympathizers in an attempt to avoid bloodshed. He had resolved never to fire upon American citizens and, unable to reconcile his duties as a soldier with his belief in the states' right of secession, he requested that he be relieved of his command, but his relief arrived too late.[8] Greatly outnumbered by secessionist militia, he surrendered his entire command to General Ben McCulloch on February 19, 1861, an action that shocked the nation. He had surrendered "the whole army, munitions of war, and all the forts, arsenals, arms, military stores, and general property within his department... almost five sixths of the whole army and field batteries of the nation."[9] Branded a traitor, Twiggs was dismissed from the army by President James Buchanan. He returned to his home state of Georgia, where he died in July 1862. On March 16, 1861, Colonel Edwin Voss Sumner, 1st US Cavalry, was promoted to brigadier general to temporarily replace Twiggs.[10]

Open Rebellion on the Frontier

By the end of March, Union forces in Texas had abandoned fifteen frontier forts and installations. As the rebellion grew into open warfare, April and May were to be difficult months for the Federal forces in the Indian Territories, as they were forced to withdraw in the face of now-hostile citizens. "After five arduous years of fighting Indians in Texas, the troopers of the 2nd (later 5th) US Cavalry found themselves being jeered and threatened by the very folk whose lives and property they had done so much to protect."[11] The 2nd Cavalry "was about to be driven out... discarded by those who ought to have been their friends."[12] In March 1861, six companies of the 2nd Cavalry "boarded steamships at Indianola, Texas, bound for New York City." Farther to the north, the 1st Cavalry evacuated Forts Smith, Cobb, Gibson, Arbuckle, and Washita: "just barely evading a force of Texans sent to seize its arms and horses. The 3rd Infantry also made good its escape, but the whole 8th Infantry was caught (though later exchanged)."[13] Events began to accelerate. On April 15, President Lincoln, having taken office in March, called for 75,000 ninety-day volunteers to suppress the Southern rebellion. On the 21st, the U.S. Arsenal at Liberty, Missouri—about fifteen miles northeast of Kansas City—was seized. On the 22nd and 23rd, the Federal Arsenal at Fayetteville, North Carolina, was taken by North Carolina troops. The Arkansas governor refuses to send troops to support the Union. Secessionist feelings were so strong in Arkansas that Washington was making plans to withdraw all Union representation from that state as early as February 1861.[14] Pro-Confederate sentiment was spreading north across the Texas border, through Arkansas and into Missouri, in a violent effort to gain the latter for the Confederacy. Lieutenant Colonel Emory, commanding 1st US Cavalry and now the senior army officer in the Territories, began to consolidate the remaining elements of the army in preparation for abandoning the forts and leaving Oklahoma Indian Territory.

The Companies of the 1st United States Cavalry

February 1861 found the companies of the regiment disbursed across the Western frontier and Indian Territories as follows: Fort Wise, Colorado Territory, was the Regimental Headquarters, with Companies F, G, H, and K, Lieutenant Albert Colburn, Regimental Adjutant, commanding; Companies C and I were posted at Fort Washita; Companies A and B were at Fort Arbuckle; and Companies D and E were at Fort Smith, Arkansas, Captain Samuel D. Sturgis commanding. Sturgis would supervise the evacuation of Fort Smith in April. As the senior captain in the regiment, he would be promoted to major in May.[15] Captain Stanley, in command of the 1st Cavalry companies in the field, refused to be bound "by the dishonored act" of Brigadier General Twiggs:

> Withdrawing Companies D and E from Fort Smith, Arkansas, he gathered the regiment at the three supporting posts of Arbuckle, Washita, and Wise and defended his honor, and the flag of his country, during the months of March and April against, not only the hostile arms, but the more dangerous seductions of the emissaries of the insurgents.[16]

Promoted to captain, Co. C, in March, Stanley would play a prominent role in the evacuation of Federal forces from the frontier forts. By June, Companies B, C, D, and I were at Fort Leavenworth under his command; they would spend the rest of 1861 fighting rebel forces in Missouri, helping to defend and eventually save that state for the Union. Stanley would be promoted to brigadier general, volunteers, in September, leaving his regiment for the duration of the war.[17]

By orders of March 18, Lieutenant Colburn, Companies G and K, Regimental Headquarters, and Quartermaster were to transfer from Fort Wise to Fort Washita.[18]

Fort Washita was abandoned by Lieutenant Colonel Emory on April 16, and these orders were not carried out. According to the monthly reports, Companies G and K left Fort Wise in November 1861; they were reported "in the field" through December, on their way to Fort Leavenworth, where they remained until February 1862.[19] Meanwhile, Lieutenant Colburn was transferred to Staff, Army of the Potomac, and would have his only field command during the war, leading a squadron of the 1st Regiment, Companies A and E, in the first major battle of the Civil War (Bull Run) July 21, 1861.[20]

Once the "Great Rebellion" was underway, there was a further delay in the redeployment of the United States Army in the West while militia-type units were raised to replace the regular army. Corporal James Larson remained in Colorado Territory with Companies F and H. The men of these two "unfortunate companies" were "very disgusted" at being left with the sole responsibility for Fort Wise and "taking care of Uncle Sam's Indians." There were over 4,000 Indians camped near the post and "a large quantity of supplies of all kinds stored in the post."[21] Captain Newby, Company H, was post commander and John A. Thompson, commanding Company F, was second in command.[22] Thompson—promoted to captain in May—would be transferred to Co. K July 1. In May 1861, the squadron was transferred to Fort Kearney, Nebraska Territory, to protect the Oregon Trail. They remained through May 1862, when they were transferred to Fort Laramie, Nebraska Territory.[23] It was not until May 1863 that they would finally receive the long-awaited orders to join their regiment in the Western Theater.

Lieutenant Colonel William H. Emory, 1st U.S. Cavalry

Lieutenant Colonel Emory is credited with being the "only officer to bring an entire command out of insurrectionary territory..."[24] Born in Maryland, he graduated fourteenth in his class from the United States Military Academy at West Point in 1831. He resigned his commission in 1836 to work as a civil engineer but returned to the army in 1838 with the topographical engineers. Emory gained a reputation for his 1848 publication *Notes of a Military Reconnaissance*, which was "considered one of the important chronicles and descriptions of the Southwest, especially for its maps."[25] In March 1855, Emory accepted a commission as major in the newly formed 2nd Cavalry, transferring to the 1st Cavalry in May. Promoted to lieutenant colonel in January 1861, he became the temporary commander of the 1st Cavalry when newly appointed Colonel Robert E. Lee resigned his commission. He also became the senior officer in command in the Oklahoma Indian Territories with responsibility for all Union troops, property, and interests of the United States, including Indian relations.

Instructions from Washington were sporadic and contradictory. As early as February 13, orders had been issued to the Department of the West to abandon Fort Smith, "as the authorities of the State of Arkansas have seized the public property."[26] These orders were subsequently countermanded by Commanding General Winfield Scott on February 22.[27] On March 13, while in Washington, Emory had been ordered to "take post at Fort Cobb," an order countermanded on the 18th when he was ordered to concentrate the regiment at Fort Washita and establish his headquarters there. He was given: "discretionary power to concentrate at or in the vicinity of the post two companies of cavalry and five of infantry, now at Fort Arbuckle and Fort Cobb, in addition to the two companies of cavalry already at Fort Washita."[28] Left with vague orders and "large discretion," Emory began his long journey back to Fort Washita sometime during the middle of March.[29] He was delayed several days, as the water in the Arkansas River had fallen, making it "difficult to procure transportation of any kind."[30] The river was also the main trade route for military supplies and would soon be controlled by rebel forces. Upon his return to Fort Washita, Emory supervised the consolidation of troops and the eventual evacuations of Forts Washita, Arbuckle, and Cobb; Captain Sturgis would evacuate Fort Smith. The urgency was evident, not only by the activities of the secessionists, but by the fact there were only enough provisions to last through May and, as he pointed out to Washington, it was unlikely rebel forces would allow more after that.[31]

With his discretionary command, Emory found himself in the position of anticipating and reacting to circumstances rather than responding to orders once he returned to the frontier. There were no contingency plans to follow. He also had to consider the fate of the Indians currently under Federal jurisdiction, but he must have known there was nothing the Federal government could do to further protect the Indians under their care.[32] From Fort Smith on April 6, Emory ordered the commanding officer at Fort Cobb to keep two companies at the fort until further notice. Ten days later, Emory abandoned Fort Washita and began the evacuation of all Union troops and personnel to Fort Leavenworth. The unusual circumstances and responsibilities of his situation were apparently taking their toll. Having returned to Fort Smith, the Lieutenant Colonel made a curious and insightful plea in a communiqué dated April 13 to the Assistant Adjutant-General, Headquarters U.S. Army:

> Owing to the turn affairs have recently taken, the position of an officer from a Southern State out here on duty has become extremely embarrassing; so much so as to impair his efficiency. Therefore, I urgently request I may be allowed to turn over this command, with my instructions, to Major Sackett, or such other officer as may be selected, and that I may be permitted to return to Washington City where I can explain my reasons for the step. If those reasons should prove unsatisfactory, I am prepared to resign my commission.
>
> I respectfully suggest it has never been the policy of any government to employ officers to operate against their own section of country.[33]

An explanation of these circumstances is found in David Stanley's autobiography. He wrote that it was believed by the senior officers present that Lt.

Colonel Emory and his wife were "extremely intimate" with Jefferson and Mrs. Davis, with whom he had visited during his recent trip east. As a Southerner, Emory's loyalties were suspect, and his officers at that time had "no confidence" in him.[34]

Over the next six weeks, under Emory's command, the Union Army evacuated the frontier. On or about April 13, Emory left Fort Smith for Forth Washita. The command at Fort Arbuckle, which included Companies A and B, was also on the move toward Fort Washita. On April 16, Emory evacuated Fort Washita with Companies C and I and moved in the direction of Fort Arbuckle to consolidate with Companies A and B and the infantry at Fort Cobb. On the 17th, Emory received orders he had already acted on—to withdraw all Union forces under his command to Ft. Leavenworth.[35] Fort Washita was occupied by Texan forces that same day. On April 23, Captain Sturgis evacuated Fort Smith with Companies D and E and met up with Emory in the field.[36] Here may have occurred one of the earliest captures of rebel troops. Sturgis had been alerted to the fact that "some 250 Texas troopers (former neighbors)" had been sent by the governor of the state "to demand possession of the post" and capture his arms and horses.[37] As reported by Lieutenant James E. Powell, 1st Infantry, who was with Captain Sturgis at Fort Smith, Sturgis apparently surprised and captured this Rebel force on the evening of the 23rd, "as they were eating dinner."[38] Since it was impractical to take the prisoners to Kansas, much less feed them, they were "immediately paroled" after Union soldiers "shaved the tails of their horses" as a humiliation, as the only possible revenge.[39] Two hours after the Union forces abandoned Fort Smith, "a body of troops" representing the State of Arkansas took possession.[40] The Arkansas Legislature voted for secession on May 7.

On May 3, Emory's command joined Companies A and B in the field about five miles from Fort Arbuckle, which was occupied by Rebel forces on May 5.[41] The Federal troops gathered near what is today Minco, Oklahoma, "to head north" to Fort Leavenworth.[42]

On May 9, Emory "found the command from Cobb (two companies on foot) thirty-five miles northeast of the post and took the most direct course to Leavenworth that the nature of the ground would permit."[43]

This arduous effort, combined with the stress generated by the sudden fracture of the nation to which these officers had sworn an allegiance, must have put a severe strain on Emory, leaving him physically and emotionally exhausted. It appears that on or about May 9, he made a rash decision to resign his commission.

He wrote his resignation letter "sent from Indian Country" and "placed in the hands of a friend," apparently to be taken to the nearest telegraph office.[44] He almost immediately regretted his action and made several futile attempts to recall the resignation by telegraph. These messages to Washington apparently never went through and, upon arrival at Emporia, Kansas, Emory learned his resignation had been accepted.[45]

Emory's command was led by an Indian guide named Black Beaver, and the path he took would become known as the Chisholm Trail after the war.[46] "The train was nearly a mile in length," consisting of "6 companies of the 1st Cavalry and 5 of the 1st Infantry, numbering 820 men, besides about 200 teamsters."[47] There were several ambulances carrying 150 women and children and "about eighty wagons containing army stores." About six hundred horses and mules followed the soldiers.[48] On May 31, Lt. Colonel William Emory completed his last assignment with the 1st Regiment US Cavalry and safely delivered all Union troops and civilians under his command to Fort Leavenworth. In his last communiqué as commanding officer of the 1st United States Cavalry, he wrote:

> I arrived here this morning, and turned over the command to Major Sackett in good condition; not a man, an animal, an arm, or wagon has been lost except two deserters.

He signed the dispatch: "W. H. Emory, *Late* Lieutenant-Colonel First Cavalry."[49]

Without taking time to bid farewell to his personal staff, Colonel Emory left immediately for Washington to personally appeal his resignation to the Secretary of War and the President.[50] Meanwhile, Mrs. Emory made a personal appeal to President Lincoln but was turned down.[51] According to Stanley, it was only after the officers of the 1st US Cavalry—apparently now satisfied with his loyalty—submitted a petition requesting Emory's reinstatement and, along with careful examination of the circumstances by the War Department, that it was determined to restore him to the army. Congress enacted legislation to increase the size of the Regular army, including one new Cavalry Regiment (the 6th), which was "temporarily entrusted to Lt. Colonel Emory."[53] It was deemed "inexpedient" to return Emory to the 1st Cavalry as "promotions had already taken place."[52] William Emory served his flag and his country with distinction during the war. He was appointed brigadier general, Volunteers, and was assigned to command the First Brigade of the newly created Cavalry Division, Army of the Potomac, in March 1862. He would be promoted to major general, volunteers, and was appointed commanding officer, 5th Cavalry, in October 1863, retiring as a brigadier general, USA in July 1876.[54]

Historian Bruce Catton attempts to explain the attitude of the government with regard to Texas and the Indian Territories prior to the declared outbreak of war:

> It is mildly interesting to note that the Federal government actually had much more at stake in Texas than it had at Fort Sumter; 2600 soldiers and a whole chain of army installations, as opposed to seventy soldiers and one unfinished fort. Logically it would seem if a stand were to be made, San Antonio rather than Charleston would be the place to make it. But Washington was marking time. It consented to the loss of Texas . . .[55]

In May 1861, the First Regiment US Cavalry lost nine of its officers to the Confederacy, including Jeb Stuart. Captain James McIntosh, Co. D, resigned to become a colonel in the Confederate Army. Both he and Stuart had been with the regiment since its formation in March 1855.[56] As previously mentioned, many of these former comrades in arms would meet in combat on a number of occasions over the next four years. One of the earliest of these confrontations would come in August 1861. McIntosh—a Floridian—had accepted a colonelcy in the Confederate forces and led a mounted rifle regiment against his former comrades, including Major Samuel Sturgis, commanding, and Captain Eugene Carr, Co. I. The incident occurred at the early skirmish at Dug Springs, Missouri, between elements of the 1st Cavalry and the rebel forces:

> As the 1st Cavalry drew near the enemy in a column of fours, one of the troopers whistled and gasped, "My God, boys, that's Captain McIntosh." At that moment, the new captain commanded a set of fours to dismount and fire their new Sharps carbines at McIntosh's party. The order was instantly obeyed, but the bullets went whistling harmlessly through the tree limbs high above their intended targets. Taking off his hat, the popular McIntosh bowed low to his old command and galloped out of range.[57]

In January 1862, McIntosh was promoted to brigadier general, CSA. "Popular with his troops, he was known as an aggressive and daring, yet alert and loyal officer." He was killed at the Battle of Pea Ridge, Arkansas, on March 7, 1862. McIntosh's brother, John B. McIntosh, became a brigadier general in the Union Army, losing a leg in battle.[58]

In many military families, these difficult decisions would haunt for a lifetime. In 1855, a young Jeb Stuart had married Flora Cooke at Fort Riley, Kansas. She was the daughter of General Philip St. George Cooke, the senior cavalry officer in the army who remained loyal to the Union. They would face each other on the battlefield.[59] The Virginia family of Major General George H. Thomas, USA, never spoke of him or to him for the rest of his life, even refusing to attend his state funeral in Troy, New York, in 1870. His sisters told their neighbors, "Our brother died to us in '61."[60]

Feelings on both sides ran long and deep. In 1886, Captain Joseph Vale, 7th Pennsylvania Volunteer Cavalry, wrote a history of his cavalry brigade, including the 4th United States Cavalry Regiment. He addressed what he considered the "flagrant, inexcusable treachery of so many of the officers in the regular army of the United States" who joined the Confederacy:[61]

> These men, in utter disregard of every principle, not only of patriotism, but as well of every sense of honor, and with the oath of supreme allegiance to the Government yet trembling upon their perjured lips, turned their swords against the very nation which had generously educated and lavishly supported them; and, using the opportunities offered by the positions to which they had been assigned, as the sworn guardians of the national territory, arms, and public property,

betrayed in one fell sweep their own honor, their entrusted stations, their confiding subalterns and dependent men; and drew their swords as patricides against the father which had begotten and nurtured them.[62]

The "Service School of the Plains"

Of all those who fought in the Civil War, the men of the Regular Army and Cavalry had a distinct advantage in training and experience, as opposed to those who volunteered, or were subsequently conscripted. Their experience was invaluable during the Civil War years, when bivouacs (camps in the wild) and military camps were temporary affairs, hastily assembled and offering only basic amenities for the troopers. The Regular Army, out of long experience:

> had fashioned a lengthy set of regulations for maintaining the health of men in the field. These required strict cleanliness in living quarters and food-preparation areas; personal bathing and regular airing of tents and bedding; careful placement and use of latrines and garbage pits, with daily applications of earth and chloride of lime; and protection of the purity of water supplies. The volunteer units generally had no such experience, or training and if their officers did not understand or like the rules, they ignored them.[63] . . . It took years for some regiments to grasp the fact that sickness might be reduced–and the potability of their water greatly enhanced – if they stopped locating their trench latrines upstream of camp. . . . An inspector in late 1861 found most Federal camps 'littered with refuse, food and other rubbish, sometimes in an offensive state of decomposition; slops deposited in pits within the camp limits or thrown out broadcast; heaps of manure and offal close to the camp.'[64]
>
> . . . [F]lies, lice and fleas swarmed all over the camps . . . bacteria and viruses carried to the soldier by insects. The carelessness compounded by ignorance led to devastating epidemics of dysentery and typhoid fever.[65]
>
> . . . Just as widespread, though less often fatal, was malaria.[66]

Men—mostly from rural areas—had rarely congregated in large groups in confined spaces and relatively few had been exposed to common urban communicable diseases; measles, chickenpox, mumps, and whooping cough were easily contracted by these men.[67] Six times as many died of disease than of wounds received in battle.[68] All of this helps to explain why the men of the Regular Army initially had such disdain for the Volunteers.

It was generally accepted that it took two years' experience to create a "seasoned" cavalry soldier. Once the nation was plunged into war, it was unprepared for the massive influx of men into the service, and many went into combat with as little as two weeks training. Many of the new volunteer cavalry recruits:

> went off to war with such poor riding skills that they often fell off their horses the first time they rode into battle. It would take many months of duty, including combat in which many of them would die, for these former civilians to become veteran soldiers who truly understood how to do the job effectively . . .

Assuming the unhealthy conditions of the outdoor environment and the unsanitary living conditions in camp didn't kill them first:[69]

> The experience gained in the twelve years from 1848 to 1860, in frequent encounters with the restless Indian tribes of the Southwest, the long marches over arid wastes, the handling of supply trains, the construction of military roads, the exercise of command, the treatment of cavalry horses and draught animals, and the numerous other duties falling to officers [and troopers] at frontier posts, far distant from railroad or telegraph, all tended to temper and sharpen the blades that were to point the 'path of glory' to thousands destined to ride under the war-guidons of Sheridan, Stuart, Buford, Pleasonton, Fitzhugh Lee, Stanley, Wilson, Merritt, Gregg and other graduates of *the service school of the Plains* [emphasis author].[70]

Major Albert Brackett wrote in his *History of the United States Cavalry*, published in 1865, that the frontier experience "made them true soldiers, than whom there were no better on earth."[71] Cavalry historian Don Caughey writes:

> ... When not actively campaigning against the Indians, many hours and days were spent in small unit drills that enhanced teamwork and obedience to orders from superiors. They returned from the frontier accustomed to a life governed by Army regulations and the articles of war. They were *trained and disciplined soldiers with high morale* [emphasis author].

When new recruits were brought into these regiments—as compared to those going into volunteer units—they had the advantage of receiving training from experienced cadres of officers and sergeants. They also had the additional pressure of living up to the history and reputation of their regiments.[72]

Twenty-Two Future Generals

It is strong testament to the old 1st Regiment United States Cavalry that "the military aptitude of the officers selected for the First (now 4th) Cavalry was conclusively proven in the Civil War when twenty-two of them became general officers": eleven for the North and eleven for the South [see Appendix B].[73]

III. The Federal Cavalry at the Beginning of the Civil War

It has often been written that Regular Cavalry forces could have been of valuable service in the early days of the Civil War if they were readily available, but they were not. As previously discussed, the companies of cavalry regiments were distributed throughout the frontier outposts west of the Mississippi.[1] When the War began, the Union had fewer than 4,000 cavalry soldiers and was severely handicapped by the resignation of some of its most experienced soldiers.[2] The *Abstract from Returns of the U. S. Army, December 31, 1860* reveals some interesting facts about the state of the United States Cavalry as of that date:

	Present	Absent	Total
Officers	82	100	182
Men	3,123	482	3,605
Aggregate	3,205	582	3,787[3]

As analyzed by Don Caughey:

> The returns for the cavalry include all five mounted regiments and those working at the general recruiting depots. . . . Even setting aside anyone who might have been stationed at one of the depots or schools, the regiments are badly shorthanded. Quick division renders the numbers to 16 officers and 624 enlisted men per regiment, and one officer and 62 enlisted men per company. The same return lists 100 officers and 482 enlisted men as absent, for an aggregate of 582. This breaks down to 20 officers and 96 enlisted men per regiment, and two officers and nine enlisted men per company.[4]

These numbers generally reflect the roster of the 4th (formerly 1st) US Cavalry during most of the Civil War.

At the outbreak of war, four of the five colonels commanding the mounted regiments resigned from the army and the regiments lost half of their senior command to the Confederacy. West Point could not graduate enough second lieutenants in 1861 to account for all the resignations; therefore, many vacancies were filled with appointees from civil life. As a result, the US Cavalry was "saddled with a large proportion of green and untested subalterns who would have to learn their profession while practicing it—a factor that was to seriously hamper its performance over the next two years."[5] Since the 4th Cavalry was on the frontier when the war broke out and was involved in some of the earliest fighting in Missouri, the few civilian appointees—some with prior military service in the infantry or cavalry—adapted quickly, and several would go on to have distinguished military careers after the war. As will be shown, the majority of new officers in the regiment came from field promotions of senior enlisted men.

While troopers in the Regular Army were not permitted to resign, it is possible that some who deserted during the first year of the war may well have joined the Confederate Army.

Desertion remained a continuous problem; there were a reported 132 desertions in the 4th US Cavalry for the year 1861.[6] Adding to the problem of attrition, a number of senior enlisted men, sergeants, and first sergeants did not reenlist in the Regular Army at the end of their terms, instead enlisting in volunteer regiments for a commission, bonus, or higher pay. As a consequence, there was a continual shortage of men, especially in the 4th Cavalry—the only Regular Army cavalry regiment in the Western Theater.

Once the need for additional cavalry regiments was recognized, the Federal government depended on the individual states to organize the hundreds of volunteer cavalry regiments that were created. Unfortunately, the six regiments of Regulars were "swamped and lost in a deluge of volunteer mounted regiments" that brought the strength of the Union cavalry to about "54,000 by the end of 1861."[7] "Recruiting for Regular Army units was extremely difficult in the face of state competition. Bounties offered by Federal officers were met and exceeded by the states."[8] Further hampering the development of an effective cavalry unit was the expense in equipping the cavalry soldier—much greater than that for the infantryman—and it took considerably longer to train the cavalryman and his mount.[9] "Equipment for a mounted regiment of 1,200 cost over $300,000 and the pay scale for cavalry personnel was higher than that of infantry."[10]

It would take two years of trial and error for the Federal bureaucracy to overcome these obstacles and for the military command in the field to recognize the real value of a strong, unified cavalry force. By war's end, the ranks of the cavalry would swell to over 272,000 men—almost ten percent of the Federal Army.[11] "A total of 250 cavalry regiments plus 170 independent cavalry troops, which were usually employed by individual states to guard important communication and supply centers," were created by volunteer and state militia.[12]

The rule of service in the Union Army during the first two years of the war was to assign one or more regiments of cavalry to each division of infantry for such duties as the division commander might order; the regiments were then broken down by companies for various duties. The 4th Cavalry was no exception; its companies were scattered from the Mississippi River to the Atlantic coast. These assignments included the traditional cavalry missions of reconnaissance and screening, as well as the more mundane functions as orderlies, messengers, and escorts for general officers, guards for division wagon trains, and pickets (guards) to protect the front of infantry lines.[13] "Cavalry officers looked with despair on their shattered squadrons and submitted in disgust to the disintegration."[14] Philip Sheridan, who would command the cavalry in the Eastern Theater, learned early on that "a brigade commanded by a colonel was liable to find itself chewed into message-bearing platoons by a major general of division."[15] In his early commands, Sheridan "fought bitterly against having his cavalry used as wagon guards as foot soldiers could do that work perfectly well."[16] "Accustomed to traveling quickly, the escort duty that troopers hated the most was to plod alongside wagons being pulled slowly by draft horses or mules." A more dangerous assignment was serving as videttes—mounted sentries who patrolled camp perimeters to prevent surprise attacks. "They were often a mile or more beyond their lines, which meant they were vulnerable to attack, including assaults by sharpshooters, who fired from hundreds of yards away."[17] As one cavalryman recounted:

> We go out upon our shivering horses to sit in the saddle for two hours or more, facing the biting wind, and peering through the storm of sleet, snow, or rain, which unmercifully pelts us in its fury. But it were well for us if this was our worst enemy, and we consider ourselves happy if the [enemy] does not creep through the bushes impenetrable to the sight to inflict his mortal blows.[18]

They also became easy prey for any rebel cavalryman needing a new mount.

> [Union] infantrymen commonly regarded the cavalry as playboys who roamed the country at will, leaving to foot soldiers the mud, misery, and peril." A typical comment was written by an infantryman while the army was en route from Mississippi to Chattanooga in 1863: "We have considerable cavalry with us but they are the laughing stock of the army and the boys poke all kinds of fun at them.

I really have as yet to see or hear of their doing anything of much credit to them.[19]

Historian Bruce Catton sums up the general attitude toward the Union cavalry during the first two years of the war:

> . . . cavalry in the Civil War was actually of secondary importance as far as fighting was concerned. It was essential for scouting and for screening an army, but as a combat arm it was declining. Cavalry skirmished frequently with other cavalry, and the skirmishes at times rose to the level of pitched battles, but it fought infantry only rarely. It enjoyed vast prestige with the press and with back-home civilians, but neither infantry nor artillery admired it. The commonest infantry wisecrack during the early years of the war was the bitter question: 'Who ever saw a dead cavalryman?'[20]

The Horse

At the beginning of the war, the South had the advantage over Northerners in the cavalry. "Southerners–many of them aristocrats bred in the gentlemanly tradition of horsemanship–[readily] adapted to the duties of mounted warfare . . ."[21] From rural Southern farm boys to the chivalry of the gentlemen farmers, "it seemed much more knightly and gallant to go off to war on horseback than in the infantry."[22] The great majority of Northern volunteers—laborers, tradesmen, and storekeepers—had never been on a horse and "it never occurred to a Northern farm boy that he could acquire social prestige simply by getting on a horse's back."[23] The inexperience of the volunteer cavalrymen and the demands that war placed on the horses took an extremely heavy toll on the animals. The simple novice mistake of allowing an overheated horse to drink too much and then cool down immediately after a long march could ruin the animal:[24]

> Troopers used the term *marching* to refer to riding, and the cavalry was always marching somewhere. Troopers marched at different gaits–the speed their horses moved. At a walk, cavalry could cover four miles an hour; at a slow trot, six miles; at a maneuvering trot, eight miles; and at an extended gallop, sixteen miles. Troopers usually rode thirty-five miles in an eight hour day, but they could cover seventy or eighty miles in twenty-four hours.[25]

During the war, cavalry raiding expeditions would greatly exceed these times and distance, to the limits of endurance of both horse and rider.

The care and feeding of the trooper's horse was perhaps his most important duty, "a task that became the credo of the cavalry: 'Take care of your horse before you take care of yourself.'"[26] As described by a Union trooper, it was a lot of additional work:

> The company must first put up the picket rope [for horses] and then the horse must be watered, fed and groomed. Then [the trooper] unsaddles, gets his coffee, and is ready to lie down an hour after the infantryman is asleep. In the morning, if the cavalry are to move at the same hour [as] the infantry they must have reveille an hour earlier than the infantry, to have time to feed, groom and saddle their horses.[27]

Caring for the horses "was far more complex than giving them food and water," especially under combat conditions, where troopers depended on their horses for survival: "a weak or sick horse increased the odds they (the trooper) could be killed."[28] Particular attention had to be paid to the horse's back to prevent sores, as well as their feet. The regimental farriers and blacksmiths were continuously dealing with maintaining the proper shoeing of the hundreds of horses in their care. Troopers were required to carry at least two fitted shoes "so the farrier will have nothing to do but nail them on" in case any were lost while marching.[29] It was the continual responsibility of the sergeants, 1st sergeants, and officers of a cavalry company to ensure that the horses were properly maintained. These responsibilities greatly intensified when on the march. Troopers in the field had to forage for their mounts. "Horses required about ten pounds of grain or hay each day . . . and it was impossible to carry those supplies on long trips," much less during the cavalry raids that became more prominent during the last years of the war.[30] These raids, covering great distances, would take a huge toll on the horses.

The loss of his horse could be a very distressing event for a trooper on a number of levels. Many cavalrymen developed a strong bond with their mount. In battle, especially during a charge, the horse and rider had to be of one mind. There was also a certain level of pride in the horse one rode. In the early months of the war, some volunteer cavalry regiments actually went so far as to have all horses the same color, but this quickly gave way to reality. To be dismounted took a trooper out of action, as Private James Wiswell, Co. C, discovered when a shell struck his horse during a cavalry charge, "tearing him into two parts." Wiswell was thrown to the ground uninjured. "I was sorry that I lost my horse," he wrote, "for it is not every horse that I would ride going into battle and furthermore the position of a trooper dismounted is not very enviable.... [W]hen the Co. goes away on a scout if I do not get a sick man's horse I stay behind and when we move camp I ride a mule."[31]

It would take months for the Federal Quartermaster Department to establish the six remount depots required, organize the logistics of procurement, and forage for the millions of horses used during the war. "The wastage during this time was fabulous. About 284,000 horses were furnished to never more than 60,000 men in the field, which was an average of about five horses per man..."[32] For the fiscal year ending June 30, 1864, "the government bought or captured a total of 210,000 horses to supply the army's need for 500 fresh horses a day."[33] The continual need for new mounts would become the Achilles heel of the Confederate Cavalry. By the last year of the war, there were simply no more horses available for the South.

The Accoutrements

In the early months of the Civil War, "the cavalry on both sides was compact, slow-moving, heavily accoutered, usually operating with the infantry." Both men and horses "suffered terribly from the weight of the extra baggage" that was initially required to be carried.[34] Strapped and strung over his clothes, the trooper carried:

> a big saber and metal scabbard four feet long, an Austrian rifle or a heavy revolver, a box of cartridges, a tin canteen for water, a haversack [cloth bag] containing rations, a tin coffee cup, and such other devices and [items] as were recommended to his fancy as useful or beautiful.[35]

From the recollections of a trooper in 1861:

> Myself, saddle, bridle, saddle blanket, curry comb, horse brush, coffee pot, tin cup, 20 lbs ham, 200 biscuits, 5 lbs. ground coffee, 5 lbs. sugar,... 6 shirts, 6 prs. socks, 3 prs. drawers, 2 prs. pants, 2 jackets, 1 pr. heavy mud boots, one Colt's revolver, one small dirk [dagger], four blankets, sixty feet of rope with a twelve inch iron pin attached [to tie horses to at night so they could graze]... and divers [sic] and sundry little mementos from friends.[36]

Troopers soon "learned from experience to cast off all unnecessary impediments."[37] "Clothing was reduced to an absolute minimum," and by 1863: "fancy uniforms were replaced by plain infantry pants, tunics and forage caps. Most cavalrymen managed to purchase or pilfer huge [pirate-like] boots into which they tucked their pants and pistols."[38] "A pair of blankets gave way to a single one... and it became a fine art to lessen the burden of the horse..."[39] Most troopers "packed a few personal items like Bibles, pictures of loved ones, and playing cards. One popular item was a 'housewife,' a small sewing kit with needle, thread, and buttons to repair clothes. The trick for the troopers was to carry as little as possible while still having everything they needed."[40]

The Evolution of Cavalry Organization and Tactics

At the beginning, no one knew how to fight this war, much less how to use cavalry effectively. Out of necessity, there was a complete evolution in its organization, use, and tactics during the Civil War. One of the earliest changes occurred on August 10, 1861, when Congress passed an act that joined the five mounted regiments—along with the newly created 6th Cavalry—into one corps to be known as "Cavalry." Regimental designations were changed in order of seniority; the 1st Cavalry, which was the fourth mounted regiment to be created, became the 4th Regiment United States Cavalry.[41] In addition, all of the mounted units were to adopt the yellow trim and cross saber insignia of the existing cavalry regiments, giving up their traditional uniforms and insignia.

This was a very unpopular decision among the three oldest regiments, because "it wiped out the time-honored regimental names with the romantic and historic history which had distinguished them."⁴²

The cavalry began as the orphan third branch of the United States Army, with little use other than as wagon guards, escorts, and a courier service. Its transformation into an effective fighting force equal to that of infantry came mostly from within. There was no single guiding force from Washington or within the military command of the Confederacy. In the extreme—as with Nathan Bedford Forrest—the Confederate cavalry functioned almost as an independent unit. Raised as volunteers and not bound to the military custom and tradition of European and US military academies, it adapted quickly as circumstances demanded and created its own rules and tactics with surprising success. This did not go unnoticed by the Federal cavalry. Union cavalry was slower to adapt, particularly in the Eastern Theater, which was more closely tied to the military traditions of the past. However, the independent spirit of the volunteers in the West—not too dissimilar to that of the South—allowed for a quicker evolutionary process. The 4th United States Cavalry, as a part of Brigadier General Robert Minty's Saber Brigade, would help rewrite traditional European cavalry doctrine and create a new, internationally recognized set of standards and tactics of mobile combat that would be used well into the twentieth century. After two years of training and practical experience in the field, "the horse soldiers began cutting loose from their base to destroy many communications and supplies."⁴³ The Federal cavalry evolved into a rapid, highly mobile fighting force that could savage the enemy's supplies and rail system and frustrate, disrupt, and demoralize the enemy's army.

For the first time in the history of warfare, railroads played a prominent role, not only in the rapid mobility and deployment of troops, but in the delivery of massive amounts of supplies needed by both armies. As a consequence, they became primary targets for the cavalry, who burned bridges, storage depots, and supplies. The cavalrymen ripped out telegraph lines, tore up railroad tracks, and "raided far behind the lines in attempts to keep the enemy so busy that he could apply only a part of his potential when battle was joined."⁴⁴

It was not until 1863 that the Federal cavalry made more than an indifferent showing in combat. On June 9, 1863, in the Eastern Theater, in the largest cavalry battle ever fought on the American continent, Union cavalry—numbering a little over 11,000—met a Confederate cavalry force of equal number. While the battle at Brandy Station (Beverly Ford), Virginia, ended in a draw, for the first time, the Union cavalry had checked their enemy.

By mid-1863, the Union cavalry "had gained the experience, organization, weapons, and remount service it needed, and from that time on its superiority grew steadily."⁴⁵ Learning from the Confederate cavalry, "Union commanders began to use their horses for swift mobility rather than for direct attacks, bringing their men close to the enemy and dismounting them for combat, with one man in each set of four acting as horse holder."⁴⁶ "Two years of training and fighting transformed the Federal cavalryman into a hardened and disciplined campaigner. The practical school of the picket and skirmish line forged volunteers into soldiers."⁴⁷

It has been said that the Confederacy had "the best cavalry leader in the entire war" in General Nathan Bedford Forrest. Unfettered by military tradition and gifted with a natural sense for combat strategy, "Forrest simply used his horsemen as a modern general would use motorized infantry."⁴⁸ He "brought a totally new concept to cavalry tactics and warfare. After the Battle of Shiloh he began employing cavalry as mounted foot soldiers–using horses to give his men maximum mobility, to close in on the enemy for surprise attacks."⁴⁹ As best described by Major General John K. Herr—"Last Chief of Cavalry"—in his 1953 *Story of the US Cavalry*, Forrest had a "primitive lust for personal combat combined with brilliant leadership and planning."⁵⁰ Forrest also understood the awful nature of warfare: to win at all cost. His famous motto summed up his tactic: "To be there first with the most." If he didn't have "the most," he would attack with a ferocity that could totally demoralize his enemy. He rewrote cavalry tactics and taught the Union by his example and successes how to use its mounted force effectively. Forrest's attitude may best be summed up by one of his peers, cavalry historian and Major, 1st Cavalry, Albert G. Brackett: *. . . without some little recklessness, cavalry can never accomplish anything* [emphasis Brackett's].⁵¹

"Soon after assuming command of the Army of the Potomac in the Eastern Theater, in January 1863, Major General Joseph Hooker authorized the formation of a Cavalry Corps. The various regiments and brigades scattered through the Army were combined into three divisions and placed in a separate command, a major step toward consolidation."⁵²

"For the first time the Union Army had a mobile strike force that could outnumber the Confederates."⁵³ In the Western Theater, Major General William S. Rosecrans created the Cavalry Corps of the Army of the Cumberland in January 1863, consolidating the cavalry under one command. He chose Captain David Stanley, 4th US Cavalry, to command his Cavalry Division.

Another Union cavalry improvement in 1863 was the establishment of a Cavalry Bureau; the chief was charged with organizing and equipping the cavalry forces and providing their mounts and remounts. He was also responsible for establishing depots for the reception of cavalry recruits and the collection and initial training of cavalry horses. The Giesboro Depot in the District of Columbia became the principal remount depot for the supply of the armies in the east; St. Louis and Nashville were the depots in the Mississippi Valley. It was a great failure of the Confederacy that their cavalry force was never as well organized and relied almost entirely on the individual cavalryman to supply his own mount.⁵⁴

As the efficiency of the cavalry force improved, the cavalryman now found himself "compelled to render service more frequent and more arduous than that asked of most infantrymen."⁵⁵ While the foot soldiers remained in camp for extended periods of time, "most troopers saw daily activity":

> When not engaged in battles or skirmishes, they rode in all directions, scouting, reconnoitering, demonstrating against enemy forces, carrying messages to headquarters, escorting field commanders, and clearing paths for movements by the main army. On the whole, they also saw more active fighting, in the form of minor engagements, outpost skirmishes, and patrol encounters, than the foot soldiers, who only occasionally took part in pitched battles.⁵⁶

Cavalry tactics "reached a peak of refinement in covering retreats. Units halted, dismounted, bushwhacked pursuing troops and then, remounting, repeated the process further down the line. Units demonstrated similar techniques and finesse in screening and reconnaissance operations."⁵⁷ A new and uniquely American system of strategy and tactics was developing.

The most unique, spectacular, and sought after cavalry mission was the raid, "one of the most important and most taxing" of assignments.⁵⁸ All major raids of the war were directed against lines of communication, railways, staging and production areas, and supply bases. As a frequent cavalry mission, the strategic raid was a new and far-reaching concept in warfare in the Western world.⁵⁹ "Troopers became raiders who boldly rode into enemy territory, attacking in unexpected, lightning-quick strikes that produced some of the war's most dramatic and memorable moments."⁶⁰

Army historian Mary Stubbs wrote: "Cavalry in the Union Army became a really effective force in 1864." Major General Philip H. Sheridan assumed command of the Cavalry Corps of the Army of the Potomac in April of that year and demanded the right to use the corps independently. "He proved that a large force of cavalry, properly organized and led, and acting as a unit, could be successful against either cavalry or infantry. Under Sheridan's leadership, the Union cavalry played a conspicuous part in numerous operations of 1864 and 1865."⁶¹ Ironically, Jeb Stuart's death at the Battle of Yellow Tavern, near Richmond, Virginia, in May 1864—against Union cavalry under Sheridan's command—would mark the turning point in the war for Union cavalry in the East. Confederate Major Henry B. McClellan—of Stuart's staff, and later Stuart's biographer—gave his evaluation of the Federal cavalry:

> From the time that the cavalry was concentrated into a corps until the close of the war, a steady progress was made in discipline. Nothing was spared to render this arm complete. Breech-loading arms of the most approved patterns were provided; horses and accouterments were never wanting and during the last year of the war Sheridan commanded as fine a body of troops as ever drew sabers.⁶²

The introduction of the seven-shot Spencer rifle, with its rapid fire and quick loading capability, combined with a fast-moving cavalry force that could charge, fight dismounted, and then remount to chase the enemy led the Union forces to victory in 1864-1865.

In the Western Theater, the role of the cavalry continued to expand under the guidance of

Rosecrans's successor, Major General George Thomas. By 1865, under Major General James H. Wilson, the Cavalry Corps became completely independent; in one of the largest cavalry raids of the Civil War—the Selma Campaign—Wilson's Cavalry Corps, with the 4th United States Cavalry as his escort, defeated and routed Nathan Bedford Forrest's Confederate Cavalry.

The Evolution of the 4th United States Cavalry

The 4th US Cavalry was composed of as gallant a body of officers and soldiers as ever mounted horse or drew saber . . .
–Brigadier General Robert H. G. Minty[63]

The contributions of the 4th United States Cavalry have long been overshadowed by events in the Eastern Theater and too long ignored by history. Operating in the homeland of the South (Tennessee, Mississippi, Alabama, and Georgia), the 4th US Cavalry fought the best cavalry the Confederacy had to offer under Forrest and Wheeler, and became one of the finest cavalry regiments of its time in the crucible of the Civil War. What distinguished it from the bulk of cavalry regiments was that the men brought to the battlefield the rigorous experience of the frontier, military discipline, and standards of command. They were skilled in horsemanship and cavalry tactics and, as will be shown, they brought the use of the saber to its maximum efficiency.

Compounding the loss of officers to the Confederacy, most of the remaining senior officers of the 4th U.S. were quickly pulled away on "detached service" to help organize and command the new volunteer cavalry units created by the states. Many of these men would rise in leadership to general officer. The burden of leadership in the 4th Cavalry fell on the remaining core of junior and noncommissioned officers. A significant number of new 2nd lieutenants would be appointed from among the enlisted ranks. Over the course of the war, no less than thirty-nine enlisted men received field commissions to 2nd lieutenant; thirty-one were promoted between May 1861 and November 1863. Of those, thirteen transferred to new assignments and eighteen remained with the regiment. They would be joined by one senior enlisted man, who transferred to the 4th Cavalry as a 2nd lieutenant in July 1862, and two other prior enlisted men who had accepted commissions in volunteer regiments and then transferred to the 4th Cavalry. The eight promotions after May 1864 all transferred to other regiments: two to the 1st United States Cavalry, three to the 138th United States Colored Infantry, and two to volunteer cavalry regiments. All of these men carried with them the *esprit de corps* of the United States Cavalry and the 4th Regiment.

Of the thirty-nine men promoted, two were sergeants major, thirteen first sergeants, eleven sergeants, five corporals, and eight privates. There were eight promotions in 1861, five in 1862, eighteen in 1863, five in 1864, and three in 1865. Three promotions taking troopers out of the Regiment were somewhat unusual: in August 1861, at the request of General John C. Fremont, Private James A. Clifford, bugler, with eight years prior service, was discharged and commissioned a captain in the 1st Missouri Cavalry.[64] Musician Charles A. Waltz, who joined the 4th Regiment in February 1864, was commissioned 2nd Lieutenant in the 7th Pennsylvania Cavalry at the request of its commanding officer in December 1864.[65] The most unusual appointment was Private James Wyatt, Company I, who joined the regiment in May 1860 and in July 1862 "was discharged to accept commission in the navy."[66]

Four companies of the 4th Cavalry participated in the activities leading up to the earliest battles of the war at Dug Springs and Wilson's Creek, Missouri, giving the officers and men early combat experience. Company I was at Fort Donelson and Shiloh, Tennessee, and Companies A and E participated with the Army of the Potomac at Bull Run and McClellan's Peninsular Campaign. Because of this, and having been thrown in with the undisciplined "90 day rabble" that represented the earliest volunteer forces, the junior officers and senior non-commissioned officers had to learn quickly and take on responsibilities beyond their rank. In order to survive, they had to hold on to all the military traditions and discipline that had served them so well on the "training school of the Plains." It was up to this core of frontier veterans to train and transform the new volunteers who began to fill their ranks and to instill in them the pride and reputation that rode with the 4th Regiment. There was continual turnover within the enlisted ranks, as those leaving at the end of their service were replaced with the constant stream of raw recruits. Before the war, there was adequate time for training; now there was little or no time, and training was a matter of life or death, especially for those who had never before ridden a horse. When all of the companies were reunited as a full regiment in August 1863, they were battle-hardened and quickly made their reputation at Franklin and Shelbyville, Tennessee, and Reed's Bridge (Chickamauga), Georgia. Five of the companies at the Battle of Franklin (April 10, 1863) were commanded by 1st and 2nd lieutenants, all former enlisted men of the 4th United States Cavalry.

In December 1862, the Fourth Regulars would become part of the First Brigade, Second Cavalry Division, under Brigadier General Stanley and eventually be assigned to Colonel Robert Minty's First Brigade. Minty—a former British Army officer who now commanded the 4th Michigan Volunteer Cavalry—quickly came to the attention of his superior officers because of his "marked attention to the organization and drill of his regiment." Along with the distinguished 7th Pennsylvania Volunteers led by Colonel William B. Sipes, Minty's Brigade would earn the rare distinction and "singular honor" of having the title Saber Brigade bestowed upon it by Major General William Rosecrans in March 1863. When Major General George H. Thomas replaced Rosecrans in 1864, he envisioned a new combat role for his cavalry. Toward the end of the war, under command of twenty-seven year old Major General James Wilson—a protégé of Grant's—the regiment helped to write the final chapter of the new cavalry manual at Selma, Alabama, in April 1865, when "the Fourth Cavalry Regiment became the only Regiment, during the war between the states to defeat superior cavalry, large masses of artillery, and entrenched infantry" in a single battle.[67]

The Awarding of Brevet Rank

"Brevet" referred to a warrant authorizing a commissioned officer to hold a higher rank temporarily, but usually without receiving the pay of that higher rank. During the Civil War, brevet rank was an honorary promotion given to an officer (or occasionally, an enlisted man) in recognition of gallant conduct or other meritorious service. Brevets were difficult to receive and were a sign of valor in combat. They served much the same purpose of recognition that medals do today. The use of medals did not come into common use until the twentieth century, although the Medal of Honor was created during the Civil War. Typically, a brevetted officer would be given the insignia of the brevet rank, but not the formal authority or pay.

The Civil War created some unusual circumstances where brevet rank carried authority. As the small Regular Army became swamped by Volunteers, situations arose where a military academy graduate could find himself under command of a ranking Volunteer officer with no military training. In these circumstances, command would go to the Regular officer, who would be given the necessary brevet rank to become the ranking, and thus commanding officer. This allowed Regular officers with experience to assume command over higher-ranking militia or volunteer officers with little or no experience.

Under this system, it was possible for a Regular Army officer to hold four different ranks at the same time. A captain in the Regular army could be "brevet Major, USA" for meritorious service. That same captain could be serving in the United States Volunteer Army with the rank Colonel of Volunteers and be "brevet Brigadier General, USV" for meritorious conduct. In this example, his pay grade would remain captain, USA, but he would always be addressed with the highest brevet rank awarded. After the war, several captains in the 4th US Cavalry would retain the honorary rank of "brevet brigadier general."

With regard to a Regular Army regiment, such as the 4th United States Cavalry, they were frequently designated "unattached" when assigned to a command where they might otherwise fall under command of a Volunteer officer with limited military experience; in those cases, they were directly under the commanding general. The exception would be when the 4th US Cavalry was assigned to Brigadier General Robert Minty's Saber Brigade. Colonel Robert Minty, USV, would be brevetted Brigadier General for valor in May 1863, but for political reasons would not be promoted to the rank normally given a brigade commander until the end of the war.

1861: A Taste for Death

I could stand and see men shot down . . . without seeming to feel or care. I was too busy loading and firing.
–James H. Wiswell[1]

I. The War Begins

"The 34 hour bombardment of Fort Sumter commences at four o'clock" on the morning of April 12, 1861, "announcing the beginning of the bloodiest and most wrenching war in American History."[2] Everything about this war is controversial, beginning with its title. As Captain Joseph Vale, 7th Pennsylvania Cavalry, wrote in his brigade history:

> There is no subject so fraught with controversy or which calls out so much of sharp criticism as that relating to the events and incidents of the War of the Rebellion. Many of the people today [1886] vehemently insist that there was never a 'rebellion' against the United States, and are wont to refer to the war as the 'late unpleasantness', the 'war between the States', or other such half apologetic terms; deprecating the while the use of the words 'rebellion' and 'rebel' ... To those who are fastidious about using the terms rebellion and rebel, I can only say, that we of the army believed we were engaged in the work of overthrowing a lawless and unjustified and unjustifiable rebellion against the peace and territorial integrity of the Government of the United States; that the soldier in arms against us was a rebel, and that those at the head of the political machinery by which the forces in antagonism to the government were organized and equipped–were traitors ...
> We never recognized the 'Confederacy' in our vocabulary during the war . . .[3]

By May 1861, most of the Federal forces in the West had withdrawn to Fort Leavenworth. For the Union, holding the "border states"—particularly Kentucky and Missouri—became critical. During the second half of the year, Companies of the 1st [later 4th] United States Cavalry B, C, D, and I played a significant role in preserving Missouri for the Union. Captain David Stanley, Co. C, would gain national recognition for himself and the Union cause by leading companies of the 1st U.S. in the earliest saber charges in the Western Theater at Dug Springs in August, and again leading General John Fremont's cavalry at Springfield, Missouri, in October.

Companies D and I would participate in the second major battle of the Civil War at Wilson's Creek, Missouri, on August 10, 1861. Companies F, G, H, and K would remain on the frontier during most of this year. Companies F and H were stationed at Fort Kearney, Indian Territory, during August, while Company K was "engaged in escorting [wagon] trains from Fort Laramie to Fort Wise."[4]

The Civil War was fought in two separate geographic areas: the Eastern Theater and the Western Theater. The Western Theater was the vast expanse of the South between the Mississippi River and the Appalachian Mountain Range to the east. This theater was largely a matter of waterways—Cumberland, Tennessee, and Mississippi Rivers—and railroad (supply) lines. The 4th United States Cavalry operated primarily in Tennessee, Mississippi, Alabama, and Georgia—the agricultural and industrial heart of the Confederacy. Companies A and E were the only companies of the regiment to participate in the Eastern Theater of the War, primarily in Virginia and Washington, DC, and would serve as personal escort to Major General George B. McClellan and his successor, Ambrose Burnside. The squadron would rejoin their regiment at Nashville, Tennessee, in March 1863.

During this time, Regimental Headquarters was in Washington, DC, staffed on paper by newly appointed Colonel John Sedgwick, Lieutenant Colonel Thomas Wood, Major Samuel Sturgis, Major George Stoneman, and 2nd Lieutenant Eugene B. Beaumont as Acting Adjutant General. All of the staff officers were on detached service with the Volunteer Army. In May, John Sedgwick—recently promoted to lieutenant colonel, 2nd Cavalry, to replace Robert E. Lee—was ordered to Fort Leavenworth to await further orders. He was promoted again to colonel, 1st Cavalry (once again replacing Robert E. Lee), and became the third commanding officer of the Regiment. As with all the staff officers, Colonel Sedgwick never actually served with his regiment during the war. By August 1861, he was brigadier general, volunteers, commanding Second Brigade—Colonel Samuel P. Heintzelman's Division—Second Corps,

Army of the Potomac. He held a number of commands in the Eastern Theater, rising to the rank of major general, United States Volunteers. He was killed in action by a Confederate sharpshooter at Spotsylvania Court House, Virginia, May 9, 1864, becoming the third and final corps commander in the Army of the Potomac to die in battle.[5]

Thomas Wood—one of the original captains of the new 1st Cavalry—was appointed lieutenant colonel, 4th Cavalry in November 1861, replacing William Emory. During the early months of the war, he helped organize, train, and equip volunteer units in Indiana, being appointed brigadier general, Volunteers. He was commanding a division at the Battle of Chickamauga when he acted on General Rosecrans's controversial order to move out of line in support of another division. This action provided the opening for Confederate General James A. Longstreet to drive through the line, dividing and defeating the Union Army. Wood subsequently redeemed his reputation, rising to the rank of brevet major general, volunteers by the end of the war.[6]

Samuel D. Sturgis, appointed brigadier general, volunteers in August, commanded the District of Kansas for a short time before being sent east, where he participated in the Second Battle of Bull Run, Antietam, and Fredericksburg. His military career is described as "lackluster" and "undistinguished."[7] George Stoneman—one of the original captains of the newly formed 2nd Cavalry—was promoted to major, 1st/4th Cavalry, in May 1861. Other than holding this position during the war, he had no prior association with the 4th Cavalry and was appointed lieutenant colonel, 3rd Cavalry by August 1864. Stoneman was brigadier general volunteers and, in November 1862, was promoted to major general. He commanded the Cavalry Corps, Army of the Potomac, and in 1863 was chosen to head the newly established Cavalry Bureau.[8] Lieutenant Eugene Beaumont distinguished himself in battle numerous times, being brevetted four times for gallantry and bravery. He was one of four members of the 4th United States Cavalry to be awarded the Medal of Honor for exemplary conduct and gallantry during the Civil War.[9]

II. The Eastern Theater

Companies A and E

General McClellan, who had previously served as a captain in the newly formed 1st US Cavalry, was operating in West Virginia under orders to clear that area of rebel forces. In June 1861, he made several requests to Headquarters Department of the Ohio for "the six companies of the First Cavalry now at Fort Leavenworth," stating, "I know I could make excellent use of them."[1] His requests were denied. However, in July, Companies A and E were called to service in the Eastern Theater and reported to Headquarters Army of the Potomac in Washington.[2] 1st Lieutenant Albert Colburn, the Regimental Adjutant since 1857, was promoted to brevet captain July 1, 1861, and accompanied the squadron. His promotion to captain was official on August 3, and as the senior officer present he would command the squadron.[3] They participated in the first major battle of the war at Bull Run and would remain in the East until March 1863, when they rejoined their regiment in Nashville, Tennessee.

Private Charles E. Bates, Co. E

Among the enlisted men in the squadron was seventeen-year-old Private Charles E. Bates, born in Connecticut in 1844. He ran away from home at the tender age of fourteen to join the cavalry in December 1857. His parents filed a petition for his discharge, but for whatever reason, he remained in the army.[4] Assigned to Company E, he was promoted to corporal in May 1859 and to sergeant in August 1860. Since holding rank at that time required the physical ability to earn respect and maintain discipline, he was apparently able to take care of himself. He appears to have been an independent, headstrong young man with a dash of common sense and an entrepreneurial spirit. However, unlike James Larson, he never quite mastered the system; rather, he seems to have played it. Twice promoted to sergeant and twice demoted to private, he could still muse: "The Army is not a prison house or a grave for every-one although many a poor fellow finds it so."[5] Surprisingly literate for his age and education, his letters are of particular interest, since there is little information about Companies A and E during this period of detached service in the Eastern Theater.

The morning of April 23, 1861, Private (formerly Sergeant) Bates was in the stockade at Fort Smith, Arkansas, awaiting sentencing from his recent court-martial. Orders to evacuate the fort were his reprieve. As he wrote his parents:

> When I wrote my last letter to you I did not think it was to be my fate to become what I now am, a General prisoner, but here I am in a cell 10 feet long by 4 feet wide, and my feet connected with a chain eighteen inches long and about as many pounds in weight.
>
> And what, you say, have I done!! I will tell you. I have acted like a man, and an action which no honest one would blame me for has made me what I am, a prisoner. The night before last some of the secessionists in town hoisted a flag opposite of the gate of the fort bearing for a device 8 stars and a pistol and bowie knife crossed. This appeared to be an insult to the soldiers and the union so I went out and pulled it down and on being ordered by my captain [James McIntyre] to put it up again I tore it into ribbands [sic] the dirty flag that's what I am in for chained like a murderer. Pray for your most unfortunate Charles.

His prayers were answered:

> The morning of the 23rd April my sentence came to fort Smith, which was six month ball and chain and along with it an order from the secretary of war for my sentence to be remitted. So I was released and that night we left.[6]

On July 2, Captain Colburn's squadron (Companies A and E) left Leavenworth—traveling by boat and railcar—and reached Washington, DC on the ninth, making camp at Arlington Heights, Virginia. On the sixteenth, they left for Manassas Gap.[7] The squadron was attached to Colonel Heintzelman's Division, Army of Northeastern Virginia, where it remained until August 1861. It was then attached to the First Brigade, Second Division of the Army of Virginia, under the command of Colonel David Hunter. Company A was commanded by 1st Lieutenant Thomas H. McCormick and Company E by Captain James McIntyre.[8] Both officers would remain with the regiment for the duration of the war.

Bull Run (First Manassas)

It was July 1861, and the war was three months old. A rebel army was camped at Manassas Junction, just twenty-five miles from Washington, and the terms of the three-month enlistments in the Union Army were running out. The pressure was on the commander of the Federal army, Brigadier General Irvin McDowell, to attack. Unfortunately, the date of the battle would coincide with the end of the ninety-day enlistments. When General McDowell "led his green army of 36,000 south from Washington in July 1861 on a vain and hasty campaign to capture the Confederate capital of Richmond, Virginia," he was accompanied by seven companies of regular cavalry under the command of Major Innis N. Palmer, 2nd (later 5th) Cavalry.[9] This included Companies A and E of the 1st (later 4th) Cavalry. They would see action in the first major battle of the war, Bull Run. As historian Bruce Catton wrote, Bull Run was "the momentous fight of the amateurs, the battle where everything went wrong, the great day of awakening for the whole nation . . . It ended the rosy time in which men could dream that the war would be short, glorious and bloodless."[10]

On the evening of July 20, McDowell's command was near the small village of Centreville, south of Washington, DC, with the Confederate forces near Manassas. The road between the two settlements ran along a ridge and crossed the stream named Bull Run about three miles from Manassas.[11] Many battles of the Civil War have dual names; Northerners tended to name their battles after the nearest body of water (Bull Run), while Southerners used the nearest town (Manassas).

When the battle was engaged the morning of the twenty-first, the "whole cavalry force was ordered to the front, and took a position on the extreme right of the line."[12] Palmer's command consisted of the squadron of the 1st US Cavalry, four companies of the 2nd US Cavalry, and one company of the 2nd Dragoons.[13] It was reported by one observer that Colburn's squadron made a charge "in the early part of the battle near the Warrenton turnpike," but for most of the day the cavalry "stood to horse, waiting and wondering" as "the sound of the battle below the stream rose and fell..."[14] The cavalrymen were eager to enter the fray and Colonel Palmer was growing impatient as the day wore on. Among the officers in the 2nd Cavalry was a young Lieutenant George A. Custer, hoping to get his first taste of battle.[15] He would be disappointed. As the battle raged on, portions of the cavalry "were detached from time to time, to support the different batteries and to examine the ground on the left of the enemy's line."[16] Around 1:30 p.m., Captain Colburn's squadron of Regular Cavalry was called in to support the placement of two batteries of artillery—Captain James B. Ricketts' 1st U.S. Artillery and Captain Charles Griffin's 5th U.S. Artillery—on Henry House Hill to "within about 1000 feet of the enemy's battery."[17] Once established, "the two batteries at once opened a very effective fire upon the enemy's left" and a fierce firefight ensued.[18] It was also about this time that Confederate Brigadier General Barnard Bee, trying to rally his troops, pointed at the Virginians and told his men, "There stands Jackson like a stone wall." Bee would be killed in the battle. At about four o'clock in the afternoon, additional Confederate reinforcements arrived led by General Joseph E. Johnston, former Lieutenant Colonel, 1st US Cavalry. Many arrived on trains. The tide of battle turned against Federal forces. Pressure was put on the Union right flank and it began to break. At about that same time, there arose a sound above the roar of the battle, an "eerie scream that struck fear into the hearts of the enemy... the rebel yell," heard for the first time. As remembered by a Union veteran, "There is nothing like it on this side of the infernal region. The peculiar corkscrew sensation that it sends down your backbone under these circumstances can never be told. You have to feel it."[19] Under heavy fire, in total confusion, and "startled by this screaming counterattack," the Union lines—particularly those of the volunteer units—began to dissolve and withdraw without orders. Major Palmer, realizing what was happening, immediately ordered his cavalry to oppose the retreat.[20] The green Federal forces were "totally demoralized." When the Confederates opened "a galling fire" from the woods in front of them, all efforts at stemming the retreat were lost.[21] The Federal regiments gave way in disorder under "a murderous fire of musketry and rifles, opened at pistol range, [which] cut down every cannoneer and a large number of horses ..."[22] Colonel Heintzelman moved up reinforcements, but "at the first fire they broke, and the greater portion fled to the rear ..."[23] At almost the same moment, they were charged by a company of secession cavalry on their rear. The rebels were immediately met by Captain Colburn's squadron of 1st US Cavalry. They killed four and wounded one before disbursing them. "Ricketts' battery had been taken and retaken three times . . . but was finally lost, most of the horses having been killed."[24] "Finding it impossible to rally any of the regiments," Heintzelman commenced his retreat at about 4:30 p.m., relying on Arnold's battery and "a few companies of cavalry" for their protection.[25] A general retreat was ordered back across Bull Run to Centreville. The retreat quickly turned into one of the most embarrassing routs of the Civil War. According to Bruce Catton, "McDowell's army had simply fallen apart." Colonel Heintzelman wrote: "No efforts could induce a single regiment to form after the retreat was commenced . . . Such a rout I had never witnessed before."[26] The Regulars found themselves literally run over by the fleeing volunteers. The Confederates were rapidly advancing upon the rear, and at Stone Bridge, crossing Bull Run, rebel cavalry met the fleeing Federal soldiers. Former 1st Cavalry Captain—now lieutenant colonel, CSA—Jeb Stuart led "a full regiment of gray-clad cavalry, the 1st Virginia, in an attack along the left flank . . . striking the main retreat column."[27] "Stuart's men shot and sabered their way through the confused mass of blue, taking numerous prisoners."[28] Stuart's reputation would grow from this day. As Palmer's battery reached the bridge, it turned to face the rebel cavalry. Two shots from Union artillery "caused them to retire."[29] The Regular cavalry was eventually able to "chase off the Rebel troopers and take a few prisoners."[30] Concerned about saving his command, Major Palmer "pushed on as rapidly as possible, reaching Centreville about 8:30 p.m. and cavalry camp, near Arlington, at 5:30 a.m. the next morning."[31] "For its part, Palmer's battalion, which guarded the flanks and rear of the retreat column, did a fine job in the only active service assigned it this day."[32]

Colonel Hunter, commanding Second Division, was wounded early in the action and was replaced by Colonel Andrew Porter, 16th U.S. Infantry. Second Lieutenant Samuel W. Stockton, Co. E, 4th US Cavalry, had been assigned as Hunter's aide and escorted him off the field.[33] Hunter recovered from his injuries and Lieutenant Stockton would remain his aide-de-camp until the end of the war. Colonel Porter praised the action of the cavalry as "all that it could be upon such a field in supporting batteries, feeling the enemy's position and covering the retreat."[34] He would be promoted to brigadier general and posted as Provost Marshal in Washington, DC.[35]

The shame of Bull Run reverberated through the Federal Army to the White House, and "Lincoln needed to take steps to ensure that there would be no recurrence." "Before there could be another campaign, a real army would have to be put together, and expert attention would have to be given to matters of organization, training and discipline."[36] "The army had nothing resembling a general staff, no strategic plans, no program for mobilization."[37]

When General Henry W. Halleck—the fourth ranking senior officer in the army after Scott, McClellan, and Fremont—wanted maps of the South, he had to buy them from a St. Louis bookstore. "Most of the arms in government arsenals (including the 159,000 muskets seized by Confederate states) were old smoothbores, many of them flintlocks of antique vintage." There was as yet no supply system, which left the majority of new recruits unequipped, unarmed, and ill trained. To overcome all of this, President Lincoln put George McClellan in command of the Army.[38] McClellan excelled at organization, and in short order the new Army of the Potomac was "armed, equipped, and instructed until it was on a par with the finest armies in the world."[39] By November, Lincoln made him "general in chief of all armies."[40]

After Bull Run, Companies A and E—along with seven companies of the 2nd United States Cavalry—were assigned to the headquarters of the army for "escort, courier, and orderly duties."[41] Captain Albert Colburn left the regiment after Bull Run to become Assistant Adjutant-General attached to the Staff of the Army of the Potomac.[42] He was promoted to major in July 1862, and lieutenant colonel, Staff, United States Army in September 1862. Colburn would die of an undisclosed illness on June 17, 1863.[43]

In Colburn's absence, command of the squadron of 1st Cavalry devolved to Captain James McIntyre, a West Point graduate, class of 1853. McIntyre and George McClellan had both joined the newly formed 1st US Cavalry in March 1855 and served together until McClellan resigned in 1857. McIntyre would command the full regiment in the field longer than any other officer during the war and was "repeatedly officially commended for special gallantry in general orders and the official reports."[44]

In October 1861, McIntyre's squadron became part of the Provost Guard for the city of Washington under the command of Brigadier General Andrew Porter, the new Provost Marshal.[45] The company was quartered within a thousand yards of the capitol and spent every other day patrolling the streets, arresting drunk soldiers and those without a pass.[46] They occasionally had a "scout into Maryland . . . never lasting more than three days."[47] During the time the squadron spent in the Eastern Theater, it consisted of four officers and approximately 104 men.[48]

In his November letter to his parents, Bates reports on McClellan's progress with the Federal Army. His company was the general's escort for a "grand review" of the troops; 70,000 soldiers in a four-and-a-half-hour parade. "They all looked like 'Regulars,'" he wrote, "everybody was in their place, and that was stranger–for Volunteers are generally not very military. Everyone kept time with the music and looked to the 'front' when they passed the reviewing staff."[49]

McClellan built an army for the Union, but didn't know how to use it. Historians have long documented President Lincoln's frustration with McClellan's Peninsular Campaign to advance on Richmond that began on March 17, 1862. Corporal Charles Bates shares this same frustration in letters to his parents. Writing from Yorktown in April 1862, he is confident the rebs will be "whipped within seven days. I think everything is ready for the ball to be opened."[50] Two months later, camped about "7 miles from Richmond: 'Mac' is making breastworks and intrenchments [sic] all along the lines on this side and will most likely advance when the works are completed, so 'wait a little longer.'"[51] While waiting, the squadron had "Smith's new patent rifles issued" on May 26: ". . . [T]hey are beauties, and J. D.'s [Jefferson Davis'] legions had better look out the day this Squadron is let loose at them."[52] On June 19: "I suppose the Grand Army is about to start, for it is time something was being done besides throwing up dirt."[53] "Our shovels have about got their part in the siege 'played out,'" he writes on the twenty-second, "and I am a false prophet if this week passes by without a grand battle."[54] On June 25, the Confederates responded to the Federal threat on Richmond and the Seven Days Campaign began. Lee succeeded in cutting McClellan's supply line, forcing the Union Army to abandon the siege of Richmond. On July 1, the Confederates attacked McClellan's Army at Malvern Hill, but were driven off by superior Union artillery. Having suffered

16,000 casualties, McClellan retreated to Harrison's Landing, Virginia. Lee, with 20,000 casualties, had lifted the siege of Richmond and "outfought and outthought" George McClellan.[55] Companies A and E did not play a significant role in these battles.

For a brief time in May, Corporal Bates was assigned as a staff orderly at headquarters. He was relieved of that duty when he was "in durance vile, sentenced to fourteen days confinement for disobeying a direct order from his 1st Sergeant, Edward E. Fitzgerald, to take care of a horse belonging to another company."[56] During the first two weeks of July, while at Harrison's Landing, Charles found time to "speculate"—i.e., make money—"in good old fashioned style. I think the fashion is about as old as the world for Christ found the greater part of his Apostles following the same business–big fishing; I got a net in an old fish house . . . fixed a boat . . . and went to work with five other men." He earned $275. Considering a corporal's pay was about $15 a month, his two-week venture was extremely lucrative.[57]

The Enlistment of James H. Wiswell, Co. C

The standing Army of the United States—referred to as the regulars—never exceeded 20,000 men during the war. As previously indicated, volunteer regiments from the various states, communities, and organizations primarily fought the war. Prior to the war, a term of enlistment in the regular army was five years. These men were referred to as Regular Army, or "Regulars." In April 1861, hundreds of thousands of eager young men answered President Lincoln's call for volunteers for three-year enlistments in the new army, and the Regular cavalry was getting its share of volunteers. James H. Wiswell joined the United States Cavalry for a term of three years; it was a subtle difference over a five-year term and may have only affected seniority and promotion.[58] Since the war lasted much longer than anyone anticipated, most of these early volunteers, as well as many of the Regulars, reached the expiration of their service months before the war ended; some reenlisted, many did not. This circumstance, along with combat casualties, illness, and desertions, led to a constant turnover of men in all of the Union regiments.

Wiswell, along with three boyhood friends from Hydeville, Vermont—James "Jimmie" Cummings, Alvy "Al" Allen, and Henry C. Parkhurst—joined the First Regiment United States Cavalry at the Albany, New York, recruiting office. They called themselves the "Hy-4." From Albany, the new recruits traveled to New York City, then to Jersey City to catch the Central Railroad for the eleven-hour ride to Harrisburg, Pennsylvania.

They arrived at three in the afternoon and switched cars for the twenty-mile ride to Carlisle Barracks, Pennsylvania. Founded in 1757, it remains the second oldest continually operating Army post in the country. In 1838, the Cavalry School of Practice and Recruiting Depot was established and was commanded by Captain Edwin V. Sumner, who would later command the new 1st Cavalry. This was "cavalry boot camp," where the "Hy-4" would train for the next four weeks.[59]

Wiswell kept up steady correspondence with his parents and sisters during the war. Based on his letters, he was a well-educated, politically aware young man, exhibiting the initial exuberance of a new recruit volunteering to fight for his country and anxious to share his experiences with his parents and sisters at home. In excerpts from his "boot camp" letters, Wiswell was philosophical about his circumstances:

> [Three] years is not a long time for a young person like me. . . . As long as I am compelled to stay in the service I may as well take things as they come, as to the growling [complaining] about them. . . . I am very satisfied so far. I find that if I conduct myself like a man I shall be treated like man.

He also shares the fact that, "The paymaster of this post, Major Rutgers, has seceded with about $40,000 of the government's money."[60] On or about June 1, 1861, Pvt. Wiswell and his mates left Carlisle Barracks with Recruit Company B for the trip to Fort Leavenworth, escorted by Captain Gordon Granger of the Mounted Rifles (later 3rd Cavalry).[61] Granger later became brigadier general, U.S. Volunteers and command the cavalry of the Army of the Mississippi. As part of the "Dragoon Detachment of Recruits," they soon found themselves in the fight to save Missouri for the Union.[62] They would not be formally mustered into the 1st (later 4th) Cavalry and assigned to companies until September.

These early volunteers in the Regular Army had two advantages over those who went into the volunteer regiments raised by the states, or those who were later conscripted: they received rudimentary training in basic military discipline and regimen that would be continued once they were assigned to their regiments. They were also always under the supervision and training of the experienced non-commissioned officers of their individual companies. After the first year, many of these men would become corporals and sergeants. Because of their early experiences, many would be assigned duties in areas that would keep them out of harm's way, e.g., wagonmasters, farriers, and quartermaster corps. The second advantage was the higher standard of health and hygiene maintained by the Regular Army, particularly in long-term winter camp situations. All of the men whose personal stories are told here remained in generally good health and survived the war.

III. The Western Theater

The State of Missouri

After the debacle at Bull Run, little of any consequence took place in the Eastern Theater until spring 1862. Meanwhile, the West was in chaos. West of the Appalachians—particularly in Missouri and along the Mississippi River—a strategy was slowly unfolding among the disorganized Union forces that would eventually have a major impact on the course and outcome of the war. The state of Missouri and the strategic city of St. Louis hung in the balance. They were in danger of being lost to the strident pro-

secessionists, who began an escalation of violence to gain their ends:

> Missouri was a keystone in the Union cause. The nation's major lines of communication and travel were anchored in the state: The Pony Express and the California, Oregon, and Santa Fe Trails. The three major waterways of the country, the Missouri, Mississippi, and Ohio rivers, either passed through or touched the state. According to the 1860 census, Missouri ranked eighth in population, making it an excellent manpower resource for the army. The state was rich in deposits of raw materials–lead for bullets, iron for cannonballs. Its agricultural production could feed an army. Missouri became the third most fought over state in the nation.[1]

By June 1861, dozens of Federal forts, ordnance, and subsistence stores were abandoned or taken over by Confederate sympathizers in Texas, New Mexico, and the Western Territories. United States property was seized, including the arsenal and barracks at San Antonio, Texas, and Federal arsenals at Little Rock, Arkansas, and Liberty, Missouri. Units of the United States Army had been captured or surrendered, and officers had been seized and held as prisoners of war. While Kansas maintained its neutrality, Missouri was up for grabs. Ten states had followed South Carolina out of the Union, and the pro-Southern states' rights sympathizers within the state government and militia were fighting to put Missouri into the Confederacy.[2] In July 1861, four companies of the 1st Cavalry (B, C, D, and I) at Fort Leavenworth came under the command of Brigadier General Nathaniel Lyon's Army of Southwest Missouri and would become instrumental in saving Missouri for the Union and establishing the reputation of Captain David Stanley.

General Nathaniel Lyon, United States Army

Forty-three-year-old Captain Nathaniel Lyon, 2nd U.S. Infantry, was stationed in Kansas and Missouri during the years preceding the war. Described as a "fiery, irascible man," he became an ardent Unionist opposed to slavery and a supporter of Abraham Lincoln.[3] His hot temperament and his willingness to allow his strong moral convictions to override his military obligations made him one of the more controversial figures of the time.[4] He came to prominence in Missouri in February 1861, when his actions saved the United States arsenal in St. Louis from the pro-Confederate State Militia.[5] In April 1861, Lyon assumed command of the Military Department of the West, which at that time included Missouri, Kentucky, Illinois, and the area east of the Rocky Mountains. President Lincoln later confirmed his position with a promotion to the rank of brigadier general. Missouri was under the direct control of George McClellan, then commanding the Western Division. He left Lyon free to conduct his own campaign in Missouri.[6] In a June 11 meeting with the pro-Southern government of Missouri, General Lyon was angered by what he felt was local intervention in orders given to Federal troops. For Lyon, described by historian Bruce Catton as "all flame and devotion, too impetuous by half," there was no compromise:[7]

> Rather than concede to the State of Missouri for one single instant the right to dictate to my Government in any matter . . . I would see you . . . and every man, woman, and child in the state dead and buried.[8]

Not surprisingly, the next day Governor Claiborne Jackson, a states' rights sympathizer, put out a call for 50,000 volunteers "to repel what he perceives as attempts by the Federals to take over the state." Meanwhile, Union troops established themselves at Jefferson City, the state capital.[9] In his June 22 report to General McClellan, Brigadier General Lyon outlined his response:

> I had, in consequence of the proclamation of Governor Jackson, of this State, which seemed to me tantamount to a declaration of war, ordered a movement of a portion of the troops under my command to Jefferson City and in the direction of Springfield, Mo., for the purpose of breaking up the hostile organizations which I had reason to believe had been formed in those parts of the State to resist the authority of the Government.[10]

Lyon also reported that on June 17, with a force of about "1700 men," he advanced in the direction of Boonville, where "the enemy were soon routed, their camp taken, and the city of Boonville occupied by our troops."[11] This early action in the Missouri River Valley—a center for Southern sympathy—"established Union control over the Missouri River" and slowed attempts to place Missouri in the Confederacy.[12] With that part of the state under control, Lyon turned his attention to the southern districts. On July 3, Lyon led his 3,300 man army out of Boonville south to Springfield.[13]

On June 17, Major Samuel Sturgis, 1st US Cavalry, led his force of "about 2000" men—"mounted and on foot and about 150 wagons"—south from Fort Leavenworth to join General Lyon.[14] Sturgis had been brevetted to major for his evacuation of Fort Smith. Included in his command were the four companies of the 1st Cavalry and the 255 new enlistees in the Dragoon Detachment of Recruits recently arrived from Carlisle Barracks, including Private James Wiswell.[15] Sturgis's command traveled down the Missouri River to Kansas City, Missouri, where it helped to "keep down rebels in that section." Portions of the command went "out on two scouts"—one to Liberty and the other to Independence—where they drove about 1,800 rebels out of camp and took sixty prisoners.[16] Leaving Kansas City on June 24 and moving south through the open prairie, they camped near Austin, in Cass County, on July 2. Wiswell described the area as "beautiful country . . . [and] Union to the back bone."[17] Sturgis "rushed two companies forward to Clinton to secure the crossing of the Grand River just south of that village." The remaining force arrived at Clinton on July 4, naming the camp after George Washington.[18]

Wiswell wrote of an issue that was to plague both Union and Confederate Armies, and particularly the citizens of the South as the war progressed—"plundering":

> We have plenty of chance to plunder when we are on the march as the rebels leave their houses wide open and take to their heels as soon as they see us coming but all plundering is strictly forbidden. Two fellows [Regulars] tried it and were caught and dealt with in the following manner–one was stripped and tied to the wagon wheel and given 39 [lashes] on the bare back and the other got 20 and was drummed out of camp with his shirt drawers and cap on as a thief [and] is not allowed to wear the Blue. Every vice of that kind is strictly dealt with in the [Regular] Army.[19]

Most of those involved in robbing or plundering the farmers around Clinton were from the volunteer troops. Their commanding officers turned them over to Major Sturgis for punishment. "They never anticipated the severity of Sturgis' response and were startled shortly thereafter when the enlisted men rose up in near mutiny." Sturgis created a furor when he applied the strict Regular Army punishment of approximately fifty lashes apiece.[20] As these men were Kansas volunteers, outrage was widespread throughout that state and media, with threats on the major's life. This was one of several unusual circumstances involving the Regulars of the 1st Cavalry that may have overshadowed their effectiveness at Wilson's Creek. The other was the unexplained arrest of Captain Eugene Carr, Co. I, by General Lyon.

Earlier, on June 21, the pro-secession state forces that had gathered at Lexington—"variously estimated from 5,000 to 6,000 men"—broke camp and "started toward the south with the intention of uniting with the troops said to be collecting in Arkansas" under Texas General Ben McCulloch.[21] If this happened, Lyon feared McCulloch would have a combined force of 10,000 or 12,000 men to invade Missouri, giving the rebels a two to one advantage over Union forces.[22] Among other actions, Lyon ordered "the force under Major Sturgis and the volunteers with him from Kansas and Iowa" to follow the rebel forces moving south in the direction of Springfield and "cut them off."[23] There were a series of minor skirmishes between groups of disorganized volunteers on both sides while their commanders attempted to consolidate their forces. Aware that rebel forces were advancing on Springfield, Lyon prepared to send his small Army of Southwest Missouri out to meet them; Major Sturgis would command Lyon's First Brigade. Captain Stanley now commanded the companies of the 1st Cavalry.[24]

On July 22, "Captain Stanley, commanding the cavalry attached to the force under Brigadier General Thomas W. Sweeny, 2nd U.S. Infantry, made an attack on a large rebel force (comprising the greater part of Sterling Price's rebel cavalry) at Forsyth, Missouri."[25] Price—a former governor of the state—was now the militia general of the Missouri State Guard. Sweeny, who lost his right arm in the Mexican War, had saved the arsenal at St. Louis and was instrumental in the organization of the Missouri three-month volunteers; he was appointed brigadier general May 20, 1861. He would be severely wounded at the Battle of Wilson's Creek on August 10.[26]

EXPEDITION FROM SPRINGFIELD TO FORSYTH, MISSOURI

On the stormy evening of July 20, Brigadier General Sweeny's command left Springfield, arriving at Forsyth about 6 p.m. on the twenty-second. From captured pickets Sweeny learned there were only about 150 men stationed at Forsyth, and he ordered Captain Stanley's cavalry and the Kansas Rangers to surround the town. Stanley was to "keep the enemy in check" if he encountered resistance, while Sweeny would advance to his support with the artillery and infantry. Aware of the Union presence and having "partially formed in the town," the rebel forces "opened a scattering of fire on the approaching cavalry" that was returned "with a well directed volley," sending the rebels scattering to the "hills and surrounding thickets." They collected in considerable numbers "under cover of the trees and bushes upon the hills to the left of the town." Sweeny attempted to dislodge the rebels "with shell and canister from the artillery" while his infantry skirmished through the woods.[27] After about an hour, "Captain Stanley, putting himself at the head of the four companies of his regiment, charged the center of the rebel lines . . . cut through them, captured two pieces of artillery and a large number of prisoners and utterly routed the whole force."[28] Stanley had his horse shot out from under him and three men from Company D were slightly wounded: Privates Francis Casey, Alexander Martin, and William Whitthorn—all veterans of the frontier and the first casualties of the war.[29] Sweeny's forces also captured "7 horses, and a quantity of arms, munitions of war, flour, meal, sugar, syrup, salt, clothing, cloth, boots, shoes, hats, camp furniture, mule and horse shoes &c [etc.]. . . . The arms and munitions of war were distributed among the Home Guards of the county," and the clothing and provisions among the volunteer troops, "of which they stood in great need."[30] As Sweeny's statement implies, Lyon's efforts were seriously hampered by the condition of his volunteer troops and a lack of adequate supplies.

THE EARLY VOLUNTEERS

At the outbreak of war, the initial volunteer forces on both sides could be best described as little more than undisciplined mobs with makeshift armaments. The majority was the militia called out by the president's proclamation of April 15, and after ninety days in the service, "all the initial enthusiasm was gone; they were largely a mutinous rabble, untrained, undisciplined, unequipped, unarmed, and unpaid."[31] Over time, this situation within the volunteer forces of the Federal Army would improve somewhat, but even at its best: "there remained a greater informality in the West at every level, in dress and behavior, in the relations between officers and enlisted men, and in a casual lack of reverence for the traditions instilled by West Point and Carlisle."[32] Even into 1863, volunteers having joined "out of patriotism and a sense of duty" had no intention of "abandoning [their] western distaste for authority or [their] spirit of self reliance. Such a man would obey an order if sensible, otherwise not."[33] This was very apparent in Lyon's assembled Army of the West:

> No love was lost between the professional soldiers and the volunteers. One of the Regulars recalled 'a mutual feeling of unfriendliness and aversion.' He believed that this 'scant civility and offishness was not confined to the ranks; officers shared it to a greater degree than the soldiers, and harbored it more tenaciously.'

In return, the Volunteers "greatly despised the young Regular Army officers . . . as they were 'snobs of the first order' who affected 'jaunty and effeminate ways.'"[34] The Regulars resented the volunteers' lack of discipline. One Regular complained that the Kansans "kept their camp in an uproar all the time, which was a nuisance and annoyance to us."[35] As Major Sturgis discovered at Clinton, "Regular Army standards were not well suited to volunteers," particularly where discipline was concerned.[36] It was with these volunteer units and under these conditions that the much more disciplined and better-equipped officers and men of the Regular Army quickly found themselves.

For the companies of the 1st Cavalry, the events leading up to Wilson's Creek, Major Sturgis's disciplinary actions, and the arrest of Captain Carr by General Lyon—for which there is no explanation—did little to improve the situation. As if to set the trend for the first two years of the war, the Federal Cavalry at Wilson's Creek was ill-used with questionable results. In the case of Captain Carr, his actions before and during this battle appear to be the only blemish on a long and distinguished military career, which may explain why so little is known of the exact circumstances. Between the core of officers and men of the 1st US Cavalry who had served before the war, contempt for the volunteer regiments, with few exceptions, would last well into 1864.

As the war waged on, the size of the Union Cavalry would grow from its initial 5,000 mounted horsemen to over 250,000. The organization, training, and equipping of such a force must have required all the expertise and patience of the seasoned Regular Army cavalrymen, although little credit has been given them.

The Battle at Wilson's Creek (Oak Hill) – August 10, 1861

Union Order of Battle (Partial)
Army of the West
Brigadier General Nathaniel Lyon [Killed]
Major Samuel D. Sturgis [Assumed command]
First Brigade—Major Samuel D. Sturgis
Company D, 1st United States Cavalry—Lieutenant Charles W. Canfield, 2nd Dragoons
Battalion of Regulars / Company of Mounted Rifle Recruits—Captain Joseph B. Plummer, commanding
Second Brigade—Colonel Franz Sigel
Company I, 1st United States Cavalry—Captain Eugene Asa Carr
Company C, 2nd Dragoons—Lieutenant Charles E. Farrand, 11th Infantry[37]

Exhausted and bloodied after the encounter with rebel forces at Dug Springs on August 2, Lyon's army reached McCulla's Farm—about twenty-four miles from Springfield—the next day. Three weeks of half rations and a diet of meat that "caused considerable diarrhea" had severely weakened his army. Lyon reported his command was "unfit to march forward and drive in the enemy's advance."[38] Writing to his superiors on August 4, he expressed doubts about his ability to "retain position in Springfield," which was strategically important for the control of southwestern Missouri. The three-month volunteer enlistments were expiring, which would reduce his force to "about 3,500 men, badly clothed," many without shoes, and "without a prospect of supplies."[39] Lyon's untenable position was summed up in a report filed by Acting Adjutant-General, Army of the West, Major John M. Schofield:

[Lyon] saw clearly the inevitable necessity of either retiring to Rolla, and abandoning to the enemy all the southwest portion of Missouri and Southern Kansas, or of risking the utter destruction of his little army and the loss of all his material of war in a desperate engagement with a vastly superior force of the enemy.[40]

Lyon withdrew to Springfield on August 5 to replenish and rest his troops. He began making plans for a direct attack on the Confederates: "I shall hold my ground as long as possible, though I may, without knowing how far, endanger the safety of my entire force . . ."[41] Under these circumstances, Lyon needed all the experienced men he could get; on August 6, he ordered Captain Carr's release from arrest. The order returning Carr to his company stated: "the subject matter of the charge against Captain Carr will be investigated at a future time." There is no record of the incident or the charges against the captain, and it is speculation how this episode affected Carr's conduct at Wilson's Creek.[42] Company C, 1st Cavalry—badly mauled at Dug Springs—was detached on escort duty "to guard a train of twenty wagons approaching from Rolla" that arrived on August 6. These supplies "allowed the men to go back on full rations for the first time in two weeks." Company B was engaged in scouting activities around Greenfield. These two companies—under command of Captain David Stanley, along with other Home Guards—would remain behind to protect Springfield and its nervous citizens. Company I and "17 members" of Co. D would accompany Lyon in the upcoming battle at Wilson's Creek. The balance of Co. D were with Stanley on escort duty, guarding the hundreds of supply wagons.[43]

Captain Carr, along with Company I, was stationed on Grand Prairie, west of town. On August 8, Carr sent a dispatch to General Lyon reporting: "an enemy force of 20,000 strong was within two miles of the Union position and advancing." Reinforcements were sent, but it turned out to be a false alarm, causing a twenty-four-hour delay in Lyon's plans to attack.[44] The next day Captain Stanley—commanding Company C—captured several rebels in a skirmish on Grand Prairie who provided information that rebels had combined their forces at Wilson's Creek, about ten miles south of Springfield.

The united Confederate forces under Texas Brigadier General Ben McCulloch and Major General

Sterling Price—commanding the Missouri State Guard—numbered a little over 12,000 men, including "2,000 unarmed Missourians, who went with the army with the expectation of getting arms after a while," usually from their fallen comrades.[45]

Lyon's combined forces numbered a little over 5,400.[46] Feeling he had no option but to engage the enemy, he made plans for a surprise attack, striking the Confederate camps simultaneously from the north and the south. Lyon divided his outnumbered army into three columns: under himself, Major Sturgis commanding First Brigade, and Colonel Franz Sigel commanding Second Brigade. Sigel—a German refugee from the failed 1848 revolution—immigrated to the United States in 1852, settling in St. Louis. A strong pro-Unionist, he was commissioned a colonel of the 3rd Missouri Infantry at the outbreak of hostilities.[47] Sigel was ordered to detach his brigade, the 3rd and 5th Missouri, one six-gun battery, and three companies of cavalry: "on a night march to flank the south end of the southern camps, while Lyon himself led the main force on a night march to attack the north end of the camp."[48] Sigel's sixty-five-man cavalry included Captain Carr's 1st US Cavalry, Co. I, along with Company C of the 2nd Dragoons (later 2nd US Cavalry) under 1st Lieutenant Charles Farrand, 11th U.S. Infantry. Farrand had served with the infantry since his graduation from the U.S. Military Academy in 1858. Unable to report to his new assignment with the 11th Infantry, he was temporarily assigned command of Company C, which was left without officers due to the number of resignations.[49] Lieutenant Charles Canfield, 2nd Dragoons, commanded the small contingent of Company D, 1st Cavalry, along with a mounted company of about sixty men of the Second Kansas Volunteers. This comprised the mounted units in Major Sturgis' First Brigade.[50] Canfield dropped out of the U.S. Military Academy in the mid-1850s, but was commissioned a 2nd lieutenant two weeks after Fort Sumter.[51] He would be mortally wounded in the largest and most severe cavalry battle of the war at Brandy Station (Beverly Ford), Virginia, in June 1863.[52]

Around sunset on August 9, Private James Wiswell—still attached to Dragoon Detachment of Recruits as part of the company of Mounted Rifle Recruits—suspected something was up when he saw "Little Red Head" (Lyon) take the lead as his battalion started to move out with "drums beating and colors flying." The new recruits were assigned to Captain Joseph Plummer's Battalion of Regulars in the First Brigade. Among the Mounted Rifle Recruits were Wiswell's three friends from Vermont, along with approximately fifty new troopers who would be assigned to the renamed 4th US Cavalry Companies B, C, and D in September.[53] They would receive a severe baptism of fire in farmer John Ray's cornfield the morning of August 10. Private Wiswell recorded that they marched about ten miles, stopping at midnight when they were close enough to see rebel campfires "gleaming among the brush." The Confederates, planning to move out the next day, had withdrawn their pickets, which afforded Lyon's army the element of surprise. The Union soldiers "laid down and slept till dawn of day," when they "advanced in order of battle."[54]

Lyon's plan had worked perfectly up to this point, affecting complete surprise on the enemy. Company I, 1st US Cavalry was the lead unit and was ordered to: "seize anyone along the route who might alert the enemy to the Federal advance and to place guards at houses in the area so word could not be sent to the Southern camp after the Federals passed by."[55] At about 5 a.m., "Sigel rode with Carr as his company moved up onto a long hill that towered above the creek's eastern side. From this high ground the two officers had a commanding view of the unsuspecting Southern cavalry camps . . ."[56]

The attack began at dawn with the sound of Lyon's artillery, followed by Sigel's. The surprise appeared to rout the Confederates, but they soon recovered and counterattacked. It was as if all the pent-up emotions from years of frustration, anger, and disappointment that led up to the war were unleashed at the Battle of Wilson's Creek. It was about the passions of states' rights. It was about the ideal of a Federal Union. It was in defense of their land and their communities. The rebels were committed to stand and Lyon had risked everything. The fierce battle raged on for six hours. As one Confederate historian notes:

> It was man to man to the death . . . they resolved to die or conquer where they stood. When one of them fell, an unarmed man stepped promptly forward to take his place and his gun. It was a succession of charges followed by a succession of repulses, with solemn intervals of silence between, as each side braced itself again for the desperate struggle.[57]

The almost two-to-one advantage the rebels had over the Federal forces may have been evened out by the fact that many Union troopers had the new Sharps breech-loading rifle, while the rebels "were armed with double-barreled shotguns," antique rifles, pistols, and knives.[58]

Lyon attacked from the north, directly across from the enemy camp on the opposite hill with Wilson's Creek and a ravine between them. Because of the undulating terrain of scrub brush, oak trees, and creeks, Lyon was unsure what lay before him and proceeded with caution. After positioning his artillery, "Lyon gave the signal to advance"; it was 5 a.m.[59] "The First Brigade, or right wing of the army, led by Major Sturgis, bore the burden of the fight, and for a time drove the rebel army rapidly before it."[60] Lyon's forces reached the top of the northern spur of what would become known as "Bloody Hill" before the day was out. At this point, Lyon took steps to secure his left flank, ordering Captain Plummer to take his battalion of about 300 Regular recruits to "carry forward the left flank of the attack."[61] Private Wiswell and the rest of the troopers "waded the creek, crossed the ravine and ascended the opposite hill."[62] At about 6:30 a.m., they found themselves in a field of "Indian corn of moderate height."[63] They were immediately under fire:

> . . . The balls came thick as hail–we had to lay close to the ground as they fired very well for green hands . . . There was 4 men killed from my side. I was surprised at myself. I expected to be excited and trembling but instead of that I took everything as a matter of course. I could stand and see men shot down . . . without seeming to feel or care one single whit for them. . . . I was too busy loading and firing . . .
>
> . . . From the cornfield it was hard to see the Confederates who were in some brush adjoining the cornfield and commenced playing upon us and we played back a little smarter than they did according to our number.[64]

Outnumbered three to one, they were engaged in a fierce, confusing, and bloody fight lasting almost an hour. Unable to clearly distinguish the enemy, becoming separated in the cornstalks, and afraid of accidentally shooting one of their own, the fight came to a standoff when the smoke became so thick it obscured targets.[65] Confederate Colonel James McIntosh—formerly captain of Company D, 1st Cavalry—concerned at the mounting casualties, ordered a charge into the cornfield with about "900 cheering rebels," driving back Plummer's battalion.[66] The casualties were heavy on both sides: The Confederates lost nearly 100 men, and Plummer lost nineteen killed, fifty-two wounded, and nine missing—almost 27% of his total force. Plummer himself was wounded during the retreat. Before turning over his command, he re-formed the battalion and it remained in reserve.[67] According to Wiswell, they formed to the right of Captain James Totten's artillery battery on Bloody Hill, which was becoming the focal point of the now-raging battle.[68]

The activities of Lieutenant Canfield and his contingent of Company D, 1st Cavalry, during the first hours of the battle are unknown. They were probably guarding the rear of a portion of Lyon's command as it maneuvered about three-quarters of a mile from its position on the northern spur of Bloody Hill to the main ridge.[69] The Federals had consolidated their position on the ridge by 6:30 a.m., with Totten's battery at the center of the line that was facing due south.[70] Hearing gunfire from the south, Schofield and Sturgis assumed that Sigel's Second Brigade had begun its attack.[71]

Earlier that morning, Franz Sigel had moved his force of about 1,200 men south—four miles down the Fayetteville road—and then, making a long detour to the left using a byroad: "arrived within a mile of the enemy's camp and rear at daylight." He had taken position on the Fayetteville road to intercept and capture fleeing Confederates. Sigel's battery now occupied a commanding position on a small knoll rising about 150 feet. His infantry extended on both sides of the road and "a company of regular cavalry was on each flank."[72] Sigel "succeeded in capturing the pickets of the enemy, taking him by surprise, and for a time sweeping everything before him with his artillery," creating considerable chaos and panic in the rebel camps.[73] Sigel had ordered Captain Carr to take a position north of the knoll closer to Wilson's Creek to defend against any rebels who might be on the eastern side of the creek.[74] Concerned that his position was now exposed, Sigel left the battery to direct his main column across Wilson's Creek and then north across Terrell's Creek into the southernmost end of the rebel camps.[75]

Captain Carr ordered Company I to dismount with one man in four holding the horses, while the rest opened fire with their carbines. Although too far away to do much damage, Carr wanted the rebels to know he was present in defense of the artillery. For unclear reasons, Carr's company then moved farther north along the creek, out of communication with the artillery on the knoll and "perilously close" to the enemy's camps. From this position Captain Carr could clearly see the rebels were rallying and posed a direct threat to Sigel's flank. He immediately dispatched a trooper to warn Sigel and began moving back toward the knoll, concerned that the enemy "were getting between me and him."[76] At about the same time, Sigel ordered the four guns on the knoll to join his main column. While his column was re-forming on the farm road, some of the Union Volunteers "may have broken ranks to loot the abandoned Southern camp."[77]

Around 7:15 a.m., Sigel resumed bombardment with his full battery. By the time Carr's company rejoined the column, the artillery had run out of targets and Sigel ordered Company I to "assume the advance" while the rest of the brigade filed back onto the farm road. At about 8:00 a.m., the column reached Telegraph (Wire) Road, turning right and halting near farmer Joseph Sharp's house.[78]

Meanwhile, Lyon had consolidated his position on Bloody Hill by 6:30 a.m., and for the next hour and a half an artillery duel raged while inexperienced officers and infantry on both sides fought to maintain or gain the advantage, with the Southerners hindered by a shortage of ammunition. There was a lull around 8:00 a.m. with the growing question on the Federal side, where was Sigel?

When Plummer's battalion was finally driven out of the cornfield and back across Wilson's Creek, the northeastern section of the battlefield was secured. General McCulloch was now free to concentrate on Sigel's command at Sharp's farm to the south.[79] It is at this point that Sigel's abilities come into question. He seemed overconfident and unconcerned that "thousands of enemy soldiers" stood between him and Lyon's forces stalled on Bloody Hill. "He became completely passive at the very moment McCulloch was working to gain the initiative."[80]

McCulloch "took command of the nearest two companies" and moved across Wilson's Creek. Colonel McIntosh joined him as they moved south down Wire Road. An artillery duel erupted when the Confederates came within range. Though a smaller force, the Confederate infantry was aided by the initial confusion of the Union troopers, who were unable to identify them as friend or foe, "as neither army wore a standard color or style of uniform."[81] They had been expecting to meet Lyon's forces at some point, and many of the inexperienced Federal soldiers hesitated to fire. Confusion mounted and the command quickly began to fall apart, "despite the fact that it outnumbered the attackers three to one."[82]

Sigel had earlier ordered Captain Carr's Company I to dismount and guard his left flank just north of Wire Road. For reasons never explained, "Carr repeated his error of earlier in the day" by moving so deeply into the wooded area that his men were "beyond effective supporting distance."[83] Sigel's panicked forces dissolved into full retreat, abandoning four guns and one of the caissons.[84] Unable to assist, Carr's company rode to catch up with the fleeing forces along Wire Road, where they formed an "impromptu rear guard" for about 150 "badly demoralized infantry, one piece [artillery] and two caissons."[85] Company C, 2nd Dragoons—commanded by Captain Farrand and also dismounted—was not in position to respond quickly and were the last to leave the field.[86] The main battle now raged on "Bloody Hill" as both sides dug in. As Major Sturgis noted, the engagement had become "inconceivably fierce all along the entire line."[87]

The enemy would charge Totten's battery and was driven back again and again. Wounded several times and with his horse shot out from under him, the shaken General Lyon insisted on leading his men in battle. "In the shadow of impending defeat [Lyon] was determined to make a supreme effort to reverse the tide that was setting strongly against him."[88] Given another mount by Major Sturgis, Lyon moved to the center of his command to rally his men. As the gallant "red-bearded Lyon" raised his hat high in the air and called to his men, a bullet knocked him from his horse; mortally wounded, he became the first Union general to die in combat.[89] It was now about 10:00 a.m. General Nathaniel Lyon's "brave little army was scattered and broken."[90] The Battle was lost.

With the general's death, command devolved to Major Sturgis, the senior Regular Army officer on the field. At about 11:30 a.m., the "almost uninterrupted conflict of six hours came to an end."[91] During a lull in the action and with no word of

Sigel's fate, Sturgis decided to withdraw from the field.[92] As he later reported, "most of our men had fired away all their ammunition and all that could be obtained from the boxes of the killed and wounded. Nothing, therefore, was left to do but return to Springfield, about twelve miles distant."[93] The order to retreat was given. "The whole column moved slowly to the high open prairie about 2 miles from the battleground," while "ambulances passed to and fro" carrying off the wounded.[94] The exhausted Confederates were just as happy to see them go.[95] Upon reaching Little York Road, Sturgis met up with Lieutenant Farrand and Co. D, 1st Cavalry "and a considerable portion of Colonel Sigel's command." After a short halt they continued the march to Springfield, arriving at 5 p.m.[96]

Sigel's southern command was in full flight toward Springfield along Wire Road. Captain Carr's little group came under fire that killed one of the wheelhorses pulling the gun and wounded the other. His men returned fire, driving off the rebels; however, they were forced to abandon the artillery. Captain Farrand, accompanied by Sergeant John Bradburn, Co. D, and two privates of the 2nd Dragoons, recovered the piece, along with a caisson "full of ammunition" belonging to Sigel's battery.[97]

Captain Carr reported finding Colonel Sigel at Moody Springs, where Wire Road crossed Terrell Creek.[98] They decided to move south on the Fayetteville road until they could "go out and circle round the enemy towards Springfield."[99] Here begins the final controversy regarding Sigel's use of the Federal cavalry and Captain Carr's actions. Just as Sigel's group reached the turnoff for Springfield, Carr's scouts discovered a "large body of cavalry" farther down Wire Road. It was "at least a quarter of a mile in length moving towards the south . . . filing into the road in front."[100] The situation called for rapid movement and the deployment of the cavalry at the crossroads as skirmishers to delay the enemy's pursuit, but Sigel did neither. In fact, the colonel asked Carr to "march slowly," so that his exhausted infantry could keep up with the mounted forces.[101] Pointing out that the enemy would surely try to cut them off at Wilson's Creek and that the infantry and artillery should at least march as fast as the ordinary walk of his horses, a frustrated Carr sought Sigel's permission to ride ahead to the creek.[102] Carr's command crossed Wilson's Creek "near its junction with the James River."[103] While watering his horses, Carr "observed a great dust coming from the enemy's camp." Concluding there was no time to delay, he moved off to a safer spot to wait for the colonel. He waited "for some time" before continuing his march to Springfield. He was not at all surprised to hear that Sigel was ambushed and again routed while attempting to cross the creek.[104] Sigel was last seen by the Confederates "when he dashed into a field and disappeared among the rows of corn."[105]

Private Wiswell's brigade was the last to leave the field, his battalion covering the retreat:

> In leaving the field I had the most trying time for I had to leave many wounded and dying friends and acquaintances laying there parching with thirst and groaning with agony. All that we could do was to give them the water remaining in our canteens and what few consoling words we could.[106]

The brigade remained in the area until 2 a.m. the next morning, when it was ordered to "pack up." The men then marched thirty miles, not arriving in camp until "9 or 10 o'clock."[107] This was a complete rout for the Union forces. The Federals, having lost heavily in the battle, were badly demoralized, and the more than 4,000 survivors had a long and difficult journey ahead of them before they could reach the safety of Rolla, Missouri, about 125 miles to the northeast of Springfield.

The "scattered and broken" Union forces reached Springfield around 5 p.m., where Major Sturgis turned command over to General Sigel. It was agreed the march to Rolla should begin at 2 a.m. "in order that the entire column, with its long train [370 wagons]" might leave Springfield to avoid a potential attack at dawn by the rebels. Major Schofield was to oversee all preparations. When he checked with Sigel's brigade at 1:30 a.m., he found the men "making preparations to cook breakfast" and the general "asleep in bed."[108] After confronting the general, Schofield began the evacuation, but it would be 6 a.m. before the rear guard was able to leave Springfield. Sigel had "arranged the order of march, his brigade and the Iowa regiment forming the advance guard, followed by the baggage train, then the main body of the army." Sturgis's brigade of Regulars was assigned "the fatiguing duty as rear guard."[109]

The road to Rolla was bogged down and "crowded with hundreds of Union refugees, with their teams and families, fleeing in mortal terror from Ben

McCulloch and his Texans."[110] For three days, without rotation, the Regulars were kept at rear guard, arriving in camp each night long after dark, unable to find their supplies in the "inextricable confusion" and catching what rest they could, frequently without food.[111] After three days of disorganization and intolerable delays, a number of the senior officers insisted that Major Sturgis resume command of the Army, using the excuse that General Sigel "acting as an officer of the army . . . had no appointment from any competent authority." In an unusual precedent, Sigel relinquished command.[112]

Marching on foot, Private Wiswell later wrote: ". . . it nearly killed me to march at the rate we did in marching that 122 miles." While Wiswell was on foot, his friend Alvy Allen—wounded during battle and with "nothing to do but plunder the 'Devils' as we politely call the rebels"—was now riding a horse.[113] Wiswell was extremely critical of the officers he saw during this period of time.[114] New to the Army, he may not have been able to distinguish between the few Regular Army officers present and the officers of the volunteer regiments. Based on the results of Bull Run and Wilson's Creek, Wiswell's observations were confirmed in the following months, as hundreds of inexperienced and incompetent officers—many who were "democratically elected" to their positions by the green troops they were to lead—were subsequently dismissed or resigned from the volunteer units under McClellan's rebuilding program. As with most Regular Army soldiers, Wiswell would share a disdain of most volunteer regiments throughout the war.

After Bull Run, the Battle of Wilson's Creek is considered the second major Confederate victory in the Civil War. However, this did not prove to be a decisive victory. By failing to pursue and destroy the retreating Union forces, the Confederates had to fight again seven months later at the Battle of Pea Ridge, Arkansas, which was a decisive victory for the Union. The battle cost the life of Confederate General Ben McCulloch, as well as Colonel James McIntosh, former captain, 1st US Cavalry. Although other skirmishes would follow, the weakened Confederates were never able to control the areas necessary to establish a political foothold in Missouri and the state was saved for the Union.

Wilson's Creek was not only the first major battle west of the Mississippi River, but one of the costliest: "Of the 5,400 Union forces, 285 were killed, 873 wounded, 186 missing, for a casualty rate of 24.5%"—higher than any single battle of the Mexican War.[115] Captain Carr reported four troopers missing from Company I, and there was one wounded and three missing in Company D. The actual casualty rate for the squadron of 1st Cavalry appears to be nine wounded—one mortally—and six missing in action. Four of those wounded would be discharged for disability. Of those reported missing in action, all eventually returned to their companies.[116]

As Major General John Schofield later commented: "The small regular cavalry force engaged shared in whatever of credit could be obtained from the mixture of glory, disgrace and disaster."[117] What there was of "glory" was shared by the 1st United States Cavalry. As reported by General Fremont: "Major Samuel D. Sturgis, First Cavalry, U.S. Army, [was] distinguished for marked intrepidity and gallantry for the highly meritorious services, both before and after the fall of General Lyon." Despite questionable actions on his part, Captain Carr was cited for "gallant and meritorious conduct . . ."[118] Both officers were awarded the "brevet" of lieutenant colonel for bravery during the battle of Wilson's Creek. Carr was promoted to colonel, United States Volunteers, commanding the Fourth Division of the Army of the Southwest at the battle of Pea Ridge in March 1862, where he was again brevetted brigadier general, USV, for "distinguished service." For his actions under fire while deploying his command, he would later be awarded the Medal of Honor.[119]

General Fremont praised Lieutenant Canfield, commanding Co. D, 1st Cavalry, for his "conspicuous gallantry and highly meritorious conduct from the beginning to the close of the battle." He also singled out Lieutenant Farrand, commanding Co. C, 2nd Dragoons, for his "gallant and meritorious service." It is important to note that when a commanding officer is singled out for his conduct, it was understood the recognition also applied to the men under his command.[120]

Colonel Sigel—promoted to brigadier general—would actually distinguish himself at the Battle of Pea Ridge, the high point of his checkered career. Although much admired by the German-American community during the war, his name would become "synonymous with controversy and defeat."[121]

As it happened, the same day the battle at Wilson's Creek was being fought, Congress passed the act that reorganized and renumbered the mounted regiments. The 1st Cavalry now became the 4th United States Cavalry.

Missing in Action

Sometime between October 14 and 23, 1861, there was an exchange of correspondence regarding prisoners of war between Major General Leonidas Polk, commanding Confederate forces, and Union commander Brigadier General John A. McClernand. On October 14, Polk wrote to Ulysses S. Grant—commanding the District of Southeast Missouri at Cairo, Illinois—proposing an exchange of prisoners based on "the principles recognized in the exchange of prisoners effected on the 3rd of September between Brigadier General [Gideon] Pillow, of the Confederate army, and Colonel [Lew] Wallace, of the U.S. Army . . ."[122] Grant, concerned that a response on his part could possibly constitute recognition of the "Southern Confederacy," passed on the correspondence to General McClernand.[123] The general responded to Pope on October 22 regarding three rebel prisoners held by Union forces:

> Sir: The chances of the present unhappy war having left in my hands a number of prisoners who have been detained at this post for some time past I have for special reasons as well as in obedience to the dictates of humanity determined unconditionally to release them.
>
> The prisoners alluded to . . . [were] all taken by a part of U.S. troops in the affair at Charleston, Mo., on the 20th of August.[124]

In authorizing the return of the rebel captives, McClernand was very careful in his instructions to the officer assigned the duty:

> In your conversation with the commandant or his representative you will avoid all discussion upon the rights of belligerents and place my action herein simply on the grounds of humanity and a desire to relieve the unhappy war now waged between kindred of peculiar and aggravating difficulties. Beyond this limit I do not deem it advisable for you to go.[125]

The three captives were delivered to Confederate headquarters at Columbus, Kentucky, on October 23. Leonidas Polk was generous in his response:

> I accept the release of the three prisoners tendered me being as your note implies all of those of the Confederate army in your possession. In return I have the pleasure of offering you the sixteen of those of the Federal army in my possession.[126]

Among those prisoners who were returned to Brigade Headquarters at Camp Cairo were two from 4th Cavalry, Company I: Privates John M. Herberich and Michael H. Lambert.[127]

For the remainder of August, the four companies of the 1st Cavalry remained at Camp Lyon, near Rolla, Missouri.[128] David Stanley—promoted to brigadier general Volunteers on August 10—was now in charge of all the cavalry in the Army of the Mississippi. Three companies of the 4th Cavalry were attached to the 5th Division (Cavalry Division), Army of the West. Companies B, C, and D were assigned "bodyguard duty" for three new brevet brigadier generals: Company B for Frederick Steele, Company C for Samuel Sturgis, and Company D for James Totten.[129] On August 28, Company I was dispatched to Paducah, Kentucky, reporting to Brigadier General Ulysses S. Grant at his headquarters at Cairo, Illinois. They would remain in that vicinity, "scouting the country and doing picket duty."[130]

During the first week of September, Companies B, C, and D were transported by rail to St. Louis, where General Fremont, Federal Commander of the West, was assembling his army. They would remain there until the ninth. During this time, the four recruits from Hyderville, Vermont, along with approximately fifty other new recruits, were assigned to their new companies: James Wiswell and Alvey Allen to Co. C, Henry Parkhurst to Co. B, and James Cummings to Co. D. The new troopers "drawed [sic] clothes, horses and arms."[131] The battalion marched to Jefferson City, where they remained for ten days before moving to Syracuse (about twenty miles due east of Sedalia), where they received their first pay on October 16.[132]

The following incident was reported in the *Grand Traverse Herald* (Traverse City, Michigan), on October 18, 1861:

> Cairo, October 10. This morning about two o'clock a large number of rebels, estimated at two thousand or three thousand strong, attacked a squad

of Federal pickets, six in number, from Company I, Fourth Regular Cavalry, stationed four or five miles from Paducah, KY., mortally wounding two, taking two prisoners and all their horses and equipage. The other two escaped.

This may have been where Privates Lambert and Herberich were captured and Private Hugh Morgan was killed.[133]

SPRINGFIELD, MISSOURI—OCTOBER 25

On October 4, by order of General Fremont, Brigadier General Frederick Steele was to organize a new brigade that would include the three companies of the 4th Cavalry commanded by Captain David Stanley. Leaving Syracuse on October 20, they made a "forced march" to join Fremont, who was advancing on Springfield.[134] The scene was now set for another highly publicized cavalry charge. As later recorded by Captain Joseph Vale, 7th Pennsylvania Volunteer Cavalry:

> Stanley, now in charge of all the cavalry in the Army of the Missouri, led two hundred and fifty men, including forty of Fremont's Body Guard, commanded by Lieutenant Charles Zagonyi, in the great charge upon the rebel rear guard at Springfield, Missouri. This, being the first occasion in the war, in which a volunteer cavalry force participated in a saber charge, attracted great attention at the time was so illustrated and advertised as to create the impression that no other troops were present. The fact is, however, that Captain Stanley led the fight, and the regulars were equal participants with the volunteers in its glorious results. In this engagement, the entire rear guard of [Sterling] Price's army, over two thousand strong, was cut to pieces and destroyed. It was a *saber* fight, and from it the old Fourth Regulars . . . *learned the lesson of the power of that weapon, which they did not forget during the whole war* [emphasis author]. . . . The importance of this conflict can scarcely be over-estimated, in its influence both on the regulars and volunteers. The boys of the Fourth never forgot that the men [volunteers] of Fremont's Guard proved equally good soldiers with themselves, and always acted in perfect accord with any body of volunteer cavalry that would fight, *while the dashing gallantry of the regulars became an inspiration for all cavalry to emulate* [emphasis author].[135]

The publicity and propaganda generated by the two cavalry charges led by Captain David Stanley as illustrated in *Harper's Weekly* may have had their desired effect. According to cavalry historian Stephen Z. Starr: "The bars were now down to the formation of mounted regiments of volunteers, with the result that within a month after Bull Run, thirty-one such regiments had been organized and mustered in, followed by fifty-one more by the year-end."[136]

SALINE COUNTY AND BLACKWATER CREEK (SHAWNEE MOUND)

The action was not quite over for the three companies of the 4th Cavalry. There would be two more scouting activities of note: the first from December 3-12, and the other from December 15-19. Major George C. Marshall, 2nd Missouri Cavalry, was ordered to take 300 men—composed of the companies of the 4th Cavalry and Colonel Lewis Merrill's Horse Cavalry—on a ten-day scout through Saline County, Missouri, which was more pro-secessionist than not.[137]

Twelve men from Company C, with Lieutenant Michael Kelly, led the advance guard. The second day (December 4), they were fired upon "by a portion of a company of 60 rebels" that quickly retired. Searching the nearby farm, they found "2 kegs of powder and a quantity of parts of cavalry equipments." The next day, after taking several prisoners, they camped on the farm of a "notorious traitor" and "raised the Stars and Stripes over his house." On the sixth, they "marched north about 18 miles through Arrow Rock," where they found more kegs of powder concealed in warehouses. They also burned a ferryboat. They were again fired upon "by a few men from across the river" without incident. At Saline City the next day they confiscated more arms and powder. On the seventh, they captured two officers "of General Clark's staff." The next day, they found "government wagons," took five along with them, and destroyed three for which there were no mules or harnesses. On the evening of the ninth Joseph Shelby—a local rebel leader—arrived with his company and tried bombarding the Union camp with a 10-inch mortar loaded with mud. They were quickly dispatched by Lieutenants Kelly and Henry Gordon, Co. D. Marching into the small town of Waverly the next day, they found the "celebrated mortar" and nine kegs of powder concealed under a platform in Shelby's store. On December 12, Marshall's command returned to Sedalia, reporting two casualties: one of the Regulars broke his leg when his saddle turned during a charge, and a trooper in Merrill's Horse Cavalry accidentally shot and killed himself.[138]

With less than three days rest, Companies B, C, and D became part of a five-day expedition under Brigadier General John C. Pope to cut Price's communications.[139] All three companies were now led by newly appointed 2nd Lieutenants: Michael Kelly, Co. C, a civilian appointed on May 8; Copley Amory, Co. B, a civilian from Massachusetts appointed on August 5; and Henry Gordon, a sergeant and ten-year veteran appointed to command Co. D on October 24.[140] Kelly, having the senior appointment, should have led the battalion, but with the disaster at Dug Springs on August 2 still fresh in everyone's memory, the command was passed to 2nd Lieutenant Amory.

"The object of this movement was to interpose between Price's army, on the Osage, and the recruits, escorts, and supplies on there way south from the Missouri River."[141] By the third day, when they reached Warrensburg, Pope's command had captured "16 wagons, loaded with tents and supplies and 150 prisoners."[142] On the afternoon of the eighteenth at Milford, a little north of Warrensburg, "a brisk skirmish ensued" with a large force of the enemy.[143] After sealing off all possible escape routes, General Pope sent his eight companies of cavalry—including the three regulars and a section of artillery—"to march on the town of Milford, so as to turn the enemy's left and rear and intercept his retreat to the southeast."[144] The enemy's camp was in the "wooded bottomland on the west side of Blackwater [Creek] opposite the mouth of Clear Creek," accessible only by a long narrow bridge "which the enemy occupied in force." 2nd Lieutenants Amory and Gordon's companies were placed in the advance, supported by the five companies of the First Iowa. After firing two volleys at the men on the bridge, Amory led the charge with Co. B, closely followed by Companies D and C. The rebels, "terrified by the suddenness and boldness of the charge," broke and fled, closely pursued by the 4th Cavalry. They soon found themselves in the main enemy camp. Quickly dismounting his troopers, Lieutenant Gordon and Company D "delivered two volleys, which the enemy returned."[145] "The bullets flew pretty fast for a few minutes," wrote Private Wiswell, "but we made short work of it."[146] Eight men of Company D and one of Company C were wounded, and Lieutenant Gordon received "several balls through his cap."[147] One of the wounded—Private Patrick Tracy, Co. D—was transported to City General Hospital in St. Louis, where he died from his wounds on February 16, 1862.[148] The support of the 5th Iowa Volunteers failed to materialize as "one of the companies had broken and were in confusion," and the commanding officer of the 5th Iowa sat waiting for orders from General Pope.[149] By the time Amory re-formed his three companies "in line of battle opposite the enemy's camp . . . a flag of truce appeared."[150] Pope's command took "1300 prisoners, including 3 colonels and 17 captains, and 1,000 stand of arms, 1,000 horses, 65 wagons, and a large quantity of tents, baggage, supplies."[151] The expedition was a success. Having marched nearly 200 miles in bitterly cold weather, Lieutenant Amory's little battalion returned to Sedalia.[152]

When General Pope delivered his official report to Major General Henry Halleck, there were two interesting omissions. He failed to credit Lieutenant Amory for any of his actions, while crediting Lieutenant Gordon with "leading the charge in person with utmost gallantry and vigor" and carrying the bridge "in fine style." Nor did he mention the failure of the 5th Iowa to provide support prior to the surrender.[153] Apparently upset at these omissions, 2nd Lieutenant Amory took the highly unusual step of submitting his own report—not through General Pope, but by way of Brigadier General Frederick Steele, commanding at Sedalia. Steele forwarded Amory's report to Major General Halleck with his comment:

> I have no doubt but that this is a correct report of the affair. Lieutenant Amory thinks that justice was not done him in General Pope's report. Lieutenant Amory's account is corroborated by Dr.

Brodie and Lieutenant Gordon. If the matter were investigated I think it would be found that there are other inaccuracies in the official report of the expedition and affair near Milford.[154]

As a civilian appointee, Lieutenant Amory may not have appreciated the fact that this was a career-ending move for a junior officer. Although promoted to 1st lieutenant in October 1862, this may explain his detached service as "Recruiting Officer" and his early resignation in December 1863.[155] John Pope was a career soldier, and a newly appointed brigadier general with his first field command in the war. He may well have favored 2nd Lieutenant Henry Gordon, the veteran 1st sergeant, over the recently appointed green civilian officer, and Pope apparently wasn't about to report any shortcomings in his first command.

Although companies of the Fourth US Cavalry did not participate, the definitive Battle of Pea Ridge on March 8, 1862, effectively ended the influence of the pro-secessionists in Missouri, Captain Stanley's battalion of 4th Cavalry, Companies B, C, D, and I, had a significant impact on the outcome of the events that kept Missouri in the Union. For their participation in the engagements at Forsyth, Springfield, and Dug Springs, the officers and men were continually recognized for their "gallant and meritorious" conduct fighting off the advances of the Confederate forces and capturing a large number of prisoners, their weapons, and supplies.

To expand on Vale's observations made after the Battle of Springfield in October, "The importance of [these] conflicts can hardly be over estimated . . ." This was the ultimate training ground for what was to come. The activities of July and August 1861 gave opportunity for these officers and men to sharpen their skills of command and tactics that would be so necessary for their future survival. Companies B, C, and D remained "in the field" in Missouri until January 1862.[156]

Company I was now on duty around Paducah, Kentucky. Late in the evening of December 28, Brigadier General Lew Wallace took a detachment of 130 men from the Second Illinois Cavalry, Co. I, 4th U.S., Co. C, 2nd US Cavalry, "and 70 men from Thieleman's dragoons [Illinois Independent Cavalry]" on an expedition "in the direction of Camp Beauregard [Mayfield, Kentucky]." This was for the purpose of "reconnoitering that camp, gaining information as to the strength of the enemy and their whereabouts, and ascertaining whether or not re-enforcements had left Camp Beauregard for Bowling Green."[157] When they approached within six miles of Camp Beauregard the next day, "where the enemy appeared to have an outpost, guarded by about 75 men," the rebels fled "helter-skelter." The following day Wallace encountered "a heavy force of infantry and cavalry," but both sides withdrew. "The country from Mayfield to Camp Beauregard," wrote Wallace in his report of January 1, 1862, "is of such a character as to render fighting with cavalry almost impossible."[158]

In 1862, Union control of the state of Missouri facilitated the evolving military strategy of the Federal Army in the West: controlling the Mississippi River from St. Louis to New Orleans, isolating Texas, and splitting the Confederacy. Company I participated in the opening battle at Fort Donelson, Tennessee, in February. They were the first company of the regiment to confront the man who would become one of the Confederacy's greatest and most notorious cavalrymen, Nathan Bedford Forrest.

1862: Finding Form

The many scouting excursions, skirmishes, and constant activity in which [the cavalry] *was kept, formed a most admirable school of training for its future operations.*
– Captain Joseph G. Vale[1]

I. The Western Theater

In early 1862, military strategy in the west centered on the Mississippi River and its tributaries. By taking control of the Mississippi from St. Louis to New Orleans, the Confederacy would be divided, the Republic of Texas isolated, and the Union Army would have access to the main arteries of the Tennessee and Cumberland Rivers. It would then have the ability to penetrate the heart of the Confederacy. The key to this plan was capturing the two Confederate forts that controlled the Tennessee and Cumberland Rivers: Fort Henry and Fort Donelson.

Throughout the year, the officers and men of the 4th United States Cavalry refined their skills and techniques, developing the form that would distinguish them as a new fighting unit equal in importance and ability to the infantry and artillery. Companies of the Fourth Regiment became field-tested veterans in an endless number of expeditions, skirmishes, and battles. As pointed out by regimental historian Captain Joseph Vale:

> . . . [T]he exigencies of the service, the topography of the country, and the

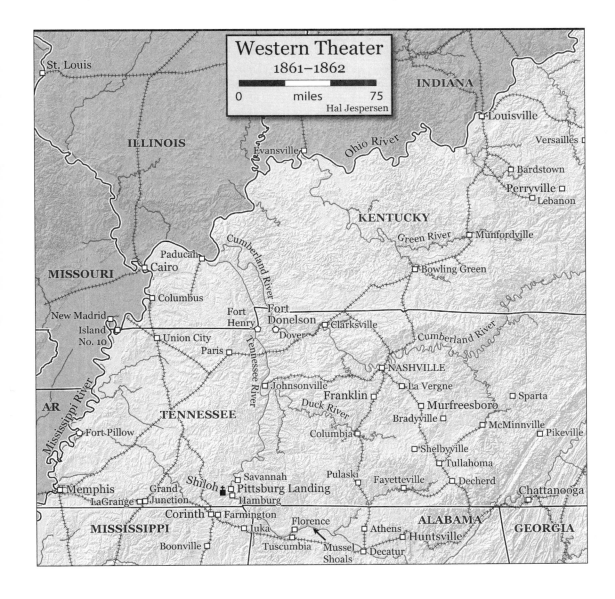

necessity of guarding and occupying so large an extent of exposed territory, as lay on the flanks and in the rear of our main army, compelled the frequent use of the cavalry in independent operations . . .²

The troopers learned picket, sentry, courier, and escort duties. They were constantly on the move, learning to travel light and move quickly in the most severe weather and over mud, slush, and frozen roads. They became accustomed to temporary bivouacs in the worst of conditions; they mastered finding shelter and building fires with wet fuel; they learned to stretch their meager rations and find forage for their mounts. They surveyed the countryside and built roads and bridges. They built earthworks and dug trenches. They trained the volunteer cavalry. The majority of the commands to which they were assigned were "composed, officers and men, of citizens, who at the time of enlistment, were entirely without military knowledge or training."³ It fell to the Regulars to provide the necessary training in the field. They fought. They fought as companies, squadrons, and battalions. They learned early "the utility and power of the saber and found, that by daring charges bringing on a hand-to-hand encounter," they were "uniformly successful" in defeating enemy cavalry "who depended mainly on the double barreled shot-gun and revolver."⁴

On a growing number of occasions, companies of the 4th Cavalry were engaged in "curbing the depredations of the Confederate Cavalry under Nathan Bedford Forrest."⁵ Forrest is considered by some to be the greatest cavalry leader of the war. Fiercely independent and a natural strategist, he was among the first to recognize that this war would not be won with the gentlemanly rules of conduct subscribed to by the old military command. The 4th U.S. and Forrest's cavalries would develop a bitter and bloody rivalry that would last until the final week of the war.

The officers and men of the 4th United States Cavalry were battle tested. Their leadership came from within: Stanley, Sturgis, McIntyre, James Oakes, Elmer Otis, McCormick, and others—in most cases under the direction of competent senior commanders Generals Granger, Rosecrans, and the newly appointed Chief of Cavalry David S. Stanley, who quickly began to see the combat value of this newest branch of the Army.

During 1862, Companies A and E remained with the Army of the Potomac, participating in the Peninsular Campaign and Antietam and serving as Major General Ambrose Burnside's escorts at the Battle of Fredericksburg in December. They would rejoin the regiment in Nashville in March 1863. In late January, Companies B, C, and D were ordered to Jefferson City and then to St. Louis for refitting and new orders.⁶ They would subsequently be assigned to Pope's Army of Virginia. Company I would be assigned to Brigadier General Ulysses S. Grant at Cairo, Illinois. In February, Companies G and K, "aggregate 88 . . . armed, equipped, and mounted," were transferred from Fort Leavenworth to Louisville, Kentucky, and attached to the Department of the Ohio, General Don Carlos Buell commanding. According to Buell, there was "no other cavalry in the department completely armed, equipped and mounted."⁷ This might explain the high desirability of having companies of the 4th US Cavalry in the advance of military movements and acting as personal escorts for the generals of the army. In April 1862, these six companies of the regiment would reunite under General Gordon Granger in the Cavalry Division of the Army of the Mississippi, participating at Farmington and Corinth, Tennessee, and the capture of Boonville, Mississippi. In June, the same six companies were with Buell's Army of the Ohio in the Northern Alabama Campaign, Middle Tennessee Campaign, Kentucky Campaign, and the Battle of Perrysville, Kentucky, in October. Companies F and H remained on duty at Forts Kearney and Laramie, Nebraska Territory, throughout 1862. Two new companies (L and M) were formed in the field near Murfreesboro, Tennessee, in November 1862. By the end of 1862, when the officers and men of ten companies of the battle-hardened 4th US Cavalry became a part of General David S. Stanley's Cavalry Brigade, they were one of the best-trained, disciplined, experienced, and equipped cavalry regiments in the Union Army.

Forts Henry and Donelson, Tennessee

Henry W. Halleck—a career officer—was appointed a major general at the beginning of the war, and his first command was to replace the troublesome Fremont in Missouri. One of his field generals was a relatively unknown brigadier general named Ulysses S. Grant, in command at Cairo, Illinois. At the junction of the Ohio and Mississippi Rivers, it was here that the Federals were concentrating an army of 11,000 men of all arms. Most of the army that had been operating in Missouri was brought to Paducah and Smithfield, Kentucky, and placed under Grant's command. This included Company I, 4th US Cavalry. It would participate in the capture of Fort Donelson in February and was with Grant's Army at Pittsburgh Landing (Shiloh) in April.[8]

By September 1861, the state of Kentucky moved from its original neutral position to siding with the Union. The Confederacy, under Major General Polk, responded by capturing the town of Columbus on the Mississippi River. "Grant countered by seizing Paducah, which controlled the mouths of the Tennessee and Cumberland Rivers."[9] Private Wiswell suspected that the "war had just begun . . . and Kentucky is to be the 'Dark and Bloody Ground' she has always been."[10]

In the first weeks of January 1862, General Halleck ordered Grant—with about 6,000 men of Brigadier General McClernand's command—to make a demonstration against Columbus, Kentucky, to prevent the enemy from sending troops from there to Bowling Green. Company I, having joined Grant's forces in November, "led the advance of this expedition and did valiant service in driving in the enemy's pickets and out-posts . . . notwithstanding the continued rain and the wretched condition of the roads . . ."[11] When Company I became a part of Grant's Army, it was originally assigned to Brigadier General Charles F. Smith's Second Division under command of 1st Lieutenant James Powell, 18th U.S. Infantry. Among the first of the enlisted men in the 4th Cavalry to receive a commission in May 1861, Powell had risen through the ranks to 1st sergeant, Company I, when promoted.[12] Company I became part of a squadron of Regular Cavalry with Company C, 2nd United States commanded by Captain Charles E. Farrand, 11th U.S. Infantry. Farrand would command the squadron leading to the surrender of Fort Henry, but was absent from the Battle of Fort Donelson because of ill health; the squadron was then led by Lieutenant Powell.[13]

Under the command of Major General Halleck, Grant led a force of 15,000 troops up the Tennessee against the strategically crucial Fort Henry. On February 6, the rebel troops at Fort Donelson—eleven miles away—were awakened by the sounds of heavy guns from Union gunboats firing on Fort Henry. They would be joined by the retreating Confederate forces within 24 hours as Fort Henry fell to the Union advance. The garrison at Fort Donelson began to prepare for the inevitable.

Captain Vale records: "After being transported 50 miles up the Tennessee River by steamer from Cairo," the squadron of Regular Cavalry landed at Fort Henry the day after it fell into Union hands. They then slogged through the mud that passed for a road to within three miles of Fort Donelson. On the seventh, they "established a strong line of pickets" and made a "complete topographical survey of the country almost to the enemy's works."[14] The next day, they found themselves "actively engaged" with four companies of Confederate cavalry under the command of Nathan Bedford Forrest. "The country being heavily wooded, the engagement was fought dismounted, and resulted in the repulse of the rebel attack and driving Forrest inside the entrenched position at Donelson."[15] Writing his regimental history years later, Captain Vale may have combined several days of skirmishes into his version of events. Forrest notes the actual date of the first encounter he had with Union Cavalry as Tuesday, February 11, with slightly different results: "We met about 3 miles from Fort Donelson . . . and after a short skirmish, pressing them hard about six miles, captured 1 prisoner and mortally wounded several others."[16]

By mid-February, Fort Donelson had been heavily reinforced by the Confederates. Not only did it guard the Cumberland River, it was also vital to the Confederacy for the defense of Nashville, a major armament and supply center of strategic importance to both sides. Although only eleven miles from Fort Henry, the winter weather and road conditions slowed Grant's progress to Fort Donelson. His army had to travel "on two primitive roads" that had been reduced to a muddy slush. Without teams and wagons to carry supplies that would have bogged down in the mud, the men had no tents or blankets and were short on rations and ammunition.[17] This delay allowed the Confederacy time for additional heavy reinforcements. By February 12, Grant's infantry and cavalry had arrived at the site of the fort and spent most of the day getting into position on the field. Grant placed his First Division, under General John A. McClernand, on his right; General Charles Smith's Second Division on the left; and General Lew Wallace's Third Division at the center. McClernand's Division was to hold the road to Nashville. The squadron of Regular Cavalry was attached to Colonel Richard J. Oglesby's First Brigade in McClernand's First Division. Under the command of Colonel Silas Nobel, 2nd Illinois Cavalry, the two companies of Regular Cavalry, along with two companies of the 2nd Illinois Cavalry, were "sent forward . . . at 8 o'clock a.m. . . . to reconnoiter to a point within 2 miles of Fort Donelson." Meeting the enemy's pickets, "they drove them back." They then moved "to the right of the Ridge road . . . to the main road leading from the Big Sandy Creek to Dover."[18] The cavalry was again "thrown forward, and occupied the heights," scouting and reconnoitering the ground in front while the Second Brigade was dragging its artillery up the steep, wooded hills.[19] With the artillery in place, the cavalry advanced "towards the enemy's center" on Indian Creek Road, where it "came in full view of the enemy's tents on the opposite hill."[20]

The Confederates had "created a semi-circular defensive position," with Fort Donelson at one end and the town of Dover at the other. The position backed to the Cumberland River. Included in the rebel force were three cavalry regiments under Colonel Forrest. His cavalry spent the day "from about 9 a.m. to near 2 p.m." harassing Federal forces, causing considerable delay in the deployment.[21] Powell's squadron of Regulars "pushed forward to the right . . . attacking the enemy works at Dover" and skirmishing with Forrest's cavalry.[22] With this effort McClernand was "able to deploy his command," get his artillery in place, and "commence at long range a slow cannonade."[23]

February 13, Grant ordered a detailed reconnaissance of the enemy position and gave orders "for probing attacks only." No general engagement was to be made.[24] Skirmishers were sent out in advance "to draw fire from, and thus detect the location of the enemy." Both sides began using their artillery. At the same time, another cavalry reconnaissance was ordered to the right of the enemy's entrenchments at Dover.[25] Noble's cavalry regiment was again attacked by Forrest near River Road, "supported by infantry and artillery." Holding their position, they were able to drive the rebels back.[26] "A counterattack was then ordered by McClernand about 11 A.M.," during which Colonel Oglesby's brigade: "captured the rifle-pits and outlying works of the enemy, driving them off the ridge while Colonel Noble, with the cavalry, advanced to within half a mile of Dover, finally establishing the line of investment clear to the over-flow of the Cumberland river."[27] The squadron of Regular Cavalry commanded by Lieutenant Powell did "gallant and effective service" under "very hazardous" conditions, opening the way to the river.[28]

McClernand took position to defend the road from Dover to Nashville, closing off possible Confederate communications and their escape route.[29] Believing that the rebel position was now weakened and acting without direct orders from Grant, McClernand ordered his Third Brigade to advance against the enemy. These actions precipitated the opening battle for Fort Donelson.[30] McClernand's Division made two valiant assaults and was repulsed both times. At the third attempt, the leaves and underbrush caught fire. "The heat and smoke became stifling." The flames crept down upon the wounded, "smothering and charring them where they lay," consuming the dead and wounded on the field of battle. Fort Donelson was becoming a nightmare for the recently recruited Union soldiers. Without shelter and scanty rations consisting of "a small allowance of hard bread and coffee," they now had to endure a "devastating blizzard." A strong wind, "bringing rain that turned into sleet followed by snow," dropped the temperature to ten degrees above zero.[31] Some of the wounded who had survived the fire now froze to death in the dark. Both sides had sharpshooters, and the men in the front lines were not allowed campfires for warmth. Drenched and chilled, they caught colds "that would bring pneumonia and death no matter how the battle went."[32]

On February 14, "the pattern of sniping and probing continued until midday," as additional Union forces continued to arrive overland and by steamer. McClernand continued his reconnaissance and repositioning of his troops, including his cavalry, which was "disposed to the rear and still farther to the right . . ."[33] A Union gunboat assault in the late afternoon failed.[34] For the third night, "Grant's soldiers endured the weather with neither food, nor shelter, nor fires for warmth." All night long they could hear the Confederates "felling trees and using picks and shovels to strengthen their defenses."[35]

Meanwhile, the commanders at Fort Donelson were slowly realizing that they could not survive a siege. They planned an attack on the Union's right wing, attempting to reopen land communication with Nashville and creating the possibility of a route for retreat.[36]

After snowing during the night, the morning of February 15 "came in clear with a wintery sunlight lying on the white hills."[37] The Confederates "stormed forth from their snow-covered trenches in a devastating surprise assault" on Grant's right flank, held by McClernand's division.[38] Colonel Oglesby's brigade, including the two companies of Regular Cavalry, took the full brunt of the attack.[39] Reveille was just being sounded, and "the numbed soldiers of the line were rising from their icy beds and shaking the snow from their frozen garments" when the pickets began sounding the alarm as the woods "became alive" with rebel infantry. The Federals fought back as Forrest's cavalry moved in to surround them. The attack quickly spread. Two Confederate charges were repulsed. Rebel artillery opened fire. Union artillery responded and "exhausted their ammunition in the duel. The roar never slacked ...":

> Men fell by the score, reddening the snow with their blood. The smoke, in pallid white clouds, clung to the underbrush and the tree-tops as if to screen the combatants from each other. Close to the ground the flame of musketry and cannon tinted everything a lurid red. Limbs shattered by shells dropped from the trees on the heads below, and the thickets were shorn as by an army of cradlers [scythes]. The division was under peremptory orders to hold its position to the last extremity . . . .[40]

By 10 a.m. the pressure was overwhelming and the Federal infantry was running out of ammunition. The Union right began to give way, and by 11 a.m., the Confederates held the ground that had been occupied by McClernand's First Division that morning. McClernand's troops were retreating by Wynn's Ferry Road and the entire brigade commanded by Colonel William H. L. Wallace was pushed back, giving the Confederates the open road to Nashville.[41] Believing they had achieved their objective, at about 1:00 p.m. "the battle began to subside, the firing ceased, and the Confederates receded."[42]

General Grant, conferring with Commodore Andrew H. Foote aboard his gunship *St. Louis*, was unaware of the disaster that had befallen his right. Rushing back to his command, he immediately ordered his Third Division, under General Lew Wallace, to reinforce McClernand, who "hastened to reorganize his beaten brigades for a counterattack."[43] In a move that was to characterize his future career, Grant would "seize the initiative and hit back harder . . . when his opponents least expected it."[44]

In this case, he also had some help from Confederate General Gideon J. Pillow, who made a critical mistake at this time. He assumed the whole Federal Army was in retreat and ordered the bulk of his army to follow in pursuit, thus weakening the defenses of Fort Donelson. Grant's immediate counterattack took the Confederates completely by surprise. Aided by the confusion and incompetent leadership in the Confederate command, "the advantage that had been won was thrown away. By night all of the rebels were back in their trenches, bewildered by the way victory had turned to defeat."[45]

Fort Donelson was now under siege, and it turned into a disastrous trap for the Confederates.[46] They had no choice but to surrender. A note was sent to General Grant, asking what terms he could give.[47] He issued his now famous response: "No terms except unconditional and immediate surrender can be accepted."[48]

Nathan Bedford Forrest and his men were trapped in the fort. Furious at the thought of surrender and ignoring his commanding generals, he gathered his troops together and made a daring escape in the dark of night, "floundering through ice-cold water in the swamps but getting out alive."[49] The surrender of the fort and its garrison of over thirteen thousand men followed the morning of the sixteenth, "the first great Union victory of the war."[50]

The loss of Fort Donelson was a major setback for the Confederates; it broke open their defensive line, forcing them to fall back through Tennessee and abandoning southern Kentucky and much of west and middle Tennessee.[51] The loss of so much territory—especially the transportation and supply center at Nashville—was a severe emotional blow to the Confederacy.[52] Success at the Battle of Fort Donelson—the North's first major victory—"made Brigadier General Ulysses S. Grant's name as a leading Union Commander" and brought a promotion to major general.[53]

The price of victory among the inexperienced troops was heavy, especially in Colonel Oglesby's First Brigade, which received the brunt of the Confederate attack on the fifteenth. Of the 2,886 Union casualties, 30% were in the First Brigade, with 184 killed, 603 wounded, and sixty-six missing.[54] There were no reported casualties in the Regular Cavalry squadron, although Private Herberich, Co. I, "received a shell wound on the right leg above the ankle."⁵⁵ This injury was not reported until after the battle at Shiloh two months later. Emergency medical treatment on the field was almost nonexistent at this early stage of the war. Grant's Chief Surgeon—an apparent alcoholic—was charged with "gross irregularities" for his alleged mistreatment of Federal wounded at Fort Donelson.⁵⁶

Nashville, Tennessee

On February 16, General Grant moved "by boat, up the Cumberland river to Nashville, while a Cavalry force, Company I, Fourth United States, in the advance, marched on the same place, moving on the river road, in active pursuit of Forrest's cavalry."⁵⁷ Captain Joseph Vale writes:

> ... the whole country was in a wild panic, and evidences of the most complete demoralization of the enemy were seen on every hand. So widespread and absurd was the panic that the people, *en masse*, were seen, men, women, and children, leaving their homes and fleeing in every direction, seeming only anxious to go somewhere.⁵⁸

The cavalry apparently played an odd role in this panic. Wild rumors had spread of "the most terrible of all the new engines of war"—gunboats. The citizens were terrified, although few knew or had any idea of what they were. When overtaken by the cavalry, they were generally in a deadly fear of the harmless bundles of blankets and extra clothing which the cavalry had strapped in the cantles of their saddles, believing they were some infernal machines or parts of the dreaded gunboats.⁵⁹

Even among rebel forces there was evidence of panic: "scattered all along the road, for ... ten miles, first hats, caps, and extra clothing," then mess kits, tents, heavy baggage, and wrecked wagons.⁶⁰ Nashville was surrendering to General Don Carlos Buell. The city formally surrendered on February 24, and the command entered Nashville on the twenty-fifth.

On March 1, Company I was relieved and returned to Fort Donelson with General Smith's corps. Companies G and K remained attached to General Buell's Army of the Ohio as his escorts.

New Madrid and Island No. 10

In early February, Companies B, C, and D—once again commanded by the young Lieutenant Michael Kelly—were ordered to Benton Barracks, St. Charles, Missouri, northwest of St. Louis on the Missouri River. They were to "proceed without delay to the seat of war in Tennessee, stopping long enough at St. Louis to obtain a full supply of ordnance stores and touching at Cairo and Paducah for orders."⁶¹ They left Sedalia "February 3, arriving in Jefferson City on the 7th and Benton Barracks on the 19th."⁶² They were to be attached "unassigned" to General Pope's Army of the Mississippi and were to participate in his Joint Operations on the Middle Mississippi River between February 29 and April 8.⁶³ Island No. 10, a fortified Confederate installation in the Mississippi about sixty miles below Columbus, became the next line of defense for control of the Mississippi River. Brigadier General Pope set out from Commerce, Missouri, laying siege to New Madrid on March 3.⁶⁴ His troops succeeded in "cutting a canal through the marshy area near Island No. 10 ... near New Madrid, thus allowing Federal gunboats to go around the island and land four regiments in Tennessee below the Confederate position on Island No. 10." By March 13, the Confederates abandoned the fort and New Madrid.⁶⁵ The Mississippi River was now open to Federal forces and traffic.

"They must have a large quantity of siege guns" wrote James Wiswell, "if they can afford to give them away as they have been doing for the past few days." He was commenting on "all of the batteries on the Kentucky and Tennessee shore" abandoned by the rebels, as well as a "large quantity of ammunition, camp and garrison equipage, quartermaster and commissary stores." The three companies of the 4th Regulars remained on duty at Pope's headquarters.⁶⁶

Having lost this vital section of the Mississippi River as a supply route, the Confederates urgently needed to establish a new line to defend the Memphis and Charleston Railroad, the only all-weather link between Richmond and Memphis.⁶⁷ Confederate General Albert Sidney Johnston concentrated his forces at Corinth, Mississippi—a major transportation center—as the staging area for an offensive against Grant's Army of the Tennessee. The two armies would meet again at the "bewildering and bloody Battle of Shiloh."⁶⁸

II. Pittsburg Landing (Shiloh) – April 6-7

In March, Major General Henry W. Halleck was put in command of all Federal forces in the Mississippi Valley. He initiated a slow advance that sent his two armies south along the Tennessee River. By early April, Grant's 40,000-troop Army of the Tennessee was near Pittsburg Landing, "on the west side of the river, from which direct roads led to Corinth, the Confederate base," close to the Tennessee-Mississippi border.[1] They were to be joined by Don Carlos Buell's 35,000-man Army of the Ohio. From there they would initiate a joint campaign to seize the Confederate rail line. Lieutenant Colonel James Oakes, assigned to the 4th US Cavalry in January, replaced Lieutenant Colonel Thomas Wood, who had been promoted to colonel, 2nd Cavalry. He led General Buell's escorts (Cos. G and K) as they moved with the advance of Buell's army from Nashville.[2] Oakes would be the highest-ranking officer of the 4th US Cavalry to lead companies of the regiment in the field during the war. Buell's advance arrived at Columbia, Tennessee, where they halted until March 31, then moved rapidly to the Tennessee River at Savannah, and on to Pittsburg Landing, "arriving on the field during night of Sunday, April 6, and Monday morning."[3]

On March 1, Company I marched from Nashville with Brigadier General C. F. Smith to Clarksville, Tennessee, to secure the grounds around Forts Henry and Donelson.[4] From Fort Henry, the troops were transported by steamers to Pittsburg Landing, where they reported on March 31.[5] Pittsburg Landing had become "an enormous army camp . . . [with] transports docked at the landing five deep." The sheer magnitude of the Pittsburg Landing encampment—42,000 men—awed recruits and veterans alike. "There is no end to the tents. We can see them scattered in all directions as far as we can see," described one army private. "Everywhere there were sounds of pounding axes, beating drums and braying mules."[6] As the spring temperatures increased, "A light foliage covered the trees, and peach orchards turned pink with blossoms. 'We have a most lovely spot here to camp. This is nice country, heavily timbered with oak, ash, maple, beach, poplar, etc. just like Indiana,' commented one soldier."[7] There was confidence of easy victory throughout the camp. Ironically, Shiloh is a Hebrew word meaning *place of peace*.[8]

Awaiting the arrival of Buell's army, "Grant entertained no thoughts of a Confederate attack."[9] Among the many errors of judgment made by the inexperienced and overconfident Grant at Shiloh was his conviction that the Confederate attack would come at Crump's Landing, about six miles north of Pittsburg Landing. Concerned that Confederate General Johnston would "make a quick dash upon the base," Grant had positioned General Lew Wallace's Third Division to guard the army's supplies.[10] On April 4, he ordered newly appointed Brigadier General William H. L. Wallace's Second Division at Pittsburg Landing, including Company I, 4th Cavalry, to be on standby to reinforce Crump's Landing if necessary.[11] The company of cavalry was used to keep the lines of communication open between the two divisions.[12]

One of the difficulties faced by Grant's command was the inability to obtain accurate information on the movements of the Confederate Army that had controlled the area for over a year. Civilians in the area who may have been sympathetic to the Union cause were reluctant to provide information, fearing retribution. Grant and Lew Wallace had to rely solely on military sources. Encamped at Crump's Landing, General Wallace had employed several scouts to operate as spies and, although he did not put his full trust in them, he was alarmed when two of them reported that "the whole Rebel army" was moving toward Pittsburg Landing. Wallace immediately wrote a dispatch to Grant. He entrusted the delivery of the note to his orderly, Private Thomas W. Simson, Co. I, 4th US Cavalry. Simson was to deliver the note personally to Grant at Pittsburg Landing or, if he was not there, put the dispatch in the hands of the postmaster. Leaving the note with the postmaster, Simson returned to Crump's Landing at 2 a.m. While there is no record of this dispatch, Grant did send a note to General Sherman the morning of April 5, inquiring about an enemy attack. "Sherman's reply was negative, and Wallace's dispatch, if received, was promptly disregarded."[13] Private Simson would later become one of the many enlisted men in the 4th Regulars to receive a field commission to 2nd lieutenant during the war.

At 7 a.m. on the morning of April 6, "thousands of screaming rebels . . . burst out of the woods near

Shiloh church."[14] The nation was about to learn the horror of a modern war. In the backwoods of Tennessee, the largest land army ever assembled on the American continent—100,000 men—participated in the greatest battle of the Western Theater of the Civil War: Shiloh. Facing the greatest concentration of field guns ever assembled with untrained green troops led by inexperienced and untested leaders, the battle at Pittsburg Landing took 23,746 casualties—more than had been lost in all previous American battles combined.

General Albert Johnston had achieved complete surprise. When informed, General Grant immediately left his headquarters in Savannah by steamer. "The din of the battle [was] steadily increasing" to a "roar" as they approached Crump's Landing an hour and a half later.[15] There was confusion throughout the Union Army and it was slow to respond to the Confederate onslaught. By 11:30 a.m. the Federal right had collapsed, and the Confederates consolidated their position, taking control of the Pittsburg-Corinth Road and pushing back Sherman's and McClernand's line.[16] "By mid-morning the Confederates seemed within easy reach of victory, overrunning one entire frontline Union division and capturing its camp."[17] "The attack pushed most Union divisions back to reform elsewhere, while others fought to hold their line." There was "mass confusion on both sides," as most of the new recruits had never been in battle and did not know their orders.[18] The rest of the day was a series of bloody assaults, charges, and countercharges. The murderous fight went on for thirteen hours. Wounded from both sides sought water from the farm pond near the peach orchard. It turned red with their blood.[19] Only the arrival of Buell's army that evening saved the Union forces from total destruction.

Lieutenant Powell's two companies of Regulars (Company I, 4th U.S. and Company C, 2nd US Cavalry) were originally assigned to Brigadier General William Wallace's Second Division, acting as couriers and escorts.[20] The morning of the attack, Powell's squadron was "deployed as a line of videttes (sentries) to keep the road open between the right of Sherman's Division and the position of Major General Lew Wallace who was to move his command from Crump's Landing to Pittsburg Landing."[21] This assignment, as well as the rough and heavily forested terrain, may well have kept the small cavalry squadron out of the main battle when Brigadier General William Wallace's Second Division was overrun. Wallace himself was mortally wounded. At about 9 a.m., Lieutenant Powell ordered the squadron to "deploy as skirmishers on the right flank . . . to annoy a rebel battery that kept shelling our camps" and at the same time keep the communications open "between the expected re-enforcements under the command of Maj. Gen. L. Wallace and the army . . ." They held their position "against superior forces" until Lew Wallace arrived and then "bivouacked for the night in the rear of [the Union] right flank."[22]

Late that evening and into the early morning, during a drenching rainstorm, Union troops established another line covering Pittsburg Landing—Grant's last line of defense. General Lew Wallace was desperately trying to move his division south to join Grant. Having just crossed Owl Creek, they moved south "along the Hamburg-Savannah [or River] Road through Russian Tenant Field." Wallace "did not know the location of the Rebel army, or, for that matter, the precise whereabouts of Grant's army." Just south of Tenant Field, he ran into a sergeant of Company I, 4th US Cavalry, in the darkness. This may have been Sergeant Albert Kaufman. The trooper informed him that his division—William Wallace's Second—was on the eastern slope of Tilghman Branch and the enemy on the opposite slope. "There," he whispered, "see the top line of the trees against the sky? Well, they [rebels] had a battery here when the sun went down." Lew Wallace's Third Division "deployed facing west along the Hamburg-Savannah Road."[23] There was no rest for the soldiers. "It was a perfectly miserable night," as reported by one Third Division soldier: ". . . [T]he water was flowing in torrents. There were no logs or stones on which to sit . . . and all that weary night I stood or walked about in the pitiless rain, soaked through and through."[24] The dead lay everywhere; neither army had as yet developed a system for gathering bodies. The wounded lay among them, crying out, "but none dare try to help them."[25] The battlefield was enveloped in a thunderstorm that night and "flashes of lightening showed vultures feeding on the dead."[26]

Confederate General Albert Johnston was killed in battle and was replaced by General Pierre G. T. Beauregard. Beauregard, unaware of Buell's arrival, launched an attack at 6 a.m. on the second day. The battle raged the entire length of the field. Despite all efforts, the Confederates were slowly pushed back. By four o'clock that afternoon, the Confederate Army retired from the field, retreating to Corinth, Mississippi.[27]

Powell's squadron of cavalry was now under General Lew Wallace's command. During the second day's fighting, the squadron supported one of Wallace's batteries, following the enemy and taking several prisoners. The squadron remained with this division during the night.[28]

With the Confederate failure to destroy the invading Union forces at Shiloh, it relinquished all hold upon western Tennessee, except for a few forts on the Mississippi that soon fell to Federal forces. The Union was now free to carry out the capture of the Corinth rail junction and move on to Memphis and Vicksburg. Both sides now knew that hope for an early or easy victory was ill founded; it was going to be a long and bloody war.

On April 8, Powell's squadron of Regulars "proceeded on the road to Corinth" where, finding the enemy in force, they "returned and reported accordingly." Casualties reported for Company I included Private Frederick Rhyman—mortally wounded—and four privates "slightly wounded."[29]

The final number of dead or missing was 13,000 on the Union side and 10,500 on the Confederate side. There were as many people killed at Shiloh as there were at Waterloo. The difference between that Napoleonic war and the Civil War is that there weren't twenty more Waterloos to come.[30]

Considering the thousands of officers and men involved in these battles from individual regiments to divisions, it was a rare and exceptional distinction to be singled out by a commanding general. At Shiloh, four present and former members of the 4th United States Cavalry were so distinguished in the after-battle reports. Major General Lew Wallace was generous in his praise of his orderly, Private Thomas W. Simson, Co. I, and Sergeant Albert Kaufman, Co. I., "who was of great service . . . and has every quality that goes to make a practical officer."[31] Both men earned promotions to 2nd lieutenant in 1863.[32] Two officers on detached service from the 4th U.S. were singled out by Major General Don Carlos Buell: 2nd Lieutenant Edward M. McCook, Co. G; and Lieutenant Colonel James Oakes. McCook—now lieutenant colonel, USV, 2nd Indiana Cavalry—was brevetted 1st lieutenant, US Army, and promoted to colonel, commanding the 2nd Indiana Cavalry, for his conduct at Shiloh.[33] Lieutenant Colonel Oakes, "inspector of the cavalry and commander of the regular cavalry, was capable and zealous, though suffering greatly from shattered health."[34] Oakes would be on "mustering and disbursing" duty for the remainder of the war and retained on the roster of the 4th Cavalry as lieutenant colonel until July 31, 1866, when he was promoted to Colonel, 6th Cavalry.[35]

III. Cavalry Division Army of the Mississippi

Fourth Cavalry Companies B, C, and D—now commanded by Captain Eugene W. Crittenden, Co. D—had been with General Pope's Army of the Mississippi since February 29, participating in the capture of Island No. 10 and New Madrid, Missouri.[1] Crittenden—one of the original 2nd lieutenants in the new 1st Cavalry in 1855—was promoted to captain in May 1861.[2] By General Orders issued from Headquarters, District of the Mississippi at New Madrid on April 1, Brigadier General Gordon Granger, "having reported for duty . . . is assigned to the command of the cavalry with this army, except the three companies of the Fourth Regular Cavalry on duty at these headquarters."[3] Companies G, K, and I were subsequently attached to Granger's new cavalry command, and in late May 1862, Companies B, C, and D were reluctantly released by Pope. As James Wiswell, Co. C, wrote: "Gen. Pope hates to let us go but he received an order from the War Dept. and was obliged to."[4] Company I was now temporarily commanded by Lieutenant Clarence Manck, a civilian appointment in March 1861 on loan from Co. K. Lieutenant Michael Kelly commanded Co. B, and newly commissioned 2nd Lieutenant Thomas Healy—a thirteen-year veteran and former sergeant in the 2nd Cavalry—was commanding Co. D.

Brigadier General Gordon Granger, United States Volunteers

Gordon Granger was an old-school cavalryman with a fifteen-year career prior to the war. A graduate of West Point in 1845, he was commissioned a 1st lieutenant in the Mounted Rifles (later 3rd Cavalry) in 1852. Until the end of 1860, his service was on the

Southern frontier. He was on sick leave when the rebellion broke out, and he immediately reported for duty and was assigned to the staff of Major General McClernand. Promoted to captain in May 1861, he was subsequently on detached service to the staff of General Sturgis and participated in the Missouri Campaigns, including the action at Dug Springs and Wilson's Creek. He was brevetted major, USA, for his "gallant and meritorious" conduct at Wilson's Creek. In recognition of his service with the Army of the Mississippi, President Lincoln commissioned Granger a brigadier general of volunteers. He would command the Cavalry of the Army of the Mississippi in the upcoming advance upon Corinth, Mississippi, and in September 1862, he would be promoted to major general, USV.[5]

On April 23, Granger's new Division was organized at Hamburg, Tennessee, on the Tennessee River near the Mississippi border. It was composed of four regiments of Volunteer Cavalry: the 3rd Michigan, 7th Illinois, 2nd Iowa, and 2nd Michigan. The six companies of Regular Cavalry were attached to headquarters.[6]

For the next six weeks, Granger's cavalry command commenced a "series of scouting and reconnaissances, embracing the whole country lying between the Memphis and Charleston Railroad on the South, and the Monterey and Hamburg road on the North."[7] The terrain was "almost impenetrable," consisting of "a succession of high rolling ridges and intermediate low swampy bottoms, all covered with a heavy timber . . . with a dense growth of

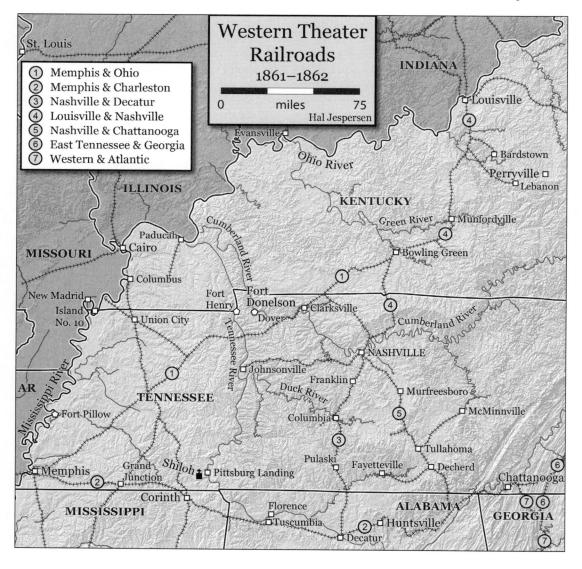

tangled vines." Recent flooding of the lowlands "made them impassable for wagons and infantry until the construction of miles of corduroy roads and bridges." Corduroy roads were temporary roadways created by logs laid side by side transversely to make a passable surface. For over two weeks, "in the frequent heavy rains," Granger's "whole division was thus laboriously employed in the advance," while almost every day "brought with it some sharp skirmish with a vigilant enemy . . ."[8] Before this expedition was over, the cavalrymen would also be engaged in the "very unusual service to mounted men" of not only building roads and bridges, but "earthworks for batteries, rifle pits, and laying in the trenches as infantry . . ."[9] Throughout the war, the men of the 4th Cavalry would frequently find themselves rendering these "very unusual services."

CORINTH, MISSISSIPPI

For the first time in history, railroads played a vital part in war. Both sides recognized they were of strategic importance in moving troops and supplies, and key railroad junctions were often the target of campaign maneuvers.[10] Two major railroads crossed paths at Corinth and they "connected the Confederate States of America from the Mississippi River to the Atlantic Ocean and to the Gulf of Mexico." They were the backbone of the Confederacy, bringing troops from the Deep South and ammunition, equipment, and supplies to the armies in the field.[11] Corinth was second only to Richmond in military importance. The Confederate brigadier general placed in command of the cavalry forces at Corinth was William N. R. Beall, formerly captain, Co. A, 1st (now 4th) United States Cavalry.[12]

Between May 9 and 12, Company I—now commanded by 2nd Lieutenant Henry Gordon, as part of a detachment made up of three battalions of Volunteer Cavalry—took part in an affair near Farmington, Mississippi. Gordon was a 1st sergeant in the 2nd Cavalry when commissioned 2nd lieutenant, 4th Cavalry, in October.[13] Confederates had "appeared in strong force" to dispute the occupation of Farmington, with two batteries at the causeway and bridge over Seven Mile Creek. The ground was "much broken by hills and ravines, and utterly unsuited to cavalry movements." Nevertheless, the small cavalry force charged the two-battery position "in splendid style, driving in the strong force of the enemy's skirmishers and battery supports with great fury, and completely silencing the fire of both batteries."[14] Forty-three Union soldiers were reported "killed, wounded, and missing," including Private William Peters, Co. I, killed in action on May 9. On May 13, Company I was part of Major General George H. Thomas' "Right Wing," Second Division. Companies B, C, and D—Captain Crittenden commanding—were part of the "Left Wing" in Major General John Pope's Army of the Mississippi, "unattached to divisions."[15]

BOONVILLE, MISSISSIPPI

On the evening of May 16, General Granger received orders from Major General Pope to have the cavalry in readiness at daylight the next morning to move on Farmington—four miles due south of Corinth— and guard the approaches. The next day, orders were to "proceed to Farmington and post the whole army on the ground indicated by him." On May 26, "Colonel [Washington L.] Elliott, commanding Second Brigade, succeeded in reaching the railroad at Boonville, thirty miles below Corinth, and after a sharp skirmish with about two hundred and fifty of the enemy's cavalry, succeeded in obtaining possession of the town." Companies of the 4th Regiment were involved in the pursuit to and capture of Boonville, May 30 through June 12.[16]

While there were a number of skirmishes on the march to Corinth, it was an "illness that overtook the Confederate troops" that forced them to withdraw.[17] Without a major battle, the Federal Army took possession of Corinth. Having seen the fortifications, James Wiswell wrote: "I think that if we had ever attacked them there we would have lost a great many men before we ever could have whipped them."[18] The Confederacy had now "conceded the northern tip of Mississippi and with it the vital Memphis and Charleston Railroad . . . not only cutting a rail artery that had pumped supplies critical to the survival of the Confederacy . . . but opening the way to a Federal advance on Chattanooga, Tennessee, gateway to the Deep South."[19]

On May 30, General Granger started from Farmington with the First Brigade in pursuit of the Confederate Army. He found the country rugged, "and the road strewn with blankets, knapsacks, small arms, carriages and wagons, broken and abandoned by the enemy in his flight." After skirmishing with the enemy near the causeway at Tuscumbia Creek eight miles south of Corinth, he bivouacked for the night. Granger's force entered Boonville at 5 a.m. on June 2.[20] Private David

Daugherty, 4th U.S., was killed in action the previous day.[21] A native son of Ireland, Daugherty left a wife and three children under the age of five back in Clarion County, Pennsylvania.[22]

In his lengthy report on the siege of Corinth, Brigadier General Stanley provided the following paragraph that gives some insight into the conditions and deprivations faced by the enlisted men of the Union Army:

> I have thus endeavored to trace out the service of this division for fifty days. Of course it is a mere outline. The labor of road making, of camp labor, of marches through heat and dust, of privations in short rations, in bad clothing, in bare feet, all I am happy to report born with patience and cheerfulness, have shown that our young soldiers already appreciate Napoleon's maxim, that 'the first quality of a soldier is constancy in enduring fatigue; that poverty and privation are the soldier's school.' Neither have they ever shown that their courage may be classed as secondary to these qualities.[23]

IV. Army of the Ohio – Major General Don Carlos Buell

In June 1862, Companies B, C, D, G, and K were attached to Headquarters, Army of the Ohio, Major General Don Carlos Buell commanding. Company I would join them by the end of the month. Lieutenant Colonel James Oakes would command the companies until ill health forced him to relinquish command in October.[1] They would participate in Buell's campaigns in northern Alabama and middle Tennessee through August 1862.

General Buell had "contempt" for volunteer soldiers and insisted that "Regular Army standards of discipline" be forced upon them.[2] Even Private Wiswell complained: "We do not have an easy time as we used to for we have four hours drill per day and Dress Parades and so forth . . ."[3] This "fundamental error" in understanding the men under his command and how they might "best be led" would eventually cost Buell his command. "During the hard and tedious marches around Kentucky, hundreds expressed their disaffection through desertion; the thousands who remained wrote home of Buell's severity."[4]

Incident at Athens, Alabama

After the capture of Corinth, the 4th Cavalry escorted General Buell to Athens, Alabama, being on duty there June 30.[5] Two companies of the Regulars accompanied Buell's advance under Brigadier General John B. Turchin. Upon entering the town:

> . . . and after its complete evacuation by the rebel cavalry, the citizens, noticing that there were but comparatively few Union soldiers present, began an indiscriminate firing on them from the houses, stables, &c [etc.]. Turchen's brigade retaliated and when General Buell arrived a day later, "the site where Athens had stood was marked by badly wrecked, demolished, and plundered buildings. The town was not burned, but it was badly torn to pieces, and every building from which a shot had been fired was demolished."[6]

Buell was not amused. It was his policy to not "violate the sanctity of private property in territory conquered by his army" under any circumstances, and he summarily dismissed Turchin from his brigade command—angering many, including his powerful enemies at the state and federal level, who were appalled by his "kid glove" policy toward the rebels.[7] War is also a political game, and Buell's days were numbered.

Huntsville, Alabama

Moving with General Buell, "the companies of the Fourth occupied Huntsville, Alabama, in July, remaining in that place until the 2nd of August."[8] "This is the healthiest country and prettiest town that I have seen since I left the Green Mts.," writes Wiswell. "The water is splendid. . . . If the balance of 'Dixie' is as pleasant as this I shall be tempted to bid the North 'Good Bye' and emigrate." He concludes: "I do not think that there is much prospect of the war ending under a year yet."⁹

From August 21 to September 26, 1862, the 4th Regiment was with Buell's Army of the Ohio in pursuit of Braxton Bragg's Confederate Army of Tennessee. From Huntsville they moved to Shelbyville, Tennessee, and then to Tullahoma, "where they remained until the 18th of September." That day, the 4th U.S. "started with army head-quarters to Nashville, and thence moved back through Kentucky to Louisville, a major Federal supply center, where they were remounted on the 30th of September."¹⁰

The Battle of Perryville, Kentucky

The Confederate loss at Fort Donelson, the Federal occupation of Nashville, and the surrender of Corinth, which conceded the northern tip of Mississippi and with it the vital Memphis and Charleston Railroad, "left the Confederate heartland vulnerable." The way was now open "for a Federal advance on Chattanooga, gateway to the Deep South."¹¹

Braxton Bragg was the new commander of all Confederate forces between Mississippi and Virginia and commander of the Army of Tennessee. He faced three immediate challenges: protect Chattanooga, reopen the Memphis and Charleston Railroad, and recover at least a portion of Tennessee. If he could move his army into Kentucky, he felt confident he would win the support of that state and from there be able to control much of Tennessee. On August 28, he marched his army out of Chattanooga, crossing the Tennessee River that same day.¹² His initial objective was Louisville, Kentucky. He reached the Union-fortified town of Munfordville, where the Louisville and Nashville Railroad crossed the Green River. The town surrendered to Bragg on September 17. Believing that Nashville was safe from Confederate threat, "the Federal forces under Buell, with 4th Cavalry companies B, C, D, G, I and K as his escort, left that city on September 12, for Louisville."¹³ With Bragg's army at Munfordville blocking the approach, Buell prepared to attack. The Confederates held the advantage, but Bragg hesitated. He was frustrated at the lack of support for the Confederacy he found in Kentucky and, believing wrongly that Buell was being heavily reinforced, began to question his entire operation. He became "determined not to expose his army to disaster nor take any chances." Choosing not to fight at this time or place, Bragg withdrew from Mumfordsville, leaving the road open to Louisville. His staff was stunned.¹⁴ Louisville was occupied by the Union army on September 28. The Federal advance continued, and the two armies finally met on October 8 at Perryville, about forty miles southwest of Lexington, Kentucky. Six companies of the 4th US Cavalry (Cos. B, C, D, G, I, and K) were part of Buell's escort. There is no record of any significant activity at Perryville.

While the battle at Perryville is considered the most significant of the battles fought in Kentucky, it has been described as an "indecisive bloodbath," with no clear winner and appalling loss of life on both sides. Both commanding generals were ineffectual: ". . . neither exerted forceful control when the armies blundered into each other," and "Buell was not even aware that a fight was going on until it was almost over." Confederate General Braxton Bragg, "concluding gloomily that he had done all he could in Kentucky, withdrew." Buell "let him go unmolested, much to the ire of the War Department."¹⁵ On October 24, Buell was relieved of his command and replaced by Major General William S. Rosecrans.

V. Army of the Cumberland – Major General William S. Rosecrans

Between October 22 and November 7, the six companies of the 4th US Cavalry marched from Green River to headquarters at Nashville, Tennessee. Major General William S. Rosecrans replaced Buell and the Army of Ohio became the Fourteenth Army Corps. On January 9, 1863, the name was again changed and remained the Army of the Cumberland.

The ineffective Kentucky Campaign and the results at Perryville exhausted and shattered the morale of the Federal forces, creating serious problems for the Union Army in the West.¹ Discipline and leadership had broken down, thousands were deserting, supply and communication lines were in shambles, and Nashville—the new headquarters—

had only minimal rations on hand.² The Volunteer Cavalry—primarily responsible for protecting the lines of communications and supplies—was described as "useless." They were untrained, undisciplined, and "fully half were without weapons of any kind."³

The dire situation of the army and the course of the war were apparent even to a disillusioned Private Wiswell:

> If I was out of the service now I would take good care they would not get me again until they took more vigorous measures to put an end to this awful war. You may be certain that I will be spared for I will not put myself in any danger that I can get rid of for the Govt. I have struck my last <u>willing</u> blow that I ever will for it. You need not think that I say this on account of not getting promotion for with Uncle John's signature I could get a commission but I would not accept it.⁴

It had been over twenty months since the first shots were fired at Fort Sumter. Tens of thousands of lives had been lost on both sides and the end was nowhere in sight. Although McClellan had amassed a huge army in the East, he lacked the ability to use it effectively. While Robert E. Lee's Antietam Campaign into Maryland was rebuffed, McClellan's procrastination—his failure to commit his troops and take the offensive to pursue the Confederate Army when he had the opportunity—finally cost him his command.

Despite the situation in the West, which saw both armies engaged "in a series of barren victories and costly defeats," the Union had gained the advantage.⁵ The Confederacy would never recover from its loss of control of the Mississippi River and its tributaries. The door was now open into the industrial and agricultural heartland of the South.

> Following Antietam and Perryville, a new kind of war began to emerge: a war of ruthless, grinding attrition, in which catchwords like honor and glory did not quite fit any more. . . . Union generals like McClellan and Buell were gone, and tenacious fighters like Grant and Sherman and Sheridan were moving toward the top. After October 1862, chances for a negotiated peace flickered out. The war could end only when the armies—and the civilians—of North or South were beaten to their knees.⁶

Cavalry Division, Army of the Cumberland

Rosecrans immediately set about rebuilding his demoralized army and instilling a sense of *esprit de corps*. He was a soldier's general who was actually concerned about the well being of his troops. "The men rapidly developed respect for their new commander," and "their respect turned to affection as Rosecrans made his presence felt in the camps."⁷ The army settled into winter camp in and around Nashville, and Rosecrans set about creating a "state of discipline at least equal to that of the Rebels."⁸ Discipline was tightened among the officer corps and the men, and a uniform daily regimen was established as Rosecrans worked to reorganize his army.

It was imperative that Nashville remain secured for Federal forces and that its supply lines, communications, and railroads be kept open and free from the harassment and embarrassment of Confederate cavalry raids. John Hunt Morgan, "the Confederate Cavalry officer whose unit was celebrated for the endurance, speed, daring and success of their raids," had just routed Union forces outside Lexington, Kentucky, and entered the city on October 18. Earlier, on October 9, Confederate General Jeb Stuart staged his bold raid at Chambersburg, Pennsylvania, crossing Federal lines and boldly riding in a complete circle around McClellan's humiliated Army of the Potomac.⁹

Rosecrans recognized he needed an effective cavalry force. He sought out a new chief of cavalry "capable of restoring order and discipline" in the Volunteer units. He found David S. Stanley, captain, 4th US Cavalry, who was then commanding a division under Grant. "Rosecrans applied for Stanley's services with annoying persistence, alternately writing Henry Halleck and [Secretary of War] Edwin Stanton." "Besides being an indefatigable soldier [he] is a thorough cavalry officer. He can do more good . . . by commanding a cavalry than an infantry division. I beg you . . . to send him to me." His request was granted in late November.¹⁰

As ordered by Rosecrans, Stanley was to organize an adequate cavalry force "to combat that of the enemy, protect our own line of communication, *and take advantage of the enemy should he be beaten or retreat* [emphasis author]."¹¹ This would initiate a whole new strategy and tactic for the cavalry. In a departure from earlier concepts of a chief of cavalry as "a combination administrative and staff officer," Rosecrans wanted his cavalry commander to *command* his cavalry division.[12] According to cavalry historian Stephen Starr:

> There had not been in October, 1862, nor would there ever be, to the end of the war, an official pronouncement defining and prescribing these fundamental changes in cavalry organization and leadership. They were tried, they seemed to work, and so the idea spread and was adopted first in one army then in another, on empirical grounds and on a voluntary basis.[13]

Starr describes David Stanley as "A radical by the standards of the day with respect to cavalry organization . . . [but] a traditionalist in another aspect." Stanley felt there had been too much dependence on the carbine rather than the saber. He believed in the saber and wanted his men to rely on "cold steel." To Stanley, the saber "represented an attitude, an expression of the 'cavalry spirit'. . . and his men were in favor of it."[14]

First Brigade, Second Cavalry Division

On December 19, 1862, General Order No. 41 created the new organization of the Army of the Cumberland. Part of this new command included a consolidated Cavalry Division commanded by Brigadier General David Stanley.[15] Stanley knew that the cavalry "had been badly neglected." As he wrote: ". . . it was weak, undisciplined, and scattered around, a regiment to a division of infantry . . . To break up this foolish dispersal of cavalry, and to form brigades and eventually divisions, was my first and difficult work."[16]

The 4th US Cavalry at Nashville was incorporated into the Cavalry Division. According to Joseph Vale, orders constituting a new cavalry brigade went into effect and " . . . the new brigade was officially given the designation of the First Brigade, Second Cavalry Division, Army of the Cumberland." It would soon come under the command of Colonel Robert H. G. Minty, 4th Michigan Volunteers, and was originally constituted of Minty's 4th Michigan Cavalry; the 7th Pennsylvania Cavalry, commanded by Colonel George C. Wynkoop; the 2nd Indiana Cavalry, Colonel Edward McCook (1st Lt., 4th US Cavalry) commanding; and the 3rd Kentucky Cavalry, commanded by Colonel Eli H. Murray.[17]

Captain Vale, 7th Pennsylvania Cavalry, saw this as the first recognition of "the importance of the cavalry arm of the service and its proper organization for effective work":

> Prior to this, we had been attached in squads and battalions to various infantry brigades and divisions; not even a single regiment operating long enough as a unit to become an effective power; while, on sudden emergencies arising, these different detachments would be thrown together, placed under the nearest unemployed infantry colonel or brigadier general, and sent on scouts, or to engage the enemy; without having any opportunity to acquire that *esprit de corps* so necessary to a successful military movement.[18]

The full power of the newest branch of the Federal Army was about to be unleashed. In the new organization of the Army of the Cumberland, Captain Elmer Otis, 4th US Cavalry, was designated as commanding Courier Lines on the staff of Major General Rosecrans:

> All such lines will be under his general direction, and his orders in reference to them are to be obeyed and respected. Commanders of corps, divisions, brigades, and detachments will immediately cause all non-commissioned officers and privates of cavalry who are mounted, but have no arms (except orderlies), to report at once to him at these headquarters, to be used in forming courier lines for carrying dispatches in a safe country. By this means effective cavalry, now performing this duty, may be sent to the front. By command of Major-general Rosecrans.[19]

Another career army officer from the 4th Cavalry, Otis graduated from West Point in 1853 and was one of the original 2nd lieutenants when the regiment was formed in 1855.[20]

Companies L and M

One of the effects of cavalry reorganization was to bring all of the cavalry regiments to a full complement of twelve companies. The two new companies of the 4th Cavalry were added in the field near Murfreesboro in November and December 1862. "Our companies have been filled up and L and M Co's added to the regt.," writes James Wiswell. "The recruits were taken from the Volunteer Infantry who wished to reenlist in the regular service." James was offered "the berth of Clerk with the rank of Sergeant in one of the new companies," but chose to stay with his original company.

His friend James Cummings went to Co. M as a sergeant.[21]

Captain Thomas B. Alexander was appointed to command Co. M and, even though 1st Lieutenant Edward McCook was on detached service commanding the 2nd Indiana Volunteers, he was posted as the new 1st lieutenant for Co. M. Newly promoted Captain Charles Bowman was appointed to command Co. L, but remained absent since his appointment. 1st Lieutenant Anson O. Doolittle and 2nd Lieutenant Douglas A. Murray, also appointed to Co. L, were also absent from the regiment at the time of formation of the new companies.[22] Thomas Bullett Alexander—a civilian appointment from Kentucky in February 1861—rose quickly through the ranks and was promoted to captain on July 17, 1862. For reasons unknown, he would defect to the Confederacy shortly after his appointment to command Co. M, the last officer in the 4th United States Cavalry to do so.[23]

The officers and non-commissioned officers of the 4th U.S. would have their work cut out for them. With the addition of two new companies, as well as recruiting to replenish the existing six companies, approximately 380 new recruits joined the 4th Regiment during this time, many from Volunteer regiments.[24] If the recruits survived their initial exposure to camp life and were not injured during their horse training, they had yet to face the hazards of their new weapons. There were numerous "accidental deaths" from cleaning or otherwise mishandling firearms.[25]

On November 5, 1862, President Lincoln removed McClellan from command of the Army of the Potomac and replaced him with Major General Ambrose E. Burnside. Companies A and E of the 4th Regulars were assigned as part of Burnside's personal escort. They would rejoin their regiment in March 1863, at Murfreesboro, Tennessee. Companies F and H remained stationed at Fort Laramie, Nebraska Territory, for the remainder of 1862.[26] They did not rejoin the regiment until August 1863, when all twelve companies of the Fourth Regiment United States Cavalry would be united for the first time in the Civil War.

While Rosecrans was rebuilding his Union Army, the whole Confederate Army in the west was now concentrated under General Bragg at Murfreesboro, Tennessee. Bragg considered this a strategic defensive position to stop any Federal advance on Chattanooga. He arrived at Murfreesboro on November 26, ordered his troops to build winter quarters, and began to reorganize his "depleted forces." He would wait for Rosecrans to take the offensive. In his last letter for the year, and in a more optimistic tone than a month earlier, James Wiswell senses a battle ahead: "Everything is as quiet as though we never expected to see a rebel. But I expect that it is the quiet that precedes a storm for when the 'General' sounds the 'Advance' we will scatter them like chaff on our march towards 'Dixie' again."

Both armies were scavenging the same countryside and Wiswell notes: "When we go out after forage we are obliged to take a whole Brigade as an escort."[27] Captain Vale writes that previous orders prohibiting the taking of any private property of citizens, "no matter if the owner was in the rebel army or what the necessity for so doing was," were rescinded. Now "everything necessary for the subsistence of the army was directed to be seized . . . and the army made to subsist, as far as possible, off the countryside."[28] This change of policy would bring the war directly to the citizens of the Confederacy with devastating results.

While all this was going on, Rosecrans found himself under tremendous pressure from Washington to mount an offensive against the Confederacy before winter set in. There was fear of foreign support for the South from England and France if the Union appeared to be faltering.

Joseph Vale provides an appropriate summary of the activities in the Western Theater to close out the year:

> The close of the campaign of 1861-62 found the Army of the Cumberland firmly holding Nashville and a large portion of Tennessee; the States of Kentucky and Missouri reclaimed; the Mississippi River freed from obstructions to Vicksburg; the Cumberland and Tennessee rivers open to the navigation of the National gunboats and transports, and the domination of the rebel authority seriously impaired in Alabama, Georgia, and Mississippi; while more than two thirds of Arkansas was in the possession of the Government.[29]

The American Civil War was just getting started. Appropriately enough, 1863 would begin in the violence of a "desperate, inconclusive battle on a desolate frozen field" known as the Battle of Stones River (Murfreesboro), December 31, 1862–January 3, 1863.[30]

1863: Stones River to Chattanooga

The Cavalryman was on duty virtually every waking minute and often grew sore, tired, dirty, hot or cold, and hungry – a far cry from the knight-errant that many a young recruit fancied he would be.
– Edward G. Longacre[1]

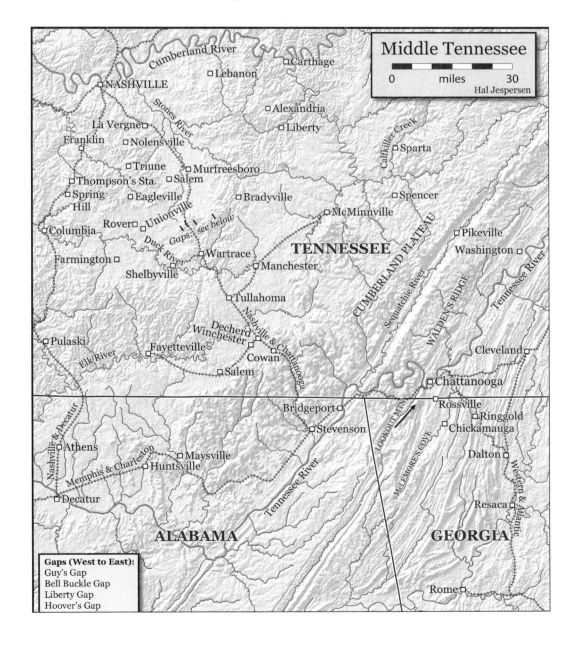

I. Middle Tennessee

For the Fourth Regiment United States Cavalry, events of 1863 would unfold in a small geographic rectangle commonly known as Middle Tennessee. The year would begin at the northwest corner with the battle of Stones River and end with the Battle of Chickamauga and the siege of Chattanooga at the southeast corner. The diagonal distance between the two is approximately sixty miles. This land would be ravaged as the men of the two great armies—Army of the Cumberland and Army of Tennessee—lived off, fought, and died over every mile of this distance.

While the armies were resting and recuperating during the harsh winter months, there would be no rest for the cavalry. The officers and men of the 4th US Cavalry would continuously be in the saddle and on the move the majority of the days and weeks of 1863. They were on foraging and scouting expeditions, endless skirmishes, and several major battles during which they would continue to rewrite the cavalry manuals while building their reputation as one of the most effective and efficient cavalry regiments in the Civil War.

As a consequence of practical evolution in the field and under the guidance of some of its most experienced cavalry officers, the Union cavalry in both the East and the West "first gained real confidence in itself and its leaders. during the events of 1863".[2]

In the Eastern Theater, the process began with General John Pope. An experienced cavalryman himself, Pope was originally assigned to commands in the West, including Fremont's command in Missouri. In February 1862, he took command of the Army of the Mississippi. Promoted to major general, he was with Grant and Buell in the October attack on Corinth, Mississippi. In June 1862, Pope was given command of the Army of Virginia in the East. Based on his experiences in the West and learning from the methods adopted by the Confederate Cavalry, one of his first orders was to direct that all cavalry units within each army corps be consolidated to serve in a single corps. He also ended the policy of encumbering cavalry operations with baggage and supply wagons that slowed the horsemen to the speed of their wagons. In the future, troops were to carry with them what they needed and take everything else from the countryside. They became lighter and faster, like their Confederate counterparts. This was also true in the West, where these changes were facilitated by new orders regarding foraging from the countryside. With greater mobility and speed, a new style of fighting evolved within the cavalry regiments. Under "light marching orders," the cavalry could cover greater distances, arriving quickly at their destination. They would dismount and one man in four would take the reins of the horses, while the other three men went into action. Learning from the Confederates and combining the bold, unrestrained tactics of Forrest, Morgan, and Stuart with the regimen and discipline of the Regulars, the Union Cavalry was now developing a new form of mobile warfare that would evolve into the raid. With the success of the Union Cavalry at Kelly's Ford on the Rappahannock on March 17 and in the largest single cavalry battle of the Civil War at Brandy Station (Beverly Ford) on June 9, 1863, the Federal Cavalry in the East came into its own. Even the enemy agreed. Major Henry B. McClellan—Jeb Stuart's adjutant and later biographer—states that the cavalry battle fought between Stuart's 10,000 cavalrymen and a Federal cavalry force of approximately 8,000 troops that ended in a draw "*made* the Federal cavalry."[3] This was the "turning point," he wrote, "in the evolution of the Federal cavalry, which had heretofore been dominated by a sense of its own inferiority to Stuart's bold horsemen."[4]

Writing about events in the Western Theater, Civil War historian General Theophilus Rodenbough, who commanded the 2nd US Cavalry at Gettysburg, notes that at about the time of the battle of Stones River:

> the Federal horse [cavalry] began to show confidence in itself, and in numerous encounters with the Confederates—mounted and dis-

mounted—acquitted itself with credit, fairly dividing the honors of the campaign. The names of Grierson, [Able D.] Streight, Wilder, and Minty became famous not only as raiders but as important factors in great battles, as at Chickamauga, where the 'obstinate stand of two brigades of Rosecrans' cavalry [Minty's and Wilder's] against the Confederate infantry gave time for the formation of Union lines.[5]

Another cavalry historian, Charles Rhodes, writes: "At Stones River, at Knoxville, at Chickamauga and other important battles, the cavalry of the West did desperate fighting and considering its numbers, was not lacking in efficiency."[6] Stones River was the turning point for the cavalry in the Western Theater.

In 1863, the Federals would "resume the advance on Chattanooga and ... continue with the drive to open the whole Mississippi Valley."[7] During the year, the companies and men of the 4th United States were engaged in no less than twenty-two fights.[8] From December 1862 through March 1863, the eight companies of the 4th US Cavalry were commanded by Captain Elmer Otis. The officers and men would distinguish themselves at the Battle of Stones River and Captain Otis would receive high praise, and a recommendation from General Rosecrans for promotion to brigadier general. Suffering from health issues, Otis would eventually relinquish command to his West Point classmate James B. McIntyre. Both officers had joined the newly formed 1st Cavalry as 2nd lieutenants in March 1855.

In March, the 4th United States was assigned to Colonel Robert Minty's cavalry brigade "unattached." A volunteer cavalryman with previous military experience, Minty would come to be regarded by his peers and future historians alike as "one of the best cavalrymen in the army."[9] During an expedition under the command of General Philip H. Sheridan, the actions of Minty's Cavalry were brought to the attention of General-in-Chief Henry W. Halleck in Washington and the brigade received the rare and distinct honor of being officially designated the Saber Brigade by General Rosecrans. By April, the 4th Cavalry would be formally attached to Minty's brigade.

Companies A and E returned from the Eastern Theater in March and the ten companies of the regiment—now commanded by Captain McIntyre—engaged in the first Battle of Franklin, Tennessee, in April. Captain Otis would return briefly in May, taking his final leave in June. McIntyre—the senior officer present—would command the regiment until October 1864. Eight of the junior officers present were former enlisted men who earned field commissions to 2nd lieutenant, five from within the ranks of the 4th U.S. commanded companies. As reported to General Rosecrans by General Stanley, chief of cavalry, the 4th Cavalry "did the most gallant service." At Franklin, McIntyre led his troops on an attack against Nathan Bedford Forrest's artillery battery that would ignite a controversy existing to the present day.

During the year, Minty's brigade was constantly engaging and more often defeating the Confederate cavalries of Generals Joseph Wheeler, N. B. Forrest, and George Dibrell. On June 27—for the first time in the war—fortified entrenchments and artillery were stormed and overridden by cavalry in a mounted saber charge, and the Confederate cavalry under Wheeler was completely routed at Shelbyville, Tennessee. In one of its most important engagements during the war at the Battle of Chickamauga in September, as part of Colonel Minty's Brigade, the 4th Cavalry would make a heroic stand at Reed's Bridge, helping to save the Army of the Cumberland from certain destruction.

In the first week of August, Companies F and H would finally return from their frontier assignment and the full complement of twelve companies of the 4th United States Cavalry would remain together for the duration of the war. The exact size of the regiment during 1863 is difficult to ascertain. It appears that the average company roster fluctuated between forty-five and fifty-five men "present and fit for duty." When the 4th US Cavalry reported for duty on September 13, it was "650 strong," at an average of fifty-five officers and men per company.[10] During this year, Minty's Saber Brigade with the 4th United States Cavalry would become Masters of the Field.

II. Stones River Campaign–Murfreesboro, Tennessee

The Army of the Cumberland and the Confederate Army of Tennessee were to meet in middle Tennessee on New Year's Eve in another of the bloody encounters of the Civil War. In December, Major General Rosecrans's refitted Army of the Cumberland was just below Nashville, Tennessee. As part of a new offensive, his army was to move against the Confederacy in a massive assault to "collapse the Confederate defenses and destroy the Confederate armies..."[1] On December 24, 1862, General Stanley, chief of cavalry, reported that he had available "about 1,300 fighting men, exclusive of the Fourth Regular Cavalry," who were to be assigned escort duty for General Rosecrans. The rest of the cavalry were in detail and foraging. This was one of the reasons for the delay of his campaign; he was unable to break camp until his foraging train returned.[2]

Union Order of Battle (Partial)
Army of the Cumberland
Major General William S. Rosecrans
XIV Corps
Right Wing – Major General Alexander McD. McCook
Center Wing – Major General George H. Thomas
Left Wing – Major General Thomas L. Crittenden
Cavalry
Brigadier General David S. Stanley
First Brigade – Colonel Robert H. G. Minty
Second Brigade – Colonel Lewis Zahm
"Unattached"
4th United States Cavalry – Cos. B, C, D, G, I, K, L, and M
Captain Elmer Otis, Commanding[3]

On Friday, December 26, a "cold and dreary day with a drizzling rain the whole army was in motion for the Stones River campaign."[4] Rosecrans sent his army in three columns to the little town of Murfreesboro, where Braxton Bragg's Confederate Army of Tennessee had been camped for a month.[5] When the Army of the Cumberland moved out of Nashville, elements of the 4th US Cavalry were assigned to accompany General Rosecrans on Murfreesboro Pike.[6] On December 28, they established general headquarters near La Vergne "on the railroad, near Concord Church," about fifteen miles north of Murfreesboro. From there, they "opened a line of couriers from that point to Nolensville," about five miles to the southwest.[7] Captain Otis, designated chief of couriers, was to "make arrangements for courier lines . . . across the country from one corps headquarters to another." The posts were to be half a mile apart, with cavalry patrolling the roads between them.[8] Second Lieutenant Elbridge Roys and his company were assigned to command the escort of the headquarters (wagon) train. Roys—a former sergeant in Company B recognized for his bravery at Dug Springs, Missouri—had been given a field promotion to 2nd lieutenant in July 1862.[9]

Rosecrans reported that they met with "a strong resistance, such as the nature of the country permits–rolling or hilly routes, skirted by cedar thickets, farms, and intersected by small streams, with rocky bluff banks, forming serious obstacles." In some places the center of the army was "engaged in cutting roads through an almost impenetrable growth of cedar" that separated them from the right, "rendering communication with them exceedingly difficult" and complicating troop placements.[10] As was often the case, terrain and wet weather dictated the actions of both the Union and Confederate armies. By December 30, Rosecrans's army, numbering nearly 44,000, faced Bragg's forces of 38,000 along the Nashville Turnpike, just north of Murfreesboro, separated by less than 700 yards.[11]

As recorded by Rosecrans: "Our small division of cavalry, say 3,000 men, had been divided into three parts of which Brigadier General Stanley, took two and accompanied General Alexander McCook, fighting his way across from the Wilkinson to the Franklin pike..."[12] General George Thomas led ten regiments of cavalry under Stanley, including a two-company squadron of the 4th Regiment (Companies G and K).[13] Company L, commanded by 2nd Lieutenant Elbridge Roys, "was detached as General Rosecrans' immediate escort."[14] On December 30, "the entire cavalry force" —with the exception of companies of the 4th US—was engaged in guarding the flanks of the army."[15] Company M—now commanded by 1st Lieutenant Tillinghast L'Hommedieu, who replaced the defecting Captain Alexander—was "strengthened by 50 men detailed from Companies B, C, D, G, I, and K and directed to establish a courier line from General Rosecrans' headquarters to La Vergne."[16]

Second Lieutenant Joseph Rendlebock was left behind at camp at Stewart's Creek to command the guard of the (wagon) train and baggage.[17] A slightly frustrated Otis writes: "These details left me with six small companies, numbering in the aggregate 260 men, rank and file."[18] Joseph Rendlebock was one of the senior non-commissioned officers, having enlisted in 1851 and rising to 1st sergeant, Co. G. He was commissioned 2nd lieutenant of that same company in November 1862.[19] L'Hommedieu—a civilian appointment from Ohio—was originally commissioned a 2nd lieutenant in the US Infantry in April 1861 and was promoted to 1st lieutenant, 4th Cavalry, in August 1861.[20]

Lieutenant Robert Burns—4th Michigan Volunteer Cavalry—who later became Colonel Robert Minty's assistant adjutant, gives a detailed description of the function of the cavalry as advance guard:

> The cavalry were of course in the advance, and the 4th Michigan [Minty's Regiment] led that, so that we were the leaders of the army. About 10 miles out, our advance guard and flankers were thrown out, which is done in this way. Four men are sent about 1/2 mile ahead of the main body [the videttes–mounted sentinels]. Then one company or about 50 men follow them 1/4 of a mile in their rear, and about the same distance in front of the main column. These are what is called the advance guard. They are to keep about that distance in front, advancing and halting when the column does. They are for the purpose of drawing the enemy's fire, etc. The flankers are from 10 to 150 men who are put in line on both sides of the road, stretching from the road for a half a mile or so each side. They should keep up with the advance guard, and should thoroughly beat up the country they go over, so that no enemy may be in the bushes.[21]

On Tuesday, December 30, Burns notes: "The army was waiting for something. Troops were shifting positions here and there, but not advancing." They remained at the ready, horses "saddled all the day and night." The remaining companies of the 4th Cavalry "proceeded to join Rosecrans on the field of battle and were drawn up in line of battle in rear of the general's headquarters."[22] While awaiting orders, a shell exploded "on the brow of the hill," killing Sergeant Joseph B. Richmond, Co. K.[23]

Rosecrans ordered Companies G and I down the road to find out the positions of the Confederates. They quickly found themselves "on top of them," wheeled around, and made their report. They were then ordered to "ascertain the position on the left, and also to select positions for the batteries." They returned at dark, "and the occasional flash of musketry and the rolling thunder of artillery indicated a fierce struggle on the extreme right."[24]

That night, "by some oversight," writes Captain Vale, "the rebel army, having during the night strongly massed and extended its left, was permitted to approach to within striking distance without being discovered."[25] In the early light of dawn of December 31, Confederate General William J. Hardee—former lieutenant colonel of the old 1st US Cavalry—struck, "catching some Federals cooking breakfast at their campsite."[26] The Federal brigade on the extreme right received the first shock: ". . . The on-rush of the rebels met with little opposition, breaking down brigade after brigade . . . carrying position after position, until the whole right wing was driven back to a line but a few hundred yards from, and parallel with, the Nashville Pike."[27] For a time, it appeared the Union army would be completely routed, but Rosecrans's center, commanded by General Thomas and his cavalry corps, "held while the shattered right was re-formed."[28]

Between seven and eight that morning, Captain Otis was ordered by Colonel Julius Garesché—Rosecrans' long-time personal friend and chief-of-staff—to "proceed with the Fourth US Cavalry to the right flank, on the line of battle" and confront any rebel cavalry he found. At about this same time, a battery of the Fifth Wisconsin, led by Captain Oscar Pinney, was reacting to the collapse of the right wing. The battery "changed from front to the right, to meet the enemy rapidly approaching by the right and rear." They opened fire with canister, temporarily checking the advance of the enemy, but their position soon became untenable. Captain Pinney was "dangerously wounded" and they lost eighteen horses and one gun.[29] As the battery was being dragged to the rear near Nashville Pike, it was charged by Confederate cavalry and partially captured.[30] Captain Otis immediately responded with his cavalry, driving off the rebels.[31] The battery was then pulled across Overall's Creek, taking a position on a hill to the right of Nashville Pike, from which it repeatedly shelled and drove back the enemy's cavalry, who were trying to take possession of the road.[32] Otis then proceeded to the right of the line, where he found the entire right flank "had given away."[33] Having been informed of the position of the rebel cavalry, he moved about one-quarter of a mile under cover of brush.

Emerging from the timber, Otis gave the command: "Front, into line, charge!" "On we came," wrote one of the 4th Regulars:

> yelling like so many savages, and scattering them like chaff. Two-thirds of our men were fresh recruits, but nobly and well did they march with the regulars. We captured three hundred of [Bushrod] Johnson's men, and brought back with us one hundred and seventy Texas Rangers and [Colonel Henry M.] Ashby's [2nd Tennessee] Cavalry.[34]

The rebels were "completely routed, with the exception of two pieces of artillery, supported by about 125 cavalry."[35] Their artillery, which was stationed between Otis's right and the Murfreesboro and Nashville Pike, had moved off before Otis could re-form his command.[36] On the performance of his command, Otis wrote:

> I cannot speak in too high terms of the officers and men. Every man charged and kept in position, taking over 100 prisoners of the enemy and releasing a large number of our own captured men. More redounds to their credit, considering that a large majority are recruits from volunteer infantry, and only *some five days drilled and mounted* [emphasis author].[37]

Rescuing McCook's Ammunition Train

After the first hour of battle, "five Union brigades were in full retreat." "Confusion and panic" gripped the Federal forces, and it didn't seem the Confederates could be stopped. While the rebels were "netting hundreds of prisoners... a far greater prize awaited them near the Gresham house... where the seventy-six heavily laden wagons of McCook's ammunition train were drawn up, ripe for the picking."[38]

Confederate cavalry was in heavy presence; Brigadier General Joseph Wheeler's, Colonel John A. Wharton's, Brigadier General Abraham Buford's, and Captain Dick McCann's rebel cavalry and artillery struck wherever they could, targeting the wagon trains. At nine o'clock in the morning on December 31, a small Confederate raiding party attacked and captured the trains of the 28th Brigade near Smyrna.[39] The trains were highly vulnerable, as they were easy targets and not well guarded. Under attack from rebel cavalry, infantry would not be able to keep up with the moving wagons. In one of his messages to General-in-Chief Halleck, Rosecrans bemoans: "We labor under great disadvantage from the inferior number of our cavalry, necessitating large detachments of infantry to guard our trains."[40]

During the initial panic, when the Right Wing of the Army of the Cumberland crumbled, Lieutenant Colonel Joseph W. Burke of the 10th Ohio Infantry discovered "the prominent movers in the panic were the quartermasters in charge of the trains."[41] Riding to the rescue of one train, he comments: "The scene on the road was indescribable. Teamsters had abandoned their wagons and came back mounted on their mules and horses; wagons were packed across the road, and many capsized on the side of the pike; horses ran wild through the woods..."[42]

It did not take long for the Confederate cavalry to discover McCook's wagons and ammunitions train. A group of rebel cavalrymen seized McCook's supply and personal baggage trains, while another made ready to seize the ordnance wagons.[43] Captain Gates P. Thurston, the Union officer in charge, used his seventy-five man infantry guard to repel the initial advance of rebel cavalry and led the train north into the cedars above Wilkinson Pike. They struggled "through a half mile of thickets, ravines, and fencerows" in utter confusion and turmoil, "before reaching the open ground south of the Widow Burris [or Burrows] farm."[44] There they found the Confederate cavalry in full force.[45] Faced with imminent loss of the train, Thurston appealed to every Union cavalry officer in the area for help. A number of regiments, including Thruston, his infantrymen, and the teamsters responded, only to be "swept from the field."[46] The rebel troopers began leading away the wagons. Suddenly, a small Federal cavalry squadron led by Colonel John Kennett, 4th Ohio, "launched a surprise counter-charge" that caught the Confederate cavalrymen unprepared.[47] Rosecrans had earlier ordered Kennett to "gather all idle cavalry from along the Nashville Turnpike and ride at once to the right." As Kennett led his "ragtag force" south across the turnpike toward the retreating Union infantry, he ran into Captain Elmer Otis "with six companies of his unattached Fourth United States Cavalry [Cos. B, C, D, G, I, and K]," as well as the retreating 3rd Ohio Cavalry. "Kennett ordered his reinforced command to dismount behind a fence south of the Nashville Turnpike," and from there they attacked and drove away the "startled" rebel troopers.[48] Thruston then "patched up the disabled wagons and reorganized the train . . . bringing his wagons safely to rest on the west bank of Stones River near army headquarters." Rosecrans, having heard that the ammunition train had been lost, was "delighted" to find it safe and promoted Thruston to major on the spot.[49]

This action, facilitated by Captain Otis and the 260 officers and men of the 4th US Cavalry, helped save the ammunition train and enabled General Sheridan's troops "to replenish their empty cartridge-boxes," thus allowing his division to "repulse the enemy . . . [and] protect the flanks of the center."[50] "The fiery Phil Sheridan" then handed Bragg "his first defeat of the day."[51] This, in turn, allowed Rosecrans time "to retain the left wing [and] support the right, until it could be rallied and assume a new position."[52]

The Confederate advance was slowed and the possible destruction of the Union Army prevented. At the end of the day, Otis was ordered to escort a train to the rear and his command spent New Year's Eve bivouacked near Rosecrans's headquarters.[53]

Captain Elmer Otis and the 4th Cavalry were later singled out as "deserving . . . of special notice" by General Stanley: "Captain Otis, Fourth US Cavalry . . . rendered important and distinguished service, gallantly charging and dispersing the enemy's cavalry in their attack upon our train Wednesday, the 31st."[54] In his after-battle report, Captain Otis singled out a number of officers and men in his command:

> Of the officers engaged it is almost impossible to particularize, they all did so well. Capt. Eli Long led his company with the greatest gallantry, and was wounded by a ball through his left arm. . . . Lieutenants Mauck [Clarence Manck], Kelly, Lee, and Healy could not have done better. First Sergt. Martin Murphy led Company G and commanded it with great gallantry. He reports having counted 11 dead of the enemy on the ground over which his company charged. Sergt. Maj. John G. Webster behaved gallantly, taking 1 lieutenant, mounted on a fine mare. First Sergt. James McAlpin led Company K after Captain Long was wounded, and reports having killed 2 with two successive shots of his pistol. First Sergt. John Dolan, Company B, captured a captain and received his sword. No one could have acted more bravely than First Sergt. Charles McMaster, of Company I. First Sergt. Christian Haefling, in charge of courier line near headquarters, proceeded in the thickest of the fire and recovered the effects of Colonel Garesché, on his body, killed in this day's fight. Our loss in this charge was trifling.
>
> Capt. Eli Long and 6 privates wounded.[55]

Captain Long would be appointed colonel, USV, commanding the 4th Ohio Volunteer Cavalry in February. In September, he would be commanding Second Brigade under General George Crook.[56] Before the year was out, Sergeant Major John G. Webster and 1st Sergeant Charles McMaster would be commissioned 2nd lieutenants.[57] Lieutenant L'Hommedieu would soon be on detached service for the remainder of the year. He would die due to illness on December 31, 1863.[58]

New Year's Day 1863

On the night of New Year's Eve 1862, Confederate General Bragg received "unusually poor intelligence from his cavalry," which appeared to support the apparent rout and retreat of the Union army. He believed victory was his and waited word of the Federal withdrawal from the field.[59] He may well have assumed this was the case. Lieutenant Robert Burns, 4th Michigan Cavalry, was up at 4 a.m. and was:

> surprised to see the road jammed with wagons, loaded and unloaded, going towards Nashville. . . . It was supposed a general retreat would take place as we had without doubt been badly whipped the day before. . . . Our wagons, with all our tents, clothes, etc., had by this time (9 o'clock) come to Stewart's Creek where we were.[60]

However, Rosecrans was making other plans. After a council with his general staff, he spent New

Year's Eve reorganizing his troops, intending to hold his ground.[61] On January 1, the Federal cavalry was "under arms all day, with two regiments on picket and skirmishing with the enemy's pickets."[62] Lieutenant Burns saddled up and rode out to find the main body of cavalry:

> We were back a little and I saw men running without arms, bare headed, teamsters cutting loose from their wagons, infantry men mounted on mules–all rushing toward Nashville in terror. We stood and watched them pass, expecting the enemy on us every moment, but none appeared that day.[63]

Burns found the Federal Cavalry "about a mile to the rear and right," about 2,500 drawn up in line of battle. Almost immediately:

> the enemy opened on us with artillery. The shells burst in all directions about us . . . two or three men were wounded. I could distinctly see the shells flying over us. I never could before. They have most persuasive voices. We were soon ordered to move back out of range, as cavalry, unsupported, can do nothing against artillery."[64]

This common assumption would be proven wrong at Shelbyville in June.

The balance of the 4th Regulars, under Captain Otis, were ordered to "make a reconnaissance on the right flank," reporting to Major Calvin Goddard, Rosecrans's acting assistant adjutant-general. That night they bivouacked near Overall's Creek, three miles east of Murfreesboro, where they remained for the next few days, "watching the movements of the enemy as far as possible."[65] As the "gloomy New Year's day" passed with a standoff, the feeling began to grow within the Confederate Army of Tennessee that "victory was slipping away . . ."[66]

Panic at Stewart's Creek

The morning of January 1, Lieutenant Rendlebock and the men of Company L were posted at Stewart's Creek Bridge, a few miles southeast of La Vergne, to guard their camp and train. The day before, Colonel Burke, 10th Ohio Infantry, had also been posted to the area to guard the headquarters train.[67] They were threatened with attack the entire day. Burke had the large train "corralled in close order, and by extreme vigilance prepared to resist any attack during the night." He was also dealing with the multitude of stragglers coming back from the front "from an early hour of the day." Burke "deployed a line of skirmishers across the country from the pike to the railroad with instructions to shoot down every straggler who attempted to force the line and marched over 1,100 of these men" back to camp.[68] Among these were "skulkers, to be found in all armies, ever ready to fall out of line of battle . . . robbing the dead and wounded."[69] Burke was again threatened by rebel cavalry and their advance guard, and they were "twice repulsed" by his pickets. At about one o'clock, remnants of the panicked and disorganized Union Army that Lieutenant Burns had observed earlier that day were upon them:

> . . . a squadron of affrighted negroes came charging at full gallop from Murfreesborough toward Stewart's Creek, and with such impetuosity and recklessness that over 100 passed the bridge before I could check the progress of the main cavalcade . . . This was the advance of what seemed to me to be the whole army–cavalrymen with jaded horses, artillery and infantry soldiers, breathless and holding on to wagons, relating the most incredible defeats and annihilation of the army and their respective regiments, came streaming down the road and pouring through the woods on their way toward the bridge. In vain did my small guard stationed on the road try to check this panic.[70]

Burke ordered his officers to draw their revolvers, "but the fugitives heeded them not." He "fixed bayonet" and "marched at double-quick to the bridge":

> and drew up a line before it, sending out, at the same time, two companies, deployed as skirmishers, on the right and left, to prevent the passing of the creek by fording. The fugitives crowded in thousands, and at one time pressed closely up to the bayonets of my men. I ordered the battalion to load, and determined to fire if the crowd did not move back; seeing which, many took flight back toward the front. At this critical moment I was rendered most valuable assistance by

Lieutenant Rendlebrook [sic], Fourth US Cavalry, and his men, who were stationed at the bridge with their camp and train. To him I assigned the duty of getting the stragglers into line, and nobly did his men execute his orders. Riding through the panic-stricken crowds, the cavalrymen drove them into a field, where a good line was formed, and every straggler taken and made dress up. When I had a regiment formed in this manner, I assigned it officers and marched it across the bridge, stacked arms, and rested it. In this manner I secured over 4,000 men.[71]

Colonel Burke concluded his report, stating: "The Fourth US Cavalry . . . were constantly on duty, reporting the movements of the enemy and assisting in effectually checking this disgraceful and causeless panic."[72] He later offered high praise for the "signal [remarkable] assistance" rendered him by Rendlebock and the non-commissioned officers and men of his command. Captain Otis also cited 2nd Lieutenant Rendlebock as "exceedingly vigilant in getting the train, and of great service in sending forward supplies."[73]

Sporadic fighting did not resume until the afternoon of January 2, when Bragg ordered a controversial failed assault on the Union Army. He began to withdraw after dark the next day. On January 2 and 3, Stanley reported the cavalry was "engaged in watching the flanks of our position . . . and making reports thereon, until January 4."[74]

The weather alternated between freezing rain and sleet, leaving the ground inches deep in mud and making cooking or sleeping almost impossible.[75] Rosecrans reported that Saturday, January 3, was spent "bringing up and distributing provisions and ammunition. It has been raining all day; ground very heavy."[76] On Sunday, January 4, "it became evident that the [Confederate] army had fled."[77]

The ammunition train arrived during the night, and Sunday "was occupied in distributing ammunition, bringing in the dead, and collecting arms from the field of battle."[78] Minty's brigade moved to Wilkinson's Cross Roads, six miles northwest of Murfreesboro, and bivouacked there with the 4th Cavalry.[79] On Monday, the 4th Regulars, as part of Minty's brigade, marched through Murfreesboro and reported to General David Stanley, who then took the lead himself with his old regiment.[80] During this march, Otis's 4th Regulars "engaged the enemy's rear guard on the Manchester Pike, driving them some 2 or 3 miles." After crossing a small creek about two miles from Murfreesboro— the bridge having been destroyed—"the enemy opened with artillery."[81] Minty sent two of his cavalry regiments to the front, keeping three in reserve.[82] Although "it was almost impossible to move because of the dense cedar thickets," the cavalry "pressed vigorously forward."[83] There was occasional skirmishing and shelling from the Confederate forces.[84] After about six miles of "driving the rebels from one hill and thicket to another," they approached Beach Grove, where they found the enemy "strongly reinforced." The rebels "made a determined stand, attacking the Seventh Pennsylvania and First Tennessee with vigor. The fight lasted nearly two hours."[85] According to Minty: "The Fourth Cavalry, First Tennessee Infantry and Seventh Pennsylvania Cavalry were chiefly engaged on our side."[86] When the fight "reached a more open country," a saber charge capturing one piece of artillery "was delivered by the Fourth United States Cavalry and the Seventh Pennsylvania; the enemy being driven completely from the field."[87] The brigade returned to within a mile and a half of Murfreesboro "and went into camp on the Manchester pike, establishing a line of pickets six miles out."[88] General Stanley, noting the "very severe character" of this skirmish, wrote: "Captain Otis' command acted independently until the 5th . . . when they came under my orders." He also described "the duty of the cavalry [as] very arduous. From December 26 to January 4 the saddles were only taken off to groom, and were immediately replaced."[89]

Once again, members of the 4th US Cavalry were singled out for special mention by their commanding general. In his subsequent reports, Rosecrans wrote about Captain Otis, "who commanded the courier line . . . most successfully, and who made a most opportune and brilliant charge–with 400 men–on Wheeler's cavalry, routing a brigade and recapturing 300 of our prisoners." He continued: "By their consent, and at their request [Captain Otis] is commanding a brigade of three regiments, each with a colonel."[90] Even Colonel John Kennett, commanding First Cavalry Division, felt compelled to remark, "Although he does not belong to my division . . . I feel it is my duty, as well as take great pleasure, in stating that [Captain Otis] is an able and efficient officer."[91] In concluding his remarks about Otis, Rosecrans wrote: "I earnestly urge his appointment as brigadier-general, in order that he may continue to command, as cavalry officers are greatly needed."[92] While this recommendation was not taken, Elmer Otis would remain in the cavalry, rising to the rank of colonel, 8th Cavalry, before his retirement in 1891.[93] Rosecrans also recognized Lieutenant Roys, "who commanded the escort of the headquarters train, and distinguished himself for gallantry and efficiency."[94] For his Chief of Cavalry, General Stanley—in command of ten regiments of cavalry—Rosecrans had high praise: "He ought to be made a major-general for his service, and also for the good of the service."[95]

Even the enlisted men were showing initiative. Private Francis H. Snow, Co. L, was assigned as orderly to General Rosecrans. On January 2, Snow was ordered to pick up fifteen Union stragglers and deliver them to a commissioned officer. This he did, but unable to find an officer, "he put them in line and brought them himself," telling them he would shoot the first one who attempted to run.[96]

It would seem the 4th US Cavalry made its reputation at the Battle of Stones River. The Regulars gained respect for the leadership of General David Stanley—one of their own—*as well as for the Volunteer Cavalry*, particularly that of Colonel Robert Minty, 4th Michigan Volunteers, and the 7th Pennsylvania Volunteers.

Writing to his father from Murfreesboro on January 8, James Wiswell has much to say:

> We were constantly fighting and skirmishing. It was the hardest fighting that I have seen since Wilson's Creek . . . our horses were not unsaddled but twice and then only long enough to groom them. . . . [T]he rebel cavalry broke around our flanks and captured our train a number of times, but as soon as the '4th U.S.' sounded the 'charge' they were obliged to leave without doing much damage.

Wiswell made an interesting comment regarding his commanding officer:

> Capt. Otis . . . anxious to have us and himself distinguished plead [sic] with the Genl. to have us relieved from Headqrs. until at last he consented and now we belong to Genl. Stanley's Cavalry Division. The work now will be a little more exciting but not so dangerous hard. I believe that there was better fighting done here than before in this war.

Wiswell also gained respect for the volunteers:

> I used to brag on the eastern 'Yankees' but these Western Volunteers with Gen. Rosecrans to lead them can whip the world–for five days they stood and fought all day and were obliged to lay down at night in mud and water–and the Pikes were so blocked up with Ammunitions Trains that for two days out of the five they had nothing to eat and there is men in my own Co. that saw them eating the dead horses killed during the day. If the boasted 'Army of the Potomac' would fight like that the 'Rebellion' might be 'crushed.' . . . As for 'Old Rosey' he is the only fighting Genl. that I ever saw–during the action he was constantly riding up and down the line cheering on his men.
>
> He lost a good part of his staff and a good many orderlies out of our regiment ... It was nothing but his own appearance and courage on the field before the troops that won the battle. I do believe that if Buell had been in command that he would have lost the field and maybe the city of Nashville.[97]

Although Stones River was a "tactical draw," it had far-reaching consequences. The impact on the Confederacy was decidedly negative. "Not only were some ten thousand irreplaceable veterans killed, wounded, or captured, but Tennessee was effectively lost and the high command of the South's principal Western army was hopelessly divided."[98] Bragg's "failure to maintain a hold on middle Tennessee cost the Confederacy rich farmland and opened a corridor for the Union army to penetrate the Deep South."[99] "The casualties had been shocking. The Federals lost 13,231 men (31%) and the Confederates 10,306 (28%)–in each case more than a fourth of the army's total strength. Few Civil War battles ever cost more or meant less."[100] Rosecrans's army was "too badly mangled to go any farther," and "six months would pass before the Union Army of the Cumberland could resume the offensive."[101]

According to the casualty reports, the Fourth US Cavalry lost three enlisted men killed, one officer (Captain Long), and nine enlisted men wounded. Twelve enlisted men were reported captured or missing for a total of twenty-five. Along with the loss of Sergeant Richmond, Company K, Private Daniel McDonell, Company D, was killed while on escort duty. Two others reported killed were Privates William H. Glynn and Commodore P. Cole of Company L.[102] Both men had enlisted at Nashville and were among the numbers of new recruits needed in November 1862 to create Companies L and M at Murfreesboro. With little time for training, they found themselves in combat in a matter of weeks. Commodore Cole, the first casualty of the new year, was killed while on escort duty on January 1, 1863, just three weeks into his enlistment. Private Glynn was actually missing in action and would return to his regiment, serving until his "expiration of service" at San Antonio, Texas, in December 1865.

One of the overlooked consequences of Stones River, as expressed by James Wiswell, was the impact on the Union Cavalry. With the exception of the 4th U.S., David Stanley's cavalry regiments were all volunteers, two of them being Minty's 4th Michigan and the 7th Pennsylvania. As reported by Major General Rosecrans, "Our ten regiments of cavalry fought the enemy's forty regiments of cavalry, and held them at bay, or beat them" wherever they were found.[103] During those arduous six days at Stones River, the volunteers fought side by side with the Regulars and won their respect. The cavalry of Stanley's Division and the regiments that would soon make up Minty's Brigade, including the 4th U.S. and 7th Pennsylvania, would coalesce into a formidable fighting force.

III. Cavalry Division, Army of the Cumberland
Rosecrans – Stanley – Minty

Colonel Robert H. G. Minty, United States Volunteers

On January 5, 1863, the Fourth Regiment United States Cavalry came under direct command of the new Chief of Cavalry, Army of the Cumberland, Brigadier General David S. Stanley. In this new Cavalry Division, the First Brigade, Second Cavalry Division, was to be commanded by Colonel Robert Minty, 4th Michigan Volunteer Cavalry. The Fourth Regulars would ride with the First Brigade in January 1863 "unattached," finally becoming a component of that brigade in April.[1]

Robert Horatio George Minty was a most extraordinary military commander to have come from the civilian side. In his own words, "I was four years, less 15 days, in the service, and never lost a flag, a guidon, or a gun." He was "personally engaged in 109 battles and skirmishes in which blood flowed ... had five horses shot under him ... and thirteen bullets pierced his clothing."[2] Of slight build, many of his men described him in diminutive terms, such as "the little Colonel" or "our little General." One comrade wrote: "Although small in stature, he was without a peer as a cavalry officer." His "clear and ringing voice" carried a heavy British accent, or perhaps a combination of British from his parents and Irish from his childhood years in his birthplace, County Mayo, Ireland. He was said to have never used tobacco or intoxicating liquors and was a practicing Episcopalian throughout his life.[3]

Minty was born into a military tradition, his grandfather and father having served in the British military. His father had been appointed Judge Advocate in Jamaica, but died suddenly of yellow fever at the age of fifty. Two months later, in March 1848, seventeen-year-old Robert was commissioned as an ensign in his father's regiment; his mother and the rest of the family emigrated to Canada. Robert served for five years before resigning his commission and rejoining his family in Canada. He married and began a new career working for a number of railway lines, which eventually led the family to relocate to Detroit in 1859. By the beginning of the rebellion they had become citizens. Since military officers were in short supply, Minty's prior military experience led him to accept a commission as major in September 1861, in the newly formed 2nd Michigan Volunteer Cavalry Regiment. Brevet

Colonel Gordon Granger, USV, formerly captain, 3rd US Cavalry, was the commanding officer. When Granger was promoted to brigadier general, he was replaced by Captain Philip Sheridan, 13th Infantry. Minty, because of his "marked attention to the organization and drill of his regiment," was quickly promoted to lieutenant colonel and assigned to the newly formed 3rd Michigan Cavalry. On July 21, 1862, Colonel Minty was given his own command, the newly formed 4th Michigan Cavalry. He would command the "Fighting Fourth" and the brigade of which it would become a part (the *Saber Brigade*) for the next two years.[4]

Major George W. Fish, regimental surgeon, rode with Minty and had this to say about the character of the man after a hard campaign that had taken a "severe toll upon the men":

> In all these long and dreary marches, the officers and men bivouacked together, and were equally destitute of tents. I have never known an officer of this regiment to enter an inhabited building to shelter himself for the night, while the men were without shelter. Colonel Minty has always shared with the men such fare and shelter as they had, and the other officers do the same.

Continuing his praise:

> The 4th Michigan is one of the best, if not the best officered regiment of the cavalry in this army . . . Much of this is due, no doubt, to the clear discrimination and impartiality of Colonel Minty, in selecting officers to fill vacancies. Few men seem better judges than he of whom is the man for the place.[5]

He concludes that Colonel Minty "was without peer as a cavalry officer."[6]

First Brigade, Second Division

The majority of days and weeks of January and February were spent in constant scouting activities and responding to the movements of the Confederate cavalry. It was in one of its first assignments that Minty's brigade would distinguish itself and set the tone for the rest of the war. At the same time, the officers and men of the new Cavalry Corps would experience some of their most difficult and challenging circumstances of the war.

In January, as part of Minty's Brigade, the 4th Cavalry was involved in a number of reconnaissance and expeditionary activities. On the thirteenth, there was a three-day reconnaissance to Nolensville and Versailles, in an area about twelve miles southeast of Murfreesboro, in the most difficult weather conditions. Captain Otis commanded a force of "about 300 of the Fourth US Cavalry and 350 of the Second East Tennessee Cavalry" under "light marching orders." As Sergeant Larson explains, this meant no trooper "should carry anything on his horse except what was actually necessary":

> Each man carried only the clothing he wore and, as protection against the rain, only his poncho which was strapped on the pommel of his saddle. Under the saddle were either two saddle blankets or a saddle blanket and bed blanket, which served as bed for the trooper whenever time and the condition of the weather would allow him to spread a bed at all, but as no tents or anything to make a shelter with was carried, the making of beds depended entirely on the weather.[7]

Leaving camp a little after 12 a.m. on January 13, Otis's command marched to the Murfreesboro railroad depot to join Colonel George D. Wagner, who was commanding the expedition. They camped that evening near Nolensville, seeing little of the enemy.[8] The following day, moving over stony roads made slick by the continuing rain, they marched to Eagleville. Believing some of Wheeler's couriers were in town, Otis gave orders for two companies to "charge the town." They met some minor resistance and the officer leading the charge had his horse shot out from under him, but they captured "some ten or twelve of the enemy."[9] That night they camped with little sleep, in the misery of the "rain and mud."[10] By the morning of the fifteenth, the rain had turned into sleet and snow.[11] Otis was instructed to "act as rear guard" as far as Salem, five miles southwest of Murfreesboro. During that scout, his men destroyed a mill owned by a Mr. Webb containing a large amount of grain on hand for the Confederate army. The troopers also captured "twenty-four horses, which were principally turned over to men whose horses had given out."[12] As a corporal in the 4th Michigan writes, that night they "camped in the snow–mighty uncomfortable." The next day there were "about 3 inches of snow . . . everything covered with ice."[13] Otis' command returned to Murfreesboro on the seventeenth.

Expedition Against Wheeler's Cavalry

There would be no rest. While Otis was out on his reconnaissance, Rosecrans received word that the Confederate cavalry, under Forrest and Wheeler—"with over four thousand of the best rebel cavalry in the department and eight pieces of artillery"—had been sent on an expedition to "obstruct the navigation of the Cumberland River and recapture Fort Donelson."[14] At twenty-six, General Joseph Wheeler was the senior cavalry commander in the West. A native son of Georgia and member of the West Point Class of '59, he served briefly with the 1st Dragoons and Mounted Riflemen. Wheeler had proven his ability when he "virtually immobilized" the Federal troops at Perrysville, Kentucky, the previous October.[15] On or about January 15, the Confederates moved against Fort Donelson and Dover, but were repulsed with heavy losses by Union forces. Rosecrans ordered a division of infantry and the First and Third Brigades of cavalry—with Colonel Minty in command—to go after them. It would turn into an arduous two-week expedition against the Confederate Cavalry, testing the endurance of man and horse.

On January 31, with a force of "1,370 men," Colonel Minty reported to General Jeff C. Davis, who was commanding the expedition. He was instructed to "take the advance, to drive the rebel forces from Middleton and Unionville, and, 'if possible, keep the enemy from all knowledge of there being infantry behind me.'"[16] The rebel cavalry was "in and about Unionville," with "strong outposts at Middleton to the east and Rover to the north."[17] On approaching Rover, Minty's advance discovered an outpost of "about six hundred rebel cavalry."[18] Minty sent one cavalry regiment "in skirmishing order across the country" to flush them out. His main column consisted of the 7th Pennsylvania and 4th Michigan; Lieutenant Nathaniel M. Newell's section of Battery D, 1st Ohio Artillery; and the 4th US Cavalry "in the order mentioned."[19] The skirmish line discovered a "considerable body of Confederate cavalry" less than a quarter mile in their front.[20]

It appeared the entire rebel force, "formed on a slight hill along a piece of woods," was developed and drawn up in line of battle.[21] A couple of freshly plowed fields were between them and the Union Cavalry.[22] Colonel Minty, on assessing the situation, "wanted to strike the first blow; not to allow the enemy to do it." Riding to the head of his column, Minty addressed Major William H. Jennings, commanding the 7th Pennsylvania: "Major, draw sabers." Jennings replied, "Colonel, my men have never used sabers; they have no confidence in them."

"In what have they confidence," Minty inquired.

"The pistol, sir," was the response.

"There was no time to lose," Minty wrote. Addressing the men of the 7th Pennsylvania, he gave the orders: "Seventh Pennsylvania, numbers one and three, draw sabers; numbers two and four, draw pistols; forward–march; trot–march," and upon reaching the skirmish line, "gallop–march." "I then ordered the 'charge' sounded, and under the soul-stirring notes of the trumpets and the cheers of the men, the gallant 7th rode down the incline and struck the Confederates who were advancing to meet them."[23] According to Captain Vale, riding with the 7th Pennsylvania:

> The movement was executed with great rapidity and dash, the last four or five hundred yards being at a charge, with drawn sabers. The rebel line was struck and the whole force utterly routed, stricken down, captured or scattered, in less than five minutes after the advance was sounded. Six officers and forty-nine enlisted men were captured; one officer and forty-three men killed and wounded on the field, every one of whom fell beneath the sabers of the Seventh; and a larger number of stragglers were gathered up in a rapid scouring of the country.[24]

The rebel cavalrymen never forgot their first experience of a saber charge delivered by Minty's brigade.

The entire Confederate Cavalry was *pursued* through Unionville and "driven in confusion toward Shelbyville."[25] Rosecrans's and Stanley's tactics for the new cavalry force were clearly demonstrated in this affair. Wheeler and Forrest escaped capture and retreated to Columbia, and further pursuit was abandoned. Minty's command marched to Franklin, arriving there on February 10. On the twelfth, "as rear guard to General Davis, it marched to Triune and camped in that place." On the thirteenth, General Davis's command marched on to Murfreesboro, arriving after dark.[26]

Writing twenty-five years later, Captain Vale described this expedition of fourteen days and 300 miles as "the most severe it is possible to conceive":

> The weather was a constant succession of rain, snow, and sleet, alternating with

the most intense cold; the roads were knee deep with mud and slush, varied at times with a crust of two or three inches of ice and frozen ground on top; not hard enough to carry a horse, but enough to make marching difficult and dangerous. The cavalry moved without tents or baggage, and the suffering was very great; many of the men had their hands and feet frostbitten, and all felt the effects for weeks and months after. There are few of the survivors, either of the National or rebel forces, who would again voluntarily pass through the experience of that terrible fortnight.[27]

The major significance of this particular fight is in the casualty reports. Minty sent to the rear "94 rebels; . . . 51 wounded . . . 13 of them with saber wounds on or about their heads . . . by the glancing of our *blunt* [emphasis author] sabers . . ."[28] Minty himself had only "2 men wounded, 1 pretty badly."[29] "What I considered of more value than all else," wrote Minty almost thirty years later, "after this successful charge, my gallant men were firm believers in the effectiveness of the saber as I was myself."[30]

Major General Rosecrans expressed his satisfaction with his new Cavalry Corps to the Secretary of War, writing that the many "spirited skirmishes" with the enemy "terminated well" for his horsemen. Commenting on Minty's cavalry charge, he particularly noted the number of injured Confederate soldiers, "*all but one . . . wounded with the saber* [emphasis author]."[31]

The Saber

Among scholars, the use of the saber in the Civil War is a controversial topic. As cavalry historian Edward Longacre points out in *Lincoln's Cavalrymen* (2000), "Over the past century and a quarter, historians have cast doubt on the Union cavalryman's faith in, and regular use of, his saber. According to this school of thought, few troopers called on their sabers in battle when a pistol was handy and loaded."[32] It was generally believed that by the beginning of the war, the saber had become a relic left over from an earlier time, worn now more by tradition and custom as a ceremonial ornament for officers and men on parade. Certainly by the mid-1800s, the almost daily advances being made by gunsmiths would seemingly have rendered the saber obsolete. It was seen as useless against entrenched ground troops, and its primary use by mounted forces was in the "slashing and thrusting" during the pursuit of broken and routed infantry. Surprisingly, sabers were not necessarily sharpened, but were blunt, and it seemed their best use was for breaking bones or beating off an individual or mob trying to dismount the rider. From the trooper in the field to high-ranking former cavalry officers—including George McClellan—it was reported that the saber had fallen out of favor and that many mounted units had abandoned it altogether. It was "annoying to ride with," and many troopers learned to strap it under the legs and leave it on the saddle when they dismounted to fight. As Longacre points out, "This theory is open to question."

One of the misleading facts that may account for this early interpretation is that four years of combat records show there were fewer than 1,000 saber wounds treated in Federal hospitals.[33] Unfortunately, there are no records for the Confederacy. Part of Longacre's thesis is that by 1862-63, the Federal cavalry became the dominant cavalry in the war and, based on his extensive research and use of new primary-source documents, he shows that the saber was used extensively and effectively. This seems particularly true in the Western Theater, heretofore largely ignored by historians. Contrary to earlier published accounts, Longacre quotes McClellan, stating, "'The strength of the cavalry is in the spurs and sabre,'" and that McClellan "filled his mounted ranks with like-minded officers."[34] Longacre continues: "Saber exercise was a ritual of Union cavalry training, one to which drillmasters devoted much time and energy":

> Troopers not only honed their blades regularly, but they used them regularly. In almost every cavalry encounter for which a written record survives, references to the use of the saber abound, along with testimonials to its effectiveness–often in sharp contrast to that of the pistol, the reloading of which while in the saddle was a nigh impossible process. One influential postwar theorist, formerly an officer in the 6th New York, claimed that in every mounted engagement between 1862 and 1865 in which he took part, saber-wielding Federals routed pistol-carrying Confederates.[35]

With the extreme difficulties in creating efficient cavalrymen for the newly formed volunteer regiments under war conditions, it would seem only logical that training for use of the saber on horseback would be about the last level of mastery, assuming the novice trooper survived his first year in the saddle. The 4th US Cavalry had a core of well trained men and non-commissioned officers, and it would have been far easier to assimilate and train the smaller number of new recruits into a Regular regiment than train an entirely new cavalry regiment of volunteers.

It would also seem logical that the level to which the saber was put to use by any cavalry regiment depended totally upon the skill and abilities of the commanding officers. Both Stanley and Minty had "full confidence" in the use of the saber and intended for their officers and men to use it. As recounted by a young 2nd lieutenant in the 4th Michigan, "The worst raking I ever received was from my colonel [Minty] . . . for retreating," without making much of a fight. "At the time he told me that sabers are intended for use, not ornament."[36] Colonel Minty always impressed upon his men, "the saber is the cavalryman's weapon and that we should never lose a chance for using it."[37] The brigade commanded by Minty—consisting of his 4th Michigan Volunteers, Colonel William B. Sipes's 7th Pennsylvania Volunteers, and the 4th United States Regulars—would quickly earn the sobriquet the Saber Brigade.

What comes to mind in any discussion of the actual use of the saber is the apparent insanity of leading a saber charge against a group of men armed with rifles and handguns. However, how the cavalry was trained, the state of arms at this time, and the general lack of military discipline and training evidenced among early Confederate soldiers must be considered. The early volunteers on both sides have already been described as "mobs," armed with little more than shotguns, knives, and "obsolete single shot flintlock pistols." This situation would eventually improve over time, along with greater use of the rapid fire revolving pistol and the Spencer rifle. However, single-shot, muzzle-loading rifles, shotguns, and handguns with limited degrees of accuracy were used well into the war by Confederate soldiers and were no match for a well disciplined saber charge. As Captain Vale described in his regimental history, the 7th Pennsylvania learned "early in the campaign the superiority of its sabers over the fire-arms and unskillfully wielded sabers and cutlasses of the enemy."[38]

It has been demonstrated how effective cavalry became in support of artillery batteries and supply wagons—both critical elements in a major battle—as well as chasing down, capturing, rounding up, and controlling the stragglers of a fleeing enemy. As Sergeant Larson points out, it was during the endless scouting expeditions and reconnaissance activities against smaller groups of enemy where the cavalry initially played its primary role, and the saber accentuated their effectiveness. Much has been made of the "rebel yell" and the fear it sent through those who experienced it. The argument could also be made that the same level of fear was experienced by those seeing a dozen or more Union cavalrymen charging on horseback, blades waving and glistening in the sun, bearing down and closing in at full force. There may have been a chance to get off one shot, but there was no time to reload. By the time the enemy started to use his weapon, he was running in panic, shooting over his shoulder.

There are several versions as to what brought about the change in the use of the saber from a blunt instrument to a *terrible swift sword*. Colonel Minty gave his account in his writings after the war:

> On the morning after our return to Murfreesboro [February 13] I directed my quartermaster to procure a grindstone for each regiment in the brigade. He secured a supply the same day from the surrounding plantations, and I ordered all sabers to be ground two-thirds of their length from the point.[39]

Under existing Federal regulations, cavalry sabers were not allowed to be ground at all. Subsequently, Braxton Bragg filed a formal complaint with General Rosecrans "by flag of truce, in which the Confederate General said he understood the Union cavalry were grinding their sabers, and he protested against it, as an act of barbarity, and contrary to the usage of laws and war."[40] Minty was called before his superiors for an explanation:

> I was directed to report in person to Gen. Rosecrans. I found the General pacing to and fro in a large parlor, his hands clasped behind him, his head bent slightly forward, a position that all who have had the privilege of meeting him will recognize. Gen. Stanley, the chief of cavalry, one of the grandest soldiers of the war, was sitting on a sofa at the side of the room. 'Well,

Minty,' asked the General, 'what is this you are doing?'

I replied, 'I don't know General, what is it?'... [H]e handed me a dispatch... [and] after reading it I handed it back and said: 'General, Gen. Bragg is correct in stating that we are grinding our sabers; but I think he is in error in denouncing the act as barbarous; in my opinion it is much more barbarous to bruise and mangle a poor fellow with a blunt weapon than it is to give him a good clean wound with a sharp one. In a charge we made a few days ago, thirteen of the enemy had chips taken out of their skulls by the glancing of our blunt sabers. This, General, was poor work and should not be.'

Both Generals laughed, Stanley said: 'That's right.'

General Rosecrans then added:

'You are quite right; make your sabers as sharp as you please–the sharper the better for such troopers as yours, who know how to use them.'[41]

Colonel Minty continues:

A few days later Gen. Stanley told me that General Rosecrans, in replying to Braggs protest, said: 'Sabers are given to the cavalry as offensive weapons, and the more effective they can be made the better they will answer their purpose; sharp sabers are much more effective than blunt ones ...'[42]

From this point forward, the regiments in Minty's brigade maximized the use of the saber as an effective offensive weapon as well as a psychological one. This turned out to be a controversial order, and it led to serious threats of retaliation by Nathan Bedford Forrest's cavalry—the immediate execution of any captured trooper from these units.

Both Larson and Vale wrote about the "tremendous furor that existed among the rebels" with regard to "reducing the thick round edge to a razor-like degree of sharpness."[43] According to Larson: "Two regiments of Forrest's cavalry, who had been roughly handled... in a saber charge by the 4th US Cavalry, were now anxiously waiting for a favorable opportunity to retaliate... and for that purpose had ground their sabers..."[44]

The use of this weapon seems to have remained a controversial issue with Larson long after the war. When writing his autobiography forty-five years later, he states that his cavalry unit was merely responding to rumors of Forrest's men having sharpened their sabers. He then makes this interesting comment:

... [I]t is highly possible that Forrest's men had never sharpened their sabers at all. Such an act did not seem at all in line with their character. We met them often and always found them fair fighters, and always eager to fight, without any need for sharpened sabers or other *discredited tactics* [emphasis author].[45]

Perhaps after the passage of time and memories of the mayhem, Sergeant Larson was reflecting the sentiment expressed by historian Edward Longacre: "Even though they engaged in considerable swordplay, Union soldiers were wont to downplay the use of edged weapons, which in some quarters carried a connotation as *primitive, terror weapons* [emphasis author].[46]

The use of the saber was never universally popular, even in Minty's own brigade. As reported by Minty's biographer:

Discovered amongst the official brigade records, was a request made by Lt. Col. Josiah B. Park... dated about the middle of May, asking that his regiment not be supplied with sabers, stating as reasons: 'This regiment was originally issued with sabers, but finding that they were constantly in the way and of no use to men issued with long guns, I turned them in prior to the battle of Stones River. I trust that no change will be made in the case of a regiment that has proved itself.' Minty declined the request.[47]

In the May 1892 edition of the *National Tribune*, Lieutenant William A. McTeer, adjutant, 3rd Tennessee Volunteer Cavalry, writing of the ill-fated Smith expedition into Mississippi in February 1864, states:

General Smith gave orders that we should all grind our sabers and make them sharp. This created considerable alarm among the men for they had the impression, from some unknown source, that it was contrary to the rules of war to carry sharp sabers; but the order was obeyed, and many sabers were made sharp enough to trim fingernails.[48]

The 4th United States Cavalry became notorious for its aggressive use of the saber.

INCIDENT WITH FORREST'S BATTERY: THE KILLING OF CAPTAIN FREEMAN, C.S.A.

Against this background of controversy and within a month, another incident was to take place that added to the animosity between Forrest's cavalry and the 4th United States—a controversy that exists to this day. It occurred on the Lewisburg Pike, a few miles south of Franklin, Tennessee on April 10, 1863, when the 4th Cavalry charged the Confederate battery of Captain Samuel L. Freeman; the event was recorded by Captain Vale in his regimental history. Although not present, he interviewed the 4th Cavalry principals involved. Freeman's battery was following Colonel James W. Starnes' 4th Tennessee Cavalry at a leisurely pace toward Franklin on the Lewisburg Pike when:

> the 4th Cav. dashed upon the center of Starnes's line, broke it, driving it demoralized from the field; then charged upon the battery. A short but desperate encounter took place over the guns. Freeman, knowing that Forrest's whole force was at hand, encouraged his men to fight to the last, and when completely overpowered endeavored to retreat with two of his guns. Lieut. Rendlebock, with two companions, dashed after and soon overtaking him demanded his own, and the surrender of his guns. Freeman refused, and urged his horses on, firing his revolver almost in the face of the Lieutenant. At his third shot, Serg't-Maj. [Sherlock E.] Strickland, with a single shot from his revolver, laid him dead on the road. The guns were brought back to where the other portion of the battery was in possession of the 4th Cavalry.

The Confederates quickly rallied and the 4th Regulars, entirely unsupported, retreated to the north side of the river. Vale reports that five men of the 4th Cavalry were killed and ten wounded. He continues with his version of the events:[49]

> As was the custom of the rebels after meeting a mishap, they, in this instance, invented a cock and bull story to the effect that Capt. Freeman was murdered by an officer of the 4th after he had surrendered, and while a prisoner in their hands, on their retreat; the object being to give a color of excuse for the atrocities committed by themselves, and to create a bitter, blood thirsty feeling on the part of their soldiers against efficient cavalry regiments in general and the 4th Regulars in particular. Serg't-Maj. Strickland killed Capt. Freeman in a fair fight, and Capt. Freeman's bravery required no false statement, such as made, to perpetuate his memory. The report was, however, assiduously circulated and generally believed in Forrest's command, and on two notable occasions afterwards Forrest's men refused to take any of the 4th U.S. Cav. prisoners. They in some way learned that it was the Sergeant-Major of the regiment who killed Freeman, and they threatened to hang him if they ever caught him.[50]

From the day Captain Freeman was killed by a member of the 4th US Cavalry until the present, the myth has persisted through a series of Southern historians that it was a cowardly act of murder committed by an officer of the 4th Regulars when a surrendering Captain Freeman refused to move fast enough to the rear. In reality, the only fact known is that the captain was shot by Strickland as reported by Vale. While the circumstances of the incident are open to question, and taking into account Vale's bias, a thorough study of supposed "eyewitness" accounts brought forward by Southern historians offers no real clues and casts doubts on the accepted Southern version of the incident. As recently as 2002, a monument was erected by a Southern organization to mark the spot where Captain Freeman was "murdered."[51]

The deadly use of the saber and the Freeman incident generated a bloody rivalry between Forrest's Cavalry and the 4th US Cavalry. Aside from the number of casualties inflicted on both sides, Forrest would lose two of his highly valued officers in fights with the 4th US Cavalry: Captain Freeman and later Colonel Starnes, as well as his younger brother, Colonel Jeffrey E. Forrest. During the final week of the war, the last encounter would be the massacre at the hands of Forrest's men of a 4th US Cavalry scouting party commanded by Lieutenant Elbridge Roys—perhaps the greatest single loss to the regiment during the war.

Permanent Camp

The Army of the Cumberland would remain in its permanent winter camp outside Murfreesboro until late June 1863 "with a strong detachment at Triune, Rover and Unionville."[52] It would be temporary quarters for nearly 70,000 men. Vale presents a "vision" of the camp at Murfreesboro:

> Standing on a knoll, midway between the Shelbyville and Manchester pikes, the observer sees, all around him, as far as the eye can carry on every road, a sea of canvas, almost hidden, however, in the mass of cedars and evergreens which the busy industry of the 'boys' have brought to camp, and wrought into a thousand picturesque and summer-house pavilions.
>
> In the center of each division extends a grand avenue, one hundred feet in width, flanked on either side with stalwart cedars; while, at each end, a gigantic arch is sprung, from which, woven in evergreens and forest creepers, hangs the name of the division commander, and the number and designation of the division. At regular intervals, down this avenue, and at right angles with it, are similar ones for each brigade, with the name of the brigade commander and its number pendant from an arch at its entrance; and, from this brigade avenue, at right angles therewith, the regimental street is laid, on which, in regular order, the company quarters are pitched.
>
> All the regimental and company streets are roofed with evergreens; this forming a clean, delightful booth in every street. No dirt of offal is to be seen in street or tent, but each man's 'traps and kit' are kept packed, and ready for instant use.[53]

While the Federal Army was recovering from the Battle of Stones River, the endless monotony of camp life for the cavalry would be "punctuated by many long scouting excursions" lasting from one to several days to weeks.[54] Larson writes about the "marching and skirmishing" that occurred with cavalry duties in the months between Stones River and the Chickamauga Campaign the following September. He also helps explain the prevailing lack of recognition for the cavalry:

> Whenever we met the enemy or could force them to make a stand, fights occurred which, although in history are called skirmishes, were often equal to big battles considering the number engaged. Many a cavalryman found his last resting place in a grave dug by the roadside where such unrecorded and unnoticed affairs took place. Sometimes several such burying places would be made in one day at a distance of ten to twenty miles apart; still, these affairs are considered of minor importance. History takes no notice of them and gives the cavalry no credit for their work. Neither do the infantry and artillery, generally. They are not really to blame for that, as those affairs were fought behind their backs, sometimes fifty to seventy-five miles back of where they were quietly resting in their tents, receiving their daily rations promptly and even their letters and newspapers from home. They did not know that the fact that there had been no break or stop in the receipt of their daily supplies was due to the vigilance of the cavalry operating in the rear of their positions, nor did they know that the men of that branch of the service had to splash along in dirt knee-deep day and night to protect their comfortable camp.[55]

The bucolic scene described by Vale changed with the unusually harsh winters of '62-'63, and again in '63-'64, that brought extreme hardship to both sides of the war. The following descriptions are taken from letters of Confederate Army soldiers who suffered through it:

> It had ceased raining, but the ground was one grand loblolly from the tramp of thousands of men and animals, and the running to and fro of supply and baggage wagons. That night the ground froze very hard, and during the remainder of our stay there . . . the ground didn't thaw. It was impossible to do any writing on account of the ink's freezing. I would put the inkstand

in the warm ashes, but when I dipped my pen in it, it would freeze before I could transfer it to paper. I never experienced such cold weather, or I never spent such a disagreeable time . . .

. . . It grew cold so fast that by the time we had made the encampment safe, the wet canvas froze stiff. The thermometer had fallen to zero . . . The soldiers in the camps had slept but little, for they were obliged to keep awake and near the fires to keep from freezing. . . [E]ntire teams of mules dead, standing frozen in their tracks.[56]

Foraging

From February 13 to March 4, Minty's Brigade lay in camp near Murfreesboro. While in permanent camp, Vale describes their daily activities:

[There was] only the usual routine of camp and picket duty; the regiments, being regarded as veterans, were not required to drill, and the general commanding the army, as well as General Stanley, not being of the kind delighting in reviews, or devoted to military pomp and pageantry, allowed the soldiers to rest and recuperate while in camp [which] was greatly appreciated by the soldiers, and endeared their commander to them, as one who cared for their comfort rather than for display.

Foraging parties, under strong guards, were, however, sent out daily in every direction, and gradually all the supplies of forage and food the county offered, for more than twenty miles around, were gathered into our lines. Thus the country was held by the National cavalry, and the long line of railroad communication with Louisville was guarded and protected.[57]

There was a fine line between foraging and pillaging. Sergeant Henry Albert Potter, 4th Michigan, provides insight into the practice of foraging and Colonel Minty's handling of it:

Colonel Minty sent out Lieutenant Carter & 20 men foraging last night. They brought us 8 sheep this morning. The boys drove about 20 pigs from a yard and delivered them to the commissary. 3 men have passed me while I have been writing, one had 4 turkeys, one had 2 turkeys & 3 chickens, and the other had some geese. If we stay here a day or two eggs will be very high here next season I fear. Colonel Minty asked very innocently of the cook this morning where he got that mutton. Cook said he didn't know. T'was brought there last night. The colonel thought it was very singular. The colonel allows the men to get supplies. He keeps an account of it so that if necessary he can sign receipts for the same. If they belong to a Union man and he makes complaint, he gets a paper to show the facts and the government will pay him for all that is taken. If it belongs to a rebel he will probably not make a complaint, for we should nab him. The colonel knows that if he did not allow the men to get forage in this way, that they would get in on their own hook and he takes a wise course.[58]

Captain Robert Burns, 4th Michigan Cavalry, was never comfortable with this activity:

Men who were in Michigan considered honest now have no hesitation in stealing, robbing, passing counterfeit money, etc. . . . A private can go foraging on his own account, which an officer can not do, and return loaded with chickens, etc. What plundering I have seen. One day last week I saw a ham brought into camp wrapped in a southern lady's wedding dress.[59]

The effect of two massive armies foraging the same countryside was devastating; the once lush and productive land was stripped bare. By mid-June 1863, after nearly six months in Murfreesboro, the country "was in a most deplorable condition, there being neither horse, forage, nor provisions of any kind left in it." During the last months of the war, troopers would have as much to fear from the desperate, starving citizens as from Confederate soldiers.[60]

The monotony of winter camp also caused other problems typical of any military encampment near a civilian town. "With many men lying idle in camp, either too ill to ride, or bored when not out on scouting duty, some attempted to steal away into nearby Murfreesboro in search of comfort and entertainment." Soldiers were not allowed to go into town without permission, however, "several men of the brigade made visits anyway." Finally, after enough complaints had been reported to Colonel Minty, he issued orders on January 27, outlining the arrest and punishment for future offenders.[61]

Continuing the pattern previously established between battles and during permanent camps, there would be no rest for the cavalry. As Vale writes, they would "continue a constant round of wearisome marches," expeditions, and skirmishes until the Army of the Cumberland struck camp on June 23, 1863. Captain Burns adds, "We are usually worn out by fatiguing marches, night raids, dashes of 40 or 50 miles, etc."[62]

Edward Longacre provides one of the best descriptions of what was expected of, and experienced by, a Civil War cavalryman. Those joining the cavalry after 1861 with romantic notions soon found that "the realities were harsher, the service more difficult and burdensome than most would-be cavaliers could have imagined." The unique mobility of the mounted cavalryman allowed for the performance of a "wide variety of functions ... in and out of combat":

> In addition to adding weight to offensives by the main army, horsemen reconnoitered the enemy's position to discover his strength and determine his intentions; performed counter-reconnaissance by foiling the intelligence-gathering abilities of opposing cavalry; guarded the head, flanks, and rear of their army on the march; rode in advance to gain a foothold on the battlefield; took the advance during pursuit, prodding the enemy into flight and preventing him from regrouping and counterattacking; bought time for their own army's retreat, falling back from point to point and offering resistance when-ever conditions permitted; and raided communications facilities, supply depots, and other strategic targets behind enemy lines. When away from the battlefield, the typical trooper was not permitted to lie idle. While infantry and artillery rested, he served on a daily basis as a vedette [mounted sentry], a courier, a member of an escort unit, a provost guard, a forager. The cavalryman was on duty virtually every waking minute...[63]

The requirements of this new war put severe pressures on cavalrymen. "Few can stand the duties of this life," wrote a lieutenant in the 3rd Pennsylvania in October 1861. A New York trooper agreed: "The cavalry is the hardest branch there is in the service ... a cavalryman is kept busy all day long." Longacre continues: "As well as being hectic and severe, a trooper's job was dauntingly complicated, especially as he and his mount had to learn by intricate and intensive training how to act as one."

An officer from Michigan noted that 'the duties of cavalry are as arduous, complex and diversified as possible for any branch of the military service to be.' ... Those who had been fascinated by the glamor and dash of the cavalry life doubtless wished many time, during those laborious days, that they had the more frequent hours of recreation granted their neighbors in the infantry. It took a special breed to embrace a life filled with so many burdens and complexities.

Capt. Charles F. Adams Jr. of the 1st Massachusetts summed up the requirements succinctly: 'Alertness, individuality, reliability, and self-reliance.'[64]

Foraging Expedition and Skirmish at Bradyville, Tennessee

Rosecrans's command "fared badly" for forage, and on March 1, he sent Brigadier General Stanley with a "foraging train of 400 wagons on the Bradyville pike as far as the village of Bradyville," about fifteen miles southeast of Murfreesboro.[65] The escort: "consisted of a part of the three brigades of cavalry at [Murfreesboro] ... and one brigade of infantry. Directing the advance himself, Stanley placed the infantry in the center, the 4th US Cavalry on the exposed flank of the train, and Colonel Minty's command as rear guard."[66] Two miles from Bradyville they met and drove in the rebel pickets. Meeting further resistance, two of Stanley's cavalry regiments "drew pistols and sabers and rushed upon [the] enemy ... routing him, and sending his men and horses flying in all directions over the rugged hills." The rebels were part of Morgan and Wharton's brigades. Four of the enemy were killed, "not less than 20 were wounded," and "83 prisoners" taken. The Union forces captured "two wagon-loads of saddles of a rough pattern (all new), one wagon-load of picket rope, some bacon, corn, and meal, and in all 70 horses and mules. The animals were poor."[67]

In his official report of the expedition, Stanley wrote: "These little affairs, though not important in results, often show the character of the officers and troops more than great battles."[68]

IV. Riding With Sheridan

Philip H. Sheridan was career army since his graduation from West Point in 1853. He was assigned to the 4th Infantry on the frontier, where he had some experience with cavalry. As a young officer stationed in the northwest, he commanded a small detachment of dragoons in forays against the Yakama Indians. Part of this command was made up of volunteer militia with whom the Regulars "didn't get along."[1] In the spring of 1856, he led his Regulars and the volunteer militia in a successful expedition out of Fort Vancouver against several local tribes in revolt. As described by cavalry historian Richard Wormser:

> It wasn't a very big campaign, not a very significant victory; but it put Sheridan of the infantry in command of cavalrymen; it showed him how to live off the country and how to keep the enemy from doing the same thing; and it reassured him that the most unpopular of soldiers [volunteers] could be honored if he moved briskly, bravely, and with ingenuity.[2]

A lieutenant when the war began, Sheridan's first assignments were merely administrative. In May 1862, he was promoted to colonel and given command of the 2nd Michigan Cavalry Regiment, in which Major Robert Minty was serving at the time. Sheridan participated at Boonville, Perryville, and Stones River. In his early commands, he "fought bitterly against having his cavalry used as wagon guards; foot soldiers could do that work perfectly well."[3] "He wanted his mounted arm to function independently and be used *en masse* against Confederate cavalry or infantry, as the situation dictated."[4] During the expedition to Unionville, he was to observe one of the best cavalry brigades in action to date, commanded by General Stanley and Colonel Minty. In April 1864, Sheridan would be given command of the Cavalry of the Army of the Potomac by General Ulysses S. Grant and would earn his reputation as one of the most successful Union generals.

EXPEDITION TO UNIONVILLE

Early on the morning of March 4, 1863, Minty led a detachment of 864 men "from the First, Second, and Third Cavalry Brigades, two companies from the Fourth US Cavalry" commanded by Lieutenants Roys and Rendlebock, and Lieutenant Newell's section of First Ohio Artillery.[5] Their objective was "to drive the rebel detachments, who had reoccupied Rover and Unionville, from these positions."[6] Under orders from General Stanley, Minty "reported to General Sheridan, then commanding the Third Division of the Twentieth Corps, or the right wing of the Army of the Cumberland."[7]

Minty found Sheridan at his camp on the Salem Pike, his division about ready to move. While Sheridan's division was to march to Eagleville, he ordered Minty to "mask my division from the enemy" and gave him "*carte blanche*" to perform that duty in his own way.[8] Minty marched immediately for Rover, where he learned a Confederate brigade led by Colonel Alfred Russell was encamped. Approaching Rover at around 8 a.m., he met about a hundred rebels who showed "a bold front" and appeared determined to make a stand.[9]

Minty sent his 4th Michigan Cavalry with orders to "gain the [Shelbyville] pike," cutting the rebels off from Unionville. Perceiving the Union objective, the rebels "commenced a retreat."[10] Minty immediately ordered the 7th Pennsylvania "to close ranks in column of fours ... draw sabers and charge."[11] He supported them with the 4th Michigan and 4th US Cavalry.[12] The Federals drove the rebels "in wild disorder, down the pike towards Unionville, the sabers of the Seventh cutting up their rear the whole distance."[13] "The rebels were rapidly driven to Unionville," where the Union forces discovered "a camp of three regiments of cavalry and one of infantry recruits or conscripts," about "600 men, drawn up in line covering their camp."[14] They attempted to make a stand, but without stopping, the Union Cavalry "rode right at them and they were soon fleeing in confusion," leaving behind many of their dismounted infantry "and camp and garrison equipage."[15] "The pursuit was continued with constant captures from the rear of the fleeing foe; until within five miles of Shelbyville, the rebel cavalry found shelter behind a division of Leonidas Polk's corps."[16] Lieutenant Vale "and four or five of the men of the Seventh, actually rode into the line of one of Polk's Divisions and received a heavy volley from a full brigade. Every man and horse in this squad was struck by the enemy's bullets, but none of the men injured."[17]

Gathering his prisoners together, Minty re-formed his command and marched to a site south of Eagleville, where he bivouacked for the night.[18] Later that night, newly commissioned 2nd Lieutenant Henry Potter, 4th Michigan, made the following entry in his diary:

"... gave a rebel lieut. cup of coffee and couple biscuits. Fine fellow. I may be taken someday."

Captain Vale later writes:

> We captured at Unionville alone fifty one unwounded prisoners, seventeen wagons, forty-two mules, thirty-one tents and a couple of wagon-loads of bacon, meal, &c.; besides thirty-one prisoners, all wounded with the saber, at Rover, and in the pursuit of that place to the camp; and twenty-seven likewise wounded in the pursuit beyond Unionville; the killed of the enemy was known to reach thirty-eight. *The Seventh used saber only, did not fire a shot* [emphasis author], and had one man wounded, which was the only casualty in the brigade.[19]

General Sheridan arrived early the next morning and "expressed himself as highly pleased" with Minty's work of the day before.[20] Sheridan reported Minty's actions to Rosecrans and followed up with a second message, stating: "I have the honor to enclose a note just received from Colonel Minty, which makes his success still greater than that heretofore reported to you."[21] Minty's report expands on this: "The fruits of this charge–in which not one shot was fired by my brigade, the entire work being done with sabers."[22] He lists:

> 151 unwounded prisoners . . . [there] would have been more, but many of the rebels disappeared into the dense brush, 28 killed, 58 wounded . . . 17 wagons, 94 horses, 12 mules, 31 tents, two portable forages, and several wagon-loads of commissary stores; all of which I sent into Murfreesboro.[23]

For the next two days, Minty "had patrols out in every direction opening communications with outposts or other expeditionary forces, and feeling for the enemy, who were impressed with the idea that the entire country was swarming with our cavalry."[24]

Thompson's Station

Word was received that the Confederates had captured Colonel John Coburn's three regiments of infantry and some cavalry units at Thompson's Station, near Franklin, Tennessee. Minty was immediately ordered there, arriving "early in the morning of March 8." Sheridan arrived later that same afternoon.[25] Colburn's brigade had originally been sent out to find and check the progress of Forrest, "who had taken position at Spring Hill with a large force."[26] Forrest's four regiments of cavalry and effective use of Captain Samuel Freeman's artillery battery quickly overwhelmed Colburn's force.[27] Forrest and Earl Van Dorn, operating in concert, threatened serious results to the right flank of Rosecrans's army and caused "no little anxiety to the Union Commanders."[28]

Under orders from General Granger, Minty marched at daybreak on the ninth to Carter Creek Pike with "Lieutenants Roys' and Rendlebock's company in the advance."[29] They made a "circuit through the country to form a junction with General Green Clay Smith's heavy column of infantry and artillery . . . moving directly down the Franklin and Columbia pike."[30] Minty proceeded with caution down the valley, as there were "numerous defiles, through which a force could easily be thrown" on their right and rear.[31] Six miles out they "met the enemy's pickets, which were rapidly driven by the Fourth Cavalry."[32] Near the junction of the roads at Thompson's station, "part of the Fourth US Cavalry had a severe skirmish," dislodging the rebels, during which two Regulars were killed: Privates Archibald B. Orr, Company I, and James Orange, Company M.[33]

Minty found a force "of about 600 rebel cavalry" in position about a mile and a half from Thompson's Station.[34] His column was "very much scattered" by their rapid march over fourteen miles of "a bad dirt road," so Minty had to delay while re-forming his men and giving the horses a breathing spell.[35] From captured prisoners, Minty learned that the rebel cavalry now in his front and moving rapidly toward Thompson's Station was Brigadier General Frank C. Armstrong's brigade, "one of the best Confederate brigades in the field."[36] This caused Minty "considerable uneasiness," since this put Armstrong's brigade in General Smith's rear, and it was not known what additional forces might be at Thompson's Station.[37] Much to his consternation, Minty soon discovered that Armstrong was now being reinforced by Starnes's brigade of cavalry, along with Van Dorn's.[38]

The Confederate line now formed: "covering the Columbia pike and the approaches to Spring Hill; holding a position on rising ground northwest of and covering the railroad."[39] Minty "moved two companies of the 4th Regulars and one battalion of the 7th Pa. well to the right, with orders to turn the enemy's left, and then with sabers to charge directly on their flank."[40] With the rest of his command, Minty "made a direct assault on the enemy's position."[41] "The 4th Cav. and 7th Pa. advanced rapidly on the right, turning the rebel left," while the 4th Mich. "dismounted, seized the hills immediately south of the station."[42] At some point during this battle, Colonel Minty had his horse shot out from under him.[43]

Even though the Union forces were outnumbered two to one, the rebels were "so disconcerted" by the vigor of the attack that they "broke in disorder" and were rapidly driven through the gap leading to Spring Hill.[44] As they abandoned their positions near the station, the rebels were "literally mowed down by the fire of the 4th Mich., while the sabers of the 4th Regulars and 7th Pa. *did terrible execution on their flank* [emphasis author]."[45] "The whole rebel force abandoned the field" and retreated "across Rutherford Creek to the south bank of the unfordable Duck River."[46] At around 4 p.m., General Smith's column arrived at Thompson's Station with Generals Granger and Sheridan riding in the lead. Sheridan, acknowledging his appreciation for the work done by the cavalry, grasped Minty's hand and said, "Well, Minty, you have taken the spots off my cavalry to-day."[47] That night, the Union forces bivouacked near Spring Hill.

While this was a significant victory for the Federal cavalry, it had little strategic value, as Spring Hill was reoccupied by Forrest two weeks later.[48] However, as stated by cavalry historian Stephen Z. Starr, Colonel Minty's reputation as a commander of cavalry was made at Spring Hill, along with Edward M. McCook, First Division, and Eli Long, Second Division, both officers of the 4th United States Cavalry, "who were to make their mark as cavalry commanders of outstanding merit in the remaining years of the Civil War."[49]

The remainder of March was consumed by minor skirmishes, surveying the countryside, and picketing the Manchester, Wartrace, and Brady roads, as well as the Shelbyville and Middleton roads.[50] An incident occurred on March 11, when Minty's command crossed Rutherford's Creek at Moore's Ford and found itself facing "Forrest's forces under Forrest in person."[51] As vividly described by Captain Vale, Minty's "whole force was ... massed on the low grounds" south of Rutherford's Creek:

> The rebels now advanced, dismounted, and, with battle flags flying, showing sixteen brigades, formed line on the crest of the hills, about three fourths of a mile distant. Minty massed the First brigade, except the Fourth Michigan, which was detached on an expedition, on the extreme right flank, in column of squadrons; formed the Third brigade in line on the right, and the Second brigade in line on the left, with a heavy line of skirmishers covering the whole front.
>
> Minty ordered the whole force to draw sabers, and moved forward up the hills in an open country, at a walk . . .
>
> . . . It is seldom that the soldier or subordinate officer in a great army has the opportunity of seeing, on the battlefield, the inspiring pageantry of large bodies of men moving to the conflict . . . a scene of rare and almost unexampled grandeur.
>
> Five thousand cavalry, mounted on exceptionally good horses, dressed in the gorgeous uniforms of that day; their bright sabers, arms, and trappings flashing in the sunlight; sweeping up the slope of the gently rising hills . . . while, on the crest, with their battle flags flying, stood in serried ranks a line in gray over a mile and a half in length; the white smoke from the scattering skirmish fire alone obstructing the view, formed a picture rarely seen, and far more easily imagined than described.[52]

It was the picture perfect scene for a battle that would not happen. Before "half the distance had been covered, the rebels suddenly disappeared from the crest of the hills . . ."[53] Nature once again played a role: "A sudden rise in the Duck river" had "broken and swept away the rebel pontoon bridges," cutting off all means of escape for the Confederates "except by White's bridge, twenty-five miles up river." Already low on ammunition, Forrest chose the wise course and made a sudden and unexpected dash to the bridge.[54]

On March 12, the command returned to Franklin, reaching Triune on the thirteenth and camp at Murfreesboro on the fourteenth.[55] On March 16, Major General Rosecrans submitted the following "laudatory message" to General-in-Chief Henry W. Halleck in Washington, DC:

> I have the pleasure to report the gallant conduct of our cavalry under the brave Colonel Minty. They drove the rebel cavalry wherever they met them, captured one of their camps, 17 wagons, 42 mules, and 64 prisoners. *They used the saber where the carbine would delay* [emphasis author].[56]

Minty had high praise for the officers commanding the companies of the 4th Cavalry, calling "attention of the general commanding to the great gallantry displayed by Lieutenants Roys and Randelbrock [sic] . . . and their brave men at Thompson's Station . . ."⁵⁷

The Saber Brigade

General Stanley was "highly pleased" with the praise General Phil Sheridan bestowed upon his cavalry, particularly Minty's brigade. So too was Major General William S. Rosecrans, who stated in his General Orders: *In recognition of the dash and gallantry displayed by his brigade on all occasions, it shall hereafter be known as the* Saber Brigade *of the Army of the Cumberland.*⁵⁸

In several articles written for the *National Tribune* years later, Colonel Minty clarifies the significance and meaning of this designation:

> . . . [W]hen a commander is named, as I was in this report of Gen. Rosecrans, it does not mean him personally; it refers to the command which is known by his name. Thus, 'the brave Col. Minty' in this case meant the brave, the gallant, the noble men whom Col. Minty had the honor to command.⁵⁹ . . . We know that if we had not earned the title by our readiness to use the saber on all occasions, Gen. Rosecrans would not have conferred it upon us . . .⁶⁰
>
> . . . [W]hen that title is bestowed or conferred by proper authority every man of that organization should feel the same honorable pride in wearing it as the individual would in wearing a medal of honor properly bestowed upon him.⁶¹
>
> . . . [I] believe that every man in 'The Saber Brigade', felt a personal pride in the grand fighting qualities of the mounted infantry and the battery, who were second to no commands in the service, and I know that the confidence each had in the other was practically unlimited.⁶²

The significance of any brigade receiving a lasting nickname as a tribute was explained in a speech given in 1900 to veterans and guests attending the dedication of a monument to Wilder's Lightning Brigade:

> It was a singular honor, a 'badge' of distinction . . . In the organization of great armies . . . a brigade was so small an item as to be generally lost sight of and it is rarely the case that a brigade ever attains any distinct identity or individuality.⁶³

Colonel Robert Minty's character and modesty are both revealed in the above quotes. His qualifications and accomplishments with his cavalry brigade could not be argued, and his promotion to brigadier general—the rank generally required to command a brigade—seemed assured. And yet, as his biographer writes:

> During the early months of 1863, Minty had acquitted himself in an outstanding manner, earning the notice and praise of nearly all of the leaders in that section, as well as those of his men. While earning the special designation as 'The Saber Brigade of the Army of the Cumberland' for themselves, Minty had also received several recommendations for promotions to the rank of Brigadier General–which everyone felt he duly deserved. Both Generals Stanley and Rosecrans had sent such endorsements in February, and again two months later when Rosecrans requested said rank be awarded to him 'for the good of the service.' But, not being a West-Pointer, having been commissioned as an officer from the volunteer forces, every recommendation seemed to fall on deaf ears.⁶⁴

"Minty's reputation and popularity among the men of the cavalry service continued to grow, and everyone thought he deserved a promotion," wrote Lieutenant Potter: "He will get a star [general rank] before long, I believe, every body likes him also and he is a rising man."⁶⁵ Another historian of the Fourth Michigan writes:

> On the 12th [of April] while the regiment was in the vicinity of Lavergne, Colonel Minty, who had been too ill to start out with his brigade, but who was afterwards telegraphed for by General Stanley, came up and took command. On his approach, the 4th Michigan was formed in line by Lieutenant Colonel Park, as an everlasting testimonial of their confidence in the hero of so many cavalry fights, as well as their appreciation of the brave soldier, the gallant gentleman, and the true friend, the men drew their sabers, and waving them over their heads, rose in their stirrups and gave three cheers for *'Our Colonel'*.⁶⁶

After a few short days rest at Murfreesboro, "Minty and his men were once again ordered into the saddle," and the Saber Brigade was engaged in several short expeditions from March 17 to April 2.⁶⁷

V. The 4th Regiment United States Cavalry

Companies A and E Return from the Eastern Theater

In January 1863, Companies A and E, 4th United States Cavalry, commanded by Captain James McIntyre, were escorts for General Ambrose Burnside and in "Camp near Falmouth, Virginia."[1] In correspondence on January 21, 1863, to "His Excellency President Jefferson Davis," Robert E. Lee reported on the activities of the men of his former regiments:

> Mr. President: A scout just returned from Washington City reports that the impression is prevalent there that General Burnside's army is preparing to advance.
>
> The river is filled with transports with supplies; lumber and forage ascending the river, provisions &c., descending–all going to Aquia and Potomac Creeks. The Fourth and Fifth Regiments US Cavalry have, within a few days, marched from Washington, via Piscataway to Liverpool Point, and thence crossed to Aquia. A large supply of mules, both for draught and packing, sutlers' wagons, &c., now take that route, either on account of better roads or safety from our cavalry.[2]

Sergeant Charles Bates wrote to his parents from "Port Tobacco, Md., Jany 26th 1863," telling about their exploits in catching deserters and smugglers:

> Our duty is to scout the country between Great Mills and Piscataway Creek to catch deserters from the other side of the Potomac and stop Smugling [sic]. The smugglers have so perfect an organization that as yet we have only caught one, but judging from the deserters we catch I should say the Army of the Potomac was rather demoralized. We have got two hundred and nine deserters since we came over last Wednesday. They come over every night, some on logs, some on rafts and a few lucky ones have managed to appropriate some of Uncle Sam's boats and get over in them. There is a suspicion that some of the ferry-boats Government employ bring loads of them over but as yet we have no proof. And 'still they come.' One of our men 'surrounded' seven of them in one party last night and marched into camp. Pretty well done for one man want [sic] it. I think of recommending him for a commission. We are having good weather now but it did rain awful last week and the roads are in good condition for a bootjack.

The squadron spent February doing duty in and around Port Tobacco, Maryland, taking quarters in the court house: "a large two story brick building . . . lately renovated inside and out."[3]

On the twenty-seventh, Captain McIntyre received orders from General Halleck directing his squadron to report to General Joseph Hooker's headquarters and to turn in its horses and equipment to the quartermaster. As Bates writes, they were to proceed "with as little delay as possible to the Army of the West there to join the rest of the regiment now serving with Genl. Rosecrans. We start from here at six o clock tomorrow, and if nothing overtakes us we shall be with the remainder of our boys in a week."[4]

On February 28, the squadron began the journey by rail, described by Bates as "a rather sloppy, slow coach affair," stopping for a few days in Cincinnati, Ohio, on March 11-12. From there they boarded a steamboat to Louisville. They eventually arrived at their destination—Nashville, Tennessee—on March 23.[5] As Sergeant Bates quickly learned, there was a "difference" between the Eastern Theater and Western Theater:

> I have at last got to the end of my journey for a time at least, and now we are all together. That is, the regiment is all here except Companies H and F who are on their way here from Fort Kearny. We got here day before yesterday and to-day commenced our duties with the regiment. Ours is the only regiment of regular cavalry in the western army, and they are considered equal to four regiments of southern men.

Everybody here talks about the gallant deeds of the 'Fourth' in the battles and skirmishes here, and laughs at the 'Army of the Potomac' and their actions. They think the eastern troops have done nothing but eat soft bread, potatoes and all the goods of the commissary, while occupying comfortable quarters, leaving the western troops to do all the fighting.

There is no use in my trying to argue with them or to mention any of the battles of the east to prove the 'Army of the Potomac' not altogether worthless. If I mention Fredericksburg they are ready to prove that the western boys done all the fighting there. Ditto for Malvern hills, Antietam, and all the rest, so at last I am half persuaded that we have been in the wrong shop all the while, and this is the true field of play.[6]

Sergeant Bates was also assigned a new duty:

I am now acting as 'Camp-Kettle-Sergeant,' or 'Cracker boss' for the Company, for that is what the men call the Commissary Sergeant, and so shall not be in much danger from losing my precious life unless Morgans guerillas get hold of the [wagon] train.[7]

Upon return of Companies A and E, the 4th Regiment was assigned to Stanley's cavalry division "unattached." Captain Otis was on sick leave during this time and the command of the Regiment devolved to Captain James McIntyre.

Expedition to Liberty and Snow Hill

Sergeant Bates and the returned squadron were soon in the field chasing Morgan's cavalry on a five-day expedition with Minty's Brigade. On the morning of April 2nd, Stanley ordered Minty "to take the advance with the First and Second Brigades of Cavalry, and to march rapidly for Liberty."[8]

Leaving camp at daylight, the 4th US Cavalry marched to Murfreesboro, reporting to General Rosecrans' headquarters. Within half an hour, Minty's command—made up of four regiments of cavalry, followed by about thirty wagons—was on the Liberty pike moving toward Liberty, a small town thirty miles to the east. "In the rear of the train came the 4th U.S., a brigade of infantry, and a battery of artillery."[9]

At about "five o'clock in the evening," writes Bates: "the skirmishers of the Tenth Ohio sighted the Secesh and the firing got a little warm":

The Waggons were Corralled, line of battery formed, skirmishers sent in all directions and everything made ready for a fight, but 'Night dropped her mantle o'er the scene,' and the troops are bivouacked for the night–Saddles left on the horses and <u>everything</u> <u>ready</u> <u>for</u> <u>anything</u>. The night wore away without much sleep on our side, and at day-light a strong party of our regiment galloped to the front and all around the lines of our pickets without meeting any of the secesh except some whom Abraham had taken to his bosom, (not Abraham Lincoln). They reported fourteen found dead, but I saw only one, he was killed enough for fourteen . . .[10]

That night, while bivouacked at Liberty, Bates found his clothes covered with "what the boys call 'beggar lice'" and discovered the next morning that his horse was so infected with them that he was forced to find another mount.[11] That day, Minty's brigade marched to Alexandria northwest of Liberty "and captured 7 waggons of Morgan (Secesh)." They camped on the ground "of a fat old secesh . . . the boys charged on his poultry. Chickens, Geese, and Turkeys disappeared like magic."[12]

The following morning, Bates was left behind with the wagons and, with time on his hands, "took one of the cooks . . . and struck off through the woods" to do some scouting. He was hoping to find a better horse:

. . . I saw some horses through the trees and <u>surrounded them</u> with the help of Soap, the cook; there was three horses tied to trees saddled and bridled, one of them had a haversack of victuals on the saddle and a bag of corn lay on the ground a little ways off. I held a council of war with the cook and we concluded to search the woods and find the riders of the horses if possible . . .

By calling out to one another and pretending there was a whole squadron in the area, they bluffed the surrender of "five of the southern chivalry, stowed away among the rocks. They surrendered without resistance . . . only one revolver in the party." Bates turned his prisoners over to Captain McIntyre. Soap kept the revolver "for a memento."[13]

Minty reported the results of the expedition to Liberty and Snow Hill: "17 confederate dead . . . 65 prisoners and 357 horses and mules. The total loss in the cavalry was two men wounded in the 4th Mich., and one killed and two wounded in the 7th Pa."[14]

Bates concludes his letter commenting on some of the differences he found between the Eastern Theater and the Army of the West and exposes his own prejudices:

> . . . if a man kills turkeys, chickens, pigs, or any such commodities he is not punished here, but if he strikes a Nigger he had better have hit his Captain. In the army of the Potomac it was different. This part of the country seems to me to be a different Government altogether, but I shall get used to it soon . . .[15]

Bates's comment on the treatment of blacks—at least by the soldiers of Minty's Brigade—appears to reflect the background and training of Colonel Minty himself. As his biographer writes:

> Regarding the Negroes, or 'Contrabands' as they were called, one must recall that during Minty's service in the British army, most of his troops were blacks, either in the West Indies or Sierra Leone in Western Africa, and he was probably completely comfortable associating with them.[16]

Major George Fish, 4th Michigan surgeon, writes: "There was no fear of 'Negro equality' on the part of Colonel Minty."[17] This attitude and experience served Minty well. As noted by Sergeant Larson: "The negroes would generally do all they could for the Union soldiers," and Colonel Minty was not above "close consultation" with any slave who had valuable information. Major Fish commented on one such event: "You ought to have seen our gallant Colonel . . . with this Negro slave. Both lying flat on the ground before our camp fire, tracing upon the map certain lines."[18] This attitude towards Negroes was not shared by all the men of the brigade, particularly Charles Bates. In several of his letters he is adamant that he will never be able to accept the black man as his equal.[19]

Blacks in Service: Jackson Kelley, 4th United States Cavalry

Early in the war, there was initial resistance to employ "contraband" (slaves) in any capacity for both political as well as practical reasons. As the war effort escalated, "the number of former slaves, the declining members of white volunteers, and the increasingly pressing personnel needs of the Union Army pushed the government into rescinding the ban."[20]

By 1863, the companies of the 4th US Cavalry had acquired a number of blacks for mostly non-combat support: to drive the supply wagons and pack mule trains, tend the herds of domesticated animals, and serve as company cooks. After the Emancipation Proclamation was issued in January 1863, "black recruitment was pursued in earnest."[21] These men, along with their white officers, served at great risk. Many in the Confederate Army maintained a policy of no black prisoners, with similar attitude toward their officers. At least one member of the 4th Cavalry—1st Sergeant Albert B. Kauffman, Co. I—"declined the appointment of Captain 1st Colored Volunteers" in October 1863.[22]

By March 1863, new regulations allowed the enlistment of "African under-cooks" for each company in a regiment. They were enlisted the same as the Regular enlisted men for a term of three years and their accounts were kept in the same way. "They are entered on the company muster-rolls, at the foot of the list of privates" and were "allowed ten dollars per month." They did not have rank and, unlike the black soldiers who enlisted in the U.S. Colored Corps, military service records were not kept on the "sub-cooks." Company cooks or "head cooks" were detailed from the Regular enlisted men on ten-day rotations, and the entire process of food preparation was supervised by the 1st sergeant or commissary-sergeant.[23]

Available records indicate at least twenty-six black "sub-cooks" were enlisted in the 4th Cavalry beginning in October 1863. Of those, there was an 80% desertion rate, with a length of service from one month to over two years. Perhaps these men sought safety by enlistment from whatever dangerous place or circumstance they found themselves in, then deserted at the opportune moment for the ultimate goal of freedom.[24]

Four men served their full three-year enlistments: James Evans, Co. H; John Johnson, Co. A; Cato Marshall, Co. F; and Perry Thompson, Co. A. One of those who deserted after eighteen months was George Slade (or Sledge), who received a "release from service" under an act of Congress in 1891.[25]

One of the "colored cooks"—Jackson Kelley, a native of Walton County, Georgia—was thirty-four years old when he enlisted in the 4th Cavalry in January 1863, serving in Co. L. He was killed in action on August 20, 1864, at the Battle of Lovejoy's Station during Kilpatrick's raid around Atlanta. His service is recorded for posterity on the monument at West Point dedicated to the Regular officers and men who were killed in service to their country during the Civil War.[26]

THE 4TH US CAVALRY AND FREEMAN'S BATTERY AT FRANKLIN, TENNESSEE

On April 9, General Stanley led a cavalry force of 1,600 men composed of the 4th US Cavalry, 4th Michigan, and the 7th Pennsylvania, along with five companies from the 3rd Indiana and 1st Middle Tennessee, plus two pieces of artillery. Colonel Minty was absent from this campaign due to illness.[27] Stanley was to "scout the country to Triune, and thence to Franklin," to give General Gordon Granger as much assistance as he might require in his operations against Confederate General Earl Van Dorn.[28]

As previously noted, creating newly commissioned 2nd lieutenants from within the enlisted ranks of the Federal cavalry was a necessity. Of the eleven officers now present with the 4th US Cavalry, eight were former enlisted men: six from the 4th Cavalry, with five of those commanding companies of the regiment. They would be involved in one of their more controversial skirmishes near Franklin, Tennessee, where General Van Dorn had concentrated "10,000 cavalry and mounted infantry."[29]

When the 4th Cavalry met Forrest's battery just south of Franklin, Tennessee, six of the eleven officers present were newly commissioned former enlisted men: 2nd Lieutenants Neil J. McCafferty, Bird L. Fletcher, Thomas Healy, Edward Fitzgerald, Joseph Rendlebock, and Thomas W. Simson. Two of the 1st lietenants were also former enlisted: Elbridge G. Roys and William H. Ingerton (see Appendix E).[30]

Nathan Bedford Forrest led an attack on Franklin on April 9. The small town is on the banks of the Harpeth River, about ten miles south of the strategic town of Nashville along the Nashville and Decatur Railroad line. The following morning Van Dorn, leading a reconnaissance expedition, advanced northward from Spring Hill, making contact with Federal skirmishers just outside Franklin. That same day, Stanley's command advanced on Franklin from Murfreesboro, taking "the direct Franklin road," with the remainder of the command on the Bole Jack road. At ten o'clock the morning of the tenth, they reached Franklin, camping four miles east of town at the brick church on the Murfreesboro road.[31] "At about 2:30 o'clock, a continuous fire to the front of Franklin, on the Columbia pike, indicated that the enemy was making an attack in force."[32] Stanley "immediately ordered a counter attack . . . at Hughes' Mill and the Lewisburg pike" by way of the ford on Harpeth River.[33] After crossing the ford the road forks; Stanley took the right fork and ordered McIntyre to take the left, telling him to "strike the Lewisburg pike" about a mile and a half away and "proceed to Franklin on that road."[34] After crossing the Harpeth, the 4th Cavalry ran into a part of James Starnes's brigade and four pieces of artillery heading to Franklin on the Lewisburg Pike. The 4th Regiment US Cavalry was about to have its first independent action of the war.

Separating from Stanley, Captain McIntyre immediately gave orders: "throwing forward Company C, under Lieutenant Fletcher, as an advance guard; Company A, under Lieutenant McCafferty, as left flankers; and Company E, under Lieutenant Fitzgerald, as right flankers."[35] Upon reaching the woods, about a hundred yards from the road McIntyre discovered a rebel battery in position on the turnpike, moving north towards Franklin with strong cavalry support. This was Captain Freeman's battery. As later described by Confederate artilleryman Lieutenant Nat Baxter: "Not suspecting the proximity of any Federal nearer than Franklin . . . we were utterly unprepared for the sudden collision with this cavalry."[36] The four guns of the battery were "strung out along the pike," with Captain Freeman at the head of the column. Baxter was casually riding "in a careless manner" with his leg "thrown over the saddle . . . about the center of the battery, behind the second gun."[37] James Starnes's cavalry regiment was ahead of them, "out of sight," and another regiment of cavalry was about a half mile in the rear.[38] On the left (west) side of the road was a "high new plank fence."[39] On the right were dense woods that concealed the presence of the Federal Cavalry.

McIntyre ordered Lieutenant Ingerton, with Companies K and B, to charge the battery.[40] As they burst out of the woods onto the pike, Captain Freeman, startled, "straightened himself in his saddle," reined his horse up quickly, and began yelling commands to get the guns in action.[41] Lieutenant Baxter looked up and "saw a squadron of Federal cavalry charging right at us from the woodland, not more than one hundred yards off . . . at full gallop."[42] Jumping off his horse, Baxter ran to the guns, trying to get them loaded. The artillerymen succeeded with one gun, but it failed to discharge because of "a faulty friction-primer which failed to explode." By that time they were overridden by the Union Cavalry, "using their sabers or six shooters . . . driving [them] for upward of a mile."[43] Baxter tried to escape by scaling the fence and running across a field but was captured before he could reach the protection of the woods.[44]

During the initial confusion, Captain Freeman was desperately trying to pull his two lead guns north along the pike toward Starnes's position. Captain McIntyre ordered Lieutenant Hedges, with Company G, to follow up the initial charge "and attack the enemy on the hill and on the right [east] of the turnpike." Freeman apparently made it "uphill about a quarter of a mile" with his guns, arriving at the top of Oden Hill at the same time as the Union cavalry.[45] At this point, Freeman and his guns were surrounded and the controversy began.

Freeman was about to lose Forrest's premier battery. Knowing that Starnes was minutes away with reinforcements, he certainly would have done everything in his power to avoid the mortal disgrace of losing his artillery. Surrender would not have been an option, nor in the character of the man. Based on extensive review of all available reports, it appears the version presented by Captain Vale is the most accurate: Captain Freeman was shot by Sergeant Major Sherlock Strickland after firing his pistol at Lieutenant Rendlebock when surrounded and asked to surrender.[46] It may well be that the time Freeman bought at the sacrifice of his own life ultimately saved his battery from total loss or destruction. It is for his determined bravery under fire that Captain Freeman should be remembered. Once the rebels learned it was Sergeant Major Strickland who shot the captain, he lived in fear of being captured and hanged by Forrest's men.[47] He took his discharge when his term was up during the Atlanta Campaign, becoming a clerk in the Quartermaster Division. He was later captured and held in rebel prisons, claiming he was a member of the 4th Michigan Volunteers.[48] He was freed at the end of the war. Lieutenant Rendlebock would be brevet major at the end of the war and would serve as captain of Company G, 4th US Cavalry, until his retirement in 1879.[49] Both he and Strickland were still alive when Vale published his version of the incident and Vale had conversations with Strickland before writing his book. It is unlikely Vale would have fabricated the story at the expense of his former comrades.

About the time Freeman was surrounded and killed, Captain McIntyre became aware that Lieutenant Roys and Company M in the rear had come under attack. Dismounted, they "were fighting on foot against a superior force and needed immediate support." He ordered Companies E, D, and I under Lieutenant Healy to their aid.[50] Rebel reinforcements continued to arrive and Lieutenant Healy, with Companies D and I, attempted to cut them off. Healey was severely wounded and the Union cavalrymen were "forced to fall back."[51] Company M was running out of ammunition and began to retreat.[52] At the same time, Starnes was moving in with a strong force to cut off the Union Cavalry's only escape route to the ford. McIntyre, finding the enemy "on my right, front, and rear," and threatening to surround his regiment, "had the rally sounded" and ordered a retreat. "Having only 150 yards of a plowed field open to retreat between a cross-fire from my rear, right, and left . . . I reached the ford and recrossed the river with but little loss . . ."[53] McIntyre had with him:

> . . . a captain, one second lieutenant, and 34 prisoners, but was obliged, by overwhelming numbers to abandon the battery and between 400 and 500 prisoners, and after having inflicted upon the enemy a loss of at least 100 killed and wounded.

Before retreating, Company A spiked four of the guns, cut the spokes and tongues, and entirely destroyed the harness, thus dismantling the battery.[54]

This entire event lasted less than an hour.[55]

Freeman's Battery was apparently well known to Union forces. In a terse, if not totally accurate report to General Rosecrans, General Granger reported: "General (S. L.) Freeman's battery was taken and destroyed by chopping it to pieces. Himself, 1 lieutenant, and several men were killed; 2 lieutenants and 29 men of the battery were taken prisoners. In other words, the battery was defunct."[56] In fact, the four guns recaptured by the artillery battery were quickly restored and back in action in a matter of days. Over the next few days there were several more skirmishes until Van Dorn retreated. The result of this expedition was that the Confederates canceled their operations in the area and withdrew to Spring Hill, leaving the Federals in control of the area.

The reputation of the 4th Cavalry was greatly enhanced, although not without cost. From General Stanley's report:

> From the circumstances, the Fourth US Cavalry did the most gallant service. The report of Captain McIntyre is called to the attention of the general commanding.
>
> Two gallant officers, old soldiers, were dangerously wounded in this regiment, leading their companies–Lieutenants Healy and Simson, the former is feared mortally.[57]

Thomas Healy, who originally joined the Second Dragoons in 1848, died of his wounds on April 23. Thomas Simson would never fully recover. He was promoted to 1st lieutenant in February 1865, but would resign "for incapacity" that same month and died in October of that year. Along with the two officers, casualties in the 4th US Cavalry were three enlisted men killed: Privates Charles Cowarden, Co. K; Nathan Writhe, Co. M; and William H. Senegan, Co. H. Private Frederick Hensinger, Co. D, was mortally wounded. Five troopers were wounded and seventeen were taken prisoner.[58]

2nd Lieutenants McCafferty, Fletcher, and Rendlebock were brevetted 1st lieutenant for "gallant and meritorious service in the cavalry action at Franklin." All three would reach the rank of captain and survive the war.[59] 1st Lieutenant Joseph Hedges was also recognized for his "gallant and meritorious" service and would ride to greater glory in 1864.[60]

Franklin was the first and only battle to be missed by Colonel Minty because of illness. In a telegraph to Rosecrans, General Stanley wrote: "If Minty is well enough, send him to me. If he had been here to-day we would have brought out those guns." Within an hour of hearing this, Minty began his return trip to his brigade.[61]

On the evening of April 17, Stanley's cavalry command returned to Murfreesboro. The 4th US Cavalry, "which up to this time had been acting under direct orders from the Chief of Cavalry, would be formally attached to the Saber Brigade." Captain Elmer Otis, having returned from sick leave and commanding the regiment, reported to Colonel Minty and "was assigned camping ground within the brigade." Writing of their meeting years later, Colonel Minty recalls:

> Capt. Otis, after reporting to me, said: 'Colonel Minty, you must allow me to say that you are the only volunteer officer in the army whom I would be willing to serve under.' I think the Regulars, at first, felt a little sore at being brigaded with volunteers, and having to serve under a volunteer, but this did not last long. The regiment was composed of as gallant a body of officers and soldiers as ever mounted horse or drew saber, and were soon proud of their brigade, proud of the regiments composing it, and proud of the soldier-like work achieved by it.[62]

With the arrival of Companies A and E, Captain Elmer Otis, suffering from ill health, relinquished command of the 4th U.S. to Captain James McIntyre, two days his junior in seniority. Otis would command the regiment in the field for the last time in May, writing his last report on May 22. His health failing, Otis convalesced while on detached service as a recruiting officer.

McIntyre was brevetted major on May 10 for his conduct at Franklin, leading the attack on Forrest's battery on the Lewisburg Pike. As described by Sergeant James Larson:

... there being no officer with the regiment bearing the title of Major, although there were several brevet Captains and brevet Majors. Officers of higher rank were serving with the volunteers. That made no difference. McIntyre, even without the title of Major, was well able to lead the 4th Cavalry.[63]

Captain McIntyre "commanded the regiment with distinction... until October 1, 1864," and was "repeatedly officially commended for special gallantry in general orders and the official reports."[64]

"Camp Minty"

The men of Minty's brigade gave their campsite near Murfreesboro the name "Camp Minty."[65] They "were continually assigned to picket duty" and to guard the approaches to the city. From April 26 to May 21, the brigade "had many affairs" that kept it "constantly in the saddle and on the alert."[66] According to Captain Vale, the brigade "mustered two thousand seven hundred effectives, mounted and equipped for duty."[67]

During the first half of 1863—"with the exception of a few minor affairs"—the infantry and artillery of the Union and Confederate armies in the West had been resting and preparing for six months. According to Colonel William Sipes, commanding 7th Pennsylvania Cavalry, "Only the Cavalry had been active."[68] Most of this time was "one continuous series of reconnoitering and raiding upon Confederate outposts and flanks. As the weather improved, Confederate activity likewise increased." Minty's brigade was frequently sent out to "drive off the enemy...[and] burn any farm out-buildings, bridges, and mills found to be utilized by the enemy." There were offensive maneuvers as well, "designed to clear the enemy's cavalry from such towns as Middleton, Eaglesville, Rover, Salem, and Versailles, among others–mostly in the area to the south of Murfreesboro."[69] All of this activity would lay the groundwork for the upcoming Tullahoma Campaign.

The Cavalry Raid

The Federal cavalry in the West began its final phase of new evolutionary tactics: the raid. As described by cavalry historian Edward Longacre, "a cavalry raid was more of a grueling test of endurance and skill rather than a highly dangerous undertaking...:

Several conditions had to exist if a mounted raid were to be conducted successfully. First of all, the officer in charge had to be bold and aggressive but also prudent, capable of exercising strict authority when necessary and allowing subordinates the discretion to launch secondary operations when desirable. He had to be adept at meeting unexpected turns of events, and implementing contingency tactics, and at fighting on the defensive as well as on the offensive, as conditions warranted. Likewise, his subordinate officers had to be enterprising and imaginative, as well as deeply committed to serving their commander faithfully in moments calling for unity of purpose and action. Then too, the common soldiers had to be adaptable and resourceful, willing to endure the acting with individual initiative but also as members as a unified team, and be able to wield axes and crowbars with vigorous precision [for the quick destruction of the railroads].[70]

To succeed, the raid had to be well planned and boldly and rapidly executed. Speed was essential to prevent capture or serious engagement. There would be no support. Severely wounded troopers would be left behind, and along with those captured in late 1864, this would mean certain death in a Confederate prison—a fate suffered by no less than twenty-eight troopers from the 4th United States Cavalry.

"The amount of destruction accomplished by this arm of the service was well-neigh incalculable."[71] A major goal of such raids was also to demoralize the enemy. Bold cavalry raiders helped create a new form of mobile combat that would be adopted and used extensively in future conflicts around the world. The full destructive force of the Federal Cavalry was about to be unleashed upon the Confederate homeland.

Between April 20 and 26, the 4th Cavalry was part of a search and destroy expedition to McMinnville with General Joseph J. Reynolds, commanding Fifth Division, Fourteenth Army Corps. This may have been one of the earliest cavalry raids for which Minty's brigade became famous—or infamous. The raiders destroyed "almost entirely the railroad from Manchester to McMinnville, a cotton mill and two other mills . . . a small mill at Liberty, captured a large amount of supplies, 180 prisoners, over 600 animals," returning to Murfreesboro with the "loss of one man wounded."[72]

Captain McIntyre was on leave and Captain Elmer Otis returned to command the 4th Cavalry in the field for this expedition. It was part of Minty's cavalry brigade of 1,708 men, composed of parts of the First, Second, and Third Cavalry Brigades.[73] With six days rations, they left camp at 12:30 p.m. on April 20. They formed on Woodbury Pike and, after marching fourteen miles, encamped two miles from Readyville.[74] In the early hours of the twenty-first, Minty dispatched the Second Brigade "to strike the railroad at or near Morrison . . . and to destroy the tressel-work at that place." At 3 a.m., Minty "marched for McMinnville with the rest of his command, taking the old McMinnville road."[75] Upon approaching McMinnville, Colonel John Wilder's brigade of mounted infantry—part of Joseph Reynold's division—with the support of the 7th Pennsylvania ran into the rebel pickets, driving them into town, where they met the balance of the Confederate forces, "about 700 men–600 cavalry."[76] Along with 4th Cavalry Companies B, G, K, and M, the Federals "charged through the town."[77]

"The [rebel] cavalry scattered in every direction, part of them retreating at a gallop on every road, 50 taking the railroad train," which started moving as the Federals entered the town. Minty sent the Third Brigade and 4th Michigan after the train, "with directions to destroy it and also the new bridge of Hickory Creek," and dispatched the 4th Regulars to support the 7th Pennsylvania on the Sparta and Chattanooga roads.[78]

"Captain McCormick, with Company A, took up a position to the left of the road leading to Chattanooga." Captain Otis, with the remainder of the regiment, "took up a position on the Chattanooga road 2½ miles from the town," which he held until ordered to fall back at night.[79]

The attack, which had taken the rebels by surprise, was a complete success. "General John H. Morgan came very near to being captured but escaped by having a fresh fleet horse."[80] The "notorious Dick McCann"—apparently acting as a diversion to enable Morgan's escape—was not so lucky, being badly wounded and captured.[81]

Minty sent out details "which thoroughly destroyed the railroad for many miles, burned the railroad buildings," and destroyed a "locomotive and train of three cars, and various other detached cars." They also destroyed a large cotton factory used in making cloth for the rebel army and two mills.[82] A considerable amount of quartermaster and commissary stores were also destroyed.[83] "Six hundred and thirteen animals were captured, and seventy-six abandoned. Large quantities of forage and wheat were discovered."[84] "30 horses, 12 mules and 3 wagons" were also taken.[85]

Omitted from all official reports, but included in letters home by the soldiers: "We captured about five thousand cigars, and about two thousand dollars worth of tobacco," which were passed out to the troops. They also "impressed a good cow . . . and now have fresh milk for our coffee." They burned the courthouse and "several houses of leading Rebels." Individual foraging was rampant among the troops, who "returned to camp well loaded."[86]

That night Minty "encamped on the hill west of McMinnville," and was rejoined early the next morning by the Second and Third Brigades and the 4th Michigan.[87] During the night Captain McCann—placed under a guard of the 4th Regulars—escaped, casting some suspicion on Captain Joseph Vale. Vale was present at the capture and intervened just as McCann was about to receive a mortal blow. He did not recognize the wounded officer and was surprised that evening to get a message that the prisoner was requesting to see him. McCann wanted to thank Captain Vale for saving his life that day. It turned out that a year earlier, Vale had been wounded and captured by McCann's men. Because of his injuries McCann paroled him. Vale, remembering the kindness shown him, "sent for the brigade surgeon to dress his wounds and promised to obtain a parole from Colonel Minty." Late that night, during the change of guard, McCann crawled away. Suspicion immediately went to Vale, but he was exonerated in a subsequent investigation of the incident.[88]

This was an arduous but profitable expedition of six days, "covering 328 miles." As Vale recorded: "By this expedition, the effort to establish the right wing of Bragg's army at McMinnville was frustrated, *his depots and supplies destroyed* [emphasis author], and over five hundred prisoners captured . . ." Vale reported total losses for the division at five men killed and three wounded.[89]

Companies D and I: Expedition to Middleton

Another significant expedition involving companies of the 4th US Cavalry occurred between May 20 and

23, when it was learned that "a large force of the cavalry of the enemy" was in and around Middleton in an area northeast of Unionville. On the twenty-first Minty—on orders from division headquarters—moved with his brigade out the Salem Pike.[90] The 4th Regiment, consisting of 320 enlisted men and fourteen officers, was again under the command of Captain Elmer Otis.[91] A portion of Brigadier General John B. Turchin's division, along with his staff, orderlies, provost-guard, and escort, rode ahead of Minty's brigade. Companies D and I—about 75 men of the 4th U.S. under command of 1st Lieutenant William O'Connell—were his advance guard.[92] Having joined the Dragoons in 1854, O'Connell had risen to 1st Sergeant, Co. B, 4th U.S., when he was commissioned 2nd lieutenant in October 1861.[93] He was assisted by newly commissioned 2nd Lieutenant Francis C. Wood.[94]

The command marched to Salem, "and thence, striking out south," marched through fields and by-roads, keeping three miles west of the Middleton Road.[95] At daybreak, it arrived within two miles of Middleton. There was some delay while they waited for "the rear of the column to close."[96] General Stanley, perhaps getting impatient, "ordered a direct attack by the entire column upon the [rebel] camp." Giving the order himself, Stanley joined the advance guard—Lieutenant O'Connell's squadron—ordering them "to run over the enemy's pickets." He then ordered his own command that included Captain Otis and Companies B, E, G, K, and M of the 4th Cavalry to "gallop" for the first mile and then to "go at full speed upon the rebels."[97]

Unfortunately, once Stanley and the advance squadron charged ahead of Turchin's escort and out of sight, no one knew which road he had taken.[98] Captain Otis was held up by General Turchin when the general ordered him to provide a squadron of the 4th to act as advance guard. "Captain McIntyre took the two leading companies and moved forward as directed."[99] Before Otis could lead the rest of his command after Stanley, "Colonel Minty ordered details of his companies to different places" until Captain Otis "found himself without a command."[100] He then joined the largest portion of the command he could find—Captain McIntyre's squadron. Musket shots in the distance "indicated the position of the enemy."[101] Minty, unsure where the action was, "followed a circuitous route," arriving when the skirmish was over.[102]

General Stanley, "having gone 1½ miles," looked back and, to his "surprise and indignation, saw no one following!" Sending out orderlies in all directions, he finally found his column. "By fours, by companies, and by squadrons" he turned them back and soon arrived at the enemy's camp, only to find that Lieutenant O'Connell:

> to whom the word gallant applies, not as a compliment, but in true old English signification, had, with his squadron, whipped the enemy out of his three camps. The rebels, with the exception of a few men . . . escaped to the cedar thicket – literally *sans culottes* [without pants].[103]

O'Connell's little squadron—Cos. D and I, reduced to about forty-five men because the horses could not keep up due to the rough roads—had overridden the enemy's pickets and completely surprised the sleeping rebels when they charged into their camp.[104] They captured the camp, "killing and wounding many, capturing arms and ammunition, all the horses and horse equipage as well as all the miscellaneous camp equipage . . ."[105] Unfortunately, 2nd Lieutenant Wood's horse was shot and Wood was mortally wounded.[106] Without pausing, O'Connell's men charged and captured a second camp, "driving the enemy . . . a distance of nearly one-fourth of a mile, over very rough and rocky country, into a forest of heavy timber . . ."[107] O'Connell dismounted Co. I and "gave battle."[108] Fortunately, reinforcements in the form of Colonel Eli Long's 4th Ohio Cavalry and the 4th Regulars, led by Captain Otis, arrived and "drove the enemy out of sight."[109] The rebels attempted to make a final stand one mile from Fosterville, but fled upon the approach of reinforcements.[110] "Sgt. Edward Owens, Co. K, 4th US Cavalry and four men of the regiment and two of the 3rd Indiana Cavalry, captured a piece of artillery. While they were moving to the rear with it, a company of rebel cavalry recaptured the pieces with all the men but two."[111]

Despite all the confusion, the expedition was successful. As Stanley reported: "We destroyed probably about 800 stand of arms, all the camp equipage and saddles, blankets, and clothing in all the camps, some wagons, and, perhaps, captured about 300 horses." He faults General Turchin for not keeping up, depriving them of "at least 600 prisoners," and accepts some responsibility "for not taking more precautions."[112]

Captain Vale reports that the number of killed and wounded of the enemy was one hundred eighteen, although Colonel Minty did not report them, "as he was not in chief command." He writes:

> This victory, though brilliant, was not so decisive in its results as it should have been, or could easily have been made, had all the forces moved forward to the work after the enemy had been driven out of their camps. Several thousand prisoners could have been secured by prompt action.[113]

Captain Otis had high praise for Lieutenant O'Connell and his squadron—Companies D and I—acting independently of the regiment.[114] General Stanley could not "speak in terms too high of the conduct of the Lieutenant and his brave squadron."

> He was well assisted by Lieutenants Rendlebrock [sic] and Wood. With such officers and men our cavalry must soon be what I know it is fast becoming – *a real terror to the enemy* [emphasis author]. To this squadron belongs whatever of the brilliance that may be attached to the affair."[115]

Francis Wood enlisted in Co. K in May 1860. He quickly rose through the ranks to sergeant major and was commissioned 2nd lieutenant on May 18, 1863. He died of his wounds on May 23; he was twenty-four years old.[116] Two men in Company D were wounded: Sgt. Daniel Gaffney (slightly) and Private Patrick Flanagan, "wounded through the shoulder."[117]

A disagreement, which was not resolved for thirty years, arose between the 4th Regulars and the 4th Michigan as to whom took possession of the standard (flag) of the 1st Alabama Cavalry. Capturing the colors of the enemy was a prize of battle, bringing honor to the individual or regiment who carried it from the field. In Colonel Minty's original after battle report, he notes that Lieutenant O'Connell requested credit for the standard. After investigating the claim made by O'Connell, Minty was persuaded that it was actually taken by three members of his own regiment, the 4th Michigan. "The stand of colors," writes Vale, "was afterwards presented by Colonel Minty 'to the people of Michigan,' in accordance with a resolution adopted by the regiment."[118] However, writing in the *National Tribune* thirty years later, Minty made the following statement:

> In my official report I made honorable mention of Lieut. O'Connell, 4th U. S. Cav. for the 'very gallant manner in which he led his squadron, driving the enemy out of both their camps;' of Serg't [Edward] Owns, Corpl's [Jerome] Bartlett and [John] Miller, privates [Charles E.] Smith and [Sylvester] Riggin, 4th U.S. Cav., who distinguished themselves by capturing the standard of the 1st Alabama Cav.[119]

It is evident from reading numerous articles written by Minty thirty to forty years after the war that he strove for fairness and accuracy. Had he been misled by his own troopers in the rivalry for recognition among the regiments of the Saber Brigade? Considering Robert Minty's character, integrity, and his desire for accuracy, this would appear to be a public correction for the record.

Captain Vale and Colonel Minty both relate the following story about a young trooper injured in the action at Middleton:

> Private [Edward] Racine, of company A, Fourth Michigan, was severely wounded in the breast, being shot through the right lung by a rebel, who rushed on him, calling out to him to surrender, instead of which, the brave little fellow, about sixteen years old, raised his carbine and shot the rebel dead. When Dr. Fish was dressing his wound, he gulped out, 'Just think, doctor, the fellow had the impudence to ask *me* to surrender!'[120]

> After dressing the wound the Surgeon said: 'Well, Racine, I think you will be all right but I don't know where your heart was when that ball went through you.' 'I guess, Doctor,' Racine replied, 'it was in my mouth about the time I was hit.'[121]

COMPANIES F AND H RETURN FROM THE FRONTIER

Companies F and H were the last squadron of the Fourth Cavalry to remain on the frontier and the last to rejoin their regiment. From April 1861 through April 1862, they were at Fort Kearney, Nebraska

Territory. Captain Edward Newby—the senior officer present, commanding Co. H—also acted as commanding officer of Fort Kearney until his transfer to Fort Leavenworth in December 1861. Newby would be promoted to major, 3rd Cavalry in July 1862, but was forced to retire in September 1863 due to serious illness.[122]

Captain John Thompson, commanding Co. F, replaced Newby as commanding officer of Fort Laramie.[123] Newly promoted Captain George G. Huntt now commanded Company H and the squadron. Huntt—a civilian appointment in March 1861—would be on detached service during the war. He would return to command the regiment at Macon, Georgia, at the end of the war. Huntt would remain in the cavalry rising through the ranks to Colonel, 2nd Cavalry.[124]

In June 1862, the men of the squadron were bitterly disappointed when ordered to Fort Laramie, Wyoming. The fort was under the Department of the Missouri, District of Nebraska, commanded by Brigadier General James Craig. Writing to his superiors in July 1862 in a desperate plea for help and supplies, he mentions the "two skeleton companies of the Fourth Regular Cavalry, about 60 men, mounted on horses purchased seven years ago..."[125]

The long-awaited orders to rejoin the regiment arrived sometime during March or April 1863. It would be four months before companies F and H reached the 4th Regiment in the field in Tennessee. The squadron left its camp in the vicinity of Fort Laramie "on the 1st of May 1863 and reached Fort Kearney on the 11th of May 1863."[126] They followed the North Platte River along a portion of the Mormon Trail, which ran between the two forts. Leaving Fort Kearney on the eighteenth, they reached camp near Omaha City on May 27, 1863, marching a distance of 408 miles.[127] Sergeant Larson, Co. H, writes:

> Omaha was reached in a remarkably short time by our brisk marching and there we found three steamboats waiting for us, and our baggage and wagons were taken aboard at once. The next morning, horses and men went aboard and soon after we cast loose from the levee and steamed down the Missouri River. The whole movement... seemed to indicate that we were needed at some particular place as soon as possible...
>
> ... The great Confederate raider, General John Morgan was raiding through Kentucky and Indiana and we were needed in that locality to help drive him out.... On our arrival in St. Louis we disembarked as soon as the boats had made fast to the levee, saddled up and marched in columns of fours through the city to camp... In marching through the streets of St. Louis we received hearty cheers on several occasions... such cheering and waving of flags for Union troops in St. Louis was encouraging and interesting... [and] it was evident that the people in St. Louis and the State of Missouri had no longer any fear of expressing their opinion plainly for the Union.
>
> A day or two after our arrival the Quartermaster sent out some sixty to seventy fresh horses and those who were riding unserviceable animals were called to the pen to pick out one in the new supply.[128]

Unfortunately for Sergeant Larson, the horse he picked balked at an attempted jump, throwing him to the ground and severely spraining both of his ankles. While "totally disabled," he was able to remain with his company and complete the trip with the help of his men. The month-long stay in Louisville helped with his recovery.[129] While at their camp outside Louisville:

> ... two lieutenants, Sylvian [sp: Sullivan] and Fletcher, arrived from Carlisle Barracks, Pa., with a small detachment of recruits. It was a sorry looking set. Evidently Uncle Sam was not as particular in picking his men as he had been before the war. Of those six or eight that were assigned to 'H' Company, there were only three who would have had a chance to pass in 1860.... [T]wo or three deserted a few days later. We had then two lieutenants in the squadron. Before that we had none. [Sullivan] was assigned to 'F' Company and Fletcher to 'H' company. Both were strangers to the squadron and soon after [they arrived] both of our captains [Thompson and Newby] left and we did not see them any more until we had taken possession of Macon, Georgia, and the war was ended.[130]

Second Lieutenant Thomas W. Sullivan, who had been wounded at Dug Springs in August 1861, was a former sergeant in Company C, having joined the 1st Cavalry in March 1857. He was commissioned in March 1862.[131] Second Lieutenant Bird L. Fletcher originally enlisted in the old 1st Cavalry in 1859 and was a corporal in Company C when commissioned 2nd lieutenant in February 1863. He participated in the Battle of Franklin in April before transferring to his new company.[132] For reasons Larson does not disclose, a strong animosity would develop between Fletcher and Larson in the months to come.

Larson was still in severe discomfort when the squadron left Louisville. "My ankles were still in a condition that would have kept a civilian in bed, but a soldier, particularly a cavalryman, must be as tough as the proverbial 'boiled owl.'"[133]

Confronting Morgan's Cavalry at Bardstown, Kentucky

In early July, Confederate cavalryman General John Hunt Morgan, "disobeying his orders which confined his raid to Louisville, swept into Ohio" on a fatal expedition that ended in his capture on July 26, with his brigade "dispersed, killed, or captured."[134] Major General Ambrose Burnside—after being relieved of command of the Army of the Potomac—was commanding the Department of the Ohio and put all of his resources into the capture and destruction of Morgan's Cavalry. On July 2, Morgan's command crossed the Cumberland River at and near Burkesville, Kentucky. On the fifth he was in Bardstown, a small community about thirty miles south of Louisville. A squadron of men from the Fourth Regulars, under the command of Lieutenant Thomas Sullivan, was sent out to patrol that area. Sergeant Larson writes of the activities of the squadron while it was stationed at Louisville, as well as the characteristics of the rebel guerrilla forces with which it had to deal:

> It seemed that the squadron was placed out there as a troop of observation to watch the movements of the Confederate General Morgan's men and to make regular reports to the commander of a larger body of Union troops stationed somewhere on the other side of Louisville.
>
> ... The state of Kentucky, like Tennessee, had by a majority vote declared for the Union and remained out of the confederacy, but there were a great many Southern sympathizers in those states. Some of them joined the Confederate Army, but many did not. They formed independent bands under desperate leaders such as [John] Mosby, [Moses] White and others, whose real object was plunder much more than the success of the Confederate cause. Those bands roamed about in the border states and harassed the Unionists, robbed, murdered, and destroyed property, and in many instances, compelled families to abandon their homes and move north. That class became somewhat difficult for the Union troops to deal with, due to the fact they roamed about as orderly citizens, singly or in groups as people generally do, and wore no uniforms or anything else by which they could be recognized as enemies, except when they were called together by their chief. Then they did not wear uniforms either, but each had his long gun, rifle or double-barreled shot gun, lying across the saddle in front of him and when we met them in that style, we know of course, what they were. They had still another advantage over the Union troops, which often saved them. If a party of those guerrillas met a body of Union cavalry too strong for them, all they had to do was to scatter in the woods, which was easy for them as they know the lay of the country in all directions and as soon as they could dispose of the long gun in a safe place, there was nothing by which they could be recognized as enemies and they might turn right around and meet the soldiers as peaceable citizens. A Union soldier would never fire upon a disarmed citizen, but if they captured a Union soldier, his time in this world was up. He would get a rope around the neck and up he went on a stout limb of a tree. That was the way they served the Rebel cause.[135]

While on expedition to Bardstown, the squadron suffered its first casualties and the regiment experienced the first of four recorded occasions during the war when members of the 4th US Cavalry were forced to surrender. Informed that a detachment of Morgan's raiders was moving toward Bardstown, Lieutenant Sullivan "took twenty-five or thirty men in that direction at once, traveling all night, striking the enemy's advance guard 6 miles out of Bardstown at 6:30 a.m. the morning of July 5."¹³⁶ They chased the rebels through the town, but had to abandon the pursuit "on account of the jaded state" of their horses, two of which dropped dead.¹³⁷ Returning to Bardstown, Sullivan was informed by some loyal citizens "that the place was completely surrounded by 300 to 400 mounted rebels." He took possession of a large livery stable and purchased provisions for his men to last as long as their ammunition would hold out. Sullivan then "threw out pickets on the corners of the main streets and waited.¹³⁸ The rebel attack began at 11:30 a.m., "the enemy advancing in three columns and from three different directions." Larson continues:

> A Young Irishman named Collins was placed alone in the main street. Of course, the party being small, only one could be spared for each post, but the main street happened to lead to the road on which the enemy was advancing. Soon they came in sight and when near enough to be effective, this brave son of Erin commenced to send them Uncle Sam's blue pills as quickly as he could load and fire his carbine, and continued to hold his post until he was pierced by several bullets and fell dead in the street. Thus Collins became the first victim of our squadron in the Civil War. He was a young and lively companion, always full of fun and jokes and was well liked by everybody and this act of his showed that he did not lack in bravery either.¹³⁹

Writing from memory fifty years after the event, Larson may have actually recorded the death of Private Bartholomew Burke, a native of Londonderry, Ireland. There is no record of a Private Collins killed at Bardstown. The rebels were "gallantly repulsed," but Private Burke, Co. H, was mortally wounded in the assault. As he lay dying, his last words to his commanding officer were, "Lieutenant, did I fall like a soldier?"¹⁴⁰

A demand for surrender was made and refused. Firing commenced on the stable and continued sporadically throughout the night. The rebels tried to set fire to the stable, "but after losing 2 men and a negro in the attempt, gave up the project." Surrender was demanded again the next morning, followed with a threat of artillery. Deeming it useless to resist any longer, Sullivan negotiated their surrender with the general's brother.¹⁴¹ As Larson writes:

> Their horses and equipment and arms were taken away and a parole agreed upon between the officers while the privates relieved our men of whatever valuables they happened to cast their eyes on.... The affair, however, did not turn out as badly as it at first appeared, as the paroling of our men proved to be worthless. Morgan was not a regular commissioned officer in the Confederate army and therefore no parole by him or any of his subordinate officers was binding.¹⁴²

Larson explains the "observed rules of civilized warfare." If Morgan had been a recognized part of the Confederate army, "those twenty-five or thirty men paroled by Morgan could have done no more fighting until they were exchanged for Confederate prisoners."

> Morgan was a sort of independent roamer. He raised his troops and equipped them himself and moved about as he pleased and made what he could by raiding on Union territory, but in a somewhat different way from the guerrillas. He made his gains principally by levying on towns and cities, which he threatened to burn and destroy if the required sum was not paid. Otherwise he observed the rules of civilized warfare to some extent, but he and his troops were not recognized as a part of the Confederate Army.¹⁴³

Finally, by late July, Companies F and H were preparing to join their regiment and their new brigade. From Louisville—led by a guide who was familiar with the route—they would march to Sparta, Tennessee. They had "nothing but two pack-mules to each company, and they were to carry only rations and camp kettles and some extra ammunition." Rations consisted of "raw bacon, black coffee and hard tack... meaning Uncle Sam's crackers." In light marching order no tents, overcoats, or extra clothing were carried. Their rubber ponchos were their only protection against the rain and cold.¹⁴⁴

It would be an arduous march in the saddle lasting over thirty-six hours, with one stretch over difficult mountain terrain. Along the way, their advance guard was fired upon by rebel videttes and they spent one long night pinned down without water, food, or fire:

> This was one of the many such occurrences which persisted in interfering with the soldier's regularity in eating and sleeping during the whole war. Here, two companies of as hungry and thirsty men as could be found anywhere were lying along that fence through the whole night within easy reach of a running creek and good camping place. It was something we now had to get used to however.

By daybreak the enemy had gone and "soon the smell of coffee boiling and bacon frying delighted the nostrils of a set of very hungry men...."[145]

It was then noticed that one of the troopers from Company F who was leading the officers' extra horses was missing and a party was sent back to hunt for him. Late that afternoon Sergeant Patrick McGorran, Co. H, and the search party returned and reported finding the soldier "hanging on a limb of a large tree." They examined the body and, not finding any bullet wounds, declared that "he had undoubtedly been murdered after surrendering... strung up to a limb like a common criminal."[146]

The squadron got "a small measure of revenge" when they camped on a large plantation owned by "one of the most notorious bandits and guerrillas in the vicinity of Sparta...." They not only helped themselves to the "plentiful supplies" of ham, flour, corn meal, and sweet potatoes, as well as chickens and turkeys and corn and fodder for their horses, but to the slaves, as well:

> As congress had passed a law providing for the enlistment of negroes as cooks and servants to lead pack-mules, they were accepted, and four enlisted in Company H ... Company F also took four. Those negroes stayed with us through the war and were very useful.[147]

One of the blacks named "Gumbo" or "Gum" became popular with his company. Larson estimates that "by the time we left the plantation . . . the owner had been punished to the amount of eight thousand dollars worth of negroes, as values ran at that time."[148] Plantations were often the targets of Union expeditions. As Dr. Fish, 4th Michigan, writes:

> When we are on scouts, we usually select a camping ground near a place where forage is to be had for the horses. 1,500 or 2,000 horses will consume a good deal of corn and fodder in a night. When we favor some rich old secessionist with a night's patronage, we always leave him in the morning a poorer if not a wiser man. For property so used our Quartermaster gives a receipt in due form, to be paid on proof of loyalty. We can always tell who is and who is not loyal, by the Negroes, before we get to their plantation.[149]

The squadron moved on in the direction of Shelbyville, where "they accidentally met the Fourth Regiment, in the saddle, on a cross roads in the woods some miles from Shelbyville":

> The regiment had been on a scout toward Tullahoma, Tennessee, and was then on the lookout for a party of Confederate raiders of Forrest's command, who were expected to try to cross the Tennessee River in the vicinity of the crossroads. . . . The next day we, now with our regiment, also came up with our brigade in camp among the tall trees in Tennessee River Bottom.
>
> We had so far, at least, reached a part of our proper organization, which when united was 1st Regiment: 1st Brigade; 2nd Cavalry; 14th Army Corps. The 1st Brigade consisted of four regiments; the 4th US Cavalry, 7th Pennsylvania Cavalry, 4th Michigan Cavalry and the 5th Tennessee Cavalry, numbering about three thousand men and commanded by General R. H. G. Minty. The Chicago Board of Trade Battery also belonged to our brigade and was with us in all affairs where the brigade was engaged, and sometimes on special occasions with the 4th US Cavalry alone.[150]

Years later, Sergeant Larson writes that "General Rosencrans had carried off the laurels of General Minty and his brigade," and expresses the pride the men felt at this designation. He then adds, "As for our squadron, we were really doing similar duty in the battle without knowing it, although further back."[151]

Chicago Board of Trade Battery, Illinois Volunteers

Minty's biographer writes: "During this period the brigade was augmented with a powerful new weapon–the Chicago Board of Trade Battery. This group of men was to become an integral and trusted part of the Saber Brigade during the remaining years of their service."[152] As described by Sergeant Larson:

> The Board of Trade Battery was composed of well drilled artillerists and it had fine guns too. It was a militia organization of the State of Illinois and was equal in every respect to the best drilled battery in the regular army and rendered Minty's Brigade great assistance in many tight places.[153]

The battery distinguished itself in their first major engagement as an entire battery at the Battle of Stones River, holding its ground "against cannon fire and repeated charges by Confederate infantry, losing three men who lay dead by their disabled guns."[154] After the battle, General Rosecrans issued a special order, giving the battery "the privilege of carrying the colors presented by the Chicago Board of Trade, this being the first time in the history of the army where a battery of artillery was allowed a stand of United States colors and a battery flag." The battery had one other singular distinction: At Stones River, the battery "brought in from between the Federal and Confederate lines a six-pounder gun to replace one that had become disabled. In recognition of this daring bravery, General Rosecrans issued an order making the battery a seven-gun battery and so it remained until after the Battle of Chickamauga."[155]

In March 1863, the battery was changed from field artillery to horse artillery. On May 16, 1863, the battery was attached to the Second Cavalry Division, Army of the Cumberland. They were then ordered to be equipped as horse artillery, the first battery in the Western Theater to do so, according to the unit historian. The battery remained with this division until the end of the war.[156]

VI. The Tullahoma (Middle Tennessee) Campaign

Events were taking place in the Eastern Theater that would lead to the most celebrated battle of the Civil War—Gettysburg. By the spring of 1863 Joseph Hooker—replacing Burnside—had restored the Army of the Potomac and had "turned his cavalry into an outfit that could fight Jeb Stuart's boys on something like even terms."[1] For the third time, the Union Army would attempt to take Richmond. An overconfident Hooker was initially successful as he moved his 100,000-man army to Chancellorsville, Virginia, where he hesitated. On May 2, Lee and Stonewall Jackson struck Hooker's army "with pile driver force . . . shattering it to pieces," forcing the Union Army to retreat with a loss of 17,000 men.[2] Although a "brilliant victory" for Lee, the loss of Stonewall Jackson—who was mortally wounded—was a severe blow to the Confederate cause. However, this victory, along with the growing pressure Grant's army was putting on the Confederacy in the Mississippi Valley, encouraged Lee to make a major strike into the North, and he began to move his Army of Northern Virginia into Pennsylvania. At this same time, Grant was moving his army across Mississippi toward the capital of Jackson, a supply base and railroad center for the Confederacy.[3] His ultimate goal was Vicksburg. Here again, the Union cavalry played a prominent role, with Colonel Benjamin H. Grierson's cavalry brigade "slicing the length of the state, cutting railroads, fighting detachments of Confederate cavalry, and reaching Union lines finally at Baton Rouge." This action, "for the few days that counted most," distracted and confused the Confederate generals as to Grant's objectives.[4] Grant occupied Jackson on May 14. On May 19 and again on the twenty-second, he attempted to "take Vicksburg by storm" and was twice repulsed. The month-long siege of Vicksburg began.

In the North, as both armies moved towards their destiny at Gettysburg: "the rival cavalry sparred and skirmished, each commander trying to get news of the enemy's army and deny to the enemy news of his own."[5] During the Chancellorsville Campaign, General George Stoneman and his detachment of Union cavalry led a raid on the Confederate Army of Northern Virginia, "destroying portions of the Virginia Central Railroad and cutting General Lee's communication lines."[6] By the end of June both armies were in Pennsylvania and Major General George Gordon Meade had replaced Hooker. With one exception, the stage was set for the great battle of July 1-3. By a questionable tactical decision still hotly debated today, Jeb Stuart's cavalry was miles away when the battle of Gettysburg started.

At the same time Lee was losing at Gettysburg, Grant obtained the surrender of Vicksburg on July 4. That same day, Lee began his long retreat to Virginia. By July 9, the entire length of the Mississippi River was in Union hands and the Confederacy was split in half. Bruce Catton summarized these events:

> Gettysburg ruined a Confederate offensive and demonstrated that the great triumph on Northern soil which the South had to win if it was to gain recognition abroad could not be won. But Vicksburg broke the Confederacy into halves, gave the Mississippi Valley to the Union, and inflicted a wound that would ultimately prove mortal. Losing at Gettysburg, the Confederates had lost more than they could well afford to lose; at Vicksburg, they lost what they could not afford at all.[7]

With the two major campaigns in the East and the West resolved and the necessary time needed for recovery, there were no more campaigns for these armies for the remainder of the year. Rather than beginning an offensive to "sweep through southern Mississippi and Alabama," Grant was "compelled to scatter his troops" as "the authorities in Washington . . . clung to the notion that the important thing in this war was to occupy Southern territory . . ."[8] The focus of the war now shifted to middle Tennessee, where Rosecrans's Army of the Cumberland faced Bragg's Army of Tennessee. At the end of June: "Rosecrans at last began to move, hoping to seize Chattanooga and thus to make possible Federal occupation of Knoxville, and eastern Tennessee–a point in which President Lincoln was greatly interested, because eastern Tennessee was a stronghold of Unionist sentiment."[9] Colonel Sipes, 7th Pennsylvania, sums up the events of the first half of 1863:

> With the exception of a few minor affairs, the infantry and artillery of the Union and Confederate armies had been resting and preparing for six months. *Only the cavalry had been active* [emphasis author] . . . The time had now come for a general advance, and on the 24th of June this forward movement was begun by Rosecrans' entire army. General Stanley was in command of all the Union cavalry, which was in good condition, not withstanding the hard service it has performed.[10]

Preparations were underway for the upcoming Tullahoma Campaign to drive the Confederates out of middle Tennessee. In Major General David Stanley's Cavalry Corps, Brigadier General John Turchin commanded the Second Division. Colonel Robert Minty commanded the First Brigade in Turchin's Division that consisted of his 4th Michigan Volunteer Cavalry, the 7th Pennsylvania Volunteer Cavalry, 4th United States Cavalry, 3rd Indiana Volunteer Cavalry, and 5th Tennessee Volunteer Cavalry.[11]

Sergeant Charles Bates wrote to his parents on May 31: "The Fourth Cavalry is only three hundred strong in the field but every man is of the Davy Crocket style and they will do something if they get the chance. Our regiment is well known in the southern army . . ." Bates was anxious for action: "I have not had the satisfaction of painting my sword with southern blood yet, only a pig which I transfixed at Franklin was a southern, so I am a little anxious to get into a fight."[12] Bates would get his wish in the forthcoming Tullahoma Campaign, when Minty's brigade would distinguish itself in the battle at Shelbyville; Charles Bates, among others, would be cited for his "gallantry and solderlike conduct."[13]

At Shelbyville, the Union Cavalry would "prove to be more" than the Confederate Cavalry could handle.[14] In the meantime, there was still more work for Rosecrans's cavalry. On June 3, Forrest's, Wheeler's, and Colonel C. P. Breckenridge's cavalries "made a demonstration on the pickets and outposts in front of Murfreesboro, from Triune to the Manchester pike."[15] Colonel Sipes writes that:

A similar attack was made the same day on a picket commanded by Lieutenant Vale, on the Wartrace road. This developed into quite an affair, in which Minty's Brigade, including [Lietenant Nathaniel] Newel's section of artillery, became actively engaged with a large Confederate force, comprising all arms. For a little while the enemy had the advantage, but in the end were forced to retreat with considerable loss.[16]

Scout on Middleton and Eagleville Pikes

On June 10, "the brigade was ordered out at 3 in the morning to meet a reported advance of the enemy on the Triune road."[17] As reported by General John Turchin: "in accordance with written instructions from Major General Stanley, Colonel Minty received orders at head-quarters at 2 a.m. this day . . ."[18] The First Brigade was to proceed to Salem, "and from there to scout the country toward Middleton and Eagleville, and, if possible, to be at the bridge on the Salem pike by 5 a.m."[19] He was to ascertain what force, if any, was moving and report by courier direct to General Rosecrans from the bridge on the Salem Pike.[20]

Minty dispatched his first courier from the brigade at 3:45 a.m. and his second from Salem at 4:30 a.m. He detached the 3rd Indiana and 4th Michigan Cavalry, under command of Lieutenant Colonel Robert Klein, 3rd Indiana, to scout the Middleton Road and then proceeded with the 4th U.S. and 7th Pennsylvania to Versailles.[21] There he "struck a cavalry picket which quickly retreated toward Rover." Minty sent a scout of fifty men to Eagleville and dispatched his third courier to Rosecrans at 5:30 a.m.[22]

At Rover, Minty found "two regiments of cavalry which were quickly driven through and beyond Unionville." Minty made his fourth report to headquarters at 7 a.m. He halted at Unionville and, "being fully satisfied that there were no force of the enemy moving," sent his last courier at 9 a.m. and began the return to Murfreesboro.[23]

Expedition To and Skirmish Near Lebanon

On June 15, it was reported that Colonel Basil Duke—"one of the best officers in John Hunt Morgan's Division"—was in Lebanon with his brigade. At 5 p.m., with 1,500 men, Minty's brigade "left Murfreesboro on the Lebanon pike with the object, if possible, of capturing the force."[24] According to Vale:

. . . Minty moved with the Fourth Michigan, Fourth United States, Seventh Pennsylvania, and Fifth Iowa cavalry–the latter regiment having been attached to the brigade about the 1st of June–out the Lebanon road to Stone's river, where he halted, at Black's crossroad, until 10 p.m.[25]

Minty ordered the horses fed and the men to "get their suppers, and made every preparation for an all-night march."[26] They resumed their march at 10 p.m., "so as to strike Lebanon by daybreak."[27] They reached Lebanon by 4 a.m., only to find that the rebels had left a day earlier. Minty moved on to Spring Creek where, "finding plenty of corn," he halted to feed the horses and "give my weary men a much needed rest." However, the men were shortly attacked by Duke's rebels, who drove in their videttes. After a brief skirmish the rebels withdrew. Minty immediately sounded "to horse" and "every man was soon in his saddle and ready for the fray." The 7th Pennsylvania, commanded by Colonel Sipes: "moved down the right side of the valley, and the 4th Michigan, commanded by Major [Frank W.] Mix down the left side, both officers with orders to keep slightly in advance of the column on the pike which consisted of the 4th U.S., 5th Iowa, and 3rd Ind., in the order named." The rebels fell back in a southeasterly direction as the Union forces advanced. Near Shop Spring—about six miles southeast of Lebanon, at the junction of the road leading to Beards Mill—Duke dismounted his men, "taking position behind the fences." They were immediately charged by a squadron of 4th Regulars commanded by Lieutenant William O'Connell, who drove them from their position and captured over twenty of the rebels before they could get back to their horses. Once mounted, the remainder were able to escape capture because the horses of the Union cavalry were "tired from their long night march."[28] After a brief halt for breakfast, "the march was resumed and the fight continued to Walter's Mill when, having marched fifty-six miles, a halt in line of battle was ordered . . . [and] strong detachments were sent out two miles toward Alexandria . . . while a heavy line of skirmishers encircled the bivouac."[29] It was about 2 a.m. when the men proceeded to unsaddle and feed their horses.[30]

Some of the men had had one hour's sleep and others no sleep whatsoever. At 6:30 a.m., Minty resumed the march for Murfreesboro, arriving at

Stones River at ten o'clock, where he halted for a couple of hours to rest the horses.[31] At about 7 p.m., Minty received word that John Hunt Morgan was in Alexandria with 5,000 men and eighteen pieces of artillery. With 1,500 men and no artillery he decided not to challenge them, withdrawing "by way of the cross-road from Shoop's [sic] Spring to Beards Mill where he arrived at 2 a.m. and camped for the balance of the night."[32] At 8:30 the next morning, Minty's brigade began its return to Murfreesboro, "arriving at 4 p.m., having marched 64 miles since leaving there 23 hours before." Minty reported that the brigade "sustained the loss of two men killed, one 4th U.S. (accidentally) and one 5th Iowa."[33] According to Lieutenant Potter, 4th Michigan, the 4th U.S. trooper—Private Patrick Craven, Co. I—was actually killed in a skirmish on the Alexandria Pike and the 5th Iowa trooper was accidentally shot by "his comrade next to him" when dismounting, "the ball passing thro' his left lung and out on the right side cutting one of the large arteries."[34]

Colonel Sipes writes that the brigade was paid a very high compliment by General Turchin. The general asked the commander of the 7th Pennsylvania "to point out, on the military map, the route" that had just been taken by the brigade on their last two-day expedition. "The distance was estimated at more than 100 miles–Vale says one hundred five."[35] The Russian-born general—"veteran of the Imperial Military School"—offered the opinion: "If an account that such a march, by a body of cavalry had been made, was published in St. Petersburg or Vienna, no officer in Russia or Austria would credit it."[36] The United States cavalry, as well as the Confederate cavalry, were rewriting the European military manuals on the effective use of mobile cavalry in modern warfare for decades to come.

General Turchin—originally given command of the Second Brigade—would be replaced by Brigadier General George Crook in late July. The brigade would remain on detached service for several weeks, temporarily assigned to the 21st Army Corps.[37] General Crook would be the most controversial general under whom Minty's brigade served, leading to the court martial of Colonel Robert H. G. Minty.

Shelbyville, Tennessee

During the winter, the Confederate Army of Tennessee established a defense line "nearly 13 miles long," from Shelbyville—under Leonidas Polk—to Wartrace and Fairfield under William Hardee.[38] Bragg's army was "covered by a range of high, rough, rocky hills" in the Cumberland Mountains made passable by a number of narrow gaps, with the Shelbyville-Murfreesboro turnpike running through Guy's Gap, about nine miles directly north of Shelbyville.[39] Two Confederate cavalry corps occupied positions on either flank: Joseph Wheeler at McMinnville and Nathan Bedford Forrest at Columbia. Confederate strength was approximately 43,000 men. It was a good defensive position with terrain that favored the Confederates:

> To traverse the Cumberland Plateau the Union army would have to move along roads that pierced the mountains by way of Hoovers, Liberty, and Guy's Gap. The railroad to Chattanooga and another road passed through Bellbuckle Gap. This latter route and the road by way of Shelbyville were well fortified.[40]

Under the command of General Rosecrans, the Federal army began a major, successful effort to harass the Confederates in the Tullahoma (or Middle Tennessee) Campaign.[41] There were a series of skirmishes and minor battles that eventually forced Bragg to pull his Confederates across the Tennessee River in a retreat from Tullahoma, while Rosecrans established his Federals at Chattanooga.[42] Generals Stanley and Granger were to take the fortified town of Shelbyville, "which shielded Bragg's main foraging area in Middle Tennessee."[43] Vale records:

> Late in the evening of June 23, 1863, sealed orders were issued by General Rosecrans to the different army camps to hold themselves in readiness to move the next morning, with two days' cooked rations in haversacks, and five days' uncooked, with twenty days' rations of hard bread, coffee, sugar and salt, in wagons; all tents and extra baggage to be packed and left in store; the transportation to be reduced to one wagon to a regiment; all extra wagons to be placed in charge of a corps wagon-master, loaded with ammunition and subsistence, and the troops to move in lightest possible marching order.

These orders, clearly foreshadowing a forward movement, proclaimed to the whole army that the long period of comparative inactivity was at an end...[44]

At 6:30 a.m. on June 24, Minty marched on the Woodbury Pike from Murfreesboro to Cripple Creek, his brigade numbering 2,522 officers and men.[45] His brigade consisted of the following:

> 7th Pennsylvania Cavalry
> Lieutenant Colonel William H. Sipes
> 4th United States Cavalry
> (Cos. B, C, D, G, I, L, and M)
> Captain James McIntyre
> 4th Michigan Volunteer Cavalry
> Major Frank W. Mix
> 1st Middle Tennessee Cavalry
> Lieutenant Colonel Robert Galbraith
> 3rd Indiana Cavalry
> Colonel Robert Klein
> 5th Iowa Cavalry
> Lieutenant Colonel Matthewson T. Patrick
> 5th Tennessee Cavalry
> Colonel William B. Stokes
> Battery D, 1st Ohio Artillery
> Lieutenant Nathaniel M. Newell[46]

At 10 a.m., General Stanley learned that General Robert B. Mitchell's First Division of Cavalry had been seriously engaged with the enemy at Rover the day before. At 1 p.m. he ordered Colonel Minty's brigade and a section of Stokes's battery—by way of Salem—to Middleton "to get within supporting distance of General Mitchell."[47] That night Minty camped within two miles of the general.[48] "A drizzling rain began to fall at noon that day and by night it rained copiously."[49]

The rain would continue for weeks, "converting the whole surface of the country into a quagmire . . . rendering this," as Stanley wrote, "one of the most arduous, laborious, and distressing campaigns upon man and beast I have ever witnessed."[50] Adding to the distress, "the road was exceedingly rough, and the rebels had made it impassable, for artillery, by rolling great rocks into it and felling trees across it."[51] The next day, "in the midst of furious thunder showers," Minty moved:

> through the fields across the country to the Shelbyville pike, skirmishing all day on the right flank and camped at Christiana on the rail line ten miles south of Murfreesboro.... Late in the evening the 4th US Cavalry picket on the Shelbyville pike was attacked and driven in; but after a sharp fight, the rebels were repulsed by the Fifth Iowa and Fourth Michigan, who pursued them into Guy's Gap.[52]

The rebel forces holding Guy's Gap and Shelbyville had to be defeated and driven off to protect the rear of Rosecrans's advancing army and the supply depot at Murfreesboro.[53] A severe storm raged on the twenty-sixth, "making military movements tedious; in fact, the army almost came to a halt."[54] Minty's brigade "demonstrated heavily on the right of Alexander McCook's Corps in front of Guy's Gap, pushing the line well up to the range of hills, threatening the enemy's positions at Wood's Gap and Hoover's Gap as well." All the while, there were "continuous heavy showers," and the whole valley was "cut and trampled into a lake of mud."[55] That afternoon, during a heavy storm, General Mitchell engaged the enemy at Middleton. The fighting ceased at about 4 p.m., with the rebels withdrawing.[56]

Perceiving that the enemy's positions were weakening, Colonel Wilder, along with his brigade of mounted infantry, "dashed forward that night, routed the enemy, and seized the entrance to Hoover's Gap . . ." By the morning of the twenty-seventh, they carried the gap "from end to end," opening the way "to turn the rebel right."[57] During the action at Hoover's Gap, Captain John Thompson—who had previously commanded the squadron of Companies F and H at Fort Kearney—now commanded a squadron of 4th US Cavalry under General George Thomas; he was brevetted major for his meritorious conduct. A six-year veteran prior to the war, Thompson would be promoted to major, 7th Cavalry, in 1867. Ironically, he would be "murdered by desperados" in Texas in November that same year.[58]

The Charge at Guy's Gap

On the morning of June 27, the Federal cavalry was poised in front of Guy's Gap, which ran a distance of about three miles. The east end was "protected by a line of trenches running along the summit of a hill, north and south, as far as the eye could see," with Wheeler's Confederate cavalry posted behind the trenches.⁵⁹ At 3 a.m., the bugle sounded reveille and Rosecrans gave the orders to dislodge the enemy from Guy's Gap. In a heavy fog, the cavalry was formed in columns of regiments in an open field. By seven a.m., the fog had disappeared, presenting "a scene of grand military pageantry, as rare as it was inspiring."⁶⁰ "The bright morning sun shone upon the seven thousand horsemen massed in the field... reflecting in full splendor the bright sabers and arms, and kissing the flags, banners, and streamers, as a harbinger of victory."⁶¹ At 8 a.m. "the entire cavalry force moved out," with Minty's brigade in the rear:⁶²

> A line of dismounted skirmishers nearly two miles in length covered the front; two thousand mounted men in columns of attack moved up the slope, on each side of the road, while on the pike, in serried [compact] ranks, pressed forward nearly three thousand more, forming a compact column over three miles in length.⁶³

It was a tediously slow movement: "advance a couple of hundred yards–halt–wait; dismount–wait."⁶⁴ At about 11:20 a.m., an aide on General Stanley's staff "came to the rear on the gallop" and told Minty that General Stanley wanted him to move up to the front of the column as the brigade in front "is so damn slow he can do nothing with it." Minty gave the order: "Mount–Forward, march–Trot, march," and they were soon leading the column.⁶⁵ As they were passing the infantry "a tall sergeant, leaning on his rifle, very audibly remarked to the men standing near him, 'Boys, there's going to be a fight. When them fellows are hurried to the front it means business.'"⁶⁶

Moving forward, Minty "found the enemy in position at the gap, with a strong force of skirmishers behind the fences on the face of the hill [and] a column moving through the woods threatening our right flank." He "deployed the Fourth Regulars to the front, and General Stanley took the 7th Pennsylvania, 4th Michigan, and 3rd Indiana to the right," driving the enemy from its position.⁶⁷ The skirmishing had commenced at Old Fosterville (about halfway between Murfreesboro and Shelbyville), and the rebel response convinced General Stanley that "the enemy was not in force of all arms at the gap." He received permission from General Granger to make a direct attack upon the pass.⁶⁸

The 7th Pennsylvania turned into a field on the right of the pike and formed a line of battle, with the Third Battalion of the regiment dismounted in front as skirmishers, as a screen to protect troop movements.⁶⁹ The 4th United States Cavalry formed on the left of the pike. The 4th Michigan was ordered to move to the right and "find a bridle path that led to the trenches about a mile beyond." The 3rd Indiana Cavalry was held as reserve.⁷⁰ Minty—with the 4th US Cavalry in advance—moved up the road with the 1st Middle Tennessee in columns of fours, at the same time "ordering up the other regiments from the right."⁷¹ When Minty gave the order for a saber charge, Colonel Galbraith, along with a dozen men of the 1st Middle Tennessee, "dashed forward and removed a barricade which the rebels had built across the road at the top of the hill."⁷² Under heavy fire of artillery and musketry, the Federal cavalry, with sabers drawn, charged into Guy's Gap.⁷³

The rebels "fled in wild confusion, artillery, mounted and dismounted men, all mixed up together, down the road toward Shelbyville."⁷⁴ Minty ordered Captain McIntyre to send a squadron to the left to strike the Fairfield road and cut off the enemy's retreat. This was effectively done by Companies D and I under Lieutenants Joseph Rendlebock and Wirt Davis, along with companies from the 7th Pennsylvania and 4th Michigan. They "cut the rebel column in two, turned the rear of the column to the left, and forced the rebel cavalry into a large field with strong fencing on three sides." With no outlet, "250 of them were easily captured."⁷⁵ Meanwhile, the 1st Middle Tennessee—supported by the remainder of the 4th U.S.—"followed the mounted forces on a run" for about three miles.⁷⁶ With his men "very much scattered, picking up prisoners," Minty halted while his command regrouped.⁷⁷ "Guy's Gap was won."⁷⁸

The Battle at Shelbyville

The advancing Union cavalry was brought to a stand about three miles from Shelbyville by the enemy opening with artillery from an entrenchment.⁷⁹ During the twenty minutes Minty took to regroup his forces, he received word from Colonel Galbraith that "the enemy had rallied and was showing him fight." He immediately moved forward with the 7th Pennsylvania, 4th Michigan, and 3rd Indiana.⁸⁰ The last barrier to Shelbyville was an abatis—a barricade of felled trees with spiked branches facing the enemy. It was constructed in a semicircle around Shelbyville, facing north.[81]

Minty "now learned that he was fighting the whole of the rebel cavalry in the Department, except Forrest's division."[82] The Confederate forces consisted of General William T. Martin's division and a part of Wharton's, all under command of Major General Joseph Wheeler. They numbered approximately "4,000 men, with artillery," while Minty's force "numbered less than 2,000 and was without artillery."[83]

A battalion from the 7th Pennsylvania dismounted and engaged the enemy, who immediately opened fire with artillery.[84] Minty ordered the 4th Michigan "to the right about three-quarters of a mile" to make a flank movement on the entrenchments. He sent the 3rd Indiana with the same instructions to the left. At the same time, Minty sent messengers to Captain McIntyre "to bring up the Fourth Regulars; to General Mitchell, asking him to send forward a couple pieces of artillery, and to General Stanley, informing him of the position of affairs."[85]

The 4th Michigan dismounted, but finding the distance too great remounted, advancing through the abatis on horseback and engaging in a "severe skirmish."[86] Minty, hearing the heavy firing on the right from the engagement of the 4th Michigan, ordered the 7th Pennsylvania and 4th United States on each side of the road with sabers drawn and charged down the pike.[87]

John A. Wyeth—a Confederate soldier in Wheeler's command that day, who later became Forrest's biographer—describes what he saw: "On either side of the highway, in columns of fours, they advanced at a steady gallop." With sabers held high in the air, they "made no sound whatever, beyond the rumbling tattoo which their horses' hoofs played upon the ground."[88] The advancing Federal cavalry "passed into the opening in the line of earth works, through which the main road led, some two or three hundred yards" from the entrenched rebels.[89] As soon as they reached the point inside the works—still on the full run—the cavalrymen "deployed from column of fours into line of battle, like the opening of a huge fan. *The movement was made with as much precision as if it had been done in an open plain, on dress parade, or in some exhibition of discipline and drill* [emphasis author]."[90]

Seeing the reinforcements, the First and Second Battalions of the 4th Michigan, joined by the 7th Pennsylvania, "charged into the enemy."[91] "Forcing their horses through the tangled abatis," the entrenchments were quickly reached. Colonel Sipes "sounded the charge and, with two battalions of his regiment dashed forward over the ditch and intrenchments into the midst of the astonished enemy."[92] As Captain Vale notes:

> *This was the first time in the history of the war, when strong lines of entrenchments, protected by an elaborate abatis, ditch and parapet, were stormed and taken by cavalry in a mounted saber charge* [emphasis author].[93]

Wyeth continues: "No more gallant work was ever done by any troops than was done this day . . . [when] the Seventh Pennsylvania and the 4th United States Regulars rode out and over us in the most brilliant cavalry maneuver the writer ever witnessed."[94]

Overwhelmed, the rebels re-formed in a field on the outskirts of the town "behind a palisade fence on the left of the pike." The fighting was ferocious. Troopers with horses shot from under them fought on foot or remounted a riderless horse. One trooper charged into the town, selected a position where the fleeing rebels would have to pass him and, "with drawn saber, hewed away at them until he was disabled." Another trooper, out of ammunition, used his carbine as a club, "and did good service among the rebels with whom he was in close contact."[95] Hundreds of the fleeing rebels were being captured.[96]

About a mile after the works Minty found himself on the outskirts of Shelbyville. He could see the courthouse with "the Confederate artillery in position in the square, ready to sweep the street, both sides of which were lined with picket fences."[97] When the Union cavalry came within range, the rebels opened up with their four pieces of artillery. Just as Minty was forming for a charge, Captain Charles Aleshire arrived with four pieces of artillery that Minty had ordered earlier.[98] As cavalry historian Stephen Starr writes, it was at this moment that Minty demonstrated "how far the officers of the Union cavalry had come in learning the tricks of the cavalryman's trade."[99]

"Captain," Minty said, "all I want now is a little smoke; place one gun on each side of the street and fire one shell from each gun; give all the room you can for my column to [move] between your guns."[100] Captain Aleshire fired as directed; the bugler sounded the charge and, "under cover of smoke," the 7th Pennsylvania, led by Captain Charles Davis, and "one squadron of the 4th U.S., led by Lt. [Neil] McCafferty were more than half way down the hill."[101]

The men "dashed forward with an impetuosity never before surpassed on any field," writes Vale. The rebels fired their guns "with all the rapidity and precision possible, hurling cannister in double-shotted charges at and through the dense ranks of onrushing cavalry."[102]

As recalled by Colonel Sipes: "Never did men move more gallantly and daringly into the face of the most imminent danger than did this little force."[103]

They were on a dead run; two artillery shots screamed over their heads. "The third shot hit . . . killing three men and a horse," but onward they charged.[104] According to Vale: "A shower of balls, pistol, and carbine slugs rained down on the charging cavalry," but they could not be stopped.[105] Resistance at the railroad depot was met and overrun by "the platoon of the Fourth Regulars led by Lieutenant McCafferty."[106]

"We saw the Confederate cavalry waver and break," writes Lieutenant George Steahlin, 7th Pennsylvania. "The artillery limbered up and joined the fleeing cavalry."[107] "Yelling like demons and spurring their horses to the wildest speed," the Federal cavalry "reached the square, leaping their horses over the guns, and sabering the gunners alongside the pieces." They captured three of the guns "in their position."[108] Captain Vale was given credit for the capture of two of the artillery pieces.[109] As the last piece of rebel artillery turned the corner of a street, it ran into two hundred Federal sabers.[110]

The 7th Pennsylvania and 4th United States were now joined by "men of other regiments who had caught the contagion of the fight." They rushed "in a wild craze of enthusiasm" after the demoralized Confederates as they tried to retreat to Skull Camp Bridge—the only bridge across the Duck River within seven miles of Shelbyville "by which escape was possible."[111]

"Shelbyville and the country of which it was the county seat, was strongly Union in politics . . ." Colonel Galbraith's regiment (the 1st Middle Tennessee) had a number of recruits from the town:

In the midst of the fierce charge upon the battery, and the hot, desperate fight from the square to the railroad depot, the loyal people recognized their men and the standard of the First Middle Tennessee, and in a wild burst of patriotic enthusiasm, dozens of ladies rushed from their houses, and, standing on the steps, porches, door stoops, and many out on the curb of the pavement in the street, waved the stars and stripes, cheering and yelling to their friends, calling to them to 'Go on! Go on! You've got the rebels! They are running! They can't cross the river! God bless our boys in blue!'

All the while, "canister . . . rifle and revolver balls, and minnie slugs were hissing through the air, and all the wild pandemonium of battle was raging around them . . ."[112] Even General William Rosecrans was compelled to write: "It is worthy of note that the waving of flags and cheers of welcome from the inhabitants . . . doubtless gave added vigor and energy to the advance of our troops."[113] This scene would be repeated for the 4th Regulars at Okolona, Mississippi, in February 1864—only the citizens would be cheering on the Confederates.

General Wheeler was desperately trying to rally his men on the bank of the Duck River to cover their crossing on the narrow wooden bridge, guarded by three pieces of artillery.[114] As the Confederates fled to the river, the 3rd Indiana and the 4th United States under Captain McIntyre: "swept down the north bank . . . driving a crowd of fugitives before them . . . making thrusts right, left, and front–dealing death at every blow, until Duck river was reached."[115] "The fight was hand-to-hand for 300 yards" when both parties reached the river.[116] One of the artillery caissons had overturned on the bridge, and Company A, 4th U.S., captured the second gun.[117] The third piece was taken by the 7th Pennsylvania.[118] Private William Sommers, Co. A, 4th U.S., captured a battle flag of Wheeler's command.[119]

The bridge was now completely blocked and the rebels were "driven into the river where they perished by the scores."[120] The Duck River "ran through a deep, narrow channel" and was "swollen almost to its full banks" by recent rains. About twenty feet deep, it was a rushing torrent, "and the finest cavalry of the rebellion . . . found a grave in the mud and slime of Duck river."[121] Once the bridge was cleared, Captain McIntyre and his command of 4th Cavalry "followed the enemy nearly 2 miles . . . and, finding no force, returned and encamped that night in town."[122]

In the fighting General Wheeler had his horse shot from under him, and he barely escaped by "mounting another horse and swimming the river."[123] Forrest's command—"floundering in the mud all day between Unionville and Middleton"—was unable to reach Shelbyville in time to support Wheeler and was now "endeavoring to escape to Tullahoma."[124] "The actual [Confederate] loss in killed, wounded, and prisoners has never been correctly stated . . . but the most disastrous loss was in morale." As David Stanley writes: *The Confederate cavalry never recovered from the demoralizing effect which it experienced of being ridden down by the Union cavalry* [emphasis author].[125]

Of the events at Shelbyville, historian Stephen Starr writes: "Minty earned in full measure this day the high praise he was to receive":

> . . . On this occasion the men of [the 7th Pennsylvania] . . . performed with spectacular bravery and skill one of the principal functions of the cavalry of tradition, a thundering charge with the saber, the 'arme blanche' of cavalry orthodoxy. And they did this after a battalion of their own regiment had demonstrated comparable skill as dismounted skirmishers, performing one of the important functions of mounted infantry.[126]

General Robert Mitchell, commanding First Division, "in a generous tribute to an officer and troops who did not belong to his division" wrote in his report: "I cannot refrain from expressing . . . my admiration of the conduct of Colonel Minty and his brigade. . . . Before the gallantry and skill of its commander and the dashing bravery and skill of his troops, all efforts of the rebels to withstand his advance were ineffectual."[127] Lieutenant George S. Steahlin, 7th Pennsylvania, put it simply: "General Wheeler's cavalry never stood our cold steel. This day they were stampeded and were totally routed."[128] Writing of the day's events years later, General Stanley states: "On the part of the Union soldiers there can scarcely be instanced a finer display of gallantry than the charge made by the 7th Pennsylvania Cavalry backed by the 4th U.S. I have read of nothing more admirable."[129]

Captain Charles C. Davis, 7th Pennsylvania, who led the charge upon the enemy's battery at the courthouse in Shelbyville, was awarded the Medal of Honor in June 1894 for leading "one of the most desperate and successful charges of the Civil War."[130]

Minty's brigade was credited with the capture of three pieces of artillery "and 599 of the enemy, including 30 commissioned officers, while their killed and wounded could not have been less than 200, including those lost in the river." Minty's command lost "2 officers and 4 men killed and 5 officers and 21 men wounded." In the 4th US Cavalry, Lieutenant William O'Connell was injured when "thrown from his horse," breaking his shoulder, and one man was wounded.[131]

Once again, the names of officers and men of the 4th United States Cavalry appear in the official records as "deserving of special mention for gallant conduct at Shelbyville": Captain James McIntyre; 1st Lieutenants William Ingerton and William O'Connell; and 2nd Lieutenants Joseph Rendlebock, Neil McCafferty, and Wirt Davis. All five lieutenants had received field commissions from the ranks of enlisted men. 1st Sergeant Charles McMaster, Co. I—"for his gallant conduct in the charge of the battery"—would receive his field promotion to 2nd lieutenant in August. Also mentioned were 1st Sergeants James Callehan, Co. D, and James Egan, Co. E; Sergeants Charles Bates, Co. E, and John Riker, Co. D; Corporals William Tudhope and John Rankin, Co. A; and Private William Sommers, Co. A.[132]

Unfortunately, with the "politics of war," full credit for the decisive victory at Shelbyville would be denied the Saber Brigade and its commanding officer. As recorded by Minty's Acting Adjutant General Robert Burns:

> After the whole thing was over General Mitchell rode up, and about two hours after him in came general Granger, and the next day it was telegraphed all over the country that General Mitchell's Division of Cavalry had taken Shelbyville, and that General Granger had entered the place a conqueror, etc., etc. All sheer humbug . . . We felt very sore when we saw the newspaper reports.[133]

Colonel Minty had earned his promotion to general. It was strongly supported by the governor of his state, among others, but Major General Halleck would deny it and Minty would "continue in command of a 'Brigade' without the rank of 'Brigade-ier.'"[134]

Aftermath

For four days the men "were compelled to 'slop around' in wet clothing, to wade and fight through the mud by day, and 'sink to sleep' in the mud by night . . .".[135] Shelbyville had been an exhausting seven hours of heavy work and the men and horses were completely worn out. Minty recalled his regiments and bivouacked on the outskirts of the town, surrendering the pursuit of the Confederate cavalry to General Mitchell's fresh troops.[136] The arduous circumstances of this expedition and the "consequent condition of the roads" rendered the operations of the cavalry "difficult and exceedingly trying to men and horses." The inability to bring up feed in the wagons and the constant rain depriving the "poor beasts" of their rest had "reduced the cavalry considerably. They now required some little rest and refitting."[137]

Adding to the misery were the fleas: "the terrible ally to the rebel army, waging . . . a general guerrilla warfare against our army," the blood-sucking mosquitos, and the "jigger . . . an original secessionist, bitter, determined and unrelenting in his attacks upon the Union army."[138]

The Confederate army was still holding Tullahoma in force and occupying Bellbuckle. On June 28: "Minty's brigade was moved to about three miles south-east of Guy's gap where it forced the rebel evacuation of Bellbuckle Gap that night. At 1 a.m. on the following day the brigade marched to Shelbyville and from there to Fairfield."[139]

That same day, Bragg and the Confederate Army evacuated Tullahoma. To facilitate the retreat to Chattanooga, Bragg sent his cavalry "out on the roads to shield his army."[140] It was during this screening action in the area of Walker Mills and the Elk River that Colonel James Starnes—one of Nathan Bedford Forrest's most valued officers—was killed in a skirmish with troopers from Minty's Brigade.[141]

With the exception of July 2, when the 7th Pennsylvania "skirmished for a short time" with a force of rebels; and July 3, when the 4th Regulars "made a dash" on Decherd—about a mile northeast of Winchester—but found no rebels, the rest of the expedition was uneventful. The brigade camped one and a half miles from Decherd that night.[142] Minty's brigade returned to headquarters at Salem on July 5.[143] Between June 23 and July 5, in continuous rain, the brigade had marched over 800 miles.[144]

Despite the daunting conditions of terrain and weather, Granger's Reserve Corps, with Minty's brigade, broke the Confederate line that had been established from Shelbyville to Manchester and pushed the Confederate cavalry out of middle Tennessee. This allowed the remainder of the Union Army under General Rosecrans to force Bragg to evacuate Tullahoma. The Confederate forces "took a strong defensive position at Chattanooga" behind the Tennessee River.[145] Colonel Sipes gives a summary that once again points out the influence of the continual rains on the outcome of the military activities. He notes that General Stanley pronounced Rosecrans's plans "perfect":

> and his orders from day to day beyond criticism, but his artillery was unable to move as directed, his supply trains were stalled, and in some instances had to be abandoned. These conditions enabled Bragg to retire across the Tennessee river, burn the bridges behind him, and secure safety in an almost impregnable position.[146]

General Rosecrans concludes:

> Thus ended a nine days' campaign, which drove the enemy from two fortified positions and gave us possession of Middle Tennessee, conducted in one of the most extraordinary rains ever known in Tennessee at that period of the year, over a soil that becomes almost a quicksand. . . These results were far more successful than was anticipated.[147]

The campaign closed and the division marched to Salem, "going into camp at that place on the 5th."[148] Celebration erupted in the camp on July 7, when a telegram from Washington announced the fall of Vicksburg on the fourth and the overthrow of Lee's army. There was "a national salute by every battery in [the] army, at sun-rise, and rejoicing without stint."[149]

Camp at Salem, Tennessee

With the retreating Confederate army having crossed the Tennessee River into Chattanooga, the Union cavalry had an opportunity for a desperately needed rest. They were to remain at Salem until August 27, when an advance began that culminated in the battle of Chickamauga in late September. During this time, it was the function of the cavalry: "to keep the rear of Rosecrans clear of Confederate cavalry and protect his communications, also to guard the crossings on the [Tennessee] river to prevent Bragg from moving any large body of troops on the flank and rear of Rosecrans' army."[150]

"Towards the middle of July" Minty's brigade moved in a "southerly direction" into Alabama.[151] They were "engaged in scouting and clearing the country between Columbia, Tennessee and Huntsville, Alabama . . . of small bodies of rebels who were maintaining an irregular or guerrilla system of warfare."[152] As described by Adjutant Robert Burns, 4th Michigan:

> We have been constantly on the move, stopping but a few hours at a time in any place, and almost every day having a skirmish with the enemy. It has been raining every day; sometimes in perfect torrents. Having no change of clothes with us, you can easily imagine how excessively dirty we are. When it don't rain it is insufferably hot, and the men and horses steam like so many soup dishes . . .
>
> . . . [On July 13] we entered Alabama and began carrying out the President's Proclamation. There is a great difference in the treatment of the States Lincoln considers out of the Union, and those accepted by him. Every able-bodied Negro, every serviceable horse and mule is seized and confiscated. The darkeys are obliged to go with us whether they wish it or not. What is to be done with them I can't tell.[153]

The Federals would have to deal with tens of thousands of blacks who sought protection by following the armies as they moved through the South.

Sergeant Larson recalls chasing Forrest's cavalry in the vicinity of Florence, Alabama.[154] It took more than two weeks to push Forrest back across the Tennessee and prevent his planned destruction of Rosecrans's supplies.[155] During continual rains, the roads were "stirred up in a thin gruel-like substance, red or black, in which the horses stepped way over the ankle joints, splashing the thin mud over the men and horses in front of them."[156] Each man was covered with his poncho, "his head stuck through the center, the brim of his hat turned down so as to shed the pouring rain."[157] Under these conditions making camp was impossible. No fires could be built, "and no cheering and invigorating cup of coffee could be had."[158] No satisfactory sleep could be obtained; only a chance for short naps under protection of their ponchos.[159] Horses could not be unsaddled or fed, and "very often in addition to the hard marching were forced to give out."[160] If it wasn't the mud, it was the dust. As Captain Burns writes: "The dust a column of cavalry raises is suffocating. Sometimes the horse immediately preceding cannot be seen. It gets into our ears, eyes, hair, and through and under our clothes."[161] Dr. George Fish, 4th Michigan, observed, "Negroes become white, and white men dark, with coats of Tennessee dirt."[162]

August 1863—Detached Duty

"August 1863 found Minty and his cavalry deployed in support operations of the Tullahoma Campaign, assisting to drive the rebel army southward" across the Tennessee River into Alabama and Georgia.[163] Minty writes that after Rosecrans drove Bragg's army out of middle Tennessee: "he established his headquarters at Winchester, Tennessee under the shadow of the Cumberland Mountains, and devoted himself actively to the work of re-opening the railroad and accumulating supplies at the front in sufficient quantities to enable him to make a further advance."[164]

On the first day of August, Minty's brigade was detached from the Cavalry Corps and "ordered to cover the left of the army in its advance to Chattanooga" and "clear the rebel cavalry out of the country." That would be the brigade of George Dibrell's cavalry, "which was then camped in the vicinity of Sparta, Tennessee."[165] Minty reported to General Thomas Crittenden, commanding the left wing of Rosecrans's Army, with the following regiments:

> The 4th United States Cavalry, Captain James B. McIntyre commanding.
> The 4th Michigan Cavalry, Major Horace Gray commanding
> The 7th Pennsylvania Cavalry, Colonel William B. Sipes commanding
> One battalion of the 3rd Indiana Cavalry, Lieutenant-Colonel Robert Kline commanding
> One section of the Chicago Board of Trade Battery, Lieutenant Trumbull D. Griffin commanding.[166]

Minty was assigned temporarily to Brigadier General Horatio P. Van Cleve, commander of the Third Division of the Twenty-first Army Corps.[167]

During this interval, his brigade was busily employed scouting the country, providing "screening and support services for the infantry," while at the same time gathering up "a large number of stragglers from Bragg's army."[168] They were also involved in opening communications with General Burnside's Army on the left in preparation for the march on Chattanooga. Minty's brigade was camped near McMinnville, Tennessee, August 5 through 17, when it began its arduous march over the Cumberland Mountains to Pikeville, arriving there on the twentieth.

During the first few days of August, the brigade was involved in a couple of night marches "for the purpose of surprising the camp of Colonel Dibrell's confederate cavalry near Sparta." In subsequent reports to Confederate authorities, Dibrell indicated "his men were encamped upon his own farm, 2 miles south of Sparta." As noted by Colonel Minty, Dibrell obviously had the advantage, as he possessed a "thorough knowledge of his own land" and the surrounding countryside and "every cowpath."[169] Minty's comments about the unfamiliarity of the terrain were a serious issue in the Western Theater, as addressed by historian Stephen Starr:

> It is not remembered as often as it should be that with the exception of General Lee's invasion of Pennsylvania, this was an advantage every Confederate force enjoyed and a handicap every Union force had to contend against throughout the war.[170]

In February 1864, hazardous and unknown terrain would help destroy Union General Sooy Smith's ill-fated expedition to Okolona, Mississippi. It allowed General Forrest—outnumbered more than two to one—to achieve one of his greatest victories over Union cavalry at a heavy cost to the 4th US Cavalry. This handicap was also discovered by Confederate cavalryman Colonel John Hunt Morgan during his ill-fated campaign into the North in July 1863, where he found "every man, woman, and child his enemy; that every hill-top was a telegraph and every bush an ambush."[171]

Adding to Minty's frustrations was the fact that "Dibrell kept moving his camp from one locality to another every day or so."[172] Having received information on August 8 that Dibrell "was camped with his brigade about two miles south of Sparta,"

Minty "moved with seven hundred and seventy-four officers and men to attack him." The brigade marched for Spencer, "situated almost directly east from McMinnville and south of Sparta." Arriving at 11:30 p.m., the men stopped "long enough to make coffee and feed horses."[173] With a guide familiar with the "rough and rugged" terrain of the Cumberland foothills, Minty "pushed forward, across Caney Fork at the mouth of Cane Creek" and at daybreak struck Dibrell's pickets "on the east bank of Calf Killer Creek, about four miles south of Sparta."[174] Aware of Minty's advance, Dibrell "took up a strong position on a hill commanding a narrow, rickety bridge, which was the only means of crossing the creek at this point."[175]

Minty sent Captain McIntyre with the 4th Regulars to cross the creek at an "ugly, rocky ford" some distance below the bridge and "sharply attack the enemy's right." Colonel Sipes, with the 7th Pennsylvania, was to support the 4th U.S. while Minty took the 4th Michigan and 3rd Indiana on a direct attack at the bridge.[176] Having drawn Dibrell's attention with "a short, but sharp, contest at the bridge," the 4th Cavalry "touched his flank" and Dibrell, although with superior numbers, "abandoned his strong position and scattered on the run."[177] The 4th U.S., 7th Pennsylvania, and 3rd Indiana "were sent out to scour the country, which they did for five miles." However, their exhausted horses could not overtake "the freshly mounted, fast fleeing foe."[178] Minty later quotes one of Forrest's biographers as stating: "The attack was made with so much dash, that escape of any of Dibrell's men was due to the fleetness of their horses."[179] Minty's command returned to McMinnville on August 10, where it remained for a week.[180]

Expedition to Sparta and Calfkiller Creek

On the morning of August 16, Rosecrans's army began its move over the Cumberland Mountains to occupy the valleys of the Tennessee and Sequatchie Rivers.

The 4th United States was to "move on the left by Sparta, to drive back Colonel Dibrell's cavalry toward Kingston"— approximately fifty-five miles due east—where Forrest's mounted troops were concentrated. The Regulars would then cover the left flank of General Van Cleve's column as it proceeded to Pikeville.[181] Based on Sergeant Larson's previous account of Companies F and H confronting Morgan's Raiders at Bardstown and their subsequent march from Sparta to Shelbyville, this may have been the approximate time and place where the squadron found the 4th Regiment. For the first time in the war, all twelve companies of the 4th United States Cavalry were riding together. Minty's brigade marched from McMinnville at 2 a.m. on August 17 and began a "slow and tedious" climb of six hours, reaching the high table land on the summit of the Cumberland Mountains about midday.[182] After a halt of two hours to "close up the column" and feed the men and horses, the brigade crossed the "broad table land of the summit" and began the "dangerous march" down the steps of the southern side," reaching the valley of the Sequatchie. Pikeville, Tennessee, "was occupied about dark."[183]

At Pikeville, Minty learned that "Dibrell was camped near Sperry's Mill, on the banks of the Calf Killer."[184] Local citizens estimated the enemy's force at 1,500; Minty's own estimate was closer to 1,200. Minty had about 1,400 in his command.[185]

It was the worst possible ground to fight over, "wooded, hilly, rocky, broken, and intersected by half a dozen branches or creeks, with plenty of good positions, all of which [the rebels] were able to take advantage of."[186] Minty sent the 7th Pennsylvania and 4th Michigan "up the east side of Calfkiller Creek to Sperry's Mill," where they found Dibrell's brigade and quickly drove it across the creek. With the 3rd Indiana and 4th Regulars, he "moved up the west side of the creek with the intention of cutting off their retreat." However, "the broken nature of the ground . . . was so much in the enemy's favor that they had no difficulty in escaping."[187] The rebels scattered and, taking advantage of every stream and cove, fought in widely detached skirmishing parties in a line nearly five miles long.[188]

This rugged terrain almost cost Colonel Minty his life. As he was moving along the Sparta Road, on the west side of the creek, he was riding about "150 feet" ahead of the 4th U.S. with Captain Burns and Captain Vale without his usual advance guard.[189]

The march was "wearisome" and progress was made slow "by the small creeks every few miles."[190] There was a "high wooded hill" on the opposite side of the "unfordable" creek, and two regiments of Dibrell's command were lying in ambush.[191] They opened fire: "Captain Vale had four holes bored across his shoulders by a raking shot from left to right, Sergeant Birch, one of the orderlies, was shot in the thigh and his leg broken, another orderly was shot in the knee, and two privates from the 4th Michigan were also severely wounded."[192] Colonel Minty's horse received three balls—the third horse shot out from under him—and the horses of both orderlies were killed.[193] The rebels were completely concealed and the initial reaction of the men under fire had been to "run the gauntlet." Finding the fire "was getting hotter" the farther they advanced, so they hit the ground and sought shelter in the brush. As Robert Burns writes: "I was never so surprised in my life as when they opened fire on us . . . it is remarkable that we were not nearly all killed."[194]

The sound of the gunfire drew the advance squadron of the 4th U.S., who dismounted and attempted to engage the rebels across the creek. They were joined by companies of the 7th Pennsylvania and 3rd Indiana and the enemy was driven off. Unfortunately, one of the 4th Regulars—Private John M. Clark, Co. B—drowned in the attempt. The brigade bivouacked for the night near Yankeetown, "it being after eight o'clock."[195]

In its last edition, the *Chattanooga Rebel* newspaper—a "sheet about twelve inches square, and printed on one side only"—declared: "In the fight at Sparta on the 17th, the notorious Yankee cavalry general, Minty, was killed."[196] It would appear that Colonel Minty and his brigade were well known by the rebel citizens of Tennessee. At least they credited Minty with the rank he deserved.

According to Captain Vale, from the number of captured rebels taken on August 17 "representing four different regiments" of Dibrell's command, the rebel troops were highly demoralized after their confrontations with the Saber Brigade.[197]

With so much time in the field covering so much of the countryside, the condition of Minty's command was deteriorating. Minty's scouts were covering "about 150 square miles daily," and together with picketing made the duty "too heavy on both men and horses."[198] His command was "so reduced with broken horses" that he had to leave 200 troopers in McMinnville and "could turn out only 1,200 men."[199] At one point, the command actually ran out of rations, causing Minty to report to his superiors somewhat sarcastically, "You ought to keep me supplied with coffee, sugar, and salt. The men are constantly worked and should be fed."[200]

Minty's brigade returned to Pikeville on the twenty-fourth, where it was resupplied, and after a short rest sent out to make a reconnaissance in the area of Smith's Crossroads, near the Tennessee

River.²⁰¹ The brigade moved east across the Sequatchie Valley and Walden's Ridge, once again under light marching orders "without tents, clothing, baggage or wagons." The men had to go "shirtless" while theirs were being washed and dried. As Captain Burns noted: "When on a campaign, we are not models of dress and good looks. We are decidedly rough and black."²⁰²

Minty halted his command at Smith's Crossroads. He sent the 7th Pennsylvania to "scout the country as far down as Sales Creek" and the 4th United States "on a like duty up the river and beyond to Washington," forty miles north of Chattanooga. Strong pickets were placed at Blythe's ferry and other threatened points along the banks of the Tennessee River. A scouting party of the 4th U.S. was sent eastward, but failed to establish communications with General Burnside, who was advancing on Knoxville. Minty's brigade remained in the vicinity of Smith's Crossroads in the Tennessee Valley, picketing and guarding different fords and ferries on the Tennessee River until September 9.²⁰³

It had been a long, hard-fought four months since the men of the 4th United States Cavalry had distinguished themselves at Franklin, Tennessee, in April. "Constantly in the saddle and on the alert" as part of Minty's Saber Brigade, they had been effective against the best of the Confederate cavalries of Wheeler, Forrest, and Dibrell, driving them out of Tennessee across the river to Chattanooga and capturing and killing a number of officers and men.²⁰⁴ The 4th United States was involved in numerous skirmishes and battles, with victories at McMinnville, Middleton, Lebanon, and Shelbyville—names and places lost to history, but critical to the Union cause.

The 4th Regulars and Minty's brigade would now face one of their greatest challenges, when their commanding generals failed to heed their warnings of impending danger, forcing the Saber Brigade to make one of their most significant contributions of the war at the Battle of Chickamauga.

VII. The Chattanooga Campaign

The Tennessee River now formed the barrier between Rosecrans's Army of the Cumberland and Bragg's Army of Tennessee.¹ On August 27, General Rosecrans began his advance eastward from Tullahoma toward Chattanooga that would culminate in the Battle of Chickamauga (September 19-20).

In preparation for this campaign, Rosecrans overcame almost impossible logistical challenges. The area he occupied around Tullahoma "afforded no supplies of any kind. Naturally poor, it had been swept over three times by advancing and retreating armies, who made 'desolation more desolate.'" Rosecrans devoted his energies "to the perfecting of his railroad communications and to the concentration of supplies."² His quartermaster estimated in early August "that he would need 48 tons of rations, forage, and stores delivered to the railheads daily to supply the army's needs. That tonnage represented sixty loaded cars per day . . ."³ Sixty train cars of supplies would then have to be disbursed by: "4,000 six-mule wagons throughout the theater of war. This required 45,000 horses and mules, which had to carry their own feed. The manpower required for this effort would reduce Rosecrans' strength at the front to an estimated 58,000 of his 80,000 men present for duty."⁴

Rosecrans's Army crossed the Tennessee River at a point about thirty miles west of Chattanooga and established a base of supplies at Bridgeport, Alabama. Union Generals George Thomas and Alexander McCook brought their corps up south of Chattanooga, attacking the Western and Atlantic Railroad—Bragg's main supply line—and forcing him to abandon Chattanooga on September 9. Up to this point, "Old Rosy had completed a brilliant and virtually bloodless campaign."⁵

Unfortunately, from here on the Union command made a series of blunders that resulted in the Federal loss at the battle at Chickamauga. Rather than consolidating his forces at Chattanooga, Rosecrans pushed his army southward through mountain passes that caused his three corps to become widely separated and unable to communicate with one another. Meanwhile, Bragg had stopped retreating and was consolidating his forces.

On September 18, the Confederates orchestrated a massive counterattack against the disorganized Union forces along the banks of Chickamauga Creek, about twelve miles below Chattanooga. Forced to retreat, the Federals found themselves trapped in Chattanooga.

Union Order of Battle (Partial)
Army of the Cumberland
Major General William S. Rosecrans
Fourteenth Army Corps
Major General George H. Thomas
Twentieth Army Corps
Major General Alexander McDowell McCook
Twenty First Army Corps
Major General Thomas L. Crittenden
Cavalry Corps
Major General David S. Stanley (seriously ill)
Brigadier General George Crook
First Brigade
Colonel Robert H. G. Minty
4th United States Cavalry
(Cos. A, B, C, D, E, F, G, H, I, L, M)
Captain James B. McIntyre
4th Michigan Cavalry
Major Horace Gray
7th Pennsylvania Cavalry
Colonel William B. Sipes
Artillery
Chicago Board of Trade Battery
Captain James H. Stokes[6]

Brigadier General George Crook had by this time replaced General Turchin as commander of the Second Cavalry Division. Due to a miscommunication between Crook and Minty in early October 1863, Minty failed to join Crook at an appointed time; as a consequence, he was arrested for disobeying orders (that Crook never gave). Minty was later cleared of all charges, but was away from his command nearly five months, most of which he spent waiting for his court martial.

During the campaign, Minty's brigade was assigned to Brigadier General William B. Hazen's force, which was "prepared to occupy the city if the Confederates evacuated it."[7] General Crittenden's corps was ordered down the Sequatchie River, "leaving the two advance brigades under Hazen and George D. Wagner with Minty's cavalry and Wilder's mounted infantry to watch and annoy the enemy."[8] Between September 6 and 10, Minty's brigade was camped six miles north of Chattanooga at McDonald's Mill, on Sale Creek.[9] The wagon trains arrived on September 7 and "the day was spent in shoeing up the command." On the eighth, all the dismounted men were sent back to Nashville for a remount.[10]

Before attempting to cross the Tennessee River, the brigades of Hazen, Minty, Wagner, and Wilder were sent to demonstrate against Chattanooga from the north side of the Tennessee, "guarding the line of the river from Washington down to Chattanooga."[11] On September 9, the reconnaissance activities of General Crittenden's command revealed the enemy had evacuated Chattanooga, and his advance "took peaceable possession at 1 p.m."[12]

As described by Sergeant Larson, Rosecrans—believing that Bragg was retreating "and leaving the country altogether"—ordered his army to cross the Tennessee at different places "and to move out to the sides like spokes in a half wheel."[13] Hazen's and Wagner's brigades, as well as Wilder's mounted infantry, "crossed into the city... linking up with Brig. Gen. Thomas J. Wood's division of the XXI Corps."[14] Wood was one of the original captains when the 4th Cavalry was formed in 1855. On September 12, after crossing the Tennessee River at Friar's Ford, Minty's Brigade joined Wood's division. Minty, along with Wagner's infantry, remained behind to garrison Chattanooga, while Wood's division moved south of the city to occupy Lee and Gordon's Mill.[15] The 4th Michigan maintained a courier line between Rosecrans and Burnside on September 1 and were then on "courier duty between Chattanooga and Rosecrans' headquarters until September 13, when Minty's brigade was reformed to march as a unit."[16]

Rosecrans was "slow to believe" that Bragg planned to give battle, "as his army had been so badly defeated at Stones River." He pushed his army southward through mountain passes that caused his three corps to become widely separated and briefly out of contact with one another.[17] Meanwhile, Bragg had stopped retreating and was consolidating his forces at La Fayette, Georgia, about twenty-five miles south of Chattanooga. There he awaited the reinforcements of General

James Longstreet that were coming from Lee's army in the East. Rosecrans was completely unaware of this activity.

On the morning of September 13, Captain McIntyre's 4th US Cavalry—"650 strong"—reported to Major General Thomas Crittenden, commanding

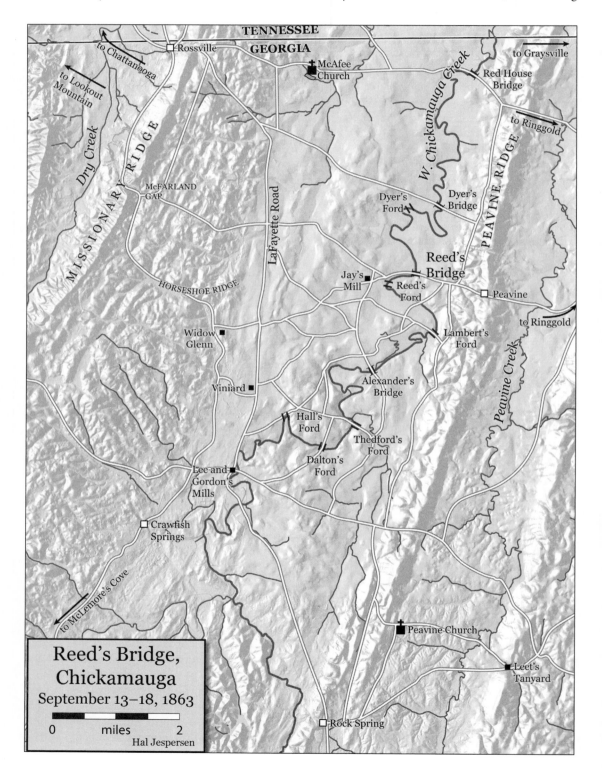

Reed's Bridge, Chickamauga
September 13–18, 1863

the XXI Army Corps.[18] The following evening Minty—with the 4th Michigan Cavalry, 7th Pennsylvania Cavalry, and one section of the Chicago Board of Trade Battery—marched from Chattanooga to Gordon's Mills and also reported to Crittenden.[19] The general, unable at the time to communicate with Rosecrans, "launched a series of probes across his front to confirm his judgment" that there were few Confederate forces nearby. On his right, he ordered the 4th United States to push southward from Crawfish Spring into McLemore's Cove. "On his left, he directed Colonel Wilder to return to the vicinity of Leet's Tanyard and Pea Vine Church to see if [Confederate General John] Pegram's cavalry was still in that area."[20] "The ride of the 4th U.S. yielded little: two prisoners gained at the cost of one Federal killed."[21] Similarly, "Wilder . . . encountered only a handful of Confederate cavalry pickets. They returned to Lee and Gordon's Mill."[22]

Meanwhile, the balance of Minty's brigade had been sent "to reconnoiter the whole front and left."[23] The men crossed the Chickamauga at Reed's Bridge and shortly before dark encamped on Pea Vine Creek, near Peeler's Mill, and sent out scouts toward Graysville, Ringgold, Leet's, and Rock Spring. At 11:30 p.m., Colonel Minty reported to General Crittenden, "the enemy was in force at Dalton, Ringgold, Leet's and Rock Spring Church."[24] Much to his surprise and consternation, Minty received the following response from Crittenden's assistant adjutant-general:

> The major-general commanding directs me to acknowledge the receipt of your report of this date informing him that Forrest is at Ringgold, Longstreet at Dalton, Pegram at Leet's and [Simon] Buckner at Rock Spring; all this would indicate infantry, which the major-general commanding cannot believe.[25]

Here begins one of the many controversies that surround the subsequent Battle of Chickamauga. In his history of Minty's regiment, Captain Vale makes the following statement:

> It will always be a source of wonder to the military student, by what, and by whose stupid blunder, it was rendered possible for an army corps of twenty thousand men, with all its artillery and transportation, to be moved from the rebel army of Virginia, not more than ten or fifteen miles in front of the Federal army of the Potomac; over six hundred miles, to the army of Bragg, on the banks of the Tennessee, without its absence being suspected, or even the movement detected, although more than a month was actually consumed in making the transfer.[26]

> . . . It was the good fortune of Minty's brigade to get and transmit the information which, though obtained when the impending blow was already descending, in some degree repaired the blunder.[27]

On September 16 and 17, Minty remained at Reed's Bridge, sending scouting parties toward Ringgold and La Fayette, where they found "large bodies of the enemy" on their front.[28] Minty's Brigade was "the only unit of consequence east of Chickamauga Creek" and, as Chickamauga historian William Glenn Robertson writes:

> . . . Minty's brigade would be the first to know if Confederate forces indeed were attempting to outflank the Army of the Cumberland in the direction of Chattanooga. Facing increasingly aggressive probes by Confederate cavalry detachments, Minty at noon [on the 17th] abandoned his advanced position at Peeler's Mill and withdrew most of his command west of Pea Vine Ridge. He retained a line of pickets along Pea Vine Creek in the valley, but saw his position becoming more precarious by the moment.[29]

According to Colonel Sipes, Minty had "uncovered Buckner's corps of Confederates, and Wilder . . . had encountered that of Polk." "Wilder and Minty united in informing Gen. Crittenden" that the Confederates were advancing, not retiring. "*Their reports were not credited*" [emphasis author].[30]

While Crittenden notes that on September 16, "nothing occurred of particular interest this day," Minty was dealing with the reality of the situation.[31] His pickets were being met by "strong scouting parties from toward Ringgold and Leet's . . . and the pickets on the La Fayette and Harrison road, which lies between Pea Vine ridge and Chickamauga, were attacked," and his rear threatened.[32] Minty "fell back to the west side of the ridge," covering Reed's Bridge.

A small party of scouts led by Lieutenant Rendlebock, 4th US Cavalry, ran into a column of Buckner's infantry moving from Rock Spring to Ringgold and lost one man "shot through the head."[33] That was Sergeant Martin J. Murphy, Co. G, who was reported killed in action "near Ringgold, Ga.," on September 16.[34] Crittenden dismissed the incident, saying, "It could be nothing but dismounted cavalry."[35] It was now obvious to Minty that "all the intelligence gathered by his trusted troopers had fallen on deaf ears at 21st Corps headquarters."[36]

On September 17, Colonel Wilder's brigade of mounted infantry, along with four pieces of artillery, took a position on the west side of the Chickamauga at Alexander's Bridge, about 1,600 yards south of Reed's bridge. On the evening of the seventeenth, Minty's and Wilder's Brigades were still the only Union forces beyond the Chickamauga.[37] Just before sunset, Wilder "climbed a tree . . . to have a look around. To the southeast he noticed a large dust cloud . . . two and a half miles from Alexander's Bridge. 'That,' he remarked, 'is the advance of Bragg's army.'" The report of large dust clouds "across the entire front" by scouts and casual observers "seemingly prompted no action by Rosecrans."[38]

That day, Sergeant Larson's mess mates "had got hold of a nice fat sheep and some sweet potatoes, cabbage and onions," but it was too late to cook that night; they "planned a great feast in the morning." At daylight they were up, caring for their horses, "while the cook fixed up the fire and began to prepare the soup." The cook called in an assistant to "make some pancakes and a more than usually large amount of extra strong coffee."

A delightful aroma began to permeate the campsite.[39] At 8 a.m., the Confederate Army struck. "All of a sudden shots were fired at our picket post on the other side of the Chickamauga . . . which rapidly increased to volleys." The men ran to their horses and saddled up without waiting for orders. The trumpeter sounded "boots and saddles" and then "to horse." Only four pancakes were done, which were quickly divided up, and with half a pancake for breakfast, Larson and his mess mates began the "great Battle of Chickamauga."[40]

September 18—Reed's Bridge

"The winding Chickamauga River coursed between the armies as it flowed north to join the Tennessee."[41] The Army of the Cumberland—in unfamiliar territory and "victimized by the confusing roads"—was separated over a wide area "which rendered them incapable of supporting one another."[42] Two divisions under General Thomas's command made their camp three miles west of Reed's Bridge.[43] Believing the Union Army was widely scattered, Confederate General Bragg created a "strategically sound plan intended to cut off Rosecrans from Chattanooga by first throwing his right across Chickamauga Creek north of Crittenden's corps, sweeping upstream along the west bank while the rest of the army attacked at Lee & Gordon's Mill, then driving the Federals into McLemore's Cove."[44] Reed's Bridge and Alexander's Bridge—approximately ten miles southeast of Chattanooga—were essential crossing points for the Confederate Army, allowing the heavy artillery and quartermaster wagons to cross the river in a timely manner. These bridges were also to be used by Forrest's cavalry, which was assigned to cover Bushrod Johnson's flanks and front.[45] General Polk was to lead this offensive, crossing Chickamauga Creek with Johnson's division, consisting of "four infantry brigades, five batteries," and supported by Forrest's cavalry in the advance. "Johnson was confident he could deal with whatever enemy force he encountered at Reed's Bridge."[46]

The attack began early in the morning of September 18, and Minty's three regiments, including the 4th United States Cavalry and Wilder's four regiments—"fewer than 3,000 Federal troops"—stood "directly in the path of Bragg's proposed three-corps juggernaut."[47] Earlier that morning, Colonel Minty placed his brigade on the east side of the bridge in anticipation of the advancing rebel army. A fierce battle ensued that intensified throughout the day. Minty's Brigade was slowly forced back across Reed's Bridge, where it made its stand. In his remembrances of the war, Robert Minty writes: "The Battle of Chickamauga, as told in history, lasted two days, the 19th and 20th of September, 1863." In reality, the battle began on the eighteenth, when the Saber Brigade and Wilder's mounted infantry held off the advance of the Confederate Army at Reed's and Alexander's Bridges. As Minty correctly points out, the "stubborn fighting on the 18th has never been properly appreciated in full value."[48]

Bragg's plans were frustrated when his advancing army was stalled at the Chickamauga. Had he succeeded, he may well have overwhelmed Rosecrans's army. The time bought by Minty's and Wilder's brigades allowed Rosecrans to reposition and concentrate his scattered forces. To have given credit due at the time would have been to admit the failures on the part of the Union general command that nearly caused the destruction of the Army of the Cumberland. It would take a century and a new generation of historians for the complete story to be told.

The Stand at Reed's Bridge

The first shots in the memorable battle of Chickamauga were undoubtedly Fired by the 4th US Cavalry . . . – Sergeant James Larson[49]

September 18, 1863, dawned "cool and cloudy–autumn weather."[50] Colonel Minty—more aware than his commanding generals of the approaching Confederate Army—prepared accordingly. In the early hours of the morning at his camp on the east side of the Chickamauga near Reed's Bridge, Minty "had the men quietly aroused before daylight, the horses fed, and the men directed to prepare and eat their breakfasts; and at daylight had the horses saddled, the artillery harnessed, and the baggage loaded up."[51]

At 6 a.m., he sent one hundred men of the 4th United States (Companies A, B, C, I, and M) toward Leet's Tanyard, about eight miles southwest of Ringgold and just east of Pea Vine Creek; another hundred men from the 4th Michigan and 7th Pennsylvania were sent toward Ringgold.[52] By 6:30 a.m., Minty was moving the balance of his brigade to the east slope of Pea Vine Ridge.[53]

Around 7 a.m., Minty received couriers from both scouting parties "with the information that the enemy was advancing in force."[54] He immediately strengthened his pickets on the La Fayette road and "moved forward with the 4th Michigan, one battalion of the 4th Regulars, and a section of artillery," taking position on the eastern slope of Pea Vine Ridge and "ready to contest the advance of the approaching enemy."[55]

All the while, Minty was busily dispatching couriers to Granger and Crittenden. "The enemy, infantry in force, was advancing steadily," driving in his skirmishers. They were followed moments later by his patrols, "closely followed by the rebels, who advanced a strong skirmish-line, followed by heavy columns, on the Ringgold and Leet's (or Lafayette) roads."[56] Newly commissioned 2nd Lieutenant Henry Potter, 4th Michigan, reported seeing the rebel line "in strong force," its artillery "plainly visible in the road."[57]

The 7th Pennsylvania scouting party ran into Bushrod Johnson's command of 4,700 at Pea Vine Creek, supported by Forrest's cavalry. A skirmish followed and "the Pennsylvanians lost five men killed by artillery and musket fire"; the first Union casualties in the Battle of Chickamauga.[58] The "outnumbered cavalry-men, popping away with their carbines were buying precious time." Temporarily held in check, the Confederate infantry halted, during which time Minty was able to position the Chicago Board of Trade Battery "and form a line of battle overlooking Pea Vine valley where the skirmish was going on."[59] Minty "again advanced and drove the rebel skirmish line over the ridge and back on their line of battle in the valley." By this time, Minty could see "thirteen sets of regimental colors" and estimated at least 7,000 men advancing toward his position.[60]

As the head of one of the columns came within range, Lieutenant Trumbull Griffin opened fire with two of his guns, doing "considerable execution."[61] This "checked the enemy" and "caused them to deploy." Believing there was a strong force opposing them, the rebels took "considerable time getting into position."[62] After "several hours," Johnson was "heavily reinforced by both infantry and artillery" and made a flank movement that "compelled Minty to retire" to the vicinity of Reed's Bridge.[63] Lieutenant Potter saw "a strong flanking party" moving to his right as he, along with the 4th Regulars, was ordered to fall back.[64] He took his men into a cornfield on their right and up a hill to support the artillery. Potter could see "the clouds of dust of a heavy column" moving toward them on the left. The Chicago Battery opened fire again and was "answered promptly by the rebels with four pieces." As the smoke cleared, the men were ordered to fall back and rejoin their regiments. Sergeant Larson's company was part of the battalion moved back towards Reed's Bridge "to prevent [the Confederates] from crossing that bridge and fording places in that locality."[65]

Bushrod Johnson "sent his entire line across Pea Vine Valley and up the slopes of Pea Vine Ridge. . . . Minty could see the strength of the force opposing him in front, as well as another dust cloud moving north toward more crossings of the Chickamauga downstream from his location." He delayed Johnson "as best he could," but was forced "to relinquish the crest of the ridge."[66] Lieutenant Potter and the men of the 4th Michigan retreated through the woods, where they encountered rebel infantry. Dismounting half of the men, they gave battle, but were driven back by "overpowering numbers." Forming in line again, they were again driven back, through their camp and "past the 'Regulars,' towards the river."[67] Minty had no illusions about the force he was facing. "Instead of standing, and fighting, [he] intended to delay the Rebels as much as possible. Each time they organized into a line of battle to attack, he gave ground."[68]

At 11:45 a.m., "Federal signalmen on Lookout Mountain continued to report [to headquarters] the progress of the massive dust cloud toward the lower Chickamauga crossings at Reed's and Alexander's bridges." At 12:40 p.m., Rosecrans's Chief of Staff, James A. Garfield, reported that Minty's cavalrymen "were heavily engaged in the vicinity of Reed's Bridge, and that a major Confederate turning movement was probably in progress."[69]

At Alexander's Bridge, Wilder's brigade "had repulsed a late morning cavalry charge near the creek" and began to destroy the bridge. "Wooden guard rails on both sides were hacked down and flooring planks pried loose . . . rendering the structure impassable." The men used the boards to construct a crescent-shaped barrier facing south, and "crowded inside the makeshift fort to await developments." By 1 p.m., the Confederates had "five regiments in a long line of battle 900 yards from the bridge" and "skirmishers were thrown out 200 yards." The Confederates began to move forward.[70] Wilder, with "less than 1,000 men to dispute any bridge crossing," realized that "his own left and rear were only secure so long as Minty held out at Reed's Bridge."[71]

By 2 p.m., Minty "had resisted Johnson for seven hours." He was "finally driven off Pea Vine Ridge." Finding his position "most perilous," Minty "decided it was time to get over the Chickamauga as soon as possible."[72] Reed's Bridge "was a narrow, frail structure which was planked with loose boards and fence-rails . . . only wide enough to allow two men to ride abreast."[73] There was also "a bad ford about 300 yards higher up" near which was the Reed house and orchard.[74] Minty sent his battery across the ford with Captain McCormick's battalion of the 4th U.S. as support.[75] The two guns were "masked behind some shrubs near the ford on high ground . . . where they could command both the bridge and ford."[76] Minty then sent his ambulances and baggage across the bridge.[77] Orders were given to "form skirmish lines by companies" facing the advancing rebels.[78] "A tremendous fusillade was opened on the enemy at once, which had the effect of checking them up short."[79] Minty gave orders for Captain McIntyre to cross the bridge with the remainder of the 4th U.S.[80] The old bridge "swayed to and fro, creaking and groaning as if ready to fall at any moment . . . crossing had to be done very slowly and carefully."[81] Just as the 4th Regulars started to cross, "the head of a rebel column, carrying their arms at right shoulder shift, and moving at the double-quick as steadily as if at drill, came through the gap not 500 yards from the bridge."[82] Lieutenant Griffin's artillery "opened on them with canister . . . which took them by surprise and immediately checked their advance."[83] As the rebels were deploying: "the 7th Pennsylvania and 4th Michigan delivered a terrific saber charge, riding into the thronging masses of their infantry and hewing them down by the score," their field of battle now "confined to a space not more than two hundred yards in greatest diameter."[84]

The balance of the 4th U.S.—with the exception of Lieutenant Wirt Davis's squadron—made it across the bridge. It was followed by the 4th Michigan as rebel reinforcements began arriving, along with artillery fire "sweeping the entire space."[85] For a moment, it looked "as if the whole brigade east of the creek would be captured or annihilated."[86] Captain McCormick's battalion that had been supporting Lieutenant Griffin's artillery "wheeled and made a most daring and desperate saber charge," clearing space and gaining time for the 7th Pennsylvania to complete its crossing.[87] It was also "most gallantly covered by Lieutenant Davis' squadron, the last to cross the bridge."[88]

Once across the bridge, Lieutenant Potter, along with men of the 7th Pennsylvania, "formed a line to cover the retreat of the 4th Regulars." Several were wounded by artillery fire before withdrawing into the woods.[89] Lieutenant Davis and a few of his men halted on the bridge that was being "raked by rebel artillery" and "tore up the rails and boards, sending them floating down the stream."[90] The rebels were making a "desperate effort to gain possession of the bridge" before it was destroyed.[91] Minty placed his artillery in a position to "dispute passage" and Lieutenant Griffin's guns returned fire "so thoroughly that the enemy had to fall back in confusion."[92] With the exception of a picket of the 4th Michigan that "made a gallant resistance and eventually swam the creek without the loss of a man," all of the Federal forces were now across the river.[93]

The 4th Cavalry at Reed's Bridge. Outnumbered seven to one, Minty's Brigade held up the advance of 7,000 rebel infantry for ten hours. From an A. R. Waud wartime sketch first appearing in *The Mountain Campaigns in Georgia* by Jos. M Brown, 1895.

It was now about 3 p.m. Minty's brigade and artillery battery held a good position "on a slight ridge 750 yards west of the bridge and prepared to continue its resistance to the Confederate advance."[94] Minty's command now had the advantage of heavy timber on their side of the Chickamauga, with the rebels on open ground in front.[95]

It didn't take long for Johnson's infantry and cavalry to reach the creek. Nathan Bedford Forrest "rode calmly across the bridge and took the measure of the defenders." Finding the bridge still serviceable, Forrest sent the 23rd Tennessee Infantry across.[96] "Raising the Rebel Yell, they rushed the damaged structure at double quick. Five Tennesseans were shot down, including the regimental color bearer."[97] Some time was consumed in getting Johnson's entire division across.[98] They "formed in an open field facing Minty's handful of cavalrymen."[99] Minty's cavalry "continued its stubborn defense for another hour, shooting over the creek at any visible movement."[100] Both sides were now firing their artillery. Two of the rebels' guns were damaged.[101]

Minty's position was untenable. At about 3:34 p.m., he received a message from the officer in charge of his wagon train at Gordon's Mill that Wilder had fallen back from Alexander's Bridge to Gordon's Mill and the enemy was crossing in force at all points.[102] The Confederate artillery battery "began to hammer Minty's position on the ridge to the west, shooting a wheel off one of the Chicago Board of Trade Battery's guns."[103] There was no option but to retreat southward toward the main army.[104] At about 4:30 p.m., Minty began to withdraw "via William Jay's stream sawmill and the Brotherton Road to the La Fayette-Rossville road, then southward in search of friendly units."[105] The enemy followed closely, "firing in their rear," with Minty's cavalrymen "continually turning back to check them."[106] "With 973 men, the First Brigade had disputed the advance of 7,000 rebels from 7 o'clock in the morning until 5 in the evening, and at the end of that time had fallen back only 5 miles."[107] By their own reports, the rebels had suffered severe losses at both Reed's and Alexander's Bridges.[108] "One hundred and two rebel graves at Reed's Bridge" and "105 killed and wounded at Alexander's Bridge" attest to the effectiveness of the cavalry's resistance to the rebel crossing of the Chickamauga.[109] Union casualties were surprisingly light at fewer than a dozen killed.[110] Of more importance, Minty and Wilder had "completely upset the Confederate plan" for a quick crossing at both points and prevented a combined sweep upstream into Crittenden's flank.[111] Crittenden's corps might have been "annihilated before Thomas could have got within supporting distance," leaving Rosecrans severely crippled.[112] This critical delay gave Rosecrans time to concentrate his corps so that, on the morning of September 19, his army was in a better position to receive Bragg.[113]

The day-long ordeal for the 4th US Cavalry and the Saber Brigade was not yet over.

The Night of September 18–19

In the early evening of the eighteenth, Bushrod Johnson's leading skirmishers "stumbled upon Wilder's videttes." Fighting continued until Wilder disengaged at 7 p.m. and retired "several hundred yards closer to East Viniard Field," where he was soon joined by Minty's Brigade.[114] Wilder was facing northeast and Minty took a position "800 yards to the right, placing his tired troopers in a field west of Hall's Ford."[115] They were soon joined by several other regiments on Minty's right "facing the Chickamauga."[116] Everyone was ordered dismounted and "took position in line as infantry."[117] "The line formed by the 4th US Cavalry ran through a large field just inside of the fence."[118] "Horses and mules were led to the rear, while a rough barricade of decaying logs, fence rails and rocks was scratched together."[119] "The crude fieldworks were completed 'not a minute too soon.'"[120] At dusk, heavy skirmishing was heard on the road.[121] The enemy was pushing forward again. A sharp fight took place, the brunt of which was borne by the 59th Ohio Infantry. Darkness "put an end to the day's work."[122] Bushrod Johnson, "surprised at the stiff opposition, believed 'the whole Yankee army was in our front,' and ordered his regiments to bivouac in place." "Pickets were posted as far forward as possible" and "one-third of the Confederates were told to remain awake while the rest of his men slept with weapons close at hand."[123]

The Federal cavalry "remained all night in line of battle as infantry," suffering from cold and hunger—"not a mouthful since breakfast."[124] Since no engagement was expected on the eighteenth, no extra rations were issued.[125] The men were allowed no fires.[126] In their "light marching order," they had no overcoats and their ponchos and extra saddle blankets were with the horses far back in the woods.[127] The men were not allowed to get up, but had to "lie close to the damp and cold ground– their gun beside them–and keep very quiet, as the enemy was within 100 yards."[128] "The usual order to keep awake was given," but there was no need, since the men "were all too busy shaking with cold to find time or inclination for sleep."[129] It was so cold during the long, starless night "that the frost fell on the leaves and grass" and the men suffered severely.[130] They could hear the noise of "thousands of troops moving into the woods," taking up positions to the north. The rebels in the woods were so close they could be heard when they spoke loudly.[131] "The rumbling of the enemy's moving artillery and ammunition wagons never ceased the whole night."[132] Many expected "at earliest dawn to be annihilated." If the enemy attacked, "very few would escape alive."[133]

Colonel Minty spent the bitterly cold night worrying about his "worn out and weary" men. At 2 a.m., in an effort to find relief for his troopers, he mounted his horse and rode back toward Gordon's Mill. They had had "no food or rest for nearly twenty-one hours."[134] General John M. Palmer relieved both Minty's and Wilder's brigades.[135] At daybreak, the infantry moved into position behind them and they "retired to the rear–to a large cornfield west from Gordon's Mill," where the horses were fed and the men received "the first mouthful of food" they'd had in twenty-six hours.[136] Minty's brigade remained at Gordon's Mill until noon on the nineteenth.[137]

VIII. The Battle of Chickamauga Creek

Saturday, September 19

Dawn of September 19 found both fronts solidly facing one another along a six-mile line.[1] The opposing forces were fairly evenly matched, with between 60,000 and 62,500 in action on each side.[2] When one of Thomas's brigades—operating under erroneous information—stumbled upon Forrest's dismounted cavalry, fighting erupted along most of the battle line. "A fierce fight ensued," with Forrest calling for infantry support and being reinforced by at least three other brigades.[3] The Battle of Chickamauga "had been joined at a time and place which caught both Rosecrans and Bragg out of position."[4] Throughout the day there was "intermittent but fierce fighting."[5] Dr. Fish, 4th Michigan, writes:

For nine hours on Saturday there was not one moment's cessation to the roll of musketry. Men who have been in twenty battles say they have never heard anything to compare with this. I am worn out, weary, and nearly sick, and my heart is sad over the gallant dead.[6]

By the end of the day losses were enormous on both sides, but neither gained any significant advantage. By nightfall, "the battle sinks to a standstill." The next day, the Confederates launched an attack against Thomas's corps and "in the confusion of sending reinforcements," Rosecrans issued a controversial order that would nearly destroy his army, cost him his command, and made the reputation of his successor, General George H. Thomas.[7]

Earlier that morning, Colonel Minty was called to Rosecrans's headquarters at the widow Glenn's house. The general told him of reports that Forrest was somewhere between them and Chattanooga, "playing havoc with our transportation." Minty was to "go out there and take care of him."[8] Since Forrest would soon be engaged in the primary battle along Chickamauga Creek near Jay's Mill, this information was apparently in error. Following orders, Minty moved his brigade "along the rear to the left to protect the [wagon] trains going into Chattanooga." He found the road to Chattanooga "entirely unobstructed by the enemy" and so reported to Rosecrans.[9] According to Sergeant Larson, that morning the 4th US Cavalry was assigned for a few hours to a duty he "always did hate, in support of the reserve artillery." The men were out of the action and "compelled to stand inactive, listening to the roar of battle and see the hospital ambulances passing slowly, one after another, each carrying its load of wounded and moaning soldiers," a sight that made Larson "sick at heart." The 4th Regulars rejoined their brigade at Rossville later that day.[10]

After reporting back to Rosecrans, Minty was sent to General George Thomas, who told him to report to General Granger, commanding the Reserve Corps in front of Rossville—a pivotal mountain pass to Chattanooga.[11] Arriving late in the evening, Minty met with Granger, who ordered him to "move to his left and to guard the fords at and near Mission Mills," and to be in position as early as possible in the morning.[12] At 5 a.m. on Sunday, September 20, the brigade marched to Mission Mills on Missionary Ridge to "watch the left flank of the army."[13] Minty's pickets took possession of the fords, and "strong patrols" were sent to Chickamauga Station and Graysville.[14] They were to hold the enemy's cavalry in check on their right, "from the direction of Ringgold and Graysville."[15] The 4th United States was "posted at Mission Mills to guard the ford at that point."[16]

SUNDAY, SEPTEMBER 20

At dawn on the twentieth, the sky was "red and sultry, the atmosphere and all the woods enveloped in fog and smoke."[17] This day would see some of the fiercest fighting experienced by either army. The battle swayed back and forth indecisively, both sides losing about twenty-eight percent of their strength.[18] "The Confederates struggled determinedly to flank the Federals but Thomas' men held at the breastworks." He called for assistance at 9 a.m.[19] Around 11 a.m., General Rosecrans, "mistaken as to the location of his divisions in the thick brush," made a "strange and fatal error."[20] In the confusion of reinforcing Thomas, Rosecrans created a gap in his center at precisely the spot where General James Longstreet's heavy assault wave struck. The Confederates sent "20,000 men charging through, cutting the Union in two by mid-day, routing the Yankees."[21] Thousands of Federals were killed or captured, and the rest were running.

Because of his position on the extreme left of the Union army, Minty was completely unaware of the disaster befalling Rosecrans. Between 2 and 3 p.m., he received orders to take possession of the position occupied by General Granger on the Rossville and Ringgold road.[22] The brigade "moved from Missionary Ridge down the road toward Ringgold."[23] Upon arriving, Minty discovered that General Granger had already "marched to the assistance of General Thomas."[24] Not knowing what was in front of him, he "pushed forward toward Red House Bridge [Ringgold Bridge]" and found Colonel John Scott's Confederate brigade of cavalry and mounted infantry "1,500 strong, moving into position" on the west side of the creek.[25] There was a "spirited skirmish of about an hour's duration," with considerable loss to the enemy. Minty's Brigade drove the rebels about two miles across the creek at Red House Bridge, taking possession of the bridge.[26] It was getting dark and Minty returned to McAfee's Church, "the position which General Granger had occupied." There were no other units in the area and the brigade "remained in position all night, sitting on the ground" holding their horses and "procuring but little rest." The men, "worn out with three days' of fighting and want of food," were thoroughly chilled.[27]

Meanwhile, General Thomas maintained firm control of his troops and assumed a virtually impregnable position on Snodgrass Hill and Horseshoe Ridge. Repulsing repeated rebel assaults while holding his position, Thomas was "facing the fight of his life."[28] His men desperately turned back wave after wave of attacks—bayonet charges and hand-to-hand fighting—as the Confederates attacked the slopes.[29] An officer with Forrest's cavalry described the scene:

> Neighing horses, wild and frightened, were running in every direction; whistling, seething crackling bullets, the piercing screaming fragments of the shells, the whirring sound of shrapnel and the savage shower of canister, mingled with the fierce answering yells of defiance, all united in one horrid sound. The ghastly, mangled dead and horribly wounded strewed the earth for over half a mile up and down the river banks. The dead were piled upon each other in ricks, like cordwood, to make passage for advancing columns. The sluggish stream of Chickamauga ran red with human blood.
> . . . I had been in 60 battles and skirmishes up to this time, but nothing like this had I ever seen. Men fought like demons.[30]

At 3 p.m., when Thomas was nearly out of ammunition and was threatened from the rear, Gordon Granger's Reserve Corps reinforced him from the north. Thomas held the position until nightfall, then began his withdrawal to Rossville.[31] The "routed Yankees streamed toward Chattanooga," carrying Generals McCook and Crittenden with them.[32] "A panicky and demoralized Rosecrans flees to Chattanooga, assuming his whole army is being destroyed."[33]

The Lost Patrol

Colonel Minty and his brigade were not the only ones "in the dark" the night of September 20. Second Lieutenant Bird Fletcher, Co. H, ordered Sergeant Larson to "take 20 men and form them into a skirmish line as far as they would reach, at a reasonable distance apart, in the woods between the cavalry and infantry position."[34] He was to hold the position until relieved:

> . . . No other orders were given and were not necessary. All soldiers know that they are to hold their ground until relieved or driven back by a superior force. But the number of men I had was not enough to form an effective line thru that woods and underwood. . . . Consequently my little party became an isolated body, standing in woods and thick bushes without any connection or view of other troops at either end.[35]

There they remained, listening to the sounds of battle all around them:

> . . . The battle raged furiously for hours. By the noise and cheering it was often evident that charges were being made by one or the other of the contending lines. From my place it was impossible to tell which was victorious . . . About the middle of the afternoon the fury of the battle subsided as if one or the other side had been victorious. The noise seemed all of a sudden to have moved far away to the right where it was still booming and roaring.[36]

The sounds of the battle gradually faded from the center toward the right, "and finally it ceased entirely . . . Night came, and the moon rose higher and higher; everything was still as death. . . . Things really looked dubious."[37] In fact, Larson's squadron had been abandoned by the routed and retreating Union forces; he was now on his own in totally unfamiliar territory. Because of his position in the forest, Larson was unable to determine the outcome of the battle: "As I had no right to leave my post... I continued to ride up and down the line wondering what it all meant."[38]

Around ten p.m., Sergeant Larson "decided to take some action on the matter." His first concern was to find out where the Confederates were. Leaving his men, he rode back in the direction of Lee and Gordon's Mill, but was waved off by a black boy who informed him that Forrest's men were there. Rejoining his squadron, he decided to move on the main road toward Rossville, where they came across a house on the right-hand side of the road. As Larson and one of his men moved cautiously within sight of the house, his companion, Corporal Edward Sweeny, whispered, "By God, Sergeant, the house is full of Rebs!"[39] Realizing they may have been spotted, and that it would be fatal to try to run, Larson—in a most audacious act of bravery— "carelessly dismounted" and walked into the house. Turning to one of the men, he asked, "Can anybody here tell me where the damn Yanks went to that were at the mill to-day?"[40] Assuming him to be "a reckless spy" dressed in a Yankee uniform, he was told, "They took the road toward Rossville about the middle of the afternoon." Larson thanked them and walked out of the room.[41]

Sergeant Larson and his men found their brigade and arrived at the camp of Co. H, 4th U.S., after midnight. The sergeant subsequently published several accounts of this event, one of which was responded to by retired Brigadier General Robert Minty on November 9, 1893, in *The National Tribune*. He registers surprise, hearing of the incident for the first time. While not doubting Larson's story, Minty wrote: "I cannot but express my surprise that such a splendid soldier as was commander of that regiment, Capt. James B. McIntyre, should have been guilty of such neglect." It may well be that Captain McIntyre was also unaware of what had happened, as Larson did not report the incident to his superiors.[42]

As previously mentioned, there was apparently some animosity between Sergeant Larson and Lieutenant Fletcher. The two men had enlisted prior to the Civil War: Fletcher in December 1859, and Larson in June 1860. Larson had been a sergeant since the spring of 1862. When Fletcher received his commission in February 1863, he was still a corporal; now he was Larson's superior officer. This may explain the apparent friction between the two.

The following statement appears in Larson's autobiography that wasn't published until 1935:

> The very first man I met was Lieutenant Fletcher and the remark he made when he saw me confirmed the opinion I had formed that I was left there purposely. I never could get myself to believe it to be by neglect or carelessness. . . . As soon as he saw me he said: 'Why, Sergeant, I certainly did not expect to see you again; at least not for a long time.' There could be no other meaning taken from those words than that it was expected that we would be killed or captured. I made no other report to him than simply that I had brought all my men in. I did not care to have anything more said about it. That was the reason it did not come to General Minty's ears until a long time afterward.[43]

Under the circumstances, this heroic act of bravery that resulted in saving the lives of twenty men in his charge would have brought a commendation, if not a promotion; Minty implied as much in his 1893 article. Larson responded in his autobiography:

> . . . As to a commission I did not care for that anyhow. I would probably have had to go into a volunteer regiment and that I would not do. I would sooner be a sergeant in the regular army than a commissioned officer in the *untrained and undisciplined volunteer service* [emphasis author].[44]

Years later, when he was the plaintiff in a lawsuit that went all the way to the Supreme Court, Fletcher's character seems to have come into question. Incapacitated for service, Captain Fletcher retired in June 1868 and was receiving retired officers pay. In 1872, he was brought up on charges of not paying his debts and of conduct "unbecoming an officer and a gentleman." He was found guilty and dismissed from the service. Sixteen years later, he petitioned Congress for "redress and restoration to the retired list," which was ultimately denied by the United States Supreme Court.[45]

Retreat to Chattanooga

The battle lost, Thomas began his slow retreat to Chattanooga, covered by Minty's Brigade and the 4th US Cavalry. Thomas's obstinate stand ensured that Union forces "still held and covered the road from Rossville" through the mountain gap to Chattanooga, making it difficult for the enemy to follow up the retreat.[46] Minty's command had taken possession of the Rossville and Ringgold road, "about a half mile in advance of the gap," at 2 p.m. September 20. Thomas began his withdrawal around 5:30 p.m. that evening.[47]

That night, after the men of the 4th Cavalry had taken care of their horses, they "gulped down a quart and a half of the black coffee quickly manufactured by Gum [their black cook]," chewed "some crackers and raw bacon," and "rolled up in their blankets and slept until about 3 o'clock [a.m.], when the brigade quietly saddled up and moved into a position in Thomas's new line as infantry."[48] With their horses taken to the rear, the men "stood in a field along a rail fence" where they "built barricades with rails and other stuff," and by "break of day stood ready for the expected advance and attack" of the Confederate Army. "The sun rose in a clear sky and climbed gradually up over the treetops; noon came and passed, but no enemy appeared."[49]

On September 21, Thomas's battered army moved toward Rossville and through the pass to Chattanooga.[50] The First Brigade guarded the gap at and above Rossville.[51] General Thomas received a message from Colonel Minty at 10 a.m. that "the enemy were advancing on him with a strong force of cavalry and infantry." Thomas directed Minty to "retire through the gap and post his command on our left flank, and throw out strong reconnoitering parties across the ridge to observe and report any movements of the enemy on our left front."[52] That night, Thomas withdrew from Rossville and, as Rosecrans writes: "took firm possession of the objective point of our campaign–Chattanooga–and prepared to hold it."[53] Thomas instructed Minty "to delay the enemy" as long as possible without "unnecessarily endangering his command."[54] He needed time to prepare his army to defend Chattanooga. "Near sunset Minty's brigade was withdrawn from the line and mounted."[55] Larson wrote:

> The 4th US Cavalry took the direct road to Rossville. . .the other regiments moved off along the ridge some distance in rear of Thomas' position and we did not see them again until late next morning. We arrived at the old Ross house, standing close by the road, a little after sundown.[56]

The 4th Regulars found themselves "at the foot of the mountain near the gap where the road to Chattanooga passes through." The men dismounted and "stood to horse." They spent the entire night standing by their horses, "rein in hand ready to mount in a moment." Another "supperless, sleepless night" without campfires:

> The balance of the brigade held similar position on the other side of the road and farther down the Mission Ridge. When night was well advanced, Thomas' retreating, but not defeated, army began to come down the road through the gap on their way back to Chattanooga. The men moved very quietly. Not a sound or voice could be heard as they passed us, and the artillery which followed in the rear of each division had the wheels wrapped with blankets so that they made no more noise than a bundle of straw coming rolling down the road.[57]

"We realized," writes Larson, "the fact that the great Army of the Cumberland had been defeated in battle . . . There was one consolation left for us, however, and that was the fact that the army had not been beaten. It had simply been outgeneraled and outnumbered."[58]

Minty was at Rossville with his brigade by 2 a.m. on September 22, and during the night, the 4th Cavalry was moved to take possession of the gap vacated by the retiring infantry.[59] At dawn, they were ordered to mount up and move into the woods, taking the most advanced position and forming "one long skirmish line."[60] As the men began moving "through the woods parallel to the road to Chattanooga," they began receiving fire from Forrest's cavalry.[61] The 4th Regulars began to withdraw, moving slowly back.[62] Hearing the firing in the direction of Rossville at around 6 a.m., Minty "marched with the 7th Pennsylvania and 4th Michigan to support the 4th Regulars." It appeared the Confederates were "advancing on the road from the battlefield and from Ringgold," and Minty found that Captain McIntyre had "judiciously fallen back."[63] According to Colonel Minty, "This was all cavalry, and consisted of Pegram's Division and Scott's and Davidson's Brigades."[64] By 7 a.m., Minty's cavalry was "showing a bold front on every possible occasion and checking the enemy as much as possible."[65] He began retreating to Chattanooga, "skirmishing sharply" with the rebels over the rough terrain.[66] Larson describes the difficulties:

> . . . skirmishing in the weeds they had an advantage over us, as they were on foot

and we remained mounted. They could take shelter behind trees so that we could seldom see any of them plainly. We had no shelter and sat high up among the leaves and limbs, which also obstructed our view; therefore our loss was heavier in going through the woods than after we got out on flat country and several of our men were left there. Those who were seriously wounded had to be abandoned to the mercy of the enemy. Cavalry, when covering a retreat, have not the benefit of hospital service; neither stretchers nor ambulances are used. A badly wounded man is simply left on the ground. His comrades are unable to give him any assistance.[67]

Even with this disadvantage, Minty's cavalry held the rebels in check. Forrest later wrote: "I vigorously attacked them with Dibrell's command dismounted, *but I could not move them* [emphasis author]."[68] At 1 p.m., Minty's brigade "passed inside [the] lines in front of Chattanooga." It had taken the rebels six hours to drive the brigade the four miles between Rossville and the advanced works at Chattanooga.[69] The men of the 4th US Cavalry finally got some desperately needed food, water, and rest. "The camp we were assigned was very handy," writes Larson:

> It was a big space enclosed by a fence, with plenty of water and the quartermaster has also provided forage, both corn and hay, and our horses were watered and fed at once. The pack mules had arrived the evening before, and old Gum was on hand with his delightful black coffee and fried bacon and had also prepared a big kettle of boiled beans. We had a very solid meal, after which we were prepared to take a good long sleep, to make up for lost time . . .[70]

Of the actions of Minty's and Wilder's Brigades on September 18, it has been written this "obstinate stand of two Brigades of Rosecrans' cavalry against the Confederate infantry gave time for the formation of Union lines," allowing Rosecrans to position his army to meet the Confederate attack.[71] Combined with Thomas's heroic stand on the twentieth that "bought an afternoons time," these actions—strongly supported by Minty's Brigade and the 4th United States Cavalry—allowed the Union army to escape total destruction and retreat to the safety of Chattanooga.[72] Rosecrans writes in his after-battle report: "On the 20th Minty covered our left and rear at Missionary Mills, and later in the day on the Ringgold road":

> On the 21st the cavalry still covered our right as securely as before, fighting and holding at bay very superior numbers. The number of cavalry combats during the whole campaign have been numerous, the successes as numerous, but the army could not have dispensed with those of the 19th, 20th, and 21st.[73]

In a later communiqué Rosecrans writes:

> As to the cavalry . . . as an arm of the service it has been equal to its duty on all occasions and on the 18th, 19th, and 20th of September it behaved with conspicuous gallantry covering our shattered right . . . and it is greatly due to the behavior of the cavalry . . . that we lost none of our wagons and that many of our ambulances and some of our artillery and caissons came safely into [Chattanooga].[74]

The heroic stand of General George H. Thomas "saved the Union forces from utter rout," and he will hereafter be known as "The Rock of Chickamauga."[75] This Confederate "victory" cost them 17,800 casualties; there were 16,000 on the Union side.[76] Stunned by his losses, Confederate General Bragg failed to take this opportunity to destroy the Union Army. Instead, his army occupied Missionary Ridge, Lookout Mountain, and Chattanooga Valley, "effectively blockading the city.[77] "The great railroad bridge at Bridgeport was destroyed, and the river and road from there to Chattanooga" was held by the Confederates. "This left no outlet for the Union forces but the steep, rocky, and almost impassable roads over the mountains to Stevenson, Alabama, to which place they had railroad communication."[78] The Union Army of the Cumberland was now trapped by the geological barriers around Chattanooga to their rear and the Confederate Army at their front. The siege of Chattanooga had begun.

IX. The Siege of Chattanooga

On September 23, after covering the retreat of General Thomas from Rossville, Minty's cavalry brigade arrived in Chattanooga and "bivouacked on the Crutchfield property, on the slope of Moccasin Hill"[1] Two of the regiments (the 7th Pennsylvania and 4th Michigan) "were put into the intrenchments to throw up breastworks."[2] Minty records that they "worked in the trenches all night, and at 5 a. m., on the 24th, crossed the Tennessee with the brigade." Minty camped on Opossum Creek—up the valley about ten miles from Chattanooga—and from there picketed the Tennessee River from Washington to Sandy Shoals.[3] According to Colonel Sipes, the Confederate Army took position south of Chattanooga:

> . . .their lines touching the river on both flanks, and including intermediately fortified positions on Lookout Mountain, Missionary Ridge, and Pigeon Mountain.
> The great railroad bridge at Bridgeport was destroyed, and the river and road from there to Chattanooga were held by them. This left no outlet for the Union forces but the steep, rocky, and almost impassable roads over the mountains–more than two score miles–to Stevenson, Alabama, to which place they had railroad communication.[4]

By late September 1863, "the entire Union army, trapped at Chattanooga, was down to quarter rations and in danger of starvation or capture."[5] Supplies were "utterly inadequate," writes Sipes, "and the privations endured by the thousands of soldiers . . . may be imagined":

> Men were seen picking up bits of moldy hard-tack where, in times of plenty, damaged stores had been thrown away, and officers turned their horses loose to die in the streets. . . . Medical stores were unobtainable, and the wounded, who were able to travel, were told to get back to Stevenson as best they could and they would be cared for there."[6]

Many died along the way. It would be late October before the Federals were able to open an adequate supply route into Chattanooga and begin to fortify the city. According to Sergeant Larson: "The enemy apparently did not intend to attack Chattanooga, perhaps because their reinforcements from Virginia were recalled."[7]

Union forces would be able to hold Chattanooga as long as communications were kept open and the supply base was protected. That duty fell to the cavalry.[8] It would be dealing with General Joseph Wheeler, who had been given instructions to cross the Tennessee River with Brigadier General Philip D. Roddey's cavalry and disrupt the Union lines of communication.[9]

Minty was ordered "to cross the Tennessee River on the pontoon bridge and march for Washington, Tennessee," near where the 4th U.S. had "joined the division, with General George Crook in command."[10] "General Crook had been stationed at Washington with a force of 2,000 effective men to guard the river for a distance of fifty miles up and down from near that place."[11] "The duty now devolving on our division," writes Minty, "was that of guarding the Tennessee River, for the purpose of preventing the crossing of the enemy's cavalry and the destruction or interruption of our line of communication."[12]

On September 25, Minty's Brigade marched to Sale Creek, where it remained until September 28, when the brigade "marched to near Washington, Rhea County" and remained there during the twenty-ninth.[13] Reports reached General Crook that "Wheeler was making for Cotton Port Ferry on the Tennessee River with 8000 men."[14] On September 30, the rebel cavalry under Wheeler crossed the Tennessee River. The Fourth Michigan and one battalion of the 4th US Cavalry were patrolling in the area, but were unable to dispute Wheeler's passage.[15] After the Confederates crossed, Minty's command was gathered together and moved to Smith's Crossroads.[16]

A Daring Escape

In late September, Cos. H and F under Captain Thomas McCormick were sent to Cotton Port Ferry to watch the ferry and report on Wheeler's movements.

They were subsequently reinforced by two more battalions, along with Major Horace Gray of the 4th Michigan Cavalry and his battalion. Meanwhile, the rest of the division under Colonel Minty was ordered to Sale Creek, a short distance north of Chattanooga.

This movement, unknown to the expedition at Cotton Port Ferry, left McCormick's and Gray's commands isolated and in danger of becoming surrounded and trapped by Wheeler's troops. Fortunately, Wheeler was unaware of the Union force, now concealed by rugged terrain and darkness of night. Pickets and videttes were placed, horses were unsaddled, and campfires were built when orders were suddenly given to Sergeant Larson: "Have these fires put out and tell the first sergeants to have their companies saddle up and mount at once, but without making any noise whatever." Having become aware of their precarious position, McCormick and Gray devised an ingenious and daring plan for escape. While mounted and waiting for orders to move, a torrential rainstorm broke out, forcing every man to put on his poncho. With their uniforms covered and only their heads showing in the darkness and heavy rain, they could not be distinguished from the rebel cavalry. On orders to move, the men were once again instructed to avoid unnecessary noise and talking, and to not answer any questions should anyone come riding alongside trying to talk to them. Moving forward slowly, "we came within hearing of a continual tramping and splashing in the mud, a sound with which we were well acquainted . . . a large body of cavalry marching on a muddy road." It was Wheeler's command. At a break in the line, "we slipped right in behind the column that had passed and followed as though we belonged to the Rebs. They moved south on the Kingston Road that was just the direction we would have to take to join the division. They were themselves leading us out of the trap in which they had placed us. It was a fine trick and well executed." When the rebel forces halted before daybreak, the Union column kept slowly moving forward, as if to picket. "At daybreak on the 27th, we struck our own picket at Smith's Crossroads . . . by a nice trick well managed by our officers and coolly carried out by the men."[17]

Fearing the worst for his men and unable to send reinforcements, Minty writes of "the joy in the ranks of the Saber Brigade before daybreak" when "Gray and McCormick, with their three battalions, rejoined us. Their escape from Wheeler's force was almost miraculous. . . . It was bravely done, all honor be yours, my gallant comrades."[18] Deception could work both ways, as Minty records in the unfortunate events of the next day:

> On the morning of the 28th, a large scouting party of the enemy, wearing ponchos, the same as those used by us, and under cover of a heavy rain storm, approached a picket of the 4th U.S. Cav., commanded by Lieutenant Stockton, and captured the entire force, 24 men.[19]

This was the second of four occasions during the Civil War that saw members of the Fourth Regulars captured or surrendering. It appears that Lieutenant Samuel W. Stockton was either exchanged or escaped, as he went on to distinguished service during the remainder of the war. Stockton was a civilian appointment to 2nd lieutenant in May 1861, and was promoted to 1st lieutenant that same month.[20] The fate of his men is not known.

Chasing Wheeler's Cavalry

From September 30 through October 17, the Union Army—particularly the Cavalry Corps—was involved in the "chase of the rebel General" during his raid into middle Tennessee and upon Federal supply lines and communications. The route taken by Wheeler in this raid was from "Cotton Port across Walden's Ridge and the Cumberland Mountains to McMinnville, thence by way of Murfreesboro, Shelbyville, Farmington, and Pulaski, to a ford of the Tennessee about 3 miles above the mouth of Elk River, which he crossed on the 9th of October."[21] While this was occurring, Major General Ulysses S. Grant was given command in the West, and on October 19, he ordered General George Thomas to replace Rosecrans as commander of the Army of the Cumberland. Thomas began to fortify the city while Grant made plans to break the Confederate siege.

Upon learning that the enemy had crossed Walden's Ridge opposite Smith's Crossroads with a force "subsequently ascertained to number from 5,000 to 6,000 men," Brigadier General George Crook, commanding the Second Cavalry Division, "collected together the First and Second Brigades" and started in pursuit.[22] For this expedition, Minty's brigade consisted of the 4th Michigan, 7th Pennsylvania, 4th Regular Cavalry, and a battalion of the 3rd Indiana.[23]

Eli Long—a captain in the 4th Cavalry—was now commanding the Second Brigade and would "serve out the remainder of the war alongside Minty." Supporting both brigades was Captain James Stokes's Chicago Board of Trade Battery, which would also remain with them until the end.[24]

Crook's command began moving over the mountains some five miles south of Smith's Crossroads, reaching the top that night. They resumed the march the next morning, "entering the Sequatchie Valley at Pitt's Crossroads."[25] Colonel Sipes summarizes the exhausting actions of these two weeks:

> Once the pursuit of Wheeler began, and for fourteen days was kept up, only ending when the Confederate raiding force had recrossed the river at Mussel Shoals, Alabama. Day after day the experience was the same. At the first peep of dawn both forces would be moving. Details from our command would scout the adjacent country, securing what supplies they could, while the command itself kept steadily after the raiders. No rest was taken or allowed, and as evening approached our advance and the enemy's rear usually came in touch, a few shots would be exchanged, and night would close the scene. Both commands stopped where they were, in or beside the road, and if they had anything to eat, ate it, and afterwards wrapped the soil of mother earth about them and lay down to dreams, pleasant or otherwise. No time was allowed the raiders to capture a square meal, much less Uncle Sam's supplies.[26]

"This chasing Wheeler," writes Sergeant Larson, "or any other raiding party from place to place . . . is badly checked when . . . rain is pouring down almost constantly, and mud is ankle-deep":

> [W]e were compelled to make forced marches every day, lasting from daylight until far into the night . . . to splash in the mud all day from early morn till late at night, every man and horse literally covered with dirt and wet as drowned rats, was very unpleasant. . . . At Pikesville we got a glimpse of the main body going up the Cumberland Mountains. We brought their rear guard to a stand and had a lively spat with them in which artillery was used on both sides, until at last, by a charge, we sent them off aflying.[27]

. . . It was not until the first days in October that we succeeded in making Wheeler fight. It occurred in the evening at the foot of Cumberland Mountains where they . . . made a stand. The fight was short and sharp, but they were driven from their position and we camped on the spot where the fight took place. The next morning . . . they had passed through McMinnville. We had been after them from about 10 A.M. until near sunset, when we ran their rear guard on a gallop through the main street of that town.[28]

The head of Wheeler's column had got in there earlier, however, and had done all the damage that could be done. They rolled all the cotton bales they could find out in the street and set fire to them. Several houses along the street were also on fire. In fact, it looked like the whole town was on fire from end to end when we entered. We did not stop to put out fires, but continued right on after them so as to bring them to a stand . . . which we succeeded in doing about sunset on some wooded hills some four or five miles from the town. On those hills was fought regular night battle, in which the men on both sides fired at the flash of the opponent's carbine. It was such an affair of such importance that daylight could not be awaited. On it depended the safety of Murfreesboro, at which place a great deal of military supplies were stored, and if Wheeler could enter that town . . . he would succeed in burning and destroying them before we could drive him out. If we could turn or flank him at this point we would be able to protect Murfreesboro. Hence, it was a severe and stubborn fight, almost equal to a regular battle, and lasted until near midnight, but when it did end General Crook's Division stood between Wheeler and Murfreesboro and that place was safe. Wheeler would now have to move toward Shelbyville and the Tennessee River, which was just the direction we wanted him to take. The next morning we moved very early . . . [and]

we came up with Wheeler at Farmington, where we gave him a severe thrashing and compelled him to retreat in haste. [29]

Lieutenant Henry Potter, 4th Michigan, writing on October 8, expressed his confidence in the final outcome: "Have had a couple of fights. Think we will succeed in gobbling [capturing] all of them. We have enough to do it."[30]

That same day, one part of the brigade under Colonel Minty remained in Murfreesboro due to a mix-up in command that left Minty relaxing, instead of joining the rest of the brigade at Farmington, where a battle was in progress. When the orders were unscrambled, Minty took off and arrived at the end of the fight. Due to his tardiness, he was ordered arrested by General Crook for disobeying orders. Minty was later cleared of all charges at a court martial and returned to the command of the brigade on March 11, 1864.[31] With his absence, the following reorganization of the Second Division cavalry command was announced: "The First Brigade will be commanded by Colonel William W. Lowe, Fifth Iowa Cavalry, and will be composed of: Seventh Pennsylvania Cavalry, Fourth Michigan Cavalry, Fourth US Cavalry, Fifth Iowa Cavalry, Third Indiana Cavalry Battalion."[32] The Second Brigade continued to be commanded by Colonel Eli Long.[33]

As Sergeant Larson notes: "This act of General Crook made him very unpopular with the men of the Saber Brigade and he was made to feel it, too."[34] Larson describes the chase of Wheeler's cavalry on October 9th:

> We again came up with Wheeler at a place called Sugar Creek, some ten miles from Elk River. Here Wheeler had made a barricade, trying to delay our advance to gain time to cross the Tennessee River. Minty's Brigade, as consolidated under Colonel Lowe, now numbering about 4500 men, had the advance that day. We struck the enemy about 10 o'clock, dislodged them, killing 13 and wounding 150, besides capturing 85, who were not wounded and put the rest to a precipitate flight.
>
> On a brisk gallop we followed up the advantage and captured many more as we rushed forward, hoping to bring the rest of Wheeler's forces to bay before they could cross the Tennessee River. We arrived at the river in quick time, but Wheeler had succeeded in crossing his troops except his rear guard and some of his baggage wagons and two pieces of artillery. The wagons and artillery and some of the rear guard we captured. That ended Wheeler's expedition.[35]

During this final skirmish, Sergeant Charles Bates "charged on two 'rebs' singlehanded and captured both, horses and revolvers and one rifle" which he kept as the "spoils of war." Shortly afterwards, he was briefly taken prisoner. He managed to escape but lost the horse. He would have to wait for over a month for a new mount.[36]

Captain Joseph Vale, 7th Pennsylvania, summarized the results of Wheeler's raid:

> The force with which Wheeler crossed the Tennessee, on the 4th, was his own cavalry corps, consisting of [William T.] Martin's and [Frank C.] Armstrong's divisions of three brigades each, and Hodge's division of two brigades, or in all nine brigades, numbering not less than six thousand men, and twelve pieces of artillery. He destroyed one hundred wagons loaded with commissary stores and forage in the Sequatchie valley, burned two small bridges, and slightly damaged about five miles of the railroad, near Wartrace, and captured one hundred and fifty infantry guards at the two bridges; this, with the scare, were all the damage he inflicted. He lost four pieces of artillery; two captured and two abandoned; over five hundred killed, nearly eight hundred wounded, and eleven hundred taken prisoners. He recrossed the Tennessee on the 8th, at Muscle Shoals, Alabama, with eight pieces of artillery; and less than three thousand dejected men, his horses broken down, and a thoroughly disorganized command. The difference is the number of deserters who were 'tired of the wah, sah;' and went home to stay. This was the last extensive raid against our rear and lines of communication Bragg attempted, he being satisfied that, as Morgan's raid into Kentucky and Ohio had cost him over four thousand, and Wheeler, in four days of that kind of

work, had lost over three thousand of his best cavalry, the raiding business, as a paying institution, was a failure . . . The loss to the brigade was, after Colonel Lowe took command, eight killed and forty-six wounded and three captured.[37]

Sergeant Larson writes of the responsibilities placed on the Federal cavalry during the past six months:

> It had taken us a good many days of hard marching and fighting to drive [Wheeler] back and the task of keeping him, as well as the other great raider, General Forrest, on their own side of the river and leaving Rosecrans' communication open, still devolved upon the First and Second Cavalry Division. Hence we could not rest and go into winter quarters, as the artillery and infantry did at that time of year. We had to keep moving.[38]

"We have marched in six days 247 miles," writes General Stanley: "Wheeler's retreat was a rout, and his command were running all day for the river, every man for himself, and hats, canteens, coats, guns, and broken-down horses were strewn along the whole route."[39]

"This pursuit is unsurpassed for its energy and the bravery and endurance of the officers and men engaged in it," writes General Thomas:

> and prevented the execution of an extensive plan of destruction to our communications, and plunder, rapine, and murder throughout Middle Tennessee and Northern Alabama . . . It cost the enemy six pieces of artillery and about 2,000 men, including the killed, captured, and deserted.[40]

From the congratulatory order of Major General William S. Rosecrans:

> The brilliant pursuit of the enemy's cavalry under Wheeler by the cavalry command of this army, especially Crook's division and Stokes' Chicago Board of Trade Battery, which were foremost in the fight, deserves honorable mention. The general commanding thanks the cavalry, and particularly General Crook, with the officers and soldiers of his division and of Stokes' battery, for their valuable services in the pursuit of the enemy which resulted in driving him in confusion across the Tennessee River. He compliments them for *inaugurating the new practice of coming to close quarters without delay* [emphasis author].[41]

Corporal James Wiswell wrote a series of letters to his family during September and October, describing his experiences at Chickamauga and Chattanooga. From "Camp in Chickamongoo Valley, East Tenn., 30 Sept 1863":

> After another hard fought battle I take the opportunity to inform you that I am safe as are the other three live yankees from Vermont.
> We are laying here about twenty miles from Chattanooga, partly to protect a ford of the river and partly because there is plenty of Forage hereabouts. We left Chattanooga on the 23rd inst., for 'old Rosy' had deemed it advisable to fall back into his works and there was no chance for Cavalry either to maneuver or Forage. I can not tell you much about the Battle excepting that it was next to Wilson's Creek for hard work. It appears that the C.S. [Confederate States] and U.S. had united–the first in sending troops to Bragg and the last in allowing them to do it–and they intended to completely anhilate 'Old Rosy' but that is more than they can do.
> Some of the rebels that we took belonging to Longstreet's Corps said that they expected that when they gave a yell and made a charge that we would break and run like the Army of the Potomac, but in the place of that our men received them on the front of the bayonet, and it rather cooled their military ardor. Now they have got a holy horror of the Army of the Cumberland and want to get back into Virginia. It is my opinion that some one around Washington had ought to be hung for letting them come here. Rosecrans is too successful and the green eyed monster has begun to work.

We fell back in good order and commenced fortifying and now they can send the whole army of Virginia here and Old Lee at their head and they cannot drive us out of here. The Cavalry is all stretched along on the north bank of the river to prevent them from cutting our communications.

Wiswell described his new job with the Quarter Master Division:

> ... I am not in any danger with the Q.M.D. only as it was in the action the other day. I had to go to the regiment out in the field and carry them supplies and the rebs tried to get my wagons but could not. My business in the Q.M.D. is nominally called clerk.
>
> I have to see that all of the property passing through the Qr.Mr. hands is accounted for–either turned over, issued, or expended. I have to make reports to Washington a good deal . . . and on the report every article has to have a column of course and as I have all kinds of articles from a Saddler's Needle to a Steam Boat you can form a slight idea of the size of my Abstracts, and besides there is so many little technical points in the regulations that it makes it very tiresome.

On October 8, Wiswell writes again from "Camp North Bank, Tenn. River, Chattanooga":

> I did not have a chance to see much of the action. I was out to the regiment on the field on the 19th alt. with part of our train but on the 20th we were ordered to recross our train on a hastily constructed bridge (we crossed it the first time by a Horse Boat) and then after the action our division under command of Gen. Crook went up the river leaving a small detachment to guard each ford as far as Washington. But the Genl. by some bad luck or other did not think of one of the fords for a day or so and then sent a battalion of our regiment to guard it and when they got there they found one division of rebel mounted infantry across and more crossing as fast as possible so we were compelled to fall back in this direction until we met reinforcements and then the wagons were sent here and the command followed the rebels into the mountains.

Writing on the effects of the siege:

> We have been here now for a number of days–rations are scarce and I have not seen any beans or peas since we left MBoro [Murfreesboro] and part of the time we could not get soap, candles, nor salt. Fresh Beef, Hard Tack and Coffee is the principal staples of the Commissary.[42]

According to Sergeant Charles Bates: "We are living on the country most of the time, having only been issued with eighteen days rations in two months."[43]

Continuing with Wiswell, writing on October 9:

> . . . I expect that this will be the last letter that you will receive from me in some time as my Co. Officer is trying to get me relieved from the Q.M.D. He and the [Quartermaster] have agreed to leave it to Capt. McIntyre the Comdg. Officer whether I shall go or stay. If I am relieved I shall not have as good an opportunity of writing you as I have at present for my part I am not particular–this is the easiest but I am afraid that I shall get so lazy as not to be good for anything when I get out of the Service. The Extra duty Pay that was allowed soldiers employed in the Q.M.D. was played out Mar. 4th '63 although the order did not come until I had been here a month or more. The man that I relieved got 40 cents per day extra duty pay and I should have got it too only for the order–which would have made me larger pay than any enlisted man in the regiment for the Hospital Steward gets but $23 per month.

Commenting on his birthday on September 19:

> . . . Tell mother that my last birthday was celebrated here by the whole army on our side and the rebel army besides and many a poor fellow bit the dust on my birthday too. I suppose that there was more guns fired on the 19th Sept than there ever was on the 4th of July.

As to the present situation in Chattanooga, Wiswell expresses optimism: "We can hold Chattanooga... we are all in good health and spirit excepting that 'grub' is a little short at present but that will all come right in the end." Colonel Sipes expresses similar optimism: "... [T]here was no thought of giving up the position. They had won it and they were going to hold it while a hand would hold a rifle or grip a gleaming blade. The army had unlimited confidence in Thomas, and know it was only a question of time when relief would come."[44]

Maysville, Alabama

Colonel Sipes writes that once Wheeler was driven across the Tennessee River, "Crook moved his command slowly eastward to Maysville, Alabama, where he went into camp to rest and recruit."[45] Maysville is about ten miles northeast of Huntsville, Alabama, near the line of the Charleston and Memphis RR. Chasing Wheeler took a heavy toll on the men and horses:

> The principal article of food for the men gathered in the pursuit of Wheeler was sweet potatoes, and this had proved neither sustaining nor healthful. As a consequence many of them were ill and unfit for duty, while the horses, living principally on green corn, were in a frightful condition.[46]

Sergeant Larson picks up the story of the 4th Regulars at Maysville and the deprivations endured by the men of the regiment for the past six months:

> At this place the 4th Michigan and 7th Pennsylvania Cavalry, both regiments of Minty's Brigade, turned in their horses and were posted in stockades along the railroad as infantry. This virtually broke the brigade up for the time. *All their best horses were issued to the 4th US Cavalry* [emphasis author]. At this place we also received new clothing, which we certainly needed, as we had thrown away all surplus clothing and for nearly six months had been in light marching order, carrying only what we wore.
>
> Our clothing was simply rags, and for underwear we had been compelled to adopt the Mexican plan of turning that once in a while to keep it from rubbing. We had no changes so that we could wash any of our clothes, so we were glad when new underwear was issued to us and as winter was on hand we drew overcoats and 'dog tents' also.[47]

The weather also added to the misery. Lieutenant Potter writes on October 25:

> We have had a very different Fall from what we had last. It has been cold, cloudy, windy and rainy mostly all the month– decidedly uncomfortable. The brigade has not seen a wagon or piece of a train since it left Washington, East Tennessee, September 30, 1863 to chase old Wheeler day and night from that place to Pikeville in the Sequatchee Valley, to McMinnville, to Murfreesboro, to Shelbyville, Lewisburg, Pulaski, from there to the Tennessee river at Lamb's Jenny 3 miles above Muscle Shoals where they got away from us. I rather think they got worsted. We captured mostly all their artillery and took about 600 prisoners and killed. I have not seen a clean shirt or pr of drawers or socks since the 30th ult. The consequences I need not tell you.[48]

In this same letter, Lieutenant Potter recounts how the cavalry lived off the land and as much as admitted that it went too far:

> I would hate to be a citizen living in this country about this time. We have moved so fast and so meteor-like Uncle Sam couldn't touch us–consequence was we didn't draw any rations and Uncle Jeff had to suffer. We had to forage on the country. We lived well but I admit the thing went almost too far with some. A great many have been ROBBED OUTRIGHT of everything but it is stopped now.[49]

Sergeant Larson recalls early orders issued by the new brigade commander, Colonel William W. Lowe, regarding the problem of foraging:

> At Maysville our new Iowa commander issued orders that foraging should be done only by regularly detailed parties under an officer. This would badly interfere with

our chance to get some fresh meat and other necessary supplies of food. This was a new feature in the rules, but the colonel and his Iowa regiment were also new in the service . . . hence, the Colonel had the same idea of supplying troops in the field as all the officers had in the beginning of the war and until Morgan, Wheeler, Forrest and other Confederate leaders had shown by their example how things should be done. Hence the colonel's order received very little attention by the men except that we made our foraging expeditions more secretly.[50]

Corporal Wiswell was still with the Quartermaster Division at Headquarters, and in his letter of November 15 from Maysville, he describes the great difficulty moving out of Chattanooga:

> On the 20th ult. [October] we left Chattanooga for the base of supplies via Stevenson, Ala. Now in common times we would consider that only a good days march but owing to the results of a civil war we were eleven days on the road for the rebel Sharpshooters command the lower or twenty eight mile road and the middle road was utterly impassable by reason of mud and therefore we were obliged to take the upper one which is eighty miles long, two miles wide, and as to the depth it has been never known. I know myself that it is more than two feet for I went that far myself without finding bottom. We had five days half rations when we left [Chattanooga] and after they run out we parched the corn that we had from our animals to keep ourselves from going hungry for there is not food enough to feed a suckling babe. Our train lost two wagons and any quantity of mules that went down and we never saw them afterwards. We arrived at Stevenson on the 31st ult. and laid over one day when we heard that our command was here and then we started again but we had good roads and arrived here [Maysville] on the 6th inst. [Nov.] and found the whole of them parching corn for dear life. This is a small place about the size of Comstocks and is twelve miles from Huntsville. The country is rich and fertile–the present inhabitants are mostly of Africa descent and guerillas abound in large numbers. The RR is completed to Flint River–twelve miles from here and as they are repairing the bridge at that place.

Commenting on the "rivalry" between the two great Union Armies:

> I saw a large part of Hookers command at Stevenson . . . our Cumberland men and they are having 'plug[?] fights' every day and we call them S.B.M. for soft bread men. Sherman's Corps is passing here every day on their way to Chattanooga. They are a fine looking set of men and look as though they had seen hard service. I could not help but notice the difference in the manner which our men treated them and treated Hooker's men–one they treat as an old soldier and the other like a recruit–that they are to learn the art of war. In fact the A.O.C. [Army of the Cumberland] has got a supreme contempt for the A.O.P. [Army of the Potomac].

Petty rivalries between commands could have dire consequences, as the Fourth Regulars would soon experience in the ill-fated Meridian Expedition of February 1864. As to the recent change of command in the Army of the Cumberland, Wiswell writes:

> I am sorry that my favorite general . . . was relieved but I am glad that we have so good a man in his place. The Army liked Rosy as a Brother but they like Thomas as a Father. I do believe that if Rosy had been relieved by any other men than Thomas and Grant that the whole army would have mutinied.[51]

There was another significant change in the command structure on November 12, when Major General David Stanley, USV, was relieved from further duty with the cavalry and assigned to command the First Division, Fourth Army Corps.[52] Suffering from ill health, he was forced to take sick leave for several months. He would return to participate in Sherman's Atlanta Campaign.

Expedition to Whitesburg and Decatur

On November 13, Colonel Lowe—temporarily commanding Second Cavalry Division—issued orders for a raiding party "to thoroughly scour the country situated between the Memphis and Charleston Railroad and the Tennessee River from Whitesburg to opposite Decatur":

> and drive out or capture the marauding rebel bands known to be roving over that country, pressing horses, mules, cattle, sheep, hogs, wheat &c., and running them across the river for Confederate use; to capture and destroy all boats and ferries on the river from Whitesburg to Decatur; to break up or capture a band of rebels, supposed to be encamped near the Tennessee River, about the mouth of Limestone Creek, and to destroy or render unserviceable a grist and saw-mill in that vicinity and in the service of the rebels . . . .[53]

This raid passed through a region called "Sandy Beat . . . a wild, comparatively desolate region; but little of it reclaimed from its natural condition and thinly inhabited by people who were hardly abreast with the civilization of 1863."[54] Colonel Sipes was ordered to take the effective men of his regiment and a detachment of 4th Regulars and "gather in all the horses and mules" that could be found in that area.[55]

Another detachment of 4th Regulars was assigned to Major J. Morris Young, 5th Iowa Cavalry, who led a command of 400 men. It left early the morning of November 14 and marched "by a circuitous route across the mountains, leaving Huntsville to the right," arriving at Whitesburg at 5 p.m. The detachment captured two Confederate soldiers "after a lively chase of some 4 miles, a drove of 29 young, fat hogs, and the ferryboat which had just come over for them." Using the ferryboat, a detachment searched a nearby island, "returning with 25 head of horses and mules. The ferry boat was then destroyed."[56] The next day Captain Charles Bowman, 4th U.S., was "detached with 150 men to make a detour northward, by way of Madison Station, down the Memphis and Charleston Railroad, and to secure a position in the rear of Limestone Creek, guarding the roads leading out by way of Mooresville and the point opposite Decatur." They were "fired upon in the rear by a small party" and chased a squad of rebels. In both cases they were unable to engage, as "the enemy's horses were too fleet."[57] On the sixteenth, Major Young learned from a captured prisoner that General Philip D. Roddey would be in Decatur by sunrise, joining a portion of General Stephen D. Lee's command that had already arrived and was engaged in "throwing up earthworks." Young sent out parties "in all directions" and reported that they destroyed a number of boats and "certain portions of the machinery" of a mill "found to be in the service of the rebels, grinding corn and sawing lumber to build boats . . ."[58] As a result of this expedition, Major Young reported:

> captured and destroyed 9 ferry-boats, 9 Confederate States soldiers, one (supposed to be) a captain, and one a sergeant, and remounted the command with from 150 to 200 fine mules and horses, with a loss of 1 man slightly wounded. . . . The Fourth United States reported having captured 5 Confederate soldiers, one of them the notorious Captain Robinson.[59]

Colonel Sipes's expedition was also successful, returning with "nearly four hundred . . . horses and mules" that "helped materially to fit out the command."[60]

With Stanley's departure, command of the cavalry in the Department of the Cumberland was turned over to Brigadier General Washington L. Elliot. Colonel Edward McCook—commanding 2nd Indiana Cavalry—succeeded Elliott to the command of the First Division. Originally commissioned 2nd lieutenant (Company G, 4th Cavalry) in May 1861, McCook would be recognized as one of the outstanding civilian appointments to the 4th Cavalry. Before his resignation from the Army in May 1866, he would receive five more brevet commendations to Major General, USV.[61]

On November 21, headquarters of the cavalry command and the First Cavalry Division—along with First and Second Brigades—marched from Winchester via Shelbyville and Murfreesboro to Alexandria, Tennessee. The First Brigade took post at the forks of Auburn and Liberty turnpikes; the Second Brigade was posted at Alexandria.[62] Lieutenant Potter records the activities of Minty's Brigade during the remaining days of November:

Our Brigade crossed the Tennessee Tuesday the 24th Nov. with Sherman's Corps and following the line of the Knoxville RR burnt the bridges and destroyed all commissary stores which we found. When we reached Cleveland 30 miles from Chattanooga, we had captured and burnt 65 wagons and taken over 200 prisoners, burnt all bridges of importance, cut telegraphic communications between Bragg and Longstreet, — which was our intention when starting on the raid. We started on the 27th, captured about 260 hogs, a first thing for us and destroying the Copper Rolling Mill, their only factory of [percussion] *caps* in the Confederacy. It was the grandest sight I ever saw, we put 50 boxes of shells and torpedoes in the walls before firing it and such explosions you never heard. The rebels hurried us out quite unceremoniously. We then went back to Chattanooga and moved out with Sherman to reinforce Burnside at Knoxville. We went as far as Loudon when hearing that Longstreet had been repulsed and was retreating, we turned off to Maryville. From there our Brigade moved over the Alleghenies in North Carolina and a hard trip it was, I tell you. Rain and cold on the mountains making things disagreeable.

We found plenty to eat in NC plenty of apples and peach brandy. No army had ever troubled them of any size. Lots of them never seen a Yankee, as they call us, before. They are ignorant and simple–but nearly all stick to the old Union, also many have been conscripted–most of them were glad to see us.[63]

The Battle of Chattanooga

Between November 23 and 25—with Hooker on the right and Sherman on the left—Grant launched a coordinated assault on Confederate positions. Sherman encountered strong resistance and Grant ordered Thomas's Army of the Cumberland to seize the rebel line at the base of Missionary Ridge. "Scorned by Hooker's Easterners and Sherman's veterans" for Rosecrans's defeat at Chickamauga and "tired of playing the poor relation in this campaign," the Army of the Cumberland was so eager for action that it not only cleared the base of Missionary Ridge, but "went straight on up the steep mountain slope without orders . . . broke Bragg's line right where it was strongest, drove the Confederate army off in complete retreat, and won the Battle of Chattanooga in one spontaneous explosion of pent-up energy and fury."[64] Chattanooga was delivered and was now the "springboard for an invasion of the South's heartland."[65] This was a decisive battle: ". . . [T]he South had definitely lost the war in the West–and when spring came, the Federals would have a chance to apply more pressure than the Confederacy could hope to resist."[66]

On December 1, 1863, General Thomas reorganized the Army of the Cumberland into three corps and three cavalry divisions; Brigadier General George Crook now commanded the Second Division. His First Brigade, commanded by Colonel William Sipes, consisted of:

> 4th United States Cavalry
> Captain James B. McIntyre
> 4th Michigan Cavalry
> Major Horace Gray
> 7th Pennsylvania Cavalry
> Lieutenant Colonel James J. Seibert
> 5th Iowa Cavalry
> Lieutenant Colonel Matthewson T. Patrick
> 3rd Indiana (3rd Battalion)
> Colonel Robert Klein
> <u>Artillery</u>
> Chicago Board of Trade Battery
> Lieutenant George J. Robinson[67]

Once again, while the armies were in winter camp there was no rest for the men of the 4th United States Cavalry. "While it was the lot of all cavalry to be constantly on the move," writes Larson:

> such activity seemed to fall to the 4th Cavalry with particular frequency. Wherever anybody needed assistance, or thought he did, it seemed *the 4th Cavalry was the old stand-by of which every commanding general thought first* [emphasis author], so that we were always on the move somewhere, even if after we got to wherever we were going, we did nothing more than turn around and go back again.[68]

James Wiswell describes this as being under "marching orders . . . such as 'Jack and Jill' made of which I read in my 'Schoolboy days,'" up the hill and down again.[69]

From Maysville, "the 4th US Cavalry was soon ordered to the Tennessee River to picket that river by companies at different fords and crossings." Larson's company was posted at a place called Love's plantation, "to guard a ford at that place and to patrol the river for twenty miles up and down." Lieutenant Bird Fletcher was absent during this time and Co. H was commanded by Lieutenant Elbridge Roys. The men found themselves in plain view of the enemy on the other side of the river, which at this point was too wide for anything other than artillery fire.[70] Larson describes the duty at this pleasant location:

> At this camp we enjoyed good quarters without having to build them. We found plenty of houses and nobody living on the place at all. Hence we took possession of them by squads, according to the size of the room. Furniture, of course, had all been removed, but there was a fireplace in every room, and furniture we manufactured out of boards and boxes found about the place. We were soon fixed so that we could sit at a table like gentlemen and eat our meals and in the evening smoke and play cards by lamplight. The oil we burned was extracted from fat bacon.[71]

After several weeks in their "comfortable quarters" at Love's plantation, the regiment "marched up the Flint River, to protect some mechanics while they were rebuilding a railroad bridge that had been destroyed by a Confederate raiding party."

The camp they went into "was a miserable one for that time of the year . . . It was in the river-bottom on low land, but almost open country." As Larson describes it: "We had no opportunity to build even the rail shelters we were able to put up in some places, for there were neither logs nor rails at hand. In fact, nothing grew there but a few bushes." On the first day of January 1864, the companies of the 4th U.S. were relieved of their duties on the Tennessee River and ordered to join General William Sooy Smith at La Grange, near Memphis, Tennessee, for duty in northern Mississippi. Larson concluded: "We did not feel sorry over being ordered to leave that ugly camp . . . feeling very certain that no worse camp could be found. Still, the long march ahead of us did not seem particularly pleasant at that time of year, when rain, mud and cold were the order of the day."[72]

Huntsville, Alabama

Colonel Sipes "took command of the city and of the country for three miles around it . . . serving as provost guard." The balance of the troops made camp "outside the three mile limit."[73] Sergeant Larson writes of the difficulties faced by the men of the 4th Regiment in the transfer to Huntsville, Alabama—a march of about 200 miles:

> After a stay of about fifteen or twenty days at this place [Maysville] the 4th US Cavalry was ordered to Huntsville, Alabama, which was then the headquarters of the division. As we started it began to rain and grow cold; the rain soon turned into fine snow and the weather was about as unpleasant and winter-like as in a northern state. The evening we arrived in Huntsville the weather had turned so intensely cold that it was difficult to keep from freezing to death during the night, and the campground assigned to us by General Crook, being on a high hill among some scattering trees where the cold wind had full force, made it still worse.
>
> We set to work at once to fix things so as to enable us to live through the night. Each mess dragged together a big pile of logs and fence rails and then began a pen with four rails (one each way) and two rails high; then a rail was laid across the pen about two feet from the side and then other tails and poles were stuck in with one end under the lowest rail in the pen and by resting them over the rail that was laid across. They stood up in a slanting manner like half of a roof. On that we fastened our 'dog tents.' This kept the snow and rain from falling in the pen. Then we scraped together leaves and small brush, snow and all, and put it in the bottom of the pen to keep us from the wet and cold ground, then saddle blankets and other stuff was spread on it and the bed was ready. Then a big fire was built in front of the open side

of this 'shanty pen' and every man in the mess, eight in all, crawled in, and of course, in such small space, we had to pack close together, but that just aided us in keeping warm with our remaining blankets and overcoats as covering. This was cavalry winter quarters, the only kind that we had then enjoyed for any considerable time. We built them on all occasions in winter when very bad weather compelled us to do so. That it was necessary that night was evidenced the next morning by the fact that a French lieutenant named Lamadue, was found frozen to death in his tent.[74]

In his final letter for the year written on December 12, Sergeant Charles Bates describes his life in winter camp at Huntsville, Alabama—which he seemed to have enjoyed more than Sergeant Larson—his views on military strategy, and on McClellan's bid for the presidency:

> I believe we are 'settled down' for the winter, and I don't want to be in a better place than this for the cold weather. Huntsville is a very pretty city and formerly contained about nine thousand inhabitants. It is celebrated for the 'big spring,' and the healthy climate in its vicinity. The spring is a <u>stunner</u>, affording more water than the Pomperary river (in dry weather) and the location of the town is so remarkably healthy that the citizens had to borrow a corpse to start a graveyard with. Our camp is situated on a beautifully wooded knoll, just such a one as Cooper would delight in assigning for the picturesque camp of some Indian tribe, or as Walter Scott would select for some story of Scottish chivalry. From the top, a fine view of Huntsville is obtained, and thanks to the warm climate of the sunny south, we are <u>comfortable</u>. I received a letter from you three days ago, but had to go on guard one day, and spent two days in fixing my quarters, so your letter had to wait a reply. I now have a very comfortable little <u>snuggery</u> built about ten feet square with fire-place, chimney, and all the <u>modern</u> —- Modern Improvements, and intend to take a good comfortable winter rest. General Grant is doing things up in a hurry and may interrupt my pleasant fancies but I hope not.
>
> There is considerable rain here, three days out of four we have been here it has rained but I dont think such weather can last forever we must have some pleasant days, and even the rain does not make the roads as muddy as they used to in Virginia. Speaking of Virginia brings me to the Army of the Potomac again and I see that Meade is at some of the incomprehensible strategy of all the other Generals; falling back to allow Lee to reinforce Longstreet, of a surety we have some chivalrous Generals they scorn to take a mean advantage of a man and when they have the Rebs at a disadvantage they hold up to show fair play. Bully for them. I suppose before you get this McClellan will be nominated for president at least I hope so. Not that I expect to see him elected for that I judge to be out of the question with as many candidates in the field as there will be for the Democratic party, but give him a try for it anyhow. I am going to vote for him a dozen times if I can.[75]

James Wiswell writes to his family on December 17 from Huntsville, telling them that he had been relieved from the Q.M.D. (Quarter Master Division):

> and almost immediately detailed in the Adjutant's office of the regiment. I do not think much of the change as I am kept busy now morning, noon and night–for all of the business of any kind in the regiment must, according to the rules of "Red Tape" pass through the A.G. and in a regular regt. those rules are pretty well "lived up to."
>
> We left Maysville on the 25th ult. and move camp to this place and before we had our camp fairly laid. The 4th U.S. and 5th Iowa were detailed from Div. H. Qrs. to picket about seventy miles of the Tenn. river and accordingly we proceeded there and

scattered ourselves along the river in squads of from eight to ten until the 8th inst when we returned to this place and formed a winter camp in the suburbs of the city. Now we have good comfortable shelters built (i.e. comfortable for a soldier) and are prepared to face the winter rains and winter cold if there is any such thing here for it has not been very cold here as yet and believe that they call this one of the worst months of the year in this part of the country.

We have begun the "Fancy work" again that is polishing every thing that we have from Boots to Buttons. We have "Division parade" every evening and "Drill Call" sounds daily but upon the whole I guess that the men are better satisfied to do that than to endure the hardships that they have undergone in the past summer and autumn campaigns. I am excused from all of the above miseries–all that I have to endure is "Muster" and that comes but once in two months. You have no doubt heard ere this of the great victory our brave Infantry men won before Chattanooga in which we did not have the honor of participating–I presume on account of the scarcity of Forage in that section. But it was a glorious thing and is another Crown of Laurels for our "Lucky" commander "Unconditional Surrender" Grant. It seems to me that a few more well directed blows of that stamp would put an end to this 'Cruel War.'

Twenty-two-year-old James Wiswell describes how he spent Christmas Day and makes an observation about the literacy of some of his non-commissioned officers:

> I spent the "Holidays" as follows. Christmas we were marching through Athens and my "Chum" and myself stopped at a citizens house to get dinner and as there was some very nice young ladies there who gave us a cordial invitation to spend the day with them. Why of course we stopped and then time passed quickly and pleasantly until twilight when we started. But then was the time that Christmas was not so "merry" for we had to gallop twenty miles against a strong west wind to join the command at Elkton and there we found the Sergt. Major calling for us like a wild man to make out a guard duty for him. For he, like most all of the Non Com [non-commissioned] officers in the army who are promoted for their military appearance has not got education sufficient to do such things themselves.

Wiswell continues with a sarcastic comment reflective of the general attitude towards General Crook, who had filed charges against Colonel Minty:

> My New Year's I passed on the top of a big hill near Pulaski called by the soldiers "Crook's Peak" in honor of our beloved Division Commander who took especial pains to camp us where we could get the full benefit of all the air that was in circulation at this season.[76]

X. Masters of the Field

The movement was executed with great rapidity and dash, the last hundred yards being at a charge, with drawn sabers. The rebel line was struck and the whole force utterly routed, stricken down, captured or scattered in less than five minutes after the advance was sounded.
– Captain Joseph Vale, 7th Pennsylvania Cavalry[1]

The Federal Cavalry in the Western Theater came of age in 1863. Beginning with the Chickamauga Campaign and during the Battle of Stones River, it made its mark and earned a place of equal standing with the infantry and artillery. From the top of the command on down—from Rosecrans to David Stanley and Eli Long, both officers in the 4th US

Cavalry, to Colonels Minty and Wilder, both volunteers—to the field-appointed 2nd lieutenants and non-commissioned officers and men of the 4th Regulars, as well as those in the volunteer cavalry, these men did all that was asked of them and more under the most difficult and challenging conditions of the war. Vale offers a "brief summary of the achievements" of Minty's brigade through 1863:

> The brigade as a body, not counting the numerous expeditions of detached portions, had marched three thousand four hundred and eighty-nine miles; it had been under the enemy's fire as an organization, counting the great battles of Stone's river and Chickamauga as one each, on fifty different occasions; had fought twenty-four engagements worthy of the name of battles; had delivered fifteen strictly saber charges; had captured six pieces of artillery; two thousand six hundred and sixty-nine prisoners, when acting independently; and in conjunction with the other brigades of the division, over eleven hundred more, making an aggregate of three thousand seven hundred and sixty-nine; besides wagons, mules, horses, and provisions from the enemy in more than sufficient quantities to have kept it in constant supply. It had killed of the enemy in battle six hundred and fifty-seven, and wounded seven hundred and seventy-three known, besides the large number of killed and wounded, who, not falling into our hands, could not even be estimated; Had been gloriously victorious in every encounter except one, [Chickamauga] and on that occasion, had withdrawn in such good order as made the *morale* of the men as good as a victory. It had *never been repulsed in a saber charge!* [emphasis Vale's]. Its total casualties were sixty killed, one hundred and seventy-four wounded, and seventy-three missing; total of twelve officers and two hundred and seventy-six men.[2]

The six companies of the Fourth Cavalry present at Stones River, acting as an "independent command," were "deserving of special notice," rendering "important and distinguished service" in saving General Alexander McCook's ammunition train, "allowing General Sheridan . . . to hand Bragg his first defeat of the day."[3]

General Rosecrans had high praise for Stanley, along with his ten regiments of cavalry, who *fought the enemy's forty regiments of cavalry, and held them at bay, or beat them wherever he could meet them* [emphasis author].[4] In his summary report for the year written in January 1864, General Rosecrans writes of his Chief of Cavalry:

> To Maj. Gen. D. S. Stanley is justly due great credit for his agency in bringing about these results, and giving firmness and vigor to the discipline of the cavalry.
>
> It requires both nature and experience to make cavalry officers, and by judicious selections and promotions this arm may become still more useful and distinguished.[5]

Considering the number of divisions, brigades, and regiments involved with tens of thousands of men in combat, it would seem a rare distinction and high honor for an officer or enlisted man to be singled out by his commanding general. In the Fourth Regiment United States Cavalry at Stones River, Captain Elmer Otis was cited by Major General Rosecrans for his "most opportune and brilliant charge . . . on Wheeler's cavalry" and was recommended for promotion to brigadier general.[6] Captain Eli Long was promoted to Colonel, USV, commanding the Fourth Ohio Volunteer Cavalry. Lieutenant Elbridge Roys, who commanded the escort of the headquarters train and accompanied General Rosecrans throughout the battle, "distinguished himself for gallantry and efficiency."[7] Lieutenants Rendlebock, Manck, Kelly, Lee, and Healy were all honorably mentioned in the official reports, as were Sergeant Major John Webster and 1st Sergeants Martin Murphy, James McAlpin, John Dolan, and Christian Haefling. Even Private Francis H. Snow, Co. L—orderly to General Rosecrans—received credit and praise for picking up fifteen Union stragglers and leading them into combat.[8]

In skirmishes at Manchester Pike, Lytle's Creek, Nolensville, Versailles, and Bradyville, the men of the Fourth United States Cavalry honed their skills and built their reputations. While temporarily assigned to Phil Sheridan's Third Division in the expeditions to Unionville and Thompson's Station in March 1863, the "great gallantry" displayed by

Lieutenants Elbridge Roys and Joseph Rendlebock at Thompson's Station was brought to the attention of Major General Rosecrans. The 4th Regulars, as part of Colonel Minty's brigade, earned their share of Rosecrans's ultimate tribute: the Saber Brigade.

Of the eleven officers present with the 4th Regulars at Franklin in April, eight were former enlisted men—six from the 4th Cavalry and five of those commanding companies of the regiment. Captain McIntyre, Lieutenants Hedges and Rendlebock, and newly appointed 2nd Lieutenants McCafferty and Fletcher were recognized with brevet rank for their exemplary conduct. Second Lieutenant Fitzgerald, 4th U.S., and Lieutenant Ingerton—on loan from the 16th Infantry—also received commendation for their charge and capture of a rebel battery. In General Stanley's report to Major General Rosecrans, he cites Captain McIntyre and notes "*the Fourth US Cavalry did the most gallant service* [emphasis author]."[9]

The 4th US Cavalry was formally assigned to Minty's Brigade in March. Under the command of Captain Elmer Otis, the regiment participated in numerous engagements during April and May. Commenting on expeditions to McMinnville and Middleton, Tennessee, General Stanley writes: "I cannot speak in terms too high of the conduct of Lt. O'Connell, Fourth US Cavalry, and his brave squadron. He was well assisted by Lieutenants Rendlebock and Wood."[10] On an expedition to Lebanon, Tennessee, Minty's command covered over 100 miles in forty-eight hours—a feat that amazed the Russian-trained cavalryman General Turchin.

The Tullahoma Campaign in Middle Tennessee began in June 1863 and, at Shelbyville, the Confederate forces were overwhelmed in a Federal cavalry charge where, *for the first time in the history of the war . . . strong lines of entrenchments . . . were stormed and taken by cavalry in a mounted saber charge* [emphasis author].[11] This was followed almost immediately by a brilliant cavalry charge on the rebel battery at the courthouse. During this same battle, Lieutenants Rendlebock and Wirt Davis, commanding Cos. D and I, "charged two regiments of rebel cavalry and completely routed them, taking between 200 and 300 prisoners."[12] Among those "worthy of special mention for their gallantry and soldierlike conduct" were Lieutenants Ingerton, O'Connell, Rendlebock, McCafferty, and Davis, as well as 1st Sergeants McMaster, Callehan, and Egan, Sergeants Charles Bates and John Riker, Corporals William Tudhope and John Rankin, and Private William Sommers.[13] "Between the 23rd of June and the 5th of July, the brigade had marched eight hundred miles, almost constantly drenched by rains . . . and had encountered the enemy, always successfully, in several severe engagements."[14] There was little time for rest.

In August, as Union forces advanced on Chattanooga, Minty's brigade was on detached duty to clear out the rebel cavalry led by General George Dibrell. The story of the Battle of Chickamauga has been told and retold. Reputations were made and lost. Only recently has the "obstinate resistance" of Minty's brigade and the 4th Regiment at Reed's Bridge been thoroughly recognized:

> Outnumbered seven to one, . . . Minty's little brigade held up the advance of 7,000 Rebel cavalry for ten hours, quite possibly helping to save the Army of the Cumberland from complete destruction.[15]

For over five months, the 4th United States Cavalry was "constantly in the saddle and on the alert," continuously on patrols, engaged in expeditions and scouting activities of two to fourteen days, and covering hundreds of miles under the worst of conditions and circumstances.[16]

With the Army of the Cumberland trapped at Chattanooga, Minty's brigade and the 4th Cavalry prevented Wheeler's cavalry from disrupting the fragile communication and supply lines. Rosecrans's cavalry was recognized by General George Thomas for its "*unsurpassed . . . energy . . . bravery and endurance*" in its effort and praised by General Rosecrans for "*inaugurating the new practice of coming to close quarters without delay* [emphasis author]."[17] Federal cavalry in the Western Theater, particularly Minty's brigade, equaled and surpassed the effectiveness of the Confederate cavalry with totally new cavalry tactics.

In completing his final reports for the General-in-Chief and War Department in January 1864, Major General Rosecrans had nothing but praise for his cavalry:

> . . . As to the cavalry, the accompanying reports are so full that I need only add that as an arm of the service it has been equal to its duty on all occasions, and on the 18th, 19th, and 20th of September it behaved

with conspicuous gallantry, covering our shattered right and protected our trains in the Valley of Chattanooga Creek on the 20th.

It was to provide for the security of these trains, which had been sent to that valley on the 18th, and that they should be moved into Chattanooga after our right was driven back on the 20th, that I directed special attention, and it is greatly due to the behavior of the cavalry on that day that we lost none of our wagons, and that many of our ambulances and some of our artillery and caissons came safely into the place.

Rosecrans concludes:

> ... *I cannot forbear calling the special attention of the General-in-Chief and the War Department to the conspicuous gallantry and laborious services of this arm. Exposed in all weather, almost always moving, even in winter, without tents or wagons, operating in a country poorly supplied with forage, combating for the most part very superior numbers, from the feeble beginnings of one year ago, when its operations were mostly within the infantry lines, it has become master of the field, and hesitates not to attack the enemy wherever it find him. This great change, due chiefly to the joint efforts of both officers and men, has been greatly promoted by giving them arms in which they had confidence, and by the adoption of the determined use of the saber* [emphasis author].[18]

An argument can be made that before the war was over, the Federal cavalry in the West—particularly the men of the 4th United States Cavalry as part of Colonel Robert H. G. Minty's Saber Brigade—performed some of the most demanding, arduous, challenging, and dangerous duties required of any soldier in the Civil War. It has been estimated that infantrymen spent approximately fifty days in camp for every day in battle. Along with artillerymen, they had long periods in camp between battles and during the winter months. This was not true for the cavalry. The itinerary for the 4th United States Cavalry for 1863 shows continual daily activities, from scouting and sentry duty to expeditions ranging from days to weeks at a time, covering hundreds of miles. During time spent away from the main camps in "light marching order" carrying the minimum of supplies, the men were frequently short of food, without tents or adequate protection from the elements, and constantly foraging for their mounts. Days without food or rest were not infrequent. It was under these conditions that they would meet and skirmish with the enemy, pushing them farther and deeper into the heart of the Confederacy. While operating independently on these expeditions or raids, the men had little or no support. Wounded were left to fend for themselves and the dead were buried in shallow, unmarked graves along the side of the road; capture by the rebels frequently led to execution or death in a Confederate prison camp. The attrition of exhausted troopers and horses was tremendous. Even when in camp, the cavalry frequently found itself "in the trenches," filling in for the infantry.

Writing in *The National Tribune* almost thirty years after witnessing the 4th US Cavalry in action at Okolona, Mississippi, in February 1864, Lieutenant William A. McTeer, Adjutant, 3rd Tennessee Volunteer Cavalry, makes the following tribute:

> The 4th United States Cav. was as fine a regiment as was ever organized in any war. The discipline, the gallantry, the bravery and prowess of that regiment was not excelled by any regiment in any department of the armies of the United States.[19]

During 1864, the 4th Regiment United States Cavalry would prove itself worthy of the title Masters of the Field.

1864: Through the Heart of the Confederacy

I would much sooner burn a man's barn and all his supplies than kill that man's son; it did more to win a war and was less brutal.
– Philip H. Sheridan[1]

I. Grant–Sheridan–Sherman–Thomas:
All the Generals who were to win for the Union[2]

In his 1996 book *Sherman's Horsemen: Union Cavalry Operations in the Atlanta Campaign*, David Evans writes that his interest evolved from the fact that "few articles and even fewer books" dealt with the cavalry under General Sherman in the Western Theater:

> Despite changes in Civil War historiography, there is still a tendency to describe campaigns and battles solely in terms of bloody clashes between rival armies of massed infantry. This is understandable. But by 1864, more than one out of every ten Civil War soldiers was a cavalryman . . . and nowhere did horse soldiers play a more important role than in William Tecumseh Sherman's Atlanta Campaign. If someone did not tell their story, it was going to be lost forever.[3]

In March 1864, Congress created the rank of lieutenant general previously held only by George Washington and Winfield Scott. Ulysses S. Grant was awarded the rank and became General-in-Chief of the Union Armies.[4] This act "transforms the way in which the war will be waged. For the first time the North's military might will be directed by a man who is capable of using it with maximum effectiveness."[5] "Grant considered the military problem to be basically quite simple: The principal Confederate armies had to be destroyed. The capture of cities and 'strategic points' and the occupation of Southern territory meant very little; as long as the main Confederate armies were in the field, the Confederacy lived, and as soon as they vanished, the Confederacy ceased to be." Grant set out to destroy the Army of Northern Virginia in the East and the Army of Tennessee—now led by former 4th Cavalry Lieutenant Colonel Joseph Johnston—in the West.[6]

Grant chose Major General Philip H. Sheridan to command his cavalry in the Eastern Theater. "The ferocious, driven, and blazingly brilliant Sheridan impressed Grant, who made him Chief of Cavalry of the Army of the Potomac."[7] Sheridan was to direct the Shenandoah Valley Campaign and deprive the Confederates of this fertile valley and "devastate the whole area." This garden spot "was to be turned into a desert."[8]

In the West, Major General William Sherman now commanded the entire theater of the war. He became an "army group commander" of the Military Division of the Mississippi with his own Army of the Tennessee. The Army of the Cumberland was now under the command of Major General George Thomas and Major General John Schofield commanded the Army of the Ohio. This created a combined force of over 100,000 men and 254 guns.[9] Sherman's assignment was to destroy Johnston's Army of Tennessee, take the city of Atlanta, and "do as much damage to the resources of the enemy as possible."[10] By early summer, Sherman had driven the Confederate Army from the Tennessee border to the edge of Atlanta.[11] By the time Sherman's Atlanta campaign began in May, the force under Thomas numbered 61,000 men, 130 guns, and all the cavalry, which was two-thirds of the entire invading force. It was "expertly trained and by far the most powerful of the three armies."[12] By September it was to be "total war," with Grant and Sherman striking directly at the Southern economy.[13] It became a war of attrition, and the primary targets for cavalry were the rail supply lines, storage depots, crops, mills, and manufacturing centers.

For the remainder of the war, three men would have a dramatic effect on the evolution of the cavalry—in particular Minty's brigade and the 4th US Cavalry—to its peak of efficiency as a fighting unit: Major General George Thomas, Colonel Robert Minty, and Brigadier General James Wilson.

Major General George H. Thomas, U.S.A.

George Thomas is considered by many of today's Civil War historians to be one of the best, most able generals of the entire war. The cavalry "was a combat arm dear to the heart of the old cavalry-man."[14] He was one of the very few senior Union officers with long field experience in cavalry arms, and he intended to use his cavalry "in an unprecedented fashion." Learning from the tactics used by the Confederate Cavalry under Nathan Bedford Forrest and the now-proven effectiveness of the mounted regiments, he wanted to use his cavalry on a much larger scale. "Thomas envisioned a decisive new role: dismounted troops with rapid-fire carbines that would overpower the muzzle-loaded rifles of the Confederate army." Once the enemy broke ranks, "the troops would *mount and pursue relentlessly, as no other army had done in the war* [emphasis author]."[15] According to Civil War historian Thomas Buell, General Thomas's Army of the Cumberland was to become "the most modern army of the Civil War, so advanced was it in technology and organization."[16]

By the end of July 1864, Union cavalry was dominating Confederate cavalry, although in the West, Forrest remained a dangerous, disruptive adversary and a thorn in Sherman's side. The Union cavalry "accomplished the destruction of millions of dollars worth of property useful to the Confederate Government . . . more than once forcing General Robert E. Lee to detach much-needed troops from his hard-pressed front."[17]

Despite these initial successes, by the end of summer, the Union campaign appeared to be a failure: "Neither Lee nor Johnston had been beaten, neither Richmond nor Atlanta had been taken."[18] President Lincoln was up for reelection, and "if the war effort was alleged to be a failure . . . by election day, it would in fact become one through the defeat of the candidate" and the party that directed the war effort.[19]

Sherman's Army took up winter quarters in Bridgeport and Huntsville, Alabama. Food and forage were still in short supply and the railroads were in need of repair.[20] During the winter of 1863-64, the army in the West was widely scattered in middle and east Tennessee. It was engaged in minor military operations: repairing railroads, building bridges, stockades, fortifications and storehouses, transporting supplies, and restoring the appointments lost at Chickamauga.[21] After the battle of Chattanooga and through April 1864, General Thomas and his Army of the Cumberland administered the Tennessee region and were involved in building up supplies and supply systems for the coming Atlanta Campaign. Lack of strong horses was one of the greatest weaknesses of the Federal Army at Chattanooga. Grain was almost unobtainable in the devastated West, and the wintery country was bare of subsistence.[22]

Thomas needed time to rebuild his cavalry.[23] Manpower was yet another problem, as "thousands of volunteer officers and soldiers were either leaving for good or taking the thirty-day furlough which had been granted those who would 'veteranize,' that is, re-enlist for the duration."[24]

On January 9, General Thomas posted his selections for his department staff, appointing 1st Lieutenant Michael Kelly, Company B, 4th US Cavalry, Chief of Couriers.[25] In the "Organization of troops in the Department of the Cumberland" promulgated on January 31, the 4th US Cavalry became part of the First Brigade, Colonel William W. Lowe commanding, as part of the Second Division, commanded by Brigadier General George Crook. The cavalry commander was Brigadier General Washington L. Elliott.[26] Captain McIntyre was on leave during this period.[27]

On the morning of January 7, the 4th US Cavalry arrived by train at Pulaski, Tennessee.[28] As reported by James Wiswell, Company C: "Every regiment in our Brigade excepting ours re-enlisted and went home on thirty days furlough . . . so that all that now remains of the 1st Brig. 2nd Cav. Div. is about 150 men of the 4th,"[29] referring to Companies C, D, and E. General Crook had sent the balance of the regiment under Captain Charles Bowman as "escort to a supply train," with rations for Brigadier General William Sooy Smith's command to Savannah, Tennessee.[30] A graduate of the U.S. Military Academy, Bowman was assigned to the old 1st Cavalry as 2nd lieutenant in May 1860.[31]

Corporal Wiswell had originally volunteered for service and enlisted in the regular army cavalry for a term of three years; his enlistment would be up in April 1864. He was not sure what he was going to do. As he wrote to his parents in his January 17 letter:

> . . . I am sure of being discharged on the 21st of April 1864. Do you think that I would be exempt from the draft if I were to come home as soon as discharged–for if I thought there was any possibility of being drafted I would re-enlist and come home with a furlough in my pocket sooner than be called a 'conscript.' I would give the Govt ten years service gratutiously.
>
> I wrote to the Hon. E. M. Stanton [Secretary of War] today asking for the Bounty of $100 provided for the 'Yahoos' who enlisted at about the same time that we did.

James took his discharge, trading his gun and saber for a pen and position with the Quartermaster Corps.[32]

According to Charles Bates, the day before Christmas companies C, D, and E of the 4th Regulars left for "a trip into western Tenn.," looking for elements of Forrest's cavalry:

> We . . . marched through Athens, Voresallie [Versailles], Rogersville, Pulaski, and half a dozen other small towns occupying two weeks in our erratic wanderings.
>
> When fifty men were sent to Columbia after rations and one hundred were sent back to Pulaski with General Crook. The remainder of the regiment under General Smith is still out on an expedition after Forrest . . . The detachment which went to Columbia joined the detachment with General Crook at Pulaski on the 9th and came to this place [Huntsville] on the 16th, I think it was . . .[33]

The 4th United States Cavalry did not rejoin the Saber Brigade until spring, when they were "called back to Chattanooga to take part in the campaign to Atlanta, Georgia."[34] The year 1864 would be the bloodiest of the Civil War.

II. Sherman's Meridian Campaign

In January, Major General Sherman launched a campaign "to take the strategic railroad center at Meridian, Mississippi" and strike a blow at General Leonidas Polk's army. Sherman advanced from Vicksburg—a distance of 150 miles—while General William Sooy Smith was to march 250 miles south from Memphis to meet Sherman at Meridian on or about February 10. Both commands were to "destroy railroads, bridges, corn not wanted, and strike quick and well every enemy that should offer opposition." Once the two columns combined at Meridian, Sherman would launch a new campaign to drive Polk's army out of Mississippi.[1]

From the very beginning this was an ill-fated expedition, in effect confirming the concerns of the officers and men of the 4th Regulars regarding riding with inexperienced Volunteer cavalry units. The 4th United States Cavalry, "a regiment of staunch, well disciplined and reliable troops," was assigned "unattached" to a command incapacitated by poor leadership, undisciplined volunteer troops, petty jealousies, illness, and alcoholism. First Sergeant James Larson later wrote of the "disgraceful" and "shameful" conduct of the volunteers he witnessed on this expedition.[2]

For the men of the 4th U.S., the battle they fought at Okolona, Mississippi, would be one of their costliest encounters with Nathan Bedford Forrest's cavalry and would also claim the life of Forrest's younger brother, Colonel Jeffrey Forrest. The stand of the 4th Regulars at Okolona and subsequent actions as rear guard during Smith's humiliating retreat may well have saved the expedition from total destruction.

General Sooy Smith's Failed Expedition

On January 5, the 4th Cavalry, with the exceptions of Cos. C, D, and E, "in compliance with orders, moved from Pulaski . . . arriving at Savannah on the morning of the 7th."[3] The next day, General Smith sent a message to General Crook, informing him that instead of sending the 4th Regulars back as he had intended, he would take them with him on the expedition.[4] Smith also indicated he was crossing the Tennessee that day with his six regiments and would arrive in Corinth the next day. Upon reaching the Tennessee River, Smith's "whole command, consisting of the Second, Third, and Fourth Tennessee Cavalry, Fifth Kentucky Cavalry, Fourth US Cavalry, and the Seventy-second Indiana Mounted Infantry was thrown across the river and moved toward Corinth."[5] The full strength of the 4th United States Cavalry available for the Meridian Expedition was thirteen officers and 378 men, for a total of 391 present and fit for duty.[6]

They arrived in Corinth, Mississippi, on January 10. On the eleventh, the regiment traveled by rail, arriving at La Grange, Tennessee, the next day. After refitting on January 26, Captain Bowman received orders to march his regiment to Collierville and await the orders of Brigadier General Smith.[7] The Regulars left the next day and remained at Collierville with Smith's command until February 11, when Smith finally moved out, arriving at New Albany, Mississippi, on the fourteenth.[8] The 4th Cavalry would be Smith's personal escort and Lieutenant William H. Ingerton was appointed Acting Assistant Adjutant-General.[9] First Sergeant Martin C. Rossmaier was assigned to General Smith's staff as provost sergeant.[10] This position—filled by the senior non-commissioned officer present — was to supervise the security of command headquarters. Brigadier General Benjamin Grierson, commanding Cavalry Division (XVI Corps), accompanied the expedition "since he was familiar with the whole country."[11] General Smith's Volunteer Cavalry force was comprised of about 7,000 men in three brigades: First, Colonel George E. Waring Jr. commanding; Second, Lieutenant Colonel William P. Hepburn commanding; and Third, Colonel Lafayette McCrillis commanding. The Fourth US Cavalry was "unassigned." Lieutenant William A. McTeer—the adjutant of the 3rd Tennessee Cavalry in the Third Brigade—provided a detailed and candid description of the events twenty-seven years later.[12]

Smith's expedition was ten days late starting. Not leaving until one day after he was supposed to have united with Sherman at Meridian, Mississippi, rendered the primary objective of Sherman's plans moot. Smith had also been instructed to "look to the greater object": to destroy the enemy's communications from Okolona to Meridian, disable the Mobile and Ohio Railroad "as much as possible," and "consume or destroy the resources of the enemy along that road."[13]

The tone of the expedition was established on the first night when pickets from McCrillis's Third Brigade "were badly posted" and several were shot and killed by the enemy. Their bodies "were mutilated and badly used. This enraged the boys so that they were *hard to control* [emphasis author], and the next day houses and barns were burned in every direction."[14] On the fifteenth, while the Third Brigade was camped on a plantation, a green trooper from the 3rd Tennessee Cavalry—in violation of policy—"went off by himself to forage." When he saw some soldiers ahead of him, he mistook them for Confederates and opened fire. They, in turn, assuming he was the enemy, returned fire. The 3rd Tennessee quickly sounded "boots and saddles," thinking it was under attack. Fortunately, before anyone was killed, it was quickly discovered they were firing at their own men.[15] These were undisciplined troops.

Sergeant Larson describes the almost impassable terrain encountered by the expedition in this low-lying, swamp-infested part of Mississippi that was much more familiar to General Forrest and his cavalry:

> Soon after we started it began to rain and continued with more or less force for several days, which made the road bad every-where. In swamps the logs in the corduroy bridges were swimming and loose so that the horses stepped in between them, and sinking in the mud, got hurt or lamed. After passing a swamp we would come on a muddy road; sticky black mud, too. . . . The prospect of having to wade through [it] for over 250 miles . . . was very gloomy . . .[16]

The green Federal soldiers became terrified at the prospect of becoming lost in the unfamiliar and forbidding swamps. This circumstance provided the perfect setting for an ambush, with "bushwackers [firing] on the rear and advance-guard," killing several troopers.[17]

Smith's command continued moving south toward Okolona, meeting little opposition. "Here began a systematic destruction of the supplies, the [rail]road, [cotton]gin houses, cotton, barns, and dwellings. Escaped slaves, mounted on their masters' stock, flocked to [Smith] to the number of three thousand"—nearly half again as many as the original military column.[18] This was an unwelcome and dangerous burden for a cavalry expedition.

On the seventeenth, the brigades that had been marching on parallel roads came together and "marched in one body through Pontotoc."[19] The next day, General Smith issued orders to Colonel George Waring, commanding First Brigade, to destroy the railroad and any government stores it found. Smith would accompany the troops, escorted by the 4th US Cavalry.[20] At daybreak on February 19, the brigade marched on the road to Egypt Station, arriving there between 8 and 9 a.m. The Federals destroyed all the government property at and near the station. From there, the brigade marched to Prairie Station, about fifteen miles north of West Point, arriving at 6 p.m. The expedition covered a distance of twenty-two miles with several "trifling skirmishes in the course of the day."²¹ Careful reconnaissance was made of the Sakatonchee Swamp on their right, the Oktibbeha at their front, and the Tombigbee on their left. "They were all found strongly held by the enemy, present in four brigades and to the number of about 6,000 or 7,000, according to the best information that could be obtained." It was also reported that General Stephen Lee was about to reinforce Forrest "with a portion or the whole of his command."²² It was one of General Forrest's tactics to see to it that through rumor spread by sympathetic citizens or "captured" rebels, Union forces always received information of greatly exaggerated Confederate forces. "Knowing that Nathan Bedford Forrest commanded the troops he was fighting . . . and not knowing how many of the enemy he faced," Smith decided to concentrate at Prairie Station.²³

On the nineteenth, the expedition arrived in Monroe County, Mississippi, described as "a beautiful place," where the land was level and very fertile. Forrest's biographer, Andrew Lytle, provides a description of the countryside:

> The dividing line between the hill and flat country was Okolona, the Indian word for Queen of the Prairie. The prairie produced corn in such abundance that it was called Egypt Land. Along the Mobile and Ohio Railroad there was hundreds of bins filled with corn for the armies of the Confederacy. Each bin belonged to a farmer, and it was his duty to keep it filled at fixed times. Besides, the depots were crammed with meal, bacon, white beans, and hundreds of thousands of bushels of corn in the shuck. . . . Two streams, the Tombigbee River and the Sakatonchee Creek bound together this granary.²⁴

"Here the Confederacy had gathered supplies in great abundance. Great piles of corn and fodder dotted thickly all over the land. Some piles of corn must have been 100 yards long, 30 wide, and 25 feet high." With the exception of what the Union troops used themselves, these were all burned.²⁵ At 3 p.m. on the twentieth, Smith reached West Point, ninety miles north of Meridian. As the expedition marched farther south, the country "became more settled, with large plantations along the road, and fields all snow-white with cotton, but no pickers in them." Larson records that at about this time, "a change seemed to come over General Smith. He did not push forward as he had been doing." Apparently, the general had taken seriously ill and was reportedly riding in a carriage.²⁶ "We made long stops every day on the march":

> while large detachments were sent out all directions to destroy everything that could be of use by the enemy, and gather all the horses and mules they could find.
>
> Every day fires could be seen in all directions, where these detachments were burning cotton and large quantities of corn. In fact, the expedition seemed all of a sudden to have turned into a raid with no other object than to destroy Confederate [and private] property.²⁷

The corn burned with an "exceedingly bright light" and intense heat. As far as the eye could see, the countryside was lit up with "wild, flashing flames." "Destruction and fury were depicted over the land" as the flames "mellowed by the clouds of smoke gave a ghost-like appearance to the men." It was "a picture of the desolation of war. . . angry and furious destruction, awful terror, ghastly and hideous specters."²⁸ The Volunteer troops were out of control. "The behavior of some of the troops," writes Larson, "was not as we had been in the habit of seeing cavalry act in our department."²⁹ Not surprisingly, the duty to "prevent the willful destruction of private homes by fire" was assigned to the Regulars. The night of the twentieth General Forrest, leading Ben McCulloch's brigade, discovered a small detachment of 4th Regulars led by Lieutenant Neil McCafferty. After a brief skirmish during which several men of the 4th Cavalry were killed, McCafferty and about twenty-three of his men were captured. Forrest "condemned McCafferty and his party to be shot, without court-martial. Only the interceding of a miller, at whose mill they were and which McCafferty had saved from burning by Union troops, saved him and his men."³⁰ McCafferty was later exchanged; the fate of the enlisted men is unknown.

Ellis Bridge

On Sunday morning, February 21, Smith's column and Forrest's cavalry had their first major encounter at Ellis Bridge, at Sakatonchee Creek, about three miles south of West Point. Colonel Jeffrey Forrest— the general's brother—had his brigade posted there to prevent the Federals from crossing.³¹ The main road in the area was bound by swamps on both sides and Ellis Bridge was the only means of crossing the creek.³² "That morning [James R.] Chalmers' Division held the crossing of the Sakatonchee, with Jeffrey Forrest's Brigade north of the stream and McCulloch's on the south bank, covering and holding Ellis Bridge."³³ After engaging the enemy for about two hours, General Smith turned his column around and began to retreat north toward Okolona. "No sooner had we turned tail," writes Colonel Waring, commanding the First Brigade, "than Forrest saw his time had come, and he pressed us sorely all day and until nightfall."³⁴

Soon Smith found himself in a difficult situation. He was bogged down in unfamiliar, swampy territory with thousands of contraband. His command was being harassed by Forrest's cavalry, whose strength he had greatly over-estimated. Fearing he was being drawn into a trap, a weary and ill General Smith seems to have lost his nerve and began to retreat. With Forrest harassing the rear of his column, Smith's Federals "marched till 2 a.m. and halted for four hours three miles south of Okolona."³⁵

Outnumbered by more than two to one, Forrest proceeded to take every advantage offered by the Union Army. Believing the attack at Ellis Bridge was "a mere feint to cover a retreat," Forrest determined the Federal forces would not leave the country without a fight.³⁶

THE 4TH UNITED STATES CAVALRY AT OKOLONA, MISSISSIPPI

> . . . *the grandest cavalry charge I ever witnessed.*
> – N. B. Forrest³⁷

Late on the evening of February 21, the Fourth Regiment took possession of the town of Okolona and "went into camp in the outskirts." Sergeant Larson described the town:

> . . . a small but nicely built railroad town located on high ground and most of the houses were two-story buildings. The railroad passed close to the place on the opposite side from where we camped. Of course a good deal of the track on the road was destroyed by General Smith's men during the night.³⁸

On the morning of the twenty-second, reveille was sounded early. The men were up before daylight and had time to feed their horses and prepare breakfast. The line of march north was taken up by daybreak.³⁹ The Third Brigade was in the rear of the column, and the 2nd Tennessee, "having but 275 men for duty," was the rear guard.⁴⁰ McCrillis received orders from General Grierson to move out and join the column on the Pontotoc Road.⁴¹ Grierson also ordered the Fourth Regulars, commanded by Captain Bowman, to relieve the 2nd Tennessee as rear guard. The 4th US Cavalry was now alone in the town of Okolona with orders "to hold the town ten minutes longer and then fall back."⁴² The men of the 4th Cavalry, writes Larson, "had not the slightest idea that there was any considerable number of the enemy's troops within fifty miles of Okolona":

> It was therefore a surprise to us when, just at daybreak, we were ordered to saddle up at once, and soon after mounted and wheeled by fours into town through the main street toward the railroad, which was on the opposite side of the town from where we had been in camp.⁴³

This activity was precipitated by the Confederates, who were also moving before daylight. A portion of the rebel force was moving to attack the Union forces at Okolona, while Forrest, with his escort company and one brigade, made a "circuit around the town" on the left flank "with the evident intention of cutting off two or three regiments in the rear."⁴⁴ The Union rear guard (the 2nd Tennessee) was the first to be hit. "They received us with a volley," Forrest later wrote, "and charged with yells, but were handsomely repulsed in the open field and forced to retreat, which they did rapidly and in confusion."⁴⁵

Lieutenant William McTeer, 3rd Tennessee, presents a slightly different version. Just as the 2nd Tennessee withdrew from Okolona to join the retreating Union forces, their rear pickets were attacked and "driven rapidly forward":

> A company was quickly thrown out in the line facing the rear and when the Confederates came in range they received a deadly volley, which checked and confused them. As that company retired another formed some distance in front and waited for the enemy. The bloody work was repeated . . . holding in check the forces of the enemy that was pressing the rear.⁴⁶

Since the Tennessee regiments had the greater firepower of the new Spencer rifles, McTeer's description might be more accurate than Forrest's. However, in the first few moments of the attack, the 2nd Tennessee lost Lieutenant-Colonel Cook (captured) and "14 men killed and wounded." The troopers quickly found themselves being flanked on the right and left by the Confederates.[47] This might help explain their subsequent actions in the ensuing panic. Lieutenant McTeer raced off to find Colonel McCrillis, who was riding at the head of his command unaware of what was happening at the rear of his column.[48] At the same time, the balance of Forrest's men "charged into Okolona . . . yelling and firing." The second battalion of the 4th Regulars (Companies F, H, and M), commanded by Captain Thomas McCormick, had the rear guard and received the brunt of the rebel attack.[49] Sergeant Larson provides a detailed description of the men of the 4th US Cavalry meeting the rebels coming through Okolona. They pushed the Confederates back into the town and made an orderly retreat that delayed the effectiveness of the enemy and helped to protect the rear of the Union column:

> All three companies wheeled about and came up alongside of each other, still retaining the formation in column of fours, then opening heavy fire on the advancing enemy, which checked their rush. Then one company fell back a short distance and wheeled about and faced the enemy again, then the next company did the same, on so on. By that means the enemy was constantly faced by all three companies. The enemy poured out of town in columns of fours and wheeled into line along the road, which was on much higher ground than where the 4th Cavalry stood. A regular fusillade then began. It was no more a matter of desultory firing or skirmish, but volleys roaring like a regular battle.[50]

All the while, the now-wakened townspeople "appeared very interested" in the pre-dawn battle raging in their streets:

> All the windows in the upper stories were crowded with ladies, young and old . . . their hair . . . flowing loose about their heads, arms bare nearly to the shoulder, [hanging] out of the windows, and [waving] small Confederate flags and handkerchiefs frantically to encourage their men to give those hateful 'Yanks' Hail Columbia![51]

From this point on, it is difficult to determine what happened next. There was considerable confusion on the field, for which Forrest and his tactics must be given credit, compounded by inexperienced cavalry regiments and very poor command on the Union side. There was also another factor apparently affecting the efficiency of the Union forces. Lieutenant McTeer, attached to Brigade headquarters, writes about the "strong jealousy" that existed within the command of the Third Brigade between the soldiers of the Army of the Cumberland and the Army of the Mississippi: "Part of the Brigade staff were determined that the Mississippi men should have the glory and the Cumberland men the cursing." McTaer cites this as the reason the 4th US Cavalry was "left in the streets of Okolona to fight Forrest's command alone and without support."[52] McTeer continues:

> The attack came with terrific fury, and the Regulars stood their ground with great bravery. The firing was heavy, and in its heat Capt. Glore of the 5th Ky., rode up to Col. McCrillis and said: "Colonel, hadn't we better reinforce our men in Okolona? They are being butchered there!"
> "Oh no!" McCrillis replied, "that is only a skirmish."
> Capt. Glore's countenance fell as he slowly rode off, replying:
> "I call it a _____ heavy skirmish!"[53]

According to McTeer: "Only one regiment at a time was thrown out to meet the enemy, and so we were cut to pieces by piecemeal. . . . Had the whole command been thrown into action at once, the result would undoubtedly have been reversed."[54] McTeer goes so far in his May 1891 remembrance as to question the sobriety of those making the decisions in the Third Brigade.[55] Meanwhile, according to acting 1st Sergeant Larson, the "skirmish" in Okolona became:

> one of the most stubborn cavalry fights with carbine and revolver at short range, at a stand and mounted, that ever occurred

on any battlefield of the Civil War. Men in the enemy's line could be seen to give a sort of spring, and tumble head foremost to the earth; horses fell, and others that had lost their riders chased about wildly. . . . I emptied and reloaded my two revolvers three times, and therefore fired forty-eight shots . . .[56]

Three Regulars near Larson were shot and killed. Unaware at the time it happened, Larson's mount had taken a bullet and was disabled, which later nearly caused Larson to be captured:

The pressure on us was getting heavier every minute. The enemy was constantly pushing troops toward their left so as to envelope our right. On our left, where the 2nd Battalion stood, was a street coming out of the town just in rear of our line, and [rebel] troops began to appear in that street where they would at once be in position to take the 2nd Battalion and the left of our line in rear, as well as in flank.[57]

At that moment, two regiments of Volunteer cavalry arrived "in columns of fours on a brisk gallop as if they meant business." When they got within eight or nine hundred yards, Larson writes, "they wheeled in line and halted":

. . . but they did not remain a minute. They saw enough at once . . . their ranks broke and they went to the rear as fast, or perhaps faster than they had come to the front. At any rate, they started a most disgraceful cavalry stampede, the only one I witnessed during the whole war.[58]

What distressed the Regulars even more was the fact that these regiments were armed with the "Spencer seven-shooting carbine, the best cavalry gun in the army."[59] Larson continues:

The country on that side of the town was an open prairie for a couple of miles, and as the enemy stood on the highest ground from where they could overlook the whole flat, they saw the two Yankee Regiments flying from the field without firing a shot. The enemy were now assured of having no other troops to deal with than the 4th US Cavalry.[60]

"The 2nd Tennessee, being in pieces, and endeavoring to form," was apparently run over by the retreating cavalry regiments. The Third Brigade was struck next, "her columns broken and driven in confusion." The enemy "saw the condition of the arrears" and took every advantage. "They pressed the rearguard and added flanking columns, thus cutting off small squads of men."[61] The 4th Regulars were now entirely on their own, and it "became necessary to begin a retrograde movement":

Both flanks had to be cleared of the Rebs that were constantly massing in those directions and that had to be done by a charge from both flanks of the regiment. The 4th Battalion being on the right, charged in that direction and the 2nd Battalion charged to the left. The moment the charging battalions rushed forward the other two battalions wheeled about and fell back slowly, firing rapidly as possible to the rear. The 2nd Battalion, Company "H" in the lead, rushed at full speed against the Rebs that were coming out of that street and ran them at once. They did not seem to relish a saber fight. We drove them away into the market square, but there we found the market-house full of infantry and so turned into an alley and left the town. The alley brought us out to a large field enclosed by a fence. There, after kicking the top rails off, we jumped the fence and were in the field when the Rebs we had driven into town, came yelling and firing out of the alley.[62]

Forrest himself supported Larson's version. As he wrote in his report, the 4th Cavalry "was forced to retreat . . . using every exertion to check pursuit by ambuscading and forming regiments on either side of the road, who would fire and retreat successively."[63] By Forrest's own testimony, the 4th U.S. did not participate in the stampede, as it would later be accused of doing.

Having "shaken the enemy off the flanks," the 4th Cavalry, "under a hale of fire," regrouped on the main road and fell back "in a regular and steady order" while "stubbornly resisting the rushing advance of the enemy."[64] "They seemed to have too much respect for us," Larson wrote, "to try to rush in on us."[65] What Larson took for respect may have had more to do with Forrest's tactics, as well as his shortage of ammunition.[66] That the 4th US Cavalry had fought an extremely hard battle is reflected in a comment made by Colonel Joseph Kargé, commanding 2nd New Jersey Cavalry: "I saw the Fourth Regulars coming from the direction of Okolona in a rather disturbed condition, exhibiting marks of pretty severe handling."[67]

An early Union casualty of the stampede was six guns of General Smith's artillery. Sergeant Larson came across the six pieces "about a half mile from where we entered the woods." They were "tumbled over in a deep gully by the roadside":

> The stampede must have been terrible from the very beginning. Artillerists are not likely to abandon their pieces if there is a chance to save them, because it is a disgrace to them similar to losing a flag by a regiment. Hence they must have been so crowded by the stampeders that they had been forced into the gully and obliged to unhitch the horses and leave the guns, wheels upwards.[68]

The Union command was desperately trying to stem the panic. Colonel Waring, commanding First Brigade, witnessed the effects of the stampede. He received a message from the rear that the 4th US Cavalry had been forced to retire "with much loss" and that the "whole of the Third Brigade" was unable to resist the onward march of the enemy and were "retreating upon the main column." Taking advantage of the road "being pretty wide and the woods open," he formed his brigade in line "with skirmishers far out on each flank" and remained in this position until the Third Brigade had passed through "in such confusion as to endanger the morale of my own command."[69]

Lieutenant Colonel Thomas Brown, 7th Indiana Cavalry, was at the rear of the First Brigade when called out to assist the 4th U.S. His regiment had moved but a few miles "when a portion of the force left in our rear came forward in the wildest disorder and confusion."[70] Adding to the chaos was the panic among the blacks, who were fearful of being captured by the Confederates. As described by Colonel Waring:

> The immense train of pack mules and mounted contrabands, which had been corralled in a field near the road, swarmed up with such force as to carry past the line the Second New Jersey and Second Illinois Cavalry, which were then marching to this position. Several regiments of the other brigades were brought to a stand at this place, and the chief of cavalry in person assumed command of the field.[71]

All attempts at reorganizing the Union troops were futile.[72] General Grierson—whose division "had not been engaged at all" — along with part of his staff officers aided by part of McCrillis' staff, tried to "check the column." At this point in the rout, "the men were mixed until companies and regiments were unknown."[73] Several officers of the 4th Cavalry arrived on the scene. Captain Bowman and Lieutenants Thomas Sullivan, Wirt Davis, and others tried to stem the panic and organize the troops but "found it only partially practicable." They would later be credited with rendering "efficient service and assistance in checking the advance of the enemy" as Union forces were eventually reorganized.[74] It took some individual acts of bravery to finally stem the tide. Captain Booth of McCrillis' staff received "an ugly but not dangerous wound across his nose":

> The blood ran down his face and over his clothes and upon his horse until he presented a ghastly appearance. In this condition he stopped at the roadside in a little field and called some men to halt with him. They did so. He placed himself at the side of the road and ordered the men as they came up to form on that line, 'Let us stop and fight them here!'
>
> The color-bearer of the 72nd [Indiana Mounted] came along with his colors rolled up and covered. Captain Booth asked him if he couldn't throw his colors, to which he readily assented. The banner was unfurled, and the men came to it like a colony of bees to their queen . . . and thus reorganization began.[75]

Forrest reported that upon "gaining the broken and hilly country on the Pontotoc road," the Union resistance became more stubborn. He was compelled to dismount most of his command and fight the last nine miles on foot. "About 5 miles from Okolona they formed and awaited us, making a determined stand... After a short but obstinate resistance the enemy gave way."[76]

The Federal forces "formed a new line on Ivey's Hill farm, near Tallaboncla, some seven miles northwest of Okolona on the Pontotoc road."[77] When the rebels attacked, they were met with "good effect by the battery of the Fourth Missouri Cavalry." A fragment from an exploding shell is reported to have killed Colonel Jeffrey Forrest, who was commanding the enemy's column.[78] As described by General Forrest, the Union forces:

> had formed in three lines across a large field on the left of the road... Their lines were at intervals of several hundred paces, and the rear and second lines longer than the first. As the advance of my column moved up they opened on us with artillery. My ammunition was nearly exhausted, and I knew that if we faltered they would in turn become the attacking party, and that disaster might follow. Many of my men were broken down and exhausted with clambering the hills on foot and fighting almost constantly for the last 9 miles.... As we moved up, the whole force charged down at a gallop, and I am proud to say that my men did not disappoint me. Standing firm, they repulsed the grandest cavalry charge I ever witnessed.[79]

What Forrest observed was the final cavalry charge of the day led by the 4th United States Cavalry. As described by Sergeant Larson:

> Major Bowman galloped out in front and gave the command, 'draw saber' and then in a thundering voice the command 'charge' followed, and away we went. There was no powder to be wasted by us this time. The saber had to do the work and did it in much quicker time than firing could have done. The charge was made in regimental front and met by a volley from the enemy's line, but only one. Then the sabers clashed among them and in a short time they were fleeing into the woods for protection.[80]

Forrest offers a slightly different version. He writes that his cavalry "drove back the advance line" and "each successive line of the enemy" until they "fled the field in dismay and confusion..." It was late in the afternoon and, owing to the exhausted condition of his men and horses, "and being almost out of ammunition," he was compelled to stop pursuit.[81] Smith's expedition retreated in disgrace.

With 2,500 men—including "new troops from Tennessee" —and with each man having "not more than 40 rounds of ammunition," Nathan Bedford Forrest managed to rout and defeat 7,000 Union cavalrymen armed with superior weapons.[82] He suffered a total of 144 casualties: seven officers and twenty men killed, seventeen officers and eighty men wounded, and twenty men missing.[83] General Smith's column, including the 4th US Cavalry, reported a loss of 388: two officers and fifty-two men killed, sixteen officers and 163 men wounded, and two officers and 153 men captured or missing.[84] Second Lieutenant McCafferty, 4th U.S., who had been captured on the twentieth while protecting private property and was later exchanged, was again captured and held for a brief time by the rebels. Five men of the 4th Cavalry were killed: Sergeant John Carmichael, Company B; Corporal Stephen Wetzberger, Company A; and Privates Frank Bars, Company H, John Baum, Company G, and Levi Pettitt, Company G. An additional thirteen were wounded and thirty-two were captured or missing for a total of fifty-one—a thirteen percent casualty rate.[85]

Forrest considered "the defeat of this force, consisted as it did of the best cavalry in the Federal army, as a victory of which all engaged in it may justly feel proud...":

> and its moral effect upon the raw, undisciplined and undrilled troops of this command is in value incalculable. It has inspired them with courage and given themselves confidence in themselves and their commanders.[86]
>
> ... [T]he moral effect of their victory over the best cavalry in the Federal service will tell in their future operations against the enemy, inspiring them with courage and confidence in their ability to whip them again. Considering the disparity in numbers, discipline, and drill, I consider it one of the most complete victories that have occurred since the war began.[87]

Sherman never forgave General Smith for the failure of the Meridian expedition.[88] For his part, Smith found no shortage of excuses, including, but not limited to, the nature of the terrain and the massive "incumbrances"—the thousands of slaves and livestock accumulated along the way. He blamed his subordinates, particularly those in McCrillis' brigade. While addressing his command, he publicly charged the officers and men of the 2nd East Tennessee and 2nd New Jersey with cowardice:

> I sent you to assist the 4th Cavalry in checking the enemy's advance because both your regiments are armed with the Spencer carbine . . . But what did you do with it? You not only rendered no assistance to the regiment . . . but without reason or cause . . . you stampeded in plain view of the enemy, and went to the rear in a complete panic that caused the loss of a battery.[89]

Then, pointing to the men of the Fourth United States Cavalry, he said:

> To that regiment . . . is due all honor and credit for the staunch, soldierly conduct that prevented this day from becoming even more disastrous. The 4th US Cavalry, armed with an inferior carbine and not even enough of them, stood firmly to their duty and prevented the annihilation of my whole column and I sincerely thank both officers and men for their gallant conduct.[90]

General Smith personally told Captain Bowman, commanding the 4th U.S.: "As soon as we arrive at Memphis your regiment will receive the Spencer. You can rely on that. Such a regiment ought to carry the best weapons that can be had, and I shall see that your men are fully equipped before they go into action again."[91]

For leading three successful charges against the rebel brigade at Okolona, Captain Charles Bowman was brevetted major and Lieutenant Wirt Davis was brevetted captain for "gallant and meritorious services" on the Meridian Expedition.[92]

First Lieutenant William Ingerton was also cited for "leading the charge of the Third Tennessee most brilliantly . . . distinguished by his skill and dashing bravery."[93]

Sergeant Larson concludes:

> For the 4th US Cavalry it had been as hard a day as any regiment, either cavalry or infantry had experienced in any of the big battles.
> . . . [W]e had made a long toilsome march of more than 825 miles and had been in an engagement as severe as any ever recorded in which we had maintained the good name of the regiment and brigade, and had added another wreath of laurels to it.[94]

III. Preparing for the Atlanta Campaign

THE SPENCER CARBINE

On or about February 26—in the aftermath of the Meridian Expedition—Sooy Smith's defeated cavalry straggled back into Memphis, where they remained for the next two weeks, "mounting, equipping and preparing" for the coming campaign.[1]

General Smith kept his word. The 4th United States Cavalry, writes Larson, "received the premium General Smith had promised us for our part in the Mississippi campaign. . .a brand new Spencer carbine for every man in the regiment":

> We were proud of them, as they were not issued as the government generally issued necessary arms to soldiers, but as reward for our conduct in the disastrous affair at Okolona. From that day on, *We . . . carried with us what was to us Medals of Honor, our Spencer rifles* [emphasis author].[2]

The new Spencer carbine—the most advanced weapon of the day—could be fired seven times without reloading. As opposed to the Spencer rifle, the carbine had a shorter barrel more suited for cavalry use and was lighter than the rifle. David Evans describes the advantages of the weapon:

> A spring-tensioned tubular magazine in the Spencer's stock held seven copper

cased .52 caliber rimfire cartridges. Pushing the gun's loading lever down lowered the breechblock, ejecting a spent cartridge. Pulling the lever back up raised the breechblock and chambered a fresh round. The hammer was cocked by hand like a regular musket, but a practiced marksman could empty the magazine in as little as ten seconds. [The men] soon learned they could keep up a withering fire by moving the loading lever just enough to unseat the spent casing and reloading from their cartridge boxes. That way, a good trooper always had seven rounds in reserve.[3]

Perhaps the most astonishing feature of the Spencer carbine was that it was waterproof and could be carried and loaded under water. Colonel Sipes described the crossing of the Chattahoochee River outside Roswell, Georgia, on July 9, 1864:

> In crossing, which was accomplished by fording the river dismounted, the men would keep down in the water, only exposing their heads, put the seven cartridges in the magazine, then raising, would pour water from the muzzle, and blaze away at the astonished enemy. Never had they seen guns that could be loaded in this way.[4]

Surgeon George W. Smith, 4th Michigan, described their confidence in the new guns:

> ... [The] regiments are well mounted and armed with a new arm, known as the Spencer Carbine (believed to be the most effective Cavalry arm ever introduced into the service) ... It is twelve inches shorter and five pounds lighter [than the Spencer rifle] and consequently much less fatiguing for the men. It carries seven cartridges instead of five and is breech loading. The cartridge is so constructed as to require no cap. The men are to carry no pistols, but each man has a good cavalry saber. *This brigade, thus armed, will be one of the finest bodies of cavalry ever sent to the field* [emphasis author].[5]

"Our Spencer rifles [carbines] are the best thing in the world," writes Charles Bates. "One man with them is equal to twenty with the old fashioned rifles. The Lord have mercy on the souls of all rebs we come across this summer for its sure death to their bodies. I expect to have the blood of a thousand on my hands."[6]

The longer and more accurate Spencer rifle—considered the best gun of the Civil War—was used primarily by the infantry, but was also issued to Wilder's Mounted Infantry.[7] Colonel Minty describes the destructive power now in the hands of the Saber Brigade:

> [T]he marked difference between our casualties and those of the enemy, invariably prevailed when we used the sabers. The dashing charge, the gleaming sabers, and the wild cheering of the horsemen always disconcerted the enemy; their fire was wild and uncertain, and when we struck them our keen sabers always did effective work. Our Spencer carbines were so effective, and we had such unlimited confidence in them, that in our dismounted fighting we always felt that we could cope with seven times our number; the confidence the men had in themselves and in their weapons rendered them cool and steady, and their fire was always destructive.[8]

The Spencer had one life-saving quality–it could be loaded from the prone position, unlike the muzzle-loading rifles that had to be loaded while the soldier was standing, making himself a better target. Unfortunately, there was an unexpected, although logical, consequence to having this superior firepower: "Once outfitted with the powerful Spencer repeating carbines, [the troopers] were often placed at the forefront of the army, thus finding themselves continuously exposed to enemy fire."[9]

After a short stay at Memphis, the 4th U.S. received orders to return to their own army at Nashville, Tennessee. Major Joseph E. Hedges, in his 1886 letter to Joseph Vale, described the trip:

> We staid [sic] at Memphis a few days, and then started back to Nashville overland, but being in the spring of the year, it proved to be marching through water most of the way. We had to abandon and burn our wagons before we had gone very far.
> We crossed several rivers by fording, swimming, and building bridges besides the Tennessee and Cumberland, which we

crossed by boat [. . .] and while we were making this trip, Forrest went up to Columbus and murdered the negro troops at Fort Pillow. How we escaped his command, was more luck than strategy. Our regiment was entirely alone–not over nine hundred strong–while Forrest must have had some ten thousand, and after he returned south of the Memphis and Charleston railroad, you will recollect that General Sam Sturgis was sent out with an infantry command of five thousand or six thousand from Memphis, and Forrest pitched into and whipped him, and drove him back into Memphis.[10]

On April 21, 1864, one of the most notorious events of the war happened at Fort Pillow, Tennessee, on the banks of the Mississippi River. While on a raiding expedition against Federal operations in Tennessee and Kentucky, Forrest's troops surrounded Fort Pillow, demanding its surrender. Originally built by the Confederates in 1861 "to assist in defending the water approaches to Memphis" and abandoned in 1862, the crude fort was now held by approximately 580 "black and white Union troops, more or less evenly divided."[11] Forrest's biographer Brian Wills provides a psychological explanation for the ensuing massacre at the hands of Forrest's men:

> In his attitude toward the members of the Union fort's garrison, Forrest exposed his deepest prejudices. As a white Southerner, he considered the white Southerners in Fort Pillow to be traitors and examples of humanity at its worst. To Forrest, it was such 'renegade Tennesseans' who violated the norms of warfare and civilization. They were the cold-blooded savages who waged war on civilians, tortured prisoners, and compounded their sins by fighting beside former slaves. And the black troops were little better. They were deluded miscreants, coerced from the fields by their new masters. But their current behavior, as misguided as it might be, could not be tolerated.[12]

Having failed to negotiate a surrender, the Confederates attacked and quickly overran the fort. The panicked Union forces—especially the black troops—began to run. While in the process of attempting to flee or surrender, white and black troops alike were shot down in a "systematic massacre."[13] While this shocked and inflamed the passions of the North, it also reverberated through the black troops of the Union Army. The repercussion of this event contributed to Forrest's greatest victory in the war on June 10, 1864, at Brice's Crossroads, Mississippi. In an effort to "cripple or destroy" Forrest, the Federals had assembled over 8,300 cavalrymen and infantrymen, of which 1,200 of the infantrymen were black troops. General Samuel D. Sturgis, USV, a major on the roster of the 4th US Cavalry, had command. Forrest, with only 4,800 troops, was aided by foul weather that mired the Union advance in mud and, using his familiarity of the densely wooded terrain as a tactical ally, he defeated the Union forces in a fierce, day-long battle. Many of the black troops panicked and ran, and Forrest took an additional toll with a "relentless pursuit" of the routed and retreating Federal army.[14]

NASHVILLE, TENNESSEE

During the last week of February, Colonel Sipes, commanding the 7th Pennsylvania, "drew from the Ordnance Department at Washington [DC] complete sets of horse equipments, Spencer carbines and sabers for a full regiment. These were shipped to Nashville, where the regiment arrived early in March."[15] On March 19, the Fourth United States joined the command at Nashville and, having received a sufficient number of recruits to make a full complement, was remounted, armed with Spencer carbines, and fully equipped and ready for the field. The 4th Michigan was likewise re-equipped.[16] The eighteen hundred men of these three regiments—temporarily commanded by Colonel Sipes—went into camp on the Franklin Turnpike, three miles south of Nashville.[17] "The army was then being prepared for the advance on Atlanta, and care was taken to mount and equip the [regiments] as completely as possible."[18]

THE COURT MARTIAL OF COLONEL ROBERT H. G. MINTY

After a frustrating five months waiting for his court martial, Minty's trial was held from February 3 to 16 at Nashville, "on the charge of 'disobedience to orders' at Shelbyville, during the Wheeler raid. "He was on the latter date triumphantly acquitted by the unanimous vote of the whole court," and eventually returned, by order of General Garrard, to the command of the brigade.[19] The following was published in the *Detroit Advertiser and Tribune* "where in fine Victorian fashion, nothing was held back in the editor's criticism of General Crook":

> Just five months from [his arrest] he was 'honorably acquitted,' and restored to his command. A few hours investigation served to satisfy the court of the entire want of foundation for the charges. They were absolutely *childish*. General Crook made a great blunder in marching on the morning of Oct. 7th without sending orders to the 1st (Col. Minty's) Brigade. He was following the enemy; overtook and fought him; wanted to use the brigade, and came near meeting with a serious disaster for want of Colonel Minty's command. He was deeply mortified, and in his vexation arrested Colonel Minty, hoping, no doubt, to divert attention to *his own culpable heedlessness*.[20]

Colonel Robert Minty was allowed to return to his own men on April 17.[21]

By the beginning of May, "Sherman had assembled three veteran armies commanded by Major Generals George Henry Thomas, James Birdseye McPherson, and John McAllister Schofield," numbering just over 100,000 men and 254 guns.[22] The Cavalry Corps, under Brigadier General Washington L. Elliott—which General Sherman assembled for his Atlanta Campaign—"numbered about fifteen thousand sabers" organized into four divisions: The First, commanded by Colonel Edward M. McCook, (1st Lieutenant, 4th Cavalry); the Second Division by Brigadier General Kenner Dudley Garrard; and the Third Division commanded originally by Colonel William W. Lowe and later by Brigadier General Judson Kilpatrick. "Major General Lovell H. Rousseau commanded a much smaller expeditionary force."[23]

In the Second Division, commanded by Kenner Garrard, Colonel Minty's First Brigade included the 4th US Cavalry, 7th Pennsylvania Cavalry, and 4th Michigan Cavalry.

The Second Brigade was commanded by Colonel Eli Long (captain, 4th US Cavalry) and the Third Brigade of Mounted Infantry was commanded by Colonel John T. Wilder.[24] Sherman's order to advance was issued on April 2, 1864, and two days later, division headquarters moved from Huntsville, Alabama, to Columbia, Tennessee, to concentrate the command at that point "predatory to its reorganization and fitting for the summer campaign."[25] "On April 19 the First Brigade joined General Garrard at Columbia," where Colonel Minty once again took command of his Saber Brigade.[26]

On the twenty-fifth, Colonels "Minty, Long, and Wilder reported with complete commands," spending the next few days "in completing arrangements for operations in the field."[27]

"On the 30th of April, 1864," writes Minty, "the First and Third Brigades of the Second Cavalry Division... marched from Columbia, Tenn., to join the army south of Chattanooga, and to take part in the coming Atlanta campaign." The three regiments (4th Michigan, 7th Pennsylvania, and the 4th Regulars), once again under the capable command of Captain James McIntyre, "mustered about 2,500 men; they were well mounted, well equipped, and well armed, and, above all, they had full and implicit confidence in themselves."[28] Cavalry historian David Evans states that Kenner Garrard's Second Cavalry Division was Sherman's "*biggest and best-equipped* [emphasis author]."[29]

This feeling was also expressed by Captain Burns of the 4th Michigan Cavalry:

> We have obtained new horses, new saddles, new everything, and the celebrated seven-shooting Spencer Carbine, the best arm in the service. The three regiments are fitted-out alike, and we never were in as good a condition. It is supposed that we shall see some hard service this summer.[30]

Burns could not have been more correct. As the "best-equipped" cavalry force, it was constantly in use during the Atlanta Campaign. "Rapport within the cavalry corps was at a zenith," writes Minty's biographer:

> The men, amongst proven veterans, with replenished ranks and fresh mounts, and provided with the latest in weapon technology, were at the pinnacle of good morale. Each trooper was filled with anticipation and an anxious yearning to return to the fray.[31]

As stated by a sergeant major in the 7th Pennsylvania, "Our brigade [Minty's] felt perfectly safe when we knew the Ohio boys [Colonel Long's] were on one flank of us and Wilder's Brigade of Mounted Infantry on the other."[32] In his letter of May 11 written from the field, "12½ miles west of Dalton," Charles Bates writes, "Our regiment is 408 fighting men strong but [paraphrasing a poem], 'their hearts are ten thousand. We are fighting men.'" He also includes "a piece of good news–let me tell you that I am appointed Sergeant again."[33]

The Secret Mission of the Horse Marines

About this time, Captain Vale reported on one of the more bizarre expeditions by members of the 4th United States Cavalry. On April 3, while the brigade was encamped near Nashville, Captain George W. Lawton, 4th Michigan Cavalry, was "ordered to take command of a sergeant and fifty men, selected from the Fourth Michigan to which was attached Lieutenant [Elbridge] Roys, Co. G, and a sergeant of the Fourth US Cavalry, with an equal number of men, and to report at army headquarters . . ."[34] They were then directed by a staff officer and conducted on board of the "quartermaster's gunboat, *Silver Wave* . . . lying in the Cumberland, with horse equipments, arms, and ammunition and thirty days' rations."[35] Major Lawton was told to "await orders." At about 10 p.m., he was joined by Brigadier General John M. Corse and instructed to take his orders from him. As Major Lawton writes: "the boat cast off, and we moved down the river with not a distant shadow of understanding of our destination, and amused ourselves in watching the lights of Nashville drop behind us and disappear."[36]

General Sherman had personally selected Corse—whom he considered one of the "finest young officers in any army"—to carry out this enterprise with "the most absolute secrecy." At Nashville, he placed at Corse's disposal "a fleet steam-boat guarded by 100 armed and dismounted cavalry."[37] Corse was to personally deliver secret correspondence to Sherman's generals in the field who were involved in the Red River Campaign in Louisiana, an ill-conceived plan "to establish Union control in Louisiana and eastern Texas."[38] Corse was also instructed to "gather all real information . . . as to forces with Forrest."[39] Sooy Smith's recently failed expedition at Okolona had emboldened General Forrest and left him in control of large parts of eastern Mississippi and western Tennessee. There was concern that he was "threatening to cross the Tennessee" as soon as he could mount his force.[40]

For several days "Horse Marines" were "winding down" the Cumberland, "noting with great interest such points as Fort Donaldon [sic]," stopping at Smithfield for coal, heading down the Ohio, past Paducah, and stopping again at Cairo on April 4 for supplies, including "a cask of 'red-head' whiskey and sundry kegs and half barrels of salt fish."[41] In the absence of any artillerymen and to keep his men busy in anticipation of any of "Forrest's or Wheeler's efforts to take us in," Major Lawton "divided the men into gun-squads and in default of other exercise . . . began to drill in the howitzer and Parrot rifle practice."[42] As the major notes, "they were now *marines*, for if whiskey and salt fish rations, and artillery drill on shipboard don't make a marine, what does?"[43] These exercises proved useful when, on the only eventful incident of the expedition, their little boat was fired upon by "rebels secreted on the bank of the river." Major Lawton was sitting in the cabin "when a crash of glass and shower of splinters, with a spent ball striking at my feet, gave notice of the assault." His men quickly returned fire, disbursing the enemy, but not before the rebels killed a member of the 4th Michigan and slightly wounded a member of the 4th Regulars. Private Andrew J. Bibb, Co. A, 4th Cavalry, was reported to have "drowned in the Mississippi River" on April 5.[44]

Lawton's command was now headed down the Mississippi, "past Island No. 10 and other points made historical by the bloody strife waged upon them. Island No. 10 was almost washed away by the river."[45] After stopping at Memphis on April 6 for more coal and stores, they continued down the river, still not knowing the reason for the expedition or their destination.[46] Arriving at Vicksburg "at about 8 a.m." on the eighth, they "were kindly allowed, by the general, to visit the bluffs, caves and dug-outs . . . and obtain a clearer impression of the great victory gained in its conquest."[47] The expedition was on its way by 11 a.m.[48] When it reached the mouth of the Red River at about 7 a.m. on April 9, they found the "locality was delightful.[49] Roses were in full bloom and most varieties of other flowers, and at the mansion-houses were ladies who, in spite of their Southern proclivities, stood to welcome the 'shoulder-straps' [officers] with smiles and cheerful hospitality."[50] When their small boat headed up the

Red River, they hoped their destination would be New Orleans. Reaching Alexandria, they were informed they were "destined to General [Nathaniel P.] Banks, wherever he might be."[51] Major Lawton believed he was to "escort General Corse to him for some purpose–to deliver dispatches, doubtless, that would not be sent otherwise."[52] However, upon reaching Grand Écore, Lawton found General Banks was in town, claiming a "glorious victory" over Confederate forces that seemed to have left him in "depressing looking circumstances," reminding Lawton of the Union forces at Chickamauga.[53] General Corse, in his report to General Sherman of April 21, described "Bank's demoralized command" as having retreated to Grand Écore "*a la* Bull Run."[54]

Whatever their original objective was, the expedition was now effectively ended and the Horse Marines were left to "wend their way from the Red up the Mississippi, the Ohio, and the Cumberland . . . back to the old wharf at Nashville."[55] Upon rejoining their command, a "show tent" was struck "near the horse corral" and the Horse Marines were persuaded to share their adventure with their fellow troopers.[56]

The Death of Major General Jeb Stuart, C.S.A.

May 1864 was to mark a turning point in the war for both the Union and Confederate cavalries. In the Eastern Theater, a seminal cavalry battle took place on May 11, when General Sheridan took a strong cavalry force of 10,000 Union horsemen, including General James Wilson's cavalry division, on a driving raid toward Richmond, "destroying large quantities of Lee's already dwindling supplies."[57] In a hard-fought battle at Yellow Tavern—a suburb of Richmond—Confederate cavalry commander General Jeb Stuart was mortally wounded, dying the next day. Stuart was one of the most revered officers of the Confederacy and this was a severe loss for the South.[58] Stuart's biographer H. B. McClellan writes: "The Federal Cavalry, up to that time . . . inferior to the Southern horsemen," gained a new "confidence in themselves and their commanders."[59] According to cavalry historian Richard Wormser:

> The day of Southern cavalry was over. There were no horses left to mount another corps or division. While there was Southern horse action for the next eleven months of the war, it was a series of small raids. The power of the cavalry as a striking force had shifted from the South to the North, from J. E. B. Stuart to Phil Sheridan.[60]

It would be the same in the Western Theater, as the growing strength and power of the United States cavalry under Minty, Thomas, and Wilson overrode the Southern Confederacy.

IV: The Atlanta Campaign–May 1864

The Atlanta Campaign provided unique challenges for the cavalry, requiring the continuing evolution of their use and tactics. The first and least desirable was acting as decoys for the infantry, i.e., occupying infantry positions, such as in trenches, while Sherman moved his infantry around, confusing the Confederates as to numbers and placements. Another new tactic was necessitated by the entrenchments and earthworks thrown up by the retreating Confederate forces. These were initially attacked by infantry supported by cavalry, but then the cavalry itself dismounted and began to act like infantry on the initial attack, then remounted to continue the attack. In the end, the cavalry alone—without infantry—would charge and take not only entrenchments and breastworks, but artillery batteries as well. In the true definition of dragoons they fought as effectively on foot as they did while mounted.[1] Colonel Sipes points out that in overcoming the new defenses created by the Confederate Army, "every command did its own engineering and pioneering."

During the last months of the war, when Major General George Thomas appointed General James H. Wilson to command his cavalry, they would initiate the final phase in the evolution of the cavalry: the immediate and continued pursuit of a fleeing command. It would all come together during Wilson's Selma-Macon Campaign in 1865.

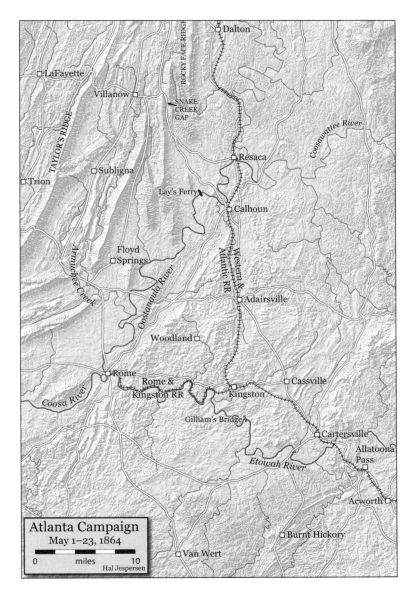

Of the three armies Sherman assembled, General Thomas's Army of the Cumberland "with 60,773 men . . . was larger than the other two combined."[2] General Garrard took two brigades of his division—Minty's First Brigade and Abram O. Miller's Third Brigade—and left Columbia, Tennessee, on April 30, "to join the army south of Chattanooga, and to take part in the coming Atlanta campaign."[3] As Minty recorded, he had "over 2,200 men, 1,994 being included in the class mounted and equipped." The brigades marched through Shelbyville, Tullahoma, and Decherd, crossed the Cumberland Mountains at Cowan, "passed through Stevenson, crossed the Tennessee River on the pontoon bridge at Bridgeport and climbed the steep and rugged Lookout Mountain." From the top they had before them "one of the grandest panoramas in the world."[4] Captain Vale described the grueling journey:

> After crossing the Tennessee, we wended our slow, weary way up the steep sides of the lofty Lookout, until, when about thirty-six hundred feet above the river, we came to the precipitous and often overhanging 'palisades,' extending perpendicularly three hundred feet to the summit above us; then turning sharply to the right passed for nearly two miles along

the base of the high, solid, giant wall, when, coming to what appeared to be a well-used footpath up a long winding stairway of high steps . . . we turned sharply to the left, and, dismounting, scrambled to the top, pulling our horses up and after us. The wagons and artillery had to be hauled, pushed, carried and lifted by hand. It took nearly an hour to get a man and horse, and about three hours to get a wagon or piece of artillery up.[5]

Descending the mountain, the men marched across Lookout Valley, Sand Mountain, and the Valley of the Chickamauga to Lafayette, Georgia, and across Taylor's Ridge to Villanow, at the northern end of Snake Creek Gap, where they arrived on May 10, joining the left wing of the army. In his May 13 letter written "near Villanow, Ga." Lieutenant Henry Potter, 4th Michigan, wrote of the eleven-mile march over Taylor's Ridge to Villanow:

We had the most terrific storm of rain, thunder, and lightning I ever experienced that night. The column marched very fast which kept the rear on a trot. The darkness was so intense you could not distinguish ANYTHING above or below. The rain pound (sic) down so that gullies were formed even under the horses feet. The road was rough, steep, and rocky. The poor horses, urged onward by the men and blinded by the vivid and incandescent flashes, were totally bewildered. When the lightning flashed and lit up the path they would make a rush for the horse ahead of them, when the darkness, thick enough to be felt or cut, closed down they would stop like stocks or, still goaded, would pitch blindly into the bush on either side. The road in the morning was strewn with hats, caps, canteens, haversacks, rubber blankets, etc., with here and there a poor horse or mule who had given up the ghost. I cannot tell you–it was the worst night I ever saw of the kind. I have suffered with cold and hunger many nights, but this was ahead in honor and grandeur, in light and blackness, in cursing and laughing that I ever saw or hope to see.

Colonel Sipes also wrote of the difficulties faced by the brigade:

The march was in impenetrable darkness, the rain pouring down, but somehow the place to be held was reached about midnight. The water on the ground where the Seventh was halted was up to the horses' knees, and most of the men remained mounted until day dawned. Then the rain ceased, and on the sloping hillsides places could be found where earth and vegetation were merely drenched–not submerged–and here the cavalry remained for twenty-four hours.[6]

According to his letter of May 11, Charles Bates put the 4th U.S. "on the extreme right of the Army and at present . . . camped 12½ miles west of Dalton." That same day, Minty's brigade was ordered "to take possession of the Rome road and cover the right flank" of McPherson's Army of the Tennessee in its passage through Snake Creek Gap toward Resaca.[7] Colonel Sipes described "the grand spectacle as seen from the position held by the cavalry" as the Army of the Cumberland passed through Snake Creek Gap:

The great army of sixty thousand men began its movement through the Gap, and down the valley, at sunrise, and all day, in solid column, it moved by. As it proceeded, the wagons attached to brigades and divisions were moved out of the marching column, and halted in the field to the right and left of the road. These wagons, numbering hundreds, dotted the fields for miles, their white covers gleaming in the sunlight; and when night descended, hundreds of camp fires were started, filling the valley with glowing stars.[8]

On May 12, Minty's scouts reported a full brigade of Confederate Cavalry north and west of Armuchee Creek. They were soon encountered and driven back to Farmer's Bridge "in possession of which they were allowed to remain."[9] According to Colonel Sipes:

. . . a scout of 200 men from the Seventh Pennsylvania, under Captain Vale, was sent toward Rome, going as far as Sub Ligna [Subligna] on the right hand and Farmer's Bridge on the main road, without meeting the enemy; its rear was, however, assailed by the enemy at the junction of the Sub Ligna road, by a regiment numbering about eight hundred poorly mounted, worse commanded, rebels, which is easily repulsed and returned without loss.[10]

During the ten-day march Minty's Brigade had "been on about half forage of grain and entirely without long forage during the march."[11] Feed for the horses, as well as their deteriorating condition, was becoming a serious problem. The brigade remained on picket duty on the Rome road until May 15.[12]

Rome, Georgia

The morning of May 14, Minty was ordered by General Garrard "to make a demonstration on Rome to cover an attempted crossing of the Oostenaula by the Third brigade." Minty moved out at 5 a.m. on the fifteenth with the 4th Michigan in the advance.[13]

At the intersection of the Dallas and Rome roads, they "found the enemy strongly posed and the brigade was again formed for the attack."[14] The 12th Alabama advanced from Farmer's Bridge, at the junction of the Rome and Sub Ligna roads, but were driven back and engaged in a sharp skirmish.[15] Having scouted a "practicable ford," Minty sent two companies of the 4th Michigan "to the right and left" and then sent the 4th Regulars to the right to get past the enemy's flank—well in their rear—and then charge with saber.[16] With the remainder of the 4th Michigan followed by the 7th Pennsylvania, Minty assaulted and carried the bridge, killing a captain of the 12th Alabama and nine men representing five other regiments.[17] Minty found the "Alabamians" at the intersection of the Dallas and Rome roads strongly reinforced. They attempted to make a stand, "showing four pieces of artillery in position."[18] Again, Minty sent the 4th Cavalry to the right with orders to get well on the flank and then charge with sabers. At the same time he advanced the 4th Michigan—dismounted—with the 7th Pennsylvania in reserve.[19] "When the enemy saw and understood the movement," Larson writes, "they fell back" without waiting for the attack.[20]

"The Spencer carbines of this gallant regiment made things too lively for them," writes Minty.[21] The Confederates "took position about three miles from Rome and it was now evident that the rebels held the town with a heavy force."[22] Minty reports that the "rebel force was Jackson's Division of cavalry . . .and Lawrence Sullivan Ross' brigade of cavalry in reserve. Vale places the Confederate loss at from 50 to 60." Minty considered this a low estimate, as he saw "23 dead, including the 10 killed in the assault of the bridge, and made 19 prisoners." Minty's brigade "took position at Floyd's Springs, north of Armuchee Creek."[23]

On May 16, Minty's brigade crossed the Oostenaula on a pontoon bridge at Lay's Ferry "and pushed forward in advance of the right flank of McPherson's army, meeting and driving Confederate General Samuel W. Ferguson's brigade beyond the Rome and Kingston Railroad." The next day it "moved on right flank of General McPherson's army."[24] By that time, according to Vale, General McPherson had:

> met and defeated the rebels in a series of great battles at Resaca, fought on the 14th and 15th, and on the 16th drove them across the river to a fortified position in front of Adair. The left flank of this position was slightly in front of Kingston, at the junction of the Rome branch with the Georgia Central [Western & Atlantic] railroad. To seize Kingston, therefore, would not only enable Sherman to turn Johnston out of his position near Adair [Adairsville], but insured the fall of Rome, with all its arsenals and machine shops.

Vale comments on the importance of Rome, Georgia:

> Situated at the junction of the Oostenaula and the Etowah, which there uniting, form the Coosa, as the head of steamboat navigation, Rome was, in point of locality, the most important place in inland Georgia, and in point of manufacturing facilities for supplying the rebels with arms and ordnance, and ordnance stores, second only in the West to Atlanta itself. But Kingston, the key to Rome, if seized at all

must be by a rapid advance of the right, while the center and left of the army held Johnston in check at Adair [Adairsville]. Hence, on the 17th, General McPherson, with the Army of the Tennessee, was deployed rapidly to the right, reaching toward Kingston, and Minty was directed to move to his right flank and occupy the place by a dash.

Minty came in collision with Ferguson's brigade about a mile and a half after crossing the Oostenaula, which, attacking vigorously, he soon brushed from his path, and pushed on rapidly to the railroad between Rome and Kingston, as by cutting the road he would isolate the force at Rome and prevent the removal of the arms and military stores at that place. After heavy fighting Minty succeeded in getting possession of the [rail]road, and destroyed it from a point about two miles out to the Kingston junction.[25]

Larson explains the importance of this action and describes the tactic used to keep local citizens (i.e., spies) off guard as to Union Army activities and movements:

> By destroying this [rail]road the enemy's forces at Rome were prevented from coming to the assistance of Johnston at Dallas and it also prevented the removal of the enemy's military stores then at Rome. It was a very important point gained in the advance of the army and successfully carried out by General Garrard's cavalry. . . . [T]o keep the enemy from becoming aware of a contemplated raid on his rear and communication, we were generally withdrawn from the line and moved some miles back in woods, apparently for a few days' rest. On the first pitchy dark and stormy night the company commanders would order their companies to saddle up at once and as quietly as possible. When everything was ready we would move out of the woods by companies in the direction of some opening or road, where we would form regiment, brigade and division, and then move off with General Garrard and his staff at the head of the column.[26]

The Federals had to rely on citizens loyal to the Union "who knew the country and roads, particularly by-roads and trails," as the army could not remain on main roads longer than necessary. By this method the army "had succeeded in passing around the enemy's flank unobserved and were well in rear of their line."[27]

Sergeant Larson provides a detailed description of the cavalry's part in the destruction of the railroads, including the making of "Sherman's bowties:"

> As soon as the railroad was reached the work of destruction commenced. If the road had to be destroyed in an effective manner, bridges, culverts and stations were burned, but to complete the work the iron rails had to be bent so that they could not be used again. In that case spikes that fastened the rails to the tie were pulled out and thrown into ponds or creeks, the ties were piled along the road bed, the iron rails laid across the piles, and fires started. The ties being dry pine wood, a roaring fire soon blazed up, heating the middle of the rails red hot while the ends remained cooler. The weight of the cooler part of the rails bent the middle and heated part into a bow so crooked that they were good for nothing but old iron. That, however, required time and hard work and could not be easily accomplished with the enemy close at hand.
>
> Another way in which we did the work when an immediate attack might be expected was to pile dry wood, logs, fencerails and brush on a bridge with plenty of good kindling wood ready to be fired. When that was being done, another part of the force would destroy as much of the track as possible, but as fire was not used, except to burn the bridge, a rail would be disconnected on each side of the track and some 50 or 75 yards farther away the same was done. Then a row of men along one side of the track took firm hold under the iron rail and the whole stretch of 50 or 75 yards of rails and ties was lifted and overturned down the embankment.
>
> In that way as much of the track as possible was destroyed and the work continued until it became evident that the

enemy was approaching, then the bridge was fired and the division formed for battle. If the enemy arrived before the fire had gained such headway that it would be impossible to put it out, a lively fight took place, which was kept up until the bridge was burned. Then of course, we had to begin the retreat, and that was the ugliest part of the whole business.[28]

On May 18, Minty's brigade was at Woodlands, Georgia, northwest of Kingston. The next day, "the Second Cavalry Division, with the Saber Brigade in advance, drove the enemy out of Kingston, and about an hour later the advance of the Army of the Tennessee marched in, and with it came Generals Sherman and McPherson."[29] Minty immediately received orders from Garrard to move to Gillem's Bridge, spanning the Etowah River, and hold the bridge at all hazards.[30] He describes the charge to the bridge:

> The Brigade was then standing in columns of fours, the orders 'Mount–' 'Forward–March'; staff officers hurrying to the rear with instructions to regimental commanders to keep their men well closed up; 'trot–March! Gallop–March!' and away went 2,000 horsemen over the rough road; the entire valley seemed to shake under the mighty tread, and the thunder of that gallop echoed far and wide among the hills and along the river.[31]

Captain Vale's version of the five-mile charge is even more romanticized:

> The road was rough, but hard, and the twelve hundred horses and men, rushing at a fast gallop, seemed to shake the very earth and cause the trees on the hillside to topple, as though bowed before the stern blast of the tempest. Certain it is, that the thunder of that gallop echoed far and wide among the hills along the Etowah. On, on we rushed! Over hills and valleys, across streams and rickety bridges, while in dust behind us, 'Far streamed a smoky cloud, Echoed the hills, The Valleys shook, The flying forest bowed'.[32]

Minty's brigade "arrived at the bridge in good time to prevent its destruction." After several hours building "a strong crown-work of rails and logs covering the north end," the Army of the Tennessee arrived and took possession of the bridge. When Minty's men returned to their horses, they found that "fully 300 had been rendered totally unserviceable" by their charge.[33]

From May 19 to 22, "the brigade lay in camp at the position on the ridge at Spring bank, near Gillem's Bridge," picketing and scouting along both sides of the Etowah River.[34] On the twenty-third, "the Second Cavalry Division, moving as usual in advance of the infantry"—Minty's Brigade leading—"arrived at Van Wert that night without causing any contact with the enemy."[35]

Early the next morning, Minty "pushed forward," striking the enemy about two miles from Dallas:

> I attacked vigorously, and drove him back to within half a mile of Dallas, where Hardee had already commenced entrenching. I was now fully 24 hours in advance of the army. As night approached I fell back about a half a mile to a small stream, and bivouacked for the night.
> On the 25th, Gen. Garrard came up with the Third Brigade and moved the division to the Powder Springs road, where he took position. McPherson's line was now in close contact with the enemy's works at Dallas; our position being on his right flank, slightly advanced.[36]

In his history of Minty's brigade, Vale made an interesting observation regarding night movements:

> During the night [of May 25] . . . the division moved to the left front, from its position of the day, for about three miles, then turning to the left or eastward advanced in the direction of the Dallas and Villa Rica road. . . . [T]he men, particularly of Minty's brigade, never took kindly to a night attack. They were always ready and willing, aye, even eager to meet the foe in open, manly conflict by day . . . but from some cause seemed particularly averse to owling it by night. . . . We don't know, but certain it is, the brigade was not as reliable by night as by day.[37]

On the morning of May 26, the 4th United States Cavalry was detached from Minty's brigade and placed "on temporary duty on the flank of McPherson's army." They were soon recalled to join the division in the trenches in front of Dallas, where it was "doing duty as infantry."[38] Meanwhile, Minty's brigade—the 4th Michigan and 7th Pennsylvania, along with the 72nd Indiana—found itself engaged with rebel forces on the Villa Rica Road and in the area of Powder Springs and Dallas roads. They drove the dislodged enemy, "cavalry fighting on foot [and] mounted," in the direction of "the heavily fortified rebel position at Dallas."[39] The brigade then withdrew "to a position about half a mile west, and a line formed parallel with the [Villa Rica] road."[40] The next day the brigade was attacked by three brigades of rebel cavalry: "the brigades of . . . Ferguson and Ross."[41] Vale provides a classic description of the use of the newly armed cavalry as he describes the "gallant attack" of the 4th Michigan, who were:

> received by a galling fire as they galloped over the open field . . . but pushing gallantly forward, soon drove the enemy in confusion from their front, while the dismounted men, pressing forward at a run, forced the enemy to retreat, *pouring the while volley after volley from their Spencer carbines* into the disordered ranks, to and beyond the road, where the *sabers* of the Seventh, coming into play, completed his discomfiture and caused him to seek shelter in disorganized flight beneath the strongly fortified infantry lines at Dallas [emphasis author].[42]

Vale's statement is reinforced by cavalry historian David Evans' writing of Wheeler's Cavalry in this campaign: "Most of Wheeler's men relied on clumsy, single-shot Springfield, Enfield, and Mississippi rifles. Only about half of them had pistols and a Confederate deserter asserted not more than three of Wheeler's regiments carried sabers."[43]

Minty "now caused strong breastworks of rails and logs to be thrown up" and called up an infantry brigade to hold it, "ordered up the artillery, and opened fire, dropping shells inside the rebel works."[44] The Confederates responded with "a heavy column of infantry . . . [and] although vigorously assailed in repeated assaults," Minty "repulsed every attack and successfully maintained his position. The enemy abandoned the contest and retreated from his front before night."[45] General McPherson, writing of the day's events to General Garrard, states: "[Minty's] brigade has done good service to-day, and drew four regiments of rebel infantry from in front of our right off towards Villa Rica to fight them."[46]

From May 28 to June 1, Minty's brigade picketed close to McPherson's right.[47] According to Vale:

> On the 28th the brigade moved close in on the right of the Army of the Tennessee, and a large portion of it was dismounted and placed inside of the entrenchments in front of Dallas, the whole army having that day taken ground to the left or east. It remained, doing the same duty as infantry, the 28th, 29th, 30th, and 31st of May and on the 1st of June, repelling repeated assaults and skirmishing constantly day and night.[48]

Infantry Duty

The 4th US Cavalry now found itself in front of Dallas, "doing duty as infantry" in the trenches.[49] "This was another manner in which the cavalry was made useful during Sherman's campaign," writes Larson:

> and at such times they did the same service as the infantry. Sherman did not intend to waste more time than necessary in driving Johnston out of his strong position at Dallas. Therefore, he put his cavalry in the trenches so as to cover his movement, and at night withdrew his infantry and appeared on the enemy's flank and rear with a large force of infantry which compelled Johnston to move out. The move, however, occupied five days during which time two brigades of the 2nd Cavalry Division, Minty's and Wilder's were dismounted and occupied a portion of the trenches vacated by the infantry, repelling assaults and skirmishing constantly day and night.
>
> In order to keep the enemy impressed with the idea that Sherman was holding his position and meant to give Johnston battle on that line, exhibitions of activity and threats of pending attacks had to be

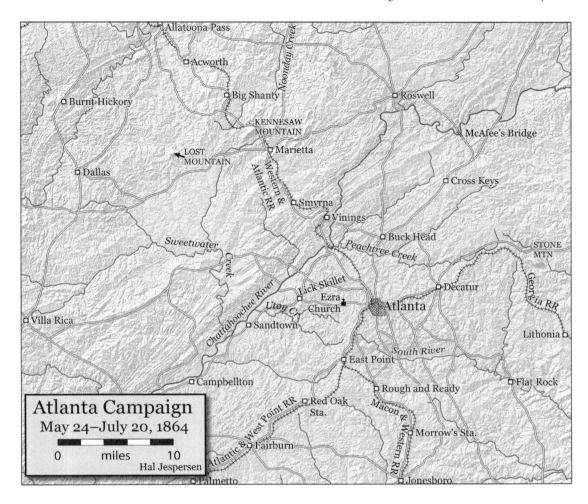

made by the cavalry holding the trenches and the skirmish line was pushed forward twice while we held the trenches to indicate that an attack in force might be expected. This is a move very difficult to execute and dangerous for the men on the skirmish line, particularly when the lines are, as they were then, within easy firing distance of each other.

The establishment of a skirmish line when the enemy is found protected by breastworks and redoubts, is done on dark and stormy nights. Each man provides himself with an empty box or barrel, which he packs full of something light and bullet-proof, such as hay or straw, which will not make his box or barrel too heavy to move easily. Then each man slings his carbine over his back, provides himself with a short-handled spade or anything that can be used for digging, and starts off on hands and knees, rolling his portable breastworks ahead of him. When the proper distance is reached, the men dig holes, packing the loose earth around the boxes and barrels, and when daylight came, the enemy would find our skirmish line much closer than it had been the night before, and so well protected.

We took the infantry's position in nearly all of Sherman's and McPherson's great flanking moves as far as our numerical strength would permit, often after having just made a rapid march of several hundred miles in rear of the enemy to destroy some important railroad or bridge which had to be done to facilitate the movement. *The cavalry was useful in the saddle and out of it* [emphasis author].[50]

Lieutenant Potter, 4th Michigan—writing "in the field" on May 30—described the fight and the cavalry's difficult circumstances:

> We are all about tired out. The Cavalry has never had such hard work or so much fighting. Our horses have not had a feed of grain in four days. They cannot go on much further. The whole rebel army is in front of us. They are determined to drive us back or die.
>
> Night before last they made an assault upon our lines but were repulsed with a loss of 800. Last night there was the most terrific fighting I ever heard. The whole rebel army I should judge was charging upon our lines. I have had no report of the result yet. Only that we held our line firmly. Their loss must be terrible. Such firing and crashing and moaning was never heard. Our Cavalry fell back to the left and we were four miles in the rear when the assault was made. The whole sky was lit up as if the world was on fire. A sullen and continuous roar was heard. The sound would rise and fall like the waves of ocean. The earth fairly trembled and shrunk from the shock of hundreds of cannon. I am confident of success. We CANNOT fail . I have not had one night's good rest in a week. We marched all last night. I am tough or I could not stand it.[51]

Sherman's Cavalry

It was June 1864, and the Union Army in the West was now in its second month of the Atlanta Campaign. Sherman's flanking movement was successful in turning the position of Johnston's army to the southwest by way of Burnt Hickory and Dallas, Georgia.[52] The cavalry had done what was asked of it in "the decidedly unglamorous" and arduous task "of protecting the flanks of Sherman's advancing armies" in terrain that was "utterly unfit for cavalry operations."[53] There was, however, growing dissension within Sherman's cavalry command. Sherman had an uneasy relationship with his cavalry corps. His own personal inexperience with cavalry, combined with a lack of "competent, aggressive" leaders among his senior cavalry officers, resulted in a cavalry force that was underutilized and overworked. Sherman failed to understand the effectiveness of cavalry when combined with infantry.[54] In the months to come, this would put a severe strain on the men and the mounts of Sherman's cavalry, pushing them to the limits of endurance with devastating results.

Corps commander Brigadier General Washington Elliott, "An old cavalryman of high character . . . rarely ventured far from his headquarters and never accompanied his troops in the field. Sherman usually ignored him." Instead, he went directly to his division commanders, particularly Major General George Stoneman, USV, commanding the Cavalry Corps, Army of the Ohio.[55] Stoneman was one of the original captains when the two new cavalry regiments were created in 1855. He was promoted to major in May 1861 and brigadier general Volunteers in August 1861. He was the "oldest and most experienced of Sherman's cavalry generals."[56] Sherman's relationship with Kenner Garrard, commanding the Second Division, was also problematic. Complaining that he moved too slowly and "belittling him as 'over-cautious' and 'timid,'" Sherman doubted that Garrard "had the dash" needed in a cavalry officer. It was a fundamental difference in style. Unlike Sherman, "Garrard was reserved and modest, and he waged war with a kid-glove gentility."[57] Their relationship became even more strained when Garrard's division failed to attack the rear of the Confederate Army as it withdrew from its entrenchments at Kennesaw Mountain and later failed to prevent the destruction of the covered bridge spanning the Chattahoochee near Roswell, Georgia.[58]

Even at the regimental level Garrard's abilities were questioned. Captain Robert Burns, acting assistant adjutant general for Minty's Brigade, wrote: "we are cursed with a very poor Division Commander, a man of neither dash, energy, nor self-reliance, but a West Pointer," textbook trained with no practical experience. "In fact, there are not many men who can command 6,000 or 7,000 Cavalry successfully." Burns even comments on Sherman's abilities: "We have our doubts about General Sherman, and say that if Rosecrans had the number of men 'S' has, he would have done as well, if not better. The Army of the Cumberland believes in Rosecrans yet."[59]

Fortunately for both Sherman and Garrard, as noted by cavalry historians Starr and Evans, the three brigades of the Second Division were "blessed with extraordinarily gifted commanders" in Eli Long, commanding Second Brigade; Abram O. Miller, commanding Third Brigade; and Robert

Minty, commanding First Brigade, ". . . three officers of intelligence and ability."⁶⁰ Evans continues: Colonel Minty was "generally regarded as *one of the best cavalrymen in the army* [emphasis author]":

> [He] taught his troopers to sharpen their sabers and to use them. He repeatedly won praise for his 'able, undaunted spirit and ability' and was three times recommended for promotion to brigadier general. . . . [A] temperate man who neither drank nor swore, . . . [he] was extolled by one of his contemporaries as 'an educated soldier of great intelligence and enterprise . . . a dandy cavalryman . . . and excellent disciplinarian.'⁶¹

Evans concludes that Minty, Long, and Miller made Garrard's Cavalry Division "*the best in Sherman's army* [emphasis author]."⁶² Major George Fish, 4th Michigan Regimental Surgeon, also writes: "there are indications of the position occupied by Colonel Minty among commanders. He is often closeted with our General, and is always consulted in regard to cavalry movements. Colonel Minty is without doubt the ablest cavalry leader of this army."⁶³ Even the enemy agreed. As one Confederate cavalryman wrote: "Col. Minty is one of the most gallant and dashing officers in the Federal army, and those who 'scare him up' may count on having to fight."⁶⁴

Dallas, Georgia

Johnston's army was forced to evacuate Dallas and the Union cavalry was once again in the saddle. On the night of June 1, the First and Third Brigades "covered the withdrawal of the Army of the Tennessee from intrenchments in front of Dallas."⁶⁵ According to Sergeant Larson, the 4th US Cavalry:

> taking the direct road to the town in a column of fours, charged into Johnston's rear guard, set them to flight and entered town running them before us. Just after entering the town we moved to the right into an open field to form line and deploy skirmishers, as the enemy was making a stand on the opposite side of a creek outside of town.

> A regiment of Colonel Wilder's brigade, coming to the town in an oblique course through the woods, saw us forming line in the fields, and as we were so covered with dust from the long charge on a dusty road that they could not see our blue uniforms, they took us to be Rebels, quickly got their battery in position and commenced to shell us lively. Shells from that side were a surprise to us, and we knew there could be no other troops there than our own. Captain McIntyre did some big swearing and hurried off a part of men to stop them. They saw the mistake themselves and stopped before there was any more harm done than killing one horse and wounding another.⁶⁶

While his regiment occupied Dallas, Larson found himself posted in town, "across the market square," where he witnessed the crude state of medical care in a field hospital:

> The left of our line stood by the court house and as my company was on the left it placed us in a position where I did not like very well to be. The court house had been a Confederate field hospital and I hated so much to witness the suffering of the wounded whether friend or foe, but our position at that time was such that it was impossible to avoid it.
>
> All the windows in the lower rooms were opened or taken out entirely so that what was going on inside was in plain view of us standing so near the house. Around the sides of the room were cots where the wounded men, both in gray and blue uniforms, were lying, each waiting his turn to be put under the surgeon's knife. In the middle of the room stood a long table and around it several surgeons, with shirt sleeves rolled up and hands and arms stained with blood, smiling and joking while at work on some unfortunate fellow, as if that was all fun for them. The wounded man was under the influence of chloroform and fastened to the table so that he did not move and only occasionally gave way to a low moan, but that did not affect the surgeons at all. They continued with their work in a very light hearted manner.

One of them, after making a cut with his knife, put the bloody blade between his teeth with the blood still dripping from it while he used both hands at something else, just as I have seen butchers do. While standing with the bloody blade between the teeth, he had a broad smile on his face. Of course, it requires such cold-blooded men at that kind of work, but it was very unpleasant to look at, particularly for me. When the leg was cut off, it was pitched out of the window where there was already a pile of legs and arms, presumably from operations done during the night. When that operation was finished one of the surgeons called 'next.'[67]

Captain Burns provides a more hopeful assessment for those who survived their wounds and operations, reflecting the major improvements in field hospitals and medical care after mid-1863:

> I was astonished to see what comfort wounded men could have so near a fighting army. Every one of them had been thoroughly washed and encased in a clean cotton shirt and drawers. Their cots had on mattresses filled with straw and covered with clean sheets. They had excellent bread, meat and soup to eat. Few of them had been as comfortable since they entered the service.[68]

Minty's brigade was beginning its second month of the Atlanta Campaign and, as noted by Colonel Sipes: "From this time on, until Atlanta surrendered, the fighting was almost continuous, and terribly severe–the Confederates resisting with all their power, and the Unionists attacking determinedly."[69] Captain Vale summarizes the advance of Sherman's army up to this time:

> During these days, the army had, by a succession of daring movements and hard-fought battles, extending along a frontage of over twenty miles, completely turned the rebels out of their fortified position at Alatona [sic] pass, and with his left now well planted on the railroad south of the pass, and Alatona itself in his full possession, Sherman now threatened to cut Johnston off from his line of retreat by seizing the bridge over the Chattahoochee. To prevent this, Johnston hastily marched from Dallas and Good Hope [New Hope], on the night of June 1, by the Marietta road, and took position on the Kenesaw and Lost mountains, northward of Marietta.[70]

On June 2, Minty's brigade marched to the west end of Allatoona Pass "without very much resistance."[71] There it remained on picket duty at "Allatoona, Cartersville, &c" through June 7.[72] On June 8, the brigade marched to Ackworth "without coming into any clash with the enemy except an occasional spat with a picket post composed principally of Georgia Homeguard." Larson continues:

> McPherson, with the Army of the Tennessee, was then on the extreme left of Sherman's army and Garrard, with the 2nd Cavalry Division, covered his left flank. The 2nd Brigade under Colonel Long, had joined us and the division then consisted of three brigades.[73]

Lieutenant Potter, writing to his parents from his camp on the Etowah River near Cartersville, Georgia, on June 5, describes their activities:

> We have been eight days without forage for our horses excepting green wheat which is bad and weakening.
>
> We are somewhat to the rear now... and are guarding an important Gap in the Allatoona Mts and protecting the RR. The cars run down to the River now. As soon as the bridge is built we will have clear sailing to the Chattahoochee.[74]

The construction of the "great bridge" across the Etowah completed, Garrard's division moved forward from Ackworth on the Marietta road at six o'clock the morning of June 9 with the Saber Brigade in the advance.[75] In many places the road was obstructed by breastworks and fallen trees. The enemy's pickets were soon encountered and driven back to a stronger, "heavily manned" position in front of Big Shanty.[76] Here a more formidable breastwork of logs and rails had been erected, with the ground in front obstructed with brush and trees that were cut down, making it difficult for a cavalry charge. The rebels had also strung telegraph wire "the entire distance in front of their position at a height of about two feet from the ground."⁷⁷ "Garrard's entire division now became engaged with the infantry, artillery, and cavalry of the enemy . . . [and] drove them from their fortified positions with considerable loss."⁷⁸ Sergeant Larson describes the events at Big Shanty and the use of dismounted cavalry acting as infantry, combined with mounted cavalry, overrunning the enemy's breastworks:

> General Garrard knowing that his men could do good work as infantry when necessary, brought the 3rd Brigade forward, dismounted, and the 4th Michigan Cavalry, also dismounted, formed on the left of the 3rd Brigade. The 4th US Cavalry formed mounted on their left and the 7th Pa. Cavalry, mounted, on the right of the line.
>
> As soon as the formation was completed the whole line rushed forward with one mighty cheer and over their breastwork, driving the enemy out in confusion, and followed by our line to the foot of some other hills, where we found two other still stronger lines of breastworks, which after a moment's delay in correcting the alignment, we charged and carried one after the other, the last being close to the edge of the woods on [. . .] Kennesaw Mountain.
>
> Some of the enemy's cavalry retreating in front of the 4th US Cavalry, and while we were banging away at them lively, too, treated us to the Song 'The Bonny Blue Flag,' and their color bearer shook the Confederate flag at us.
>
> The two first lines of the enemy's works were defended by William Martin's Division of cavalry and the third line was occupied by a brigade of infantry reinforced by the dismounted cavalry driven back from the other two lines. The loss in our brigade in that affair was 30 killed and wounded. At night we fell back again in line with the main army. We had found the enemy and tried strength with him and defeated him too, but to remain on the field over which we had fought seemed not to be the plan, though why not, no one but our general knew.⁷⁹

With his last line, Sergeant Larson hints at the growing dissatisfaction within the ranks of the abilities of Division Commander Kenner Garrard.

Big Shanty, Georgia

While Sherman was setting up his new headquarters at Big Shanty, the Confederate Army was re-establishing defensive positions north of Marietta. Sherman ordered Garrard to cross Noonday Creek and confront Wheeler's cavalry, known to be in the area of McAfee's Crossroads. A series of skirmishes and battles were fought between June 9 and July 3 in the area of Noonday Creek (Lattimer's Church) as the Union army pushed south to Marietta via Big Shanty and Kennesaw Mountain. The most significant of these battles occurred on June 20 between Minty's Saber Brigade and Wheeler's Confederate Cavalry.

Minty quotes from Sherman's memoirs: "On the 10th of June the whole combined army moved forward six miles to Big Shanty. McPherson had the left, following the railroad, which curved about the north base of Kennesaw." Minty continues:

> Early on the morning of the 10th I received orders from the General commanding the division to proceed to McAfee's Cross-roads, the crossing of the Canton and Marietta and the old Alabama roads, and from thence open communications with the Second Brigade, which would be moving on the Big Shanty road. I crossed Noonday Creek, on the old Alabama road, and at 10:30 a.m. my advance regiment, the 7th Pa. drove in the enemy's advance at McAfee's Crossroads.⁸⁰

According to Larson, "another severe skirmish took place between a part of the division and some of the enemy's cavalry . . . [but] the 4th US Cavalry did not become engaged that day . . ."⁸¹ At the time, the 4th U.S. was holding the Woodstock Road and covering the artillery and pack train.⁸² Larson continues: "In the afternoon those regiments that had crossed and met the enemy at McAfee's Crossroads retired across Noonday Creek and took a position in the high ground, parallel to the creek in line with us."⁸³ As described by Larson, Noonday Creek:

> . . . ran through the middle of an open and marshy swamp about 700 to 800 yards broad, where the ground was so soft that a man could not walk on it, far less a horse, and the only place where it could be crossed . . . was on a corduroy bridge, located just opposite the position held by the 4th US Cavalry.⁸⁴

The rebels had built "a good barricade" at the middle of the bridge and there was some minor skirmishing. A Confederate officer rode out on a white horse on the opposite side of the marsh and was brought down by "one of the division sharpshooters," but the 4th U.S. took no action to cross. On June 11, Minty found the bridge abandoned by the enemy during the night. A battalion of the 7th Pennsylvania crossed and established a picket post on the other side of the marsh.[85] That same day, the Union Army "advanced to the front of the rebels' strong position" at Kennesaw Mountain.[86] Minty's brigade, now "on the extreme left" of the Union Army, marched to McAfee's Crossroads, where the road from Marietta to Roswell crosses the road leading from Ackworth to Latimer Mills. Later that day the advance regiment (the 7th Pennsylvania) became "heavily engaged" at McAfee's Crossroads with "Martin's Division and the whole of Ferguson's Brigade of cavalry," during which it lost five men killed and seventeen wounded.[87]

Minty brought up the 4th Michigan and 4th U.S. for support, and after skirmishing for approximately an hour he saw the opportunity for a saber charge. "[Minty] formed the 7th Pennsylvania in column and let it loose," writes Vale:

> Charging directly on the center of Ferguson's brigade, it cut through the rebel lines, and then making a half wheel to the left swept like a tornado through the crowd of affrighted fugitives. The Fourth Michigan and Fourth United States, now advancing on a run, firing heavy volleys from their repeating carbines, completed the rout of the heavy rebel force . . .[88]

"The Union Cavalry," writes Sipes, "sent [the rebels] flying from the field in wild disorder."[89] Vale acquaints his readers with a realistic description of a cavalry charge, as opposed to "the pageantry of perfect military drill and manual." It is, "on the contrary":

> a wild rush forward, at a full, running, racing speed, in loose formation, with far more attention to who would first strike the enemy than whose buttons he aligned with or whose file he covered, or whose stirrup he touched. There was no such thing as riding stirrup to stirrup, mounted, or standing shoulder to shoulder, dismounted, in any of our fights in the Western cavalry, or, at least, in Minty's brigade. In our mounted saber charges, our favorite formation was in columns of four, of platoons, of companies, battalions, or regiments, in single rank, taking distance to the right and left about four paces, or ten feet, the sets being about six paces, or fifteen feet, apart. In fighting on foot or dismounted, the formation was generally in line, or rather, a succession of two or more lines, single rank, and what we called half skirmishing distance, i.e., each man in line, about four paces, or ten feet, from his comrade.[90]

For Minty's Brigade, the days between June 11 and June 20 were involved "picketing, scouting, and skirmishing" almost daily with the enemy around McAfee's Crossroads and to the south on Bell's Ferry and Marietta Road.[91]

Sergeant Charles Bates writes on June 20 from Big Shanty—"just 22 miles from Atlanta"—that "Captain McIntyre has been publicly complimented by General McPherson for meritorious conduct with his Regiment at Dallas and afterwards at the left of Big Shanty." He also reports that as of that date, "not a man had been hit in our Regiment":

> The health, too, of the men is remarkably good, not only in my regiment but the whole army and the sick are, with the usual cases of "Cannon Fever," (or scheming sick to get away from the front) remarkably healthy; for a wonder the whole line of Rail Road from here to Nashville is in complete repair and supplies are furnished in abundance if I except forage for animals . . .[92]

The young sergeant describes his new duty assignments which keep him from the front lines, as well as the activities of the previous day:

> I have got a 'non-combatant' appointment now–Regimental Ordinance Sergeant and am having, or have had until today very easy times, but to-morrow I have to commence the preparation of Quarterly returns from the first of January

and I expect to be busy for two or three weeks.... [T]he whole Division yesterday dismounted, and left their horses behind, drove the rebs from their position on the Ackworth and Marietta road and captured ninety prisoners with one small field piece, with a loss of thirteen wounded and five killed in the Division, but not a hurt from our regiment.

Commenting on the activity at the front, Bates wrote:

> The action has become pretty hot ... the guns are keeping up an incessant roar like dropping peas into a pan, and the cannons are giving the 'embellishments,' [Confederate fortifications at Kenesaw Mountain] thick and fast. I hope for luck to our arms, and pluck to the troops for it is a terrible place to storm ... It seems there was a continual stream of Confederate prisoners being moved to the rear: Several hundred of the Southern Chivalry have just passed in on their way to make an 'inspection tour' of the northern fortifications at Camp Chase, Johnson Island [both in Ohio], and other places of resort for prisoners of war; they were closely attended by a body guard of Yanks and seem down in the mouth. The boys say theres more of the same sort coming ... for Uncle Sam is rich enough to give them food and lodging for a while.[93]

BRICE'S CROSSROADS, MISSISSIPPI, JUNE 10, 1864

While Sherman's army was slowly grinding its way south toward Atlanta, the general was also paying attention to activities in Mississippi, 300 miles to his rear. Nathan Bedford Forrest was planning a raid into Tennessee to strike at the tenuous Union supply lines.[94] Sherman ordered General Samuel Sturgis to move his troops south from Memphis to head off the potential Confederate raid. In what Bruce Catton describes as "Forrest's supreme moment of glory," 8,000 Union troops under Sturgis's command were "badly beaten" at Brice's Crossroads on June 10 by Forrest's 3,500 troopers.[95] Already exhausted from a forced march in extreme heat and unfamiliar terrain when attacked by Forrest, the two armies "fought with the ferocity of wild beasts ... so close that guns once fired were not reloaded, but used as clubs."[96] In one of his classic maneuvers, Forrest succeeded in flanking the Union column on both sides, forcing the Federal troops to panic and flee in one of the "most humiliating Union defeats in the western theater."[97] While the battle did keep Forrest from the rail lines in Tennessee, an angry General Sherman ordered another expedition out of Memphis to "follow Forrest to the death, if it cost 10,000 lives and breaks the Treasury."[98]

With this defeat, Samuel Sturgis—the hero of the early battles in Missouri—would be sidelined for the rest of the war. He would later be appointed colonel, commanding the 7th US Cavalry; his lieutenant colonel was the flamboyant George Custer. After Little Big Horn, in which Sturgis's son was also killed, Colonel Sturgis would rebuild the 7th Cavalry and personally lead it in campaigns against the Indians in the 1870s.[99]

THE BATTLE AT NOONDAY CREEK

Early in the afternoon of June 20, Minty received orders from General Garrard to move his entire brigade across Noonday Creek and establish camp on the east side. When Minty informed Garrard that "the whole of Wheeler's force was 'within striking distance,'" the general "replied very positively: 'There is no part of Wheeler's command nearer to us than Marietta.'"[100] Minty was "so positive of the correctness" of his information that he sent one battalion of the 7th Pennsylvania Cavalry to the north "to occupy the position at Mud creek" and sent the two other 7th Pennsylvania battalions south to the crossing of the Big Shanty road.[101] "At 10 A. M., ... the Fourth Regulars were sent across Noonday Creek to guard the Canton and Marietta road." They reported "parties of the enemy moving all through the country." After driving the rebel outposts from near the creek, the 7th Pennsylvania was formed on the Marietta road.[102] One battalion of the 4th U.S. formed a skirmish line "holding the junction of the Big Shanty."[103] Around 4 p.m., Minty received orders from Garrard to move his entire brigade across the creek.[104] While the 4th Michigan was in the process of crossing, Minty received a report that "the battalions of the 7th Pa. on the Marietta road ... had been attacked in force from the direction of McAfee's."[105] As Minty later wrote, they "were attacked by 6,000 rebel cavalry under our old

Shelbyville friend, Wheeler."[106] General Wheeler, outnumbering Minty more than six to one, was aware that Minty's Brigade was in the area. Still smarting from the rout at Shelbyville, he would make a determined effort to capture or destroy it.[107]

Of the four-hour battle that followed, Larson wrote it was "one of the sharpest cavalry engagements of the Civil War."[108] A general and later historian who witnessed the battle from the hills near Kennesaw wrote that it was "one of the most hotly contested cavalry fights of the war."[109] The 7th Pennsylvania battalion under attack on the Marietta road was quickly supported by a battalion of the 4th Michigan. While they held their positions, two more battalions of the 4th Michigan moved in line on the rising ground to the left of the road and two battalions of the 4th U.S. "covered a county or neighborhood road half-way between the 4th Mich. and Noonday Creek."[110] One battalion of the 4th U.S. formed a skirmish line connecting Minty's position on the right flank and the 7th Pennsylvania, holding the junction of the Big Shanty road. Two guns of the Chicago Board of Trade Battery were posted in the angle created by Minty's formation.[111] The two battalions of the 4th Michigan (288 men) and the battalion of the 7th Pennsylvania (170 men) bore the brunt of the charge made by the 800 men of Colonel Robert Anderson's brigade charging with sabers, "supported by 300 or more of the 5th Ga. with pistols."[112] Minty described a "very severe fight," during which there were a total of three charges; each time the rebels were repulsed and "driven back in confusion."[113] Minty's brigade "maintained a desperate fight for a full two hours," wrote 4th Michigan Regimental Surgeon Major Fish:

> charging upon the enemy, and standing to their carbines in fine style. Our men of the 7th Pennsylvania and 4th Michigan were for some time engaged in a hand-to-hand fight. The ground was soft and miry, so much so that the horses frequently floundered and fell, leaving the men to scramble out the best way they could.[114]

Overwhelmed by his opposition, which he later estimated at "31 regiments...a total of nearly 10,000" men, Minty was forced to withdraw under the protection of cannon fire from the Chicago Board of Trade Battery.[115] The cannons "kept up a steady shelling of the enemy and checked their advance."[116] Meanwhile, Minty began receiving the assistance of "at least three regiments of mounted infantry"[117] "The battle continued until dark and defeated all efforts by the enemy to get possession of the corduroy bridge," which was the only crossing for miles, thus protecting all of the Union Army on that side of the creek.[118] Continuing with Major Fish, "as night was closing in, the recall was sounded, and our men fell back, and here we met our heaviest loss. We had to fall back over a low, swampy field, and ford a creek, where many of the horses stuck fast and had to be abandoned."[119]

During the retreat, Sergeant Larson was "placed in charge of the skirmish-line to cover and keep time with the retrograde movement of the 4th U.S. Cav." along the road to the marsh while "falling back toward the old corduroy crossing," which the Confederates were determined to possess. The 4th Regulars were the last to cross the bridge that night when the guns from Minty's battery "lit up the horizon" and the shells "whizzed over" their heads.[120] Minty quickly re-formed the six guns of the Chicago Board of Trade Battery and loaded with canister. The advancing Confederates demonstrated their intentions with a "sheet of flame...and storm of lead" combined with the "rebel yell."[121] At Minty's command, "the volley from the six Parrots made the welkin [heavens] ring. Volley after volley pounded into the enemy's ranks and this, supplemented by the fire of the Spencers, was more than the men in front of us could stand; they broke and quickly disappeared in the darkness of night."[122]

> The magnificent work done by Lieut. Griffin's section of the Chicago Board of Trade Battery...was the salvation of my command.... The steady, soldierly manner in which Lieuts. Fitzgerald and Davis, with their squadrons, 4th U.S., retired before Allen's Brigade gave me time to form my command in the final position near Noonday, and the timely arrival of the mounted infantry brigade on the field insured the final repulse of the enemy.[123]

Colonel Sipes had even more praise for the officers and men of the 4th United States Cavalry who rallied to their assistance:

> [The] Seventh did some heroic fighting, particularly a detachment of it led by Capt. [Cyrus] Newlin, of Company F, which

gallantly charged a vastly superior force of the enemy, engaging them in a hand-to-hand contest for half an hour... [until] attacked in flank by [William W.] Allen's brigade. Newlin... unable to repel the over-whelming numbers, he, with five of his men, were taken prisoners. *In fact, this entire force of the Seventh was only saved from capture or destruction by the gallantry of the Fourth Regulars* [emphasis author], who, perceiving the peril in which the Seventh was involved, rushed to their succor, under Lieutenants Fitzgerald and Davis, and after an hour's fighting, succeeded in driving back the enemy.[124]

One of the Confederate soldiers in the 51st Alabama—a part of Allen's Brigade—Private Cicero C. Bain, would become a future in-law of 1st Sergeant John M. Herberich, Co. I, 4th US Cavalry, when their children married.[125]

While Minty's casualties were high—"sixty-five killed, wounded and missing, of which the 4th [Michigan] has to bear forty"—Wheeler's losses were higher, "the heaviest that they had ever experienced."[126] In a letter to his adjutant in Michigan, "Minty rather sarcastically offered an indictment of General Garrard, in placing them at that place, stating: 'This is another case of throwing a couple of regiments in where the whole Division should have been.'"[127]

It rained heavily throughout the night, and the dreary dawn unveiled the aftermath of the battle. Captain Burns, "with a small party and a flag of truce," went to look for the dead and wounded, bringing back four dead. "Lieutenant Davis of the 4th Regulars went out with another party and brought in four more. The poor fellows were lying as they fell. Some of them had been stripped by the rebels. All had their boots taken off."[128] Sergeant Larson was sickened "when the long train of mules came back across the bridge, each carrying a perfectly nude corpse fastened across the pack saddle."[129] Dr. Fish was more graphic and disgusted, writing that "some other barbarities too revolting to describe had been perpetrated on our brave dead, indicating the utter relapse into barbarism of the slave minions..."[130]

Colonels Minty and Sipes, Captain Vale, and Sergeant Larson all quote editions of a leading Confederate newspaper giving the Southern version of what happened, indicating that the Saber Brigade had been the specific object of the attack. From the afternoon edition of the *Memphis Appeal*, published in Atlanta, Georgia, June 26:

> On the 20th instant, two divisions... and one brigade... of our Cavalry, went round to the left flank and rear of Sherman's army it was said, to capture a brigade of Yankee cavalry stationed at McAfee's. We succeeded in getting to the right place, where the enemy, Minty's Brigade, was vigorously attacked by [John S.] Williams and a portion of Anderson's Brigade.
>
> After a sharp conflict the enemy was driven from the field, [Moses W.] Hannon's Brigade having come up and attacked them on the flank. The Yankees fought desperately and fell back slowly, what loss we are unable to ascertain, as they carried off their wounded and most of their dead.[131]

The article continues with what may only be considered a tribute to the men of the Saber Brigade that also implies they were well known to the citizens of Georgia:

> To one who was an eye-witness, but not one so adept in the 'art of war,' it seemed very strange that the whole Yankee force was not surrounded and captured. Dibrell's Brigade was drawn up a few hundred yards from and in full view of the battlefield, with Martin's whole division immediately in the rear.
>
> This is one of the best fighting brigades the Yankees have, and to have captured or routed it would have added a bright feather to the plume of the successful hero accomplishing the feat.[132]

Minty's biographer concludes:

> For their part in fending-off superior forces at Noonday Creek [and later at Covington], and supporting the army's march toward Atlanta, Minty and his men earned the praise of General Sherman himself, who made specific mention of them in... [a] letter written to General Garrard: '... I beg you will convey to Colonels Minty, Long and Miller the assurances that I fully appreciate the services recently rendered.'[133]

A Lonely End

A cavalry regiment does not usually suffer a heavy loss in any one engagement; it is one here, two or three there–a constant attrition that is ever wearing away the substance . . .
– Stephen Z. Starr[134]

Sergeant Larson recorded the following incident in the days after the battle at Noonday Creek:

> During the next five or six days we had a little rest; that is, we remained in a stationary camp but scouting parties were sent out at different times and small skirmishes took place. We had a chance to take better care of our horses by getting plenty of forage for them and also something for us, and as I have stated we were a good deal like the Indians. We feasted and lived high whenever there was a chance, knowing very well that the time would come again when there would be nothing to feast on for days. One day we organized a foraging party of some eight or nine men and started off towards the left, clear of both the Union and Confederate lines.
> After riding some six or seven miles we came to a place where the road forked and a halt was made to consider which would be the best to follow. Two of our party, John Aaron, a young Pennsylvanian, and Otto von Louby, [Otto Lauby] a German nobleman, insisted on taking the left hand road . . . and that was the last we saw of them. They were both members of 'H' Company and mess-mates of mine. A few days after when scouting in that direction, we found the place where they had been buried near the road by some people living near by. The people gave a good description of both of them and said that they had fought like tigers against a Confederate scouting party and were killed fighting.[135]

Larson apparently never knew that Privates Aaron and Lauby were actually captured and died as prisoners of war at Andersonville. No less than twenty-nine other members of the 4th Cavalry would suffer the same fate in Confederate prisons.[136]

It had been a very difficult month for the cavalry. As the Saber Brigade continued its scouting operations, providing cover for Sherman's main infantry advance, the men were kept constantly in the saddle.[137] In his June 30 letter to his parents Charles Bates wrote:

> For the past two weeks it has been about a continued battle with the "rebs" and although no general engagement has taken place, there has not been a day or an hour but firing could be heard. The casualties have not been as numerous on our part as the Secesh, but many a poor fellow has gone to his long home since Sherman started from Chattanooga.[138]

"What a life we have had," writes Captain Robert Burns, 4th Michigan:

> Since the first of May we have been continually on the move. Have not been clean once since. Have been heavy fighting almost every day. Can get no clothes, hats nor boots. We are ragged, black and uncombed. Have not received a cent of pay since Dec 31st.
> To crown it all, there is a little insect in the woods here, called "chickor" or "Jigger" which now torments us out of our senses. It is so small that it is almost imperceptible.
> It pierces the skin and makes a terrible itching. My body is covered with the marks of the remorseless little monster. . . . We are also troubled with wood ticks, scorpions, and all sorts of accursed bugs. The other night a snake ran across my body when asleep, scaring Captain [Heber S.] Thompson out of his . . . senses.[139]

Major Fish, 4th Michigan, writes that this was "about the worst country for cavalry to operate in that I have ever seen."[140] And, as Colonel Sipes explains, it wasn't just the natural topography that Sherman's army and cavalry had to deal with:

> The entrenchment's so frequently mentioned, were a distinguishing feature of the Atlanta campaign, just as the campaign itself was, in some respect, peculiar. Johnston knew the route by which Sherman must advance, and chose, at his

pleasure, the places he would defend. These he fortified at his leisure. When Sherman's army ran against the enemy, they knew that a line of defensive as well as offensive works were before them, and the soldiers at once threw up covers for themselves. Every command did its own engineering and pioneering. Where they were halted by coming in contact with the foe was the position to be held until their opponents were dislodged, and they knew just what was required.

It may be asked what cavalry had to do with earth-works? And the answer is that they were compelled, by the extengencies of the service, at times to help make them and help to defend them. *In fact, there was hardly any limit to the duties the men on horseback had to perform* [emphasis author].[141]

Minty's biographer writes:

> By day the men endured hot and dusty marches, often moving from one flank to the other. By night they were often found in the same manner, mounted and making their way through the darkness.... Fish, observing the men, wrote that they were 'melting under the fierce rays of the Southern sun.'[142]

"We ... now carry all our little worldly possessions on our saddles," writes Burns. "One blanket and one poncho to a man. We have no tents, and are as near the primitive man as health and decency will allow."[143] According to Colonel Sipes, this was part of Sherman's strategy: "Everything outside of absolute necessares were eliminated from [his] army." He quotes General Sherman:

> 'I made the strictest possible orders in relation to wagons, and all species of incumbrances in impediments whatever. Each officer and soldier was required to carry on his horse or person food and clothing enough for five days.... Georgia has a million of inhabitants. If they can live, we should not starve ...'[144]

But the war had ravaged northwest Georgia and its population was starving. As described by Dr. Fish, the area north of Atlanta was:

> a poor country.... The soil is mostly stingy and barren. The wheat is short, thin and poor.... Whatever there was of beauty or prosperity had departed. The men of wealth have left. They are refugees, having gone south with their human and other cattle, and all property that could be conveyed away. The men of this country have all been taken south. There is not an able-bodied man left, not one. Women and children are plenty, and such hard abject misery I have never seen in any country, or among any people ...
>
> The poor whites–the wives of those now in the rebel army–and the widows and children of those who have died or been killed in the service, are in a pitiable condition. We are often applied to by a poor forlorn woman, with many haggard and half-naked children, for protection for some miserable apology of a crop ... And our authorities have been feeding thousands of such ...[145]

Colonel Sipes continues with a sobering statistic:

> Constant movement through a rough wooded country told upon the cavalry, and the strength of the division diminished rapidly. It was impossible to find sufficient food for the horses; what little forage the country contained was swept away by the mounted forces of the enemy; and, as a result, in a month's time the strength of the brigade was reduced *fifty per cent* [emphasis author]. Still it had to perform its duties, and it evinced no indication of weakness.[146]

"I knew my horse was starving," writes Sergeant Larson, and a starving horse was a dangerous mount.[147] As David Evans notes: "Sherman had seriously underestimated the availability of forage, and his horses suffered terribly ... from hunger, disease, wounds or neglect."[148] Colonel Sipes also writes of the "sufferings to which the horses of the cavalry were subjected," and of the relationship between the troopers and their mounts, upon whom their lives often depended:

These sufferings were unavoidable, and resulted from the duties performed and the nature of the country traversed, not from any neglect or cruelty on the part of the men. A cavalryman, if he is worthy of the name, becomes attached to the animal that shares his dangers and privations, and upon which his usefulness and safety depend; and he will risk much and labor hard to secure comfort for his inseparable equine companion. Instances have been known in the Seventh Pennsylvania where, in severe weather, a man has put his only blanket on his horse, that he might be comfortable, and suffered himself through a shelterless night. . . . Every effort was made to save the lives and alleviate the sufferings of these animals, but the task was impossible of performance.[149]

In his book, Sergeant Larson recounts a number of occasions where he and his fellow troopers quite literally risked their lives foraging for their horses. Colonel Sipes mentions "paying a silver dollar for a pint cup full of wheat" for his horse, and of men from his company walking eight miles to bring corn to their animals. Throughout the written history of the Civil War, there are numerous stories of the strong bond formed between rider and mount.

Kennesaw Mountain

Minty's brigade remained in the vicinity of Noonday Creek until July 2, when Garrard's division was assigned to protect the left flank of Sherman's army that was "then operating against Joseph Johnston's entrenched forces on Kenesaw Mountain."[150] "Sherman's left flank was completely in the air," writes Vale:

> and exposed to serious danger from attack by the large cavalry forces of the enemy, and it was the duty of Garrard's division of cavalry, operating nearly ten miles to the front and left, to head off these threatened assaults and protect that flank, and the rear of the army.
>
> . . . These operations were purely *cavalry*, [emphasis Vale's] for while in many places over the whole miles of country, the dense forests and thickets of undergrowth required him to fight on foot, yet, wherever and whenever a cleared field or open round offered the opportunity, the cavalryman's most effective weapon, *the saber, was called into requisition and the 'charge' relied on to obtain the greatest result with the least possible loss* [emphasis author].[151]

Colonel Minty's report indicates "picketing and scouting" on June 21 and 22. On June 23, "in connection with the Second and Third brigades," demonstrations occurred across Noonday with "light skirmishing." From the twenty-fourth to the twenty-sixth, squadrons of the brigade continued these activities. On June 27, "the division (dismounted) made a demonstration across Noonday . . . to cover the left of the army during the assaults on Kenesaw by McPherson's and Thomas' armies."[152] As Minty writes, his brigade:

> . . . took position on the brow of a hill with open ground in front, built a line of rail breastworks, and threw forward a very light line of skirmishers, who advanced into the wood beyond the open ground. We lay in this position for several hours, and were during the entire time most industriously shelled at long range by the enemy.[153]

Sergeant Larson's Company H was attached to one of two sections of the Chicago Board of Trade Battery as they "took a position on the highest ground there and opened fire on the enemy at long range."[154] When guarding a battery, the cavalry had little to do "except to be ready at any moment" if the enemy attempted to charge the guns. The men could "sit, lie or stand as we pleased," as long as they were on hand if needed.[155]

That same day, the morning of June 27, after "three weeks of mist, drizzle, shower, and storm," Sherman "hurled eight brigades at the Confederate trenches girding Kennesaw Mountain . . . The attackers were shot down, bayonetted, and hurled back, leaving 3,000 casualties in their wake." This battle would prove the futility of frontal assaults, forcing Sherman to resort "to the old flanking tactics that had served him so well."[156] He was forced to begin "a hard and protracted struggle in flanking Johnston out of his position."[157]

On the night of July 2, the left of the Union Army "moved in from in front of Kenesaw with [Garrard's] Second Cavalry Division covering the movement."[158] Sherman "pulled McPherson's troops out of the trenches north and east of Kennesaw and circled them behind Thomas and Schofield to threaten the crossings necessary for Johnston's retreat across the Chattahoochee River," the "last great natural barrier between Sherman and Atlanta." Garrard's cavalry was left behind "dismounted" to replace the infantry in the trenches.[159] This maneuver forced Johnston to retreat southward to the town of Roswell, where one of the few remaining bridges across the river was located.[160]

Around 11 a.m. the morning of July 3, Garrard's cavalry division marched into Marietta, described by Lieutenant Henry Potter as "a handsome place built in a grove of trees."[161] The division was greeted by an angry General Sherman, who had arrived several hours earlier, demanding to know where Garrard's division was. As General Johnston began his retreat through Marietta the night before, Sherman ordered his whole army in pursuit "and fully expected to find Garrard's cavalry snapping at the heels of the Rebel rear guard."[162] After publicly berating Garrard for his delay, Sherman ordered him to pursue the Confederate Army, "sending Garrard and his men down Main Street at a prudent trot."[163] Five miles southeast of Marietta, on the north side of Rottenwood Creek, Garrard's three brigades "encountered dismounted cavalry screening the right flank of the Rebel army." On July 4, Minty reported "picketing and skirmishing on the left."[164] Later that evening, Sherman sent orders to Garrard, directing him to "move his division north and east, to capture the bridge at Roswell" before it could be destroyed by the retreating rebel army.[165] "Buglers sounded the brassy notes of 'Reveille' at 2:00 A.M.," writes David Evans:

> rousting tired troopers from their bedrolls. Yawning, stretching, hitching up their trousers, the men stumbled into line in the predawn darkness to stand for roll call. Sergeants droned down the long list of names, issued orders for the day, then dismissed the companies to feed and groom their horses.
>
> The division wagon trains, escorted by the 1st Ohio Cavalry, had trundled into camp during the night with rations and forage, and once the animals had been fed, the dark woods began to glow with the pale light of hundreds of cooking fires. Breakfast was usually a meager affair in the cavalry. Three or four men, sharing a sheet-iron frying pan, a two-quart pail, and maybe a small kettle, huddled around a flickering blaze. Blinking the smoke from their eyes, they fished greasy slabs of bacon onto battered tin plates with knives and forks, filled their blackened cups with scalding hot coffee, and rounded out the bill of fare with a couple of pieces of hardtack, plain or fried in bacon grease. Once they had eaten, the men gave their dishes a perfunctory swipe with a handful of leaves or a quick rinse in a nearby stream and hurried to get everything packed away before the bugles sounded 'Boots and Saddles.'[166]

The division began the eighteen-mile march up the Chattahoochee River to Roswell. On July 5, Minty's brigade took the lead as Garrard's division, accompanied by the 1st section of the Chicago Board of Trade Battery, moved north on the Pace's Ferry Road:[167]

> Two miles east of Marietta, Minty's advance guard turned to the right on the Roswell Road. The morning air was already hot and oppressive, but it was caution, not the heat, that compelled Garrard to call a midmorning halt after an easy six-mile march to Sope Creek. While the 2nd battalion of the 4th Michigan [Cavalry] moved a mile ahead to picket the road in front of the column, he sent Major [Jacob G.] Vail's 17th Indiana Mounted Infantry and Major William H. Jenning's 7th Pennsylvania Cavalry riding south and east with orders to converge on Roswell.[168]

"With the Seventh Pennsylvania in the advance," writes Minty, they "moved upon and captured that place, driving out the rebels and securing the crossing of the [Chattahoochee] river."[169] This is not quite accurate; Garrard's division failed to save the bridge from destruction. "At about 11:00 A.M.," writes Evans, a detachment of Confederate cavalry patrolling the Roswell road "collided with the advance guard of... the 7th Pennsylvania two or three miles west of town":

Outnumbered and outgunned, the Rebel horsemen fled through Roswell at a gallop. When they tried to make a stand at the south end of town, the pursuing Pennsylvanians drew sabers and charged. The glimmer of cold steel sent the Tennesseans flying, but not before they set fire to the covered bridge over the Chattahoochee... The bridge was gone.[170]

An angry General Sherman, upset with the delay caused by the failure to save the bridge, charged Garrard with the primary activity to "select a ford" and make a lodgement on the other bank of the Chattahoochee "as soon as possible anywhere from Roswell down to the vicinity of Sope Creek."[171]

Captain Vale describes the first Union troops attempting to ford the Chattahoochee on July 9 and the surprising effect of the new Spencer carbine:

> The First and Third brigades crossed the Chattahoochee river in the face and under fire from the enemy, by wading it, while skirmishing, from shore to shore. At first the fire was heavy, and the undertaking seemed hazardous, but after getting well into the stream [...] the scene assumed the ludicrous.
>
> As before stated, the brigade [...] armed with the Spencer repeating rifle and carbine, using a metallic water-proof cartridge. The river was very rocky, and in many places the channels between the rocks were found to be 'over head' in depth. As the rebel bullets began to splash around pretty thick, the boys sought to keep in this deep water with only the head exposed; they soon discovered that they could throw the cartridge from the magazine into the chamber of the piece, by working the lever, as well under water as in the air; hence, all along the line you could see the men bring their guns up, let the water run from the muzzle a moment, then taking a quick aim fire his piece and pop down again with only his head exposed. Now, the rebels had never seen anything of this kind before, nor, for that matter, had we, and their astonishment knew no bounds. We could hear them calling to each other, 'Look at them Yankee Son's-o-bitches, loading their guns under water.' 'What sort of critters be they now?' 'It's no use to fit agin fellus that'll dive down to the bottom of the rivah and git that powdah and ball;' their curiosity so far got the better of their devotion to the 'cause' that nearly the whole line, something over two hundred in number, remained on the bank, quit firing, and surrendered as soon as we got on the south side, anxious only to see the guns that could be loaded and fired under water.[172]

Lieutenant Henry Potter relates a similar story to his parents: ". . . they said the Yankees were the 'goldarndest gelleas they ever seed' they would fire and then dive to load, then fire and dive under again . . ."[173] Colonel Minty continues with the events of the day:

> On climbing the southern bank we captured between 40 and 50 of the enemy, took position about a quarter of a mile from the river, and erected barricades, which we held until dark, when Newton's Division of Infantry, of the Fourth Corps relieved us.[174]

Roswell, Georgia

Roswell—a thriving town of about 4,000 inhabitants—was described by a Yankee lieutenant as "perhaps the neatest and prettiest manufacturing town in the country" with "an uncommon amount of industry, including a machine shop, a cotton gin, a grist mill, a tannery, two shoe factories, two smithies and three stores. On the east side of town, three sprawling factories perched on the banks of Vickery's Creek, where spindles whirled and looms shuttled, eleven hours a day, six days a week," all for the Confederacy.[175]

General Garrard established his headquarters two and a half miles from Roswell on the west bank of Willeo Creek, "the only stream capable of watering all their thirsty horses." The First and Second Brigades also made camp on the west bank, and from July 10 to 16, the cavalrymen were "engaged in manning outposts from the Ivy Mill and all the way down to the mouth of Sope Creek," while patrols ranged upriver, looking for fords and ferries.[176] Lieutenant Potter was "up at 8 o'clock" the morning of July 10 and "had a breakfast of pork, potatoes, onions, coffee, and lots of blackberries . . ." It was extremely hot. "I never saw such heat," he writes in a letter to his parents. "The Army seems to stand it firstrate–hardly any sickness... The harvest apples sweet and sour were getting ripe," and the bountiful agriculture of the countryside provided assorted vegetables. For once, even the horses "had their fill of corn and wheat."[177] "We are 20 miles above Atlanta. A Division of Infantry came up at dusk [on the 9th] and we recrossed and came to camp where we are now. Very hard work. Yesterday no breakfast. Ford the river–climb the steep bluff and build works."[178]

The Federal forces quickly began the systematic destruction of Roswell's industries... and the forced evacuation of its terrified residents. Employees of the mills were sent to Marietta as prisoners of war.[179] Over the next several days, "the extensive cotton mills engaged in manufacturing cloth for the rebel government, were seized, and with all the machinery, destroyed by order of General Sherman."[180]

Around noon on July 14, the 4th U.S. which had been on picket duty at McAfee's Bridge since July 10, was relieved and, "Saddling their horses, the Regulars moved north to join the 4th Michigan, which left Lebanon Mill at 2:00 P.M. and moved two or three miles east to camp in some woods on the Warsaw Road."[181]

Sherman ordered the advance towards Atlanta on the sixteenth, that night Garrard's cavalry camped near Newtown Crossroads.[182] On the seventeenth, "still operating on the left of Sherman's army," Minty's brigade crossed the Chattahoochee on McAfee's Bridge and "pushed forward toward Cross Keys."[183] During the night of the seventeenth, Minty marched "about twenty miles east of Atlanta with the First and Third Brigades" reaching the Atlanta and Augusta Railroad. After driving off the rebel guards, they destroyed five miles of track, "including bridges."[184] The next day, "Garrard roused his troopers at 3:30 a.m." Leaving the sick and dismounted men and the First Brigade Band in camp with the pack mules and led (spare) horses, "the rest of the command swung into the saddle at 5:00 a.m., carrying two days rations." Minty's First Brigade and the 2nd section of the Board of Trade Battery, with companies of the 7th Pennsylvania in the advance, moved east on the Peachtree Road.[185] At approximately 1 p.m., "Garrard's skirmishers struck the Georgia Railroad about a mile west of the Stone Mountain depot" and began "tearing up rails and ties."[186] Moving down the railroad on the nineteenth, Decatur was occupied by Sherman's infantry on the 19th "after some skirmishing, and the Confederate forces driven about ten miles south-east."[187] The troopers then destroyed the railroad "as far as Stone Mountain, and thoroughly scouted the country for over 10 miles in every direction, making it decidedly unhealthy for the roving scouting parties of the enemy."[188] They began the process of destroying the railroads:

> Laying down their carbines, Minty's 1st Brigade lined up shoulder to shoulder along one side of the track. At an officer's command, the men grabbed the near rail with both hands, and heaved rails, crossties, and all over to one side. Prying the crossties loose, they piled them up with any other wood they could find, balanced rails across the top of the heap, and set it on fire. 'The boys engaged in [the] destruction resembled fiends,' declared a private of the 4th Michigan.[189]

At 5:00 a.m. on the twentieth, Garrard's cavalry broke camp at Cochran's house and moved to cover the left flank and rear of Sherman's army. Robert Minty's "4th Regulars and the 7th Pennsylvania were in the saddle at 6:00 a.m.... heading north" to picket the Peachtree Road at Buchannan's with the 1st section of the Board of Trade Battery.[190] Later that day, Sherman approved the request Garrard had made the previous evening "to burn McAfee's Bridge and shorten his lines":

> Anxious to regroup his scattered detachments, he issued his Special Field Orders Number 2, directing Minty to move his entire 1st Brigade to New Cross Keys and cover the roads to the south and east, and north to Roswell Bridge. These same orders instructed Ed Kitchell's 98th Illinois to destroy McAfee's Bridge and join the rest of the division at Decatur....[191]
>
> ... By 4:00 p.m. the 1st Brigade was assembled at Buchannan's farm. There was a brief halt while the Regulars and Pennsylvania troopers dozing by the roadside stirred from the shade and the artillerymen reharnesed their horses. Forming ranks, Minty's three regiments followed the Peachtree Road westward for another seven miles before halting at 8:00 p.m. to picket the roads converging at New Cross Keys.[192]

In his July 19 letter from Roswell, Georgia, Sergeant Bates has high praise for his commanding general: "I have no doubt but Sherman is the right man in the right place, here, for a wonder and if he is not relieved, nor his troops taken from him, he will clear Georgia this season. He has conducted this whole advance beautifully to my thinking . . ."[193]

Garrard's Raid to Covington

Sherman would later regret the order he gave General Garrard's division on the night of July 20, which would leave General McPherson's flank unprotected by the cavalry. Garrard was to immediately proceed to Covington—thirty miles east—"to burn two important bridges across the Olcofauhatchie and Yellow River, to tear up the railroad" and damage it as much as possible "from Stone Mountain eastward . . ."[194] On the evening of July 21, Minty's Brigade marched from New Cross Keys to Decatur, arriving late the next afternoon.[195] "The eastern sky was beginning to pale by the time Bob Minty's 1st Brigade reached Rockbridge," writes David Evans:

> His men had made consecutive marches from New Cross Keys and Decatur, a total of thirty-two miles, to overtake the division. Dead tired, they stripped the saddles off their weary mounts and lay down to sleep. Within an hour heavy-handed sergeants were shaking them awake. Orders were to mount up . . . Garrard ordered his column forward at 5:00 a.m. The Georgia Railroad trestle over the Yellow River lay only five or six miles to the right, and in the dawn's gray light he sent two companies of the 98th Illinois Mounted Infantry riding south to destroy it.[196]

Garrard ordered Minty to send a brigade "straight into Covington." By this time, the citizens of Covington "had seen the pillars of smoke billowing from the burning bridges over Yellow River, and heard the Yankees had captured the westbound train at Conyers." There was "a veritable stampede of 'wagons, buggies, cows, hogs, folk, women and children in terror'" as the Yankees approached the town.[197]

Presley Jones, a fifty-nine year old farmer, left his plow in the field and went home to get his squirrel rifle, vowing to kill the first "damn Yankee" he saw. One of two lead scouts and the first Union soldier to enter the town was Private William Travellion of the 4th US Cavalry; the other was Private John Williams of the 17th Indiana Mounted Infantry. "[If] nobody will fight for my country, I will," Jones shouted as he leveled his gun. His first shot "lifted" Private John Williams "out of his saddle." His second shot wounded Private Travellion. Both were mortally wounded. Jones was almost immediately brought down "in a hale (sic) of bullets" as other Yankee troopers arrived.[198]

At the railroad lines two miles west of Covington, Minty's brigade formed a skirmish line to protect the troopers of the Third Brigade, who "dismounted and began pulling down fences along the right of way." They "soon had dozens of fires blazing at the joints in the track" and steadily worked their way eastward until they reached the railroad depot on the north side of Covington at 2:00 p.m.[199] Later that evening, Garrard's Division retired through Oxford. Minty's Brigade was only six and a half miles north of Oxford when Garrard called a halt at Sardis Church at 10 p.m.[200] Garrard's troopers were exhausted:

> 'Of course we were tired and hungry,' noted one trooper, 'and sadly needed our coffee, as that above everything else was a panacea for all our ills; but we had to lie down without it, not even unsaddling our horses, and were soon sleeping the sleep of the innocent.'[201]

As Colonel Minty recalled in his published recollections: "after some spirited conflicts with the enemy" at Covington, his brigade destroyed extensive cotton factories and a large quantity of rebel Commissary, Quartermaster and ordnance stores, and tore up five miles of track "east and west of Covington."[202] He also reports that "Between Olcofauhatchie and Yellow Rivers the Second Brigade captured two railroad trains."[203] According to Sergeant Larson, the trains and "two important bridges crossing those rivers" were burned. He wrote:

> By that time the enemy had become thoroughly aroused and the attraction we were expected to create was in full force. There was probably not a force of mounted troops of any considerable strength within 50 or 75 miles that were not hurried out after the Yankee raiders. They were after us like

bees after a person who has accidentally upset their hive. Fighting was kept up constantly in front, behind and at times also on our flanks, and many a brave cavalryman of Garrard's division was buried by the roadside...[204]

This statement points out one of the weaknesses with Sherman's cavalry strategy. Without support and deep in enemy territory, the attrition rate for both man and horse was high. By 6 a.m. on the twenty-third, Garrard started his column northward again. Some of his troopers "had risen early enough to breakfast on some potatoes they dug up along the roadside, but most...began this second day of the raid just like the first, on an empty stomach."[205] Evans continues:

Two miles north of Sardis Church, the column passed through the little crossroads community of Walnut Grove. The rear guard paused long enough to burn three or four hundred bales of cotton, but the destruction was not just confined to Garrard's immediate line of march. Each brigade sent detachments ranging down the side roads to round up horses and mules and burn all the cotton they could find.

...Nine and a half miles north of Sardis Church, some of Minty's troopers charged into Loganville capturing a Rebel private and a lieutenant of engineers.

...Garrard lingered in Loganville long enough to burn another three or four hundred bales of cotton and scatter some Rebel rice. His troopers also emptied corncribs and hauled freshly shocked oats out of nearby fields, feeding their horses in the middle of the road while officers sat down to dinner in the homes of several reluctant Southerners. After an hour's rest, Garrard divided his command, sending Minty's 1st Brigade north toward Lawrenceville...[206]

Late that afternoon, having been warned of the Yankee advance:

a hastily assembled force of perhaps fifty Confederates confronted Minty's column near Tilford McConnell's farm, four miles southeast of Lawrenceville, only to scatter before a charge of the 4th US Cavalry that chased them all the way back to town...Minty's men captured a captain, four sergeants, a corporal and twelve privates representing fourteen different regiments, batteries, and battalions. They also arrested five civilians..."[207]

Captain Heber Thompson—Minty's Inspector General—comments on the behavior of some of the division:

Lawrenceville has been a really nice little place. In Covington, Oxford and indeed all the towns in Georgia, the conduct of our Division has been disgraceful - houses plundered, women insulted and every species of outrage committed.

In Lawrenceville on the contrary, when our Brigade was alone nothing of the kind occurred. The people, especially the ladies, and the town contained some really nice ones, were very much pleased with our orderly conduct.[208]

Continuing with David Evans' account of the raid:

Marching his brigade out of Lawrenceville, Minty halted for the night about three miles out of town on the banks of Yellow River.... The men not assigned to picket duty dismounted stiffly and unsaddled their horses for the first time since leaving Decatur on July 21.... While sentries stood watch on the picket lines and tired, hungry troopers huddled over flickering fires, dozens of runaway slaves peered from the dancing shadows.

'They were all intelligent looking people,' observed a Michigan trooper. 'What pleased me most was to see those who had been most against the freedom of the slave. The impulse to help the helpless was too much for Yanks, and in spite of principles they divided their rations, and it seemed as though they could not do enough to make them comfortable. If a person wants to become fixed against slavery, he wants to go on a raid into slave lands. These same negroes tell us they had been made to believe that the Yanks killed all the niggers. But they preferred death by the Yanks than longer to live with their cruel masters, in slavery. Is not that enough of an argument against slavery, when the slave prefers to go where he has been made to believe he will meet certain death, to longer remain in bondage?"²⁰⁹

On his return to Decatur, Garrard "brought in 151 prisoners and 200 Negroes." In his report to Sherman, he "commended the 'zeal and promptness' of his whole command for making the raid a success." "Since leaving Marietta," Garrard concluded, "the division has been so constantly in motion, it is now very much out of condition, and I would be pleased to have a few days' quiet, to shoe horses and repair equipments."²¹⁰ While Garrard's raid could be deemed a success, and while Sherman had succeeded in severing Atlanta's direct rail connections to the east and west, there would be a heavy price for these victories.

"Minty's brigade rode in at dark, after a twenty-seven mile march via Flint Hill Church and New Cross Keys." He brought in another 100 contrabands (blacks) and twenty-one more prisoners.²¹¹ Arriving at Decatur at about midnight, the brigade learned of the "death of that splendid soldier" Major General James B. McPherson two days earlier.²¹² As Sherman writes in his memoirs, "Unlucky for us...McPherson had no cavalry in hand to guard that flank. The enemy was thus enabled, under cover of the forest, to approach quite near without being discovered . . ."²¹³ Colonel Minty writes:

> This was the first time during the campaign that the flank of the army had been unprotected by cavalry, our absence leaving it entirely in air [exposed]. Hood [who had replaced Johnston] quickly took advantage of the fact, and it cost us 3,521 men killed, wounded and missing, including the noble McPherson, one of the most promising commanders of the war.²¹⁴

The Second Division remained in camp near Decatur on July 25 and 26. Colonel Sipes cites Kenner Garrard's July 24 report to get an idea of the extent of the destruction during this raid:

> Results: Three road bridges and one railroad bridge, (555 feet in length) over the Yellow river, and one road and one railroad bridge (250 feet in length) over the Ulcofauhatchee, were burned. Six miles of railroad track between the rivers were well destroyed. The depot and considerable quantity of quartermaster and commissary stores at Covington were burnt. One train and locomotive captured at Conyers and burnt. One train (platform) was burnt at Covington, and a small train (baggage) at station near the Ulcofauhatchee captured and burnt. The engine to the last train was detached across the river. Citizens report a passenger train and a construction train, both with engines, cut off between Stone Mountain and Yellow river. Over 2,000 bales of cotton were burnt.
>
> A large new hospital at Covington, for the accommodation of 10,000 patients from this army and the Army of Virginia, composed of over 30 buildings besides the offices, just finished, were burnt, together with a very large lot of fine carpenters' tools used in their erection. In the town of Oxford, two miles north of Covington, and in Covington was over 1,000 sick and wounded in buildings used for hospitals. The convalescents able to walk scattered through the woods while the firing was going on in town, and I did not have the time to hunt them up before dark. Those in hospital, together with their surgeons, were not disturbed.²¹⁵

David Evans summarizes the results of this raid:

> Kenner Garrard's destruction of the trestles over the Yellow and Alcovy rivers on July 22 . . . had important results. His raid, when combined with Sherman's presence on the east side of Atlanta, denied the Rebel defenders direct access to reinforcements and munitions from Virginia and the Carolinas and put the Georgia Railroad out of commission for the rest of the war.
>
> In less than two weeks, at a cost of less than a hundred casualties, [Major General Lovell H.] Rousseau and Garrard effectively crippled two of the three railroads supplying the Confederate army

in Atlanta. The results also inspired Sherman to plan another raid sending Stoneman and McCook to cut the tracks south of Atlanta on July 27.[216]

Lieutenant Henry Potter writes to his family of the previous two-week period in his August 1 letter from "Camp 5 miles from Atlanta":

> The last I wrote we had not crossed the Chattahouchee river. My health is good as ever. Two weeks ago yesterday our Division crossed the river. Since that time we have done a great deal of service and hard work but not much fighting. The next day after crossing we moved down and struck the Charleston RR from Atlanta about 12 miles between Decatur and Stone Mountain. Tore up 3 miles of track thus effectively cutting communications on that line–without any loss on our side. And our Army followed up the advantage and moved after us capturing Decatur the next morning. Six miles east of Atlanta on the RR. In a day or two we started on another raid to Coventry [Covington] a place on the same road 42 miles S.E. from Atlanta and 60 across to Macon. Our object to cut the road farther away and hinder their retreat via Augusta, if such might be their intention. We succeeded in effecting our object without serious loss. Burnt the bridges, tore up the track and burnt ties. Captured over 200 prisoners, two trains of cars, a large amount of horses, mules and cattle. Gone four days. While we were gone the rebels pitched on our left which was left exposed by our absence, with nearly their whole army, but they got enough and too much for them. But we lost one of our best Generals. McPherson was killed instantly by a volley of rebel muskets from an ambush. His loss was no sooner known than our men, maddened, rushed like an avalanche upon them and drove them back. Our loss was about 2000, rebel loss 5000.[217]

Despite these Union setbacks, Confederate General Joseph Johnston found himself in the untenable position of continually withdrawing as Sherman's Army rolled into Georgia. President Davis began to doubt the general's ability to defend Atlanta and Johnston, who "despised Jefferson Davis," was not forthcoming in explaining his plans of operation.[218] On July 17, Davis relieved Johnston, replacing him with John Bell Hood. Hood, whose left arm was crippled at Gettysburg and who had previously lost his right leg at Chickamauga, could only ride strapped to his horse. In many ways he symbolized the dying Confederacy: his body was broken but his spirit was still strong. Upon hearing of the change, Sherman asked General Schofield if he knew Hood. "Yes," he replied, "I know him well and I will tell you what sort of man he is. He'll hit you like hell now, before you know it." Hood, McPherson, and Schofield had all been classmates at West Point, and George Thomas had been one of his instructors. Sherman "concluded his new opponent was 'bold even to rashness, and courageous in the extreme.' Obviously, the change in Confederate commanders meant 'fight' . . ."[219] True to Schofield's prediction, General Hood lost no time making his presence felt, as he attacked George Thomas's Army of the Cumberland at Peachtree Creek, Georgia, on July 20. "Thomas's line held, but at a cost of 1,800 killed, wounded, and missing. Confederate casualties numbered between 2,500 and 5,000."[220] This was followed by a massive Confederate assault on July 22. McPherson was killed while trying to organize reinforcements. He was immediately replaced by Major General John A. Logan, and what followed was "some of the fiercest fighting in the war . . . leaving 3,722 Federals and fully 5,000 Confederates killed, wounded or captured . . ." By sundown the Union Army of the Tennessee "had won its greatest victory and suffered its most grievous loss," the loss of their general.[221] "For the next month Sherman and Hood would use cavalry to fight skirmishes around the city."[222]

Sherman seriously underestimated the ability and speed with which the Confederacy rebuilt their rail and supply lines once the Yankee raiders had left. Worse yet, on July 27, Sherman sent two columns of Union cavalry on a major raid to "wreck the vital railroads that supplied the Confederate Army defending Atlanta." Both McCook's and Stoneman's divisions suffered serious defeats, forcing Sherman to abandon his efforts to use cavalry to cut Atlanta's railroads and "compelled him to begin a lengthy siege, the very thing he had hoped to avoid."[223] Sieges took time, and that was a luxury Sherman did not have.²²⁴ "The Federal army was wholly dependent upon one long line of railroad, passing through an enemy's country where the people were hostile, and that only certain important points could be guarded," and Sherman was "130 miles deep in Confederate territory and absolutely dependent on the single-track railroad stretching back to Chattanooga."²²⁵

As early as May, forage for Sherman's horses began to be a problem and they "suffered terribly. . . 'They ate dried leaves . . . chewed the bridle reins and the [rope] picket lines.'" Things had gotten so bad that McCook advised General Elliott, "my horse are absolutely dying from starvation . . ." "Hundreds of otherwise healthy troopers had to be sent to the rear or reassigned to infantry commands because their horses had died of hunger, disease, wounds, or neglect."²²⁶

While Sherman crossed the Chattahoochee river and reached the outskirts of Atlanta by the middle of July, he had by no means done what he set out to do: destroy the Confederate Army. The Army of Tennessee, picking up reinforcements as it retreated, was probably stronger now than when the campaign began, and Sherman for the moment was at a standstill.²²⁷ He had suffered heavy casualties with no significant results and he was frustrated with his generals.²²⁸ To add to his pressure, the war in the East was going badly: Grant and Gordon Meade were stalled at Petersburg and Richmond had not been taken. "The Confederate strongholds were unconquered and . . . the people of the North were getting very war weary as the month of July ended" and Federal elections approached.²²⁹

Stoneman's Raid: The Battle at Flat Rock (Shoals)

Within hours after Minty's Brigade returned to camp near Decatur, on July 25, Major General George Stoneman informed Garrard of a raid Sherman was planning; he would use Stoneman's and McCook's cavalry divisions to disrupt Confederate supply lines around Atlanta. This time Sherman "wanted to bring all four divisions together at the same place, at the same time, to do the same thing: wreck the Macon railroad."²³⁰ Both McCook and Garrard had reservations about the plan, and Garrard was resentful at taking orders from Stoneman. This reflected continuing "problems in the Yankee cavalry's chain of command" and a "decided lack of coordination."²³¹ George Stoneman was a "no nonsense . . . old army" officer and did not have an easy relationship with the Volunteers.²³² It is interesting to note that in correspondence with General Sherman on July 5, Stoneman closed with, "I wish I could get my regiment, or rather the regiment to which I belong (the Fourth), with us. Can't you manage it?"²³³

"Tired and haggard after three days in the saddle," Garrard said he would try to carry out all orders. "The next day, after assessing reports from his subordinates":

> he wrote to Sherman, 'It will take three or four days to put my command in order. My wagons are not up, and I do not know where they are. I have also over 1,000 horses unshod.' [Garrard] did, however issue his Special Field Orders No. 4 on July 25 directing 'that every effort be made to get the command in as good condition as possible without delay.'²³⁴

As Sherman explained his raid, Thomas and Schofield's armies were to keep Hood busy on the north side of Atlanta while the Army of the Tennessee "quit the trenches east of the city" and moved westward "to threaten the junction of the Montgomery and Macon railroads at East Point." Meanwhile, "the entire cavalry corps, almost 10,000 strong, would move out at daylight on July 27."²³⁵

It seemed the preparation had hardly begun when reveille was sounded in Garrard's camps at 4 a.m. on July 27.²³⁶ "On the Rampage again!" writes 4th Michigan Private John Lemmon.²³⁷ Garrard's Second Division, which was to be held in reserve because of "their recent forays," marched east through Decatur to Flat Shoals to "occupy the attention of Wheeler's cavalry and thus cover the movements of Stoneman's Division of Cavalry, which . . . marched directly for Macon."²³⁸ Colonel Minty took the advance of the column with his First Brigade, followed by the Board of Trade Battery, Eli Long's Second Brigade and Abe Miller's Third Brigade, approximately "4,000 officers and men and six pieces of artillery."²³⁹ Crossing Snapfinger Creek, Garrard's division reached Latimer's Crossroads about 1 p.m.²⁴⁰ After conferring with Stoneman, "Garrard's three brigades turned to the right toward South River" to protect Stoneman's right as his column continued toward Lithonia.²⁴¹ At around 2 p.m., "Minty's advance guard approached Flat Rock; or Flat Shoals as the locals called it, and they surprised and burned six Rebel wagons and an ambulance, and captured three or four Confederate soldiers":242

Upon reaching South River, the column halted. As was customary when going into camp, the leading brigade stopped, allowing the others to pass. This reversed the next day's order of march, so that Minty's brigade became the rear guard and Eli Long's two Ohio regiments took the advance near the bridge at Flat Shoals. Troopers in both commands unsaddled their horses under threatening skies and began the familiar camp routine.... [T]he men cooked their suppers over smoky little fires and pitched their tents. They were only nine miles from the Macon railroad.243

"We went into camp about 12 m [midnight]," writes Lieutenant Potter, when "the rebs run upon our pickets . . . [and] we were ordered out."244 According to Minty, it is Allen's brigade of rebel cavalry that attacked his pickets who "were driven in from both flanks and the front; our rear was protected by the river."245

The 4th Michigan dismounted, moved to the front, driving the enemy back, and began erecting breastworks.246 The 4th Cavalry also "spent a good part of the night in building breastworks of logs, rocks and fence rails to assist us," writes Sergeant Larson, "in case the enemy should storm us early in the morning."247 "Our line was like a horse-shoe," explained Lieutenant Potter:

Minty's 1st Brigade and the 1st section of the board of Trade Battery held the left shank . . . [the] 3rd Brigade and the 3rd section of the battery anchored the right, while . . . the 2nd Brigade and the 2nd section formed their line near the bridge over South River.248 . . . We expected to have a big fight. Our whole Division was out and built works.249

"For half the night," Minty writes, "the regimental band, one of the best in the service, was well to the front, playing National airs, all of which were cheered to the echo by both sides."250

Everyone knew they were "in a tight place." Garrard convened a council of his senior commanders. It appeared they were surrounded by seven brigades of Wheeler's cavalry "and Rebel infantry might already be closing in . . ."251

At 8 a.m. "fighting erupted on all sides, . . . and Garrard had orders to hold the crossing at Flat Shoals until noon at all costs."252 "At break of day on the 28th," Minty writes, "we found nine brigades of rebel cavalry surrounding us":

As our object was to hold Wheeler long enough to let Stoneman get out of his reach, this was very gratifying. We made demonstrations, or rather videts in various directions, thus keeping the enemy on the *qui vive* until about 10 o'clock, having secured for Stoneman a good 24 hours start.253

Around 10 a.m., a Rebel officer approached Colonel Minty's Brigade carrying a white flag. His mission, he explained, was "to demand Garrard's immediate and unconditional surrender and save the unnecessary effusion of blood."254 Sergeant Larson provides an interesting description regarding negotiations for surrender:

The enemy had formed the idea that General Garrard's division was then in such a fix that it could be captured without a fight and so they opened with a slight skirmish all around early in the morning just to show us that they had us completely surrounded and then sent in a flag of truce and demanded the surrender of the whole division. This party of surrender, General Garrard made good use of by delaying his final answer as long as possible, so as to gain time for Stoneman. He managed to keep the Confederates in talk until near 10 o'clock, when he turned to the officer in charge of the flag of truce and said: 'My men do not know what surrender is and I will not teach them such a lesson. Tell your general that as soon as I get ready I will walk out of here.' With that instruction the flag of truce departed. When General Garrard gave his final answer he had already made preparations to burst through the enemy's line. The 3rd Brigade, one regiment being mounted infantry, had been formed across a large cornfield just below the old log house wherein Garrard's headquarters were and where the negotiations for surrender were going on. Our Chicago Battery stood limbered up right behind the brigade, and ready to blow open a path through which it could pass on a charge.

All this the enemy's officer could have seen if he had been allowed the use of his eyes, but that is a matter so important that great care is always taken to prevent the bearer of a flag of truce from gaining any information while inside the line, so he is blindfolded. The conference between our general and the Confederate officer was held in a small room in the old house, the small windows screened with blankets and the door closed and guarded so that the visitor could not get a view of anything outside. General Garrard and the Confederate officer conversed pleasantly together as if they were old friends and even passed jokes on each other.

The 4th US Cavalry had been moved into the woods where our horses were tied, by small parties so as to avoid notice and there mounted and formed into two battalions of six companies each. When the Confederate officer was gone these two battalions quickly took position, one on each flank of the line already formed in the cornfield and at the command 'forward march,' took the double-quick. After breaking down the fence we ran right through the rebel line and drove them back in confusion from the Lithonia Road.[255]

David Evans gives greater detail of the following action:

> The 4th Regulars mounted, deploying two battalions of six companies each to cover Miller's flanks. The 4th Michigan and 7th Pennsylvania formed ranks behind Miller's led horses and drew sabers. Wagons, ambulances, and pack mules followed with the rest of the artillery, while Eli Long's 3rd and 4th Ohio brought up the rear. . . . As the last preparations were being made, Colonel [Jonathan] Biggs asked his men, of the 123rd Illinois, 'Boys, which is your choice–to cut the way out or be captured?'
>
> 'Cut our way out,' his regiment roared back.
>
> A few moments later, the two ten-pounder Parrotts behind Miller's line boomed, sending a pair of shells hurtling up the Lithonia Road. Biggs' skirmishers leaped over their breastworks and broke into a run. A bugle blared and the rest of the brigade surged after them, a great blue phalanx sweeping across the broad fields with parade ground precision. The 4th Regulars threw down an intervening fence and quickly aligned themselves on either flank.
>
> On they came, irresistible, grim, and silent except for the jostling of accoutrements. Fifty yards passed, a hundred and more before the first flicker of flame rippled down the Rebel skirmish line.[256]

Sergeant Ben Magee, Co. I, 72nd Indiana Mounted Infantry describes the advance:

> We opened on them with our Spencers, killed a few and captured others. They were taken so completely by surprise that many of them never even fired a single round, but skinned out for Atlanta as fast as their legs could carry them. We now raised a cheer and charged right into the main line along with their own skirmishers. Never was a surprise more complete. We are sure that not half of the main line ever fired a shot, and those who did were so badly scared that scarcely a shot took effect. The last mother's son of them ran away . . . we never saw men make better time. Had our cavalry been there mounted and ready to follow us we could have captured the whole force of rebels in front of us; but the cavalry were engaged in the rear, and by the time we had run 600 yards we were all given out, and were still 600 yards from the rebel lead horses; the best we could do was for our battery to throw shells into them as they were mounting.[257]

Evans continues:

> In less than twenty minutes, it was over. Miller's winded troopers halted after a half mile and waited for the number fours to bring up their horses. Minty's

brigade passed through their ranks and pressed on toward Latimer's Crossroads. The rebels did not pursue, and shortly after noon Garrard halted the division on a three-mile stretch of road between Latimer's Crossroads and Lithonia. There, he waited.[258]

"Night came. Pickets kept their sleepless vigils, but no shots broke the stillness, no bugles sounded 'To Arms.'" The twenty-ninth was quiet, as Garrard waited for word from Stoneman. His delay and failure to take aggressive action to find and assist McCook or Stoneman would be the last straw for Sherman.

The afternoon trembled with the distant thunder of Sherman's guns. That evening a slow drizzle brought some relief from the heat, and foragers returned with welcome supplies of corn, oats, meat, molasses, flour, eggs, preserves, potatoes, apples, and watermelons. 'Had a good supper,' noted one trooper in his diary before turning in for the night.[259]

Reveille sounded at 4 a.m. the morning of July 30, and Garrard finally made a decision. At 6 a.m., his division left Lithonia on the Lawrenceville Road... The column kept this northeasterly course for about an hour, then turned northwest on the Rockbridge Road, leaving Stone Mountain's sugar-loaf silhouette towering to their left.[260] "A brief morning shower soaked everyone as the column toiled through... 'flat, open, rough country,' strewn with slabs of granite." About midday, the advance guard reached the intersection at Choice's Store. Hearing reports the rebels had reoccupied Decatur, Garrard detoured north for another six miles until the division reached Flint Hill Church. There the column turned left on the Peachtree Road, passing Buchannan's and New Cross Keys before halting in the rain at 6 p.m. after a twenty-five-mile march.[261]

Dark clouds still hung low overhead when Garrard's troopers broke camp and climbed into the saddle at 6:30 the next morning.... The column plodded six miles south, past Buckhead and across Collier's Bridge. Just beyond the bridge, not far from Sherman's headquarters, the welcome orders to halt and dismount brought their four-day journey to an end.[262]

Captain Vale summarizes the results of the raid:

Having thus completely opened the way for Stoneman by drawing the rebel cavalry far to the east of his proposed line of march, and being under orders to return to the left of the army immediately on this being done, Garrard moved the division to Lithonia, where he camped that night. Next day, the 30th, after pushing strong scouting parties out on the Flint road without developing the enemy, he marched to Cross Keys, and on the 31st went into camp near Buckhead.[263]

In his May 31, 1894, *National Tribune* article of the events, Minty quotes Thomas B. Van Horne's *History of the Army of the Cumberland*:

Gen. Garrard engaged successfully two divisions of cavalry at Flat Rock, and then returned to Atlanta. Gen. Stoneman went farther and fared worse. [He]... moved through Covington and down the Ocmulgee to East Macon. In endeavoring to return he was hemmed in and captured with 700 of his command, the remainder escaping.[264]

Minty concludes: "... what a miserable failure Stoneman–the great cavalry failure of the war–made of the expedition."[265] Adding to this humiliation, Stoneman became the highest ranking Union officer to be captured during the war. He was exchanged in three months and redeemed his reputation in the later months of the war, being brevetted major general, USA.[266] To make matters worse, Colonel Sipes reports that "General McCook's division, operating against the same railroad, was at first successful, but finally was repulsed; and, as Sherman expressed it, two of his cavalry divisions were badly demoralized."[267] "The raid resulted in utter failure," writes Vale.[268]

On July 30, Minty's brigade marched the thirty miles from Lithonia to Cross Keys. On the thirty-first, they "went into camp near Buck Head."[269] Their supply trains had arrived from Marietta "bringing forward rations and forage . . . and a good supply of horseshoes."

Garrard's three brigades "spent the rest of the afternoon refilling haversacks and cartridge boxes. Quartermasters had supplied each man with a day's rations and one hundred rounds of ammunition by the time buglers sounded 'the General' at 5:00 p.m."[270]

In the history of the 4th Michigan Cavalry it is written: "When Minty's Brigade reaches Atlanta in August, its men and mounts had been worked to the limits of endurance."[271]

As noted by Captain Burns:

> Our cavalry is now pretty well used up, that of Stoneman and McCook having been pretty badly demoralized in the recent raids. As far as we can make out, neither man of them is fit to command a platoon. McCook allowed his men to get drunk on the fruit of the vine, etc, they had captured from the rebel officers, and a great many were made prisoners. The raid of Stoneman on account of the inefficiency of himself and another General I could name was also a total failure. You may see glowing accounts of the two raids in our papers, but we consider them a disgrace, and an idle waste of men and horses . . .[272]

Burns was repeating the popular rumor about McCook's troopers being drunk, which is vehemently denied by the men of his command and others who were present.[273]

Such activity does not seem within the character of this civilian appointed officer, considering his six brevets during the war for "gallant and meritorious services," including major general, USV prior to his resignation in May 1866.[274]

A Well-Deserved Leave

Sergeant Larson writes that earlier in the year Congress had passed an act "by which all soldiers who were enlisted in the regular army for a term of 5 years and had less than one year of that enlistment still to serve, could re-enlist for another term of three years, the remainder of the 5 year term to be canceled and a furlough for 30 days would be granted at once." The soldier could also "credit themselves to any of the loyal states and receive the state bounty."[275] He continues:

About 80 of us, all from the 4th Cavalry, took advantage of the offer and re-enlisted. There were some ten or fifteen more that could have done the same but they preferred to stay the 5 years out and then quit Uncle Sam. My object was not the bounty, but I needed some rest.

The place itself where I made my second contract with Uncle Sam would have been far from enticing to raw recruits. Our position at that time was very close to Kennesaw Mountain, which was yet in possession of the enemy and they were constantly shelling us with their heavy artillery. Lieutenant Sylvan [Sullivan] had put up a tent under some trees where he had constructed a table of cracker boxes on which to write out our enlistment papers . . .

The next day we turned in all government property, including arms and ammunition, boarded a train that stood ready for us at Big Shanty and started for the North. This of course, ended our service with Sherman's army as Atlanta fell before we returned and Sherman had started on his march to Savannah.

The trains used nothing but box cars filled with wounded Union and Confederate Soldiers, with some infantry sent along as guard. We cavalry recruits had to go on top of the box cars as there was no room inside for us, but that was all right with us. We could ride a box car also.[276]

. . . Some six or seven of us had given our re-enlistment to New York and we took cars for that city . . . We had money in our pockets now and could afford it. What did we care about money? When our furlough was out we were going back and we, or at least some of us, might not need any more at all. We had seen that the chances ran very much in that direction. We wanted to see everything that was to be seen . . .[277]

After enjoying all that New York had to offer, James Larson traveled to Chicago, thence to Milwaukee and Green Bay City. From there, he took the mail coach to his boyhood home in Wisconsin to visit his father. On his return in September, he took the train from Chicago to Louisville, Kentucky, to rejoin his regiment.[278]

At least eleven troopers of the 4th US Cavalry who took advantage of this offer—including three sergeants—deserted while on furlough or sometime after their return.[279]

V. The Siege of Atlanta–August 1864

The city of Atlanta was one of the South's most important industrial, logistical, and administrative centers. With the convergence of four railroad lines, it bound together practically all of the Confederacy east of the Mississippi.[1]

Both sides dug in to their extensive breastworks and trenches. It was some of the bloodiest fighting of the year, and the cavalry found itself in the trenches along with the infantry. The "Yankees held on, sometimes rolling from one side of their earthworks to the other to halt consecutive Confederate charges from front and rear." One Federal corps had beaten off twelve Rebel assault waves in a single week.[2]

Atlanta would finally fall on September 2 "in the very nick of time when a victory alone could save the party of Lincoln" in the upcoming election.[3] In evacuating the city, Hood was forced to blow up twenty-eight carloads of ammunition in the rail yard that "precipitated the great fire that destroyed Atlanta." Sherman felt the explosion in Jonesboro, fifteen miles south and "wondered what it meant."[4]

Fighting in the Trenches

From August 1 through 14, "the First and Third Brigades, dismounted, relieved the Twenty-third Corps in the trenches on the extreme left of the army."[5]

Along with orders to act as decoys for the infantry, Sherman ordered Garrard's division to "patrol the roads around Decatur, picket toward Roswell, and 'be prepared to sally out as cavalry from his trenches in case of necessity.'"[6] At the time these orders were received, Garrard's three brigades were "bivouacked on both sides of Peachtree Creek."[7]

After half a day's preparation and a four-mile march, Minty's First Brigade and the rest of Garrard's Third Brigade "turned into a large field about 9:00 p.m." Orders were given to dismount. The number one, two, and three troopers in each rank "shouldering a rattling assortment of rifles, carbines, haversacks, and canteens," swung down from their saddles. The number threes handed their reins to the number fours, who remained mounted. The number twos tied their reins to number threes' bits, and number ones tied theirs to number twos' bits. Both brigades formed ranks. "Leaving the artillery and the number fours to guard the horses, they started down the rough and rutted road to the southeast."[8] "The mud was very deep & tenacious," complains Private John Lemmon of the 4th Michigan:

> As we floundered along, the great and unusual exercise caused curses loud & deep to rend the midnight air for the boys feet were blistered. We soon began to pass in the dark what seemed to be in-trenchments–deep ditches & high banks (with slippery sides) . . .[9]

The "swearing, mud-spattered troopers slogged through the muck in their heavy high-topped boots for three miles before orders halted them at midnight behind the trenches that Schofield's XXIII Corps had vacated earlier that evening."[10] "A more tired lot of fellows you never saw," writes Lieutenant Henry Potter.[11] "Both brigades posted a regiment on the picket lines. The rest of the men tumbled into the muddy red ditches or sprawled by the roadside."[12]

> A ditch, about two and a half feet deep and four feet wide was dug out, the earth being thrown to the front, forming the breastwork. This breastwork would be but about three feet high from the outside, but about five feet from the inside, standing in the ditch. Then on top of the breastwork

a 'head log' was laid parallel to the work, supported on cross pieces. The guns were fired under this head log, which served as protection.[13]

"We are soldiering now with a vengeance," writes Captain Burns, "and we today are doing infantry duty in the dirt . . . surrounded by the debris of an exceedingly dirty infantry camp."[14] Nearby was the July 22 battlefield described by an infantryman of the 72nd Indiana:

> It is an awful sight . . . Thousands lie comparatively unburied. I saw one . . . poor fellow [who] had been standing behind a tree in the act of loading, when the fatal ball reached his heart and he still stood leaning against the tree with his hand extended holding the rammer and the other holding the gun-barrel.[15]

Minty's Brigade "manned an angle in the works investing Atlanta, in front of the Howard house."[16] One portion of the line faced southwest, toward the city, facing the Georgia Railroad.[17] Another line:

> ran nearly north-east, with a strong skirmish line, in riflepits, pushing up on the former face to within about two hundred yards of the rebel works, and outlying skirmishers on the north-east, also sheltered in strong riflepits, extending to the Augusta railroad, at the Red House, east of the city, and for a considerable distance along the railroad.[18]

They were occupying fortifications "about 1 1/3 miles northeast of Atlanta" and were "daily and nightly engaged with the enemy," taking fire from the heavy guns in the city of Atlanta.[19]

From the "left flank, in earthworks," Lieutenant Potter found the time to write letters to his father and sister:

> Our batteries are playing hot . . . cannon and small arms have been crashing away all day at the rebel stronghold. . . . The skirmishers have kept up a continual rattle night and day since we have been here. . . . Our boys in the treetops . . . can see all the city the forts and batteries. . . . I could see the City, its spires and domes, encircled by its defenses and forts.[20]

Potter had some good personal news to share with his family:

> And now I will tell you something pleasing to you as well as gratifying to my humble self. I was promoted this a.m. to Captaincy in my own company. . . . It was an entirely novel thing to me and unexpected as there are three 1st Lieutenants who had commissions older than mine. . . . In every promotion I have had I have jumped from three to half a dozen officers who ranked me and I have never been jumped. I do not tell you this in a bragging spirit, but merely to give you an idea of my standing in the regiment. I have no more responsibility now than I had before, for I have been commanding (H) Company and responsible for Property some time. It only puts one more bar on my shoulder and changes my title.[21]

For the cavalrymen wallowing in the trenches, "the novelty of foot soldiering was rapidly wearing thin. . . . It rained every day . . . [as] the two opposing armies glared at each other from their muddy trenches, each waiting for the other to make the first move. At times the stench of rotting flesh from the nearby battlefield was almost unbearable."[22] "'Everything seems covered in mud,' wrote a trooper in his diary. 'We sleep in mud, eat in mud, walk in mud . . .'" Foraging details wandered as far as ten and twelve miles from camp, searching ravaged fields and orchards for apples, sweet corn, and peaches. As the Union forces moved through the South to the war's inevitable conclusion, foragers faced increasing danger from civilians desperate for food; several troopers of the 4th Cavalry were killed by citizens.

Orders on August 10 cut their already meager rations in half.[23] Officers and men shared equally in the misery. As Captain Burns writes, for two full weeks the men and officers passed their days "lying in the trenches . . . the men burrow in their holes like foxes and not a head can be shown that is not shot at":

> ... I am sitting in a kind of arbor made of the branches of oaks (we have no tents or shelters), writing on a table made of cracker boxes which we fixed up this afternoon. In one corner of our arbor are lying Captain [Heber] Thompson and Lieutenant [Samuel C.] Dixon on their ponchos, smoking, laughing, talking, being 'jolly under creditable circumstances.' Colonel Minty is looking over and comparing a monthly return I have just made out . . . Our darkeys are outside singing and humming 'nigger' songs, and a little farther off is another crowd of them, dancing their liveliest to a sort of chant they have. A few rods from us the band of an infantry brigade is playing infantry waltzes and other airs, which strangely mingles with the bray of mules. . . . Crickets and tree toads also keep their perpetual chatter.[24]

Morale started to decline as the men's health began to suffer because of the unsanitary conditions. According to Burns, the common complaint is "Diarrhea." "Everyone here has it, semi-occasionally and it is not considered a cause for going on the sick list. It is disagreeable and weakening."[25] Colonel Sipes, 7th Pennsylvania, writes of his regiment "being almost constantly under fire from a Confederate battery of sixty-four pound siege guns. The shells thrown into the trenches from this and some invisible batteries made things lively, but little damage was done by them, and the majority buried themselves in the sand without exploding."[26] Captain Vale further describes their situation:

> About one hundred and fifty yards to the right of the bivouac of the brigade, was a hill on which, in a strong fort, a battery of heavy siege-guns was mounted, and on an opposite hill one of the strongest of rebel forts of defense was constructed, also armed with heavy (sixty-four-pounder) siege-guns: Our bivouac, located in the angle, was directly in the line of fire from this rebel fort, and almost daily the big shells from Atlanta, passing over the fort on our right, dropped down among us, sometimes exploding, but generally harmlessly burying themselves in the sand. Our acquaintance with, and experience of, these visitors began on the night of the 3d, when the rebels opened a converging fire on the battery to our right from five heavy batteries, located within easy range. The shells dropped into our camp at a lively rate, half a dozen coming at a time, and as all the boys not on duty at the line of breast works were sleeping in their little shelters at the time, they got 'waked up' rudely enough! Shelters were knocked down, cook-tents demolished, camp-kettles scattered and destroyed with a good deal of din, and the boys promptly seeking cover in the trenches, without much regard to the completeness of their uniform, presented somewhat the appearance of Falstaff's regiment of ragamuffins.[27]

Several days later a rebel fort opposite the Howard House "suddenly loosed a thunderous salvo at 9 p.m." One of the shells struck the shelter of Major Jennings, 7th Pennsylvania, exploding as it hit the log breast works . . . mortally wounding one soldier and severely injuring another.[28]

Colonel Minty writes that early in the morning on August 9, his advanced skirmishers at the "Red House" and along the Augusta Railroad were attacked by the rebels, who were driven back. ". . . The great superiority of our arms–the Spencers–over the infantry rifle was made very apparent on this occasion; the enemy could not stand before our fire."[29] Years later, Minty would write that "no portion of the line held by the dismounted cavalry was at any time carried by the rebels."[30]

On August 14, the Second Division was relieved from duty at 4 p.m., "very well satisfied" to be out of the muddy trenches. It was daylight in the early morning on the fifteenth before Minty's brigade was relieved in front of the Howard house, "and a more pleased set of men you never saw," noted a Michigan cavalryman. Their spirits were raised by the first clear skies in a week and many were drying out their sodden blankets.[31] "At 6:00 a.m. Minty's mud-stained column started back to the horse camp on the Peachtree Road with the 1st section of the Board of Trade Battery."[32] As the men moved back to their horses, "the number fours quickly saddled the horses that had been left in their care and led them out to meet the column."[33]

In a sobering assessment that underlines the gravity of the situation for the cavalry horses, Vale writes:

> While the men were thus employed in the trenches, the horses were entirely without exercise and destitute of long forage, but, on the whole, rather improved in condition. In reality, it was this rest of fifteen days which prevented the Second division from being wholly dismounted.[34]

Minty's brigade had barely returned to camp—dirty and exhausted—when the call came from division headquarters, "Send the cavalry . . ."[35] It was reported that 500 rebel cavalry were threatening Vining's Station, and General Elliott wanted a cavalry force sent there immediately. Without enough time to clean up or have a hot cup of coffee, the 7th Pennsylvania was dispatched to Vining's station and the 4th Michigan and 4th U.S. were to relieve Eli Long's pickets guarding the roads back to Roswell. It turned out to be a false alarm.[36]

The July and now August campaigns proved to be disasters for both Sherman and his cavalry. "When company clerks prepared the muster rolls, 1,230 of the 3,000 officers and men who had started with McCook were listed as dead, wounded or missing." Stoneman's losses were even worse. While there were a number of reasons for such a poor showing on the part of his cavalry, Sherman chose to direct his anger at "the overcautious" Garrard.[37]

On July 22, Brigadier General Hugh Judson Kilpatrick—recently recovered from an injury—returned to take command of the Third Division. He established his headquarters at the junction of Powder Springs and Sandtown roads. The evening of August 14, Kilpatrick received orders from General Sherman to "make a bold reconnaissance in the direction of Fairburn to railroad if you can reach it . . ." Kilpatrick wasted no time, striking the West Point railroad "about halfway between Fairburn and Red Oak, cut the telegraph wire, and began working their way south, tearing up track as they went." In Fairburn, they chased the telegraph operator out of town, set fire to the depot, water tank, and woodshed, and tore up about three-quarters of a mile of track.[38] Sherman was delighted: "He acts in earnest. I believe General Kilpatrick, with his own and General Garrard's cavalry, could go straight for Rough and Ready, and break the Macon road all to pieces."[39]

Bogged down in what he least wanted, Sherman was desperate to break the siege of Atlanta. The Confederate cavalry was raiding his supply lines and "he had had his fill of intractable, insubordinate, and insipid officers."[40] Sherman believed the quickest way to end the siege was "a deliberate attack" on the Macon Railroad, south of Atlanta, "for the purpose of so disabling the road that the enemy will be unable to supply his army in Atlanta."[41] Judson Kilpatrick proposed such a plan, and on August 16, in a telegram to General Thomas, Sherman proposed Kilpatrick be given two of Garrard's brigades to lead such an attack.[42] Since Kilpatrick ranked Garrard, it provided a diplomatic way of moving Garrard aside.

Given the nickname "Kill Cavalry" by men under his command, Kilpatrick had a reputation of "wearing out his troopers and their mounts on long rides and getting them slaughtered in furious charges."[43] "He had always been an aggressive officer, but as a division commander his hilt-to-hilt, hell-for-leather style had its limits."[44] He could be a "formidable adversary," wrote Major General Jacob D. Cox, who had observed Kilpatrick during the Atlanta Campaign. If attacked suddenly, "he was quite capable of mounting bareback the first animal, horse or mule, that came to hand and charging in his shirt at the head of his troopers with a dare-devil recklessness that dismayed his opponents and imparted his own daring to his men."[45] He was the opposite of Garrard and "had to be kept on a tight rein" by his superiors.[46] Sherman was later quoted as saying "I know that Kilpatrick is a hell of a damned fool, but I want just that sort of man to command my cavalry on this expedition."[47] Preparations were begun at once for Kilpatrick's raid around Atlanta.

VI. Kilpatrick's Raid

Sherman wanted more than a "raid." This was to be "a deliberate attack for the purpose of so disabling the [railroad] that the enemy will be unable to supply his army in Atlanta." Sherman expected Kilpatrick "to work, not to fight.... Kilpatrick could not tear up too much track or twist too much iron."[1] Assured that Kilpatrick understood the mission, Sherman sent him back to his camp with the Third Division and immediately issued Special Field Orders No. 6 for General Thomas to dispatch two of Garrard's brigades of cavalry and a battery of artillery to Sandtown "by the nearest possible routes."[2]

Colonel Robert Minty was assigned to command the division consisting of the First and Second Brigades and the Chicago Board of Trade Battery.[3] Command of a division would normally require the rank of brigadier general, which Minty had consistently been denied for reasons not based on his abilities or performance.[4] Even though not given the rank, he obviously earned and deserved being given command

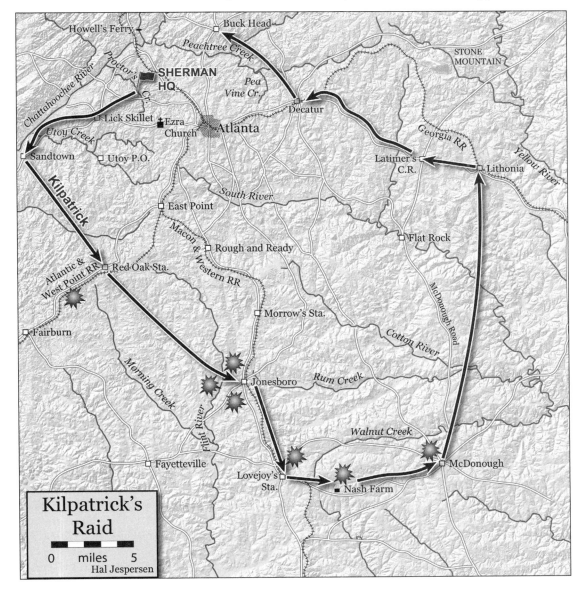

of a division for the purpose of this raid and it can be considered recognition of his leadership and an acknowledgment from his superiors.

Before Sherman decided on Kilpatrick to lead his raid, Colonel Eli Long—a captain in the 4th U.S. Regulars now commanding Second Brigade—was considered. "Several colonels in Garrard's division were senior [to Long] and the only way to get around that was to have him promoted" to brigadier general Volunteers.[5] The appointment was granted on August 18, but by that time Sherman had settled on Kilpatrick. Long's promotion over Colonel Minty—which did not become known until Kilpatrick's men returned from the raid—was a bitter disappointment for Minty.[6] Ever the soldier, he dutifully accepted the decision of his superiors. Major Frank Mix, commanding 4th Michigan Cavalry, writes that Robert Minty "left a record behind him as a cavalry officer *second to none* in the West."[7] Major Mix also provides insight into the relationship between officers of the Voluntary regiments and those of the Regular Army:

> I was in command of the 4th Mich. Cav., and was the ranking officer of the First Brigade, Second Division, and when Gen. Minty, our brigade commander assumed command of the division, I should have assumed command of the brigade, but I urged Minty to also retain command of the brigade, as he could well enough do so; being brigaded with the 4th Regular Cav., and holding only the rank of Major myself, *I did not care to take the command over Capt. McIntyre, of the 4th Regulars,* unless it was necessary, as he was a good fellow, a good officer, and commanded a good regiment, and one we always worked with in perfect harmony. *Yet there was a little feeling among their officers as to the merit of their rank as Regulars,* and on this ground I preferred not to take command of the brigade unless it should become necessary [emphasis author][8]

Having just returned from duty in the trenches and their uneventful reconnaissance to Decatur, Garrard's exhausted and dirty troopers "settled into their old camps along Peachtree Creek" and spent the time they had "bathing and washing their clothes."[9]

On the morning of August 17, the men were instructed "to have horses shod and everything prepared for 'active operations.'" "Pickets had to be relieved . . . horses inspected, mules packed, and wagons sent to the rear."[10] "Kilpatrick had ordered his troopers to "draw one hundred rounds of ammunition, one day's forage, three days' rations of hardtack, a six-day supply of sugar and coffee . . . to be carried on pack mules . . . and to be ready to march at 6:00 p.m."[11] Shortly before 6 p.m., Garrard met with Minty and gave him orders to march out at 10 p.m.[12] With delays in procuring rations, "it was 1:00 a.m., August 18, before the column got started." Major Frank W. Mix's 4th Michigan—nineteen officers and 231 men—led the way, followed by eleven officers and 262 men belonging to Captain James B. McIntyre's 4th Regulars. Then came Major William H. Jennings's 7th Pennsylvania with sixteen officers and 313 men. Together with eight staff officers and sixty-five enlisted men attached to Minty's headquarters, the 1st brigade fielded fifty-four officers and 871 men.[13]

Eli Long's Second Brigade (1st Ohio, 3rd Ohio, and 4th Ohio) "brought up the rear. Lieutenants George Robinson and Henry Bennett and 88 artillerymen accompanied the column" with four guns from the Chicago Board of Trade Battery. "Teams of eight horses pulled each of the 10-pounder Parrotts, while six-horse hitches towed the limbers packed with shell and canister."[14] Colonel Eli Murray—now commanding Kilpatrick's Third Division—also brought along a battery of four guns.[15]

This would be the last time the three regiments of Minty's Saber Brigade would ride together. It is fitting that they were about to participate in one of the greatest cavalry charges in the Civil War while rescuing Kilpatrick's expedition.

Minty's division—a total of 2,398 men—marched southwest, crossing the Western and Atlantic Railroad, "past Sherman's headquarters and down the south side of the Chattahoochie" to meet General Kilpatrick at Sandtown, a small outpost on the east bank of the Chattahoochie River directly west of Atlanta.[16]

After the all-night march from Buckhead: "Minty halted his column at 6:00 a.m., August 18, on the banks of the Utoy Creek, keeping the command under cover of the hills."[17] "Leaving instructions for his men to unsaddle, water, feed, and groom their horses, he and his adjutant, Captain Burns, rode on to Sandtown with a couple of orderlies."[18] It was the first of three nights that Minty's division would go without sleep. While the officers met with General

Kilpatrick to plan the raid, the men were kept busy.[19] During the "long, hot afternoon at Utoy Creek . . . Minty's men packed an additional sixty cartridges into their saddlebags to go with what they already had in their cartridge boxes." With the hot weather, "the flies and insects were swarming and the surroundings were anything but inviting for a good day's rest." They received orders at 5 p.m. "to feed and water their horses, eat supper, and be ready to saddle in an hour. At 6 p.m., Minty's headquarters bugler sounded 'Boots and Saddles.'"[20]

"It was a bright, beautiful, moonlight night," recalls Captain Burns, "when the column set out." The Second Brigade in the lead was followed by artillery, ambulances, and then the First Brigade. "The movement was commenced under cover of darkness to prevent, if possible, any information obtained by the enemy . . ."[21] "Unfortunately, the rebels were aware of the size and destination of Kilpatrick's command [and] would bring them a few surprises before their march was over."[22] Prior to the departure, a circular to be read to the troops that afternoon from Brigadier General Kilpatrick was distributed to every regimental commander:

> Soldiers!
> You have been selected from the Cavalry Divisions of the Army of the Cumberland.
> You have been well organized, equipped and rendered formidable at great expense to accomplish an object vital to the success of our cause. I am about to lead you, not on a raid, but in a deliberate and well combined attack upon the enemy's communications in order that he may be unable to supply his army in Atlanta. Two expeditions have already failed. We are the last cavalry troops of the army. Let each soldier remember this and resolve to accomplish the great object for which so much is risked or die trying.
> (Signed) J. Kilpatrick, Brig. Genl. Comdg. Expedition[23]

As Captain Burns writes:

> Two well-equipped expeditions, Stoneman's and McCook's, had been totally ruined in attempting the same thing. We, however, imagined we were made of sterner stuff, and started off in good spirits. . . .
> The whole was commanded by General Kilpatrick, and a good deal of a little man he is too; not at all afraid to be in the fight himself. Away we went . . .[24]

Evans describes the sight as General Kilpatrick's command moved out:

> They came down the road at a swinging trot, 4,500 men and eight pieces of artillery. Seven of the fourteen regiments carried Spencer rifles or carbines slung from their shoulders. It was more men, more firepower, and more formidable than any mounted column Sherman had ever assembled. From head to tail, the serpentine column stretched for two and a half miles.[25]

The flamboyant Kilpatrick also brought along several regimental bands.[26]

Bringing up the rear of the column, it was sometime between 8 and 9 p.m. before the three regiments of the Saber Brigade moved out under the clear sky and full moon.[27]

"This was their second night in the saddle," writes Lieutenant George Robinson of the Board of Trade Battery, "and it showed. . . . You might have ridden up and down the column . . . and not found a half-dozen men . . . but that were soundly asleep . . ."[28] Lieutenant William W. Webb, temporary commander of the 3rd Battalion, 4th US Cavalry, recalls:

> Even at this early stage of affairs the men, tired and sleepy, were nodding on their horses; and some who had been riding all the previous night were sitting bolt upright, but with their eyes shut, and evidently fast asleep, as I have seen men when thoroughly exhausted ride that way for miles.[29]

Recalling that night, Lieutenant Robinson writes:

> Up and down the column of the second division, as far as we could hear, the clicking of the sabre-scabbards against the stirrup, the jingle of the flying ends of the traces of the artillery harness, the dull rattle of the wheels of the gun carriages and limbers, and the low pattering of the horses' hoofs on the hard dirt, were the only sounds to break the otherwise almost breathless silence.[30]

"The entire night," notes Minty, "was passed in that most tiresome of all experiences to an active soldier–halt, dismount, wait, mount, advance a few hundred yards, halt, dismount, wait, and so on."[31] "Despite these frequent halts," writes Webb, "companies at the rear of the column were kept at a trot for much of the night, and often would have to close up at a gallop, as no falling back or intervals between the different regiments or brigades were allowed."[32]

The Federals met "stern resistance" almost from the start, writes Webb, "growing stronger and more determined with every mile advanced.... After the first few miles out there was no time in the following four days and nights but what some portion of the command–often the greater part–was in a fight."[33] "The advance would often be briskly engaged with the enemy," but because of the length of the column, which Captain Burns describes as "four or five miles long, ... the rear or front might be fighting briskly and the other end know nothing about it, except when the artillery was opened," or by the "halts and hitches" in the column.[34] The troopers would see the files in front "light out at a trot or gallop to close up, following in the movement by all, on to the rear, until close order was again resumed."[35] Just before daybreak on the nineteenth Kilpatrick, frustrated by the slow progress, called for Minty's division to move to the front and take the advance. "Here are men coming who will not be delayed by trifles," he is quoted as saying.[36]

The first serious meeting with the enemy was just at daylight that same morning, after crossing the Atlanta and West Point Railroad "near Fairburn, at Red Oak." "We had torn up about half a mile of track," writes Webb, "and were moving on, when the rear battalion of the 7th Pennsylvania was suddenly attacked by a force of dismounted men and artillery."[37] "The enemy, under cover of a slight fog, pushed up to within 200 yards of our left flank; and the first knowledge we had of their presence was a furious artillery fire, almost at point-blank range."[38] "They opened up on us with their artillery," writes Potter, "and shelled us rather too close for comfort ... the bullets were flying thick and fast."[39]

The 4th Regulars were following the Board of Trade Battery, crossing the tracks when a rebel shell "hurled overhead, crashed through the trees on their right, and ploughed into the ground. A second shell struck even closer."[40] "As can be well imagined," notes Webb, "there was a general waking up and straightening up."[41] Minty sent the 7th Pennsylvania and 4th Michigan to repulse the rebels, and Captain McIntyre sent a battalion of 4th Regulars under Lieutenant Elbridge Roys to attack the enemy's rear. Captain Burns describes the results of this first skirmish:

> Just back of where the rebels struck our column were the ambulances and the darkies leading officers' horses, pack-mules, &c. They, of course, skedaddled, each nigger and ambulance driver bolted for the woods. Several shells exploded among the colored brethren, and they thought the kingdom had come. Three ambulances were smashed to pieces ... I thought my lead horse was gone, but finally my contraband [negro servant] came crawling out of the woods, scared almost white.[42]

Four hundred tenacious Texans under the leadership of Brigadier General Lawrence Sullivan "Sul" Ross were all that stood between Kilpatrick's forces and the railroads south of Atlanta.[43] Captain McIntyre—"a Tennessee born Texan"—now found himself fighting a number of his former West Point classmates in Ross's brigade. McIntyre had finished "five places behind John Bell Hood" in his class.[44] For the greatly outnumbered Texans, it appeared their only strategy was to try to slow down Kilpatrick's advance by forcing the Union cavalrymen to dismount, "to feel the woods on both sides" for rebel pickets.[45] "'Delay ... was their great object,' asserted a captain of the 1st Ohio."[46] "Time was precious," writes Robert Burns, "and we could not halt for slight 'scrimmages.'"[47]

Webb writes that the objective was:

> to strike the railroad in rear of Atlanta as soon as possible. General Kilpatrick paid but little attention to the force that was now following us, giving them battle only when it was necessary to clear the road in our front, and when their flank attacks were severe enough to threaten disaster if not attended to.[48]

Colonel Minty was given orders to "push the [Texans] ... to Jonesboro."[49] The 4th Regulars and 4th Michigan, together with the Second Brigade, were to force the passage of Flint River near the small railroad town of Jonesboro.[50] "The rebels got possession of the road which we wanted," writes Potter, "and the 3rd battalion was ordered to advance in line and retake it-- which we did in good style but I lost my sergeant Cole . . . shot through the lungs."[51] The woods made it impractical for cavalry and the roads were obstructed by barricades. Minty ordered his advance regiment (the 3rd Ohio) to dismount, handing the reins to the number fours who remained with the horses, and "it moved forward as infantry, steadily driving the enemy before it."[52] It would "drive the rebels from the rail breastworks they had thrown up, mount again, and . . . find them in the same position a half mile further on."[53] Over a distance of about five miles, in mid-day temperatures in excess of 100 degrees, the regiment made at least three charges against Ross's brigade in this manner.[54] When it reached the valley through which Flint River runs, the men came under direct artillery fire from Ferguson's brigade positioned on the opposite bank. The rising bank was also "honeycombed with rifle-pits." "The shells and bullets rattled . . . around us," writes Burns, "knocking the bark and dirt in close proximity to our heads."[55]

As the 4th Regulars and 4th Michigan dismounted and hurried through the woods to support the 3rd and 4th Ohio, "Lieutenant Henry Bennett's section of the Board of Trade Battery wheeled into position on some high ground to the left of the road and began hurling shells across the river. The very first shot struck a rebel artilleryman," notes Captain Burns, "burst in him, and blew him to atoms."[56] The skirmish line "advanced steadily, driving the enemy, and was closely followed by the 1st Ohio and the 4th Regulars in line, dismounted, with the two guns, worked by hand, on the road between them . . ."[57] Kilpatrick ordered more guns on the line and the entire battery let loose "with a noise like a thunderclap."[58] For the next fifteen minutes, there raged what Ohio Captain John Rea called "as pretty a little artillery duel as I ever witnessed."[59] "After four salvoes, the guns fell silent. As the last rolling echoes faded away, the 3rd and 4th Ohio sprang to their feet with a ringing cheer and rushed to the riverbank . . . closely followed by a second line composed of the 1st Ohio and the 4th Regulars."[60] Their carbines quickly drove the enemy from the pits on the opposite banks, forcing Ross into the town of Jonesboro, where his men took shelter in the buildings.[61]

Kilpatrick ordered Minty to "bring up the balance of his command and drive the rebels out of Jonesboro." The bridge across the river was partially destroyed, and the Second Brigade, along with the 4th U.S. and 4th Michigan, "crossed the river on the stringers of the ruined bridge" on foot to continue the advance.[62] "Fence rails were thrown on the bridge as planking" and Lieutenant Robinson's gunners "wheeled a section of the Board of Trade Battery across by hand."[63] The bridge was quickly repaired, allowing the whole command to continue the advance. Meanwhile, Minty, "getting his artillery in position, formed storming columns and ordered an advance on Jonesboro at double quick."[64] It was now 4:30 in the afternoon.[65]

The Destruction of Jonesboro, Georgia

Resistance was light as Minty's skirmishers approached the outskirts of Jonesboro "just before dark."[66] The remaining rebels—Sul Ross' Texans—were "manning a hastily constructed barricade of cotton bales and fence rails between the depot and the iron water tank."[67] They were quickly dealt with by the artillery. As described by Lieutenant Webb:

> . . . as we approached the little town of Jonesboro, on the railroad we were so anxious to reach and sixteen miles in rear of Hood's army, the enemy took shelter in the railroad depot and other buildings, behind cars, etc. Our brigade was here dismounted, and marched on the town as infantry. The artillery also came up, and shelled the buildings in which the enemy had taken shelter, in volleys. The effect of the shelling by these eight guns was tremendous. The enemy retreated, leaving the town and railroad at our mercy.[68]

"We moved across to the Macon RR towards Jonesboro," writes Potter, "[and] drove out about 400 rebels." Five minutes later, Minty's skirmishers were standing on the Macon Railroad.[69] "Thus," writes Captain Vale, "Minty and his cavalry were the first of the Union army to stand on the only remaining link of supplies and communications uniting Hood's army and Atlanta with the Confederacy."[70] Shells from the artillery:

> had wrecked the big water-tank near the depot, letting the water loose in a perfect flood over the level ground in front. Another shot had struck the iron safe in the depot, completely demolishing it and distributing

innumerable accounts, vouchers and railway tickets broadcast . . . to be seen by the hundred scattered about on the ground.[71]

"The mayor of Jonesboro and several frightened civilians soon appeared in the main street waiving a white flag."[72] For the next six hours, the command was engaged in tearing up and burning about three miles of the Macon Railway and burning large amounts of supplies in the Jonesboro supply depot.[73] Minty sent McIntyre's 4th US Cavalry to burn the depot and begin destroying the railroad. Setting their Spencers aside, the Regulars lined up along the track and laid hold of the rail. As one mounted infantryman notes: "No time to wait–no time to eat–no time to rest–the whole command fell to work."[74] Once again, Lieutenant Webb describes the scene:

> . . . the dismounted men of the First Brigade were scattered along one side of the track. Each man seizing hold of the end of a tie, to the encouraging words of, 'Now, then, men, altogether! Heave ho!' one side of the track was raised and thrown down the opposite side, bottom up. The work of destruction now went rapidly on. The track was thrown over, then the ties were fired, the heat warping and twisting the rails so as to render them forever useless.[75]

"A plume of smoke spiraled from . . . the depot roof. Flames appeared, rapidly engulfing the whole building, as well as a large stone warehouse filled with cotton and three railroad cars loaded with leather and furniture."[76] "The scene now presented literally 'beggars description,'" writes Webb:

> The shouts, cheering and tumult generally were deafening. Two bands were playing 'Bully for You,' and some other equally classic airs; the roar of burning buildings, the sharp firing still going on, the occasional boom of our artillery, altogether produced a scene of wild riot and hubbub![77]

"As the Regulars bent to their work, Kilpatrick sat astride his dappled Arabian, Spot, and watched, surrounded by his staff."[78] Webb continues:

> General Kilpatrick . . . probably becoming excited and somewhat overconfident by the success that had attended us so far, as well as by the bedlam of noises raging on all sides, raising himself in his stirrups, swung his hat over his head and shouted, 'Damn the Southern Confederacy; I can ride right through it!'
> Lieutenant [Joseph] Hedges, of the Fourth Cavalry, who was standing close by me and who generally took a rather practical view of things, remarked: 'We may sing a different tune to-morrow.' Kilpatrick, who overheard him, turned quickly, asking: 'What's that my man?' 'I was merely remarking,' replied Lieutenant H., 'that when infantry begins to come down from Atlanta we will not have it all our own way.' 'Oh,' said the general, 'we will not fight their infantry–we will run away from it; but we can lick hell out of their cavalry. Don't you see?' The lieutenant said he did see; but for all that, he, as well as many more, had their thoughts on the morrow and the day after, and wondered what the end would be.
> . . . [I]n our inmost hearts lurked a vague dread that possible disaster and an introduction to southern prisons–equivalent to a lingering death–was to be the end of it all, as was the case of those who had gone before.[79]

Troopers not assigned to wrecking the railroad moved down the main street, looting and torching the courthouse, jail, the provost marshal's office, and two tax-in-kind warehouses. Their enthusiasm may have been fueled by the barrels of whiskey found earlier in one of the rail cars.[80] "A brisk wind sprung up and very soon the flames spread to stores and other buildings, and over two-thirds of the town was burned to the ground, together with considerable public property and effects of the citizens."[81] There was also looting of private residences and businesses. Private Isaac Sollars, 4th US Cavalry, managed to liberate some "good tobacco and good old whiskey."[82] While not officially condoned, looting was difficult to control. The Union soldiers had been through hell, and many felt the Southern citizens were traitors. As one defensive Union soldier later admitted, "We set fire . . . to *one house* because the owner cut the well rope and dropped both bucket and rope down the well. He ought to have been shot."[83] For Southern citizens at this stage of the war, there was no law.

They had as much to fear from their own desperate Confederate army, not to mention bands of marauders, deserters, stragglers, displaced civilians, and mobs of freed blacks swarming the countryside.[84]

"Sometime after 8:00 p.m., the 4th Regulars and 4th Michigan mounted and moved into a field on the north side of town. Joined by the 7th Pennsylvania... they unsaddled and fed their horses in the glare of the burning buildings and then began putting up barricades along the crest of a ridge running at right angles to the railroad."[85] At approximately 10 p.m., part of Kilpatrick's command was attacked by rebel forces one mile south of town.[86] Minty's brigade "abandoned their unfinished barricades on the north side of town and moved about a mile down the railroad" to guard the left flank. "By 11:00 p.m., Kilpatrick had his entire force in line of battle."[87] "It was a wild night and most graphic scene," recalls Lieutenant Will Curry of the 1st Ohio:

> The sky was lighted up with burning timbers, buildings and cotton bales; the continuous bang of carbines, the galloping of staff officers and orderlies up and down the streets carrying orders or dispatches, the terrified citizens peering out their windows, the constant marching of troops changing position... all made up a weird scene never to be forgotten...[88]

"The full moon slid behind a thick bank of clouds," writes David Evans:

> Lightning flickered overhead. Thunder rumbled and rain was pouring down when the 8th Indiana and 2nd Kentucky quitely got up and warily approached the unseen Rebel barricades 250 yards away. They had gone about a hundred yards when the opposing skirmishers opened fire. Both regiments cheered lustily and charged riddling the night with rapid volleys from their Spencers. Rushing blindly through the rain and darkness, they closed to within forty yards of the Rebel works, only to falter in the face of heavy fire.[89]

The troopers were forced to dive for cover. As his men "hugged the muddy ground," Kilpatrick brought the 92nd Illinois band right up behind his lines and ordered them to play.[90]

Lieutenant Potter and his men were caught off guard when the fighting erupted at around 11 p.m.:

> We were resting... you must know we were all very tired-- when you march all night in your saddle without any sleep. It was like a thunderbolt. I jumped and you ought to have seen... everyone fly to our horses-- but our line stood like a rock unyielding... and to show contempt for the rebs Kilpatrick brought out his band to the line... no doubt to their supreme disgust.[91]

> ... Mounted on milk-white horses, the musicians raised their German silver instruments to their lips and launched into a rousing rendition of 'Yankee Doodle,' followed by 'The Star Spangled Banner' and 'Dixie.'

"The effect was almost magical," declared one captain. "Cheer after cheer arose along the entire line."[92] "It was as much to say," writes Potter, "come and take us if you can, but you can't–they thought they had us tight but they were mistaken..."[93]

At about this time, writes Minty, "One of our men, an old telegraph operator, caught a message on the fly, which gave the information that Pat Cleburne's division of infantry and William Martin's division of cavalry were en route to reinforce Sul Ross."[94] This information was apparently false, although it continued to be believed and reported by the officers participating in Kilpatrick's Raid well into the 1890s.[95]

With the rain making further destruction of the railroads impossible, Kilpatrick convened a meeting of his officers. The decision was made to flank the rebel forces and "strike the railroad somewhere farther south, beyond the reach of the rebel infantry."[96] The general ordered the evacuation south, "placing one of Minty's brigades at the head of his column and the other at the rear." "Nearly every officer in Minty's command took 'quiet exception' to his plan, realizing if there was any fighting to be done, they would have to do most of it."[97]

"Some of Minty's pickets and vedettes had scarcely gotten into position when the order came to fall back on the number fours. After a half hour's delay, the 4th Regulars mounted and began retiring down the rubble-strewn streets at 2:00 a.m.," followed by the 7th Pennsylvania and the 4th Michigan. Bob Minty and Eli Long's Second Brigade remained in the rear to confront the Confederate infantry.[98]

It was 4 a.m. and, "like most of the men, Captain Robert Burns . . . had been awake and in the saddle for the better part of seventy-two hours." "Exhausted . . . he lay down on the rain-soaked ground and . . . fell fast asleep," only to awaken at dawn to find himself alone. He had to scramble to catch up with his regiment.[99]

Fortunately for the Federals, there was some confusion among the commanders of the Texas cavalry. Believing that the town was surrounded, they waited for a signal to attack that never came. This left an escape route open for the Union cavalry and "4,000 Yankee cavalrymen marched out of Jonesboro unmolested."[100]

Towards daylight on the twentieth, Kilpatrick moved in the direction of McDonough and then back to the railroad near Lovejoy's Station, reaching that point about 11 a.m.[101]

Burns' account describes the Union forces being followed from Jonesboro by several rebel brigades, but he may have been mistaken, as there is no evidence of this occurring.[102]

Lovejoy's Station–Nash Farm

Minty's Brigade made the finest cavalry charge I ever saw.
– Brig-General Hugh Judson Kilpatrick[103]

Kilpatrick ordered Minty to send his Saber Brigade in the advance to Lovejoy's Station and to remain with the Second Brigade "to hold [Daniel H.] Reynolds, Ross, and Ferguson in check."[104] The 4th Regulars, 4th Michigan, and 7th Pennsylvania approached the village of Lovejoy from the northeast, arriving at the intersection of Lee's Mill and the Fayetteville-McDonough Road at about 11 a.m.[105] Minty, leading the Second Brigade, skirmished briefly with the enemy before joining his First Brigade. He immediately detached the 4th Michigan to the right "with orders to make a break in the [rail]road."[106] The rebels "attempted to make a stand, and opened fire from a line extending on both sides of the road."[107] A dismounted battalion of the 7th was sent to drive them from their position. When they met with stiff resistance, Minty ordered a saber charge that drove the Confederates about half a mile until "they developed too heavy a force for the advance to deal with."[108] "The entire line of the 7th Pennsylvania," writes Minty, "was at once moved to the front, dismounted and deployed as skirmishers":

> They advanced steadily, driving the enemy's skirmish-line ahead of them, until within [80 to 100 yards] of the railroad, where the enemy's fire showed a line extending beyond both flanks of the 7th. I sent a mounted squadron of the 4th U.S.–William Webb's 3rd battalion–to cover the left flank, and ordered that regiment forward to extend my line on the right. The regiment formed line on the gallop, and Capt. McIntyre gave the command, 'Prepare to fight on foot,' and the men moved forward on the double-quick.[109]

The railroad in front of them "ran through a long cut from three to four feet deep . . ." Minty, was unaware of the fact that shortly before, a train with freight cars full of Confederate soldiers rolled in from Jonesboro. Captain Thomas McCormick's 2nd Battalion of the 4th Regulars was attempting to "gain their position in line with the 7th Pennsylvania" when Reynolds' Brigade of six regiments, hidden in the cut, "sprang to their feet, fired a withering volley, and with the old 'rebel yell' charged over Minty's skirmish line."[110]

Minty's horse was shot from under him and the troopers of the 7th Pennsylvania and Cos. G, H, and A of the 4th U.S. "were exposed to a terrific fire."[111] For a moment, Minty feared his two regiments had been annihilated.[112] The rebels "rushed forward" over the Federal line "of less than 300 men, killing, wounding, or capturing 5 officers and over 60 men."[113] Captain McCormick was captured, and among those "very seriously wounded" was Lieutenant Thomas Sullivan, Co. F, adjutant of the 4th Regulars. Captain McIntyre "ran forward, placed him on his shoulder, and carried him back to his regiment."[114] Lieutenant Joseph Hedges, commanding Co. G, and his 1st Sergeant John Harner struggled against the onslaught, trying to "keep every man in his place," ably assisted by Sergeants James Fay and James Walsh of Co. A and Sergeant John Cody of Co. G. The Second Brigade and the Chicago Board of Trade Battery quickly formed to check the rebels while the 7th Pennsylvania and 4th Regulars were re-formed.[115]

Meanwhile, a train packed with 300 Confederate infantry rolled into Lovejoy; the troops were quickly deployed. When the 7th Pennsylvania approached the depot, "a devil of a fusillade took place."[116] At almost the same time, the Texas cavalry attacked the Federal rear and Kilpatrick's column was caught in a crossfire. Minty's men rapidly returned fire, "emptying the last rounds from the seven-shot magazines of their Spencers. Before they could reload, howling Rebels were on them with fixed bayonets."[117]

"A fierce battle seemed now to be going on in every direction," writes Lieutenant Webb, "but which was the front or main point of the attack I could not for the life of me tell. If pandemonium reigned at Jonesboro, chaos certainly had the upper hand at Lovejoy's":

> Artillery and small musketry were pouring their deadly missiles into our front, rear and both flanks. I could find for the moment no one to report to, and was uncertain and somewhat bewildered as to what I should do with my handful of men. Finally, I recognized the lead horses of the Fourth Cavalry in the distance, and hastening to join them, discovered that the balance of the regiment were fighting on foot somewhere, but where, no one could tell me. Just then an aid from the general dashed up to me, and directed that I should take my men to a piece of rising ground to the left, and make a rail barricade, and to defend it until relieved. In my bewilderment I asked, 'Which way shall I face it?' as bullets and shells were coming from all directions and it would have puzzled the ablest soldier to decide how to build a barricade under such circumstances. The aid seemed equally at sea, but settled the matter, as far as he was concerned, by shouting as he rode off, 'Suit yourself.'[118]

Finding it impossible to construct any sort of barricade, Webb instructed his men to "lie as low as possible in the grass... [firing] at every enemy with our seven-shooters in whatever direction he showed himself, and were [fired] at in return from all sides."[119]

"Confusion reigned and the Union forces were in danger of breaking..."[120] "The blue line staggered. The men were falling back, firing their carbines as they went before pausing to rally on either side of the Board of Trade Battery."[121] It was not a moment too soon for Lieutenant Webb:

> Suddenly an exclamation from someone called my attention to the fact that the whole command appeared to be mounting and concentrating a short distance off to our right, faced to the rear. Although ordered to remain where I was until relieved, there was not enough of the Roman soldier of romance about me to remain where I knew I could do nothing, especially when I could shortly be left alone, food for Southern prisons.
>
> I therefore gave the order to mount, and joined the regiment...[122]

Captain Potter, along with the balance of the 7th Pennsylvania and 4th Regulars, found themselves:

> driven back... [leaving] one piece of Artillery in the ground but not so far but that our skirmishers covered it with their fire and with some loss we got it back.... Shortly we began to hear firing in our rear. It increased, and soon we found we had their cavalry in our rear and infantry in front — in fact we were surrounded.[123]

The Union command now believed that a division of infantry was closing in on their right, and that two divisions of cavalry were "in rear of their left," and that Reynold's regiments of infantry was at their front. While they may have, in fact, overestimated the strength of the Confederate forces, they were still in a dire situation.[124]

"The 4th Regulars were reforming their ranks to the right and rear of the guns when someone noticed Captain McIntyre was missing. Word quickly passed down the line and instantly... 'every man seemed to have the fury of a demon.' With carbines blazing, they rushed into the woods and soon brought their captain back in triumph."[125]

Giving orders to reunite his brigade, Minty "galloped to the rear and reported to Gen. Kilpatrick." With his column being attacked from the rear, Kilpatrick ordered Minty to "form for a charge on the attacking force."[126] "Our only recourse is to cut our way out," Kilpatrick told Minty. "You will form your division in line on the right of the McDonough road, facing to the rear. Colonel Murray will form in the same manner on the left, and you will charge simultaneously." Minty pointed out the difficulty of the terrain: "a deserted plantation [the Nash Farm], crossed in every direction by rain gullies, and two rail fences between us and the enemy." And the rebels were at work building barricades. He offered a suggestion to General Kilpatrick:

> General, I would not charge over this ground in line. If we ever strike the enemy, it will be a thin wavering blow that will amount to nothing.
> 'How would you charge?', he asked.
> In column, sir. Our momentum would be like that of a railroad train, when we strike, something has to break.
> 'Form in any way you please,' the General replied.[127]

Minty "ordered in the 4th Michigan, mounted the 4th Regulars and 7th Pennsylvanians, and moved into the field south of the McDonough road, facing east."[128] "All who did not have sabers were sent to the rear of their companies, and all pack mules to the rear of their regiments."[129] Minty's brigade, "now reduced to a little over 700 of all ranks," was formed in regimental columns of fours, "the 7th Pennsylvania on the right, the 4th Michigan in the center, and the 4th Regulars on the left."[130] Captain McIntyre and Lieutenant Hedges were at the head of the column of the 4th Regulars.[131] Colonel Long was directed to form his brigade to the rear of Minty's center, "in close column, with regimental front, . . . to sweep up whatever [Minty's brigade] broke through."[132] The remaining Ohio regiments brought up the rear, with the 4th Ohio as skirmishers:[133]

> Getting the different regiments into position took time. . . . Horses snorted and stamped their feet impatiently in the sweltering heat. Men shifted uneasily in their saddles. . . . They tightened their saddle girths, reloaded revolvers, checked their spurs, and nervously readjusted their saber belts. 'The men threw away all extra . . . trap of all kinds, horseshoes, blankets, haversacks, ammunition, carbines, camp utensils and clothing.'[134]

A lieutenant who witnessed the scene wrote: "the little General and Minty were everywhere and as pleasant and cheerful as in the midst of a tea party." Another witness later wrote: "I happened to be in the vicinity of Captain McIntyre, who commanded the 4th US Cavalry, and Major Jennings, of the 7th Pennsylvania Cavalry, in the charge, and saw them follow the illustrious example of their leader, [Minty] of whom I may say every man in the first Brigade, then as now, loved and honored."[135]

The Federal position was being shelled by two Confederate gun batteries.[136] "Occasionally there was a jarring blast as a Rebel shell burst overhead." Private Isaac Sollers, who was waiting with the 4th U.S., describes the deadly results:

> We were formed in a cornfield fronting the way we had just come from . . .
> While standing waiting orders, a ball came from the front, passing all of the brigade standing in front of us, and hit Private [George] Cassell in the breast. He fell forward on his horse and was dead before we could take him down and lay him out between two rows of corn.[137]

Captain Henry Potter was standing just six feet away from Private Cassell:

> There is a certain feeling which I cannot tell you of, when a man stands waiting the word, which perhaps will send him to Eternity . . .
> You never will know or feel it until you are there yourself . . . There is a sort of instinctive bracing of the nerves and an air of sternness in a brave man's looks which soon tell you his calibre. This is the place to detect a coward — I pity them — they dodge at every sound and sight they see like a turkey looking for bugs. It is laughable as well as sober.[138]

"[E]very officer and man in the whole command," writes Major Frank Mix, commanding 4th Michigan, "had been informed what was expected of us."[139] Kilpatrick's men were completely surrounded. "There was no salvation but to cut their way out. Visions of Libby, Andersonville and starvation flitted through their imaginations, and they saw that the deadly conflict could not be avoided."[140]

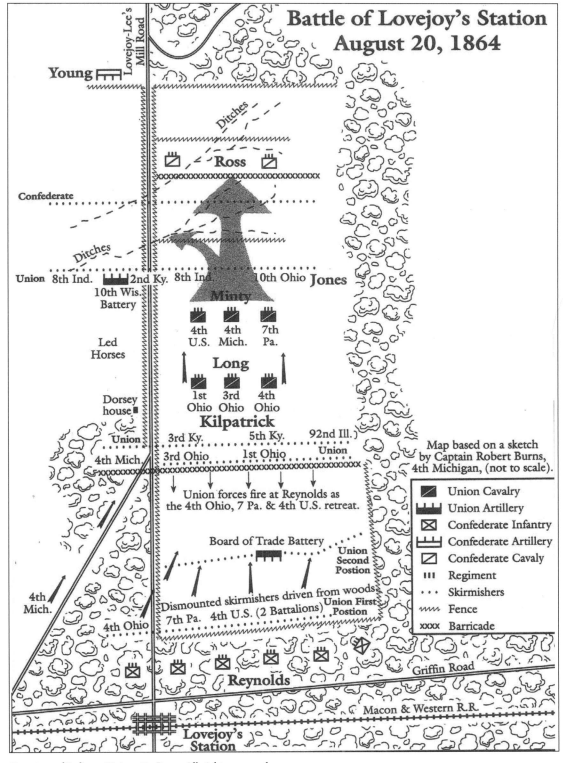

Courtesy of Indiana University Press. All rights reserved.

Minty's brigade was forming in an open field, "just behind the brow of a hill."[141] When all was ready, the "three compact columns of fours"—twelve across and approximately seventy horsemen deep—moved slowly forward until the head of the column "nearly reached the top of the hill," keeping out of sight of the rebel forces they were preparing to charge. Colonel Long brought his Second Brigade in behind Minty's column.[142]

The ground between Minty's brigade and the rebels it was facing was a deserted plantation known today as the Nash Farm, about "two miles square, thickly strewn with patches of potatoes, woods, deep water cuts, fences, ditches and grasses"[143]

Colonel Minty rode to the head of the column on his big sorrel mare, taking his position with his staff.[144] He drew his saber and "sang out in his clear, ringing voice, 'Draw Saber.'... As if by magic, every saber leaped from its scabbard."[145] Minty's bugler rode to the top of the hill to sound the charge.[146] "Silhouetted against the summer sky, he lifted the bugle to his lips and sounded 'Forward.' Red, white, and blue guidons unfurled overhead as all three regiments started up the slope..."[147] Dismounted troopers designated from each column ran ahead as skirmishers to "remove portions of the first fence."[148] Private Isaac Sollars—still attending to his fallen comrade—heard the order, "Draw sabers and six shooters–charge!" and quickly remounted.[149]

"The charge started in a corn-field," writes Lieutenant Webb:

> the high stalks almost hiding us from view. The rapid gait through this field brought the stout corn-stalks against our legs with such force, and seemed to cause the horses so much distress, that by common consent the Fourth Cavalry obliqued to the left and struck the dirt road, down which we went at break-neck speed.[150]

"What a sight it was!" writes Burns. "We drew sabers, trotted until we came to the hill, and then, with cheer upon cheer, started at the gallop."[151] As the sound of the bugle rang out, the Federals "charged for their lives... yelling like devils."[152] "As we raised that hill," writes Captain Potter, "a shower of shot greeted us —":

> but with a yell enough to wake the dead — we spurred on their line, their artillery belching forth grape and canister into our line. The Regulars were directly in front of the battery and suffered badly... a file of men... were mowed down by one shot. The ground grew rough and stony. On we pressed — keeping up that deafening yell — our sabers flashing in the sun a thousand rays of light...[153]

"Between us and the timber was quite a ravine," recalls Major Mix:

> ... the hills on both faces were badly slashed and gullied by rains, so that it was lookout and jump pretty often.
> ... Everything we possessed in the world was on our pack mules, and they were in the column with about as scared a set of darkies as ever led a mule or rode a horse.
> But we were in for it, and the cheer and yell which our boys set up, with the clanging of the camp-kettles on those mules, beat any noise I ever heard.[154]

Leaping fences, ditches, and barricades, they were among the rebels and "in an instant all was confusion."[155] On a hill to Minty's left, "a battery of three guns was pouring canister into our ranks as rapidly as they could load and fire, while four guns on a hill in front of my right was shelling us at long range."[156] At the same time, "bullets of the skirmishers and dismounted men whistled freely."[156] "The yells of the horsemen were drowned in the clashing of steel and the groans of the dying."[158]

One fence still remained between the charging Federals and the rail barricades from behind which the rebels were firing.[159] "At the bottom of the hill which we were to charge down," writes Major Mix, "was a heavy rail fence, and behind which was a heavy line of infantry [Ross's dismounted cavalry] as thick as they could stand, with still another line in their rear."[160] In "less than five minutes," writes Private Sollars, "we were huddled up against the rail barricade Ross's men had prepared for us to run against, and the [rebel] battery... throwing grape and canister over our heads, completely riddling a big mulberry tree standing inside the fence on our right."[161]

Minty continued his pursuit: "his [dismounted cavalrymen] men's sabers striking right and left, and cutting down everything in their path. The rebel horsemen were seen to reel and pitch headlong to the earth, while their frightened steeds rushed pell-mell over their bodies. . . . The terror-stricken enemy could not withstand the thunderous wave of men and horses that threatened to engulf them. They broke and ran just as Minty and his troopers were urging their horses for the decisive blow."[162]

The rebels, "trying to dodge the flailing hooves of their frightened mounts, threw up their hands to surrender, only to be cut down by the Regulars' slashing blades."[163]

"The rebel artillery was very hot at this time," writes Burns. "I could almost feel the balls as they swept by." Minty's horse was hit but was able to continue. Lieutenant Elbridge Roys, 4th U.S., was dismounted when his horse was killed by a shell.[164]

Captain Heber Thompson, 7th Pennsylvania, was dismounted when his horse was shot and was last seen "trying to rally some men to take the rebel battery."[165] As they continued to charge, leaping over the ditches and fences, a number of men became dismounted, now fighting on foot.[166]

Two of Texas General Ross's dismounted cavalry regiments took the brunt of the charge and were overrun. The Texans behind the barricade "emptied their pieces at the head of the column." This created a "momentary flutter without checking their speed," writes a Lieutenant of the 3rd Texas, "*and on they came in fine style* [emphasis author]."[167]

"As we got within 30 rods [160 yards] of their works," recalls Potter, "they threw their arms down and run —":

> but on we go dashing over their works. The work commences — they surrender by dozens — but many of them were cut down without mercy. For my part I could not strike them after they had given up and but very few did hit them in our regiment — *but the Regulars slashing right and left and many a poor devil's brains lay scattered on the ground* [emphasis author].[168]

"The charge of the Federals was irresistible," wrote an observer from the *Cincinnati Commercial*:

> Many of the rebels defended themselves with superhuman strength; yet it was all in vain. . . . The heads and limbs of some of the rebels were actually severed from their bodies.

The individual instances of heroism were many. Not a man flinched, and when the brigade came out, most of the sabers were stained with human blood.[169]

After striking the first fence, the charge of the 4th Regulars was diverted to the McDonough road.[170] Sergeant John Rose of Co. L found himself in the lead and almost single-handedly cut a path for the charge.[171] The 4th Regulars, now charging down the dirt road, "slammed into [the rebels] at a dead run. The impact was terrific":

> The enemy's lead horses were all in this road, as were also their ambulances and caissons. When we met the column of horses in this place, the shock was so terrific and the impetus so tremendous as to completely overthrow every vestige of organization or discipline remaining to the enemy, and to crowd pell-mell men and horses, ambulances and caissons upon and over each other in such inextricable confusion as to cause a jam or blockade, which for a few moments brought every one to a halt. The horses, wild with terror, must have trampled upon scores of the enemy in their mad attempts to get away and the late riders, with blanched faces and hands thrust upward, were dodging about and frantically trying to make us understand they wished to surrender; but we had no ability or wish just then to take prisoners.
>
> . . . All the time we were detained in this road . . . many fierce hand-to-hand encounters took place.[172]

The white horse Captain McIntyre was riding:

> collided with an artillery limber, hurling him head-long into the fence. An orderly retrieved the runaway and the captain quickly remounted. Brandishing his saber, he charged into the wild melee as men and horses, limbers and ambulances, hemmed in by high fences on both sides of the road, piled together in 'inextricable confusion.'[173]

"The enemy's battery on our left," writes Webb:

> and so near that we could feel the rush of hot air at each discharge, at once took advantage of the blockade, and poured a murderous volley into us, which must have done as much injury to friend and foe. Finally the road was opened, and we went on, trampling upon the bodies of men and horses and wreckage of all descriptions, but getting through at last, thank Heaven! and the battery that had done us so much damage brought off as a trophy.[174]

Lieutenant Ed Fitzgerald of the 4th Regulars, along with some of the officers and men of the 4th Michigan, "rode through the . . . gun battery . . . on the left of the road . . . sabering the gunners, but no sooner had [they] passed than the rebels again seized the cannon and, reversing them, poured grape and canister into the charging columns."[175] Major Mix, 4th Michigan, remembers as the head of the charge reached the timber line:

> On my left, between where the 4th Regulars and my regiment had entered this timber, was a piece of their artillery, which had fired on us from the start. It was stationed near the road, and was still firing upon some force coming up the road.[176]

The Texans "stood manfully and fought like madmen . . ."[177] Twice Sul Ross sent messages urging his artillery officer to "leave the gun and save his men."

"Not while I have a shot left!" was the reply.[178]

A piece of canister struck a mounted trooper in the neck. A Third Ohio trooper was hurled ten feet in the air when a shell struck his mount and exploded. Another trooper was pinned under his horse as it fell dead to the ground from shell fragments.[179] The "force" Major Mix saw approaching the rebel battery may have been General Kilpatrick accompanied by his staff officers and orderlies:

> A Rebel shell ripped through Kilpatrick's personal flag . . . hurling the color-bearer to the ground. Kilpatrick and about 30 horsemen veered to the left, spurring straight toward the smoking mouth of the gun. . . . Having fired their last round, the Rebel artillery men fled, just as the Yankees opened a hole in the fence . . .[180]

Private William Bailey, 4th Michigan—Minty's Indian orderly who was with General Kilpatrick—tore down the fence and "spurred through the gap." Kilpatrick followed his men through the opening, "brandishing his saber and yelling at the top of his voice," capturing the battery.[181] Private Bailey shot and killed the rebel captain "who was endeavoring to rally his men after Minty and his men had swept past in the charge."[182] Bailey then dismounted and "took off [the rebel captain's] saber, belt and pistols, and proceeded on after his commander."[183] "From there it was nothing but panic," writes Captain Potter:

> . . . their Battery we got, spiked the guns except the 12 LB Howitzer which we brought along. The rest after spiking we tumbled into a ditch. They had but one Inf. Brigade got in position in our rear but they were hurrying up and we were just in time — as we got the order to charge, a flag of truce we seen coming from the Infantry for our surrender — but we didn't wait. Well we only picked up 100 of them the rest got away. We were getting away ourselves and didn't stop to pick up much. The brigade we run over was Texans. We captured their battle flag.[184]

The 4th Regulars "hacked their way through" the rebel forces:[185]

> Private Thomas Douglas and Captain McIntyre . . . charged side by side, killed four or five with the saber, captured a captain and lieutenant and 13 men, who were turned over to Douglas by the Captain, who again rushed forward into the fray. After the charge was over, Douglas rode up to Colonel Minty, saluted him, turned over his 15 prisoners–four of whom were commissioned officers–and remarked, 'Here, Colonel, are 15 Jonnies, the trophies of Captain McIntyre and Private Douglas, 4th Regulars.'[184]

"Private Isaac Sollers of the 4th Cavalry captured a Rebel officer's dress cap, trimmed in gold lace. Another Regular rode away with the battle flag of the 3rd Texas Cavalry."[187] As Colonel Minty later writes:

> The 4th Regular Cavalry came nearer to the enemy's center than any other charging body. The entire [rebel] line, from the front of the 7th Pa. on my right to in front of the 4th U.S. Cav. on my left, was broken and crushed. I do not believe there were 15 of their men together in any one place, except where we held them as prisoners.[188]

After charging through the open fields and across the barricades and fences, they reached the woods, where they "could not go so fast and could not keep in column."[189] "The troops became scattered, chasing dismounted and demoralized rebels in every direction."[190] "After leaving the cornfield," writes an officer of Eli Long's Second Brigade, "no regular alignment was possible, and it soon became a charge of squadrons, companies, squads, and single riders."[191] "The race and slaughter through the wood and field continued for about three miles," writes Minty, "when I collected and reformed my command."[192]

Years later, General Judson Kilpatrick would publicly state that Minty's brigade made the finest cavalry charge he ever saw.[193] As told by the officers and men of Kilpatrick's division after their return to Atlanta, "Colonel Minty cut a hole for us and we followed him out."[194]

There was "ghastly evidence of the deadly nature of the struggle," writes Dr. Fish:

> Horses and riders together lying stark dead–with feet in stirrup, rein in hand, and saber clasped tightly, while the countenance of the dead warrior showed the fierceness of his passion. The clean blades of our sabers left many foemen dead, cloven down — literally through and through.[195]

David Evans describes the scene:

> The ground was covered with guns, pistols, sabers, sacks of corn, oats, coffee, cooking utensils, cups, pans, buckets, cartridge boxes, ammunition, blankets, overcoats, and saddlebags. Horses, some trailing skewed saddles behind them, stood in suffering silence or struggled violently, crazed with pain and fear. Others sprawled glassy-eyed and still, the flies already swarming over torn bodies and protruding entrails. Nearby lay their riders, some in ashen-faced agony, others to rise no more.[196]

Colonel Minty later reported:

> Not less than 500 of the enemy were sabered . . . the three-gun battery was captured together with three stands of colors and over 600 prisoners. The 4th Regulars captured the colors of the 3rd Texas and the Benjamin Infantry, and the 4th Mich. that of the Zachary Rangers.[197]

According to historian David Evans, the "casualty lists left no doubt who had done most of the fighting." Minty's First Brigade counted 106 killed, wounded, or missing.[198] The Fourth United States lost ten men killed and one officer and ten men wounded. One officer and four men were wounded and missing, and an additional sixteen men were missing for a total casualty count of two officers and forty men.[199] Lieutenant Thomas Sullivan survived his injuries but "never rejoined the regiment afterwards," resigning his commission in February 1865.[200] Captain Thomas McCormick was returned to his regiment as part of a prisoner exchange arranged between Sherman and Hood in September, as was the wounded Captain Heber Thompson, who recuperated as a prisoner of war at the 1st South Carolina Hospital near Charleston.[201] Losses totaled ninety-four in Eli Long's brigade and seven in the Board of Trade Battery.[202] As the war grew more desperate for the Confederacy, enlisted Union prisoners were no longer exchanged as had been done in the past, but were sent to the ever-growing prisoner of war camps at Cahaba, Alabama; Danville, Virginia; and Andersonville, Georgia.

Kilpatrick's "entire command was badly disorganized. Troopers who had lost their mounts were chasing runaway rebel horses and mules. Men were looking for their officers. Officers were looking for their regiments. Pack mules and supply wagons were scattered . . ."[203] Many of the wounded were still "lying on the battlefield, but Kilpatrick could not stop to collect them. He had to keep moving, and he was not going to make the same mistake McCook and Stoneman had made." He turned his re-formed column east toward McDonough, leaving Minty's two brigades to bring up the rear.[205] The 4th Regulars were now completely out of ammunition, and Minty sent them ahead with Kilpatrick's column while he organized his remaining regiments to protect the rear of the retreat.[205] They were "almost immediately attacked by reinforced rebel forces."

Eli Long's horse was shot in the head and he was "shot twice, in his right thigh and forearm."[206] The battle raged for almost two hours until around 6 p.m., when the rebels withdrew. Kilpatrick's retreating column was now safely ahead, and "the rear guard wearily climbed into their saddles to follow, dark clouds rolled in from the west. Thunder rumbled across the slate-gray sky and the rain slanted down in torrents":[207]

> ... The balance of Kilpatrick's plodding column was strung out for miles. The two brigades in front had not slept for two nights. The two in the rear had not slept in three. As darkness descended from the stormy skies on the night of August 20, the Rebels abandoned their pursuit and from that point on, noted Captain John Rea [1st Ohio] 'It was a column of sleeping horsemen...'[208]

Lieutenant Webb describes the bone weary physical and mental exhaustion:

> None but soldiers, I believe, know what it is to be thoroughly tired. We of the Fourth had been four nights without sleep, and had eaten no regular meal, but just when and how we could. That mind and body were exhausted and could stand no further tax was plainly evident.... Added to the bodily fatigue natural to so long a march without rest and with little food, was the great mental strain we were constantly under. The incessant fighting kept us wrought up to the highest pitch of excitement, every nerve strung to the utmost tension. Not only all this, but our anxiety for the success of the expedition, and a foreboding of disaster probably consequent upon the knowledge that two other expeditions on the same errand had come to grief... Altogether, the brain, like the body, could stand no more, and when the pursuit ceased, every one seemed to collapse. The spectacle of a body of 5,000 men marching along through torrents of rain, and four-fifths of that number sound asleep, some sitting bolt upright, others with their arms crossed on the necks of their horses, as a support to their heads, must have been a novel sight to any one who could have gazed at us as we passed; but there were no spectators, and when we came to where it was considered safe to halt for a short rest, the horses lay down as well as their riders, and snored in unison.[209]

"I fell asleep on my horse for two hours, during ... a terrible storm of rain," recalls Captain Burns. "I knew nothing of it until I awoke and found myself in a strange crowd." Some riders literally fell to the ground asleep, only to be awakened by the rearguard...[210]

It was around 6 a.m. on the twenty-first when the command and Minty's brigade reached the rain-swollen Cotton Indian Creek, "usually an insignificant stream, but now flooded, and not fordable at any point," the bridge having been destroyed.[211] As Evans writes, "troopers who had braved a hundred battles quailed at the sight ... a raging torrent three times its normal size... 'It was the most formidable torrent I have ever met,'" noted one officer. "The current rushed down between high, steep banks, that made the channel appear like a great trough through the earth, with a swiftness that appalled us all..."[212] As Minty remembers: "This entire force (about 4,000 men) had to swim, in doing which we lost one and about 50 horses and mules." He continues: "the most difficult and trying work was getting our poor wounded comrades across, [but] ... I saw my 98 wounded officers and men safely on the north side of that stream..."[213]

If Judson Kilpatrick had not won the approval of his troops for his gallantry in leading them in battle, he certainly endeared himself with his actions at Cotton Indian Creek. The crossing was reported in the Detroit *Advertiser & Tribune*:

> It was impossible to ford it. No! Nothing was impossible with General Kilpatrick. The command crossed, but with a loss of three men drowned, many horses, ammunition wagons, headquarters

wagon and ambulance. The General lost all of his personal property.... There he stood, waist deep in the water, with a rope and helping hand for the [lowest] private whose horse, born away by the strong current, came plunging down the stream. Once an ambulance containing a wounded Captain was turned downstream and capsized. Kilpatrick plunged into the water, and with the aid of the driver rescued the officer from a watery grave. Colonel Minty was there, cheering the timid and guiding the weak across that terrible stream.... [T]he writer will never forget it, for he was one of those who were so unfortunate as to be carried down stream, but fortunately escaped with everything but a dry skin...[214]

At about 7 p.m. on the twenty-first, Minty's exhausted brigade bivouacked at Lithonia, on the Georgia Railroad, "and oh! how grateful we were for our first sleep since leaving Sandtown on the evening of the 18th."[215] Captain Potter's regiment made camp at about 3 a.m. on the twenty-second:

> It rained nearly all night and we were wet as rats. Soon we come to a creek which was swollen so we had to swim across. Two of our men drowned there and some negroes. I came very near losing a man there... were out five days and nights and went entirely around the whole rebel Army going out on the right and coming in on the left. In all that time I got about nine hours sleep as I calculated.[216]

"On the afternoon of August 22," writes Colonel Minty, "Kilpatrick's mud-splattered, bone-tired, and hollow-eyed horsemen":

> ... marched to camp near Buck Head via Decatur, having made the circuit of Atlanta and both armies since 12 o'clock on the night of the 17th, and having marched and fought every day and night during that time with the exception of the night of the 21st, when we lay at Lithonia.[217]

Kilpatrick's Raid generated a considerable amount of newsprint on both sides of the war. The following dispatch appeared in a Detroit newspaper:

> This raid is the first in this department which has succeeded in passing successfully round the rebel army.... Two hand in hand fights with a force far superior to our own; destroying three miles of railroad, water tanks; depots and stores; cutting our way through five times our number, and capturing a battery of artillery, in one of the grandest charges of the war, and passing entirely around the rebel army, with but a loss of four or five hundred, (the greater share captured,) we call a success.[218]

Debate continues as to what effect the raid may have had in the eventual fall of Atlanta just weeks later. At the end of his article written twenty-five years later, William Webb writes: "... the results were barren of any permanent benefit." Robert Burns summed up his feelings with the simple statement: "We did not do all that we had hoped when we started, but we did all we could." Writing years later, Private Isaac Sollars, Co. M, 4th US Cavalry, probably spoke for Minty's brigade when he comments: "It was one of the hardest raids made during the war, *and less has been said about it* [emphasis author]."[219]

What may have actually been more important was the demoralizing effect on the Confederacy at this point in time. Minty quotes the following from the *Memphis-Atlanta Appeal* (an unverifiable source):

> When the Yankees charged they came in a solid column, ten or twelve lines deep, running their horses and yelling like devils. They didn't stop to fire, but each fellow for himself rushed on, swinging his saber over his head. They rode right over Ross's and Ferguson's men in the center, over and through Cleburne's lines, one after the other, on the left. Cleburne's first line tried to use their bayonets, but the Yankees cut them to pieces.[220]

Kilpatrick's cavalry not only rode completely around Atlanta, it rode right through the Confederate Army that was there to stop them. They rode through the heart of Georgia and the Southern cause. They could not be stopped. In fact, whatever the argument, it was, as reported by the *Cincinnati Commercial*, "one of the grandest cavalry charges of the war" and in the history of the United States Cavalry.[221] While in history it is remembered as "Kilpatrick's Raid," the *Cincinnati Commercial* concludes with, "The praises of Minty and his command are upon every tongue."[222] One wonders what would have been the results without Colonel Robert H. G. Minty and his Saber Brigade.

General Kilpatrick was generous with his praise of Colonel Minty "for his untiring energy throughout the march":

> and the consummate skill displayed at the moment when we were repulsed at Lovejoy's Station, and the subsequent gallant ride of his command over the enemy's barricades–the most perfect rout any cavalry has sustained during the war ... [He] *deserves immediate promotion* .[223]

Colonel Minty was justifiably proud of the performance of his command, writing that, "Every officer and soldier in the command acted so well, so nobly, so gallantly, that under ordinary circumstances they would be entitled to special mention."[224] He singled out Captain James McIntyre, "as gallant and thorough a soldier who ever drew saber."[225] Minty also called attention to two other members of the 4th United States Cavalry: Lieutenant Wirt Davis and Colonel Eli Long, who was brevetted colonel, USA, for his "gallant and meritorious" service at Lovejoy's Station.[226]

A Question of Facts

David Evans's research refutes the claims made by officers of Kilpatrick's raid—including Kilpatrick, Minty, Vale, Burns, and Webb, among others—regarding the Confederate forces they believed they were facing at Lovejoy's Station. Their claims would persist unchallenged in various published articles and books into the early 1900s, until Evans's research ninety years later. He believes their reports "grossly" overestimate the size of the Confederate force and that, in fact, Cleburne's infantry, Martin's cavalry, and a brigade of Georgia Militia were not present that day. This is difficult to reconcile unless one assumes that the officers actually *believed* it. Why else would they *all* have misrepresented these basic facts?[227]

This may be a case of perception displacing reality, greatly enhanced by the sheer physical and emotional exhaustion of three sleepless nights, limited food, and the adrenalin of constant combat, all combining to take their toll on the accuracy of reported events. Their circumstances cannot be denied; they were surrounded and in danger of being killed or captured.

Once reports are issued they are rarely, if ever, retracted, and are often embellished and perpetuated by future writers. Kilpatrick and Vale can be cited for their known embellishments, Minty and Burns cannot. However, in 1890, Minty did use Vale's 1886 book as a source to quote an article supposedly from the September 1864 *Memphis-Atlanta Appeal* supporting the presence of Cleburne and Martin. Evans could find no verification of this article in his investigation, but does produce evidence that Cleburne and Martin could not have been present. Whatever the reason for this discrepancy, it should not detract from the daring and heroic act of the cavalry charge led by the Saber Brigade that saved Kilpatrick's expedition.

VII. The Fall of Atlanta

After their return to Atlanta on August 22, Minty's brigade spent the next thirteen days picketing and scouting around Atlanta. On August 25, "Sherman's last great flank movement ... culminated in the fall of Atlanta."[1] On September 2, "the 'Gate City' of the Confederacy–the last stronghold of the last interior line of defense," was occupied by Federal forces.[2]

On August 26, the brigade fell back north of the Chattahoochee River, and on the twenty-seventh "marched to Sandtown and camped near Sweetwater Creek, where it remained until September 10, picketing and scouting from Campbellton to Marietta."[3] As Minty notes: "During the entire campaign, the 13 days we remained in this camp was the only time we had full forage for our horses."[4]

The campaign had taken its toll on the Saber Brigade. They left Columbia, Tennessee, "with 2,500 horses and men" and were now reduced to "about 1,000 sabers."[5] Captain Vale details the cost of victory:

> We started from Columbia, Tennessee, with seventy-one officers, twenty-four hundred and forty-four men, twenty-two hundred and seventy-nine serviceable horses, and two thousand and one carbines. We now had, at the front, forty-nine officers and six hundred and eighty seven men for duty, eight hundred and eleven serviceable horses, (ten officers and seventy men at head-quarters), and one thousand and one carbines.[6]

They had marched a total of 925 miles, "fought 31 battles, besides constant skirmishing and on three occasions doing duty as infantry in the trenches, on one occasion for 14 consecutive days":[7]

> During the campaign, as men became dismounted by the loss or breakdown of their horses–or became sick or disabled– they were sent back to Columbia, Tenn., and from there were detached as guards in the block-houses built for the protection of bridges and trestles along the line of the Nashville & Decatur Railroad. In this way a large portion of the brigade had been sent to the rear.[8]

An additional factor affecting the manpower of the brigade, as reported by Captain Vale, was the fact that "the time of service of all who had not reenlisted was now about expiring; hence many changes occurred in the regimental organizations."[9]

Colonel Robert Minty took his first leave of the war, leaving for twenty days on September 17; he would rejoin his regiment on November 14 at Louisville.[10] Major William H. Jennings, 7th Pennsylvania, would take temporary command of the Saber Brigade. "Within two weeks, the remnant of the brigade, not to exceed 500 men, was hard at work again."[11]

Chasing Hood–October 1864

The remaining members of the Saber Brigade rode together for one last time during a series of engagements and skirmishes through the month of October. On the second and third, "it engaged the rebel rear in a lively skirmish on the Sweetwater Creek, driving them constantly before it." On October 4, they joined the division at Marietta, Georgia, moving out the next day. While the battle of Allatoona Pass was going on, they attacked the rebel rear guard, "crushed it in, and captured over one hundred prisoners." The following day, the division "overtook the rebel army returning from Allatoona, and by a vigorous charge of the 4th Michigan and 4th United States, cut to pieces a whole brigade, capturing the commanding brigadier general and over five hundred prisoners."[12]

The activities of the Saber Brigade during this period are based primarily on information provided by Captain Robert Burns as recorded in his diary, as "no reports were ever made."[13] Relying on Burns, Minty writes that on October 7—near Lost Mountain, with the 4th United States in advance—they marched to "near New Hope Church [and] about 1:30 p.m. struck the rebel pickets, driving them along before us until they got in their barricades and intrenchments near them":

> Lt. William Webb, Co. K, 4th U.S., with the advance, captured Gen. [William H.] Young, of Texas, and Colonel [John L.] Camp, of the 14th Tex. We skirmished awhile with the rebels, when Miller's Brigade came up, dismounted, and with a yell and fusillade drove the rebels from their works. We encamped there during the night. We had skirmished with [Frank C.] Armstrong's Brigade of cavalry.[14]

After a two-day rest, the division moved out at 6:30 a.m. on October 10. Their original destination was Stilesboro, but while making camp three miles from there, they received orders from General Sherman at Cartersville to "move on to Rome, Georgia, and see what we could do there." After an all-night march of about thirty miles, they ran into rebel pickets nine miles from Rome, driving them back. "The whole rebel army," writes Burns—including Wheeler and his cavalry—"was reported to be south of Rome, and General Garrard decided to follow the road near the river." After a march of fourteen miles, the division reached the outskirts of Rome a little before dark and bivouacked on the south side of the Etowah River. At 8:30 a.m. on October 12, the division passed through Rome, "crossed the

Etowah and Oostenaula Rivers, and were forming on the west bank of the latter, when their pickets were attacked on the Coosaville road, about a quarter mile ahead of the division." Minty's First Brigade, now commanded by Major Jennings, was in the advance and was sent forward to feel out the enemy. The rebels were in breastworks and too strong to be attacked by a mounted force. Dismounting, the Federals formed a line with the 4th United States on the right, 4th Michigan center, and 7th Pennsylvania on the left. "Having not more than 300 men," they were outnumbered "at least four to one." They successfully "drove out of the works two rebel brigades–[Thomas] Harrison's and Armstrong's." "We sent them flying," writes Burns, ". . . the field before us was filled with dismounted cavalry and horses in confusion."[15]

At 6:30 a.m., Thursday, October 13, the division was out once again, leaving all wagons and pack mules behind. Eli Long's Second Brigade was in the advance, Wilder's brigade was next, and Minty's First Brigade was in the rear. As they came in sight of the rebels at the top of a hill, they were immediately fired upon. Moving forward "at a walk about one-third of a mile . . . we were ordered to charge. Away we went, with the most infernal yelling and cheering, the 7th Pa. in advance." They quickly overran the battery "and had it in their possession, having cut down or captured the gunners." The battle now devolved into numerous small skirmishes as the rebels were driven into the woods. "They scattered and so did we. We shot and cut. . . . They were on the full run [and] were badly demoralized."[16]

Captain Burns "chased them to the place where the road forks, one branch or line going down the river bank, the other to Millville. The most of the rebels went down the latter road." Burns and his men had to turn back near Missionary Station, as their horses were "nearly used up." Later that day, Burns found the place where Hood and his rebels had crossed the Coosa on Tuesday. The pontoon bridge they had used was now gone. "This was the first positive information Sherman (or at least Generals Garrard and Cox) had when and where the rebels crossed."[17]

"We had done well," writes Burns:

> We had totally routed and scattered two brigades of rebel cavalry (1,600 men, the prisoners say), captured two pieces of artillery, about 70 prisoners, . . . must have killed 125, if not more; destroyed many hundred stand of arms. One stand of colors was picked up by Wilder's men. The ground was covered for miles with hats, coats, blankets, guns, etc. I myself charged at least 12 miles. The 4th Regulars nearly all struck a road running to the right and drove the rebels in confusion about 12 miles. We lost only one (7th Pa.) killed, two wounded; Capt. [Clarence] Mauck and two 4th U.S. wounded.[18]

The Atlanta campaign was over. Captain Vale summarizes the events and accomplishments of Minty's Saber Brigade:

> The campaign of 1864, now closed, had thrown Minty's brigade from Nashville, Tennessee, to McDonough, Georgia, thence on its return by way of Gadsden, Alabama, to Little river, making a mounted march of the brigade head-quarters of over one thousand eight hundred miles, while the various movements of the regiments compelled each to march from two thousand three hundred to two thousand five hundred miles! It had captured ten pieces of artillery, and taken and turned in over nine thousand prisoners! Had killed of the enemy, in the field, nine hundred and forty-five, or nearly two hundred more than its effective force! Had inflicted a loss to the enemy in killed, wounded, and captured of twelve thousand, and had been engaged in fifty-two battles, besides almost daily skirmishes. Two of its regiments had twice charged mounted, and with the saber alone captured hostile batteries, by riding in column directly into the teeth of the guns; and each of its regiments had three times rode, saber in hand, upon the bayonets of serried lines of infantry, broken them to atoms, and cut them to pieces![19]

Minty's brigade bore the heavy cost of the campaign. As Captain Burns writes:

> We started with 2,400 men, and have (now only) 800 with us, having lost two thirds of our numbers. Of course, they were not all killed, but have been sent back

sick and dismounted. We have lost 250 in battles . . . We [are] . . . being sent back to Nashville soon, to be remounted, as nearly all of our horses have been killed or worn out.[20]

Disbanding the Saber Brigade

The old Saber Brigade was dissolved and never organized again.
– Sergeant James Larson[21]

Captain Vale concludes this portion of his history of Minty's brigade:

> The division followed the rebel army closely, hugging its rear and making daily captures of men and wagons; marching through Kingston, Adairsville, and Resaca, then to Summerville, as far as Galesville, Alabama. . . . The pursuit of Hood's army here stopped and the brigade remained until [October] 26th, when the Fourth United States proceeded, under orders, to report to General James Wilson at Nashville, Tennessee. The Seventh Pennsylvania and Fourth Michigan turned their horses over to Wilder's brigade, and the old First brigade, Second cavalry division, was broken up.[22]

Colonel William Sipes—commanding 7th Pennsylvania and the historian of his regiment—sums up the history of the Saber Brigade:

> For two years the Fourth Regulars, Fourth Michigan and Seventh Pennsylvania had camped together, marched together, fought together, and endured many hardships together. They had been faithful to each other in many trials, and together *they had won a reputation for gallantry second to no regiment in the great army to which they were attached* [emphasis author]. Now the time for separation had come.[23]

By Special Orders No. 1, issued from Headquarters of the Military Division of the Mississippi at Gaylesville, Alabama, October 25, 1864, the 4th Cavalry was relieved from duty with Minty's First Brigade and ordered to Cavalry Corps Headquarters at Nashville, Tennessee, for duty and refitting.[24] Having experienced minimal casualties during the last month of the recent campaign, the 4th Regulars would lose two veteran troopers on this march: Sergeant John Griddle and farrier William Griffin, who drowned during the crossing of the Collins River near McMinnville, Tennessee, on November 9.[25]

The remainder of the Second Division of Cavalry, including Minty's brigade, were required to turn over their serviceable mounts to Sherman's other commands and were ordered to rendezvous at Louisville, Kentucky, for remount and reorganization of the new cavalry command. "Great difficulty was found at Louisville in procuring horses for the remount. Virtually all of the cavalry and mounted infantry belonging to the three armies under Sherman in the Atlanta campaign were unhorsed." Only Kilpatrick's small division remained in the field.[26]

At about this same time, Sergeant James Larson and a number of other 4th Regulars returning from their reenlistment furloughs met at Louisville. "We had a very lively time there for a few days," he writes. The men then boarded rail cars for the 175-mile journey south from Louisville to Nashville, where they "reported at the cavalry reconstruction camp, which had been established just outside the city."[27]

Major General James H. Wilson, U.S.A.

In the reorganization of the Federal cavalry in the West, Brevet Major General James Wilson, who had commanded a cavalry division in Sheridan's Army of the Shenandoah and had been instrumental in raising the efficiency of the cavalry service through the Cavalry Bureau, was ordered to report to General Sherman "for the purpose of completing the cavalry reorganization and assisting in the operations of General Thomas against the rebels under Hood."[28] The new Chief of Cavalry was assigned to command all of the cavalry in the Military Division of the Mississippi. "Wilson's most urgent task," according to cavalry historian Stephen Starr:

> was to make ready Kilpatrick's division for the March to the Sea by getting it fully mounted and armed (which he was only able to do by taking horses and arms from Garrard's and McCook's divisions) and supplied with ammunition, clothing, wagons, and whatever else it needed. His next job was to prepare for the field the rest of the cavalry of the military division,

wherever found, 'and help Thomas as best as . . . (he) could to defeat and destroy Hood.'"²⁹

The Cavalry Corps, Military Division of the Mississippi—consisting of seven divisions—was organized from the mounted forces of the Armies of the Ohio, the Cumberland, and the Tennessee to constitute one new command.³⁰ Newly appointed Brigadier General Eli Long now commanded the new Second Division. In that division, Colonel Robert Minty commanded Second Brigade, including his own 4th Michigan and the 7th Pennsylvania, as well as the 1st, 3rd, and 4th Ohio Cavalry.³¹ The 4th US Cavalry would remain with the Cavalry Corps, Military Division of the Mississippi, until May 1865.

General Wilson arrived in Nashville on November 6 and immediately "began a thorough reorganization, a remounting and re-equipping of the cavalry corps of Sherman's army."³²

Writing on November 15, Sergeant Charles Bates tells his parents:

> I have just arrived from the front . . . The Regiment is <u>way down in Dixie</u> that is the small minority remaining in the field. But about 200 men are here encamped waiting to be remounted and refitted, when they will be attached to General Wilson's headquarters for duty as escort.³³

VIII. The Franklin–Nashville Campaign

The Defeat of Hood's Army

Although Sherman had taken Atlanta, he had failed General Grant's first directive to destroy the Army of Tennessee. "Hood's army remained dangerous and unpredictable . . . because it was free to maneuver and to strike where it chose."¹ Hood's Confederate forces—30,000 infantry and 8,000 cavalry—were refitting in Florence, Alabama, in preparation for a northward invasion into Tennessee. Hood was hoping that by threatening Nashville, Sherman would be forced to withdraw his advance into the Deep South.

Hood's army wasn't the only opposition facing the Federal forces. After the fall of Atlanta, Nathan Bedford Forrest "assumed the offensive on and near the Tennessee River, his object being the harassment and capture of Union outposts, thereby retarding Thomas' efforts at concentration and at the same time opening the way for Hood's advance on Nashville."² In late September, Forrest, "with a large force of cavalry," attacked and defeated a large Federal force at Athens, Alabama. In the process the rebels captured arms, ammunition, and six pieces of artillery. "Thus equipped . . . and his offensive power largely increased," Forrest "continued to plague Union forces in Sherman's rear."³ As the war drew to its inevitable conclusion, Forrest intensified his efforts and rebel cavalry would take its revenge wherever opportunity allowed, particularly on the members of the 4th Michigan and 4th United States Cavalries.

An old but ever-growing threat to Union forces—particularly those outside the protection of the major camps or occupied cities—was the ever more violent rebel guerrilla forces pillaging the countryside and murdering civilians and military alike.

In most cases, these rebel forces were operating independently of the Confederacy, many of its members deserters. It had reached the point where Colonel Minty was sending out patrols "with orders to kill" any guerrillas they found.⁴ It became personal in late December 1864 when two of Minty's staff officers "were brutally murdered by [Henry C.] Magruder's gang of guerillas while they were sitting in the parlor of Mr. Grigsby's house, Miss G playing the piano."⁵ As Captain Burns notes: "The guerillas now take no prisoners. Every one captured by them is murdered."⁶ Civil War historian Freeman Cleaves writes that "roving Confederate 'cavalry'–any outlaw with a horse and a gun" was "the scourge of the South."⁷ Adding to the danger, the rebel "irregulars" were now armed with the new Spencer carbines taken from killed or captured Union soldiers.⁸

Defending Nashville

During this time, General George Thomas worked to improve his defenses and strengthen his army in and around Nashville. He also reinforced Federal outposts at Pulaski and Columbia, Tennessee, from possible assault by Hood.[9] Thomas had been in Nashville since October 3 "... to coordinate operations against the [cavalry] raids of Forrest and Wheeler ... and defend the line of the Tennessee [River]."[10] As General Wilson would later write in his biography, "Nashville was the center of rail, river, and telegraphic communications for that entire theater of war."

It was also the principal national depot south of the Ohio, and it was Thomas's duty to make Nashville secure against every possible attack.[11]

The exact whereabouts of Hood's army remained unknown to the Union command until it was reported by Captain Burns after the brigade's expedition to Rome in mid-October. General Hood's army crossed the Tennessee and "were making their way toward the Nashville and Decatur Railroad."[12] On November 16, believing that Thomas could defend Nashville, Sherman—"with his 62,000 tough veterans"—began his "March to the Sea."[13]

In the meantime, Hood was ready to "retake Tennessee and Kentucky ... to do something that would so shock and demoralize Northerners that they would turn Lincoln out of office and elect a president with a mandate to negotiate peace." On October 22, he began his advance.[14] On November 18, Forrest's 5,000 man cavalry joined forces with Hood's advancing Army of Tennessee, moving towards Columbia. At the same time, Union General John Schofield, with his army of 32,000—under pressure from the advancing rebels—was slowly retreating from Columbia to reinforce Thomas at Nashville. Hood hoped to prevent this, and the two armies met at Franklin, Tennessee, on November 30. In the bloody battle that ensued, Confederate soldiers made thirteen separate assaults on Union forces. A Union officer later wrote: "It is impossible to exaggerate the fierce energy with which the Confederate soldiers, that short November afternoon, threw themselves against the works, fighting with what seemed to be the very madness of despair."[15]

Hood finally withdrew, suffering huge losses—6,252 men, including six generals killed, five wounded, and one captured—the "worst such loss suffered by either side in a single attack during the war."[16] The Union casualties were 2,326. As historian Thomas Buell graphically summarizes:

> Some sixty five division, brigade, and regimental commanders became casualties

in the firestorm that swept away the leaders of the Army of Tennessee and shattered its soul. Its remnants were a shell. Franklin was the last Confederate attack of any consequence in the war.[17]

Union cavalry, now under General Wilson's command, played a prominent role at Franklin, "scoring a decisive victory over Forrest's cavalry and pressing the foe so closely that the Confederate troopers were actually driven into the Harpeth River."[18] While the victory at Franklin had been won by the infantry, Wilson credited the "services of the cavalry in covering the retreat, in divining and giving timely notice of Hood's movements, and finally, in defeating and driving back Forrest."[19] "This was the first time Forrest was beaten by a smaller force in a standup fight."[20]

After the loss at Franklin, the battle-weary Hood waited for Thomas to make the next move. At 6 a.m. on December 15, in a dense fog, Thomas began his attack.[21]

While the Lincoln administration had been frustrated at his delay, the ever-cautious Thomas devised a "brilliant offensive plan" to defeat Hood's army, and it proved a resounding defeat for the Confederacy. A demoralized and disconsolate Hood admits: "I beheld for the first and only time a Confederate army abandon the field in confusion."[22] "And the war in the West, for all practical purposes, was at an end."[23]

Some historians suggest that the Confederate Army in the West was defeated at Franklin, thus taking away the significance of subsequent battles fought by the Federal cavalry. However, based on the ferocity of the fighting to follow and the severe losses to be faced by Wilson's cavalry—particularly Minty's 4th Michigan and the 4th United States, among others—it would be months before Confederate forces in the Western theater were finally destroyed.

"When General Wilson reorganized the Federal cavalry in the West, he resolved that his force would be second to none in firepower. His objective was symbolized by the cavalry emblem chosen: Above crossed sabers it bore the profile of a breech-loading Spencer carbine." In Wilson's view, "the Cavalry is useless for defense. Its only power is in a vigorous offensive."[24] It would not be until the spring of 1865 that Wilson's new Cavalry Corps would "fully recover from the losses of the Atlanta campaign." General Wilson would then lead an army "of 13,000 mounted men in a massive raid across Alabama and Georgia," playing a "significant role in the war's final campaign."[25] It seems only fitting that the general who maximized the effectiveness of the Union cavalry to its greatest potential in the closing months of the war, and perhaps for all time, chose the 4th United States Cavalry to be his personal escort.[26]

"THE LITTLE REGIMENT"

The 4th US Cavalry, which had been drastically reduced in strength to about "175 men," was to be remounted in Nashville on the serviceable horses turned in by other regiments.[27] As Larson explains: "The 4th United States Cavalry had been so reduced by losses and receiving no recruits, as no bounty was paid by the Government [as was by the States] that it was a very small regiment."[28] From this point on, the 4th Cavalry was known as the *Little Regiment*.[29] Wilson's reports throughout the following campaign "praises the splendid work" of the 4th US Cavalry and its men.[30]

Captain James McIntyre, who so gallantly led the 4th Regulars for the past two years, took leave of absence due to illness on October 1, 1864. He would not return to his regiment, spending the final months of the war on recruiting duty in Baltimore, Maryland. In July 1866, he would be promoted to major, 3rd Cavalry, prior to his untimely death in May 1867.[31] From December 1, 1864, to February 1, 1865, the regiment would be under command of Lieutenant Joseph B. Hedges. He was brevetted captain on December 16 for "gallant and meritorious service during the pursuit of the rebel forces under General John B. Hood."[32] Sergeant Larson comments on the "great scarcity of officers in the 4th US Cavalry," while again giving his opinion of the volunteers:

> Captain McIntyre was on sick leave, some of the officers had been taken to command volunteer cavalry, and even some sergeants had been given commissions in the new regiments raised by Governor Johnson in East Tennessee. I had seen enough of them at Okolona, Mississippi. On account of the use made of our officers in other regiments there was not even a captain in the whole regiment ... but as we were Wilson's bodyguard, and were always with him, we did not need any other commander. He was always at the head of the regiment and always with the advance, even on the skirmish line, and was with us when we went into action.[33]

With this last sentence, Larson explains how General Wilson, after getting off to a rather bad start with his men at the beginning of his new command, eventually gained the strong admiration of his troops once they were in action.

THE ELECTION OF 1864

Sergeant Larson writes: "the month of November came, and with it, the election for President of the United States, and I cast my vote for Abraham Lincoln. This was a new feature in the army life, as soldiers were otherwise not allowed to vote, but because the voters were nearly all in the army, an act of Congress was passed for that purpose."[34]

Captain Henry Potter seemed unsure of his choice when he writes to his father: "You must consider the matter well this fall before you cast your vote for Uncle Abe — I must admit that things look different than they did six months ago — to me." While he did not agree with Lincoln on a number of issues, in his October 26 letter he wrote: "When called upon to choose between Lincoln and McClellan I will vote for Lincoln":

> I dare not risk Mac upon such a platform and I think a change would be injurious to us and encourage the rebels and it might be taken in the eyes of foreign powers as a backing down. And this might possibly lead to a recognition of the South. And if so an attempt to raise the blockade. ... I shall vote for Lincoln and four more years of war with the rebels rather than McClellan and the recognition of the South by England and France and consequently a war with these powers.[35]

Over 77% of the active duty soldiers supported "Old Abe" in his reelection.[36]

Writing in November, Captain Potter has high praise for "our gallant army" and what it had gained through experience. He goes on to accurately predict the future course of the war:

> You have no idea of our Army. ... No letters and newspaper correspondence can give you a correct impression of the numbers

and determination. Sherman, I think, intends to evacuate Atlanta and cut loose from all supplies and sweep a broad track thro' Georgia and the Confederacy, leaving Thomas to look after Hood and make our line the Tenn River for future operations. Nothing would demoralize the South more in her present state than such a raid as you may call it thro' her heart. Rumor says the Cavalry goes to Louisville to remount.[37]

Sergeant Bates offers a dissenting view on the politics and affairs of the times when writing to his parents on November 15:

> There is wild times here now, Lincolnism and Niggerism is in the ascendant and a poor fellow like me with McClellan in his mind stands a good show for being shot. The Darkies got up a procession here on the night of the 12th in honor of Old Abe's re-election and paraded in front of Governor Johnson's house where he made a speech to them in good old abolition style; one of the 13th Infantry who hurahed "three cheers for McClellan," was shot with 13 balls by the Nigs.[38]

At his headquarters, "four miles east of Columbia, Tenn.," Wilson seemed anxious for the arrival of the 4th United States. On November 22, he writes to Major Eugene Beaumont, 4th Cavalry—now assistant adjutant-general at Cavalry Corps Headquarters in Nashville—"I want the 4th Cavalry as soon as possible with all its men."[39] Again on the twenty-fifth: "Send all of the Fourth Cavalry to the front to report to me as soon as you can get it ready."[40] At this time, there were "7 officers and 265 men" of the 4th U.S. present for duty.[41]

The delay seems to have been in finding enough horses in and around Nashville suitable for the coming campaign. As Beaumont writes Wilson on the twenty-sixth: "I do not think we can supply first rate stock to mount the Fourth United States, but will soon as horses arrive."[42]

While waiting for the proper mounts, the 4th Regulars were kept busy. On November 22, brevet Captain Hedges was given an order with a precaution:

> . . . proceed with your command to White Bluffs on the line of the Nashville and Northwestern Railroad; examine the country closely in the vicinity of the summit; break any organized band of guerrillas you may encounter. Seize all the inhabitants suspected as being engaged in the destruction of the railroad train on the 20th November. Take every precaution you may deem necessary for the safety of your command . . .[43]

On November 25, Lieutenant Hedges filed the following report:

> In compliance with our instruction and order, I proceeded with my command to the Summit . . . arriving there at noon on the 23rd, and camped within three miles south of the place, and sent out a scouting party with instructions to scour the country for a distance of eight or ten miles in the direction the guerrilla party had retreated. The scouting party returned at night, and the officer in charge reported that no guerrillas or any suspicious citizen to be found. . . . Not deeming it prudent to chase after [Frank] McNairy and his party with my small force and his advantage of being two days in advance, I returned to camp at this place.[44]

On November 26, Major Beaumont "had the city [Nashville] patrolled to-day by fifty men of the Fourth United States, and cleaned the town of officers and men."[45] On the twenty-eighth, perhaps frustrated by the delay, Wilson tells Beaumont to "execute the order in regard to the use of serviceable horses by gentlemen on the peace establishment [presumably private citizens]. Put the Fourth Cavalry at this work till they are all mounted, but don't delay sending it to the front any longer than absolutely necessary."[46] In this same correspondence Wilson states: "Our force is now getting to be very respectable, and if Forrest will only wait for us, we shall soon be able to cope with him."[47]

In a short message to Beaumont on December 1, Wilson orders the Fourth US Cavalry out on the Nolensville Pike to join him at Thompson's Chapel, near Brentwood, where the enemy had been skirmishing with his rear guard.[48] That same day, Wilson sent a message to Major General Thomas, stating: "I occupy a most excellent position. . . . If you can protect my right flank by infantry we can beat Forrest's whole force."[49] Continuing with General Wilson's report:

> Early in the morning of December the 1st the cavalry withdrew from its exposed position on the Nolensville pike and marched through Nashville to camp, at Edgefield, on the north bank of the Cumberland River. During the ensuing ten days every effort was made to put it in an efficient condition for active service. Horses were seized, arms, clothing and equipments were issued, and the dismounted men organized into brigades. . . . Horses were shod; extra shoes were fitted; and every horse that could be drawn from corrals of broken-down stock, or reached in Tennessee or Southern Kentucky was taken.[50]

As Minty recalls: "Horses were found in the most unlikely places–down stairs in cellars, upstairs in parlors and bedrooms, in private offices; in fact, in any and every place it was possible to hide an animal."[51]

On December 4, Captain Hedges received orders from Major Beaumont to report to General Wilson "with the 4th US Cavalry, at an early hour to-morrow, at his headquarters in Edgefield."[52] While the 4th Regulars were properly mounted, there was still a shortage of horses for Wilson's cavalry. Sergeant Larson writes:

> While preparations were in progress for active work, the 4th Cavalry camped on the Granny White Pike, about a half mile from Nashville, and was then a sort of independent body, as we were out of brigade organization and were bodyguard for General Wilson whose headquarters were in the city. The regiment furnished the orderlies and couriers daily, but we also had to take our part in picketing the roads to town.[53]

Captain Vale describes the drastic action taken to procure horses needed to remount the cavalry:

> During the evening of December 7, 1864 we received orders from General Long to pen and seize all the horses in the city of Louisville. Very early on the morning of the 8th the Fourth Michigan was sent out to picket every road leading into the city with orders to allow all horses and wagons to pass through into town, but to permit not one to go out. The Third Ohio and Seventh Pennsylvania were then ordered into the city, with directions to seize every serviceable horse they could lay their hands on, and bring them to our camp.
> When the citizens found out what was going on, they were 'in a piece of mind' about it, and attempted to hide all the good horses they could. Horses were taken out of stables, street-cars, wagons, and busses; and in the afternoon they were found in cellars, parlors, garrets, and all sorts of out-of-the way places where the owners had hidden them.[54]

On December 8, Lieutenant Colonel A. J. Alexander, chief of staff, ordered Captain Hedges to "send fifty men from your command, under a competent officer, with instructions to take all the hack, omnibus, and carriage horses in Nashville that are suitable for cavalry purposes. Adams Express Company horses were exempted. These horses will be brought to these headquarters."[55] Captain Potter comments on these activities in his December 20 letter:

> We have pressed a great many horses in the City. Before I got back our regiment was stationed on every road leading out of the city to take all horses coming out or going in and all we could find in the stables anywhere in the city. . . . The livery stables were all gutted of their fast stock and Uncle Sam's boys are now riding them by their old owners doors in triumph. Government pays about $150 now for horses.[56]

Under a New Command

The veteran cavalrymen of the West being gathered together for the new Cavalry Corps had reservations about their new commander, General James H. Wilson. Dr. Fish provides some insight with this lukewarm introduction:

> The whole cavalry of this army is at present commanded by a youth of twenty-five summers, doubtless a *smart* young man. He has been at West Point, is a Lieutenant in the regular army, promoted to a Brigadier in the volunteer service.

Everybody was surprised when he came here to command this cavalry. He will, however, have the *cordial* support of officers and men . . .⁵⁷

Captain Burns—a confidant of Minty's—may have expressed both their opinions when he wrote:

There is . . . a vast deal of swearing here, at the manner in which we have been treated. When a General of the Potomac fizzles, then he is sent *here* to command our cavalry, and experiment with it. We think we have Colonels and Generals of our own who know much more about this cavalry, and how to manage western fighting, than the men who have been beaten so many times in front of Richmond. We won't grumble, however. *Regular Army rules now* [emphasis author] and it is useless for *volunteers* to kick against it.⁵⁸

Burns may have been closer to the reality of the situation than he knew. Stephen Starr writes: "except for six months in command of a cavalry division in the field and three months in command of the Cavalry Bureau in Washington, Wilson brought no cavalry experience to his new post."

What he brought west instead were 'certain conclusions, not only from the study of military history, but from observation in the field, as to the proper functions of cavalry and the necessity of handling it in masses against the enemy's front, flanks, and communications.' *He would now have the opportunity to put these conclusions into practice* . . . [emphasis author].⁵⁹

Wilson also brought a strong sense of Regular Army organization and discipline.

The twenty-six year old West Point graduate "ordered all of the units to commence a daily regimen of marching and drill." Naturally, this order did not sit well with the men, many of whom were experienced old veterans. Minty himself complains in his diary: "Have had three years practice in cavalry service, [and] have now to try theory drill," and that "Brigade and Div. commanders have to act as inspectors or police officers."⁶⁰

The strain between the cavalry and its new commander would worsen in January, when the brigade arrived at Gravelly Springs, Alabama. "They learned that rations were short and that hunger would be a way of life. . . . Combined with the seemingly pointless orders to spend so much time in drill, the hunger of the men nearly drove them to mutiny."⁶¹

THE BATTLE OF NASHVILLE

The activities of the 4th Cavalry leading up to and including the Battle of Nashville are documented primarily by Sergeant James Larson and Lieutenant Joseph Hedges. As Larson writes:

The camp at Nashville was not pleasant. The weather was generally bad; either rainy, cloudy or cold, and as the country for miles around Nashville was an open rolling prairie, the cold winds were very disagreeable. Besides all that, the time seemed dull and lonesome, as nothing at all was going on. No attacks were being made by the enemy and we remained equally quiet. It seemed both Hood and Thomas were busying themselves with making preparations for something great to come . . .

. . . A severe northerner set in on the 13th day of December, the day that Thomas intended to advance on Hood. Rain soon followed, which made the roads bad. This, we found later, was both to our advantage and disadvantage because it had swelled the streams between Nashville and the Tennessee River. . . . At daylight on the 15th the rain had stopped and frost had set in so that the ground was frozen and the whole country covered with ice and sleet, and a cold wind swept over us as we moved out to take our place in the line of battle. The sun was then just beginning to redden the eastern horizon.

The work cut out for us according to the wording of General Thomas' order of battle, was as follows: 'General Wilson commanding Cavalry Corps will move with his three divisions on the right of General Andrew J. Smith and assist in carrying the left of the enemy's position and be in readiness to throw his whole force on the enemy's flank and rear the moment a favorable opportunity occurs.' The 4th US Cavalry as usual, was in the honorable position as Wilson's bodyguard and of course, was leading regiment, with the general at the head we moved out. Later we were most of the time with General Garrard's [2nd Infantry] Division.[62]

From General Wilson:

> In obedience to orders from the major-general commanding, on the 12th of December, the corps marched to the south side of the river, crossing on the railroad and pontoon bridges, and massed between the Harden and Charlotte pikes. The effective force was 12,500 men, 9,000 horses, 2,000 of which were scarcely fit for service. At 6 a.m. of the 15th of December . . . the corps was ready to move, but owing to the foggy weather and the delay of Smith's corps could not advance until about 10 a.m.[63]

In a letter Lieutenant Joseph Hedges sent to Captain Vale in 1886 he writes:

> Our regiment was acting singly, reporting directly to General J. H. Wilson, chief of cavalry before the battle. We were first encamped on the river above the city. Then, a day or two before the battle commenced, we moved to the west side of the city, and all the cavalry were on the right flank of our army. We moved out with the rest of the line early in the morning of the first day's fight, but did not get engaged that day, but in the evening we took a part in capturing a redoubt, or little fortification, on a hill, by getting around in the rear of it. Our simple part in the engagement was after the enemy had all started on retreat [at the end of the second day of the battle].[64]

Larson continues with the events of the day:

> In moving out we passed closely in the rear of our infantry line, already formed. Their advanced skirmishers had already engaged the enemy's skirmishers and a desultory pop, pop, pop was going on along the line, which as usual, meant that a storm would soon follow.
>
> The whole cavalry corps moved rapidly to the position assigned us on the right of General A. J. Smith's corps and then began the move to turn the enemy's left flank, which carried some of the enemy's advanced positions by compelling him to vacate them, and one fort was carried by direct charge, simultaneously with a charge made by the infantry on the main line. General Garrard's division with which the 4th US Cavalry was then operating, carried a position and a fort in which there were four guns, on the left of Hillsboro Pike and then immediately moved forward to attack the enemy's second line. Our regimental band, which for the first and only time during the war happened to be near us on the battlefield, rushed into the captured fort and played the 'Red, White and Blue,' the 'Star Spangled Banner' and everything except 'Dixie.' That was something new on the line of battle. Bands were generally kept back with the reserve artillery and pack train.[65]

Sergeant Larson recalls a very unusual movement of the 4th United States Cavalry against Union infantry:

> In moving on the second line there was considerable straggling in one of the infantry regiments, which was said to be partly composed of drafted men and substitutes from New York and New Jersey. The 4th US Cavalry was ordered to drive them up with the saber and to use revolvers if necessary. When they saw us coming at them with sabers they took the double-quick to the front at once. That about ended the first day's battle on our right flank.[66]

It was a rough night for the men of the 4th Regulars. Wet, cold, and hungry, they stretched themselves out "on the cold wet ground to pass a long and sleepless night." And "worst of all," writes Larson:

> our pack mules had not been able to find us, or perhaps had been prevented

from moving so far out by the officer in charge of the pack train. Anyhow, Gum was not on hand with his invigorating quart cup full of black coffee, and bacon and hard-tack were not available that night, just when they were so badly needed. There was nothing for us to do but put up with it as best we could. The horses were not unsaddled, so we could not make use of the saddle to sit on and the saddle blanket to draw around us as protection against the wind, and we carried no overcoats or extra clothing of any kind.

Daylight of December the 16th came at last and the regimental pack train came up just at daybreak. Gumbo, as black as he was, appeared a real angel to us. He jumped about lively, building a big fire and getting his black kettle in position. His fire was soon surrounded by shivering men and some more were built. We had not been allowed to have fire during the night, as the position of the enemy was not well known and our position should not be known either.[67]

The Battle of Nashville–Day Two

No other pursuit of the war had so promptly begun nor pushed so far without pause or halt . . .
– General James H. Wilson[68]

The morning of the sixteenth began with skirmishes. The Confederates spent the night strengthening their breastworks and waiting for the Federal assault. Wilson's Cavalry, "with its right on the Granny White Pike hacked away at the enemy's left, making slow progress." Thomas waited patiently for Wilson's cavalry to get around Hood's left, and when the moment was right, Wilson and Schofield attacked simultaneously, crushing the rebels and cutting them off from the Franklin Pike—their main escape route south. Late in the afternoon, General Wilson sought out Thomas and Schofield with an intercepted dispatch from Hood to General James Chalmers: "For god's sake drive the Yankee cavalry from our left and rear or all is lost."[69] Standing with the two generals, Wilson could see his "dismounted men, the guidons fluttering in the air, flanked and covered by two batteries of horse artillery . . . in plain sight moving against the left and rear of the enemy line."[70] Wilson urged Thomas to begin the final attack. "At about four o'clock a blast of artillery fire opened all along the line. . . . Inspired soldiers raced up the slopes, broke down tangled barricades and entered the Confederate works as the hills quaked and roared."[71] As recalled by a general on the battlefield:

> grape and canister shrieked and whizzed; bullets in a perfect hailstorm . . . The whole battlefield at times was like the grisly mouth of hell, agape and aflame with fire and smoke, alive with thunder and death-dealing shots. The hills and slopes were strewn with the dead; ravines and gorges crowded with wounded. I saw men with their heads or limbs shot off; others blown to pieces.[72]

The 4th United States Cavalry—as part of Wilson's dismounted cavalry corps—"gallantly stormed the strong Confederate earthworks side by side with their comrades of the infantry."[73] "Indeed," writes General Thomas in his official record, "the dismounted cavalry seemed to vie with the infantry who should first gain the works; as they reached the position nearly simultaneously, both lay claim to the artillery and prisoners captured."[74] Larson writes:

> The left wing of the second line of the enemy's breastworks and forts was carried in the same manner by the co-operation of Smith's infantry and Wilson's cavalry, and was done in such a manner that sometimes both claimed the captured guns. Thomas decided that they were common property.[75]

When Wilson's "five mounted brigades, for the first time united into a compact mass nearly ten thousand strong pushed to the front," along with [John] McArthur's infantry hitting "the Confederate left flank on the second afternoon, Hood's army collapsed like a house of cards."[76] In an uncharacteristic outburst of excitement, General Thomas galloped up to Wilson and "shouted so that he might have been heard a quarter of a mile: Dang it to hell, Wilson, didn't I tell you we could lick 'em, didn't I tell you we could lick 'em?"[77] Within an hour it was over. "Hood's soldiers would never fight again as an army."[78] Wilson continues:

... for the first time on any American battlefield all the available mounted force, a full army corps in strength, were massed on the flank of an advancing army, making a turning movement of the first importance against an enemy occupying a strongly fortified position. For the first time in our country the horsemen on foot had charged side by side with the infantry, carrying the enemy's entrenchments, taking his field guns, and capturing the detachments held off for their support [emphasis author]. *For the first time they had planted themselves in force behind the enemy's flank on one of his main lines of retreat in exactly the position for which they had started.*[79]

For Wilson's cavalry, the results at the two-day Battle of Nashville are described by one cavalry historian as "a grand achievement":

> When Major General George H. Thomas flattened the Army of Tennessee outside of Nashville on 15 and 16 December 1864, Wilson's troopers went charging in on foot on the right flank of the infantry, swinging around the Rebel left and rear. They took two redoubts, thirty-two guns, eleven caissons, twelve battle flags, one general and 3231 other prisoners, one pontoon bridge train and 125 wagons. Wilson's total casualties were 902.[80]

The 4th US Cavalry helped turn the Confederate flank, sending them into retreat, and would now participate in the "pursuit phase" of General Thomas's "master plan." Thomas "left one escape route open" and Wilson's cavalry, led by the 4th United States, "charged into the darkness" after the retreating rebels "with [Thomas J.] Wood's infantry close behind. The pursuit would continue for twelve days and a hundred miles. Only the weather and General Forrest prevented the annihilation of Hood's army."[81]

General Wilson ordered his men to "mount up and pursue the enemy south on the Granny White Pike to its junction with the Franklin Pike, where he hoped to intercept the fleeing Confederates." In anticipation of this, Confederate General Chalmers "set up a barricade of logs, fence rails, and brush across the Pike, and from behind it he brought the Union cavalry to a halt."[82] "We found them on the turnpike near Franklin," writes Larson, "where they had two pieces of artillery in position on the road . . . They began shelling us lively as soon as we came within range." Artillery shells were bursting in the air and striking the ground in front of the stalled Union forces, with one fragment finding Sergeant Larson's horse, "dropping him on the spot." While Larson was securing a new mount, another portion of the cavalry "gained a position a distance to the right of the main road, from which they charged the enemy in flank."[83]

"It was a scene of pandemonium," writes Wilson, "in which flashing carbines, whistling bullets, bursting shells, and the imprecations of struggling men filled the air. . . . My own staff, carried away by the excitement, threw themselves into the melee . . . with drawn saber and flashing repeater, one and all rushed into the fight . . .":

> There were neither laggards nor horseholders that night. Every officer and man, mounted and eager for the fray, did his full duty in the headlong rush which broke line after line, carried layout after layout, captured gun after gun, and finally drove Chalmers and his gallant horsemen from the field, in hopeless rout and confusion. They . . . were overborne at every turn and at every stand by the weight and fury of the Union onset.[84]

"We . . . thundered down the turnpike, saber in hand . . .," recalls Larson, "capturing their guns and taking prisoners." A Confederate artilleryman, "with one leg shot off . . . was as brave as a lion," rose to a sitting position, "lifted his hat and hallooed: 'Hurray for the Bonnie blue Flag.'"[85] The charge was kept up for "four or five miles," scattering the enemy "in all directions" and leading to the capture of Colonel Edmund W. Rucker. With night closing in and the men and horses "being worn out and hungry . . . the pursuit was necessarily discontinued."[86]

The Battle at West Harpeth River

[Hedges'] *gallant little command charged, with sabers drawn, breaking the enemy's center . . .*
– Major General George H. Thomas[87]

At 5 a.m. on the seventeenth, with only a brief rest that night, Wilson embarked upon a "most vigorous pursuit." With Union cavalry "charging at every opportunity and in the most daring manner . . . it was apparent," writes one Confederate general, "that they were determined to make the retreat a rout if possible."[88] "As it turned out," writes Wilson, "Forrest had rejoined the retreating army" the afternoon of the sixteenth "and had assumed the task of covering the retreat." He reorganized the remnants of his cavalry—"about 3,000 of his own men and 1,850 infantry" —and "managed somehow to keep the pursuit in check day after day, stopping to fight wherever the terrain gave him a reasonable chance to do so . . . It was killing work for both sides."[89]

The Confederates continued their retreat southward in the direction of Columbia, Tennessee; there was heavy skirmishing and fighting all along the Franklin Pike. There was a battle at Hollow Tree Gap—four or five miles north of Franklin—in which the rebel position "was handsomely carried," capturing "three colors and 413 prisoners." Franklin was occupied by Union troops late in the afternoon. The retreating army left "his hospitals, about 2,000 wounded, and 17,000 rations" at Franklin. "The pursuit was immediately continued," writes Wilson.[90]

By this time, the "disorganized and flying mass" of the retreating army, "apparently exhausted with rapid marching . . . took a strong position in the open fields about a mile north of the West Harpeth." There the rebels re-formed a line of defense and put their batteries into position. By now it was "almost dark from fog and approaching night."[91] "In the gloom which was now rapidly settling upon both sides," Wilson writes:

> I was close enough to see plainly that the soldiers at the front, although clad in bluish overcoats, were really the enemy. Without an instant's hesitation, I ordered my bugler to sound the charge, sang out for [Edward] Hatch and [Joseph F.] Knipe to advance on both flanks, and ordered Lieutenant Hedges, commanding my escort, the Fourth Regular Cavalry, two hundred strong, in column of platoons, to charge the enemy's center, head on with drawn sabers.[92]

"General Wilson shouted to me to take my regiment," recalls Hedges:

> and charge the line, which was then formed, supporting the battery. I moved out of the field by fours into the pike, and started at a gallop, with drawn sabers and revolvers– the first company sabers, and the balance revolvers. We rode straight into their lines.[93]

As Wilson himself records, the 4th Cavalry charged "straight against a field battery in action at the center of the line of infantry . . . and was one of the most successful charges of cavalry it was ever my fortune to witness."[94]

"The enemy opened up with artillery and tried their best to work the guns as quickly as possible," recalls Larson. The shells passed harmlessly, as the rebels did not have the time to "cut and regulate their fuses or aim their guns properly."[95] The charge by Knipe and Hatch struck the rebel line at the same time as the 4th U.S., "scattering their whole command and causing them to abandon their artillery."[96] "We killed a good many of their gunners and horses," writes Hedges, "and for a few moments it was a very hot place":

> There were, perhaps, not only forty of our men who got inside of their first line. The infantry fire went over the heads of the front of the column, but the rear caught it and was repulsed. I was asked by a mounted officer to surrender, and being almost alone, and surrounded by scores of the enemy, I threw down my saber on the ground, but just then one of my men placed the muzzle of his revolver at the head of the officer, who had demanded my surrender. His attention was withdrawn from me, and I saw a gap in the fence, spurred my horse over into the field, and riding out pretty rapidly, soon arrived at the extreme end of their flankers.[97]

"Hedges, outstripping his men, was captured three times," writes Wilson, "but waiving his hat and yelling as though frightened out of his wits: 'The Yankees are upon us, run for your lives,'" succeeded in escaping in the confusion and rejoining his command before his men missed him from the front. The raging battle started about one-half mile south of Coleman Road and ended at the West Harpeth bridge, two and one-half miles farther south.[98]

"Pressed in all directions," Forrest's artillerymen "left their guns and saved themselves as best they could; the infantry scattered in all directions . . ."[99] Hedges "continued his pursuit, spreading terror and confusion among the enemy until stopped by darkness."[100] "The rout was instantaneous and complete

...."[101] "We got the four guns," writes Lieutenant Hedges: "We lost (killed, wounded, and missing) about thirty":

> Lieutenant Fitzgerald's horse fell with him, and he was hurt on the knee, either from the shell of the enemy, or from the falling off his horse, and died a short time later from the effects of the injury. Some fifteen or twenty of the men were captured, and marched all the way to the Tennessee on foot, and were not exchanged until the war closed.[102]

General Wilson concludes his report on the incident with the following: *It is the only case I know of in which a cavalry regiment charged and broke through a Confederate line of battle composed of infantry and artillery in action and captured the guns* [emphasis author].[103]

For his exemplary conduct in the Battle of West Harpeth River, Lieutenant Hedges was subsequently awarded the nation's highest recognition for valor, the Medal of Honor.[104] In its early inception, it was not unusual for groups of men in a unit to be recognized with the Medal of Honor for their actions. Under the circumstances, the high recognition and distinct honor bestowed upon Major Hedges could well be shared with the 200 officers and men of *The Little Regiment* who were with their commanding officer that day.[105] This was the second occasion during the war in which men of the 4th United States Cavalry were involved in heroic actions resulting in a Medal of Honor citation for the officer commanding their unit during combat, the first being the cavalry charge at Shelbyville, Tennessee, in June 1863, led by Captain Charles Davis, 7th Pennsylvania Volunteer Cavalry.[106]

Lieutenant Colonel Eugene Beaumont, 4th United States Cavalry—then a captain in the volunteers—was also awarded the Medal of Honor for "his most distinguished gallantry in action" in the Battle of West Harpeth River and for his subsequent action in the Battle at Selma, Alabama.[107]

"The conduct of the troops in this affair was most admirable," writes General Wilson:

> particularly that of the Fourth US Cavalry, my escort, under the daring Lieutenants Davis, O'Connell, and Rendlebock, every one of whom gave assurance of success. They had been burning bridges, stations, and cotton warehouses and tearing up railroads all day, but were as eager as fresh troops for the fray.[108]

General Wilson requested brevet appointments for 1st Lieutenant Joseph Rendlebock and 2nd Lieutenants John Webster, James Callehan, and William Bayard "for gallantry in the pursuit of Hood after the battle of Nashville." Sergeant Martin Rossmaier, 4th U.S., Company H—also cited for bravery during the action at Little Harpeth River—was one of only four enlisted men mentioned by name in General Wilson's reports.[109]

The pursuit of Hood's infantry and Forrest's cavalry continued "with the country getting wilder and more desolate . . . with rain and frost to chill and distress both horses and men . . . and winter and its floods upon us." It continued across the Duck River through Lynnville, "driving the stubborn and still unshaken Southerners beyond Richland Creek."[110] With minimal food, fodder, or rest, the men and horses were once again being pressed to their levels of endurance.[111]

"Every afternoon," writes Larson, "we found the enemy in position in some place easy to defend, trying to delay us to give their train and artillery a chance to bog through the muddy road which was probably the worst road ever seen in that country":

> The rain constantly falling and the heavy trains and artillery and bodies of men passing over it made it almost impassable. And we, who were following the enemy were of course, wallowing in mud. Even on the graded turnpike the mud was ankle deep.[112]

The pursuit continued until December 20, when Wilson sent two commands back to Nashville and, with his escort (the 4th Regulars), went on with the remainder.[113] On the twenty-third, Wilson "was occupied crossing his command over Duck River, but took the advance on the 24th, supported by General Wood, and came up with the enemy just south of Lynnville, and also at Buford's Station." At both places the enemy "made a short stand, but was speedily dislodged . . ."[114] "In that spirited affair," recalls Wilson, "[we] routed [Abraham] Buford's cavalry and drove it from the field in confusion, capturing Buford's battle flag, wounding him through the leg, and taking many of his escort and fighting force, prisoners of war."[115]

The Confederates continued their retreat, their line stretching to the Tennessee River.

On Christmas morning, the rebels evacuated Pulaski and were "pursued toward Lamb's Ferry." They were then driven across Sugar Creek to Muscle Shoals, where "Forrest's cavalry and his eight brigades of infantry" crossed the river.[116] "Experience had by that time taught even the common soldier," writes Larson, "that preparations to destroy the [Rockland Bridge at Pulsar] were already made and a moment's unnecessary delay would ruin our chance to save it." Three of Wilson's brigades made a charge for the bridge that was already on fire when they arrived. The flames were quickly extinguished and the bridge was saved. A great number of prisoners were also taken. However, between December 25 and 28, Hood and Forrest "got most of the army over a floating bridge . . . snatching up their pontoons behind them."[117]

The Nashville campaign was at an end. It was a grueling chase "over 120 miles of soggy roads and a dozen swollen streams in an implacable chase through rain, snow, darkness, and frozen mud."[118] As one historian writes:

> The ten day pursuit was mostly a fight against exhaustion. Wilson wore out 5,000 horses before his pressure began to diminish against last-ditch defense by Forrest and the dauntless rear guard of cavalry and infantry, many of the latter fighting barefooted.[119]

During these operations, the cavalry captured "32 guns, 11 caissons, 12 colors, 3,232 prisoners (including 1 general officer), and compelled them to abandon or destroy over 100 wagons, 8 ambulances, and 1,348 mules." One hundred twenty-two officers and men were killed, 521 wounded, and 259 were missing.[120]

"I know of no battles in the war where the influence of cavalry was more potent, nor of any pursuit sustained so long and well," notes Wilson. "The results . . . clearly demonstrate the wisdom of massing the cavalry of an army . . ."[121] According to Stephen Starr: "Wilson would demonstrate in another four months that his cavalry could accomplish this and more, *entirely on its own and without the support of infantry* [emphasis author]."[122]

When Sherman's troops arrived in Savannah on December 22, 1864, the city surrendered at once. On December 29, General Thomas announced the end of the campaign against Hood and the Army of Tennessee and gave directions for the disposition of his commands. Wilson's cavalry was to concentrate ". . . at or near Huntsville . . . with a single cavalry division left at Eastport."[123]

> *The Southern vision of victory which had sustained them throughout 1864 was now gone . . . gone forever despite the desperate efforts of desperate men to revive it, gone amidst the red clay and green forests of Georgia.*
> – Albert Castel.[124]

1865: The Beginning of the End

No other mounted invasion force even came close to amassing such a record of success. . . . [Wilson] led the first and only self-sustained mounted campaign of the Civil War.
– Edward Longacre[1]

I. The Last Campaign

Reflecting back on the significance of the Battle of Franklin for his cavalry division, General James Wilson wrote:

> For the first time all the available cavalry in the west was united upon one battlefield, and, although it numbered actually present less than five thousand men, its proportion to the infantry was relatively great, while its actual service was of unusual importance. Considered from a military point of view the incidents so far related gave unmistakable indication of the great part the new cavalry corps was to play in the decisive battle and campaign which were soon to follow.[2]

In the east, Grant sent Sheridan's veteran cavalry corps to join the Army of the Potomac in front of Petersburg, Virginia, for the final campaign against Lee. In the west, Sherman and his army moved north from Savannah, Georgia, and the war "shuddered toward its conclusion."[3]

In late March, General Wilson began his Selma–Montgomery Campaign—a drive through Alabama to capture the Confederate supply depot at Selma and destroy everything along the way that could benefit the Confederate cause. As one military historian writes:

> This great raid, which severed the main arteries supplying life-blood to the Confederacy, was destined to be the culminating blow by the Federal cavalry inflicted on the already tottering military structure of the Southern Confederacy.[4]

George H. Thomas—a major general in the volunteers—finally received his promotion to major general in the regular army on December 24, 1864. Having been passed over more than once in favor of less qualified commanders, it was the final recognition of his years of dedicated service to the Union. However, it was a hollow promotion; the Army of the Cumberland would not fight again under its own leader or as a single unit.

For a number of reasons long debated by Civil War historians, Thomas was never able to gain Grant's favor. During the winter of 1864-65, Grant was busy restructuring his armies with units taken from the Army of the Cumberland. The situation puzzled Wilson:

> Just what they counted upon or expected from Thomas, whom they had promoted to major general of the regular army... was never made clear... They scattered [the] infantry around as well as the splendid body of cavalry I had got together with so much trouble.... The dispersal of Thomas's army continued throughout the winter and early spring.[5]

"Finding himself immobilized," Thomas, the consummate soldier, was directed by Grant to prepare a cavalry expedition to penetrate northern Alabama and "move on Tuscaloosa, Selma, and Montgomery."[6] This campaign was originally to be a "subordinate role" to Sherman's western campaign of 1865.[7] Fortunately, as his biographer writes: "Thomas had a very able and skillful cavalry commander, a man young in years, but larger in experience and good judgment, brave, dashing, and ambitious to excel in everything he undertook."[8] What appeared to be a setback for General Thomas became an opportunity for General James H. Wilson and his new cavalry division.

At the end of February "Thomas went down to Eastport, Mississippi, about 25 miles east of Corinth, near the Alabama border, to see the state of readiness of Wilson's command." What he saw was to his liking, "the largest body of cavalry ever collected on the American continent." When Wilson "passed 17,000 troopers before Thomas in a review":

> it was a sight never seen by any other American army commander. It convinced Thomas that with the use of such a concentrated mobile force he could break

the enemy's last interior railway, destroy their last depots and knock Forrest out of the war. This was to be a campaign in its own right . . .⁹

"After the cavalry got fairly under way south of Columbia," writes Wilson, "no part of the infantry ever caught up with it again in that theater of operations":

> As it is well known, it acted thenceforth as an *independent body* . . . an invincible mounted army, which played a separate and conclusive part not only in defeating the Confederate cavalry, but did much in destroying the resources of the Confederacy and in bringing the Civil War itself to a glorious conclusion.¹⁰

By the end of December 1864, the 4th US Cavalry—temporarily unattached—was still in Nashville, preparing to join General Wilson at his headquarters. "After seeing Hood across the river with what he had left of his once great army," writes Sergeant Larson, "we moved to Gravelly Springs, Alabama, where we remained until near the middle of March 1865. Here we built winter quarters and for the first time enjoyed the use of them and a rest of more than a month of easy times and good living":

> . . . Although we had such good times at Gravelly Springs, the monotonous camp life became tedious and tiresome toward the beginning of March and we began to wish for orders to move somewhere. We knew that although we had demolished one of the main and best armies of the Confederacy, the war was not over yet. There was more work of the same kind in store for us. In fact, we were getting restless, being now used to roaming about constantly and hailed with delight the order received about the middle of March to get ready for a forward movement.¹¹

Shortly after joining Wilson's command, Sergeant Bates writes to his parents on January 18, 1865:

> We are at General Wilson's Head Quarters yet and likely to remain so for he thinks a great deal of the Regiment and Officers. The whole Regiment is together now. The party which were with Sherman having left him . . . and come back <u>alone</u>. They lost eleven men on the return trip and brought seventy-four prisoners into Chattanooga.
>
> We have had a very exciting time since Hood 'raised the siege of Nashville' but not a very dangerous time. Our Regiment made one charge between Franklin and Spring Hill, Tenn. and took three pieces of Artillery with slight loss.
>
> . . . We are now in what is called permanent camp, that is, we expect to stay here until the Spring Campaign opens and every-body is engaged in making himself comfortable. This is a very easy job for the weather is so mild we go about in undress uniform, i.e.–shirt sleeves and slippers all day long. Wood is plenty and easy obtained, cheap as dirt too. We ran away from the Paymaster at Nashville just as he got ready to exhibit his dexterity in giving away treasury issues, but I hope he will come around before long–better later than never.
>
> . . . The people in this country are starving to death, that is what they all tell us but somehow it is rather difficult to look at a big robust, hearty, corn eating darky and reconcile his appearance with his story of starving.
>
> . . . If you look for this place on the map you wont find it I think–but find Florence and then find a place sixteen miles below, on the same side of the river and you have it. We first went to a place opposite Eastport in Mississippi but there was no favorable place to encamp as large a force of cavalry as General Wilson has pressed (about 25 thousand) so the command moved up here–Gravely Springs, Lauderdale County, Alabama is our address.¹²

Writing on February 8, Captain Henry Potter allowed himself the luxury of thinking that the end might be near:

> . . . I have thought this matter over about resigning and concluded it is my duty and interest to stay with the regiment until our time is out and go home honorably with the old and true veterans of the glorious 4th [Mich.] Cavalry. It will be a proud day

for me ... if I live to march at the head of my Company thru the streets of Detroit next August. With the Stars and Stripes floating triumphantly over our whole country. May the Lord grant that it may be so–for all of us.[13]

Unfortunately, many more lives of the old Saber Brigade, and particularly the 4th United States Cavalry, were yet to be lost.

Colonel Robert Minty now commanded the Second Brigade of Wilson's Second Division—consisting of his 4th Michigan, the 7th Pennsylvania, and the 1st, 3rd, and 4th Ohio—and was preparing to leave Louisville. Minty's brigade would continue to play a prominent role in the upcoming campaign. In the absence of the wounded Brigadier General Eli Long, Minty temporarily commanded the Second Division—once again given that responsibility without the promotion to brigadier general. At seven o'clock on the morning of December 28, Minty's Brigade "broke camp and marched south."[14] It was while passing through Bardstown on the afternoon of the twenty-ninth that two of his staff—Captain Robert McCormick and Dr. John L. Sherk of the 7th Pennsylvania—left the column to visit a doctor in the town. During this visit the two men were brutally murdered in Grigsby's parlor by Confederate guerrillas as previously reported. An enemy growing ever more desperate was exacting its last full measure of vengeance.

It was a difficult and dangerous passage. "Roads were in deplorable condition, and the movement was time-consuming and tiresome," writes Minty. "Finding forage ... was difficult. The elements were a constant aggravation; if it was not snowing it was raining":

> Camp mud almost to the knees. Snowed heavily all night, very hard on men and horses.... Bitterly cold all day. Many men had their feet frozen.
> ... At Three Springs learned that six men of the 1st Brigade who had been straggling were captured by guerillas, tied and shot.[15]

On the twelfth, "the Division crossed the Cumberland River and marched through Nashville":

> Rained heavily all night. Camp almost afloat this morning. Has continued raining all day. We have marched 217 miles coming from Louisville to this place.... Ordered to prepare for march to Eastport, Mississippi, to leave here on Thursday the 12th.[16]
> ... Following the line of Hood's retreat, we passed through Franklin, Springfield, and Columbia, where we turned southwest, and arrived at Gravely Springs, Ala, on the Tennessee River, on the evening of Jan. 25, 1865.[17]

Captain Burns describes the devastation of war they saw as they passed through Franklin and Nashville:

> The country is much changed since we passed over last Spring. It is now almost ruined. Fences are down, houses deserted, the roads lined with the carcasses of horses and mules. Graves are to be seen every mile. Almost every field is a cemetery, and every inhabited house a hospital.[18]

Having joined Wilson and his escort—the 4th US Cavalry—Minty describes the activities at their new headquarters:

> The design being to remain in camp until the weather was sufficiently settled to admit of active operations, quarters for the men and sheds for the horses were constructed; charcoal pits were burned, forges erected, and the ring of the farriers' hammers sounded from daybreak till dark, and before the end of February the 7,000 horses in the Second Division were well shod and ready for an offensive campaign.[19]

"About the middle of February," writes Minty, "Gen. Wilson, our corps commander, reviewed the Second Division; over 6,000 fighting men in line; as magnificent a body of men as could be found in the armies of the Union, confident of their ability to perform good and efficient service."[20] On February 23, 1865, Major General Wilson paraded his "seventeen thousand Federal cavalrymen" in review before Major General George H. Thomas:

> The soldiers carried sabers that had been sharpened almost to a razor's edge and carbines and pistols so polished as to

catch the reflection of the sunlight. Behind the long columns rolled hundreds of well-stocked supply wagons and three batteries of horse artillery, whose cannoneers rode proudly upon the limbers and caissons that trailed the guns. Bugles blared up and down the lines and short-tailed guidons rippled in the frosty breeze.[21]

"My God, gentlemen, did you ever see such a magnificent division?," exclaimed Wilson to his staff.[22]

By the end of February, "the organization of Wilson's Cavalry Corps at Gravely Springs was comprised of three divisions, each consisting of two Brigades. . . . The Second fell under command of Brigadier General Eli Long"—having recovered from his injuries—and contained Wilder's brigade of mounted infantry (now under Col. Abram O. Miller) and Minty's Saber Brigade "appended by the 3rd and 4th Ohio, with the Chicago Board of Trade Battery still assigned to their support."[23]

While Wilson was rebuilding his Cavalry Corps, General Sherman, from his headquarters in Savannah, was making preparations for his campaign through the Carolinas. He moved his headquarters to Beaufort, South Carolina, where he began his campaign in February. Vengeance did not belong solely to the South, as Sherman himself writes:

> . . . As the army begins its march through South Carolina, many of the soldiers seem determined to make the state, which they see as the heart and soul of secession and rebellion, suffer for its treason. Aside from the official work of destruction, the Federals also burn and destroy much private property.[24]

Although such destruction was against orders, Sherman seems to have anticipated South Carolina's fate in a letter he had written to General Halleck in December: "The whole army is burning with an insatiable desire to wreak vengeance upon South Carolina, I almost tremble at her fate, but feel that she deserves all that seems in store for her."[25]

When Sherman complains to Confederate cavalry General Wade Hampton of the murder of Union foragers by Southern soldiers, Hampton replies that, while he is unaware of the specific episode to which Sherman refers, he has ordered his men to shoot on sight any Northerners caught burning people's homes.

And ". . . this order shall remain in force so long as you disgrace the profession of arms by allowing your men to destroy private dwellings."[26]

Columbia, South Carolina, surrendered and was occupied on February 17. Within twenty-four hours two-thirds of the town of 20,000 "will lie in smoldering ashes." All railroad depots, supply houses, and industries were destroyed.[27] Sherman's army resumed its march northward toward Goldsboro, North Carolina.

Meanwhile, Hood's shattered Army of Tennessee was at Tupelo, Mississippi, being depleted by troops sent to reinforce General Hardee in his operations against Sherman in the Carolinas. Hood was dismissed and General Richard Taylor assumed command of an army numbering less than 18,000 soldiers.

On March 17, Union forces numbering about 45,000 began the Mobile Campaign to capture the city of Mobile, Alabama. At about the same time, General James Wilson's independent Cavalry Corps moved on Selma, Alabama: "Selma is one of the last remaining manufacturing centers left to the Confederacy. By depriving the South of its munitions factories, Union officials believe they can significantly handicap the enemy war effort. Thanks to the efforts of the North's numerous blockade squadrons operating along the coast, the South is already short of raw materials."[28]

What Wilson had planned was a "full-scale campaign rather than a typical cavalry raid":

> . . . He was aiming to destroy the military potential of whole states by surmounting all manner of defensive works and overpowering every defender who crossed his path. He would continue his journey as long as any objective of strategic importance remained before him.[29]

Unlike a number of Union commanders before him, Wilson was not "paralyzed by fear" at the thought of confronting Nathan Bedford Forrest, as he had already defeated him once before at Franklin.[30] In preparation for the move all sick men were sent to the hospital boats, and on the morning of March 22, Wilson's divisions broke camp:

> . . . [with] approximately thirteen thousand five hundred cavalrymen, about one thousand five hundred of them still without mounts and serving on foot as wagon guards. . . . Wilson rode alongside

the column on his dapple-gray gelding, 'Sheridan.' The young commander made an imposing picture in his trim blue uniform, topped by a heavy cavalry greatcoat, an ornate forage cap, and long black jackboots.[31]

As the general and his staff, escorted by the 4th United States Cavalry, passed the brigade headquarters, General Wilson saluted his brigade commanders.[32] "Never can I forget the brilliant scene," recalled a Federal officer:

> as regiment after regiment filed gayly out of camp, decked in all the paraphernalia of war, with gleaming arms, and guidons given to the wanton breeze. Stirring bugle songs woke the slumbering echoes of the woods; cheer upon cheer went up from joyful lips.[33]

"The corps moved out in three divergent columns, for Wilson believed this would confuse enemy observers."[34] This proved correct. Dr. Fish gives a more practical description of his brigade:

> The men may be said to be stripped for the march. Officers and men start with a single blanket and a change of under clothes–all else is packed and ready to send back . . .
>
> The men start light–only wagons enough to carry a few rations such as the country will not be likely to furnish, ambulances and a few hospital stores for the sick and wounded, and plenty of ammunition. Each man carries one blanket on his horse; and coffee, sugar and salt for a march of five days. Even the officers carry nothing but a change of under clothes. All else has been packed up and sent to the rear–doubtless to be lost, as those who turn over such articles never expect to see them again.[35]

Captain Vale provides additional detail:

> With this corps was a park of some twenty pieces of artillery, a pontoon train of fifty wagons, and a train of one hundred and fifty wagons of ammunition and supplies, the whole under the command of Major General James Wilson . . . a natural cavalry leader. Each man had five days' rations in his haversack, and on his horse two days' forage. With each regiment was transported on pack-mules ten days' rations of hard bread and meat, and sixty days rations of coffee, sugar, and salt.[36]

". . . We left Gravelly Springs for *an entirely independent campaign or raid* [emphasis author] through Alabama and Georgia," writes Sergeant Larson. "That is, we cut loose from all and any correspondence with other bodies of our troops and relied on ourselves for protection and on the country for subsistence. . . . Our final destination was Macon, Georgia, but the most important point on the way was Selma, Alabama, a distance of about 175 miles from Gravelly Springs . . ."[37]

The weather was not cooperating, as the continual rains during the first week of March caused the Tennessee to "rise so high," as Minty wrote, "that some of the camps are underwater, the men having to move in the midst of the rains."[38] As Minty's command moved out, it was difficult going at first, with "the continuous burden of rain and poor roads. Along the route they were forced to ford high streams by day and spend pitch black overcast nights in muddy, wet and miserable camps." On crossing the Black Warrior River, Minty writes: "Ford deep and very bad, thirty or forty men were dunked, and one man . . . was drowned."[39]

"During our marches," writes Dr. Fish, "I doubt not this command has built fifty miles of corduroy road":

> Coming to a swamp, the command would dismount and march to the nearest plantation and return, each man with from one to three rails on his shoulders. 4,000 men would soon construct a passable 'rail way.'[40]

Of this phase of the march, one cavalry historian writes:

> . . . Wilson pushed his men swiftly through the swamplands and forests of upper Alabama, over quagmires and around quicksand pits and across so many rivers and creeks that he later termed his march

'the most remarkable naval expedition ever undertaken by cavalry.'[41]

Even with all of these difficulties, "the invaders covered sixty miles during the first three days of their journey."[42] Major Burns "eagerly anticipated the daily opportunities to 'see what we could do in the *smashing* line," as he phrased it, as the troopers "fanned out all along the route," burning iron works, foundries, and rolling mills in every direction.[43]

Sergeant Larson describes the advance of Wilson's cavalry into the heart of the Confederacy:

> The enemy's force in our front was Forrest's division, Buford's division, [Philip D.] Roddey's division, [William H.] Jackson's division and [James R.] Chalmers' division, one brigade of Texas cavalry, one brigade of Kentucky cavalry and [Thomas J.] Taylor's brigade of infantry. A person would naturally suppose that such a force as the enemy then had to meet us would be strong enough to capture or drive Wilson's corps back again over the Tennessee River, but the outcome of the campaign proved the contrary. Perhaps that was due to the exultant spirit and morale of our men.

> Fighting was of daily occurrence from the time we crossed the Tennessee River until we reached Macon. The three columns, or divisions, moving independently of each other on different routes, struck successfully at Frankfort, Russellville, Jasper, Elyton and Montrevallo [sic Montevallo], leaving in their paths ruin and blackened walls. Everything that could be of any aid or help to the Confederacy was given to the flames. The Red Mountain Ironworks, the Central Roller Mills and other feeders of the Confederacy, such as Bibbs Roller Mills, were all destroyed. Although these were not fortified places, except where occasionally a temporary breastwork had been quickly erected on our approach, we had a good deal to contend with. Streams to cross over which bridges had been destroyed, or a fight for the possession of a bridge. Hence it was daily fighting and marching with us, and our advance was not more than 13 miles a day on an average and it was not until the 2nd day of April that we arrived in the vicinity of Selma, Alabama the objective and most important point in the campaign.[44]

II. Wilson's Selma–Macon Campaign

> *... Twelve thousand veteran horsemen, marched o'er the mountain wall,*
> *And struck the heart of rebeldom, like thunderbolt let fall.*[1] - 1872 reunion poem

"Under the personal command of General Wilson"—writes Minty—the First, Second, and Fourth Brigades, "numbering about 15,000 fighting men":

> ... formed the flying column... which pierced the Confederacy from Eastport, Miss., captured Selma, Montgomery, Columbus, West Point, and Macon, destroyed an incalculable amount of Confederate property, and finished the good work with the capture, by the 4th Mich. Cavalry, of Jefferson Davis.[2]

After marching for "almost 150 miles," Wilson crossed the Black Warrior River on March 29 and was in Elyton (present day Birmingham) the next day. From that point Wilson dispatched 1,100 men under General John Croxton to march to Tuscaloosa, where they were to burn anything of supposed military value, including the University of Alabama.[3]

When Forrest learned of Wilson's advance on March 26, he "immediately sought to concentrate his forces against it." He finally met his match in a Union commander who "moved with a swiftness that had not characterized other generals' movements" against him.[4]

City of SELMA, ALA. and its DEFENSES

Forrest's initial delaying tactics were "brushed aside" by Wilson's cavalry. He had developed an "elaborate plan to thwart the Union invasion," but unfortunately, those plans fell into the hands of General Wilson "sometime on the night of March 31 or early in the morning of April 1." Wilson now knew where Forrest's small command was and that he was awaiting the reinforcements of Jackson and Chalmers. These reinforcements would have to cross the Cahaba River over the bridge at Centerville. Wilson dispatched Edward McCook with a brigade to destroy the bridge. This temporarily separated the Confederate forces and allowed Wilson time to "concentrate his efforts almost exclusively on defeating the Confederates in front of him and pushing his way into Selma."[5]

Forrest made one last stand at Bogler's Creek, near Ebenezer Church. In the hand-to-hand combat that followed, Forrest was charged by a Union captain who slashed at him with his saber, wounding him in the arm before Forrest was able to kill him with a shot from his pistol and make his escape.[6]

Selma, Alabama

With his brigade in the advance, Minty reached the outskirts of Selma at 3 p.m. on April 2, and with his dismounted cavalrymen "formed in line behind a slight elevation," where a skirmish line had been "thrown forward." He was joined by Generals Wilson and Long. "Lying on our faces," Minty writes, "we examined the enemy's position."[7]

"This was the strongest and best fortified place we had met with on the campaign," writes Sergeant Larson. "It had a naturally strong location, being in the great bend of the river, which was high and unfordable at the time. Hence it was impossible to get a force to the rear of the place."[8] As described by one historian:

> Selma was protected by a formidable conglomeration of abaits [barricades], palisades [fences], sharpshooters' platforms, star-shaped forts, water-filled ditches, and gun emplacements stocked by a wide assortment of artillery, heavy and light.[9]

"The works extended from the Alabama River above the city to the Alabama River below," Minty recalls:

> and consisted of an outer line of bastions connected by curtains [concealments]. On this line the distance from the bottom of the ditch to top of the parapet was 14 feet. In front of the ditch, except at two points covered by swamp, a well built palisade [fence] extended, and between that and our position was a partial abatis made by felling the trees and shrubs so as to give a clear sweep to the artillery. The bastions were mounted with field artillery. An inner line of detached works was mounted with heavier guns; all the works were well manned.[10]

The outer works "extended in a half circle above the city for a distance of three miles, and where no defense existed, the river and an almost impassable swampland protected the garrisons."[11] The first line of defense "was about a quarter mile from town," recalls Minty:

> ... Plenty of artillery appeared on the first line and about 50 yards in front of it stood a line of palisades (posts about 7 or 8 feet high) set in the ground so close together that no man could pass between; but the defenders could send their bullets through.... The second line was close to town, and this strong position was held by three brigades of Confederate troops, Roddey's, Forrest's and Chalmers', with some regiments of homeguards.[12]

"Within these barriers were some seven thousand Confederates, led by Forrest and a half-dozen other generals."[13]

As formidable as these physical barriers appeared, they were poorly manned. Forrest's biographer Brian Wills describes the condition of the Confederates defending Selma and puts the number at about half the Union estimates:

> Forrest . . . attempted to create a credible defense of the city from the resources on hand. By putting every available man in three and a half miles of earthworks surrounding the city, Forrest succeeded in compiling a mixed force of about three thousand men. But he had to spread the men thinly to cover the length of the works. Doing so not only greatly reduced his firepower, but meant that he had to rely on militia who had already broken twice before the enemy or upon impressed civilians who had never before faced the Federals. If they broke this time, all would be lost.
> Forrest worked to shorten the lines by constructing a second set of entrenchments closer to the city . . .[14]

After making a "careful reconnaissance of the works," General Wilson turned to Minty and Long and said, "The assault will be made right here."[15] What Minty does not mention, nor may have known at the time, was that Wilson "had received one last piece of good fortune." An "English civil engineer who had helped lay out the Selma defenses" had fallen into Federal hands and "was easily persuaded to sketch a map of works" that Wilson found "surprisingly accurate."[16] Wilson and his subordinates now had a "clear idea of how to approach and attack the city." "Given the condition of Forrest's defenders," writes Wills, "and the confidence the Union troopers had after repeatedly beating them, the intelligence was probably not even necessary." Wills continues: "Pressing his advantage with precision, Wilson promptly prepared to attack Selma."[17]

General Long was to "develop his line . . . in front of the works"; General Emory Upton was "directed to move on the Range Line road, sending a squadron on the Burnsville road"; and Lieutenant Rendlebock, with a battalion of the Fourth US Cavalry, "was instructed to move down the railroad, burning stations, bridges, and trestle-works as far as Burnsville." Wilson's army was in sight of the town and "mostly in position by 4 p.m."[18]

The Final Battle at Selma

"We were looking for a fight," recalls Major Burns. "All pack mules, sneaks, crooks and cowards were ordered to the rear, and none but effective men allowed in the column. . . . It looked like a pretty tough thing to attempt, to drive such a number of men from so strong a position, but it must be done that night, or we might find it still more difficult in the morning."[19] "As General Wilson left us," Minty continued, "the rebel General Chalmers, with his division, came up in our rear and attacked the 3rd Ohio. . . . A movement in the rebel lines indicated that they purposed making a sortie. The gallant Long decided not to wait for Wilson's signal, but to forestall the enemy and assault at once."[20] "At approximately 5 p.m.," writes Brian Wills, "Long and Upton charged across the plain."[21] Minty continues:

> The absence of the four detached regiments and the horse holders left us only 1,483 men for the assault. Our estimate gave Forrest over 9,000 men. In a paper published at Cahaba few days later, Gen. Forrest contradicted our estimate, but acknowledged that his strength exceeded 7,000.
> Millers brigade (mounted infantry) was armed with Spencer rifles; my brigade with Spencer carbines, and the men of both brigades had unlimited confidence in themselves and their leaders.
> The moment Gen. Long gave the order we moved forward. Our thin, blue line advanced steadily until we reached the top of the elevation behind which we had formed, when we dashed forward on the run, and in less time than I can tell it we were in full possession of the outer line of works.[22]

"The whole plain for a mile and a half was covered at once with a whirlwind of battle," writes General Wilson in the gallant prose of the day. "Without waiting for the result, I promptly dismounted the horse I had been riding all day, sprang onto my splendid gray gelding, "Sheridan," and, turning to the Fourth Regulars, bade them follow at the charge":

> Regarding it as one of those emergencies which occur but once in a soldier's life and realizing that I had not another man to put in, I felt it my duty to show myself on my most conspicuous horse with staff, escort, and red battle-flag in the thickest of the fight.[23]

The moment of the assault was announced "by the roar of musketry and artillery and the cheers of our gallant men."[24] "Not a man faltered," writes Wilson. "Straight down the turnpike [Range Line Road] through the first line of works we rode all together, every man with saber drawn and nerves strained to the utmost, as though his personal example was essential to victory":

> My escort [4th U.S.] was badly scattered in the charge, but, responding to the stirring calls of my Indian bugler, it reformed at once and followed me at a rattling pace through the entrenchment's at the highway. As the guard was clear of obstructions from that point, I sent the regiment again headlong after the enemy and had the satisfaction of seeing it disappear in the mass of broken and fleeing Confederates. . .[25]

"Although the Southern fire was heavier and more effective than might have been expected," writes Wills, "the Federals soon drove their opponents out of the first line of works and into the second."[26]

According to General Wilson: "The only mounted men that actually got into the melee were the Fourth Regulars, who were always kept at hand for such purposes."[27] The 4th Cavalry was immediately followed by the remainder of the Union cavalry, dismounted. "We gave a cheer," writes Captain Burns, "and made a rush. The rebels opened on us with artillery and small arms, but did not stop us":

Our battery from behind was pitching the shell and shot over our heads, our men cheering, hurrahing, firing and running. I never shouted so. It was a *perfect pandemonium*. Our men were falling wounded and dead on every side.

No one cared; all went forward, we must take the works, or we should be awfully cut up. My own sensations were those of perfect recklessness. I expected to be shot, but really did not care. A shell bursting in front would not even make one wink. On we went, got through or climbed over the palisades, how I don't know, waded through the ditch, and were over the embankment among the rebels. As they saw us jumping in among them, they fled, the most of them towards the left. Our men pursued, driving them from their forts and capturing their artillery.[28]

Wilson—with the 4th US Cavalry—found Minty "in possession of the outer line and in the act of assaulting the inner works," and ordered them forward. Without waiting for them Wilson led his escort in an assault on a redoubt in the inner line. "The 4th Regulars recoiled for an instant from the heavy fire which they received from the enemy; but [with] their old comrades of the 4th Mich. coming up, the redoubt was carried with a rush."[29] Wills writes that their attack:

> succeeded in forcing that line as well, when the militia broke for the final time. For Forrest and the rest of his men, the battle degenerated into hundreds of individual combats as the Confederates struggled to escape or gave in and surrendered.... There was little for Forrest to do except complete his escape, fall behind the Cahaba River, and pull together the scattered remnants of his command."[30]

Colonel Minty was among the first men "to gain the works," recalls Dr. Fish. "A corporal Booth, and three or four more of the 4th Ohio, reached the works about the same moment–but they were all either killed or wounded–leaving the Colonel for a brief moment the only living Yankee within. Our men soon swarmed over."[31] All of the other works forming the inner line had now been captured.[32] Standing in the fortification on the Plantersville Road that had just been captured, Minty counted "five pieces of heavy artillery, some of which were still loaded, the enemy not having had time to discharge them ... Our victory was complete," writes Minty:

> We captured 26 pieces of artillery in position, and made over 3,000 prisoners. The loss in the assaulting force of 1,483 men was 324 killed and wounded, or 22 percent, in half an hour. The only men of the rank of division, brigade, or regimental commanders engaged in the assault who were left untouched were Col. [Jacob] Vail, of the 17th Ind., and myself. Five out of seven had fallen. Our brave division commander, Long, was seriously wounded in the head before we reached the outer line and I assumed command of the division. Col. [Abram] Miller was shot through the legs, Col. [Jonathan] Biggs through the right lung, Col. [Charles] McCormick through the leg. and Col. [George W.] Dobbs killed.

> General Forrest escaped with 28 men of his escort. Gens. Buford and [Daniel W.] Adams, with their commands, made their escape from the upper portion of the town, retreated toward Burnsville, and were followed by Upton who captured two guns and several prisoners during the night.[33]

Shortly after entering the works, Captain Burns was ordered to return to the hill and order up the led horses. He did so and then joined the 4th Regulars "who had just come on the field with Gen. Wilson, who had been with General Upton during the attack." Burns continues:

> The 3rd Ohio and 4th Mich. were also ordered up to the front, and followed at a little distance the 4th Regulars. We again entered the works and moved over to the right to cut off the retreat of the rebs. Our men had driven them over to the left towards the Plantersville Road, and captured everything there, when Gen. Upton came in with his Division, and struck them in flank and rear, driving them pell mell to the right again.

> We had reached near the fort ... when a perfect storm of bullets and grape opened on us. Gen. Wilson then ordered the 4th

Regulars to draw saber and charge, and directed me to have the 3rd Ohio support them (the 4th Mich. had not yet come up). I gave Gen W's orders to Col. [Horace N.] Howland, and then started for the head of the 4th Regular column.[34]

The objective of this charge, recalls Sergeant Larson, "was to draw their artillery fire if there were any guns in the fort."

"In a loud voice" former 1st Sergeant, now Lieutenant William O'Connell—commanding the 4th Cavalry—held his saber high in the air and "gave the command 'draw saber' and out flew the shining blades":

> ... A portion of the road was sheltered on our left side by a row of trees and the enemy held their fire until a good part of the column had passed the sheltered part, but then all at once the whole top of the embankment was one sheet of fire, flame and smoke and bullets fairly piped and screamed through the air; all musket balls however.... The fort had all of a sudden become choked full of gray uniforms and bristling with muzzles of guns and bayonets. They were infantry and were there to give the 4th US Cavalry 'Hail Columbia.'
>
> Onward we rushed and when some 20 or 25 yards from the ditch, Lieutenant O'Connell, who had adopted the Indian method of dodging the bullets by hanging down on the side of his horse, fell to the ground and one or two sets of fours passed over him. He rose all right, having the rein still in hand, vaulted into the saddle and took his place.[35]

Another eyewitness report—probably more accurate—has it that Lieutenant O'Connell's horse was killed and after the line was "gallantly carried . . . we approached the works [and] had the satisfaction of seeing the bulky form of O'Connell rise from behind his dead horse, where he had been lying to avoid the enemy's fire. He was bruised but unwounded." O'Connell and Lieutenant Webster, who was shot in the arm, were both cited for their actions.[36]

"We were all then going on the full run," writes Captain Burns, describing his efforts to catch up with the 4th Regulars:

> Our artillery by that time was then up near or right and blazing merrily away. The rebel artillery from the fort in front was answering too briskly for safety. The bullets were falling in the road about and in front of us, just as the first drops of a heavy storm, knocking up little clouds of dust in the same way. I remember noticing the same thing when we were coming down the hill in the first charge. I had nearly reached the head of the 4th Regular column, being on a very fast horse, and riding a little to one side, when they were driven back in the wildest confusion. They had run onto a deep ditch, over which their horses could neither climb nor leap. From the fort on the other side, the rebs were firing wickedly with all the weapons known to civilized warfare. They (our men) might have, but turning a little distance to the right (as we afterwards discovered) gone around the ditch. As it was, around they came on the run. I was nearly knocked off my horse, running full against one of them.[37]

Leading the charge, General Wilson "was sent sprawling to the ground when his favorite horse was wounded. He quickly remounted his stricken mount and ordered a dismounted assault by several regiments."[38] "For a moment there was a horrible confusion," recalls Burns:

> The 3rd Ohio, which was following on a jump, was nearly run over. Then Gen. Wilson ordered the 3rd Ohio and 4th Mich. (which had just come up) to dismount and storm the fort on foot. This was done as quickly as possible. I went in with them again, though this time I kept my horse. We approached the fort and made a rush over the ditch and embankments, but the rebels had vamoosed, excepting a few stragglers, leaving their artillery in our hands.[39]

The battle now moved into the town of Selma. Burns, with "two or three others who happened to be mounted, rode into the city firing at and capturing a few rebels who had not taken their departure speedily enough":

We then went to the other side of the town, which was already in possession of that portion of our men who had turned to the left, and Gen. Upton's division. There Hell had broken loose.

The darkies were standing in the streets with pitchers and pails of whiskey, which they were distributing to the men. (At this time it was just about dark). Our men, half drunk, were breaking open stores, plundering, robbing, firing buildings, and conducting themselves like *devils*. They had made a glorious fight of it, and thought themselves entitled to a full serving. We had captured 2,300 prisoners, 26 pieces of artillery in the works, and about 70 in the arsenal. Forrest himself, escaped with about 200 men, and the rest of his command was scattered all over the country. He told one of our surgeons afterwards, that he never had been *so whipped*.[40]

Selma was in chaos:

... the militia had thrown away all their arms, and were swiftly seeking their horses and divesting themselves while they fled of all that would betray their late connection to the defense of Selma. ... [T]he streets were choked with horses, soldiers and citizens hurrying wildly to and fro. Clouds of dust rose and it was difficult to distinguish friend from foe. From the houses came the wails and lamentations of terrified women and children, about to be left to the tender mercies of a storming enemy.[41]

Sergeant Larson writes of what he saw at Selma after the fighting was over late that afternoon:

... [As] we rode along we were delighted to see the Star Spangled Banner ornamenting the enemy's earthworks in different places along the whole line, but very sorry to see our loss in the affair. In many places, especially in front of the palisades, the dead and wounded lay so close together that a person could step from one to the other. Many of our old friends of the Saber Brigade, the 7th Pennsylvania and 4th Michigan Cavalry laid down their lives in front of those breastworks. Such is war.[42]

... The prisoners were confined in a large stockade, which the Confederates had kindly built for the reception and accommodation of the boys in blue, whom they intended to catch by the hundreds as soon as they made their appearance, but when the grays were marched through the gate in their place some of them remarked: 'By thunder, caught in our own trap.'[43]

... From what was told us afterwards, it had not been expected by the Confederate commanders such as Forrest and Chalmers, that the Yankee cavalry could break through their palisades and other obstructions and rush over their breastworks in such a remarkably short time or even that they would be able to do it at all. ... Hence there had been no preparations made by the citizens and non-combatants to move their families across the Alabama River to a place of safety, but the capture of the first line so quickly by the boys in blue made the situation clear to them and created a terrible rush of people and baggage over the only bridge crossing the river.[44]

... I encountered a small squad of our men who were making very free with a wholesale liquor store, and who urgently invited me to join them. No soldier needs a second invitation of that nature at the end of a campaign such as we had just completed.[45]

Forrest biographer Brian Wills concludes: "By the end of the day, Wilson securely held the industrial center and some 2,700 Confederate prisoners, at a cost of 46 killed, 300 wounded, and 13 missing":

As night fell Forrest and his companions made their way around the eastern side of the city. They cut their way through a force of Union troopers who were attempting to block their escape. In this fighting, Forrest killed the last Federal soldier attributed to him–the thirteenth man he killed in personal combat during the war. As the beaten Southerners continued their escape from Selma, they captured a picket from the

Fourth United States Cavalry. Learning that other Federal troopers occupied a nearby house, the Confederates decided to strike a final blow at Wilson's cavalry. But the men refused to attack until Forrest agreed to stay with horse holders, where he would not put his life at risk in the night fighting. Atypically the tired general complied.[46]

General Wilson, upon meeting with Forrest a week later after the surrender, noted that the general "carried his left arm in a sling and moved with cautious deliberation."[47]

It appears that Forrest did not personally participate in what followed.

The Massacre at Goodwin's Farm

Lieutenant Elbridge Roys and his scouting party would suffer the last full measure of vengeance of a defeated Southern cavalry. Sergeant Larson writes: "On the evening of the first day of April the column with which General Wilson had been marching, and of course also the 4th US Cavalry, camped some 15 miles from Selma":

> The general had from the beginning of the campaign established an independent scouting party of 25 men, mostly of the 4th US Cavalry under Lieutenant Noyes [sic: Elbridge Roys] of my company. This scout was to roam about at pleasure and watch the enemy's movements and report to the general when there was anything of importance going on. The lieutenant and party came to camp that night and made some report and then left immediately after. I mention this, not because it had anything actually to do with us, to my knowledge, but it was the last time that we saw that lieutenant and his men alive, except one of my company, who escaped and joined the company some three or four days after.[48]

Forrest biographer Robert Selph Henry offers this account of the final fight between Forrest's cavalry and the 4th Regulars after escaping from Selma the evening of April 2:

> . . . as [Forrest] and the escort picked their way around the town through unfamiliar country byways illuminated by the glare on the sky from the buildings burning in Selma, Forrest retained the aggressive spirit. Surprising and capturing a picket of the Fourth United States Cavalry [Private Henry J. Preas, Co. A], he learned that a larger body was at the near-by home of Mr. Goodwin. Forrest decided to surround and capture them . . . The attack was led by Lieutenant George Cowan, who had succeeded to the command of the escort . . .

Private Preas was summarily executed by Forrest's men.[49]

As indicated, the wounded and exhausted Forrest himself did not participate in this attack, as "his men refused to make the attack unless he would stay with the horse holders a quarter of a mile in the rear, which he did." Apparently, with his recent wounds and with the end near, his men were trying to protect him. Henry continues:

> The affair that follows appears in Federal accounts as an unprovoked attack upon men asleep, who were killed and wounded in spite of 'their cries for surrender.' One account, indeed, says that 'Forrest fell upon the party with the ferocity of a wild Indian and killed every man of it.' Cowan, who himself was wounded in the fight, and the other Confederate officers involved, insist that the first shot was fired by Lieutenant Royce's [sic] Union detachment which resisted with great courage and almost with success until a squad detached to charge them in the rear came into action, and that 'not a single man was killed after he surrendered.' Both sides were hard and veteran fighters and there was every circumstance that would lead to a bitter battle in the dark, but it is unlikely that there was such a thing as a planned massacre. If there was, the plans were not carried out, for the Confederates took a number of prisoners.[50]

Published in 1944, Henry repeats the standard Southern version that prevailed until Brian Wills' 1992 biography of Forrest, in which he writes:

> When the Confederates burst upon their sleeping opponents, the startled Federals barely had time to awaken and defend

themselves. Although only one Southerner suffered a wound, the Union detachment lost thirty-five men killed and wounded and five captured.[51]

Other than the battle at Okolona, Mississippi, for which casualty figures are not available, this represents the single greatest loss of men of the 4th US Cavalry in the war. It seems highly unlikely that these thirty-five "veteran fighters" had any opportunity to "resist with great courage," having been surrounded while sleeping. While it may not have been planned, this was a massacre at the hands of Forrest's rebels. "Such incidents as this were far too frequent with Forrest," writes General Wilson:

> He appears to have had a ruthless temper which impelled him upon every occasion where he had a clear advantage to push his success to a bloody end, and yet he always seemed not only to resent but to have a plausible excuse for the cruel excesses which were charged against him.[52]

As implied by Brigadier General Minty and confirmed by cavalry historian David Evans almost 130 years later, the events in the Western Theater of war were long overshadowed by the events in the east. What happened at Goodwin's farm was never addressed and almost immediately forgotten with the end of the war. However, there was one eyewitness report that may not have become known until Sergeant Larson's regimental history was published in 1935, although the following small notice of the incident was published in the April 27, 1865, Nashville *Daily Union* under the heading "Killing of Lieutenant Royce and Squad of Men":

> On the morning of the 3rd inst. Lieutenant Royce [sic], of the Fourth Regular Cavalry, with a squad of about twenty men dressed in butternut clothes, passed out to reconnoiter the country and ascertain the direction of the enemy's retreat. They suddenly found themselves surrounded by about four hundred rebels, surrendered, and were all shot by the rebels, save one, who fortunately escaped.

According to Sergeant Larson:

> The next afternoon [April 3rd], Julius Davenport, a member of Company H, 4th US Cavalry, and one of the men of Lieutenant Roys scouts, came into camp and reported that Roys and his whole party had been killed on the night before while in camp at a plantation about 20 miles below Selma, near the Alabama River and he, Davenport, was the only one who escaped.
> It appears from Davenport's statement that Lieutenant Roys had gone into camp at this plantation, making his headquarters at the dwelling house, and the men had taken possession of the barn. Lieutenant Roys was never very careful, and on this occasion it appeared he went into camp without putting out a picket or even a guard around the place. The consequences were that the enemy, exasperated over their defeat at Selma and on their retreat from the town found this small camp of Union soldiers unguarded and easily surrounded the houses—everybody being asleep—and demanded a surrender. Of course, the small party, being taken by surprise, was powerless to do anything and complied with the enemy's demand.
> Then followed a repetition of the "Fort Pillow" act and scene, but entirely without the cause or reason the Rebs then claimed as an excuse for their barbarous and murderous conduct against prisoners of war; this party consisted entirely of white men. After surrendering, they were ordered to step out in the yard and were shot down at once. Davenport, although a very large man—the biggest and heaviest in the party—managed to escape by dropping on the ground in some high weeds and in the excitement the Rebs apparently thought he was killed. He crawled through the weeds to a fence and climbed over into a field, then ran across the field into the woods and started for Selma on foot. The lieutenant was killed in the house.
> . . . This report greatly exasperated Wilson's men, especially the 4th US Cavalry, as the Lieutenant and most of the men were of that regiment. The party that was sent down the next day to bury our commander and comrades, after performing that sad service, ordered the people to leave at once and then burned everything on the place,

houses with their contents, fodder, haystacks and fences. Everything that would burn was given to the flames so that the owner of the place, who was suspected to have had a hand in the murders, suffered a great loss by his act.[53]

"The fighting was over, the town was won, but the price was terrible," writes Minty's biographer. ". . . [M]any brave men, who had ridden behind their Colonel for nearly three years, lay motionless on the marshy ground, their blood staining the soil of Alabama."[54] Just one week later, Lee surrendered and the war was over.

Writing one of his final articles on the Civil War thirty years later, Brigadier General Robert H. W. Minty states that he considered Major General James H. Wilson "to have been the most accomplished cavalry officer in either army . . ."[55] As to the attack on Selma, it was the "grandest and most successful cavalry expedition ever told in history":[56]

> . . . and if our campaign had not been overshadowed by the surrender of Lee's and Johnston's armies and the termination of the great struggle, the country would have rung with the achievements of Wilson's Cavalry Corps of the Military Division of the Mississippi and the fact would have generally been recognized that cavalry, when properly handled and led, can do anything that man can do.[57]

In this same article, Minty recalled the bravery and distinguished service of the men of the 4th United States Cavalry who served under his command, writing: "I cannot remember how often it was my pleasing duty to make honorable mention of Lieutenants Davis, Roys and Rendlebock."[58]

Cavalry historian Stephen Z. Starr writes that it is his "conviction (as it was General Wilson's)":

> that this campaign, its planning, organization, tactics and operations, from the departure of the corps from the Tennessee River on March 22 to the capture of Selma eleven days later, are a *model of their kind* and show the officers and men of the Union cavalry in the Civil War *at the height of their powers and effectiveness* [emphasis author]. They show, too, the Union Cavalry in the West reaching, as did their colleagues in the East under Sheridan at nearly the same moment, the culmination of a grim, costly four-year apprenticeship, in the course of which they had to learn a trade for which there were practically no native precedents, and what precedents were imported from abroad were largely misleading.[59]

As recorded in the Official History of the Fourth Regiment United States Cavalry:

> *With its victory at the Battle of Selma, the Fourth Cavalry Regiment became the only Regiment, during the war between the states, to defeat superior cavalry, large masses of artillery, and entrenched infantry.*[60]

III. Up in Smoke

Wilson's cavalry remained at Selma through April 10, 1865, "resting his command and completing the destruction of the immense workshops, arsenals, and foundries . . ."[1] As described by Sergeant Larson:

> The next day began the destruction of the immense supply of military stores collected at Selma. The torch was applied to everything that in any way could be of use to the Confederate army. Large warehouses filled with provisions of all kinds, buildings 150 feet long and 20 feet high filled with corn and oats in white cotton sacks; arsenals, rolling mills, foundries with all their contents were given to the flames. In burning the arsenal, which contained a great supply of fixed ammunition such as loaded shells, the town

and, especially our camp, became nearly untenable. Shells and pieces of shells were flying in the air over us all the time. The thundering explosion of these combustibles made a sound as if a big battle were going on.

The railroad property, depot buildings, cars and locomotives were all served the same way. Standing in several places on the tracks at the depot were long trains, loaded with war materials which had been prevented from going out on account of the burning of a bridge by a brigade of Long's division, which made a raid on the railroad during the night before we arrived at Selma. These trains all had their locomotives attached and ready to go.

Some of our men who understood engineering got up steam on one train after another, then set the woodpile in the tender on fire and when it had a good start, opened the throttle and let her fly at full speed. The force of the wind created by the fast running train carried the fire to the cars and soon the whole train was on fire and then followed terrific explosions, one after another as long as there was anything left of the powder and ammunition. The trains, if the fire on one did not take effect, were nevertheless doomed to destruction by crashing into the wreck of others lying on the track, or if the bridge was reached, by jumping into the river.

The work of the destruction continued for several days and during that time we rested in camp looking on and listening to the roar of flames and explosion of powder and shells. The town and the whole valley were enveloped in a heavy cloud of smoke night and day and the air was almost suffocating. While this was going on the 4th US Cavalry had sent out parties of men to scout the country for horses to take the place of those that were killed and wounded.[2]

A week after capturing Selma, Wilson's cavalry marched towards Montgomery through country "Yankees had never been in before."[3] The distance—about fifty miles due east—was difficult "over very bad roads" that they had to "corduroy in some places for a distance of 200 to 300 yards." As many as 300 to 500 men were required to carry rails to build the roads, on one occasion finding the planks by "pulling a barn to pieces."[4] The passage of "thousands of horses and numberless wagons" made road conditions even worse for those regiments in the rear.[5] Wilson's command passed "through the planting villages of Benton, Churchill, and Lowndesborough" with little opposition.[6] Major Burns describes the countryside as "some of the most beautiful and horrible country I ever saw. For miles the roads would be lined on both sides with hedges of roses, and then we would plunge into impassible swamps."[7] Divisions in the rear were ordered to "destroy all bridges in their wake." One of the reasons for this was to stop the "swarms of slaves and refugees" following the Union soldiers.[8]

Montgomery, Alabama

On April 12, Wilson's cavalry reached Montgomery, "and they captured the capitol of Alabama without firing a shot."[9] The 4th Cavalry was sent in advance as provost guard, and the Union Army entered Montgomery "with all the decorum and ceremony possible to a fighting force in the heart of a hostile country." General Wilson writes:

> With perfect order in column of platoons, every man in his place, division and brigade flags unfurled, guidons flying, sabers and spurs jingling, bands playing patriotic airs, and the bugles now and then sounding the calls, the war-begrimed Union troopers, batteries, ambulances, and wagons passed proudly through the city. . . . It was an example of discipline, order, and power lasting nearly all day and constituting a far more impressive spectacle than a bloody battle would have been.[10]

General Wilson was determined that his men understand that "having surrendered without a fight," the city now belonged to the commanding general, "and that every soldier was in honor bound not only to respect his truce, but to show the highest discipline of which he was capable."[11] Aware that "pillaging and robbing the country" was getting out of hand, General Wilson issued Special Field Order No. 20, that henceforth such conduct by his soldiers would be punishable by death. He halted his command about four miles outside of

Montgomery, not allowing any enlisted men to enter the city.[12] The next day, Wilson's cavalry "marched through the town of 20,000 souls . . . without stopping." As Major Burns notes, "We destroyed nothing there."[13] Marching at the rear of the column of Union cavalry were captured Confederate prisoners. The somber citizens of Montgomery waved their handkerchiefs and shouted encouragement to them: "We're not whipped yet . . ." All the while, the advancing Union column was "continually involved in seeking out and destroying any and all railroads, cotton mills, and other industrial assets discovered in the region."[14]

Arriving at Tuskeegee—a town of nearly 4,000—Wilson was met by the mayor and leading citizens, who immediately surrendered, "begging only protection for person and property."

Wilson granted their request and told the "trusty Fourth Cavalry . . . to guard the town and maintain order."[15]

COLUMBUS, GEORGIA

Wilson's cavalry then moved on to Columbus, Georgia. "From then on," writes Larson, "the skirmishing again became constant and daily. The enemy's cavalry hovered on our flanks and opposed our advance, making their stands at all naturally strong positions . . ."[16] On April 17 they reached Columbus, Georgia, on the Chattahoochee River, where the only remaining bridge "had to be taken by storm." Its destruction by rebel forces would have caused a "long and severe fight" that was fortunately avoided.[17] The destruction of war materiel continued. As Minty records:

> While at Columbus, the Federals destroyed huge amounts of confederate war material. In Wilson's report, he listed the destruction of 'the rebel ram *Jackson*, nearly ready for sea, mounting six 7-inch guns,' in addition to 15 locomotives, 250 cars, the railroad and foot bridges, 115,000 bales of cotton, 4 cotton factories, the navy yard, foundry, armory, sword and pistol factories, accouterment shops, 3 paper mills, over 100,000 rounds of artillery ammunition, and 'immense stores of which no account could be taken.'[18]

Major Burns adds: "Columbus was nearly destroyed; factories and mills burned. Upton had had a sharp fight the night before, the effects of which were visible in the streets. Unburied rebels were lying where they fell."[19]

MACON, GEORGIA

The distance from Columbus to Macon, Georgia, is "about 85 miles on a straight line."[20] The men were all aware that "near Macon was the notorious 'Andersonville bull pen' [prison]" where, as Larson writes, "so many thousands of our men had suffered death from starvation and ill treatment . . ."[21] Wilson's Corps met surprisingly light resistance. Arriving at the Ocmulgee River—"some distance below Macon"—they went into camp.[22]

Colonel Minty, commanding Second Division, was in the advance on the approach to Macon. By April 18, they had reached and captured the Double Bridges over the Flint River.[23] "Leaving their camp near Double Bridges, three miles east of Flint River, the division 'marched through Thomaston and camped three miles east of that place the next day." On April 20, the First Brigade was sent forward "to press the rebel defenses near Macon."[24] Minty reports they met a rebel force "estimated at about 400" that was "driven by a series of brilliant charges . . .":

> . . . About three miles from Tobesofkee Creek the advance was met by Brigadier-General [Felix H.] Robertson, of the rebel army, with a flag of truce, bearing a dispatch from General [Howell] Cobb, stating that an armistice had been agreed on between General Sherman and the rebel General Johnston. This document was delivered by General Robertson to Captain [Philander B.] Lewis, of my staff, and his receipt taken there-for.[25]

"As this information came from the enemy's side," writes Larson, "no attention could be paid to it."[26]

Because of his isolation, "over five hundred miles behind Sherman and as many in advance of Thomas," General Wilson and his officers were unaware of the events that had been set in motion for Lee's surrender at Appomattox on April 9.[27] Minty sent the dispatch to General Wilson, but the general remained skeptical:

General Robertson's course led me to believe that he was merely endeavoring to delay my column. He had already succeeded in doing so for nearly an hour, and I feared I would be unable to save the bridge over Rocky Creek.[28]

Major Burns, who was with Minty, recorded his thoughts on the legitimacy of the dispatch: "Col. Minty, suspecting a ruse, *'couldn't see it,'* and ordered the truce men out of the way... Our men had been skirmishing and driving the rebs all day up to the moment of the appearance of the flag and *it did look suspicious*."

Minty directed Colonel [Frank] White "to give the flag of truce five minutes' start, and then to push forward, and if General Robertson and his party did not keep out of the way, to take them prisoners":[29]

> After the expiration of the given time, Colonel White rushed rapidly forward, succeeded in saving the bridge, which the rebels were about to burn, and continuing his pursuit, entered Macon with them. The city and defenses were immediately surrendered by General Cobb.[30]

Wilson received word on April 21 to suspend his operations pending the result of peace negotiations. The war was finally over.

Without Wilson's cavalry raid, which so completely destroyed the ability of the Confederacy to continue waging war, General Lee might not have been forced to surrender when he did, and perhaps more importantly, it convinced those like Nathan Bedford Forrest and other potential guerrilla fighters that *there was nothing left to fight with or for* [emphasis author]. It had taken a long time to acknowledge, but the war in the Western Theater was now at parity with the war in the east, and it took both to finally defeat the Confederacy. Major General James H. Wilson writes in his autobiography:

> ... [T]he campaign from the Tennessee River through Selma, Montgomery, and Columbus may be fairly claimed as the most rapid, far-reaching, and successful cavalry campaign of modern times. The complete destruction of the iron works, foundries, colliers, factories, and boat yards with their supplies and provisions, as well as the principal lines of railroad communications, connecting the armies under Taylor, Beauregard, and Johnston was an irreparable blow to the Confederacy.
> ... [T]he great mass of the enemy's armed force was in our hands as prisoners of war or had deserted their colors and taken to the woods. The means of transporting troops, food, arms, and military munitions having been effectually destroyed, there was nothing left for the Southern leaders east of the Mississippi but to lay down their arms, disband their organizations, and return to the walks of peace.[31]

In his book *Mounted Raids of the Civil War*, Edward Longacre states:

> Wilson's expedition was destined for a place in history as the most tactically successful of the war.... No other mounted invasion force even came close to amassing such a record of success.... Wilson's soldiers not only surmounted heavy opposition from infantry, artillery, and cavalry but also conquered cities and towns defended by almost every conceivable form of protection. By fighting his twenty-three regiments dismounted as often as mounted, making the most of each method's advantages, the young cavalry leader had rewritten the books that set standards for cavalry deployment. In effect, he had led the first and only self-sustained mounted campaign of the Civil War.[32]

Cavalry historian Gregory Urwin writes in his evaluation that Wilson's cavalry corps had created an unprecedented and impressive record:

> In less than a month, he captured five fortified cities, twenty-three enemy banners, 6820 soldiers and 288 fieldpieces. He had 725 killed, wounded and missing,

but he dealt out 1200 casualties among those who opposed him. And then to top everything off, on 10 May 1865, some of Wilson's troopers [Minty's 4th Michigan] captured President Jefferson Davis and snuffed out the last significant hopes of continuing Southern resistance.[33]

Even European military historians recognized the significance of what Wilson had accomplished with his cavalry. Colonel George Dennison, in his *History of Cavalry* (London, 1878), concludes:

This is one of the most remarkable cavalry operations of the war, for, as we have said, it was not a mere raid or dash, but an invading army determined to fight its way through . . . It is certainly one of the most extraordinary affairs in the history of the cavalry service . . .[34]

The Confederacy and the old South were gone. The physical battle was over, but the political and social struggles were just beginning and would last well into the twentieth century.

IV. The Final Days

Your deeds have contributed a noble part to the glorious result . . .
– Major General James H. Wilson[1]

"Macon, with all the Confederate troops in and about it," writes Larson, "(and there were a great many) became ours without firing a shot":

A day or two after this General Wilson communicated with Washington over Confederate wire, and the rumor we had heard became known as a fact.
. . . That tremendous war was over at last. That was good news and it can easily be imagined how it gladdened the hearts of the men who had followed the Star Spangled Banner in victories and defeats, through thick and thin, in rain and mud, through the long and terrible war for the sake of holding together and preserving the union. Peace with victory was the end desired by the boys in blue and it was sweet because it brought with it quietude and rest from battle and strife.
Viewing the matter from the Southern side, the boys in gray might also have a reason to be satisfied that the war was ended . . . The point for which they had fought was largely a question of personal interest, in which the rank and file, the common soldier, of the army had little or no interest. As many of our prisoners had told us, they considered it 'the rich man's war and the poor man's fight.'
And then came the terrible news: While Wilson's tired and worn out men were rejoicing over the happy termination of the war, another telegram brought us the news of the assassination of President Lincoln. That cast a dark shadow over the joy of the men, and of course threw a shroud of sorrow over the entire country. Even in the Southern states people with real knowledge of affairs were deeply distressed over the entirely inexcusable act of the fanatical actor, Booth.[2]

With the end of the war, "Things had taken a sudden . . . change," writes Larson. Union soldiers now found themselves "mingling freely with the men in the gray uniforms with whom a few days before we had fought wherever we met."[3] Newly promoted Major Burns, writing to his brother, commented on the "rather strange sort of life we are leading now. Howell Cobb, and General Wilson hob-nobing. A rebel officer and your brother amicably discussing the late war."[4]

A private in the 4th Michigan later writes: "The conduct of the Cavalry Corps while at Macon redounded to the highest credit of the Union Army." The citizens of Macon "were duly impressed . . . [with] the perfect discipline of the men and their unfailing courtesy. Every man in the ranks was on his good behavior. Ladies could walk about the streets in the most absolute peace and confidence . . ."[5] Sergeant Larson continues:

> We enjoyed rest and quiet and that was very pleasant for a while . . . We had nothing but guard duty and then a half hour stable duty, morning and evening. The rest of the day we spent reading, sleeping, or card playing. We enjoyed a special privilege, however, which is not otherwise permitted in garrisons; we could leave camp mounted or dismounted and return when we felt like it when no duty was neglected by it, but Macon was a dull town and there was not much enjoyment or excitement except such as we made ourselves.[6]

Even peacetime proved hazardous. Horse racing down the main street was one of the pastimes engaged in that unfortunately took the life of 4th US Cavalry soldier Private Richard J. Perciville when he was thrown. Private Daniel Higgins died of knife wounds received while visiting "a house of ill fame." On the more domestic side, 1st Sergeant John Herberich apparently spent his spare time courting his future wife, twenty-three-year-old Zelina Roscinski, from the small German-Jewish community of Macon.[7]

One of the primary tasks now facing the Union occupiers was "the work of hunting up important men of the now defunct Confederacy."[8] One of those captured was the governor of Georgia, Joseph E. Brown. He was arrested on May 9 at Milledgeville and escorted by Lieutenant William Bayard with a guard from the 4th US Cavalry to Atlanta, and then Dalton.[9] On May 10, Jefferson Davis, his family, and some of his cabinet members and aides were captured by members of the 4th Michigan Cavalry. Captain Potter writes of the event to his family on May 14, mostly expressing regret that he was not with those members of his regiment who participated in the capture to "share the honor." On May 19 he writes:

> . . . the great Slaveholder's rebellion is over and its leaders are nearly all in our possession. I have seen and talked with the biggest one among them all–Jeff Davis.

> We all think he will be hung and hope so too. I feel sorry for his wife and children– not so much for her as the children, for she is haughty, scornful and insulting as any woman I ever saw. If she is a lady I failed to discover it. But the children are pretty and innocent as yet and I pity them. I have seen Howell Cobb [former Secretary of Treasury in Buchanan's administration, early secessionist, and Brigadier General, CSA] also an ugly looking old devil–needs hanging.[10]

They were not hanged, but another notorious captive who, at his own request, was "turned over to the 4th United States Cavalry for his personal safety" would be. That was Captain Henry Wirz, commander of the notorious prison camp at Andersonville. As Sergeant Larson recalls:

> He did not trust us either. He feared poisoning and would not eat anything, except what was brought to him by the adjutant's cook. In our adjutant, Major Wirt Davis, he seemed to have full confidence, but any other soldier wearing the blue uniform seemed to appear to him to be as dangerous as a rattlesnake. A heavy conscience undoubtedly smote the keeper of the 'bull pen.' If only half of what was laid at his door was true he certainly had his conscience well loaded.
>
> In appearance he looked like a man well able and suited to carry our the plan of killing as many Yankees as possible while he had them in his power unarmed. Later on he was tried by a military court in Washington, and found guilty of the charges against him and sentenced to hang.[11]

Four of the 1st sergeants of the 4th Regiment were called to the office of the provost marshal in Macon and charged with locating and apprehending the former Confederate secretary of state who, it was believed, was hiding in or near the city. Whoever succeeded in capturing him was to be rewarded with a lieutenant's commission. Larson did arrest a gentleman with striking similarities, but it turned out to be the wrong man, as the former secretary of state had already left Macon.[12]

The end of the war brought an additional burden to the 1st sergeants of the regiment, including Larson and Herberich—"the straightening up of the company books and accounts," which Larson describes as "a trouble I had always feared . . . a difficult task . . . as I was not a scribe or an accountant either":

> Of course, I had the services of a good clerk or matters would have gone badly.
>
> Being on the move constantly through the whole war, no time or opportunity was given for accounts and bookkeeping. A few books and papers were found, principally bills of ordnance and quartermaster stores received, but no accounts of what had been lost in battle or necessarily left behind, stored at some particular place. Capt. [George G.] Huntt had joined the company and was in command, ordered an inspection of all company property to compare property on hand with the requirements of the books.
>
> The result was that in many articles, especially of ordnance, a big deficiency was discovered and in others, a surplus was found. But as surplus articles of one kind could not be used to make up for deficiencies in others, the book account was in a bad condition and Captain Huntt, who had been the captain of Co. H during the whole war, although not with the company, was several hundred dollars in debt to the government.
>
> It was found, though, that all the companies of the 4th US Cavalry were in the same fix. One good thing in favor of the captain was that the War Department was not as strict and as much in a hurry to have accounts settled as before the war, and I, with the assistance of my clerk, managed by exchanging my surplus property with other companies for things in which I was short, to straighten out a good part of it. As the rest was done by degrees, so that the captain did not have to pay a cent for lost property.[13]

During his last months in the Federal Army, Colonel Minty—now commanding Second Division—oversaw the issuance of "over 60,000 paroles to former confederate soldiers . . . who descended upon Macon on their own accord in search of a parole and release . . ."[14]

Toward the end of May, preparations were being made to move the Volunteer armies "to the rear" to begin the process of discharge and dissolution of the units. This would be a difficult and disappointing process for General James Wilson. "They can not be excelled," he wrote in a letter to General Sherman on May 8. "I regard this corps today as the model for modern cavalry in organization, armament, and discipline . . ."[15]

In one of his final reports to the adjutant-general US Army, the general has high praise for his personal escort, the Fourth United States Cavalry:

> I have the honor to recommend and request brevet appointments for the following named officers: First Lieut. Joseph Hedges . . . to be captain and brevet major for conspicuous gallantry during the pursuit of Hood after the battle of Nashville charging the enemy's rear guard on the West Harpath River, leading his regiment, capturing three pieces of artillery. First Lieut. Joseph Rendlebrock [sic], Second Lieut. John G. Webster, Second Lieut. James Callehan, and Second Lieut. William Bayard . . . to be captains and brevet majors for gallantry during the pursuit of Hood . . . and the charge of the regiment against the earth-works at Selma, Ala. First Lieut. William O'Connell, commanding Fourth US Cavalry, for conspicuous gallantry during the charge of his regiment upon the enemy's earth-works at Selma, Ala., to be captain and brevet major. Second Lieut. Wirt Davis . . . to be captain and brevet major for conspicuous gallantry during the charge of his regiment against the earth-works at Selma, Ala., and for good conduct on all occasions. First Lieuts. John Lee, Edwin J. Conway, and Sebastian Gunther, Fourth US Cavalry, to be brevet captains for faithful and intelligent discharge of duty during the pursuit of Hood and throughout the present campaign . . . The officers of the Fourth US Cavalry have been distinguished throughout the war for gallantry and faithful discharge of duty.[16]

To the men of the 4th United States Cavalry who fought the battles from "Stones River, Shelbyville, Chickamauga, Dallas, Atlanta, Lovejoy and every fight in between" to the final battle at Selma, Alabama, General Wilson writes that their deeds "contributed a noble part to the glorious result."[17]

On July 2, 1865, a formal order dissolving the Cavalry Corps, Military Division of the Mississippi was issued by Generals Thomas and Wilson.[18] The Fourth United States Cavalry—now under the command of Captain George Huntt—as Regular Army would remain behind at Macon as "occupation troops" until December, awaiting their reassignment.[19] They would spend the rest of 1865 guarding and assisting in reconstruction.[20] In late November, the regiment received orders to Texas, where ten companies were to be stationed at Fort Sam Houston, San Antonio, and two companies were sent to the Rio Grande.[21] The commander of the occupying forces in Texas was General David S. Stanley. Stanley, who led the "splendid charge" of the United States Cavalry at Wilson's Creek at the beginning of the war, rose to the rank of major general and corps commander in the Army of the Cumberland under Major General William T. Sherman. He would be awarded the Medal of Honor in 1893 for leading a successful assault at a critical moment in the Battle of Franklin on November 30, 1864.[22]

Sergeant Larson describes the activities of the 4th US Cavalry as it prepared to leave the southern theater of the war:

> Preparation was made for us to take the train for New Orleans. Everything not needed on the way was turned in at Macon, including all our horses, except the officers' private horses. Pack mules, with their whole rig, were turned in also and the old army wagon took their place. In fact, everything was turned in except our arms and ammunition and clothing . . . and we boarded the cars and bade good-by to the state in which we had seen so much hard marching and fighting.
>
> We had marched and fought through that state in almost every conceivable direction under Rosecrans, Sherman, Thomas and Wilson.[23]

V. The Casualties

> . . . *Did I fall like a soldier?*
> – The last words of Private Bartholomew Burke, Company H, 4th US Cavalry

According to Frederick Dyer's "Compendium of the War of the Rebellion" (1908):

> The Fourth Regiment United States Cavalry lost during service in the Civil War, 3 officers and 59 enlisted men killed and mortally wounded and one officer and 108 enlisted men by disease, for a total of 171 men.[1]

This report reflects the difficulty in giving a final assessment of the losses suffered by the 4th United States Cavalry. As already reported, the following officers were either killed or mortally wounded in combat: Francis C. Wood, Thomas Healy, Edward E. Fitzgerald, and Elbridge Roys. Three former enlisted men of the 4th US Cavalry who were promoted out of the regiment were killed in combat: 1st Lieutenant Isaac M. Ward, 6th US Cavalry; 1st Lieutenant Charles McMaster, 2nd US Cavalry; and Captain Henry Kerner, 4th Tennessee Cavalry. Second Lieutenant Thomas W. Simson died of his wounds eighteen months after the Battle of Franklin. Former 1st Sergeant, Company K—now 2nd Lieutenant—Andrew Stoll, 6th US Cavalry, was captured and died as a prisoner of war. Two officers originally with the 4th Cavalry died of illness: Lieutenant Albert V. Colburn, the recruiting officer in St. Louis in 1860—subsequently promoted to lieutenant colonel, staff, United States Army—died in June 1863. First Lieutenant Tillinghast L'Hommedieu died in October 1863.[2]

There were additional casualties among the original officers of the 4th US Cavalry serving with the United States Volunteers: the Colonel of the 4th Cavalry John Sedgwick (Major General, USV) was the final corps commander in the Army of the Potomac to be killed in action at Spotsylvania. Captain George D. Bayard—an academy graduate—became a brigadier general in the volunteers and was mortally wounded at the Battle of Fredericksburg.[3]

There were approximately 234 deaths reported for the 4th United States Cavalry.[4] Ascertaining exact losses among enlisted men is difficult because of inaccurate or missing records. When General James Wilson was ordered to report to General Sherman in Atlanta to reorganize and command his cavalry division, he was "greatly hampered . . . by a lack of reliable records." "*No one*," writes Wilson, "*pretended to know how many men were actually with the colors* [emphasis author] . . ."[5]

Sixty-eight troopers were killed or mortally wounded in battle; eight others were reported missing and presumed dead. Six were reported captured, with status unknown and presumed dead. Approximately thirty men were killed at Goodwin's Farm.[6] This gives a total of approximately 112 deaths in combat. No less than twenty-nine troopers from the 4th US Cavalry were captured and died as prisoners of war, all but two at Andersonville. Four survived their imprisonment: Privates Valentine Market, Company C; Henry F. McClure, Company B; and Ambrose Henshaw, Company L. Private Charles E. Smith, Company K, gave testimony at the trial of prison commandant Captain Henry Wirz.[7]

Three deaths of "unknown cause" were reported. There were nine "accidental" deaths and seven non-battle related deaths: four by drowning and three "murdered by citizens." Ninety-one troopers died of disease or illness.[8] One trooper died of a "skull fracture" and one was stabbed to death in a house of prostitution. This gives a total of 251 deaths.

Ninety-eight troopers were discharged due to disability from injuries or illness.[9] Two of those were reported "insane" and one wounded trooper committed suicide. This brings the total casualty figure to 349. Adding the four officers who were killed in action or mortally wounded while with the 4th US Cavalry and one who died of illness, this brings the total casualty figure of officers and men to 354. Based on the maximum figure of approximately 1,300 officers and men in the Regiment during the Civil War, this would represent a minimum casualty rate of twenty-seven percent.

Toil and risk are the price of glory, but it is a lovely thing to live with courage and die leaving an everlasting fame.
 – Alexander the Great

Epilogue

At the end of the Civil War, survivors of the Union Volunteer regiments returned home to family and friends to resume their lives and civilian occupations. They formed associations, held reunions, and recorded their wartime experiences. Monuments were erected and names were etched into stone or bronze.

The professional soldiers of the 4th United States Cavalry for whom the military was home continued their service. This time it was for the western expansion of the nation they had helped preserve. Their homecoming was the next barrack or command, often in desolate isolation. They would receive little recognition from family, community, or a grateful nation. Their monuments, if they were lucky, were headstones in isolated fort cemeteries. It would seem that they and most of their accomplishments disappeared in the dust of the Great Plains and vast expanse of the West.

In reality, the influence of the officers and men of the 4th Regiment United States Cavalry continued for decades. Eight officers—Sturgis, Emory, Wood, Oaks, Otis, Carr, Huntt, and Davis—commanded cavalry regiments in the decades after the war. Frank Wheaton would command the 2nd Infantry Regiment, retiring as a major general. Two—John Wilcox and former Sergeant Albert Coats—retired with the rank of lieutenant colonel, US Cavalry. Four others—McIntyre, Thompson, Crittenden, and McLaughlin—were promoted to major of their cavalry regiments. These veteran officers were more than ably assisted by the number of civilian commissioned officers who remained in the regiment after the war. A core of senior non-commissioned officers, such as 1st Sergeants Larson and Herberich, provided the necessary basic training and military discipline at the company level in the most difficult and hostile of circumstances to help rebuild the depleted cavalry regiments on the Western frontier. The thin ranks of the cavalry were gradually filled with new recruits, as well as a number of former members of the now disbanded Voluntary cavalry regiments.[1] Among the veterans joining the regiment were former Confederates:

> many of them former officers who, for many years were not permitted to hold commissions but joined the Cavalry as sergeants and corporals. They were men who had been squadron commanders but who found no hope for a living in a prostrate South and who could not endure the carpetbagger regime. There were also former Union officers of the Civil War among the enlisted ranks.[2]

The lands west of the Mississippi were utterly lawless after five years of Civil War and lack of Indian supervision. A strong military presence was required to restore order, establish forts and outposts, and protect the trails that in the years following the war would allow the great westward expansion and future development of the United States.

During the Civil War, the 4th United States Cavalry reached the zenith of professionalism and skills for a cavalry regiment. The men fought equally well mounted or dismounted. They used their primary weapon, the saber, as no other cavalry regiment had before or since. Combined with the Spencer carbine, they became an almost undefeatable force.

Unfortunately, these skills did not transfer successfully in the following decades to the new circumstances of the Indian engagements. While advances in weaponry finally rendered the mounted saber regiments useless, the tactics and maneuvers developed by the cavalry during the Civil War carried over into the mechanized cavalry of future wars of the twentieth century, and history's romance with the cavalryman lives on. "Well done, gentlemen, well done."

1st Sergeant John M. Herberich married Selina Roscinski in San Antonio, Texas, on March 3, 1866. They would eventually settle in San Antonio and raise four children.

Herberich took his final discharge at Fort Concho, Texas, on January 1, 1872. The captain of his company, brevet Brigadier General Napoleon B. McLaughlin—a highly decorated veteran—wrote the following on his discharge paper regarding his service:

> Excellent . . . is sober and trustworthy in every way–one of the best noncommissioned officers in the Army.

On October 15, 1872, Herberich was admitted to be a citizen of the United States of America in the State of Texas, District Court of Bexar County, San Antonio, Texas.

He died January 2, 1904, at age 63, and is buried in the San Antonio National Cemetery.

Appendix
A. Staff Officers of the Fourth Regiment United States Cavalry

March 3, 1855 to June 1, 1865

COLONELS	DATES	CIVIL WAR RANK
†Edwin Voss Sumner	3 Mar 55 to 16 Mar 61	Major General, USA
Robert E. Lee	16 Mar to 25 Apr 61	General, CSA
†John Sedgwick	25 Apr 61 to 9 May 64	Major General, USV
Lawrence P. Graham	9 May 64 to 15 Dec 70	Brigadier General, USV

LIEUTENANT COLONELS	DATES	CIVIL WAR RANK
Joseph E. Johnston	3 Mar 55 to 28 Jun 60	General, CSA
William J. Hardee	28 Jun 60 to 31 Jan 61	Lieutenant General, CSA
William H. Emory	31 Jan to 9 May 61	Major General, USV
Thomas J. Wood	9 May to 12 Nov 61	Major General, USV
James Oaks	12 Nov 61 to 31 Jul 66	Lieutenant Colonel, 4th Cavalry

MAJORS	DATES	CIVIL WAR RANK
John Sedgwick	8 Mar 55 to 16 Mar 61	Major General, USV
William H. Emory	26 May 55 to 31 Jan 61	Major General, USV
Delos B. Sacket	31 Jan to 3 May 61	Colonel, Inspector General, USA
Thomas J. Wood	16 Mar to 9 May 61	Brigadier General, USA
Samuel D. Sturgis	3 May 61 to 27 Oct 63	Brigadier General, USV
George Stoneman	9 May 61 to 30 Mar 64	Major General, USV
Richard W. Johnson	17 Jul 62 to 12 Oct 67	Brigadier General, USV

ADJUTANTS[1]	DATES	CIVIL WAR RANK
Robert Ransom	25 May 55 to 7 Feb 57	Major General, CSA
†Albert V. Colburn	Feb 57 to 24 May 61	Lieutenant Colonel, Additional Aide-de-Camp, USA
*George G. Huntt	14 Dec 61 to 17 Jul 62	Captain, 4th US Cavalry
*Edward D. Baker	30 Nov 62 to 1 Apr 63	Captain, Assistant Quartermaster, U.S. Army
Thomas W. Sullivan	13 Aug 63 to 6 Feb 65	1st Lieutenant, 4th US Cavalry
Wirt Davis	1 Mar 55 to 19 Jun 68	2nd Lieutenant, 4th US Cavalry

QUARTERMASTERS		
†J. E. B. Stuart	5 Jul 55 to 1 Jun 57	Major General, CSA
James B. McIntyre	15 Apr 58 to 3 May 61	Captain, 4th US Cavalry
Walter M. Wilson	5 Mar to 30 Nov 62	Captain, 4th US Cavalry
John Lee	30 Nov 62 to 11 Aug 66	1st Lieutenant, 4th US Cavalry

COMMISARIES		
†T. L'Hommedieu	8 Jan 30 to 31 Dec 63	1st Lieutenant, 4th US Cavalry
Sebastian Guenther	31 Dec 63 to 30 Nov 67	1st Lieutenant, 4th US Cavalry

† Sumner died March 31, 1863, at age 66. Sedgwick and Stuart were killed in combat, while Colburn and L'Hommedieu died of illness.
[Transferred to another cavalry regiment]
* On detached service, not with the regiment during the war.
1 Assistant to commanding officer

B. "Twenty-two Future Generals"

The following list of officers served with the Fourth Regiment United States Cavalry prior to the outbreak of the Civil War.

Edwin V Sumner	Major General USV, commanding corps
Joseph E. Johnston	General, C.S.A
William H. Emory	Major General, USV, commanding corps
John Sedgwick	Major General, USV, commanding corps

CAPTAINS:

George B. McClellan	Major General, commanding U.S. Army and Army of the Potomac
Thomas J. Wood	Major General, USV
Samuel D. Sturgis	Brigadier General, USV
William S. Walker	Brigadier General, CSA
George T. Anderson	Brigadier General, CSA
Robert S. Garnett	Brigadier General, CSA

FIRST LIEUTENANTS:

William N. R. Beal	Brigadier General, CSA
George H. Stuart	Brigadier General, CSA
James McIntosh	Brigadier General, CSA
Robert Ransom, Jr.	Major General, CSA
Eugene A. Carr*	Brigadier General, USV
Alfred Iverson	Brigadier General, CSA
Frank Wheaton	Brigadier General, USV
Eli Long	Brigadier General, USV

SECOND LIEUTENANTS:

David S. Stanley*	Major General, USV, Brigadier General, USA
James E. B. Stuart	Major General, CSA
Francis L. Vinton	Brigadier General, USV
George D. Bayard	Brigadier General, USV
Lindsey L. Lomax	Major General, CSA

*Medal of Honor. Also awarded to Joseph B. Hedges and Eugene Beaumont, 4th United States Cavalry.

1. Taken from Theophilus Rodenbough's *Army of the United States* 1789-1896.
   Brigadier General Eli Long was not on Rodenbough's original list.

C. The Officers of the 4th United States Cavalry During the Civil War

Because of the unusual circumstances of the 4th United States Cavalry, it was difficult to create a roster of the officers who were with the regiment prior to the war and remained with the regiment for a significant period of time during the war. The number of resignations, rapid promotions, and detached duty assignments, as well as the arrival of new civilian appointments and the field commissions of enlisted members of the regiment, all created a continual turnover of officers. Disregarding all of the officers who resigned their commissions to join the Confederacy, there were twenty-one officers attached to the 4th Cavalry at the beginning of the war. Of those, only three—Captains Charles Bowman, James McIntyre, and John Thompson—remained with the regiment. Captain Elmer Otis was promoted to major 1st Cavalry in May 1864. James Oaks was appointed lieutenant colonel in November 1861, and became the highest ranking officer to lead companies of the regiment in combat.

Civilian Appointments to the Fourth Regiment United States Cavalry

Between February and May 1861, there were thirteen civilian appointments of 2nd Lieutenants to the 4th Cavalry; six were subsequently on detached service. Seven (Hedges, Kelly, Manck, McCormick, Webb, Wilson, and Wilcox) remained with the regiment during the war. Three were promoted to 1st lieutenant, four to captain.

Of the three 1st Lieutenants, all were promoted to Captain by July 1866. Three remained in the cavalry after the war: Webb retired in May 1873; Manck retired as Major, 9th Cavalry, in 1879; and Walter M. Wilcox, after serving his country for thirty-one years, retired as Lieutenant Colonel, 3rd Cavalry, in 1892.

Enlisted Men With Field Promotions to Second Lieutenant

Thirty-nine enlisted men within the regiment were promoted to Second Lieutenant. Seventeen served with the regiment prior to the war and remained with the regiment through May 1865; the remaining transferred to regular or volunteer regiments. Four enlisted men were promoted into the 4th Cavalry from other regiments; two of those never reported for duty. Three—1st Lieutenant Elbridge Roys and 2nd Lieutenants Thomas Simson and Francis Wood—were mortally wounded or killed in combat. Seven resigned their commissions between 1868 and 1871. Three—Captains Joseph Rendlebock, William O'Connell, and John Lee—retired in 1879. Captain Sebastian Gunther retired in 1884, and Albert B. Kauffman retired as a major in the 4th Cavalry in 1892. After forty years of service to his county, Wirt Davis retired as the colonel of the 3rd Cavalry in 1901.

D. Enlisted Field Commissions by Date of Commission

Name	4th Cav. Enlistment	Age	Highest Rank	Co.	Date of Commission	Highest Rank	Mustered out † date died
Powell, James	17 Nov 56	—	1st Sgt.	I	14 May 61	Capt., 18th U.S. Infantry	— Jan 68*
Egan, James	21 Jun 58	—	1st Sgt.	E	10 Aug 61	Capt., 2nd US Cavalry	09 May 79
Clifford, James A.	12 Aug 58	31	Pvt.	D	—Aug 61	1st Lt. 3rd US Cavalry	09 Jun 68•
Coats, Albert	08 Dec 56	20	Sgt.	C2	6 Oct 61	Lt. Col. 6th US Cavalry	25 Jan 66
Ward, Isaac M.	26 Jan 57	23	1st Sgt.	A	23 Oct 61	1st Lt., 6th US Cavalry	09 Jun 63†
O'Connell, William	24 Nov 54	24	1st Sgt.	B	24 Oct 61	Capt., 4th US Cavalry	02 Apr 79
Gordon, Henry	26 Jul 60	31	1st Sgt.	D	24 Oct 61	2nd Lt. Co. H. 4th U.S.	02 Dec 62

Name	4th Cav. Enlistment	Age	Highest Rank	Co.	Date of Commission	Highest Rank	Mustered out † date died
Stoll, Andrew	01 May 56	—	1st Sgt.	K	05 Nov 61	2nd Lt. 6th US Cavalry	23 Sep 64†
Sullivan, Thomas W.	10 Mar 57	—	Sgt.	C	24 Mar 62	1st Lt., 4th US Cavalry	06 Feb 65
Burnham, Frank	23 Nov 59	24	Sgt. Maj.	F/S	01 May 62	1st Lt., 2nd US Cavalry	25 Nov 63
Roys, Elbridge	02 Dec 56	21	Sgt.	B	17 Jul 62	1st Lt., Co. M. 4th U.S.	02 Apr 65†
Wyatt, James	18 May 60	33	Pvt.	I	22 Jul 62	[Navy-status unknown]	
Rendlebock, Joseph	16 Aug 56	33	1st Sgt.	G	29 Nov 62	Capt., Co. G, 4th U.S.	23 Jul 79
McCafferty, Neil J.	26 Apr 58	21	1st Sgt.	A	19 Feb 63	Capt., 4th US Cavalry	10 Jun 70†
Fitzgerald, Edward	09 Jan 58	21	1st Sgt.	E	19 Feb 63	1st Lt., 4th US Cavalry	17 Dec 64†
Webster, John G.	31 Aug 58	—	Sgt. Maj.	I	19 Feb 63	1st Lt., Co. F, 4th U.S.	08 Mar 66†
Conway, Edwin J.	28 Nov 59	—	Pvt.	B	19 Feb 63	Capt., 4th US Cavalry	31 Dec 70
Fletcher, Bird	27 Dec 59	—	Cpl.	I	19 Feb 63	Capt., Co. H, 4th U.S.	19 Jun 68*
Conway, Edward J.	28 Nov 59	—	Pvt.	B	19 Feb 63	Captain, 4th US Cavalry	— Dec 70
Simson, Thomas W.	19 Oct 58	—	Cpl.	I	27 Feb 63	2nd Lt., 6th US Cavalry	10 Apr 63**
Davis, Wirt	12 May 60	21	1st Sgt.	K	22 Apr 63	Major, 5th US Cavalry	26 Apr 01
Wood, Francis C.	30 May 60	21	Pvt.	K	18 May 63	2nd Lt., Co. L, 4th U.S.	23 May 63†
Kerner, Henry	05 Nov 58	22	Sgt.	A/D	25 Jun 63	Capt., 4th Tenn. Cavalry	07 Sep 64†
Humphrey, Clark M.	11 Apr 61	29	Pvt.	C	23 Jul 63	2nd Lt., 1st Neb. Cavalry	(unknown)
Gunther, Sebastian	27 Aug 55	23	Sgt.	B/F/S	10 Aug 63	Capt., 4th U.S.	26 Nov 84
McMaster, Charles	22 Nov 58	21	1st Sgt.	H/I	10 Aug 63	1st Lt., 2nd US Cavalry	25 Sep 64†
Callehan, James	25 Jul 60	28	1st Sgt.	D	10 Aug 63	1st Lt., 4th U.S.	25 Mar 70†
Kauffman, Albert B.	12 Dec 60	18	Sgt.	I	14 Sep 63	Major, 4th U.S.	01 Jan 92
Keirwan, John S.	23 Sep 58	21	Sgt.	K	21 Oct 63	Lt. Col., USV	07 Oct 65
Bayard, William	02 Feb 63	22	Cpl.	G	31 Oct 63	Capt. 9th US Cavalry	01 Jan 71
Haynes, John	21 Dec 59	23	Pvt.	I	— Nov 63	Capt., 9th Tenn. Cavalry	03 Jun 65
Boland, Sater	21 Jun 60	—	1st Sgt.	K	24 Nov 63	Major, 12th Tenn. Cav.	13 Dec 64†
Donnoghue, Dennis	10 Jul 60	19	Pvt.	C	24 Nov 63	2nd Lt., U.S. Volunteers	(unknown)
Harris, Moses	19 Mar 57	18	Sgt.	G	18 May 64	Capt., 1st US Cavalry	07 Mar 93
Bendire, Charles	08 Jun 60	26	Cpl.	D	18 May 64	Capt., 1st US Cavalry	24 Apr 86
Hough, Romaine	23 Jun 60	22	Cpl.	B	15 Jul 64	1st Lt., 138 U.S. Colored Inf.	06 Jan 66
Cavendish, Frederick A.	01 May 55	21	Sgt.	H	19 Nov 64	1st Lt., 12th Tenn. Cavalry	07 Oct 65
Waltz, Charles A.	21 Jun 61	23	Pvt.	Band	01 Dec 64	2nd Lt.,7th Penn. Cavalry	23 Aug 65
Johnson Garrett V.	17 Dec 62	—	Sgt.	B	04 Jun 65	1st Lt., 138 U.S. Colored Inf.	06 Jan 66
Rush, Andrew	02 Dec 62	—	Sgt.	B	30 Jun 65	1st Lt., 138 U.S. Colored Inf.	06 Jan 66

Four former enlisted men were transferred into the 4th Cavalry after their appointments to 2nd lieutenant. Thomas Healy had twelve years prior service in the army and was a sergeant in the 2nd Cavlary at the time of his appointment on July 17, 1862. He was mortally wounded in combat and died on April 23, 1863. John Lee had prior enlisted service from August 1850 and was sergeant major, Co. K, 6th US Cavalry when appointed 2nd lieutenant, 4th Cavalry, on July 17, 1862. He would remain with the regiment until 1884. Two others—Anson O. Doolittle and Douglas A. Murray—were assigned to the 4th Cavalry but did not report for duty.

† Died while in service. Killed or mortally wounded in combat: Boland, Fitzgerald, McMaster, Roys, Ward, and Wood. Stoll died while a prisoner of war at Libby Prison.
* Retired due to "incapacity."
** 2nd Lieutenant Simson was severely wounded at Franklin April 10, 1863, while still with the 4th U.S. He transferred to the 6th US Cavalry but was eventually forced to retire and he died of his wounds October 26, 1865.
• James A. Clifford's real name was Clifford Ingram.

E. 4th U.S. Cavalry Officers at Franklin, Tennessee, April 10, 1863

Showing commissioned enlisted men and date of promotion.

Co. A	2nd Lieutenant Neil J. McCafferty	19 Feb 63
Co. C	2nd Lieutenant Bird. L. Fletcher	19 Feb 63
Co. D	2nd Lieutenant Thomas Healy	17 Jul 62
Co. E	2nd Lieutenant Eugene E. Fitzgerald	19 Feb 63
Co. G	1st Lieutenant Joseph Hedges	05 Aug 61
Co. M	1st Lieutenant Elbridge G. Roys	17 Jul 62

Also present:

2nd Lieutenant Joseph Rendlebock	Nov. 29, '62
2nd Lieutenant Thomas W. Simson	Feb. 27, '63

1st Lieutenant William H. Ingerton, 16th U.S. Infantry, was on temporary assignment with the 4th US Cavalry. A drummer boy before enlisting in the infantry in 1850, he would receive several brevet ranks and be promoted to captain, USA, in October 1864. Two months later he was shot by an assassin at Knoxville, TN. Heitman, 563; Henry 2:113.

F. Civil War Roster of the Fourth United States Cavalry

A diligent attempt has been made to find every soldier who rode with the 4th United States Cavalry during the Civil War. Because the original ten companies were disbursed throughout the frontier prior to the war, their continuous independent activities in the field during the early months of the war, and the fact that all twelve companies of the regiment were not united until August 1863, all contributed to the poor quality or lack of adequate hand written records. Enlistment records were more accurate and complete for those men enlisting at cavalry recruiting stations in major cities. Unfortunately, this is not true for those enlisting in the field, particularly at Nashville between November and December 1862. During the refitting of the regiment and the formation of two new companies, L and M, approximately 385 men were enlisted into the regiment, many transferring from volunteer regiments. Some records are simply no longer available. In some cases, the recording of a death was the only indication of service in the regiment. Even then, the names were often misspelled, i.e., Sennegan, Sonigan, Sonnigan, and Jarnagan for the same trooper. Where there were multiple spellings of surnames, the most logical was chosen from the available records. The following codes will serve to provide as much individual information as possible.

† Killed/mortally wounded in action
MIA: Missing, presumed dead
* Died while in service
POW: Prisoner, presumed dead
RA: Regular Army, 5 year enlistment
Dd: Disability discharge
All others three year enlistments
Surname all capitalized: field commission

IC: Trf. to Invalid Corps (est. 1863)
P: Prior military service
Disc.: Discharged (unknown reason)
+: Reenlisted
D: Deserted after minimum
FC = Field commission 12-18+ months service
Company S: Staff

Unless otherwise noted, the 1,187 men listed below served their full three or five year term of enlistment between April 1861 or earlier and May 1865. Highest rank earned is shown.

Name	Age	Birthplace	Rank	Company	Enlisted	Status
A						
*Aaron, John A.	21	Georgia	Pvt.	Co. H	28 May 60	
Abbott, Henry L.			Pvt.	Co. C	02 Dec 62	
Abbott, Julius			Pvt.	Co. K	29 Nov 62	
Abernathy, Robert W.			Cpl.	Co. D	29 Nov 62	P
Abernathy, William H.			Pvt.	Co. L	28 Nov 62	
Adams, Andrew	30	Ireland	Sgt.	Co. C	30 Jun 60	RA
*Agnew, Hugh	31	Ireland	Cpl.	Co. I	15 Jun 60	
Ahrens, Frederick			Pvt.	Co. I	18 Apr 61	
Allen, Alvy	21	New York	Pvt.	Co. C	27 Apr 61	
*Allen, Rufis P.			Pvt.	Cos. I/H	29 Nov 62	
Allen, Thomas D.	21	Missouri	Pvt.	Co. C	14 Dec 59	RA
Allison, Jacob			Pvt.	Co. D	01 Dec 62	
Altman, Levi			Pvt.	Co. D	01 Dec 62	
Amann, Joseph			Cpl.	Co. D	28 Nov 62	
Anders, John O.	26	Germany	Cpl.	Co. K	30 May 60	RA
Anderson, Andrew	26	Ireland	Pvt.	Co. A	12 May 64	
Anderson, William	21		Pvt.	Co. D	01 Apr 61	
*Armstrong, James	21	England	Pvt.	Co. B	25 Jan 61	
Arnold, William H.	23	Penn.	Pvt.	Co. H	02 Jun 63	
Arthur, Isaac			Pvt.	Co. F	21 Jan 62	
Atherton, James			Pvt.	Co. M	06 Dec 62	
Atkins, Robert	24		Pvt.	Co. B	21 Apr 61	
Auer, Christian	31	Germany	Sgt.	Co. E	30 Nov 61	
*Austin, James		Ohio	Sgt.	Co. K	23 Jan 60	
*Axe, Charles	22	Penn.	Pvt.	Co. A	02 Mar 57	
Axt, Herman	21	Ohio	Sgt.	Co. I	10 Sep 61	
B						
Bagowski, Albert A.	22	Prussia	Pvt.	Co. D	11 Jun 60	+RA D
Bailey, John			Bugler	Co. D		
Balch, Manning B.	24		Pvt.	Co. C	22 Apr 61	
Baldwin, John	20	Ireland	Cpl.	Co. K	12 Sep 60	RA
Baldwin, William F.			Pvt.	Co. C	28 Nov 62	
Bale, Philip			Pvt.	Co. G	27 Nov 62	
Ball, Horace E.	21		Pvt.	Co. I2	4 Mar 59	RA
Ballard, James	18		Pvt.	Co. K	01 Dec 62	
Ballinger, John W.	21	Kentucky	Pvt.	Co. M	05 Dec 62	
Balmas, John	23	Germany	Trumpeter	Co. G	21 May 60+	RA
Bannersfeld, Richard			Pvt.	Co. L	02 Dec 62	
Barber, Emery	24		Musician	Co. D	10 Dec 61	
Barber, John	28		Pvt.	Co. D	08 Apr 61	
Barchell, Edwin G.	27	New York	Pvt.	Co. F	03 Jun 62	
*Barclay, Kendall			Pvt.	Co. G	26 Nov 62	
Bargarow, Augustus			Pvt.	Co. K	26 Nov 62	
Barker, Theodore P.	21		Sgt.	Co. H	01 Nov 62	
Barlow, John J.				Co. M	06 Dec 62	D
Barnard, James			Sgt.	Cos. G/M	20 Jan 62	
Barrett, Michael	22	England	Pvt.	Co. Bo	9 Jul 60+	RA D
*Barry, Daniel	38	Ireland	Farrier	Co. H	18 Apr 60	
†Bars, Frank	26	Wisconsin	Pvt.	Co. H	25 May 60	
Bartlett, Edward	30	England	Pvt.	Co. D	08 Jun 60+	
Bartlett, Jerome			Cpl.	Co. K		
Bassnet, Robert			Pvt.	Co. I	03 Dec 62	
Bastwick, Richard			Pvt.	Co. I	28 Nov 62	
Bates, Charles E.	14	Conn.	Sgt.	Co. E	30 Dec 57+	RA

Appendix 261

Name	Age	Birthplace	Rank	Company	Enlisted	Status
†Baum, John			Pvt.	Co. G	29 Nov 62	
Baxter, Edward T.	22	New York		Co. K	14 May 60	D
Baxter, Joseph W.	21		Pvt.	Co. E	09 May 64	
BAYARD, William	22	New York	Cpl.	Co. G	02 Feb 63 P	FC
Baylor, Leander			Pvt.	Co. K	02 Dec 62	
*Bears, George H.			Pvt.	Cos. G/L	05 Dec 62	
Bell, George	22	England	Pvt.	Co. A	28 May 64	
Bell, Robert M.			Pvt.	Co. B	28 Nov 62	
Bell, William H.	22	Penn.	Pvt.	Co. E	23 Oct 62	
BENDIRE, Charles	26	Germany	Cpl.	Co. D	08 Jun 60 P+	FC
Bent, John A.	21	Maryland	Pvt.	Co. E	11 Dec 62	
*Benton, John	31	Penn.	Pvt.	Co. A	07 Dec 59	RA
Benton, Thomas	21	Penn.	Pvt.	Co. H	01 Jun 63D	
Berg, Peter			Musician/Band		23 Feb 62	
Bergen, William	32	Ireland	Pvt.	Co. A	02 Aug 61	
Berzett, George			Pvt.	Co. D	03 Dec 62	
*Bibb, Andrew J.			Pvt.	Co. A	22 Jul 63	
Billow, Henry A.	21		Pvt.	Co. C	06 May 61	
Billow, John S.	18	Penn.	Bugler	Cos. F/C	24 Oct 61	
Billow, Joseph A.	16	Penn.	Bugler	Cos. E/F	10 Nov 62	
Bird, Abraham A.			Hosp. Steward	Cos. K/F/S	28 Nov 62	
†Birmingham, Martin	21	Ireland	Cpl.	Co. E	18 Dec 52	RA
Blew, Samuel L.			Pvt.	Co. L	04 Dec 62	
Blair, James			Pvt.	Co. G	27 Nov 62	
Blair, William			Pvt.	Co. F	12 Mar 58	RA
Black, Robert	28	Ireland	Pvt.	Co. K	08 Nov 59	D
Bliss, Joshua P.	23		Pvt.	Co. B	23 Apr 61	
Blodgett, John M.			Sgt.	Co. B	27 Jan 62	
Blood, Augustus			Pvt.	Co. G	25 Nov 62	
Bocroc, Samuel			Pvt.	Co. M	08 Dec 62	Dd
Bode, Henry	24		Pvt.	Co. C	08 Dec 64	
BOLAND, Sater	23	Kentucky	1st Sgt.	Co. K	21 Jun 60	RA FC
Boner, Marcus A.			Artificer	Co. M	03 Dec 62	
Bonner, Alexander			Pvt.	Co. I	01 Feb 62	
Bonnett, Peter	42		Pvt.	Co. C	15 Apr 61	
Boring, Thomas J.			Pvt.	Co. I	28 Nov 62	
Borner, William	31		Band Leader	Cos. F/S	22 Nov 61	
Bouse, Noble			Pvt.	Co.M	05 Dec 62	
Bowe, James			Pvt.	Co.G	15 Dec 62	
*Boyd, Stewart	28	Ireland	Cpl.	Co. C	18 Jul 60	RA
Brace, Charles P.			Pvt.	Co.M	19 Dec 62	
Brand, Joseph	19	Germany	Sgt.	Co. I	12 Sep 61	
Bradburn, John	23	Delaware	Sgt.	Co. D	31 Nov 56	RA
Breen, Joseph			Pvt.	Co. D	03 Dec 62	Dd
Breen, Thomas	30	Ireland	Pvt.	Co. I	17 Mar 58	RA
Brehme, Adolphus			Pvt.	Co. M	29 Nov 62	Dd
Brennan, Matthew	21	Ireland	Musician	Co. D	11 Mar 61	
Bresler, David			Cpl.	Co. L	03 Dec 62	
Brewer, Hiram H.	23	Mass.	Pvt.	Co. F	17 Nov 62	
Brick, Charles			Sgt.	Co. D	27 Nov 62	
Brill, Malick	23	Ireland	Sgt.	Co. D	28 Jan 57+	RA
Brissendine, Philip H.	24	Georgia	Cpl.	Co. C	22 Jun 60	RA
Bristol, John	28	Ireland	Pvt.	Co. K	24 My 60	RA
Browell, Andrew J.	22	Penn.	Pvt.	Co. F	06 Apr 63	
Brown, Archibald			Pvt.	Co. C	01 Dec 62	

Name	Age	Birthplace	Rank	Company	Enlisted	Status
Brown, Charles F.	25	Mass.	Pvt.	Co. A	23 Oct 62	Dd
Brown, William	26	So. Carolina	Farrier	Co. F	06 Jul 60	RA
Browne, Thomas	25	Ireland	Q.M. Sgt.	Cos. A/F/S	19 Mar 60	RA
†Bryan, John Milton	19	Ohio	Pvt.	Co. L	12 Dec 62	
Bryant, John			Pvt.	Co. C	01 Dec 62	
Bunn, Andrew J.		Ohio	Cpl.	Co. D	01 Dec 62	
*Bunn, Charles	23	New York	Sgt.	Co. C	07 Jul 60	RA
Burgen, John C.	24		Pvt.	Co. B	21 Apr 61	
*Burger, Racthles			Pvt.	Co. H	Unknown	
*Burke, Bartholomew	27	Ireland	Pvt.	Cos. I/H	25 May 61	
Burke, James			Pvt.	Co. C	01 Dec 62	D
†Burke, James H.	30	Ireland	Cpl.	Co. H	16 Apr 63	
Burke, John	23	Ireland	Pvt.	Co. A	21 Jun 64	
Burke, Walter	22	Ireland	Pvt.	Co. D	12 May 61	Dd
Burkhart, John	21	Maryland	Sgt.	Co. I	15 Mar 59	RA
Burne, Patrick	26	Ireland	Sgt.	Co. A	03 Sep 60+	RA
*Burnham, Alfred W.			Bugler	Co. E	05 Mar 61	
BURNHAM, Frank	24	New York	Sgt. Maj.	Cos. F/S	23 Nov 59	RA FC
*Burns, James E.			Pvt.	Co. D	29 Nov 62	
Burr, Frank A.	19	Maine	Pvt.	Co. B	13 May 61	D
Burroes, James			Pvt.	Co. M	29 Nov 62	D
Busch, Louis	21	Germany	Sgt.	Co. I	16 Sep 61	
Butler, Adam			Pvt.	Band	03 Nov 58	RA
Butler, James			Pvt.	Co. M	16 Dec 62	
Butterfield, Richard			Pvt.	Co. L	26 Nov 62	
Byrne, William L.	29	Maryland	Pvt.	Co. B	27 May 62	

C

Name	Age	Birthplace	Rank	Company	Enlisted	Status
CALLEHAN, James	28	New York	1st Sgt.	Co. D	25 Jul 60	RA FC
Callenbrach, Gerhard	21	Germany	Pvt.	Co. D	06 Jun 60	RA Dd
*Campbell, Henry			Pvt.	Co. ?		
*Campbell, James	31	Ireland	Pvt.	Co. F	30 Nov 63	
Campbell, John S.			Cpl.	Co. G	26 Nov 62	Dd
Canady, Seth M.			Pvt.	Co. C	02 Dec 62	
Cander, Peter L.	26	Germany	Pvt.	Co. B	25 Nov 59	RA
Canfield, Daniel	20	Ireland	Pvt.	Co. C	12 Nov 60	Dd
*Cantilion, John	32		Cpl.	Co. H	07 May 63	
Carey, James	21	Ireland	Sgt.	Co. F	04 May 55+	RA D
Carey, George W.			Pvt.	Co. I	01 Dec 62	
Carlin, Hiram			Cpl.	Co. G	04 Dec 62	
Carman, John C	26	Maryland	Pvt.	Co. C	23 May 61	Dd
†Carmichael, John	26	Ireland	Sgt.	Co. B	26 Jun 60	RA
*Carnutt, William W.	23	Tennessee	Pvt.	Co. I	03 Aug 55	RA
Carr, Charles M.	26	New York	Pvt.	D/F/S/M	22 May 58+	RA
Carr, Charles W.	21		Bugler	Co. D	20 May 58	RA
Carr, James	21	Ireland	Pvt.	Co. I	12 Aug 60	RA
Carr, John L.			Pvt.	Co. L	04 Dec 62	
Carroll, Andrew	30	Ireland	Pvt.	Co. A	20 Jun 64	
Carroll, James			Pvt.	Co. M	08 Dec 62	D
Carroll, Michael			Pvt.	Co. G	04 Dec 62	
Carroll, William	30	Penn.	1st Sgt.	Cos. E/M	20 Jul 60 P	RA
Carter, William H.			Pvt.	Co. C	29 Nov 62	
Carver, James	21	New York	Sgt.	Co. B	17 Mar 60	RA
Casey, Francis	21	Ireland	Pvt.	Co. D	07 Jul 58	RA
Cass, Thomas E.			Pvt.	Co. M	27 Nov 62	
†Cassell, George	24	Ohio	Pvt.	Cos. K/M	08 Dec 62	

Name	Age	Birthplace	Rank	Company	Enlisted	Status
Cassidy, James			Pvt.	Co. C	01 Feb 62	
Cassidy, Patrick J.			Pvt.	Co. C	13 Mar 60	Disc.
Caster, James R.	14	Penn.	Bugler	Co. H	03 Aug 61	RA
Castillo, James	26	Ireland	Sgt.	Cos. D/E	13 Jul 60	RA
Cattenhorn, Frederick	18		Pvt.	Co. D	12 Jul 58	RA
Caufield, John	23	Maryland	Sgt.	Co. F	25 May 60	RA
CAVENDISH, Frederick A.	21	England	Sgt.	Co. H	01 May 55+	RA FC
Chadwick, Charles N.			Wagoner	Co. K	26 Nov 62	
Chapman, Jacob			Pvt.	Co. D	03 Dec 62	
Christy, James Y.	26	Penn.	1st Sgt.	Co. F	16 Aug 64 P	
Chryst, D. F.	23	Penn.	Pvt.	Co. B	02 Jun 61	
Clarence, Charles	24	Penn.	Pvt.	Co. A	07 Dec 59	RA
Clapp, Quartus	21	Michigan	Cpl.	Co. E	04 Jan 60	RA
Clarey, Richard	26	New York	Pvt.	Co. M	05 Feb 63	D
Clark, Asa			Pvt.	Co. A	26 Nov 62	
Clark, Edward	23	Ohio	Bugler	Cos. F/K	14 Feb 63	
Clark, George W.			Pvt.	Co. K	01 Dec 62	
Clark, James C.	25	Illinois	Pvt.	Co. B	19 Mar 60	D
*Clark, John M.			Pvt.	Co. B	03 Dec 62	
Clark, John L.			Pvt.	Co. K	28 Nov 62	
Clark, Jonathan L.			Cpl.	Co. K	29 Nov 62	
Clark, Jos.			Sgt.	Co. I	29 Nov 62	
Clark, Newton	21	New York	Farrier	Co. E	21 Oct 62	
Clark, William			Pvt.	Co. K	26 Nov 62	
Clark, William H.			Pvt.	Co. D		
Claypool, James W.			Sgt.	Co. K	29 Nov. 62	
Cleghorn, Benjamin	24	England	1st Sgt	Co. K	04 May 60 P	RA
Clements, Matthew	21	Penn.	Sgt.	Co. E	16 Mar 59	RA
Cleveland, David	22	Ohio	Sgt.	Co. L	14 Mar 60	RA
CLIFFORD, James A.	31	Ireland	Pvt.	Co. D	12 Aug 58 P+	FC
Clingsmidtch, Franklin			Pvt.	Co. L	03 Dec 62	
Clink, William M.		Michigan	Pvt.	Co. L	12 Dec 62	
Coale, John G.			Pvt.	Co. B	02 Dec 62	Dd
COATS, Albert	20		Sgt.	Co. C	08 Dec 56	RA FC
Cody, John F.				Co. G		
Codey, John T.	32	Penn.	Pvt.	Co. G	28 Mar 62	
Cody, Morris	29		Pvt.	Co. D	05 Dec 57	RA
Coe, Wallace A.	19	New York	Pvt.	Co. A	22 Oct 62	
Coffman, Henry	29	Germany	Pvt.	Co. B	30 Jul 64 P	
Coffman, Samuel	26	Virginia	Sgt.	Co. G	24 Dec 61	
Coggans John	26	Ireland	Pvt.	Co. B	11 Oct 61	RA
Coggins, Daniel	31	Ireland	Pvt.	Co. D	21 Apr 60 P	Dd
Colbert, Edward	24	Ireland	Pvt.	Co. A	28 Sep 61	
Colbert, Thomas	25	Ireland	Sgt.	Co. H	26 Jul 64 P	D
†Cole, Commodore P.			Pvt.	Co. L	18 Dec 62	
Cole, Samuel L.			Pvt.	Co. L	17 Dec 62	
*Colean, Michael	25	Ireland	Pvt.	Co. H	28 Apr 63	
Collins, John			Pvt.	Co. M	12 Dec 62	
Collins, George			Cpl.	Co. K	01 Dec 62	
Collins, George W.			Pvt.	Co. K	01 Dec 62	
Collins, John			Pvt.	Co. M	12 Dec 62	
Condon, Michael	23	Ireland	Pvt.	Co. B	17 Apr 61	
Conkle, Amos			Pvt.	Co. G	26 Nov 62	D
Conn, James E.			Bugler	Co. G	08 Feb 62	
Connor, Hugh O. [See O'Connor]						

Name	Age	Birthplace	Rank	Company	Enlisted	Status
CONWAY, Edwin J.		Ireland	Pvt.	Co. B	28 Nov 59+	RA FC
Conway, Francis	18	Louisiana	Sgt.	Co. L	19 Jul 60	RA
Cook, James M.	32		Sgt	Co. F	01 Jul 60 P	RA
Coppell, John			Pvt.	Co. D	29 Nov 62	
Corken, Arthur J.	18	Ohio	Pvt.	Co. D	28 Mar 61	
Corlan, Michael	21	Ohio	Pvt.	Co. B	27 May 61	Dd
*Corlew, Presby					16 Apr 61	
Costillo, James	21	Ireland	Pvt.	Co. D	19 Apr 60	RA
Cotton, George H.	19	Maryland	Pvt.	Co. E	23 Oct 62	
Cotton, John T	29	Penn.	Sgt.	Co. F	19 Jan 60	RA
Coulter, Josiah H.			Sgt.	Co. M	27 Nov 62	
†Cowarden, Charles M.		Ireland	Pvt.	Co. K	27 Nov 62	RA
*Cowder, Joseph A.			Pvt.	Co. I	29 Nov 62	
Cowling, James			Wagoner	Co. A	11 Mar 61	
Crampton, Francis			Pvt.	Co. L	15 Dec 62	
Cranford, Joseph	22	Penn.	Pvt.	Co. C	15 Jul 60	RA
†Craven, Patrick	22	Ireland	Pvt.	Co. I	18 May 61	RA
Crisfield, William B.	19	England	Pvt.	Co. F	21 Oct 58	RA
Cree, John M.	22	Ohio	Pvt.	Co. H	13 Oct 62	
Crock, James	34	Maryland	Pvt.	Co. F	01 Jun 63	Dd
Croft, James	29	England	Pvt.	Co. B	26 Jun 60 P	RA
*Cronan, Cornelius	30	Ireland	Pvt.	Co. F	29 Apr 63	
Cronin, Patrick	37	Ireland	Pvt.	Co. H	18 Apr 60 P	D
*Cross, Patrick	26	Ireland	Pvt.	Co. A	23 Nov 61	
Crows, Pleasant			Pvt.	Co. M	05 Dec 62	
†Cuddehy, Patrick			Cpl.	Cos. F/I/S	01 May 63	
†Cullan, Phelix	22	Ireland	Cpl.	Co. H	02 Jun 60	RA
Cummings, James	21	Ireland	Sgt.	Cos. D/M	27 Apr 61	
Cunningham, Peter	21		Pvt.	Co. D	27 Apr 61	
Cunningham, Wm.	21	Ireland	Pvt.	Co. D	27 Apr 61	
*Curry, John	21	Ireland	Pvt.	Co. D	20 Jul 58	RA
Curtin, Cornelius	20	Ireland	Pvt.	Co. A	21 Aug 61	
Curtin, Patrick	20	Ireland	Pvt.	Co. C	29 Jan 61	
Curtis, Archibald			Pvt.	Co. B	04 Dec 62	
D						
Daily, John M.	21	Penn.	Pvt.	Co. C	21 Feb 61	
Daily, Andrew	21		Pvt.	Co. D	12 May 58	RA
†Dalrimple, Madison			Pvt.	Co. L	28 Dec 62	MIA
*Dalton, James	22	Ireland	Pvt.	Co. E	13 Jul 60	RA
Dalton, William			Pvt.	Co. C	23 Apr 62	
Damon, Albert F.	20	Mass.	Pvt.	Co. E	23 Oct 62	
Daniels, Hibbard C.	18	Illinois	Fifer	Co. D	29 Nov 62	D
Darey, Garret			Pvt.	Co. K	01 Dec 62	
†Daugherty, David	26	Ireland	Pvt.	Co. G	14 May 60	RA
Davenport, Julius R.	29	Miss.	Sgt.	Co. H	29 Mar 60+	RA
Davidson, James	21		Bugler	Co. B	17 May 61	
Davis, Charles W.			Pvt.	Co. M	03 Dec 62	
Davis, Edward			Sgt.	Co. C	28 Nov 62	
Davis, Giles	22	Virginia	Pvt.	Co. L	28 Nov 62	D
Davis, Ira W.		Vermont	3rd Cl. Musician	Cos. F/S	12 Dec 61	
Davis, Josiah	22	Michigan	Pvt.	Co. F	01 Mar 61	
Davis, Stanley			Pvt.	Co. M	11 Dec 62	
Davis, William J.	25	Maryland	Pvt.	Co. B	29 Jan 61	Dd
DAVIS, Wirt	21	Virginia	1st Sgt.	Co. K	12 May 60	RA FC
Dean, John			Cpl.	Co. M	01 Dec 63	D

Name	Age	Birthplace	Rank	Company	Enlisted	Status
*Dean Samuel (Lewis)			Cpl.	Co. B	25 Jan 62	
Dean, William H.	31	Ohio	Pvt.	Co. F	27 Dec 61+	RA
Dearth, William C.			Pvt.	Co. D	28 Nov 62	D
Debitzen, John J.	20	Penn.	Cpl.	Co. E	23 Oct 62	
Delaney, John	24	Mass.	Pvt.	Co. D	07 Jul 58	Dd
Denny, Peter J.			Pvt.	Co. B	06 Nov 60	RA
Denton, William J.	21		Sgt.	Co. H	14 Apr 63	RA
Derush, John H.	21	Ohio	Pvt.	Co. F	29 Jan 61	
Detheridge, Robert M.	26	England	Pvt.	Co. B	03 May 61	
†Devlin, Edward	27	Ireland	Pvt.	Co. C	12 Jan 57	RA
Devlin, John	27	Ireland	Pvt.	Co. A	21 Aug 61	
Diamond, Charles			Pvt.	Co. G	29 Nov 62	
Dickey, George W.			Pvt.	Co. M	03 Dec 62	
Dieter, George	21	Germany	Pvt.	Co. D	01 My 61	
Dillon, Edward	26	Ireland	Pvt.		28 Apr 60	Dd
Dillon, William A.			Pvt.	Co. G	17 Dec 62	
Dixon, William H.			Pvt.	Co. B	05 Dec 62	D
Dodd, Henry J.			Pvt.	Co. I	29 Nov 62	
Doherty, Partick	25		Pvt.	Co. B	26 Nov 60	D
Dokey, Stephen			Pvt.	Co. K	26 Nov 62	
Dolan, John	33	Ireland	1st Sgt.	Co. B	20 Jul 64 P	
Dolan, Joseph J.	26		Sgt.	Co. D	22 Feb 58+	RA
Dolan, Patrick J.			1st Sgt.	Co. D	22 Dec 62	
Dollinger, Jacob	24		Pvt.	Co. D	21 Apr 60	RA
Domhoff, Charles	18	Kentucky	Pvt.	Co. C	28 May 61	
DONNOGHUE, Dennis	19	Ireland	Bugler	Co. C	10 Jul 60	FC
Doogan, Charles	16		Bugler	Co. G	15 Oct 57	RA
Dooley, Thomas	26	Ireland	Pvt.	Co. F	09 Dec 61+	
Doty, Joseph			Pvt.	Co. K	27 Nov 62	
*Dougherty, David	28	Ireland	Pvt.	Co. G	14 May 60	
Dougherty, Edward	22	Ireland	Pvt.	Co. C	02 May 55+	RA Dd
*Dougherty, Michael	22	Penn.	Sgt.	Co. I	15 June 60	RA
Douglas, Thomas	27		Pvt.	Co. C	29 Mar 60	RA
Downey, Jonathan			Pvt.	Co. K	26 Nov 62	
Downey, Timothy	22		Pvt.	Co. D	07 Aug 58	RA
Doyle, Denis	19	Ireland	Sgt.	Co H	07 Nov 59+	RA D
Doyle, John	22		Cpl.	Co. D	29 Apr 61	
Doyle, Michael	24		Pvt.	Co. D	15 Jun 58	RA
†Doyle, Robert P.	21	Ireland	Pvt.	Co. D	07 Jul 64	
Doyle, Thomas			Pvt.	Co. D	01 Nov 61	Dd
*Drain, Harrison			Pvt.	Co. H	01 Apr 62	
Drake, Elias Jr.	27	Ohio	Pvt.	Co. H	24 Dec 62	
Drake, John	29	Ohio	Pvt.	Co. H	24 Dec 62	
Dresher, August A.	24	Germany	Cpl.	Co. G	11 May 60+	RA
Drevenstat, Alfred A.	21	Penn.	Saddler	Co. F	07 Nov 62	
Drought, John	29	New York	Cpl.	Co. A	11 Nov 61+	
Duffield, William	23		Pvt.	Co. M	04 Dec 62	
Dunlap, John	22	Penn.	Pvt.	Co. A	27 Feb 61	
*Dunn, John	18	New York	Pvt.	Co. I	16 Jan 58	
Dunning, Abram			Pvt.	Co. I	01 Dec 62	D
Dustin, Franklin	23		Pvt.	Co. D	20 Oct 57	RA
Dwire, Benjamin			Pvt.	Co. L	11 Dec 62	

E

Name	Age	Birthplace	Rank	Company	Enlisted	Status
Earley, John	22	New York	Pvt.	Co. C	25 May 61	
Eaton, Henry			Pvt.	Co. G	04 Dec 62	

Name	Age	Birthplace	Rank	Company	Enlisted	Status
Eckstein, John	21		Trumpter	Co. H	17 Apr 63	RA
EGAN, James		Ireland	1st Sgt.	Co. E	01 Mar 60 P	RA FC
*Eichoff, Francis			Pvt.	Co. G	01 Dec 62	
Elair, Edward	27	Canada	Pvt.	Co. B	01 Jan 61	
Elder, Joseph			Cpl.	Co. B	02 Dec 62	
Ellis, Robert T.	21	Penn.	Pvt.	Co. I	18 Feb 61	D
Ellis, Thomas L.			Pvt.	Co. G	29 Nov 62	
*Ellis, William			Pvt.	Co. K	26 Nov 62	MIA
Elshire, Joseph	26	Indiana	Pvt.	Co. M	16 Jan 62	D
Endress, John T.	32	Germany	Pvt.	Co. F	28 Nov 61	D
Ennis, William	27	Georgia	Cpl.	Co. C	13 Feb 60+	RA
Enright, Jeremiah	21		Pvt.	Co. C	11 Apr 61	
Esminger, Philip			Pvt.	Co. M	12 Dec 62	
†Entwhistle, John			Pvt.	Co. I	28 Nov 62	
Essley, Henry C.	23		Pvt.	Co. G	01 Dec 62	
Evans, Thomas B.			Pvt.	Co. M	04 Dec 62	D
Everett, David			Pvt.	Co. G	18 Dec 62	Dd
F						
Fabre, Benjamin		Germany	Sgt.	Co. A	14 Jan 62	
Fair, George	16	Germany	Pvt.	Co. E	10 Mar 63	D
Fairchilds, Charles			Sgt.	Co. F	22 Jun 63	
Farley, Andrew			Pvt.	Co. L	29 Nov 62	
Farn, Solomon			Pvt.	Co. L	15 Dec 62	D
Farrell, Michael	26	Ireland	Pvt.	Co. B	07 May 61	
*Fay, Daniel	21	England	Pvt.	Co. B	15 Mar 58	RA
*Fay, James	23	Ireland	Sgt.	Co. A	09 Dec 59	RA
Feather, Stephen				Co. M	28 Nov 62	D
Feeley, John C.	21	New York	Pvt.	Co. H	11 May 60	D
*Fell, Adam			Pvt.	Co. K	26 Nov 62	
Fell, Robert			Q.M. Sgt.	Cos. K/F/S	26 Nov 62	
Fennessy, Andrew	22		Pvt.	Co. D	15 Apr 61	
Ferguson, Charles E.			Pvt.	Co. K	26 Nov 62	Dd
Ferral, James	21	Indiana	Sgt.	Co. I	22 Dec 59+	
Fie, Christian	23	Germany	Cpl.	Co. E	06 Jan 58	RA
Filson, Sylvester H.			Pvt.	Co. M	15 Dec 62	D
Fisher, Edward J.				Co. C	29 Nov 62	D
Fiste, Edward			Pvt.	Co. C	29 Nov 62	D
FITZGERALD, Edward E.	21	Ireland	1st Sgt.	Co. E	09 Jan 58+	RA FC
Fitzgerald, Patrick	31	Ireland	Cpl.	Co. E	20 Nov 61+	RA
Fitzgerrold, Robert M.			Farrier	Co. M	28 Nov 62	
Fitzpatrick, John	22	Ireland	Pvt.	Co. D	11 Apr 61	Dd
Fitsh, Charles	25	Germany	Pvt.	Co. E	13 Jul 60	Dd
Fleming, Archibald B.			Pvt.	Co. M	28 Nov 62	
*Flanagan, Patrick	22	Ireland	Sgt.	Co. D	26 Jul 60 P	RA
FLETCHER, Bird		Vermont	Cpl.	Co. I	27 Dec 59+	RA FC
*Fletcher, Patrick B.	34	Ireland	Pvt.	Co. H	17 Feb 63	
Flichman, Mathew	24	Germany	Pvt.	Co. I	09 Sep 61	
Forester, James R.	24		Pvt.	Co. C	03 Mar 60	Dd
Forster, Charles	27		Pvt.	Co. D	26 Jul 60	RA
Forsyth, George	32	Ireland	Cpl.	Co. A	01 Jul 64 P	Dd
*Fought, Charles	18	Germany	Pvt.	Co. A	13 Sep 60	RA
Fought, John	20	"At Sea"	Pvt.	Co. A	14 Sep 60	RA Dd
Fox, Richard M.			Pvt.	Co. K	28 Nov 62	
Foy, George W.			Pvt.	Co. L	26 Nov 62	
Frame, Thomas	30	Ireland	Pvt.	Co. F	14 Feb 60	RA

Name	Age	Birthplace	Rank	Company	Enlisted	Status
Franklin, Hiram	20		Wagoner	Co. F	10 Dec 61+	RA
Frazer, John			Hosp. Steward	Co. H	21 Jan 62	
Freadel, Esidore	18	Ohio	Sgt.	Co. I	19 Sep 61+	RA
Frey, John	23		Pvt.	Co. C	06 Mar 60	Dd
Fugit, Edwin			Pvt.	Co. G	26 Nov 62	
G						
Gaffney, Bartholomew	21	Ireland	Pvt.	Co. D	21 May 61	Dd
Gaffney, Daniel	23	Ireland	1st Sgt.	Co. D	23 Apr 60+	
*Gainer, Thomas	21	Penn.	Pvt.	Co. F	03 Jun 63	
Gallagher, Daniel	27	Ireland	Pvt.	Co. A	23 Oct 62	
Galligar, John	29		Pvt.	Co. D	12 Apr 60	
Galvin, John			Pvt.	Co. C	03 Nov 62	
Gannon, Matthias	21	Mass.	Pvt.	Co. E	13 Jan 58	RA Dd
Gardner, Amos H.	25	Ireland	Pvt.	Co. B	16 Apr 61	
Gardner, Lewis J.	21	New York	Sgt.	Co. A	25 May 60+	RA
Garlock, James	25	New York	Pvt.	Co. B	01 Jul 64 P	
Garraty, Thomas	23	Ireland	Sgt.	Co. E	01 Mar 59	RA
Gates, Nicholas	22	Germany	Pvt.	Co. B	27 Nov 60+	RA D
Gaty, Barney		Illinois	Pvt.	Co. L	04 Nov 62	Dd
Gauthier, Charles H.	18	Mass.	Pvt.	Cos. H/M	13 Apr 63	RA
Geier, Johann	21		Pvt.	Co. D	09 Apr 61	
Geraghty, Patrick			Pvt.	Co. G	14 Mar 62	
Gerstung, John S.	33	Germany	Pvt.	Co. E	15 Jun 60 P	Dd
Gettere, Nicholas	19	New York	Pvt.	C/F/I/B	18 Jun 63	RA
Getz [see Gaty]						
Geyer, Francis Joseph	19	Prussia	Pvt.	Co. G	13 Jan 60	
†Gibbons, John Austin	23	Iowa	Pvt.	Co. C	16 Mar 60	RA
†Gibon, Calvin F.			Pvt.	Co. D	09 Nov 62	
Giles, George			Pvt.	Cos. C/M	12 Dec 62	
Giles, Thomas W.			1st Sgt.	Co. L	12 Nov 62 P	
Gill, Elijah				Co. L	27 Nov 62	
Gill, James			Pvt.	Co. G	08 Nov 62	
Gilmore, Patrick	25	Ireland	Pvt.	Co. B	05 Apr 61	
Gilmore, William M.				Co. I	27 Nov 62	
Glynn, William. H.			Pvt.	Co. L	12 Nov 62	
GORDON, Henry	31		1st Sgt.	Co. D	26 Jul 60 P	FC
*Gordon, Joshua M.			Pvt.	Co. K	26 Nov 62	
Gorman, John	37	England	1st Sgt.	Co. F	19 May 59	RA
Gosser, Peter			Saddler	Co. K	26 Feb 61	
Gould, John	22	Penn.	Pvt.	Co. B	20 Feb 61	
Gourney, Dallas M.			Pvt.	Co. A	25 Sep 61	
*Goyner, Ozias			Pvt.	Co. D	01 Nov 62	
*Granger, James	30		Pvt.	Co. D	19 Jun 58	RA
Green, John			Pvt.	Co. F	13 Oct 61+	
Green, William H.	21	Kentucky	Pvt.	Co. B	19 Jun 60	Disc.
Greene, Hugh	21		Pvt.	Co. C	12 May 61	
Grehling, Henry	21		Pvt.	Co. D	18 Apr 61	
*Grenem, Joseph	22	Ireland	Pvt.	Co. C	13 Nov 59	RA
Grew, William	21	Ireland	Pvt.	Co. E	14 May 58	RA
*Griddle, John	29	Penn.	Sgt.	Co. H	09 Jun 63 P	
Griffin, Caleb			Pvt.	Co. K	26 Nov 62	D
Griffin, John A.	25	N. Carolina	1stSgt.	Co. C	01 Jul 60 P+	
Griffin, Peter	21	Ireland	Bugler	Co. C	27 May 61	
*Griffith, William A.	26	Georgia	Farrier	Co. I	25 May 60	RA
Grim, John	22		Cpl.	Co. F	19 Mar 64 P	

Name	Age	Birthplace	Rank	Company	Enlisted	Status
Grundig, Agustus	21	Germany	Pvt.	Co. B	01 Feb 61	Dd
Guenther, Philip					06 Nov 62	D
*Gullaver, David B.			Pvt.	Co. L	04 Nov 62	
Gundel, Lenhard	20	Germany	Pvt.	Co. F	27 Jul 61	
GUNTHER, Sebastian	23	Germany	Sgt.	Cos. B/F/S	27 Aug 55+	RA FC
Gunnels, Andrew J.	29	Georgia	Pvt.	Co. C	20 Feb 60+	RA
Gunning, Thomas	25	Ireland	Pvt.	Co. D	25 Mar 61	
Gurney, Dallas M.	19		Pvt.	Co. A	23 Oct 62	
Gysi, Charles H.	27	Switzerland	Pvt.	Co. D	13 Nov 60	Dd
H						
Hack, John Jacob	24	Germany	1st Sgt.	Co. E	27 Jan 58+	RA
Hackett, William	25	Ireland	Pvt.	Co. A	20 Jun 64	D
Hadder, Leonard J.	32	Ohio	Saddler	Co. L	05 Dec 62+	
Haefling, Christian			1st Sgt.	Cos. B/K		
Hagmann, Joseph			Musician	Cos. F/S	01 Oct 62	
Hall, Charles	28		Sgt.	Co. G	05 Jul 60 P	RA
†Hall, Frederick	23	England	Cpl.	Co. K	07 Jan 63	
Hall, George K.	21	Vermont	Pvt.	Co. D	23 Apr 61	
Hallabough, Henry			Pvt.	Co. B	03 Dec 62	
Hamilton, James M.			Cpl.	Co. L	04 Dec 62	
Hand, John	25	Germany	Cpl.	Co. K	21 May 60	RA
Handy, Thomas	22		Pvt.	Co. D	16 Apr 61	
Hanish, Ernest				Co. A		
Hanley, Michael	22	Ireland	Pvt.	Co. D	21 Jun 58	RA Dd
Hanna, John	32		Pvt.	Co. C	13 Dec 59	RA
Harbert, William			Pvt.	Co. C	28 Nov 62	
Harbin, Robert	21	Georgia	Pvt.	Co. C	17 Aug 55+	RA IC
Hardy, Frederick			Pvt.	Co. C	28 Nov 62	
Hareld, Jonah	20	Tenn.	Sgt.	Co. M	16 Jan 63	RA
Harner, John	21	Penn.	1st Sgt.	Co. G	29 Nov 56	RA
Harrington, George A.	23		Pvt.	Co. D	21 Apr 60	RA
Harriott, James A.	18	New York	Pvt.	Co. C	15 Apr 61	
Harris, Francis M.			Bugler	Co. L	04 Dec 62	
Harris, Guy	26		Pvt.	Co. D	13 Nov 60	
Harris John	22	England	Pvt.	Co. D	14 Jul 58	RA
HARRIS, Moses	18	New Hamp.	Sgt.	Co. G	19 Mar 57	RA FC
Harrison, Charles E.			Pvt.	Co. M	04 Dec 62	
Harrison, Thomas B.	23	England	Musician	Cos. F/S	10 Dec 61	Dd
Harrison, William J.	18	New York	Pvt.	Co. B	07 Apr 57	D
Harsh, Harry			Pvt.	Co. L	05 Dec 62	
Hart, Jacob J.	24	New Jersey	Sgt.	Co. K	30 Aug 58	RA
Hartman, David M.			Saddler	Co. B	01 Dec 62	
Hartzell, Samuel	24		Pvt.	Co. B	09 Apr 61	
Harwick, James			Pvt.	Co. K	26 Nov 62	
†Hashberger, James	18	Indiana	Pvt.	Co. L	10 Dec 62	
Hastings, Rufus D.	23	New York	Pvt.	Co. A	21 Oct 62	Dd IC
Hastings, Warren	21	Wisconsin	Pvt.	Cos. I/M	21 Dec 59	RA
Hatch, Horace A.	27	New Hamp.	Sgt.	Co. E	18 Dec 62	P
Hayden, John			Pvt.	Co. B	02 Dec 62	
Hayes, Daniel H.			Pvt.	Co. L	04 Dec 62	
Hayes, Edward	22	Ireland	Pvt.	Co. C	22 May 61	
Hayes, Michael	26		Cpl.	Co. D	03 Mar 57	
Hayes, Wilson G.			Pvt.	Co. K	01 Dec 62	
HAYNES, John	23	Ireland	Pvt.	Co. I	21 Dec 59	RA FC
Haynorth, Charles K.			Pvt.	Co. I	29 Nov 62	

Name	Age	Birthplace	Rank	Company	Enlisted	Status
Heany, Michael	29	Ireland	Pvt.	Co. C	01 Jul 64 P	
Hearn, Patrick	29		Pvt.	Co. B	06 May 61	Dd
Heath, Charles K.				Co. K	27 Nov 62	
Heegard, Frank W.	34	Denmark	Pvt.	Co. H	29 May 60	RA
Heider, Charles	23	Germany	3rd Cl. Musician	Cos. I/F/S	10 Sep 61	
Henshaw, Ambrose			Pvt.	Co. L	10 Dec 62	
Herberich, John Martin	19	Germany	1st Sgt.	Co. I	19 Dec 59+	RA
Herdkorn, John	18	Penn.	Pvt.	Co. H	01 Jun 63	
Hering, Samuel	23	New York	1st Sgt.	Co. I	27 Jan 62 P	
Hertzler, Samuel	21		Pvt.	Co. I	07 Sep 61	
Hess, Charles A.	30	Switzerland	Band	Co. B	31 Jul 64 P	
Hesse, Charles H.	26	Germany	Pvt.	Co. B	21 Jun 60+	RA
Hesse, John	26	Germany	Pvt.	Co. I	02 Sep 61	
†Hessinger, Frederick	21	Germany	Pvt.	Co. D	19 Apr 60	
Higby, Frank T.	24	New York	Sgt.	Cos. H/M/S	26 May 60+	RA
Higden, Eli W.			Pvt.	Co. G	27 Nov 62	
*Higgens, Daniel			Pvt.	Co. K	25 Nov 62	
Higgens, Peter	35		Pvt.	Co. D	18 Mar 60	RA
Higgens, Theodore	21	Canada	Pvt.	Co. B	13 Apr 61	
Hildebrand, Andrew	28	Germany	Ferrier	Co. D	12 Jan 58	RA
Hill, Edward			Cpl.	Co. G	27 Nov 62	
Hill, Edward P.	35	Conn.	Hosp. Steward	Co. A	01 Jul 64 P	
Hill, Isaiah L.	33	Vermont	Pvt.	Co. A	27 Oct 62	
*Hill, John D.	21	Germany	Pvt.	Co. I	11 Sep 61	
Hill, Josiah S.			Pvt.	Co. A	11 Nov 61	
*Hill, William M.	19	Virginia	Pvt.	Co. H	02 Apr 63	
Hillard, Joseph	20	Ohio	Pvt.	Co. B	29 Jan 57	RA
Hills, Edward P.	35	Hosp	Steward	Co. A	01 Jul 64	
*Hireman, John H.	34	Germany	Pvt.	Cos. F/E	29 May 63	
Hock, Louis	27	France	Pvt.	Co. I	10 Sep 61	Dd
*Hoelzle, Adolph	21	Germany	Pvt.	Co. B	24 Nov 59	RA
Hoffman, Edward J.	21	Penn.	Musician	Cos. E/F/S	21 Oct 62+	
Hoffman, William	36		Pvt.	Co. D	01 Jan 60	RA
*Holly, James H.	18	New York	Sgt.	Co. I	12 Feb 57	RA
Holt, William P.			Pvt.	Co. F	09 Jan 62	
Hommes, Jacob	34		Pvt.	Co. A	05 Dec 59	RA
Hoolihan, Michael	29	Ireland	Pvt.	Co. E	23 Oct 62+	D
Hootzler, Michael			Pvt.	Co. C	01 Dec 62	
Hoppe, John			Pvt.	Co. G	03 Dec 62	
Horrigan, Martin	26		Pvt.	Co. C	13 May 61	
Horstmeyer, Christian	24		Pvt.	Co. I	16 Sep 61	
Hotze, John R.	31	Switzerland	Pvt.	Co. H	21 My 63	Dd
HOUGH, Romaine S.	22	New York	Cpl.	Co. B	23 Jun 60+	FC
House, George W.			Pvt.	Co. L	10 Dec 62	Dd
Howard, Thomas	26		Pvt.	Co. C	14 May 61	
*Hoxworth, Charles C.			Pvt.	Co. L	29 Nov 62	
Hubner, Joseph	21	Germany	Pvt.	Co. C	02 Nov 64	D
Hughes, James	22	Ireland	Pvt.	Co. D	25 May 61	
†Hughes, James	25	Ireland	Pvt.	Co. F	26 May 63	
Hulbert, Costas R.			Pvt.	Co. M	22 Dec 62	
HUMPHREY, Clark M.	29	New York	Pvt.	Co. C	11 Apr 61	FC
Humphreys, Joseph S.	24	Ireland	Pvt.	Co. C	25 May 61	
Hunt, Charles	23	England	Pvt.	Co. H	20 Apr 63	Dd
*Hurd, Andrew			Pvt.	Co. F	12 Nov 62	MIA
Hush, Jacob			Pvt.	Co. G	27 Nov 62	D

Name	Age	Birthplace	Rank	Company	Enlisted	Status
*Hutton, Elijah	18	Maryland	Pvt.	Co. H	21 Apr 63	
Hyer, Frederick	34	Germany	Sgt.	Co. D	01 Jul 64 P	Dd
I						
Ingram, Clifford [see Clifford, James A.]						
*Ireson, J. [Iverson, I.]			Pvt.	Co. A	Unknown	
J						
Jackson, Hayes St. C.			3rd Cl. Musician	Cos. F/S	11 Nov 58	RA
Jackson, Joseph	21		Pvt.	Co. B	12 Dec 60+	RA
Jackson, Thomas A.	26	N. Carolina	Pvt.	Co. C	04 Sep 60+	RA
Jackson, William	23	Kentucky	Cpl.	Co. L	28 May 60	RA
Jacobs, Charles	21	Penn.	Pvt.	Co. C	10 Jul 61	Dd
Jacobs, Z. W.	27	Ireland	Sgt.	Co. F	29 Jan 61	
Jarnigan, William H.			Pvt.	Co. K	25 Nov 62	
Jeffers, Emil			Teamster	Co. L	06 Dec 62	
Jeffrey, George			Pvt.	Co. I	01 Dec 62	
Jenkins, John W.	30	Penn.	Pvt.	Co. I	06 Dec 56	RA
Jenkins, Marian	25	New York	Sgt.	Co. F	06 Oct 61+	
†Jennett, August	26	Germany	Pvt.	Co. L	04 Dec 62	
Jesse, Joseph L.			Pvt.	Co. L	11 Dec 62	
JOHNSON, Garrett V.			Sgt.	Co. B	17 Dec 62+	FC
Johnson, George W.	28	Ohio	Pvt.	Co. F	29 Jan 63	Dd
Johnson, Laurantine			Pvt.	Co. M	19 Dec 62	D
Johnson, Lewis W.			Pvt.	Co. L	19 Dec 62	
Johnson, Orlando D.	22		Pvt.	Co. D	21 Apr 60	RA
Johnson, William	22		Pvt.	Co. D	25 Mar 61	
Johnson, David P.	22	Penn.	Pvt.	Co. D	17 Apr 61 D	
Johnson, Francis	22	Scotland	Pvt.	Co. K	23 May 60	RA
Johnson, Jacob			Pvt.	Co. K	28 Nov 62	
Johnson Joseph S.			Wagoner	Co. M	04 Dec 62	
Johnson Lewis W.			Pvt.	Co. L	19 Dec 62	
Jones, William	27	Ireland	Pvt.	Co. G	01 May 60+	D
Jones, William	21	Ireland	Sgt.	Co. A	23 Nov 60+	RA
Jordan, George	19	Germany	Pvt.	Co. I	12 Sep 61	
Jordan, Stanislas	45	Poland	Chief Bugler	Cos. F/S	23 Jun 60	RA
Jordens, Heinrick	27		Pvt.	Co. C	05 May 65	
Jubart, Napoleon	19	Canada	Pvt.	Co. C	27 Apr 61	
Judd, William	27	New York	Sgt.	Co. H	31 Jan 60	RA
K						
Kane, William	28	Mass.	Pvt.	Co. K	26 May 60	RA
KAUFFMAN, Albert B.	18	Penn.	Sgt.	Co. I	12 Sep 60 P+	RA FC
Kearney, Philip	29	Canada	Pvt.	Co. E	03 Jan 60+	RA D
†Kelly, Jackson	34	Georgia	Pvt.	Co. L	17 Jan 63	RA
Kelly, Michael	25	Ireland	Pvt.	Co. C	27 May 61	
Kemper, John	37	Germany	Sgt.	Co. A	10 Dec 59 P	RA
Kendall, Joseph F.	21	Maine	Sgt.	Co. F	15 Nov 62	
Kennedy, John D.	25	New York	Sgt.	Co. M	31 May 60+	RA D
Kennedy, Martin	27	Ireland	Pvt.	Co. K	14 May 60	RA Dd
Kenny, Felix	25		Pvt.	Co. D	03 Feb 57	RA
Kenny, James	21	New York	Pvt.	Co. A	21 Jan 61	
Kenny, Neal	21	Ireland	Pvt.	Co. H	06 Jun 57	D
Kernan, John	27	Ireland	Pvt.	Co. C	28 My 61	Dd
†KERNER, Henry	22	Germany	Sgt.	Cos. A/D	05 Nov 58+	RA FC
Kestner John			Musician	G/F/S	29 Nov 62	
Ketron, Samuel	21	Penn.	Pvt.	Co. H	26 May 63	RA
Kimball, Lorenzo A.	24	New York	Cpl.	Co. K	25 Nov 62	Dd

Name	Age	Birthplace	Rank	Company	Enlisted	Status
King, Jacob			Pvt.	Co. G	06 Dec 62	
King, John	32	Ireland	Pvt.	Co. I	29 May 64	
King, Julius A.	23		Cpl.	Cos. E/I	17 Sep 61+	
†King, Napoleon M.	30	Ireland	Pvt.	Co. L	03 Dec 62	
King, Thomas	18	Penn.	Pvt.	Cos. H/F/S	25 May 63	
Kinneson, Justice			Pvt.	Co. I	28 Nov 62	
Kinsella, John			Sgt.	Co. B		
Kirkman, George	22	Indiana	Pvt.	Co. G	09 May 60	RA D
KIRWAN, John	21		Sgt.	Co. K	23 Sep 58+	RA FC
†Klein, Frederick W.	24	Germany	Cpl.	Co. C	21 Mar 57	RA
Knudson, Henry	19	Sweden	Pvt.	Co. K	25 Nov 62	Dd
Koenig, Frederick W.	34	Prussia	Pvt.	Co. F	11 Jul 64 P	
Kohler, Joseph	31	Germany	Pvt.	Co. G	10 Feb 60	RA
Kost, Martin	26	Germany	Pvt.	Co. D	01 Oct 60 P	RA Dd
Kroft, John T.	23		Pvt.	Co. C	29 Mar 61	
Kroosse, William H.	29	Germany	Sgt.	Co. I	05 Apr 60	RA
Kutzendofer, John			Pvt.	Co. G	27 Nov 62	
L						
Lachtrup, Henry	21	Germany	Bugler	Co. I	16 Sep 61	
*Lake, Horace			Pvt.	Co. K	01 Dec 62	POW
*Lamb, Benjamin F.			Cpl.	Co. L	03 Dec 62	MIA
Lambert, Michael M.	21	Maryland	Pvt.	Co. I	25 Mar 57	RA
Landgogt, Harry	23		Pvt.	Co. D	11 Dec 56	RA
Lannon, Edward	21		Pvt.	Co. D	24 Apr 60	RA
Lansen, Welleon	21	Denmark	Pvt.	Co. H	29 May 60	RA
Lapoint, Adolphus	22	Canada	Bugler	Co. E	21 Oct 62+	RA
Larsen, James	27	Denmark	1st Sgt.	Co. H	29 May 60+	RA
†Latti, Peter	21	Germany	Cpl.	Co. D	12 Jun 60	RA
*Lauby, Otto	21	Switzerland	Pvt.	Co. H	14 May 60	
Lawless, James	27	Ireland	Pvt.	Cos. F/E	06 Jun 63	Dd
Lawn, John	24	New York	Sgt.	Cos. G/L	31 May 60	RA
Lawrence, Alexander C.		New York	Pvt.	Co. B	09 Dec 62+	
*Lawrence, Joseph	22	France	Pvt.	Co. F	15 Jun 60	RA
Lay, James A.			Pvt.	Co. C	02 Dec 62	
Lee, James	18	Ohio	Bugler	Co. F	29 Jan 63	
Lee, John J.			Pvt.	Co. M	04 Dec 62	
Leitz, Alexander	25		Sgt.	Co. D	02 Mar 57+	RA
*Lemon, John R.	22	Michigan	Pvt.	Co. K	26 Nov 62	
Lemons, George D.		Ohio	Pvt.	Co. G	10 Jan 63	
*Lennox, Jeffrey	27	Ireland	Pvt.	Co. B	11 Dec 60	MIA
Lewis, Stephen			Pvt.	Co. I	01 Dec 62	
Liebert, Lawrence			Pvt.	Co. G	29 Nov 62	
Light, William H.	25		Cpl.	Co. D	31 Jan 61	
Limberger, Charles	21	Germany	Artificer	Co. L	29 Nov 54	RA
Linch, Jeremiah	26	Penn.	Pvt.	Co. E	14 May 60	RA
*Linder, Emil	21		Pvt.	Co. I	14 Sep 61	MIA
Lindsay, Edwin B.	21	Germany	Pvt.	Co. D	31 Jul 60	RA
Lindsey, Cornelius W.			Pvt.	Co. M	02 Dec 62	D
Livingston, Clay			Cpl.	Co. K	01 Dec 62	
Loask, John	24	Germany	Pvt.	Co. D	14 Mar 61	
Long, Gerome S.			Pvt.	Co. M	27 Nov 62	D
Long, John	21	Ireland	Pvt.	Co. I	17 Mar 59	RA
Long, Samuel E.	18		Pvt.	Co. M	28 Nov 62	
Longbough, Henry	21	Penn.	Pvt.	Co. A	24 Jul 60+	RA D
Longdorff, James W.		Ohio	Pvt.	Co. M	03 Dec 62	

Name	Age	Birthplace	Rank	Company	Enlisted	Status
Loucks, Alonzo L.	23	New York	Pvt.	Co. B	29 Apr 61	
Loyd, Benjamin F.	23	Ohio	Sgt.	Co. F	29 Jan 61	
*Lucas, Otavius A.	43	Virginia	Pvt.	Co. I	18 Jun 64	
Lutton, Charles	21	Ireland	Sgt. Maj.	Cos. B/F/S	16 Apr 61	
Lyker, William F.			Pvt.	Co. I	29 Nov 62	
Lyons, Wickliff	31		Sgt./Saddler	Co. B	06 May 60+	RA
M						
Macy, Abijah			Pvt.	Co. D	28 Nov 62	D
Maguire, John	22	Ireland	Pvt.	Co. G	07 May 60+	RA D
Maher, James	26	Ireland	Pvt.	Co. G	25 Apr 59	RA
*Mahern, Charles			Pvt.	Co. C		
Mahon, Thomas	22		Pvt.	Co. H	30 Oct 62	
†Mahoney, Andrew J.			Pvt.	Co. M	04 Dec 62	
Maloughney, Patrick	23	Ireland	Sgt.	Co. C	20 Jun 60	RA
Malott, Stanley			Pvt.	Co. G	27 Nov 62	
Mann, Henry	20		Pvt.	Co. D	16 Dec 56	RA
Mara, Michael	21	Ireland	Pvt.	Co. C	03 May 61	
*Marbach, Max			Sgt.	Co. C		
Mardin, Charles F.	35		Sgt.	Co. D	13 Nov 60	RA
Maris, Enoch	21	Indiana	Pvt.	Co. F	30 Oct 62	
Market, Valentine		Germany	Pvt.	Co. C	28 Nov 62	
Markham, Richard	28	England	Pvt.	Co. C	07 Jul 60	Dd
Marky, Christopher	27		Pvt.	Co. I	11 Sep 61	
Marshall, John	30	England	Sgt.	Co. I	28 Nov 64	
Marteeny, Singleton A.	21	Penn.	Sgt.	Co. F	13 Aug 62	
Martin, Alexander	28	Scotland	Pvt.	Co. D	03 Jun 58	RA
Martin, Joshua R.			Pvt.	Co. D	01 Dec 62	
Martin, William	28	Germany	Sgt.	Co. A	28 Apr 58	RA
*Masch, Frederick	28	Germany	1st Cl. Musician	Cos. F/S	01 Jul 64 P	
Massey, James	33	Ireland	Pvt.	Co. B	15 Sep 64 P	
Mauck, Emil R.	25	Germany	Pvt.	Co. E	16 Jul 60+	RA
Mayhew, Prosper			Pvt.	Co. M	28 Nov 62	D
McAdams, John	18		Pvt.	Co. B	17 Feb 63	Dd
McAlpin, James H.	14		Trumpeter	Co. D	07 Mar 64	
McALPINE, James	40	Mass.	1st Sgt.	Co. K	19 Oct 58+	RA FC
McAnulty, Hugh	26	Ireland	Cpl.	Co. F	13 Jun 60+	
MCCAFFERTY, Neil J.	21	Ireland	1st Sgt.	Co. A	20 Apr 58+	RA FC
McCall, William H.	19	Arkansas	Pvt.	Co. C	20 May 61	
McCanaha, Samuel F. M.				Co. M	03 Dec 62	D
McClure, Henry F.			Pvt.	Co. B	28 Nov 62	
McCormick, Jacob A.	28	Penn.	Pvt.	Co. D	09 Jan 60	RA
*McCoy, Josiah	21	Virginia	Pvt.	Co. F	12 Nov 62	
*McCulling, William M.	43		Pvt.	Co. D	01 Dec 62	
McDermot, John	30	Ireland	Pvt.	Co. F	04 May 60	RA
†McDonell, Daniel	21	Ireland	Pvt.	Co. D	25 Apr 61	
*McDonald, James	25		Pvt.	Co. E	03 Jan 60	RA
†McDonald, Michael			Orderly	Co. E		
McDonald, Samuel J.			Cpl.	Co. I	01 Dec 62	
McDonough, Patrick	23		Pvt.	Co. I	11 Dec 61	
*McElroy, Peter D.			Pvt.	Co. L	03 Dec 62	
McFarland, Thomas	21	Ireland	Pvt.	Co. H	01 Nov 62	
McGarry, Patrick	31	Ireland	Pvt.	Co. B	23 Apr 58+	RA
McGee, Francis	27	Ireland	Pvt.	Co. E	30 Dec 62 P	
McGee, William	23		Pvt.	Co. D	15 Feb 57	RA
McGorran [see McGowan]						

Name	Age	Birthplace	Rank	Company	Enlisted	Status
McGowan Patrick			Sgt.	Cos. H/B	27 Sep 58+	RA
McGrath, William	20	England	Pvt.	Co. E	23 Oct 62	
McGraw, James			Pvt.	Co. I	20 Dec 62	
McGuinty, Hugh	26	Scotland	Pvt.	Co. K	09 Nov 59	RA Dd
McHugh, Peter			Pvt.	Co. F	11 Aug 63	RA
McIlvaine, John	29	Ireland	Pvt.	Co. C	16 Jan 57+	RA
†McKay, John	21	Ireland	Pvt.	Co. C	24 Apr 61	
*McKinney, Michael			Pvt.	Co. G	28 Nov 62	
McKnight, John	23	Ireland	Pvt.	Co. B	03 May 61	Dd
†McKutchen, Alexander			Pvt.	Co. C		
McLain, Daniel	23	Penn.	Pvt.	Co. F	29 Jan 63	Dd
McLaughlin, James			Pvt.	Co. H	25 Jan 61	RA
McLaughlin, Michael H.	22	Ireland	Bugler	Co. H	11 May 61	
McMannus, Charles		Maryland	Pvt.	Co. B	01 Sep 60	Dd
MCMASTER, Charles	21	Ireland	1st Sgt.	Cos. I/H	22 Nov 58	RA FC
McMillan, Orlando L.			Pvt.	Co. B	02 Dc 62	
McNally, John	24	Ireland	Pvt.	Co. D	24 Apr 61	
McNeal, Daniel			Pvt.	Co. M	05 Dec 62D	
McNight, John	23	New York	Pvt.	Co. B	03 May 61	Dd
McWilliams, Joseph	19	Ireland	Pvt.	Co. I	15 Apr 61	
†Megan, Hugh	28	Ireland	Pvt.	Co. I	25 Mar 58	RA
Meltzer, Louis	21	Germany	Pvt.	Co. K	15 May 60	D
Merchant, Caleb W.	27	Kentucky	Sgt.	Co. C	14 Feb 60	RA
Merrick, Charles			Cpl.	Co. E	26 Feb 61	Dd
Meyer, Nickolaus	26	Germany	Pvt.	Co. D	16 Apr 61	Dd
Michsell, Charles	25	Ireland	Sgt.	Co. C	03 Jul 60+	RA
Middleton, James A.			Pvt.	Co. M	22 Dec 62	
Miers [see Myers]						
Miller, Anthony	25	Germany	Pvt.	Co. K	21 Nov 59	RA
Miller, Charles	22	Germany	Pvt.	Cos. E/K	17 Mar 57	RA
Miller, Edward	21	Germany	Sgt.	Co. A	29 Mar 60	RA
Miller, Henry F.	19	Penn.	Pvt.	Co. M	28 Nov 62	D
Miller, Jacob	32	France	Farrier	Co. C	02 Aug 60+	RA
*Miller, James			Pvt.	Co. C	29 Nov 62	
Miller, Jesse			Pvt.	Co. K	26 Nov 62	
*Miller, John			Pvt.	Co. K	03 Dec 62	
Miller, John	24	Germany	Pvt.	Co. I	09 Sep 61	
Miller, John	20	Penn.	Cpl.	Co. E	23 Oct 62	
Miller, William			Pvt.	Co. D	01 Dec 62	
*Miller, William A.	20	Penn.	Pvt.	Co. F	29 Jan 63	
Mills, Ephram			Pvt.	Co. M	29 Nov 62	D
†Millwright, Alexander	24	Scotland	Farrier	Co. C	01 Dec 57+	RA
Milner, Grammar B.			Pvt.	Co. I	02 Dec 62	
*Milliner, Vincent C.	20	Illinois	Pvt.	Co. L	04 Dec 62	
Mitch, Charles			Pvt.	Co. M	08 Dec 62	
Mitchell, Charles			Pvt.	Cos. C/M	08 Dec 62	
Mollan, William J.	23	New York	Pvt.	Co. D	17 Apr 61	Dd
Monahan, Michael	25	Ireland	Pvt.	Co. E	30 Mar 63	RA
Montgomery, Charles A.	21	Ireland	Bugler	Co. A	28 Jul 62	
*Moore, Albert A.	21	Illinois	Pvt.	Co. L	12 Dec 62	
Moore, Edward H.			Pvt.	Co. L	15 Dec 62	
*Moore, John	41	Ireland	Pvt.	Co. E	27 Aug 60 P	
*Moore, Thomas			Sgt.	Co. L	20 Dec 62	
*Moran, James	21	Ireland	Pvt.	Co. D	26 Mar 61	
Morehead, John	26	Ireland	Pvt.	Co. E	10 Mar 63	RA

Name	Age	Birthplace	Rank	Company	Enlisted	Status
†Morgan, Hugh			Pvt.	Co. I		
Morgan, James			Pvt.	Co. G	28 Nov 62	
Moriarty, John	18	Penn.	Trumpeter	Co. F	03 Jun 63	
Moroney, Michael	21	Ireland	Pvt.	Co. D	01 Apr 61	Dd
Morrison, Leonard	38		Pvt.	Co. M	29 Jul 64	Dd
†Muldowny, Timothy	22	Ireland	Blacksmith	Co. C	10 Dec 59	
Mulhern, Charles	21	Ireland	Sgt.	Co. C	26 Apr 55+	
Mullaney, Barnard F.			Sgt.	Co. C	24 Dec 62	
*Mullen, Thomas			Pvt.	Co. M		MIA
Mulleneaux, James A.			Pvt.	Co. M		
Mulvihill, Morris	20		Pvt.	Co. D	08 Jun 60	RA
Munn, William H.	32	Ireland	Cpl.	Co. K	31 Jul 64 P	
*Murphy, Andrew W.			Pvt.	Co. K	01 Dec 62	
Murphy, John	29	Ireland	Pvt.	Co. C	29 Apr 61	
†Murphy, Martin J.	29	Ireland	Sgt.	Co. G	01 Nov 61	RA
Murphy, Thomas J.			Pvt.	Co. K	01 Nov 62	
Murray, John	26	Ireland	Bugler	Co. A	08 Aug 62	
Murray, Louis C.	21	New York	Pvt.	Co. B	29 Apr 61	
*Myers, Frank	27	Germany	Pvt.	Co. F	16 Jun 63	
N						
Namie, Francis	30	Switzerland	Pvt.	Co. G	04 Jul 60	RA
Narragon, Ross C.			Pvt.	Co. L	12 Dec 62	Dd
Nauck, Emil R.	25	Germany	Pvt.	Co. E	16 Jul 60+	RA D
Neff, Reuben	22	Penn.	1st Sgt.	Co. C	11 Jul 60+	RA D
Nelb, Jacob			Pvt.	Co. I	28 Nov 62	
Nettlejohn, Aaron			Pvt.	Co. K	25 Nov 62	
Newhaus, Charles	28	Prussia	Sgt.	Co. H	25 Mar 60+	RA
Newman, Charles	37	Prussia	Pvt.	Co. F	01 Jul 60	RA
Newman, Joseph			Pvt.	Co. I	03 Dec 62	
Newslak, Lewis			Pvt.	Co. L	04 Dec 62	D
Newton, William			Sgt.	Co. C	03 Dec 62	
Niscon, William			Pvt.	Co. K	26 Nov 62	
Noble, James	21	Canada	Pvt.	Co. G	31 May 60+	RA D
Norris, John S.			Pvt.	Co. L	06 Dec 62	
O						
Obay, Alexander	25	Canada	Pvt.	Co. F	15 Dec 62	
Obladen, Joseph	21	Germany	Sgt.	Co. I	27 Dec 59	RA
O'Brien, Dennis	21	Penn.	Pvt.	Co. H	17 Jun 63	
O'Brien, Henry	22	Ireland	Sgt.	Co. G	25 May 60+	RA
O'Connell, John			Pvt.	Co. B	16 Mar 62	Dd
O'Connell, Michael			1st Sgt.	Co. H		RA
O'CONNELL, William	24	Ireland	1st Sgt.	Co. B	24 Nov 54+	FC
O'Conner, John	21		Pvt.	Co. D	14 Jan 57	RA
O'Connor, Festus			Pvt.	Co. C	28 Nov 62	
*O'Dell, George C.		Ohio	Pvt.	Co. K	25 Nov 62	
*O'Conner, Hugh	24	England	Pvt.	Co. D	02 Jun 58+	RA
Olerich, John M.	23	Germany	Pvt.	Co. B	11 Jun 60	RA
O'Hanlin, Terrnace	24	Ireland	1st Sgt.	Co. A	01 Mar 64 P	RA
Olinger, John W.			Cpl.	Co. M	06 Dec 62	
O'Mally, Patrick	31	Ireland	1st Sgt.	Cos. D/L	13 Jun 60	RA
*O'Neal, Hugh			Pvt.	Co. H		
O'Neil, John	22	Ireland	Cpl.	Co. F	21 Feb 59	RA
*O'Neil, Uriah	24	Illinois	Pvt.	Co. H	18 Feb 63	
Orange, Andrew			Cpl.	Co. K	26 Nov 62	
†Orange, James			Pvt.	Co. M	06 Dec 62	

Name	Age	Birthplace	Rank	Company	Enlisted	Status
†Orr, Archibald B.			Pvt.	Co. I	28 Nov 62	
*Osmus, John C.	18	Penn.	Pvt.	Co. I	06 Sep 61	
†Owens, Edward	28	Ireland	Sgt.	Co. K	25 May 60	RA
Oxford, Henry	19	England	Cpl./Trumpeter	Cos. E/F	14 Nov 62+	
P						
Pair, William	28	Georgia	Chief Waggoner	Cos. I/F/S	31 May 60+	RA
*Palmer, George C.			Sgt.	Co. K	03 Dec 62	
Parker, B.			Cpl.	Co. H	01 Jan 63	
Parkhurst, Henry C.	21	Vermont	Pvt.	Co. B	27 Apr 61	
*Parsons, Alandon D.	27	Ohio	Pvt.	Co. L	16 Dec 62	
†Parsons, John	33	Ohio	Pvt.	Co. H	03 Apr 62	
Parsons, George	32	New York	Pvt.	Co. F	18 May 60	Dd
Partello, Alvin	27		Pvt.	Co. D	25 May 61	
*Patterson, James D.	21	Penn.	Pvt.	Co. D	20 Dec 57	RA
Patterson, Newton			Pvt.	Co. C	03 Dec 62	
*Patterson, John	24		Sgt.	Co. B	28 Nov 59+	RA
Patton, John	23	Ireland	Sgt.	Co. B	28 Nov 59+	
Paugh, Henry			Sgt.	Co. L	02 Dec 62	
*Perciville, Richard J.	21	New York	Bugler	Cos. C/H	01 Feb 58+	RA
Perrigo, Stephen			Pvt.	Co. B	04 Dec 62	
Perry, Hugh				Co. I	01 Jun 62	Dd
Perry, John C.	27	Ohio	Cpl.	Cos. G/F/S	16 Nov 59	
†Peters, William	28	Germany	Pvt.	Co. I	10 Jan 60	RA
†Pettitt, Levi L.	27	Ohio	Pvt.	Co. G	02 Dec 62	
Phelps, Herbert N.			Sgt.	Co. L	17 Dec 62	
Pherson, Elinah C.			Pvt.	Co. L	04 Dec 62	
Phfiloon, James	20	New York	Pvt.	Co. L	17 Feb 63	
Philes, George	29	Germany	Pvt.	Co. F	01 Apr 63	D
Phillabrick, John			Cpl.	Co. G	22 Dec 62	
†Phillips, George	30	Germany	Cpl.	Co. I	28 Nov 62	RA
Pierce, Samuel D.			Pvt.	Co. I	25 Nov 62	
Pile [see Prile]						
Pilgrim, William	21	Germany	Pvt.	Co. D	05 Jun 60+	RA
Pinnmil, Henry			Pvt.	Co. K	25 Nov 62	
Pitcher, Andrew J.	25		Pvt.	Co. D	02 Feb 57	RA
Plum, Henry S.			Pvt.	Co. G	02 Dec 62	
Podrabsky, Anthony	23		Pvt.	Co. D	13 Apr 60	RA
Poole, Frederick R.	25		Pvt.	Co. I	21 Dec 59	Disc.
Porchett, William			Pvt.	Co. M	20 Nov 62	
Porthouse, Thomas	35	England	Pvt.	Co. D	11 May 62	
Post, John W.			Pvt.	Co. E	27 Nov 62	
Potts, Mariam R.			Pvt.	Co. M	20 Nov 62	
POWELL, James		Maryland	1st Sgt.	Co. I	17 Nov 56 P+	FC
*Power, Maurice	26	Ireland	Pvt.	Co. D	11 Apr 60+	
†Pratt, Friend	21	New York	Pvt.	Co. A	23 Oct 62	RA
Pratt, Josiah J.	25		Pvt.	Co. D	10 Jan 60	
†Preas, Henry J.	21	Germany	Pvt.	Co. A	24 May 60+	RA
Preston, John D.			Artificer	Co. E	01 Jun 61	
†Prile, Charles	21	Germany	Cpl.	Co. I	06 Apr 60	
Probert, George W. L.	22	England	Pvt.	Co. B	26 Nov 62	Dd
Prot, Franz			Pvt.	Co. B	21 Mar 61	
Prowell, Andrew S.	22	Penn.	Pvt.	Co. F	07 Jun 63	
Purves, Alexander	18	Penn.	Pvt.	Co. F	20 Apr 63	Dd
Putman, Albert J.	21	Mass.	Pvt.	Co. C	11 Apr 61+	

Name	Age	Birthplace	Rank	Company	Enlisted	Status
Q						
Quattlandery, Paul	21	Germany	Pvt.	Co. C	14 May 61	
Quilty, James	20	Ireand	Pvt.	Co. A	23 Oct 62	
Quinn, Edward	43		Ordnance	Co. L	07 May 63 P	RA
Quinn, Michael			Bugler	Co. D	02 Dec 62	
†Quirk, James	28	Ireland	Cpl.	Co. C	25 Jan 58+	
Quirk, James	19	New York	Pvt.	Co. C	19 Jun 62	D
R						
*Ramo, Antonin			Pvt.	Co. K	26 Dec 61	
†Rankin, John	33	Scotland	Sgt.	Co. A	01 Jul 64 P	
Rankin, William H.	24	Penn.	1st Sgt.	Cos. E/F	15 Jul 60 P+	RA
*Ratlesburger, Hermon	21	Switzerland	Pvt.	Co. F	13 Jul 63	
Reese, Louis A.	29		Hosp. Steward	Co. C	28 Dec 56	RA
Reid, Alexander	34	England	Sgt.	Co. K	24 May 60	RA
*Reigilmien, William			Bugler	Cos. G/F/S	29 Nov 62	MIA
RENDLEBOCK, Joseph	33	Prussia	1st Sgt.	Co. G	16 Aug 56+	RA FC
Rengey, James	26	Ireland	Pvt.	Co. H	20 Apr 63	Dd
Rensell, John			Sgt.	Co. B	09 Dec 62	
Reppen, Alfred			Sgt.	Co. K	25 Nov 62	
†Rhyman, Frederick	21	Ohio	Pvt.	Co. I	09 Sep 61	
Rice, Daniel C.	29	Vermont	Pvt.	Co. E	21 Oct 62+	
Rice, Rufus			Pvt.	Co. G	04 Dec 62	
Richards, David	22	England	Pvt.	Co. D	01 Mar 55+	Dd
†Richmond, Joseph B.	21	Virginia	Sgt.	Co. K	12 Nov 58	RA
Richter, Otto	26	Germany	Sgt.	Co. I	03 Jan 62+	
Ries, James K.	26	New York	Cpl.	Co. C	19 Mar 60	RA
Riggin, Sylvister			Pvt.	Co. K	28 Nov 62	
Riker, John			Sgt.	Co. C	01 Jun 61	
Ripin [see Reppen]						
Rish, Adam			Pvt.	Co. M	20 Dec 62	
Ritter, John F.	21	Penn.	Pvt.	Co. A	10 Oct 61+	
Roberts, Frederick	24	Penn.	Pvt.	Co. F	14 Apr 61	D
*Roberts, Jacob	21	New Hamp.	Pvt.	Co. H	02 Mar 57	RA
†Roberts, Richard	28	England	Pvt.	Co. F	19 Jul 62+	
Robertson, Henry B.	26	Wash. D.C.	Pvt.	Co. H	31 Dec 56	RA
Robertson, James	27	Indiana	Pvt.	Co. F	07 Dec 61 P	
Robinson, Joseph R.	23		1st Sgt.	Co. D	13 Mar 57	RA
Roch, Patrick	30	Ireland	Pvt.	Co. I	17 Jan 62	
*Rodgers, Solomon	25	Ohio	Pvt.	Co. K	01 May 60	RA
Rogers, Ransom	26	S. Carolina	Pvt.	Co. C	27 Feb 60+	RA
Roland, Jacob			Pvt.	Co. M	05 Dec 62	
Rollin, Gilbert			Pvt.	Co. L	29 Nov 62	
*Roof, John C.			Pvt.	Cos. D/L	01 Dec 62	
Rora, Christ H.			Sgt.	Co. I	01 Dec 62	
Rose, Frank	28		Pvt.	Co. C	14 Feb 61	
Rose, John C.			Sgt.	Cos. C/L		
Rose, William	26	Germany	Pvt.	Co. I	06 Sep 61	
Rosmin, Henry	23	Germany	Pvt.	Co. D	19 May 61	
Rossmaier, Martin G.	31	Germany	Cpl.	Co. H	04 Sep 57 P+	
Roy, Willis			Pvt.	Co. M	25 Dec 62	
ROYS, Elbridge G.	21		Sgt.	Cos. B/L	02 Dec 56+	RA FC
Ruger, Johann			Pvt.	Co. D	01 Jun 61	
Rupell, William	26		Pvt.	Co. D	25 Nov 57	
RUSH, Andrew			Sgt.	Co. B	02 Dec 62	FC
Russell, Henry	19	Conn.	Pvt.	Co. A	23 Oct 62+	

Name	Age	Birthplace	Rank	Company	Enlisted	Status
Russell, William	29	Scotland	Commissary Sgt.	Cos. D/F/S	01 Nov 62+	
Rutherford, Isaac	29	England	Pvt.	Co. H	05 May 60	RA
Ryan, Gavin W.			Sgt.	Co. D	28 Nov 62	
S						
*Saddler, James			Pvt.	Co. K	27 Nov 62	MIA
Sager, George W.	21	Ohio	Pvt.	Co. B	22 Nov 59	RA
†Saller, Philip H.			Pvt.	Co. K	26 Nov 62	
Sanders, William			Pvt.	Co. M	18 Dec 62	
Sargent, Enoch R.		Mass.	Pvt.	Co. G	26 Feb 59	RA
Sassaman, Jacob	21	Ohio	Hosp. Steward	Cos. E/F/S	23 Oct 62+	
†Sawyer, William	33	Mass.	Pvt.	Co. F	14 Apr 63	
Schaeffer, John M.			Pvt.	Co. M	05 Dec 62	
Scherer, Martin	36	Germany	Cpl.	Co. I	06 Sep 61	
Scherr, Louis	20	Germany	Pvt.	Co. H	09 Apr 63	D
Schirle, Franz J.	24	Germany	Pvt.	Co. A	22 Sep 58	RA
Schlagel, William	22	Germany	Wagoner	Co. I	03 Sep 61	
Schmidt, Charles	22		Pvt.	Co. D	11 Dec 57	RA
Schoefer, Frederick	22	New York	Pvt.	Cos. H/G	18 Jun 63	Dd
Scholl, Frederick	25	Germany	Sgt.	Cos. I/M	12 Sep 61	
Schorling, Edward	25	Prussia	Farrier	Co. K	08 Nov 58+	RA
Schotthoffer, Bartholomew	24	Germany	Pvt.	Co. E	08 Jan 58	RA Dd
Schueffer, John W.			Pvt.	Co. M	05 Dec 62	
*Schwager, Henry			Pvt.	Co. D	08 Oct 60	RA
Schwanke, Fredrick	21	Germany	Cpl.	Co. I	12 Sep 61	
Scott, Abraham			Pvt.	Co. G	22 Nov 62	Dd
Scott, Alexander	24	Vermont	Pvt.	Co. C	16 Apr 61	Dd
Scott, George	21	Ireland	Pvt.	Co. F	14 Apr 63	D
Scott, Henry H.	20		Pvt.	Co. H	22 Apr 63	D
Scott, Patrick	23	Ireland	Sgt.	Co. K	15 Nov 58	RA
†Scott, William	26	Illinois	Pvt.	Co. D	24 Feb 60	RA
Scott, William J.			Sgt.	Co. M	17 Dec 62	
Seberean, Lyman	22	Canada	Pvt.	Co. I	16 Mar 60	RA Dd
Sebree, William K.			Pvt.	Co. D	06 Dec 62	
Secrist, Robert B.	24	Penn.	Pvt.	Co. A/L	21 Feb 64 P	D
Seely, Thomas			Pvt.	Co. L	06 Dec 62	Dd IC
†Sennegan, William H.			Pvt.	Co. K		
*Shafer, Frederick			2nd Cl. Musician	Cos. E/S/F	02 Aug 62	RA
Sharon, James			Pvt.	Co. G	25 Nov 62	
Shaw, Henry	21		Pvt.	Co. C	04 Apr 61	Dd
Shaw, John	23	Ireland	Pvt.		21 Mar 61	
Shaw, John S.	32	Ireland	Pvt.	Co. F	13 Apr 63	Dd
*Sheldon, Robert	28	Maryland	Sgt.	Co. F	14 Aug 60+	
*Sherman, Moses D.	18	New York	Pvt.	Co. E	21 Oct 62	D
Sheron, Nicholas				Co. I	28 Nov 62	
Shields, James		Ireland	Musician	Band	21 Mar 61	
Shively, William			Pvt.	Co. G	28 Nov 62	
†Shoomaker, Avram M.	21	New York	Pvt.	Co. E	01 Dec 57	RA
Shultz, William			1st Cl. Musician	Band	29 Feb 64	
Sidler, Gabriel			Cpl.	Co. L	13 Dec 62	
*SIMSON, Thomas W.		New York	Cpl.	Co. I	19 Oct 58+	RA FC
*Simson, William	21	New York	Bugler	Cos. F/S	19 Jun 60+	RA
Sisk, Jones			Pvt.	Co. G	26 Nov 62	D
*Sisson, Joseph			Pvt.	Co. D	03 Dec 63	
*Slayton, George			Bugler	Co. K	26 Nov 62	
Slogan, Thomas	21	Ireland	Pvt.	Co. B	20 Nov 58	D

Name	Age	Birthplace	Rank	Company	Enlisted	Status
Sloughund, Louis G.				Co. B	29 Apr 61	
Smassal, John	27	Germany	Farrier	Co. H	01 Nov 64 P	
Smith, Charles			Pvt.	Co. B	01 Dec 62	
Smith, Charles E.			Pvt.	Co. K	25 Nov 62	
Smith, James R.			Saddler	Co. G	28 Nov 62	
Smith, John	29	Wash. D.C.	Pvt.	Co. G	24 Feb 57+	RA
Smith, John L.	36		Pvt.	Co. A	13 Feb 60+	RA
Smith, Julius H.	26	Virginia	Pvt.	Co. C	20 Sep 60	D
Smith, Louis H.			Pvt.	Co. D	29 Nov 62	
Smith, Walter H.			Pvt.	Co. K	26 Nov 62	D
Snow, Francis H.	18	Indiana	Pvt.	Co. L	04 Dec 62	
Snyder, Thomas E.			Pvt.	Co. M	28 Nov 62	D
Sollers, Isaac			Pvt.	Co. M	09 Dec 62	
Sommers, William	29	Germany	Pvt.	Co. A	27 Sep 58	RA
*Somers, Patrick			Pvt.	Co. C	01 Dec 62	
Sonigan [see Sennigan]						
Soporling, Edward			Farrier	Co. K	08 Nov 58	RA
Spangler, Samuel	21	Penn.	Pvt.	Co. H	16 Mar 59	RA
Spencer, Uriah	33	Penn.	Pvt.	Co. I	15 Mar 58	RA
Speierer, Xavier	27	Germany	Pvt.	Co. I	14 Sep 61	
Stack, Patrick E.	24	Ireland	Pvt.	Co. M	02 Jun 60	RA
Stafford, John			Pvt.	Co. K	26 Nov 62	
Stahl, Samuel			Pvt.	Co. L	01 Dec 62	D
Stampley, Frederick			Pvt.	Co. D	13 Dec 62	
Stanley, John	23	New York	Pvt.	Co. C	15 Apr 61	
*Starkey, William			Pvt.	Co. L	04 Dec 62	
St. Clair, George W.	21	Kentucky	Pvt.	Co. A	15 Feb 60	RA
Steenrod, Louis D.			Pvt.	Co. M	28 Nov 62	Dd
Steinmetz, William	26	Germany	Sgt.	Co. G	14 May 60+	RA
Stephenson, Charles W.			Pvt.	Co. K	25 Nov 62	
†Stettler, Adolph	27	Switzerland	Pvt.	Co. A	29 Oct 58	
Steven, George H.	28	Penn.	Musician	Co. K	01 Dec 62	
Stevens, Stephen B.	23	Austria	Pvt.	Co. F	16 Nov 58	RA
Stevenson, Samuel H.	28		Musician	Co. K	01 Dec 62	
Stillwell, James			Pvt.	Co. G	03 Dec 62	D
Stitzer, John T.	22	Penn.	Sgt.	Co. E	21 Oct 62	
Stoffer, Anton				Co. E		Dd
†Stokes, Roger	25	Ireland	Pvt.	Co. C	02 Jan 57	RA
STOLL, Andrew W.			1stSgt	Co. K	01 May 56 P+	RA FC
Stoll, Labo	26	"At sea"	Farrier	Cos. C/D	16 Sep 61	
*Stone, Charles W.	25	New York	Pvt.		06 Sep 64	
Stone, Walter R.	21	Vermont	Pvt.	Co. C	05 Apr 61	Dd
Stonebach, Peter			Pvt.	Co. A	27 Jun 61	
Stoner, Nathan	28	Penn.	Pvt.	Co. H	15 Apr 63	RA
Stopper, Anthony	33	Germany	Pvt.	Co. E	12 Jul 60 P	Dd
Stout, John W.			Cpl.	Co. L	04 Dec 62	
Strang, James	21	New York	Pvt.	Co. C	01 May 61	
Striblin, Henry			Pvt.	Co. K	27 Nov 62	
Stricker, Michael			Farrier	Co. G	28 Nov 62	
Stricker, Peter A.			Sgt.	Co. G	27 Nov 62	
Strickland, Sherlock	22	Canada	Sgt.	Co. G	08 Feb 59	
Stroup, Julius			Farrier	Co. K	26 Nov 62	
Strunk, Charles			Pvt.	Co. E	11 Aug 63	
Struthers, William R.			Pvt.	Co. F	11 Oct 61	
Stump, David			Sgt.	Co. L	04 Dec 62	

Name	Age	Birthplace	Rank	Company	Enlisted	Status
Stutson, James			Sgt.	Co. C		
SULLIVAN, Thomas	W.	Ireland	Sgt.	Co. C	10 Mar 57+	RA FC
Swart, Peter			Pvt.	Co. K	27 Nov 62	
Sweeney, Edward	26	Ireland	Pvt.	Co. H	04 May 60	RA
Sweeney, Edwin P.			Bugler	Co. K	28 Nov 62	
Sweeney, Patrick	24	Ireland	Pvt.	Co. D	19 Apr 60+	RA
Swisher, William			Cpl.	Co. L	28 Nov 62	
Swords, James			Sgt./Bugler	Co. L	06 Dec 62	
T						
*Tapling, Robert	23	Mass.	Pvt.	Co. G	04 Nov 58	RA
Tarrant, Peter A.	24	New York	Sgt.	Co. H	12 Jul 64 P	
Tate, Samuel G.	22	Illinois	Pvt.	Co. I	28 Nov 62	Dd
Taylor, Elijah C.	20		Pvt.	Co. M	08 Dec 62	
Taylor, Lenonngrd M.			Pvt.	Co. M	08 Dec 62	
Taylor, Lycurgus			Pvt.	Co. M	08 Dec 62	
*Thatcher, William			Pvt.	Co. F	28 Jan 62	
Theile, Herman			Pvt.	Co. I	09 Nov 58	RA
Theiss, Frederick	25	Germany	Pvt	Co. G	04 Jul 60+	RA
Thomas, Albert M.	35	Vermont	Pvt.	Co. A	22 Oct 62	
Thomas, Edward			Pvt.	Co. G	01 Dec 62	
Thomas, John	32	Maryland	Pvt.	Co. G	01 Jul 59+	RA
Thomas, Kelly			OrdSgt.	Co. D	17 Feb 59	RA
Thomas, William	22	England	Pvt.	Co. G	23 Jan 60	RADd
†Thomi, Christian	26	Switzerland	Pvt.	Co. G	03 Nov 62	
Thompson, Benjamin F.	21	Maryland	Pvt.	Co. B	16 Aug 60+	RA
Thompson, Joseph			Pvt.	Co. L	23 Dec 62	
Thompson, William	21	Ireland	Pvt.	Co. H	07 May 58	RA Dd
Thorne, Elijah			Pvt.	Co. L	10 Dec 62	Dd IC
Thornton, William			Pvt.	Co. C	24 Dec 62	
Tibbal, Levi			Cpl.	Co. G	01 Feb 62	
Tinley, John	21	Ireland	Pvt.	Co. D	16 May 61	
Tobias, Peter	22	New York	Pvt.	Co. B	14 Mar 61	
Tompkins, David	23	England	Pvt.	Co. B	28 Nov 59	RA
Tormey, Nicholas			Pvt.	Co. F	16 Nov 58	RA
Townsend, Luther	27	Mass.	Pvt.	Co. G	25 Nov 58	RA
*Toy, Alfred S			2nd Cl. Musician	Co. M	05 Dec 62	
Toy, John	21	Ireland	Pvt.	Co. K	27 Aug 61	
Tracy, Leonard B.	27	Penn.	Co. C	26 Apr 61	D	
†Tracy, Patrick	21	Ireland	Pvt.	Co. D	18 Dec 60	
†Travillion, William			Pvt.	Co. G	28 Nov 62	
Trontner, Thomas			Pvt.	Co. L	01 Dec 62	
Truesdels, James			Sgt.	Cos. C/L	12 Nov 62	
Tudhope, William	18	Scotland	Sgt.	Cos. A/D	24 Jan 57+	RA
Tulley, Richard			Pvt.	Co. M	06 Dec 62	D
Tullis, John M.			Cpl.	Co. K	01 Dec 62	
*Turner, Donald			Pvt.	Co. I	01 Dec 62	MIA
*Tuttle, John E.			Pvt.	Co. L	05 Dec 62	
Twining, William			Pvt.	Co. B	02 Dec 62	
Twist, Stephen F.	28		Pvt.	Co. C	22 Dec 60 P	RA Dd
U						
Uhlhorn, Samuel B. P.	28	Maryland	Pvt.	Co. C	08 Feb 61	Dd
Unterriener, Mick	21	New York	Pvt.	Co. C	21 Mar 61	
V						
†Vallandingham, John			Pvt.	Co. G	05 Dec 62	
*Vallandingham, William			Pvt.	Co. G	26 Nov 62	

Name	Age	Birthplace	Rank	Company	Enlisted	Status
Vallery, Bernard	21	New Jersey	Pvt.	Cos. A/L	15 Feb 59	RA
Van Buskirk, Henry	21	New York	Pvt.	Co. D	23 Apr 60	D
Vance, Eli			Sgt.	Co. K	14 Jun 61	
Vandenburg, Henry	19	New York	Pvt.	Co. A	23 Oct 62	
Vaness, Ephraim			Pvt.	Co. G	28 Nov 62	
Van Horn, Charles	22	Virginia	Sgt. Maj.	Co. H	05 Oct 64 P	
Vallerly, Bernard	21	New Jersey	Pvt.	Co. A	15 Feb 59	RA
Varley, John			Pvt.	Co. L	02 Dec 62	
Varley, Miles	30	Ireland	Sgt.	Co. E	19 Jul 60+	
Venemon, William H.	19	Ohio	Pvt.	Co. F	29 Jan 63	
Vernon, Thomas	22	Ireland	Sgt.	Co. F	27 May 63	RA
Vetter, William			Bugler	Cos. F/S/G	09 Nov 58	RA
Vince, Allen			Sgt.	Co. L	01 Dec 62	
Von Segger, John T.			Farrier	Co. I	23 Sep 58	RA
W						
Wagoner, Jacob			Cpl.	Co. K	26 Nov 62	
*Wallace, Berry F.			Farrier	Co. K	27 Nov 62	MIA
*Wallace, William M.	21	Penn.	Pvt.	Co. H	02 Jun 63	
Wallack, Charles	22		Sgt. Maj.	Cos. F/S/G	11 Nov 57+	RA
†Walsh, James	27	Ireland	Sgt.	Co. A	03 Nov 61	
Walter, Aloys L.	32	France	Sgt.	Co. A	25 Jan 62+	
Walter, Louis			Pvt.	Co. G	29 Nov 62	
Waltman, Hiram	27	Penn.	Pvt.	Co. A	09 Dec 59	RA
*Walton, Thomas	29	England	Pvt.	Co. B	24 Nov 59	MIA
WALTZ, Charles A.	23	Germany	Musician	Band	12 Jun 61+	FC
WARD, Isaac M.	23	Kentucky	1st Sgt.	Co. A	26 Jan 57+	RA FC
Ward, John			Pvt.	Co. D	29 Nov 62	D
Ward, Walker			Pvt.	Co. G	28 Nov 62	D
Ward, William B.	24	New York	Saddler	Co. A	20 Jul 60	RA
Warner, William	30	Maryland	Pvt.	Co. E	14 Jun 62 P+	
Waterbury, William			Pvt.	Co. G	28 Nov 62	
Watham, William			Pvt.	Co. G	26 Nov 62	
Watson, John A.			Sgt.	Co. A	01 Jul 61	
Weaver, Elmodam			Cpl.	Co. K	26 Nov 62	
Weaver, William C.			Cpl.	Co. B	01 Dec 62	
Webb, William			Pvt.	Co. L	27 Nov 52+	
WEBSTER, John G.		England	Sgt. Maj.	Co. I	31 Aug 58+	RA FC
Webster, James P.				Co. M	25 Nov 62	D
Welch, John	19		Pvt.	Co. A	23 Oct 62	
Weller, James			Pvt.	Co. M	23 Dec 62	
Weller, Thomas	28	New York	Pvt.	Co. F	15 Jul 60+	RA
Welling, George			Pvt.	Co. M	04 Dec 62	
Wells, Henry			Sgt.	Co. B	25 Jan 62	
Welch, John	19	Maine	Pvt.	Co. A	23 Oct 62	
Welsh, John			Pvt.	Co. G	28 Nov 62	Dd
Welsh, Michael			Pvt.	Co. A	11 May 61	Dd
*Wentz, Charles	21	Germany	Pvt.	Co. C	15 Apr 61	
Werntz, George N.	24	Penn.	Pvt.	Co. F	13 Dec 62	
West, William			Pvt.	Co. G	01 Dec 62	
†Wetzberger, Stephen	23	Germany	Cpl.	Co. A	21 Nov 60	RA
Wetzel, Casper	31	Germany	Pvt.	Co. F	03 Nov 64 P	
Whalon, James			Pvt.	Co. M	05 Dec 62	
Wheeland, William			Sgt.	Co. I	09 Mar 63	
Whetzel, Ambrose	25	Ohio	Pvt.	Co. G	27 Nov 62	

Name	Age	Birthplace	Rank	Company	Enlisted	Status
Whetzel, Ambrose	23		Cpl.	Co. A	21 Nov 60	RA
White, Eli H.			Sgt.	Co. C	02 Dec 62	
White, William	24	New York	Pvt.	Co. F	11 Sep 61	
*Whitney, John W.			Cpl.	Co. K	28 Nov 62	
Whitney, J. W.	25	Ohio	Pvt.	Co. G	27 Nov 62	
Whitney, Mark J.			Pvt.	Co. K	26 Nov 62	
Whitthorn, William	27	Ireland	Commisary Sgt.	Co. D	26 Jul 60 P +	RA
Wiggins, Samuel F.			Pvt.	Co. M	04 Dec 62	
Wiley, Francis A.	21	Indiana	Pvt.	Co. A	11 Jun 60	Dd
Wilkey, Alexander	29	Scotland	Farrier	Co. B	12 Mar 60+	RA
†Wilkins, John	24	Illinois	Pvt.	Co. E	26 Sep 60	
Wilkins, John			Cpl.	Co. K		
*Wilkinson, Charles			Pvt.	Co. K	25 Nov 62	MIA
Williams, Charles F.			Cpl.	Co. H	29 Jan 63	
Williams, Charles T.	46	Penn.	Pvt.	Co. H	01 Mar 64 P	D
Williams, Francis	27	Penn.	Pvt.	Co. F	09 Apr 63	D
Williams, George				Co. F	28 Jul 63	D
Williams, George W.	24			Co. E	26 Sep 60	
Williams, James	25		Pvt.	Co. F	01 Feb 64	
Williams, John	26	England	Pvt.	Co. F	28 Apr 63 P	
Williams, John N.	18	Ohio	Pvt.	Co. F	29 Jan 61	
Williams, Nicholas B.			Pvt.	Co. L	05 Dec 62	
Williamson, Andrew J.	28	New York	Sgt.	Co. G	12 May 60 P+	
Willison, Charles H.	31		Pvt.	Co. I	03 Jan 60	RA
Willison, John C.			Pvt.	Co. L	05 Dec 62	Dd
Wilson, Charles H.	22	Kentucky	Pvt.	Co. I	09 Jun 60+	RA D
Wilson, Charles H.	22	Ireland	Pvt.	Co. I	09 Jun 60+	Dd
Wilson, Eaton	29	Switzerland	Farrier	Co. G	01 Jul 60+	RA
Wilson, James	22		Pvt.	Co. A	07 Feb 60	RA
Wilson, John	21	Germany	Pvt.	Co. D	11 Mar 61	
Wilson, Robert M.			Pvt.	Co. M	17 Dec 62	
Winkle, Samuel	21		Pvt.	Co. D	26 Dec 56	RA
Winson, Peter			Saddler	Co. K	27 Nov 62	
Wolf, Jacob W.	24	Ohio	Pvt.	Co. D	16 Mar 61	D
Wolford, Charles			Pvt.	Co. B	01 Dec 62	
Wood, Charles W.			1st Sgt.	Co. K	28 Nov 62	
†WOOD, Francis C.	21	Vermont	Pvt.	Co. K	30 May 60	RA FC
Wood, Isaac M.			Farrier	Co. L	23 Dec 62	
Woodward, Philip			Pvt.	Co. K	27 Jan 62	
Wrieden, Ernst L.	24		Cpl.	Co. I	14 Dec 57	RA
Wright, Clesson	23	New York	Musician	Band	08 Apr 60	RA Dd
Wright, John	24			Co. M	24 Nov 64	
Wright, John P.	27		Pvt.	Co. D	02 Dec 62	Dd
Wright, William	30	Ireland	Pvt.	Co. B	11 Apr 64 P	
†Wright, Nathan			Pvt.	Co. M	05 Dec 62	
Wroton, Thomas	20		Pvt.	Co. L	26 Nov 62	Dd
Wurm, Daniel	24			Co. H	03 Nov 64	
WYATT, James	33	England	Pvt.	Co. I	11 May 60	
Y						
Young, Richard W.			Sgt.	Co. E	01 Dec 61	
Yount, David			Pvt.	Co. L	03 Dec 62	
Z						
Zane, William			Pvt.	Co. G	28 Nov 62	
Zollinger, Morris			Pvt.	Co. G	25 Dec 62	

G. 4th United States Cavalry Regulars on the Battle Monument at West Point

Dedicated to the men of the Regular Army killed in the Civil War

Colonel John Sedgwick, Major General Volunteers
Captain George D. Bayard, Brigadier General Volunteers
First Lieutenant Elbridge Roys
Second Lieutenant Thomas Healy
Second Lieutenant Francis C. Wood

Sergeants

John Carmichael
Martin Murphy
John Rankin
Joseph B. Richmond
James Walsh

Corporals

Martin Birmingham
Patrick Cuddehy
Phelix Cullan
Frederick Hall
Frederick W. Klein
George Phillips
Stephen Wetzberger
Farrier Alexander Millright
Second Class Musician Frederick Shafer
Second Class Musician Alfred S. Toy

Privates

Frank Bars	Archibald B. Orr
John Baum	John Parsons
George Cassell	Levi L. Pettitt
Commodore P. Cole	Friend Pratt
Charles Cowarden	Henry J. Preas
Patrick Craven	Frank Rhyman
David Daugherty	Phillip H. Saller
Robert P. Doyle	William Sawyer
John Entwhistle	Adolph Stettler
Napoleon M. King	Roger Stokes
Andrew J. Mahoney	Patrick Tracy
Daniel McDonell	Nathan Writhe
James Orange	Colored Cook Jackson Kelley

Endnotes

PROLOGUE

1. Theophilus Rodenbough and William Haskin, eds., "The Fourth Regiment Cavalry." *The Army of the United States Historical Sketches of Staff and Line With Portraits of Generals-in-Chief* (New York: Maynard, Merrill, & Co., 1896), 213. Statement attributed to Major General John M. Schofield, USA Commander-in-Chief of the Army (1888-1895), and Medal of Honor recipient for "conspicuous gallantry at the Battle of Wilson's Creek, Mo. August 10, 1861."
2. The author came across several Civil War references describing a rout as "*A la* Bull Run."
3. W. Clark Kenyon, "Skirmish at Dug Springs, Missouri, August 2, 1861." *The Trans-Mississippi News*, Vol. 1, No. 1. Fall, 1995.
4. National Archives, Washington, DC, *U.S. Returns from Regular Army Cavalry Regiments*, 1821-1916, Record Group 744 (40 & 41), Combined Records of the Fourth United States Cavalry, hereafter cited as "Returns."
5. U.S. War Department, *The War of the Rebellion: A Compilation of the Official Records of the Union and Confederate Armies*, 128 Vols. Washington, DC: United States Government Printing Office, 1880-1901. Series I, Vol. 3, p. 47, hereafter cited as "*OR*," all references are to Series I unless otherwise noted.
6. Kenyon.
7. Ibid. Quotation from Thomas Knox's 1865 book *Campfire and Cottenfield*, "How Hot Was It?"
8. Kenyon, quoting Knox.
9. Ibid.
10. OR 3, 47-48.
11. OR 3, 48-50.
12. Kenyon; OR 3, 49.
13. OR 3, 49.
14. OR 3, 47.
15. OR 3, 49.
16. OR 3, 47.
17. Joseph G. Vale, *Minty and the Cavalry: A History of Cavalry Campaigns in the Western Armies* (Harrisburg, PA: Edwin K. Meters, 1998 reprint of 1886 edition), 12; OR 3, 49.
18. OR 3, 49.
19. E. R. Hagemann, *Fighting Rebels and Redskins: Experiences in the Army Life of Colonel George B. Sanford, 1861-1892* (Norman: University of Oklahoma Press, 1969), 129. In the renumbering of the Cavalry Regiments in August 1861, the 1st Dragoons was renamed 1st Cavalry.
20. "The Battle of Dug Springs." *Harper's Weekly*. Aug. 24, 1861, 535.
21. *Harpers Weekly*, 533.
22. OR 3, 50.
23. "Iowa Old Press." *Iowa City Citizen*. November 3, 1917.
24. Kenyon.
25. Returns; Kenyon; "Casualties for the Battles of Carthage and Dug Springs," http://chrisanddavid.com/wilsonscreek/rolls/CASUALTICAR.htm. Also killed or mortally wounded from Co. C were Privates Edward Devlin, John Wilkins, and Roger Stokes. Six men from Co. C were reported wounded: Sergeant Thomas W. Sullivan, and Privates Edward Dougherty, John Frey, Charles Jacobs, John McIlvaine, and Jacob Miller. Dougherty, Frey, and Jacobs were subsequently discharged for disability.
26. In July, Stanley's four companies comprised "250 officers and men," approximately sixty per company. Kenyon reports "approximately 40 troopers" were involved in the charge; the *Harper's Weekly* article cites "twenty men."

1855-1860: PRELUDE TO WAR

I. ORGANIZATION AND OPERATIONS PRIOR TO THE CIVIL WAR

1. Charles Morton, Captain, 3rd U. S. Cavalry, "History of the 3rd US Cavalry," http://www.usregulars.com.UScavalry.3us_cav.html.
2. George T. Ness Jr., *The Regular Army on the Eve of the Civil War*. (Baltimore, Maryland: Toomy Press, 1990), 1; James M. McPhearson, *Battle Cry of Freedom: The Civil War Era* (New York: Oxford University Press, 1988), 313. Gregory Urwin, in his 1983 history of the US Cavalry writes: "On paper, it was supposed to number 18,093 officers and men, but in January 1861, its actual strength ranged from 13,024 to 16,367." Gregory J. W. Urwin, *The United States Cavalry: An Illustrated History, 1776-1944* (Norman, Oklahoma: University of Oklahoma Press, 1983), 107.
3. Albert G. Brackett, Major, USA, *History of the United States Cavalry, From the Formation of the Federal Government to the 1st of June, 1863* (New York: Argonaut Press, 1965 reprint of 1865 edition), 140.
4. Edward G. Longacre, *Lincoln's Cavalrymen: A History of the Mounted Forces of the Army of the Potomac, 1861-1865* (Mechanicsburg, PA: Stackpole Books, 2000), 5.
5. Mary Lee Stubbs and Stanley Russell Connor. *Armor Lineage Series: Armor - Cavalry,* Part 1: *Regular Army and Army Reserve* (Office of the Chief of Military History, United States Army. Washington, DC 1969), 8.
6. Longacre, 5.

7. Francis B. Heitman, *Historical Register and Dictionary of the United States Army, from Its Organization, September 29, 1789, to March 2, 1903*, 2 vols. (Washington, DC: U.S. Government Printing Office, 1903), vol. I, 578, all references are to volume I unless otherwise indicated.
8. Ibid., 499.
9. Urwin, 96.
10. John K. Herr, Major General USA (Retired), Last Chief of Cavalry, and Edward S. Wallace, *The Story of the US Cavalry 1775-1942* (Boston: Little, Brown, 1953), 74.
11. Urwin, 197.
12. Heitman, 240.
13. Ibid., 872; "John Sedgwick (1813-1864)," http://www.civilwarhome.com/sedgwickbio.htm. Robert E. Lee is still listed as the second colonel of the 4th Regiment US Cavalry, from "16 Mar to 25 Apr 1861." Heitman, 70.
14. Ibid., 405-6.
15. Herr, 78; Heitman, 656.
16. James Larson, *Sergeant Larson 4th Cav.* (San Antonio, Texas: Southern Literary Institute, 1935), 98.
17. Brackett, 327-37. All 227 regiments are listed in the back of his book.
18. Urwin, 112.
19. S. E. Whitman, *The Troopers: An Informal History of the Plains Cavalry, 1865-1890* (New York: Hasting House Publishers, 1962), 38.
20. United States. Army. "Fourth Cavalry United States Army, 1855-1930," *4th Cavalry Regiment, 1855-*, Army Heritage Collection OnLine, http://www.cahco.army.mil.
21. Stubbs, 10.
22. Brackett, 316.
23. Ibid., 316.
24. Whitman, 38.
25. James M. Merrill, *Spurs to Glory* (Chicago: Rand McNally, 1966), 77.
26. Harold McCracken, *The Frederic Remington Book: A Pictorial History of the West* (Garden City, New York: Doubleday, 1966), 143. During the Civil War, this was extended to rivalries between "regulars," "volunteers," and "conscripted," as well as how the Army of the Potomac and Army of the Cumberland viewed each other.
27. Dee Brown, "War on Horseback." *The Images of the War: 1861-1865, vol. 4: Fighting for Time*. William C. Davis and Bell I. Wiley, eds., The National Historical Society (Garden City, New York: Doubleday, Inc. 1983), 308.
28. Earl J. Coates and John D. McAulay. *Civil War Sharpes Carbines and Rifles* (Gettysburg, Pennsylvania: Thomas Publications, 1996), 7; Urwin, 114.
29. Merrill, 78.
30. Whitman, 74.
31. Merrill, 78.
32. Urwin, 93.
33. Whitman, 74-75.
34. Ibid., 75.
35. National Archives, Washington, DC, *Register of Enlistments,1798-1914*. Hereafter referred to as Register of Enlistments.

PREWAR ENLISTMENT AND TRAINING

36. Larson, 44.
37. Ibid., 45.
38. Ibid.
39. Urwin, 56.
40. Whitman, 83.
41. Larson, 46-47.
42. James I. Robertson Jr., and editors. *The Civil War: Tenting Tonight* (Alexandria, VA: Time-Life Books, 1984), 44.
43. Ibid.
44. Merrill, 127.
45. Larson, 49.
46. Ibid.
47. Ibid., 50.
48. Ibid., 51.
49. Ibid., 70-71.
50. Ibid., 50.
51. Ibid.
52. Ibid., 53.
53. Ibid.
54. Ibid.
55. Ibid., 54.
56. Ibid.

SERVICE ON THE FRONTIER

57. John G. Keliher, 25th Infantry Division Association. "The History of the 4th US Cavalry Regiment," http://www.25thida.com/4thcav.html. The 1st [now 4th] Cavalry had a long association with Fort Leavenworth. It was the staging ground for a number of expeditions against the Plains Indians as well as the civil unrest in Kansas prior to the outbreak of war.
58. Richard Wormser, *The Yellowlegs: The Story of the United States Cavalry* (Garden City, New York: Doubleday, 1966), 135.
59. "The Fourth Regiment of Cavalry." Compiled in the office of the Military Service Institution, www.history.army.mil/books/R&H/R&H/-4CV.htm.
60. Stubbs, 8; Keliher.

FORT LEAVENWORTH, KANSAS TERRITORY

61. Merrill, 103.
62. Ibid., 103-4.
63. Larson, 55.
64. Ibid., 56.
65. Ibid.
66. Ibid., 73.
67. Ibid., 81.
68. Ibid., 73.
69. Ibid., 81.

Fort Wise, Colorado Territory

70. Larson, 83.
71. Ibid.
72. Merrill, 82; Michael V. Uschan, *The Cavalry During the Civil War* (San Diego, California: Lucent Books, 2003), 85.
73. Larson, 83.
74. Larson, 85; Guy V. Henry, *Military Record of Civilian Appointments in the United States Army*, 2 vols. (New York: D. Van Nostrand, Publisher, 1873), 1:174. The "cool" reception was probably due to the high rate of desertion of new recruits. They had yet to prove their worth.
75. Ibid., 86.
76. Ibid., 87.
77. Ibid., 84.
78. Ibid., 87.
79. "History of the 4th US Cavalry."
80. Larson, 85.
81. Ness, 108-9.
82. Larson, 95.
83. Ibid.

Oklahoma Indian Territory

84. "Fort Arbuckle," http://www.rootsweb.com/~okmuray/ft_arbuckle.htm.
85. Ibid.
86. "Fort Cobb," http://www.fortours.com/pages/ftcobb.asp.
87. "Official Records Related to Fort Washita," http://www.civilwaralbum.com/washita/OR.htm.

Expeditions Against the Kiowa and Comanche

88. Stubbs, 8.
89. United States. Army.
90. Returns, June 1860.
91. Ibid., "Field Report Southern Column Comanche & Kiowa Expedition" filed by Captain Samuel Sturgis.
92. Returns, July 1860.
93. Ibid.
94. Returns, September 1860.
95. Brackett, 205.
96. Returns, October 1860.
97. Returns, August 1860.
98. Brackett, 205; Herr, 81-82. David S. Stanley writes in his autobiography: "One poor no-account fellow, named [2nd Lt. Oliver H.] Fish, a graduate of West Point, resigned, went home, took neither side, and was never heard from again." David Sloan Stanley, *An American General: The Memoirs of David Sloan Stanley* (Santa Barbara, CA: The Narrative Press, 2003), 100.
99. William H. Powell, *Powell's Records of Living Officers of the United States Army* (Philadelphia: L. R. Hamersly, 1890), 657-58.
100. Heitman, 200. Cavalry historian Stephen Z. Starr stated that Bayard "was one of the most promising officers of the mounted arm." Stephen Z. Starr, *The Union Cavalry in the Civil War*, 3 Vols. (Baton Rouge: Louisiana State University Press, 1979-1985), 1, 326.
101. Herr, 82. As recorded in the official history of the "Fourth Regiment of Cavalry," this incident occurred "on the North fork of the Solomon River, in what is now Norton County, Kansas."

Fort Smith, Arkansas, New Years Eve 1860

102. National Park Service (hereafter cited as "N.P.S."), Fort Smith National Historic Site, http://www.nps.gov/fosm/history/2ndfort/.
103. Heitman, 934.

II. Surrendering the Frontier

1. Larson, 95.
2. Brackett, 210.
3. Alfred E. Bates, Major, USA "History of the 2nd US Cavalry." http://www.usregulars.com/UScavalry/2us_cav.html.
4. Larson, 99; John S. Bowman, ed. *The Civil War Almanac* (Barns and Noble, 2005), 383. In March 1861, Stuart "obtained a two months' leave of absence" to await the decision of his home state, Virginia. H. B. McClellan, *Life and Campaigns* of Major General J. E. B. Stuart (Boston, 1885 – Reprinted by Secaucus, NJ: The Blue and Grey Press, 1993), 31.
5. Larson, 99.
6. Bowman, 383.
7. Larson, 99. In writing his memoirs nearly fifty years later, Larson appears to have confused some names with specific events. In this particular case, he may have used a fictitious character to describe the actions of Captain George H. Steuart, Co. K. While on leave, and still in uniform, he conspired against the Union in his home state of Maryland, actively promoting secession. He resigned his commission on April 22, 1861, and became a brigadier general in the Army of Northern Virginia.

The Republic of Texas Secedes

8. Handbook of Texas Online, s.v. "Twiggs, David Emanuel." http://www.tshaonline.org/handbook/online/articles/TT/ftw3.html.
9. Vale, 8.
10. Heitman, 70.

Open Rebellion on the Frontier

11. Urwin, 107.
12. Brackett, 208-9.
13. Urwin, 107.
14. *OR* 1, 654

The Companies of the First U. S. Cavalry

15. Heitman, 934.
16. "Official Records Related to Fort Washita."
17. Heitman, 915; Powell, 560.

18. *OR* 1, 656.
19. Returns.
20. Heitman, 315.
21. Larson, 100-101. Larson erroneously reports Company I, rather than Company G.
22. Ibid., 101.
23. National Park Service. "Fort Laramie," http://www.nps.gov/fola/units.htm.

LIEUTENANT COLONEL WILLIAM H. EMORY, 1ST US CAVALRY

24. The University of Arizona Press review of *William H. Emory Soldier-Scientist*. David L. Norris and James C. Milligan (Tucson: University of Arizona Press), 1998, http://www.uspress.arizona.edu/Books/bid1212.htm.
25. Handbook of Texas Online, s.v. "Emory, William Helmsley," http://www.tsha.utexas.edu/handbook/online/articles/EE/frm3_print.html.
26. *OR* 1, 654.
27. *OR* 1, 656.
28. Ibid., 656; "Fort Washita Official Records."
29. *OR* 1, 659-60.
30. Ibid., 660.
31. Ibid., 668.
32. Ibid., 662. On April 30, 1861, President Lincoln ordered all Federal troops to evacuate Indian Territory forts, "leaving the Five Civilized Nations - Cherokees, Choctaws, Creeks, and Seminoles - virtually under Confederate jurisdiction and control." Bowman, 53.
33. Ibid., 665-66.
34. Stanley, 103. Emory and Davis were cadets together for two years at West Point.
35. *OR* 1, 648-49.
36. Ibid., 652.
37. Ibid., 651.
38. Stanley, 103; Heitman, 803; Wikipedia. "James Edwin Powell," http://en.wikipedia.org//wiie,James_Edwin_Powell. This article seemed well documented and referenced and concurred with other sources available to the author. Charles Bates' letter of March 8, 1861, indicates that Fort Smith was abandoned on the evening of the twenty-third. This reported "capture" of Rebel troops may have occurred that evening. Charles E. Bates, *Civil War Letters of Charles E. Bates*. Virginia Historical Society. This will account for all future references, hereafter cited as "Bates Letters."
39. Stanley, 103; "James Edwin Powell."
40. *OR* 1, 651.
41. Ibid., 648-49.
42. Bowman, 56; "James Edwin Powell."
43. *OR* 1, 648-49.
44. Ibid.
45. Stanley, 104.
46. "James Edwin Powell."
47. "Arrival of U. S. Troops." *Fort Leavenworth Daily Times*, June 1, 1861, Kansas Historical Society, Topeka, Kansas.
48. *OR* 1, 648-49; "Arrival of U.S. Troops."
49. Ibid., 648-49.
50. "Papers of William Emory, May 1861 - September 1862." University of Maryland. This file also contains a letter written to Lt. Col. Emory by 1st Lt. Albert V. Colburn after Emory left Fort Leavenworth. He mentions Emory's abrupt departure, expressing his "deep regret" at the resignation. He cites their "long and intimate acquaintance" and expressed his desire that Emory would be able to recall his resignation. He has nothing but the highest praise for the conduct of his commanding officer.
51. Stanley, 104.
52. "Papers of William Emory."
53. Longacre, 16.
54. Heitman, 405-6.
55. Bruce Catton, *The Coming Fury* (Garden City, NY: Doubleday, 1991), 235-6.
56. Heitman, 669.
57. Urwin, 108.
58. Heitman, 669; HistoryCentral.com: ConfederateGenerals, s.v. "General James McQueen McIntosh, CSA," http://www.historycentral.com/bio/CWcGENS/CSAMcIntosh.html.
59. Herr, 89-90.
60. Freeman Cleaves, *Rock of Chickamauga: The Life of General George H. Thomas* (Norman: University of Oklahoma Press, 1948), 307-08.
61. Vale, 7.
62. Ibid., 7-8.

THE "SERVICE SCHOOL OF THE PLAINS"

63. Robertson, 78.
64. Ibid., 82.
65. Ibid., 83.
66. Ibid., 85.
67. Ibid., 80.
68. Ibid., 78.
69. Uschan, 25.
70. Theophilus F. Rodenbough, Brigadier General, United States Army (Retired), "Cavalry of the Civil War - Its Evolution and Influence." *The Photographic History of the Civil War In Ten Volumes*. vol. 4, "The Cavalry." Francis Trevelyan Miller, Editor-in-Chief. (New York: The Review of Reviews, 1912), 24.
71. Brackett, 196.
72. Don C. Caughey, "Regular Thoughts," *Crossedsabers.blogspot.com*, May 5, 2009. Don, a retired Army officer, has recently co-authored a book with Jim J. Jones, *The Sixth United States Cavalry in the Civil War* (Jefferson, North Carolina: McFarland, 2013). Don has published his blog site since 2007.

TWENTY-TWO FUTURE GENERALS

73. Theophilus F. Rodenbough, "Fourth Regiment of United States Cavalry," *Army of the United States 1789-1896* (New York: Maynard, Merrill, 1896). The complete list is in the Appendix.

III. The Federal Cavalry at the Beginning of the Civil War

1. McPhearson, 313.
2. "History of the 4th US Cavalry."
3. *OR*. Series III: 1, 22.
4. Caughey, "Starting in the Hole," *Crossedsabers.blogspot.com*, March 3, 2007.
5. Urwin, 107-8.
6. National Archives, Washington, DC, *Returns from Regular Army Cavalry Regiments, 1833-1916*. RC 94 "Annual Return of the Alterations and Casualties incident in the Regiment during the year 1861." Hereafter referred to as Returns.
7. Herr, 116; Uschan, 15. Figures tend to vary widely depending on the date of publication.
8. Stubbs, 10.
9. Ibid., 9.
10. Merrill, 123.
11. Uschan, 15; David Evans. *Sherman's Horsemen: Union Cavalry Operations in the Atlanta Campaign* (Bloomington and Indianapolis: Indiana Universithy Press, 1996), xvii.
12. Angus Konstam, *The Civil War: A Visual Encyclopedia* (New York: Barnes and Noble, 2001), 112.
13. Stubbs, 10.
14. Merrill, 131.
15. Wormser, 233.
16. Ibid., 241.
17. Uschan, 32.
18. Ibid., 32.
19. Ibid., 83.
20. Bruce Catton, *The American Heritage Picture History of the Civil War* (New York: American Heritage, 1960), 359.

The Horse

21. Longacre, 16.
22. Catton, *American Heritage*, 357.
23. Ibid., 358.
24. Brackett, 164.
25. Uschan, 28.
26. Ibid., 37.
27. Ibid., 38.
28. Ibid.
29. Brackett, 166.
30. Uschan, 37.
31. James H. Wiswell Letters, "Camp 4 miles from Corinth May 12th 1862." *James H. Wiswell Letters, 1861-1867*. Special Collections Library, Duke University. This will be the reference for all Wiswell letters, hereafter cited as "Wiswell Letters." Recalling this incident years later, Wiswell would write: "I have distant recollection of that bright may morning as my horse was shot under me just as we started the charge, and as I meandered to the rear with carbine revolver and saber intact, but wondering how I would ever 'account' for saddle, bridle, nose bag, etc." *National Tribune*, June 4, 1903.
32. Herr, 118.
33. Ibid., 121.

The Accoutrements

34. Merrill, 130, 134.
35. Uschan, 28.
36. Ibid., 29.
37. Ibid.
38. Merrill, 130, 133.
39. Ibid., 130.
40. Uschan, 29.

The Evolution of Cavalry Organization and Tactics

41. Urwin, 112.
42. Longacre, *Lincoln's Cavalrymen*, 16.
43. Merrill, 134.
44. Ibid.
45. Stubbs, 10.
46. Brown, 308.
47. Merrill, 133.
48. Catton, *American Heritage*, 358.
49. Ibid., 520.
50. Herr, 100.
51. Brackett, 222.
52. Stubbs, 10.
53. Brown, 308-9.
54. McClellan, 259. As McClellan writes: "By far the greatest evil of the system was the fact that whenever a [Confederate] cavalryman was dismounted, it was necessary to send him to his home to procure a remount. To accomplish this required from thirty to sixty days. The inevitable result was that an enormous proportion of the command was continuously absent."
55. Longacre, 11.
56. Ibid., 11-12. It has been estimated that the infantry spent fifty days in camp for every day in battle.
57. Merrill, 134.
58. Longacre, 12.
59. Ibid., 134.
60. Uschan, 41.
61. Stubbs, 11.
62. Rodenbough, "Cavalry of the Civil War - Its Evolution," 83.

The Evolution of the 4th United States Cavalry

63. Robert H. G. Minty (Colonel, 4th Michigan Volunteer Cavalry), *National Tribune*, January 26, 1893. Minty commanded the First Brigade, Second Division, Army of the Cumberland, which became known as the Saber Brigade. The brigade also included the 4th United States Cavalry and the 7th Pennsylvania Volunteer Cavalry. The *National Tribune* was originally founded as a monthly newspaper for Civil War veterans and their families in 1877. In time it became a weekly forum for "discussion, debate and

reminiscence for veterans around the country." Beginning in the 1890s and continuing into the early 1900s, Minty wrote a series of letters to the editor recalling his activities and those of the Saber Brigade. "About the *National Tribune*. (Washington, DC) 1877-1917," http://chroniclingamerica.loc.gov/lccn/sn82016187/issues/.

64. Heitman, 310; Monthly Returns August 1861. Clifford was born in Ireland and his given name was Clifford Ingram.
65. Starr I, 162; William B. Sipes, *The Saber Regiment: The Seventh Pennsylvania Veteran Volunteer Cavalry* (1906: Reprint by Huntington, WV: Blue Acorn Press, 2000), 365. Starr cites as his source: Benjamin E. Dartt to E. B. Beaumont, January 27, in 7th Penn. O&L Books, RG 64, NA.
66. Register of Enlistments; Monthly Returns June 1862.
67. United States, Army.

1861: A Taste for Death

1. Wiswell Letters, August 31, 1861.

I: The War Begins

2. Urwin, 108.
3. Vale, Preface, xi-xii.
4. Returns, August 1861
5. Heitman, 872; "John Sedgwick Biography," http://www.civilwarhome.come/sedgwickbio.htm.
6. Powell, 657. For more on Wood's response to Rosecrans controversial order see Peter Cozzens, *This Terrible Sound: The Battle of Chickamauga* (Urbana: University of Illinois Press, 1991), 363.
7. Heitman, 934: Starr, 3: 254 n. 13.
8. Starr, III, 357.
9. In March 1898, Congress awarded then retired Lieutenant Colonel Eugene B. Beaumont the Medal of Honor for his "most distinguished gallantry in action" at Harpeth River, Tennessee, on December 17, 1864, and in the battle at Selma, Alabama, April 2, 1865. Heitman, 204; Powell, 50. The other recipients are David S. Stanley, Eugene Asa Carr, and Joseph B. Hedges.

II. The Eastern Theater

1. *OR* 2, 194. This sentiment was originally expressed in correspondence dated June 11, 1861, *OR* 2, 674.
2. Bates Letters, "July 16, 1861, Camp on Arlington Heights."
3. Heitman, 315. Captain James B. McIntyre, Co. E, was senior to Colburn and would command the squadron when Colburn left. It is probable that McIntyre was on leave or detached service during this time.

Private Charles E. Bates, Co. E

4. Bates Letters, "Camp on Arlington Heights, Va. July 16, 61."
5. Ibid, "August 10th 1862, Harrison Landing Va."
6. Ibid, "Fort Smith, Ark. March 8, 1861."
7. Ibid, "Camp on Arlington Heights, Va. July 16, 61."
8. Vale, 9.

Bull Run (First Manassas)–July 21, 1861

9. Urwin, 110.
10. Catton, *American Heritage*, 93.
11. *OR* 2, 317.
12. Ibid, 393.
13. Ibid.
14. Longacre, *Lincoln's Cavalrymen*, 25. The observer was George A. Custer, writing his "War Memoirs" in *Galaxy Magazine*, Vol. 0021, Issue 5, May 1876, 629. There is no other account of this action.
15. Longacre, 25-26.
16. *OR* 2, 393.
17. Ibid., 402.
18. Ibid., 2, 345.
19. McPherson, 344.
20. *OR* 2, 393.
21. Ibid.
22. Ibid., 385.
23. Ibid., 402.
24. Ibid., 403. This may have been the cavalry action witnessed by young Lt. George A. Custer, 2nd (later 5th) Cavalry, which he mentions in his postwar memoirs in *Galaxy Magazine*.
25. Ibid., 403-404.
26. Ibid., 404
27. Urwin, 110.
28. Longacre, 25-26.
29. *OR* 2, 393.
30. Longacre, 25-26.
31. *OR* 2, 393.
32. Longacre, 25-26.
33. *OR* 2, 339; *OR* 2, 383-84. Colonel Hunter reported that Stockton's conduct "under heavy fire was perfectly beautiful."
34. *OR* 2, 386.
35. *OR* 5, 15, 575.
36. Longacre, 26.
37. McPherson, 313. Ironically, as McPherson points out, "the manifestation of state's-rights sentiment . . . handicapped the early attempts at centralized control of both the Union and Confederate governments. Enterprise and vigor at the local and state levels degenerated into confusion at the national level." Pages 321-22.
38. Catton, *American Heritage*, 95.
39. Longacre, 26.
40. Catton, *American Heritage*, 114.
41. Longacre, 66.
42. *OR* 5, 575.
43. Heitman, 315.
44. Vale, 535.
45. *OR* 5, 15; Bates Letters, "October 14th, 1861, Washington, DC."
46. Ibid.
47. Ibid.

48. *OR* 11, Part II, 53; *OR*. 11, Part III, 184, 238, 312, 367. The aggregate present and absent for this period ranged from 143-145. Returns for August 1862 show "5 officers, 125 enlisted men present for duty."
49. Bates Letters, "November 21, 1861, Headquarters, Washington, DC."
50. Ibid., "April 13th 1862, Camp before Yorktown."
51. Ibid., "June 14th 1862, Richmond side of the Chickahominty."
52. Ibid., "May 27th 1862, Camp 7 miles from Richmond."
53. Ibid., "June 9th 1862, Camp Lincoln, Va."
54. Ibid., "June 22nd 1862, Camp Lincoln, Va."
55. Catton, *American Heritage*, 165.
56. Bates Letters, "June 13th 1862, Camp near Richmond," and "June 19th, 1862, Camp Lincoln, Va."
57. Ibid., "July 24th 1862" and "August 10th 1862, Harrison's Landing Va."

The Enlistment of James H. Wiswell, Co. C

58. Benson J. Lossing, *Mathew Brady's Illustrated History of the Civil War* (Avenel, NJ: Gramercy Books, Random House Value Publishing, Inc., 1994), 512. Regular Army officers and men who lost their lives in the Civil War are memorialized on the Battle Monument at West Point, dedicated in 1897, hereafter referred to as "West Point Monument." Among the names are five officers and forty-two men of the 4th Regiment United States Cavalry. See Appendix.
59. Wiswell, "Carlisle Barracks, May 12, 1861."
60. Ibid. James was always careful about what he wrote since it was read by his mother and sisters. He spared them the true horrors of this war. While he wrote in his letter "five years is not a long time," his term of enlistment was actually for three years. In his January 17, 1864, letter he writes, "I am sure of being discharged on the 21st of April 1864," and he was.
61. Piston, 167.
62. Wiswell, "Springfield Mo Nov 6 1861."

III. Western Theater
The State of Missouri

1. "Civil War in Missouri Facts," http://home.usmo.com/~momollus/MOFACTS.HTM.
2. The seceding states were Alabama, Florida, Georgia, Mississippi, and Louisiana in January 1861, Texas in February, Virginia in April, and Arkansas, North Carolina, and Tennessee in May.

General Nathaniel Lyon, United States Army

3. Brigadier General Nathaniel Lyon, Commander, Department of the West, Union Army, http://www.civilwarfamilyhistory.com/new_page_141.htm. See also "Nathaniel Lyon," http://ehistory.osu.edu/worldPeopleView.Cfm?PID=76.
4. "Blind, Mad or Foolish: Nathaniel Lyon, Part II," http://www.suite101.com/article.cfm/civil_war/103088.
5. "The St. Louis Arsenal contained 60,000 muskets, 90,000 pounds of powder, 1.5 million ball cartridges, 40 field pieces and the machinery for manufacture of arms. Also located downtown was the Federal Sub-Treasury which housed over a million dollars in gold and silver. These facilities were both severely under guarded." "A Brief Biography of General Nathaniel Lyon," http://www.lyoncamp.org/lyon.htm.
6. Edwin C. McReynolds, *Missouri: A History of the Crossroads State* (Norman: University of Oklahoma Press, 1962), 224.
7. Catton, *American Heritage*, 62.
8. John C. Moore, Colonel, CSA. *"Missouri in the Civil War,"* vol. 9, Chapter IV, Confederate Military History, http://www.civilwarhome.com, s.v. "Missouri in the Civil War," http://www.civilwarhome.com/missouri7.htm.
9. Bowman, 57.
10. *OR* 3, 11.
11. Ibid.
12. N.P.S. CWSAC Battle Summaries. *Boonville*. CWSAC Reference #: MO001, http://nps.gov/history/hps/abpp/battles/mo001.htm.
13. Brigadier General Nathaniel Lyon, Commander, Department of the West, Union Army, http://www.civilwarfamilyhistory.com/new_page_141.htm.
14. Wiswell Letters, "Camp near Austin, Mo., June 29, 1861."; William Garrett Piston and Richard W. Hatcher, III. *Wilson's Creek: The Second Battle of the Civil War and the Men Who Fought It* (Chapel Hill & London: The University of North Carolina Press, 2000), 69.
15. Piston, 69. They were escorted by Lieutenants George O. Sokalski and John Van Duesen Du Bois.
16. Wiswell Letters, "June 29, 1861."
17. Ibid. Although referred to as "rifle recruits," they were armed with smoothbore muskets. Piston, 69.
18. Piston, 70.
19. Ibid.; Wiswell Letters, "June 29, 1861."
20. Piston, 70-71. Regular army officers were often subjected to charges of "brutality" in trying to enforce regulations on volunteers. Stanley, 118.
21. *OR* 3, 12.
22. Ibid.
23. Ibid.
24. *OR* 3, 406; "History of the U. S. Cavalry."
25. Vale, 10. Vale's early history of the 1st/4th U S. Cavalry is not as accurate as his later history when the 4th U.S. and his 7th Pennsylvania Volunteers rode together in Minty's Saber Brigade.
26. "Thomas William Sweeny," http://www.virtualogy.com/thomaswilliamsweeny/.

Expedition from Springfield to Forsyth, Missouri

27. *OR* 3, 44.
28. Vale, 10.
29. *OR* 3, 45; "U.S. Regulars at Wilson's Creek," http://www.chrisanddavid.com/wilsonscreek/roles/SOLDIERSUSREG.html. These are extensively compiled rosters of United States Regulars and have

been cross-referenced with the Union casualty list and the Springfield Hospital list.
30. Ibid.

THE EARLY VOLUNTEERS

31. Starr, 3: 6.
32. Ibid., 5-6.
33. Peter Cozzens, *No Better Place to Die: The Battle of Stones River* (Urbana and Chicago: University of Illinois Press, 1990), 12.
34. Piston, 73.
35. Ibid., 69.
36. Ibid., 73.

THE BATTLE AT WILSON'S CREEK (OAK HILL) – AUGUST 10, 1861

37. Piston, 337-38.
38. *OR* 3, 47.
39. *OR* 3, 47; *OR* 3, 57.
40. *OR* 3, 57.
41. Ibid.
42. Piston, 169. Piston and Hatcher are extremely critical of Captain Carr, "whose poor performance at Wilson's Creek was mixed with a suggestion of cowardice, or at least loss of nerve . . ." Page 330. This characterization does not fit Carr's reputation either before the war or after.
43. Returns, August 1861; Piston, 168 & 185; *OR* 3, 69.
44. Piston, 174.
45. Ibid., 337; Moore, "Missouri in the Civil War."
46. Ibid., 338.
47. Heitman, 886
48. N.P.S., Midwest Archeological Center, Wilson's Creek National Battlefield, http://www.cr.nps.gov/mwac/wier_peri/wilsons_creek.htm.
49. Heitman, 414; Caughey, "Fiddler's Green: Charles E. Farrand," Crossedsabers.blogspot.com, February 10, 2009.
50. *OR* 3, 64; Piston, 183.
51. Piston, 184.
52. Heitman, 280.
53. Wiswell Letters, "August 31, 1861, Camp Lyon, near Rolla"; "U.S. Regulars at Wilson's Creek."
54. Wiswell Letters, "August 31, 1861"; Piston, 216.
55. Piston, 190.
56. Ibid., 191. Piston and Hatcher describe the phenomenon known as "'acoustic shadow,' a term used when people who should be able to detect noise fail to do so. It is caused by thick woods, terrain features, wind, or 'acoustic opacity' due to varying densities of air from location to location." It played a significant factor in a number of Civil War battles.
57. Moore, "Missouri in the Civil War."
58. Joseph Young Bates, "A Sketch of the Service of Joseph Young Bates as a Confederate Soldier." Washington County Historical Society (Fayetteville, Arkansas), *Flashback*, March 1862, 31-32.
59. Piston, 197-98.

60. N.P.S., *"Wilson's Creek National Battlefield."* @ www.cr.nps.gov/mwac/wicr_peri/wilsons_creek.htm.
61. Piston, 199.
62. Wiswell Letters, " Camp Lyon near Rolla Mo August 31, 1861."; *OR* 3, 72. Plummer described the terrain in this area as a "deep jungle" with an "impassable lagoon."
63. Piston, 212; *OR* 3, 72.
64. Wiswell Letters, "August 31, 1861." According to Wiswell, this would be the hardest fighting he was engaged in until the Battle of Chickamauga, September 1863. Wiswell Letters, "30 Sept 1863."
65. Ibid.
66. Piston, 215-16.
67. Ibid., 216.
68. Piston, 219-20.
69. Wiswell Letters, "August 31, 1861."
70. Piston, 199-200.
71. Ibid., 205.
72. Ibid., 232.
73. William M. Wherry, Brevet Brigadier-General, USV, 6th U.S. Infantry. "Wilson's Creek and the Death of Lyon," *Battles and Leaders of the Civil War*, Robert U. Johnson & C. C. Buell, eds., (New York: Century, 1887-88), 289-97; Piston, 221.
74. *OR* 3, 96-98; Piston, 222.
75. Piston, 222.
76. Ibid., 228.
77. *OR* 3, 89-90; Piston, 229.
78. Piston, 230; *OR* 3, 71. This may be a mild understatement. Some of the after battle reports fault the plundering for the breakdown in Sigel's troops, giving the Confederates time to rout them in the process.
79. Piston, 230.
80. Ibid., 220.
81. Ibid., 250.
82. Ibid., 255.
83. Ibid., 256.
84. Ibid., 247.
85. Ibid., 256.
86. *OR* 3, 89-90; Piston, 257.
87. Piston, 247.
88. Ibid., 263.
89. *OR* 3, 64-71.
90. Ibid.; Piston, 267-68; Bruce Catton, *American Heritage*, 88.
91. *OR* 3, 67.
92. Ibid., 70-71.
93. Piston, 283.
94. *OR*, 3, 70-71.
95. Ibid.
96. Piston, 286.
97. *OR* 3, 70-77; Piston, 286.
98. *OR* 3, 92; *OR* 3, 70-71; Piston, 258. In their reports, both Major Sturgis and Brigadier General Schofield accuse Sigel of abandoning his artillery and the field "when there was no enemy in sight."

99. *OR* 3, 89-90; Piston, 259.
100. *OR* 3, 89-90.
101. *OR* 3, 89-90; Piston, 259.
102. Piston, 259.
103. *OR* 3, 89-90
104. Piston, 261.
105. *OR* 3, 89-90.
106. Piston, 261.
107. Wiswell Letters, "August 31, 1861."
108. *OR* 3, 67, 69; *OR* 3, 57-64.
109. *OR* 3, 64.
110. Moore, "*Missouri in the Civil War.*"
111. *OR* 3, 64.
112. *OR* 3, 93-98
113. Wiswell Letters, "Camp Lyons near Rolla Mo Aug 31st 1861."
114. Ibid. Wiswell had a totally different view of the controversial General Sigel: "I saw letters in the paper you sent me rather derogatory on the character of Gen. Sigel. I will admit that he used us rather hard on the march from Springfield but for all that he is a braver and better officer than any regular officer that is or has been in this command excepting Gen. Lyon who is a true hero in every sense of the word. I should hate to have any regular officers see this letter for he would tie me up for running them down so."
115. Piston, 287. McCulloch's army suffered a twelve percent casualty rate (277 dead, 945 wounded), higher than in any single battle of the Mexican War.
116. *OR* 3, 72; "U.S. Regulars at Wilson's Creek." Wounded: Company D, Privates Walter Burke, William H. Clark, James Costillo, Thomas Porthouse. Company B, Privates Patrick Gilmore, Augustus Grunding and John McMannus, Bugler. Company C, Privates Albert J. Putman and Henry Shaw. Burke, Costillo, Porthouse, Grundig, and McMannus, were subsequently discharged for disability. Also wounded was one of James Wiswell's hometown friends, Alvy Allen, still with the Dragoon Detachment of Recruits. Wiswell, "Aug. 31, '61." Three reported missing from Company D, Farrier Andrew Hildebrand, Privates Thomas Doyle and William Peters, later returned to their regiment.
117. Attributed to Major General John M. Schofield, USA, Commander-in-Chief of the Army (1888-1895), and Medal of Honor recipient for "conspicuous gallantry at the Battle of Wilson's Creek, Mo. August 10, 1861"; "History of the U. S. Cavalry."
118. *OR* 3, 55.
119. Powell, 112. The Medal of Honor was awarded on June 16, 1894.
120. *OR* 3, 55.
121. Piston, 308.

Missing in Action

122. *OR* Series II. Vol. 1, 511.
123. Ibid.
124. Ibid., 512.
125. Ibid.
126. Ibid, 513.
127. Ibid. Twenty-one year old Michael Lambert enlisted on March 25, 1857. He apparently had enough of war and was discharged "by expiration of service" at Paducah, Kentucky, March 25, 1862. It is not known if he served again in any other capacity. Register of Enlistments.
128. Wiswell Letters, "Camp Lyons near Rolla Mo Aug 31st 1861."
129. Ibid., "Springfield Mo Nov 6th 1861."
130. Vale, 14.
131. Wiswell Letters, "Springfield Mo Nov 6th 1861."
132. Ibid.
133. Returns, October 1861.

Springfield, Missouri, October 25

134. Wiswell Letters, "Springfield Mo Nov 6th 1861."
135. Vale, 11. Cavalry historian Stephen Z. Starr, using this paragraph in his book, *The War in the West: 1861-1865*, Vol. 3, cites Joseph Vale as "a generally reliable regimental historian," 38.
136. Starr, 3:4.

Saline County and Blackwater Creek (Shawnee Mound)

137. *OR* 8, 34. This was the father of the twentieth century soldier-statesman George C. Marshall, Jr. Unfortunately, father and son had a very difficult relationship. The senior Marshall was bitter at not having achieved a greater Civil War record, and frequently expressed little confidence that his namesake would ever accomplish anything.
138. Ibid.
139. Ibid., 38.
140. Amory: Heitman, 1:162; Gordon: Heitman, 1:465; Kelly: Henry, 1:163.
141. *OR* 8, 38.
142. Ibid.
143. *OR* 8, 42.; *OR* 8, 37.
144. *OR* 8, 38.
145. Ibid., 40.
146. Wiswell Letters, "Sedalia Mo Dec 25th 1861."
147. *OR* 8, 38.
148. Annual Returns; Register of Enlistments.
149. *OR* 8, 40.
150. Ibid.
151. *OR* 8, 37.
152. *OR* 8, 38.
153. Ibid.
154. *OR* 8, 42.
155. Heitman, 162.
156. At the end of each year, regimental commanders were required to submit an "Annual Return of the Alterations and Casualties incident in the Regiment." This year's return showed the following: Nineteen officers resigned,

to be replaced by twenty new, inexperienced officers, eighteen from civilian life. Eighty-five new troopers joined the Regiment by "enlistment, re-enlistment, and transfers. Seventy-eight were discharged for "expiration of service" and fouteen for "disability." There were eighteen "miscellaneous discharges" by court martial or civil action, for a total of 110 troopers discharged from the Regiment for the year. There were fourteen deaths. Of those, four were "killed in action" and one died "of wounds received in action."

157. *OR* 7, 66. 158. Ibid.

1862: FINDING FORM

I. THE WESTERN THEATER

1. Vale, 6.
2. Ibid.
3. Ibid.
4. Ibid.
5. Charles D. Rhodes, Captain, General Staff, United States Army. "Cavalry Battles and Charges." *The Photographic History of the Civil War in Ten Volumes*. vol. IV, "The Cavalry." (New York: The Review of Reviews, 1912), 254.
6. *OR* 8, 535.
7. *OR* 7, 611. Buell's note to McClellan continues: "Carbines received yesterday for one regiment; nine other regiments are mounted and partially armed; three of them under tolerable discipline, the other six raw and uninstructed. Pistols and carbines are wanted for nearly all."

FORTS HENRY AND DONELSON, TENNESSEE

8. Vale, 42-3.
9. Catton, *American Heritage*, 114.
10. Wiswell Letters, "February 1, 1861, Sedalia, Mo."
11. Vale, 14.
12. Heitman, 802. Powell was one of the senior enlisted men in the old 1st Cavalry, having joined the army in 1848. In November 1856 Powell transferred to the 1st (later 4th) US Cavalry.
13. *OR* 52, 7.
14. Vale, 14-15.
15. Ibid. This would be the first of a continuing series of engagements between the 4th US Cavalry and Forrest's cavalry.
16. *OR* 7, 383.
17. Buell, 163.
18. *OR* 7, 183.
19. Ibid., 192-198.
20. Ibid., 170.
21. Ibid., 384; Kevin J. Dougherty, Martin J. Dougherty, Parker Hills, Charles McNab, Michael F. Pavkovic, *Battles of the Civil War, 1861-1865* (New York: Metro Books, 2007), 40-41.
22. Vale, 15.
23. Vale, 15; *OR* 7, 383-84.
24. Dougherty, 41.
25. *OR* 7, 172.
26. Vale, 15.
27. Ibid.
28. *OR* 7, 185; *OR* 52, 7.
29. Lew Wallace. "The Capture of Fort Donelson," in *Battles and Leaders of the Civil War*, Ned Bradford, ed., (New York: Appleton-Century-Crofts, 1956), 66-67. Lew Wallace became famous years later for his historical novel *Ben-Hur*.
30. Ibid. Bruce Catton describes John A. McClernand as "a mediocre general with delusions of grandeur." *American Heritage*, 82.
31. *OR* 7, 174; Bruce Catton, *The Centennial History of the Civil War*, vol. 2, *Terrible Swift Sword* (Garden City, NY: Doubleday & Company, Inc., 1963), 156.
32. Catton, *Terrible Swift Sword*, 156.
33. *OR* 7, 174.
34. Dougherty, 42.
35. Buell, 163.
36. Dougherty, 42.
37. Catton, *Terrible Swift Sword*, 157.
38. James M. McPherson, ed. *The Atlas of the Civil War* (New York: McMillan, 1994), 47; Wallace, 66-67.
39. Wallace, 66-67.
40. Ibid,, 74.
41. Ibid., 75.
42. Buell, 164.
43. Catton, *Terrible Swift Sword*, 158.
44. Buell, 165.
45. Catton, *Terrible Swift Sword*, 158.
46. Ibid.
47. Ibid., 159.
48. Ibid.
49. Ibid.
50. Vale, 16.
51. Konstam, 195.
52. Catton, *American Heritage*, 115.
53. Konstam, 194.
54. *OR* 7, 167.
55. National Archives, Washington, DC. Records of the Veterans Administration, 1866-1869. RC 15. Hereafter referred to as Records of Veterans Administration. While in regular engagement on the firing line at the battle of Fort Donelson, TN, Feb. 15, 1862, Private John M. Herberich received a shell wound on the right leg above the ankle. In 1903, at the age of 63, First Sergeant John M. Herberich applied for a partial pension under the "Invalid Act" of June 27, 1890. The application required a physical. The May 6, 1903, Surgeon's Certificate states that, "he received shell wound on right leg above ankle. Did not appear to be serious at the time and he did not go to hospital . . . but later abscess formed . . . and has continued ever since. Tried many medicines and physicians but he suffers and has suffered ever since. Leg is weak and claimant walks with a cane."
56. Larry J. Daniel, *Shiloh: The Battle That Changed the Civil War* (New York: Simon & Schuster, 1997), 108. That officer was Chief Surgeon Henry C. Hewitt.

Nashville, Tennessee

57. Vale, 17.
58. Ibid.
59. Ibid.
60. Ibid.

New Madrid and Island No. 10

61. *OR* 52, Pt. I, 214.
62. Wiswell, "Benton Barracks Feb. 23d 1862."
63. *OR* 8, 94; Vale, 18.
64. N.P.S., "New Madrid/Island No. 10." CWSAC Battle Summaries, http://www.nps.gov/history/hps/abpp/battles/mo012.htm.
65. "New Madrid/Island No. 10."; Bowman, 94.
66. *OR* 53, Pt. I, 517; Wiswell Letters, "April 9, 1862, camp near New Madrid." David S. Stanley writes, "The ordnance stores abandoned were immense." Stanley, 118.
67. Konstam, 397.
68. Catton, *American Heritage*, 115.

II. Pittsburg Landing [Shiloh]

1. Catton, *American Heritage*, 123.
2. Heitman, 754; Powell, 432. A career officer, Oaks graduated from the Military Academy in 1846. By March 1855 he was a captain in the new 2nd Cavalry. In April 1861 he was promoted to major, 5th Cavalry and in November to lieutenant colonel, 4th Cavalry.
3. Vale, 18.
4. Daniel, 109.
5. Vale, 18-19; Daniel, 110.
6. Daniel, 109.
7. Ibid., 110.
8. "The Battle of Shiloh," http://www.geocities.com/shiloh.html.
9. "Description of the Battle of Shiloh," http://www.civilwarhome.com/shilohdescription.htm.
10. Daniel, 139.
11. Ibid.
12. Ibid., 174.
13. Wiley Sword, *Shiloh: Bloody Shiloh* (Dayton, Ohio: Morningside House, 2001), 118-119.
14. McPherson, 408.
15. Daniel, 175.
16. Ibid., 185.
17. "Description of the Battle of Shiloh."
18. "The Battle of Shiloh," http://www.geocities.com/shiloh.html.
19. Albert Dillahunty, *Shiloh National Military Park, Tennessee* (National Park Service, Historical Handbook Series No. 10, Washington, 1955), 33.
20. Daniel, 319.
21. Vale, 18-19.
22. *OR* 10, Pt. I, 169; Vale, 19-20.
23. Daniel, 266-67, quoted from Lew Wallace, *An Autobiography*, Vol. I, 473-74.
24. Ibid., 267, quoted from "The War Album of Henry Dwight," Albert Castel, ed., *Civil War Times Illustrated*, vol. 18, February 1980.
25. Ibid.
26. "The Battle of Shiloh."
27. Ibid.
28. *OR* 10, Pt. I, 169.
29. Ibid. The four "slightly" wounded privates were: Fred Ahrens, Warren Hastings, John M. Herberich, and Joseph McWilliams. It appears that the wound suffered by Private Herberich may actually have occurred earlier at Fort Donelson.
30. Dillahunty, 17.
31. *OR* 10, Pt. I, 169; Vale, 19.
32. Kaufman would remain in the Army after the war, retiring as major, 4th US Cavalry, in 1892. Heitman, 586.
33. Henry 2:303; Heitman, 659.
34. *OR* 10, Pt. I, 677; Henry 2:324; Heitman, 802-3.
35. Heitman, 754.

III. Cavalry Division Army of the Mississippi

1. *OR* 8, 95.
2. Henry 1:145.
3. *OR* 53, Pt. I, 517.
4. Wiswell, "June 3, 1862, Camp near Corinth, Miss."

Brigadier General Gordon Granger, United States Volunteers.

5. *New York Times*, January 12, 1876, "Obituary: Major Gen. Gordon Granger," http://query.nytimes.com/gst/abstract.html?res=F70C14.
6. *OR* 10, Pt. I, 726; Vale, 22.
7. "American Civil War: Brigadier General William N. R. Beall," http://www.factasy.com/civil_war/southern_leaders/william_beall.shtml.
8. *OR* 10, Pt. I, 726.
9. Ibid.

Corinth, Mississippi

10. Konstam, 366.
11. Ibid., 142.
12. *OR* 10, Pt. I, 726.
13. Heitman, 465. Henry Gordon was another career enlisted man, having joined the 2nd Dragoons as a private in December 1849 and rising through the ranks to 1st sergeant in the 2nd Cavalry. Gordon was commissioned 2nd lieutenant Co. H, 4th Cavalry, in October 1861. With that company still on the frontier, he was temporarily assigned to Co. I.
14. Vale, 24 quoting Granger's Report.
15. *OR* 10, Pt. I, 185. Companies G and K were also present at Corinth. Rodenbough, "History of the 4th US Cavalry."

Boonville, Mississippi

16. *OR* 10, Pt. I, 726.
17. Konstam, 142.

18. Wiswell, "June 3, 1862."
19. Cozzens, 2.
20. Vale, 26.
21. Monthly Returns December 1862
22. 1860 Census for Farmington Township, Clarion County, Pennsylvania.
23. OR 10, Pt. I, 720-723.

IV. Army of the Ohio - Major General Don Carlos Bruell

1. Heitman, 754; Powell, 432.
2. Cozzens, 12.
3. Wiswell Letters, "June 3, 1862, Camp near Corinth, Miss."
4. Cozzens, 12.

Incident at Athens, Alabama

5. Vale, 28.
6. Ibid.
7. Cozzens, 13.

Huntsville, Alabama

8. Vale, 29.
9. Wiswell Letters, "July 17, 1862 Huntsville, Ala."
10. Vale, 28-29.

The Battle of Perrysville, Kentucky

11. Cozzens, 2.
12. Ibid.
13. OR 16, Pt. I, 1033
14. Cozzens, 5; Catton, *American Heritage*, 245.
15. Cozzens, 13; Catton, *American Heritage*, 245.

V. Army of the Cumberland – Major General William S. Rosecrans

1. Cozzens, 18.
2. Ibid.
3. Cozzens, 19.
4. Wiswell Letters, "Nov. 24, Nashville, Tenn." This letter and subsequent complaints of dissatisfaction with military and government policy would strain relations between James and his father, an ardent Unionist and Lincoln supporter.
5. Catton, *American Heritage*, 247.
6. Ibid. 257.

Cavalry Division, Army of the Cumberland

7. Cozzens, 20.
8. Ibid., 19.
9. Edward G. Longacre, *Mounted Raids of the Civil War*, "Second Time Around - Stuart's Chambersburg Raid" (Lincoln: University of Nebraska Press, 1994), 21-45. As the title implies, this was the second time Stuart had ridden around McClellan's army.
10. Cozzens, 21.
11. OR 23, Pt. I, 403.
12. Starr 3: 112.
13. Ibid.
14. Ibid., 113.

First Brigade, Second Cavalry Division

15. OR 20, Pt. I, 206.
16. Stanley, 132.
17. Vale, 108.
18. Ibid., 107-8.
19. OR 20, Pt. I, 23.
20. Powell, 437-8.

Companies L and M

21. Wiswell Letters, "Nashville Tenn Dec 22d 1862"; "Camp near Murfreesboro Tenn January 8th 1862 [sic - 1863]."
22. Annual Return. Of the last three officers mentioned above—Bowman, the only Military Academy graduate—joined the 1st/4th Cavalry in December 1860, was promoted 1st lieutenant in April 1861, and captain July 12, 1862. He would be with the regiment for the duration of the war and was brevetted major February 20, 1864, for his "gallant and meritorious service" in the cavalry expedition to Mississippi. He died of undisclosed cause in 1868, Heitman, 235. Doolittle, originally a lieutenant in the 2nd Wisconsin Volunteer Infantry in June 1861, was appointed 2nd lieutenant, 4th US Cavalry in August 1861 and promoted to 1st lieutenant in July 1862. His name does not appear on rosters of the 4th U.S. He may have remained on detached service, as he was a lieutenant colonel in the 37th Wisconsin in April 1864, Heitman, 379. Douglas Murray, born in England, originally joined the artillery branch of the Army in 1850, serving two five-year enlistments. From October 1861 to June 1863, he served as a lieutenant colonel, 3rd Ohio Volunteer Cavalry. During that time he was appointed a 2nd lieutenant in the 4th US Cavalry in July 1862. He resigned both positions in June 1863, Heitman, 738.
23. Heitman, 156. Alexander was appointed 2nd Lt., 1st/4th Cavalry, on February 21, 1861, 1st Lt., May 1, 1861, and captain, July 17, 1862. Heitman's notation indicates, "dropped 14 Mar 1865, (joined CSA)."
24. Annual Return. The Annual Return indicates there were thirty-one deaths reported and forty-six desertions among the enlisted men of the 4th U.S. Eleven new commissioned officers were appointed, three from the Military Academy and eight from "civilian life." Second Lieutenant Henry Gordon, former 1st sergeant, Co. I, was "mustered out" of service on December 2, 1862.
25. OR 5, 713. From the Medical Director's Office, Headquarters, Army of the Potomac, dated February 6, 1862: "In the cavalry regiments the sick report is swollen considerably in consequence of injuries to the men received from the horses." A number of accidental gunshot injuries are reported by James

Wiswell and later in the letters of Captain Henry Potter.
26. *OR* 13, 811.
27. Wiswell Letters, "December 22nd, 1862 Nashville, Tennessee."
28. Vale, 107.
29. Ibid., 105.
30. Catton, *American Heritage*, 266.

1863: STONES RIVER TO CHATTANOOGA

1. Longacre, 28.

I. MIDDLE TENNESSEE

2. Rhodes, "Cavalry Battles and Charges," 224.
3. McClellan, 294.
4. Ibid.
5. Rodenbough, "Cavalry of the Civil War," 34.
6. Rhodes, 254.
7. Catton, *American Heritage*, 213.
8. United States. Army.
9. Evans, 409; Rand K. Bitter, *Minty and His Cavalry: A History of the* Saber Brigade *and Its Commander* (Michigan: Rand K. Bitter, 2006), 36, quoting Major George W. Fish, Regimental Surgeon, 4th Michigan Volunteer Cavalry.
10. *OR* 20, 604. March 1863 returns indicate an "aggregate" of 843 men in the 4th Regiment.

II. STONES RIVER CAMPAIGN - MURFREESBORO, TENNESSEE

1. Catton. *American Heritage*, 265.
2. *OR* 20, Pt. 2, 227.
3. Cozzens, 219-227.
4. J. C. Reiff, Adjutant, *The 15th Pennsylvania Volunteer Cavalry – The Combatant's Story*. "Fifteenth Pennsylvania (Anderson) Cavalry at Stones River." Hereafter referred to as "Reiff Report." http://www.swcivilwar.com/15CombatantsStonesRiver.html.
5. Catton. *American Heritage*, 283.
6. *OR* 20 Pt. II, 241.
7. Ibid., 257.
8. Ibid., 241.
9. Henry 1:183.
10. *OR* 30, 184.
11. Catton, *American Heritage*, 283.
12. *OR* 20, 191.
13. Kelihr.
14. *OR* 20, 649.
15. *OR* 20, 618.
16. *OR* 20, 649.
17. Ibid.
18. Ibid.
19. Heitman, 823; Henry 2:328.
20. Henry 2:300.
21. Bitter, 46-47.
22. *OR* 20, 648.
23. Anonymous, "The Story of a Cavalry Soldier: The Fourth Regular Cavalry at Murfreesboro." *Lancaster Daily Evening Press*, January 28, 1863. This article was written by an unnamed trooper in Company G.
24. Ibid.
25. Vale, 118.
26. Catton, *American Heritage*, 284.
27. Vale, 118-19.
28. Catton, *American Heritage*, 266.
29. *OR* 20, Pt. I, 236.
30. Ibid.
31. Ibid.
32. Ibid.
33. Ibid.
34. Anonymous. "The Story of a Cavalry Soldier."
35. *OR* 20, Pt. I, 649.
36. Ibid.
37. Ibid.

RESCUING MCCOOK'S AMMUNITION TRAIN

38. Cozzens, 105.
39. *OR* 20, Pt. I, 654.
40. Ibid., 185.
41. Ibid., 655.
42. Ibid., 656.
43. Cozzens, 105.
44. Ibid. This is shown as the "Widow Burns" farm in the *West Point Atlas of War: The Civil War*, Brigadier General Vincent J. Esposito, chief editor, (NY: Tess Press, 1995), 65.
45. Cozzens,105.
46. Ibid., 106.
47. Ibid.
48. Ibid.
49. Ibid., 108; *OR* 30, 79.
50. *OR* 20, Pt. I, 194.
51. Cozzens, 108.
52. *OR* 20, Pt. I, 184.
53. Ibid., 650.
54. Ibid, 620.
55. Ibid., 650. Clarence Manck was brevetted captain for "gallant and meritorious service."
56. Henry 1:166; Heitman, 639.
57. Webster: Heitman, 1013; McMaster: Heitman, 677, Henry 2:306.
58. Murphy: Muster Roll September 1863; L'Hommedieu: Heitman, 631, Henry 2:300. *Xenia Sentinel* (Xenia, Ohio), January 19, 1864: "Lt. T. L'Hommedieu, son of S. S. L'Hommedieu, President of the C. H. & Dayton Railroad, died in Tennessee on January 1st of pleurisy."

NEW YEAR'S DAY 1863

59. Cozzens, 174-75.
60. Bitter, 49.
61. Cozzens, 174-5.
62. *OR* 20, Pt. I, 625.

63. Bitter, 49.
64. Ibid.
65. *OR* 20, Pt. I, 650.
66. Cozzens, 175.

PANIC AT STEWART'S CREEK

67. *OR* 20, Pt. I, 655.
68. Ibid.
69. Cozzens, 102.
70. *OR* 20, Pt. I, 655.
71. Ibid. 72.
73. *OR* 20, Pt. I, 650.
74. Ibid.; *OR* 20, Pt. I, 618.
75. *OR* 20, Pt. I, 618; *OR* 20, Pt. I, 185.
76. *OR* 20, Pt. I, 185.
77. Ibid., 618.
78. Ibid., 185.
79. Ibid., 625.
80. Ibid.
81. *OR* 20, Pt. I, 625; Vale, 121.
82. *OR* 20, Pt. I, 625.
83. Vale, 121.
84. *OR* 20, Pt. I, 625
85. Vale, 121.
86. *OR* 20, Pt. I, 625.
87. Vale, 121.
88. Ibid.
89. *OR* 20, Pt. I, 618.
90. *OR* 20, Pt. I, 199; *OR* 20, Pt. I, 188.
91. *OR* 20, Pt. I, 620.
92. Ibid., 188.
93. Heitman, 762.
94. *OR* 20, Pt. I, 199.
95. Ibid., 198.
96. *OR* 20, Pt. I, 650.
97. Wiswell Letters, "January 8, 1863, Murfreesboro, Tenn."
98. Cozzens, x.
99. N.P.S., "Stones River - Reading 1."
100. Catton, *American Heritage*, 267.
101. Ibid. Perhaps more shocking than the tragic loss of life was the incompetence of both command structures, particularly the Confederacy. The most recent and meticulously detailed account is in Peter Cozzens *No Better Place to Die: The Battle of Stones River*.
102. *OR* 20, Pt. I, 214; Annual Returns.
103. *OR* 20, Pt. I, 198.

III. CAVALRY DIVISION, ARMY OF THE CUMBERLAND
ROSENCRANS - STANLEY - MINTY

1. The Civil War Archive. "Union Regimental Histories. United States Regular Army." 4th Regiment Cavalry. http://www.civilwararchive.com/Unreghst/unrgcav,htm # 4th cav. Unless otherwise noted, this citation will account for all future references to the activities and location of the regiment and units of the 4th Cavalry during the Civil War.
2. Bitter, 391.
3. Ibid., iv.
4. Ibid., 12.
5. Ibid., 36.
6. Ibid., iv.

FIRST BRIGADE, SECOND DIVISION

7. Larson, 167.
8. *OR* 20, Pt. I, 984.
9. Ibid.
10. Henry Albert Potter, Henry Albert Potter's Diary - 1863. Archives of Michigan. Civil War Manuscripts, Michael P. Ruddy, Editor, hereafter cited as "Potter Diary," http://haldigitalcollections.cdmhost.com/seeking_michigan.
11. Ibid.
12. *OR* 52, Pt. I, 59.
13. Potter Diary.

EXPEDITION AGAINST WHEELER'S CAVALRY

14. Vale, 124.
15. Bowman, *Civil War Almanac*, 391.
16. Minty, *National Tribune*, September 22, 1892.; *OR*, 23, 25. See Appendixes for the makeup of the First and Third Brigades.
17. Minty, *National Tribune*, September 22, 1892.
18. Vale, 126.
19. Minty, *National Tribune*, September 22, 1892.
20. Ibid.
21. Vale, 126.
22. Ibid., 127.
23. Minty, *National Tribune*, September 22, 1892.
24. Vale, 127.
25. Minty, *National Tribune*, September 22, 1892.
26. Vale, 130; *OR* 23, 27.
27. Vale, 130-31.
28. Minty, *National Tribune*, September 22, 1892.; *OR* 23, 25.
29. Larson, 167.
30. Minty, *National Tribune*, September 22, 1892.
31. Starr, 210; *OR* 23, 26.

THE SABER

32. Longacre, 43.
33. Brown, "War on Horseback," 308.
34. Longacre, 43.
35. Ibid., 44.
36. Bitter, 61.
37. Vale, 130-31.
38. Ibid., 61; Gervase Phillips, "Saber verses Revolver: Mounted Combat in the American Civil War," http//:mmu.academiaedu/GervasePhillips/Papers/131153/Sabre_verses_Revolver_Mounted_Cpmbat_in_the_American_Civil_War.
39. Minty, *National Tribune*, September 22, 1892. The exact date is taken from Potter's Diary 1863. Minty, *Los Angeles Times*, September 21, 1901.
40. Minty, *National Tribune*, September 22, 1892.
41. Ibid.
42. Ibid.

43. Vale, 148-49.
44. Larson, 215; Vale, 148.
45. Ibid., 216.
46. Longacre, 44.
47. Bitter, 61.
48. William A. McTeer, "Smith's Raid," *National Tribune*, May 28, 1892. McTeer had originally enlisted as a private, Co. H. 3rd US Cavalry.

Incident with Forrest's Battery: The Killing of Captain Freeman, CSA

49. Vale, 146.
50. Ibid., 146-47.
51. "*The Civil War News*," http://www.civilwarnews.com/archive/articles/shiloh_relic_hunt.htm>.

Permanent Camp

52. Vale, 133.
53. Vale, 172.
54. Bitter, 52.
55. Larson, 166-67.
56. Larry M. Strayer and Richard A. Baumgartner. *Echoes of Battle: The Atlanta Campaign* (West Virginia: Blue Acorn Press, 2004 ed.), 12, 14.

Foraging

57. Vale, 132.
58. Bitter, 34.
59. Ibid., 34, 53.
60. Richard A. Baumgartner, *Blue Lightning: Wilder's Mounted Infantry Brigade in the Battle of Chickamauga* (Huntington, WV: Blue Acorn Press, 2007), 84. Quoting William Cole, first assistant surgeon of the Indiana 72nd. In April 1865, two 4th Cavalry troopers were "killed in the field by citizens" while foraging: 2nd Class Musicians Alfred S. Toy and Frederick Shafer. Register of Enlistments.
61. Bitter, 54.
62. Vale, 171; Bitter, 51.
63. Longacre, 28.
64. Ibid., 29.

Foraging Expedition and Skirmish at Bradyville, Tennessee

65. *OR* 23, 65
66. Ibid.
67. Ibid., 66.
68. Ibid.

IV. Riding With Sheridan

1. Wormser, 228.
2. Ibid. 229.
3. Bowman, 375.
4. Kurt Hamilton Cox and John P. Langellier, *Longknives, The US Cavalry and other Mounted Forces, 1845-1942, The G. I. Series: The Illustrated Histories of the American Soldier, His Uniforms and His Equipment*, Vol. 3 (Pennsylvania: Stackpole Books, 1996), 6.

Expedition to Unionville

5. Minty, *National Tribune*, December 15 & 22, 1892; Vale, 134.
6. Vale, 134.
7. Minty, *National Tribune*, December 15 & 22, 1892.
8. *OR* 23, Pt. I, 129.
9. Minty, *National Tribune*, December 15 & 22, 1892; Vale, 134.
10. *OR* 23, Pt. I, 130.
11. *OR* 23, Pt. I, 130; Vale, pp. 134-35.
12. *OR* 23, Pt. I, 129.
13. Vale, 134-35.
14. Minty, *National Tribune*, December 15 & 22, 1892; Vale, 134.
15. Ibid.
16. Vale, 134.
17. Ibid., 135.
18. Ibid., 136.
19. Ibid., 135.
20. Minty, *National Tribune*, December 15 & 22, 1892.
21. *OR* 23, Pt. I, 127.
22. Minty, *National Tribune*, December 15 & 22, 1892.
23. Ibid.; Vale, 135.
24. Minty, *National Tribune*, December 15 & 22, 1892.

Thompson's Station

25. Bitter, 67, quoting Minty.
26. Sipes, 55.
27. Starr, 3:229.
28. Sipes, 56.
29. *OR* 23, Pt. I, 135; *OR* 23, Pt. I, 130.
30. Vale, 137.
31. Ibid., 138.
32. *OR* 23, Pt. I, 130.
33. *OR* 23, Pt. I, 134; Register of Enlistments; Charles W. Larned, *History of The Battle Monument at West Point*. (New York: Battle Monument Association, West Point, 1898), 121, 137-38. Cited as "West Point Monument" for future references.
34. *OR* 23, Pt. I, 130.
35. *OR* 23, Pt. I, 130; Vale, 138.
36. Minty, *National Tribune*, December 15 & 22, 1892.
37. Ibid.
38. Minty, *National Tribune*, December 15 & 22, 1892; Vale, 138.
39. Vale, 138; Bitter, 68, quoting Minty.
40. Minty, *National Tribune*, December 15 & 22, 1892.
41. Ibid.
42. Vale, 138.
43. Potter Diary.
44. Minty, *National Tribune*, December 15 & 22, 1892.
45. Ibid.
46. Vale, 138; Starr, 231.
47. Minty, *National Tribune*, December 15 & 22, 1892.
48. Starr, 232.
49. Ibid., 233.
50. *OR* 23, Pt. I, 135.
51. Ibid.

52. Vale, 140-142.
53. Ibid., 141.
54. Ibid.
55. Ibid., 142.
56. *OR* 23 Pt. I, 127.
57. Ibid., **131**.

The Saber Brigade

58. Minty, *National Tribune*, December 15 & 22, 1892.
59. Ibid.
60. Minty, *National Tribune*, January 12, 1893.
61. Ibid.
62. Ibid.
63. Baumgartner, 92.
64. Bitter, 89.
65. Bitter, 76.
66. Ibid.
67. Ibid., 71.

V: The 4th Regiment United States Cavalry Companies A and E Return from the Eastern Theater

1. *OR* 21, 925, 987.
2. Ibid., 1103.
3. Bates Letters, "Port Tobacco Md, February 1st 1863."
4. Ibid., "Port Tobacco", undated letter, possibly Feb. 27.
5. Ibid., "Cincinnati, Ohio, March 12, 1863."
6. Ibid., "Camp near Murfreesboro, March 25th 1863."
7. Ibid.

Expedition to Liberty and Snow Hill

8. Bitter, 71.
9. Bates Letters, April 7, 1863.
10. Ibid.
11. Ibid. "Beggar lice" are described as Velcro-like seeds with small hooks that embed themselves on whatever they come into contact with.
12. Ibid.
13. Ibid.
14. Minty, *National Tribune*, January 26, 1893.
15. Bates Letters, April 7, 1863.
16. Bitter, 82. The Federal government realized that as long as slaves were considered "property" they could be legally seized as "contraband" of war and were not subject to return to their owners as was customary prior to the war.
17. Ibid., 81.
18. Ibid., 81-82. Surgeon Fish goes on to tell what they believe happened to the slave: "In the morning the old black man was allowed to go back to his master. I asked him if he was not afraid to go lest they should punish him. He replied that he did not believe they would touch him; if they did he would come to us. His family being back, he preferred to run his risk. (We never advise the slaves to run away, as it is not in our power to provide for only a limited number of them.) Some days later we returned by the same route. Inquiry was made at the plantation as to what had become of this man. His brother told us that he was taken out and whipped five hundred lashes on his bare back, having in the intervals of his whipping all the hair pulled out of his head, a little at a time. He had been conveyed away from the plantation, and his brother told us he had no doubt he was dead. It was well for that master that we were on a hurried march, and had no time to stop . . ."
19. In his July 24, 1862, letter to his parents Charles writes: "I don't know where my aversion to a nigger comes from, but it is of no use for me to try to think of them with the 'brotherly regard'. . . I just can't do it. They don't look right."

Blacks in Service: Private Jackson Kelly, 4th United States Cavalry

20. Elsie Freeman, Wynell Buroughs Schamel, and Jean West, "The Fight for Equal Rights: Black Soldiers in the Civil War." *Social Education* 56, 2 (February 1992): 118-120.
21. Ibid.
22. Henry I:163; Heitman, 586. Kauffman had a 45-year long career in the army, beginning in 1848 as a private in the 6th Infantry, ending with his retirement in January 1892 as major, 4th United States Cavalry.
23. August Kautz. *Customs of Service Non-Commissioned Officers and Soldiers* (Philadelphia: J. B. Lippencott & Co., 1864), Paragraphs 110, 111, 269, 270, 271.
24. Register of Enlistments.
25. Ibid.
26. Ibid. Jackson's last name is spelled both Kelly and Kelley. On this form his date of death is listed as August 21, 1864; U.S. Register of Deaths in the Regular Army, 1860-1889. This register shows his death on August 20, 1864. His name is spelled Kelley on the West Point Monument. There are two records of Kelly's enlistment. The first shows him enlisted at Big Shanty, GA, August 14, 1863, by Lt. Gauther. The notation "Error at Enlistment" is printed on this record. The second shows an enlistment "in the field, Georgia," on January 17, 1863 by Lt. Sullivan.

The 4th US Cavalry and Freeman's Battery at Franklin, Tennessee

27. Bitter, 73. Minty was "under the Surgeon's care" for a serious injury received during a saber charge in May 1862. The injury sustained was described as the "rupture or prolapse of the ani (collapse of the sphincter)." This could also be described as a protruding of the bowels. He would suffer from this for the remainder of his life. The only treatment at the time was "to bathe the parts with cold water." Considering the time spent in the saddle, this must have been a source of immense pain and suffering. A lieutenant in his regiment, aware of Minty's condition, wrote years later that Minty ". . . was one of the bravest officers I ever knew, and one who never complained unless compelled to." Bitter, 23.

28. *OR* 23, Pt. I, 230.
29. Ibid., 231. See Appendix for the roster of officers.
30. Bitter, 72, quoting Minty, *National Tribune*, January 26, 1893.
31. *OR* 23, 230.
32. Ibid.
33. Ibid.
34. *OR* 23, 232.
35. Ibid.
36. John A. Wyeth, MD, *That Devil Forrest: The Life of General Nathan Bedford Forrest* (New York: Harper & Brothers Publishers, 1899), 182. Lieutenant Baxter's first name appears as "Ned," but may actually have been "Nat."
37. Wyeth, 182; Robert Selph Henry, *"First with the Most" - Forrest* (Indianapolis: Bobbs-Merrill, 1944), 136-7. Freeman's Battery consisted of six guns, two of which were in action at Franklin at the time.
38. Wyeth, 182.
39. Ibid.
40. *OR* 23, Pt. I, 232.
41. Wyeth, 182.
42. Ibid.
43. *OR* 23, Pt. I, 232.
44. Wyeth, 182.
45. Thomas R. Tullos, "When Capt. Sam Freeman was Killed," *Confederate Veteran*, August 1913, 407.
46. Vale, 145-46.
47. Ibid., 147.
48. Ibid. Rand Bitter's research confirms that Vale and Strickland discussed this incident after the war during the writing of Vale's book. This story may explain why Stickland's records show two first names: Sherlock and Sylvester. It is not known if Vale had any postwar communication with Major Rendlebock.
49. Heitman, 823; Henry 2:328.
50. *OR* 23, Pt. I, 232.
51. Ibid.
52. Ibid.
53. Ibid.
54. Ibid. To "spike" a cannon is to make it unusable by driving a spike into the touchhole - where the fuse is. According to the eyewitness account of Thomas Tullos, of the cannons captured at the top of the hill, "all the wheels were cut down and they had to be hauled off on wagons."
55. *OR* 23, Pt. I, 231. One Confederate eyewitness recalled it lasting about thirty minutes. J. G. Witherspoon, "The Killing of Captain Freeman," *Confederate Veteran*, vol. 21, 1913, 410.
56. Ibid., 227.
57. Ibid. General Stanley seems to have personally regretted the loss of two "old soldiers" with whom he had served on the frontier. 2nd Lt. Thomas Healy was mortally wounded at Franklin, 2nd Lt. Thomas Simson was severely wounded, never fully recovering.
58. *OR* 23, Pt. I, 231; McIntyre's handwritten list, National Archives. Combined Records. Two of the wounded (Privates Lorenzo A. Kimble, Company K; and Jacob McCormick, Company D) were subsequently discharged for disability. Register of Enlistments.
59. Heitman, 563; Henry 2:113.
60. Heitman, 520.
61. Bitter, 73.
62. Minty, *National Tribune*, January 26, 1893.
63. Larson, 163.
64. Vale, 535.

"Camp Minty"

65. Bitter, 75.
66. Minty, *National Tribune*, March 2, 1893.
67. Vale, 159.
68. Sipes, 62.
69. Bitter, 90.

The Cavalry Raid

70. Longacre, 12.
71. Uschan, 41, 56.
72. Thomas B. Van Horn, *History of the Army of the Cumberland*. 2 vols. (Cincinnati: Robert Clarke, 1875), 1:287.
73. Minty, *National Tribune*, March 2, 1893.
74. *OR* 23, Pt. I, 276; Minty, *National Tribune*, March 2, 1893.
75. *OR* 23, Pt. I, 271.
76. Ibid.
77. *OR* 23, Pt. I, 276. It appears that there was a "friendly rivalry" among the regiments of the Saber Brigade when it came to taking or giving credit for participation in various battles and skirmishes, particularly when written thirty years after the event. There is almost no mention of the participation of the 4th U.S. in the Official Reports or subsequent regimental histories.
78. Minty, *National Tribune*, March 2, 1893; *OR* 23, 271.
79. *OR* 23, Pt. I, 276.
80. Ibid., 267.
81. Ibid., 272, 274; Vale, 157-59.
82. Vale, 154; *OR* 23, Pt. I, 269.
83. Vale, 154.
84. *OR* 23, Pt. I, 269.
85. Ibid., 272.
86. Sipes, 52-3. Footnote reference: Sidney A. Speed to his sister, April 30, 1863, in *The Soldiers of Indiana in the War for the Union*, vol. 2:204.
87. *OR* 23, 272.
88. Vale, 158-59.
89. Ibid., 155. On April 30, 1863, Pvt. Philip H. Saller, 4th US Cavalry, Co. K, was killed in a skirmish near Washington, TN. Register of Enlistments; West Point Monument.

Cos. D and I: Expedition to Middleton

90. Vale, 159.
91. *OR* 23, Pt. I, 338.
92. Minty, *National Tribune*, March 2, 1893; *OR* 23, 338, 339.

93. Heitman, 756.
94. *OR* 23, Pt. I, 339.
95. Ibid., 334.
96. Ibid., 338.
97. Ibid., 335.
98. Ibid., 336.
99. Ibid., 338.
100. Ibid.
101. Ibid.
102. Ibid., 336.
103. Ibid., 335. Pvt. Allen, Co. E., 4th U.S., "A Daybreak Dash Into a Rebel Camp," *National Tribune*, April 7, 1887. Allen writes: "They were in all sorts of dress and undress, some without even 'unmentionables,' running for the woods . . ."
104. Ibid., 339.
105. Ibid.
106. Ibid.
107. Ibid.
108. Ibid.
109. Ibid.
110. Ibid., 335.
111. Ibid., 337.
112. Ibid., 335.
113. Vale, 162.
114. *OR* 23, Pt. I, 338.
115. Ibid., 335
116. Henry 2:227; Heitman, 1054.
117. *OR* 23, Pt. I, 340.
118. Vale, 161.
119. Minty, *National Tribune*, March 2, 1893.
120. Vale, 161.
121. Minty, *National Tribune*, July 6 & 13, 1893.

Companies F and H Return from the Frontier

122. Henry I:174; Heitman, 744.
123. Larson, 145; *OR* 22, 893; *OR* 22, Pt. II, 131.
124. Larson, 145; Heitman, 559; Powell, 303.
125. *OR* 13, 468. An obviously frustrated Craig had his note personally delivered by 1st Lieutenant John Wilcox, 4th US Cavalry.
126. "Field Return of a Squadron of the 4th Cav. for the month of May 1863." Combined Records.
127. Ibid.
128. Larson, 140-41.
129. Ibid., 142-144.
130. Ibid., 145-46. Larson described the men: "A Pennsylvanian named Parker; Otto von Louby [Otto Lauby], a German nobleman, and John A. Irwine, whom I later saved from drowning in a river in Georgia and who has visited me several times here in Fredericksburg. The others were John Hartcorn, Samuel Kittron and two or three others who deserted a few days later." Page 146.
131. Heitman, 935.
132. Heitman, 424, Henry 2:271.
133. Larson, 149.

Confronting Morgan's Cavalry at Bardstown, Kentucky

134. Andrew Nelson Lytle, *Bedford Forrest and His Critter Company* (Nashville: J. S. Sanders, Southern Classic Series, 1992 edition), 187.
135. Larson, 146-47. In fact, Morgan was a commissioned officer in the Confederate Army.
136. *OR* 23, Pt. I, 652; Larson, 147.
137. *OR* 23, Pt. I, 652.
138. Ibid.
139. Larson, 147-48. Sergeant Larson, still recovering from his ankle injuries, was not present at Bardstown and the death of a "Private Collins" does not appear in Lieutenant Sullivan's official report.
140. *OR* 23, Pt. I, 652.
141. Ibid.
142. Larson, 148.
143. Ibid.
144. Ibid., 153-55.
145. Ibid., 159.
146. Ibid., 159-60.
147. Ibid., 161.
148. Ibid.
149. Bitter, 82.
150. Larson, 162-63.
151. Ibid., 164.

Chicago Board of Trade Battery, Illinois Volunteers

152. Bitter, 115.
153. Larson, 179.
154. Caughey, "Crossed Sabers Blog." October 6, 2008, quoting from *Historical Sketch of the Chicago Board of Trade Battery* (Chicago: Andrew Finney Co., 1902).
155. Ibid.
156. Ibid.

VI. The Tullahoma Campaign (Middle Tennessee)

1. Catton, *American Heritage*, 291.
2. Ibid., 292.
3. Ibid., 293.
4. Ibid., 293.
5. Ibid., 294.
6. Bowman, 143.
7. Catton, 295.
8. Ibid., 419.
9. Ibid., 419.
10. Sipes, 62.
11. *OR* 23, Pt. I, 423.
12. Bates Letters, "Murfreesboro, May 31, 1863."
13. *OR* 52, Pt. I, 423.
14. Starr, 3:242.
15. Minty, *National Tribune*, July 6 & 13, 1893.
16. Sipes, 60.

Scout on Middleton and Eagleville Pikes

17. Sipes, 60.
18. *OR* 23, Pt. I, 373.
19. Ibid.
20. Ibid.
21. Ibid.
22. Ibid., 374
23. Ibid.

Expedition to and Skirmish Near Lebanon

24. *OR* 23, Pt. I, 393-94. Minty, *National Tribune*, July 6 and 13, 1893.
25. Vale, 164.
26. Ibid.
27. Minty, *National Tribune*, July 6 & 13, 1893.
28. Ibid., 85.
29. Vale, 165.
30. Minty, *National Tribune*, July 6 & 13, 1893.
31. *OR* 23, Pt. I, 394.
32. Minty, *National Tribune*, July 6 & 13, 1893; Vale, 165-66.
33. Minty, *National Tribune*, July 6 & 13, 1893.
34. Henry Albert Potter, Letter No. 22, "Camp Park, June 17/63." The Letters of Henry Albert Potter, captain, 4th Michigan Cavalry, Michael Palmer Ruddy (great grandson), ed. Michigan Historical Collection, Bentley Historical Library, University of Michigan, Ann Arbor, hereafter referred to as "Potter Letters"; Register of Enlistments; West Point Monument.
35. Sipes, 61-62. There is a discrepancy in the distance traveled as reported by Minty, Vale, and Sipes.
36. Ibid., 62.
37. Bitter, 89.

Shelbyville, Tennessee

38. N.P.S. Historical Handbook: Chickamauga and Chattanooga Battlefields. "The Tullahoma Campaign," http://www.nps.gov/history/history/online_books/hh/25/hh25c.htm
39. *OR* 23, 404.
40. "The Tullahoma Campaign."
41. Bowman, 155.
42. *OR* 23, Pt. I, 402-09.
43. Ibid.
44. Vale, 168-69.
45. *OR* 23, Pt. I, 556.
46. Vale, 182; *OR* 23, 418; "History of the 4th US Cavalry."
47. *OR* 23, Pt. I, 538; *OR* 23, Pt. I, 556.
48. *OR* 23, Pt. I, 556.
49. George F. Steahlin (1st Lieutenant and Adjutant for the 7th Pennsylvania Cavalry), *National Tribune*, May 27, 1882.
50. *OR* 23, Pt. I, 538.
51. "The Tullahoma Campaign."
52. Vale, 175-76.
53. Ibid., 174.
54. Steahlin, *National Tribune*, May 27, 1882.
55. Vale, 175-76.
56. Ibid.
57. Ibid.
58. Heitman, 957.

The Charge at Guy's Gap

59. Steahlin, *National Tribune*, May 27, 1882.
60. *OR* 23, Pt. I, 539; Steahlin, *National Tribune*, May 27, 1882; Vale, 175.
61. Steahlin, *National Tribune*, May 27, 1882; Vale, 175.
62. *OR* 23, Pt. I, 556.
63. Vale, 175.
64. Minty, *National Tribune*, May 8, 1890.
65. Ibid.
66. Sipes, 63.
67. *OR* 23, 556.
68. Ibid., 539.
69. Steahlin, *National Tribune*, May 27, 1882.
70. Ibid.
71. *OR* 23, Pt. I, 539; Vale, 175-76.
72. *OR* 23, Pt. I, 557.
73. *OR* 23, Pt. I, 539; Vale, 175.
74. Vale, 175.
75. *OR* 23, Pt. I, 561.
76. *OR* 23, Pt. I, 566; Vale, 176.
77. *OR* 23, Pt. I, 557.
78. Vale, 175.

The Battle at Shelbyville

79. Vale, 175-76;
80. *OR* 23, Pt. I, 557.
81. Ibid.
82. Vale, 178. Forrest had been seriously wounded "in a disgraceful brawl with a disgruntled lieutenant of artillery, and was still recovering when the Federal cavalry was advancing toward Shelbyville." Starr, 242.
83. Minty, *National Tribune*, August 3, 1893; Vale, 178.
84. *OR* 23, Pt. I, 557.
85. Ibid.
86. Ibid., 539.
87. Vale, 177-78.
88. Sipes, 64, quoting John A. Wyeth, *Harpers' Weekly*, June 18, 1898.
89. Ibid.
90. Ibid.
91. *OR* 23, Pt. I, 561.
92. Vale, 177.
93. Ibid.
94. Sipes, 64, quoting Wyeth.
95. *OR* 23, Pt. I, 562.
96. *OR* 23, Pt. I, 557-58; *OR* 23, Pt. I, 556.
97. Minty, *National Tribune*, May 8, 1890.
98. *OR* 23, Pt. I, 557.
99. Starr, 3:245.
100. Minty, *National Tribune*, May 8, 1890.
101. Ibid.; Steahlin, *National Tribune*, May 27, 1882.

102. Vale, 179.
103. *OR* 23, Pt. I, 565.
104. Steahlin, *National Tribune*, May 27, 1882.
105. Vale, 179.
106. *OR* 23, Pt. I, 557-558; Vale, 181.
107. Steahlin, *National Tribune*, May 27, 1882.
108. Vale, 179.
109. *OR* 52, Pt. I, 423-24.
110. Steahlin, *National Tribune*, May 27, 1882.
111. Vale, 179; Minty, *National Tribune*, August 3, 1893.
112. Vale, 185. Captain Vale dedicated this passage "To the perpetuation of the memory of their unparalled devotion, on this 27th of June, 1863."
113. *OR* 23, Pt. I, 408.
114. Vale, 181.
115. Vale, 181; OR 23, 558; Minty, *National Tribune*, May 27, 1882.
116. *OR* 23, Pt. I, 559.
117. Vale, 181; Minty, *National Tribune*, May 27, 1882.
118. Minty, *National Tribune*, May 27, 1882.
119. *OR* 23, Pt. I, 566.
120. *OR* 23, Pt. I, 558; Minty, *National Tribune*, May 27, 1882.
121. Vale, 181.
122. *OR* 23, Pt. I, 567.
123. Minty, *National Tribune*, May 27, 1882.
124. *OR* 23, Pt. I, 540; Vale, 181; Starr, 242. Starr writes, "Ignoring his unhealed wounds," Forrest had "started off at once for Shelbyville," but was unable to assist Wheeler in time.
125. Stanley, 146.
126. Starr, 3:244, 246.
127. Ibid., 246.
128. Steahlin, *National Tribune*, May 27, 1882.
129. Stanley, 146.
130. United States. Army. "Medal of Honor." U.S. Army Center of Military History @www.history.army.mil/moh.html; Boston Publishing Company, editors. *Above and Beyond: A History of the Medal of Honor from the Civil War to Vietnam* (Boston: Boston Publishing Company, 1985), 8-55.
131. *OR* 23, Pt. I, 557.
132. *OR* 52, Pt. I, 423-24.
133. Bitter, 100; Vale, 182.
134. Bitter, 102. Aside from being a "mere volunteer," Minty's former service in the British military may have been held against him as Britain was considered sympathetic to the Confederacy.

Aftermath

135. Vale, 188.
136. Minty, *National Tribune*, May 8, 1890.
137. *OR* 23, Pt. I, 541.
138. Vale, 189-92. Vale devoted four pages of his text to this plague.
139. Ibid., 186-87.
140. Bryan Steel Wills, *The Confederacy's Greatest Cavalryman: Nathan Bedford Forrest* (Kansas: University Press of Kansas, 1998), 129.
141. Ibid.; Vale, 187.
142. *OR* 23, Pt. I, 558.
143. Bitter, 102.
144. Sipes, 72; Vale, 188.
145. Sipes, 72.
146. Ibid.
147. *OR* 23, Pt. I, 403-9.
148. Vale, 188.
149. Bitter, 102.

Camp at Salem, Tennessee

150. Larson, 166.
151. Bitter, 102.
152. Ibid.; Minty, *National Tribune*, August 3, 1893.
153. Bitter, 102.
154. Larson, 166.
155. Ibid., 170.
156. Ibid.
157. Ibid.
158. Ibid., 171.
159. Ibid.
160. Ibid.
161. Bitter, 111.
162. Ibid.

August 1863 - Detached Duty

163. Bitter, 103.
164. Minty, *National Tribune*, February 25, 1892.
165. Ibid.
166. Ibid.
167. Ibid.
168. Ibid; Vale, 214.
169. Bitter, 109-10; Vale, 208.
170. Starr, 3:70.
171. *OR* 23, Pt. I, 644.
172. Vale, 201.
173. Minty, *National Tribune*, February 25, 1892.
174. Ibid.
175. Ibid.
176. Ibid.; Vale, 201.
177. Minty, *National Tribune*, February 25, 1892.
178. Vale, 202.
179. Minty, *National Tribune*, February 25, 1892; Vale, 202. The Southern historian was John A. Wyeth.
180. Bitter, 110.

Expedition to Sparta and Calfkiller Creek

181. *OR* 30, Pt. I, 51.
182. Vale, 210-11; Wiswell Letters, "Camp at Pikeville, Tenn., 24th August 1863."
183. Vale, 211.
184. Minty, *National Tribune*, February 25, 1892.
185. *OR* 30, Pt. I, 920.
186. Ibid.
187. Ibid.
188. Vale, 206-07; Minty, *National Tribune*, February 25, 1892; *OR* 30, Pt. I, 920.
189. Minty, *National Tribune*, February 25, 1892; Vale, 206.

190. Vale, 206.
191. Ibid.
192. Minty, *National Tribune*, February 25, 1892.
193. Vale, 206-07.
194. Bitter, 111.
195. Vale, 207; Register of Enlistments; *OR* 30, 920.
196. Vale, 207. *OR* 30, Pt. I, 921; National Archives. US Registers of Deaths in the Regular Army, 1860-1889. RG 94. Hereafter referred to as Registers of Deaths.
197. Ibid., 208.
198. Minty, *National Tribune*, February 25, 1892.
199. *OR* 30, Pt. I, 921.
200. Ibid.
201. *OR* 30, Pt. I, 924, 926; Wiswell Letters, "August 1863, HeaqdQrs, 4th US Cavalry." Camp near McMinnville, Tenn"; Bitter, 111.
202. Bitter, 111.
203. *OR* 30, Pt. I, 925; Vale, 211.
204. Minty, *National Tribune*, January 26, 1893.

VII. THE CHATTANOOGA CAMPAIGN

1. Sipes, 73.
2. Ibid.
3. William Glenn Robertson, "The Chickamauga Campaign." *Blue & Gray* Magazine. Fall 2006, 12.
4. Dave Roth, editor, *Blue & Gray* magazine. Fall 2007, 5.
5. Catton, 420.
6. Powell, 273.
7. Robertson, *Blue & Gray* magazine. Fall 2006, 26.
8. *OR* 30, Pt. I, 51.
9. Ibid., 925.
10. Ibid., 891.
11. Richard W. Johnson, *Memoir of Maj. Gen. George H. Thomas* (Philadelphia: J. B. Lippincot, 1881), 88.
12. *OR* 30, Pt. I, 53.
13. Larson, 172.
14. David A. Powell, *The Maps of Chickamauga*. (New York and California: Savas Beatie, 2009), 23.
15. Ibid., 24.
16. Potter's Diary. @ http://freepages.geneology.rootsweb.ancestry.com/~mruddy/chicka.htm.
17. Larson, 172.
18. *OR* 30, Pt. I, 604.
19. Ibid., 922-23, 925.
20. Robertson, *Blue & Gray*, Fall 2007, 21.
21. Ibid.
22. Ibid.
23. *OR* 30, Pt. I, 605.
24. Ibid., 922.
25. Ibid.
26. Vale, 217.
27. Ibid., 219.
28. *OR* 30, 922, 925.
29. Robertson, Fall 2007, 40.
30. Sipes, 79. As difficult as this situation is to believe, it serves to emphasize the general lack of communication and information that existed. As Rand Bitter points out, since Longstreet had been exclusively involved in the east, "it seemed too incredible to believe" that Lee would send Longstreet westward into Georgia. Bitter, 124.
31. *OR* 30, Pt. I, 605.
32. Ibid., 922.
33. *OR* 30, Pt. I, 922; Vale, 220.
34. Monthly Returns September 1863.
35. *OR* 30, Pt. I, 922.
36. Baumgartner, 194.
37. Vale, 220.
38. Robertson. Fall 2007, 41-2.
39. Larson, 174-75.
40. Ibid.

SEPTEMBER 18 - REED'S BRIDGE

41. Cleaves, 158.
42. Richard O'Shea, *American Heritage: Battle Maps of the Civil War* (New York: Smithmark Publishers, 1992), 119.
43. Cleaves, 158.
44. Baumgartner, 187.
45. Ibid., 195.
46. Robertson. Fall 2007, 44.
47. Ibid.
48. Minty, *National Tribune*, March 3, 1892.

THE STAND AT REED'S BRIDGE

49. James Larson, *National Tribune*, September 19, 1912. This is confirmed by William Glenn Robertson, *Blue and Gray*, Fall 2007, 44. David A. Powell's *The Maps of Chickamauga*, published in 2009, is the definitive source for the action at Chickamauga.
50. Potter Diary.
51. Vale, 224.
52. *OR* 30, Pt. I, 922.
53. Minty, *National Tribune* March 3, 1892; "History of the 4th US Cavalry."
54. *OR* 30, Pt. I, 922.
55. Minty, *National Tribune*, March 3, 1892; *OR* 30, 922.
56. Minty, *National Tribune*, March 3, 1892.
57. Potter Diary.
58. Baumgartner, 196; Sipes, 79.
59. Sipes, 79.
60. Minty, *National Tribune*, March 3, 1862; *OR* 30, 923.
61. Minty, *National Tribune*, March 3, 1862.
62. Ibid.
63. Sipes, 79.
64. Potter Diary.
65. Larson, *National Tribune*, September 19, 1912.
66. Robertson. *Blue and Gray*, Fall 2007, 45.
67. Potter Diary.
68. Powell, David, 40, 69. Robertson. *Blue and Gray*, Fall 2007, 44.
69. Baumgartner, 203.
70. Baumgartner, 203.
71. Ibid.
72. Minty, *National Tribune*, March 3, 1892; Baumgartner, 199.

73. *OR* 30, Pt. I, 923; Minty, *National Tribune*, March 3, 1892.
74. Ibid.
75. Minty, *National Tribune*, March 3, 1892.
76. *OR* 30, Pt. I, 923; Minty, *National Tribune*, March 3, 1892.
77. Minty, *National Tribune*, March 3, 1892; Vale, 226.
78. Larson, 177.
79. Ibid.
80. Minty, *National Tribune*, March 3, 1892.
81. Larson, 177
82. *OR* 30, Pt. I, 923.
83. Vale, 226-27; *OR* 30, Pt. I, 923.
84. Vale, 226-27.
85. Ibid., 226.
86. Ibid.
87. Ibid., 227.
88. Ibid.
89. Potter Diary.
90. Vale, 227; Minty, *National Tribune*, March 3, 1892; Larson, 178; *OR* 30, 925.
91. Minty, *National Tribune*, March 3, 1892.
92. Ibid.
93. Ibid.; *OR* 30, 923.
94. Larson, 179; Robertson, Fall 2007, 45.
95. Larson, 179.
96. Robertson, Fall 2007, 45.
97. Baumgartner, 200-01.
98. Robertson, Fall 2007, 45.
99. Ibid.
100. Baumgartner, 200-01.
101. Larson, 179.
102. *OR* 30, Pt. I, 923; Larson, 179.
103. Robertson, Fall 2007, 46.
104. Ibid.
105. Robertson, Fall 2007, 46; Minty, *National Tribune*, March 3, 1892.
106. Minty, *National Tribune*, March 3, 1892; Potter Diary.
107. *OR* 30, Pt. I, 923.
108. Minty, *National Tribune*, March 3, 1892.
109. Ibid.; Baumgartner, 210.
110. Baumgartner, 200-01.
111. Ibid., 210.
112. Minty, *National Tribune*, March 3, 1892.
113. Robertson, Fall 2007, 48; *OR*. Vol. 30, 79; Catton, *American Heritage* 431; "Cavalry of the Civil War, It's Evolution and Influence."

The Night of September 18-19

114. Baumgartner, 213; *OR* 30, 920, 923, 925.
115. Baumgartner, 213.
116. *OR* 30, Pt. I, 923; Baumgartner, 213.
117. Baumgartner, 213; Larson, 179-80.
118. Larson, 179-80.
119. Baumgartner, 213.
120. Ibid.
121. Potter Diary.
122. Ibid.; Bitter, 213.
123. Baumgartner, 213.
124. Larson, 180; Potter Diary.
125. Baumgartner, 214.
126. Bitter, 125.
127. Larson, 180.
128. Larson, 180; Baumgartner, 214; Bitter, 125, quoting Burns.
129. Larson, 180.
130. Baumgartner, 214.
131. Larson, 180.
132. Baumgartner, 214.
133. Bitter, 125, quoting Burns.
134. Minty, *National Tribune*, March 3, 1892.
135. Ibid.
136. Ibid.
137. *OR* 30, Pt. I, 925.

VIII. The Battle Of Chickamauga Creek

1. Bowman, 169.
2. Cleaves, 163.
3. O'Shea, 119; Bowman, 169.
4. Cleaves, 159.
5. Bowman, 168.
6. Bitter, 126.
7. Bowman, 169.
8. Catton, *American Heritage*, 429.

Saturday, September 19

9. Minty, *National Tribune*, March 3, 1892.
10. Ibid.
11. Larson, 181.
12. *OR* 30, Pt. I, 57.
13. Minty, *National Tribune*, March 3, 1892.
14. *OR* 30, Pt. I, 923; Minty, *National Tribune*, November 9, 1893.
15. *OR* 30, Pt. I, 57; Minty, *National Tribune*, March 3, 1892.
16. Minty, *National Tribune*, November 9, 1893.

Sunday, September 20

17. *OR* 30, Pt. I, 59-60.
18. Bowman, *Almanac*, 169. "Rosecrans reported 16,179 killed, wounded, and missing. Bragg reported 17,804, but 18,500 is probably a more accurate estimate for the Rebel army." Powell, *The Maps of Chattanooga*, 256.
19. *OR* 30, Pt. I, 58; Catton, *American Heritage*, 429.
20. Bowman, 169; Catton, *American Heritage*, 429.
21. Ibid.
22. *OR* 30, Pt. I, 924.
23. Ibid., 925-26.
24. *OR* 30, Pt. I, 924; Minty, *National Tribune*, November 9, 1893.
25. Ibid.
26. Ibid.
27. Minty, *National Tribune*, March 3, 1892.
28. Catton, *American Heritage*, 430.

29. *OR* 30, Pt. I, 252-53; *OR* 30, Pt. I, 60.
30. Catton, *American Heritage*, 430.
31. *OR* 30, Pt. I, 253.
32. *Catton, American Heritage*, 429.
33. Bowman, 169.

THE LOST PATROL

34. Larson, 184.
35. Larson, *National Tribune*, September 19, 1912.
36. Larson, 184-85.
37. Larson, *National Tribune*, September 19, 1912.
38. Larson, 185.
39. Ibid., 188.
40. Larson, *National Tribune*, September 19, 1912.
41. Larson, 191; Larson, *National Tribune*, September 19, 1912.
42. Larson, *National Tribune*, September, 19, 1912.
43. Larson, 193.
44. Ibid.
45. United States v. Fletcher, 148 U.S. 84 (1893). http://supreme.vlex.com/vid/united-states-v-fletcher-20058867.

RETREAT TO CHATTANOOGA

46. Larson, 193.
47. *OR* 30, Pt. I, 254.
48. Larson, 194.
49. Ibid.
50. *OR* 30, Pt. I, 924.
51. Ibid.
52. *OR* 30, 254; *OR* 30, 924, 926.
53. *OR* 30, Pt. I, 61.
54. Minty, *National Tribune*, March 3, 1892.
55. Larson, 194.
56. Ibid., 195.
57. Ibid.
58. Larson, 195.
59. *OR* 30, Pt. I, 924.
60. *OR* 30, Pt. I, 924; Minty, *National Tribune*, March 3, 1892; Larson, 195,
61. Larson, 195; Sipes, 81.
62. *OR* 30, Pt. I, 924; Minty, *National Tribune*, March 3, 1892.
63. Ibid.
64. Ibid.
65. Ibid.
66. *OR* 30, Pt. I, 924.
67. Larson, 195-96.
68. Sipes, 81.
69. Minty, *National Tribune*, March 3, 1892.
70. Larson, 197.
71. Rodenbough, "Cavalry of the Civil War - It's Evolution and Influence," 34.
72. Catton, *American Heritage*, 431.
73. *OR* 30, 61.
74. Ibid., 79.
75. Bowman, 170.
76. O'Shea, 119.
77. Catton, *American Heritage*, 431.
78. Sipes, 81.

IX. THE SIEGE OF CHATTANOOGA

1. Bitter, 127.
2. *OR* 30, Pt. I, 925.
3. Ibid., 924, 926.
4. Sipes, 81.
5. Catton, *American Heritage*, 432.
6. Sipes, 81-2.
7. Larson, 199.
8. Ibid.
9. *OR* 30, Pt. II, 665.
10. Larson, 199.
11. *OR* 30, Pt. II, 664.
12. Minty, *National Tribune*, August 31, 1893.
13. *OR* 30, Pt. I, 926.
14. Larson, 199.
15. *OR* 30, Pt. I, 926; Wiswell Letter, "October 8, 1863, Camp North Bank Tenn. River, Chattanooga."
16. *OR* 30, Pt. I, 926.

A DARING ESCAPE

17. Larson, 199-202.
18. Minty, *National Tribune*, August 31, 1893.
19. Ibid.
20. Henry 2: 341; Heitman, 927. In November 1862, Stockton was a captain in the US Volunteers, and served as aide-de-camp on the staff of General Hunter. He returned to his regiment and in March 1865 was promoted captain, USA. He would resign his commission in September 1866.

CHASING WHEELER'S CAVALRY

21. *OR* 30 Pt. II, 665.
22. *OR* 30 Pt. II, 644, 684.
23. Bitter, 141.
24. Bitter, 141.
25. *OR* 30 Pt. II, 684-85.
26. Sipes, 84-85.
27. Larson, 205.
28. Ibid., 206; *OR* 30, Pt. II, 692.
29. Larson 206.
30. Potter Letters No. 26, "Murfreesboro Oct 8th 1863."
31. *OR* 30, Pt. II, 668; Bitter, 143. Rand Bitter covers this entire sorry episode in his chapter, "Under Arrest."
32. *OR* 30, Pt. III, 109.
33. Ibid.
34. Larson, 206.
35. Ibid., 207.
36. Bates Letters, "Brownsville, Alabama, November 5, 1863."
37. Vale, 249-50.
38. Larson, 207.
39. *OR* 30, Pt. II, 668.
40. Ibid., 665.
41. Ibid., 667.
42. Wiswell Letters.

43. Bates Letters.
44. Wiswell Letters.

Maysville, Alabama

45. Sipes, 86.
46. Sipes, 86.
47. Larson, 207. Larson describes "dog tents": "Each man was issued a piece of very light canvas, about four and one-half feet long and four feet broad. One man received a piece that had buttons on one side, while its mate had buttonholes, and they were used together to make a war tent for two men. We called them 'dog tents' because a dog might be comfortable sheltered under one, but it made a very poor shelter for two men. When stretched out under one of them, either the head or the legs had go be exposed to the rain." Larson, 151.
48. Potter Letters No. 27, "Camp near Maysville, Alabama, Sunday Oct 25th 1863."
49. Ibid.
50. Larson, 209.
51. Wiswell Letters.
52. *OR* 31, Pt. III, 126.

Expedition to Whitesburg and Decatur

53. *OR* 31, Pt. I, 567.
54. Sipes, 87.
55. Ibid.
56. *OR* 31, Pt. I, 568.
57. Ibid.
58. Ibid., 569.
59. Ibid.
60. Sipes, 87.
61. Henry, 2: 303; Heitman, 659.
62. *OR* 31, Pt. I, 436.
63. Potter Letters No. 30, "Courier Station near Cleveland, Friday Dec 18th 1863."

The Battle of Chattanooga

64. Catton, *American Heritage*, 421.
65. Ibid., 439.
66. Ibid.
67. *OR* 31, Pt. I, Part III, 556.
68. Larson, 215.
69. Wiswell Letters, "Huntsville Ala, Jany 17th 1864."
70. Larson, 210. Larson incorrectly identifies Lt. Roys as "Lt. Noyes."
71. Ibid.
72. Ibid., 214-15.

Huntsville, Alabama

73. Sipes, 88.
74. Vale, 210.
75. Bates Letters, "Huntsville Alabama December 12th 1863."
76. Wiswell Letters, "Huntsville, Ala Dec 17th 1863."

IX. Masters of the Field

1. Vale, 127.
2. Ibid., 264-65.
3. *OR* 20, Pt. I, 620; Cozzens, 108.
4. *OR* 20, Pt. I, 198.
5. *OR* 30, Pt. I, 79-80.
6. *OR* 20, Pt. I, 199; *OR* 30, Pt. I, 188.
7. *OR* 20, Pt. I, 199.
8. Ibid., 649.
9. *OR* 23, Pt. I, 230.
10. *OR* 23, Pt. I, 335.
11. Vale, 177.
12. *OR* 23, Pt. I, 566.
13. Ibid.
14. Sipes, 72-73.
15. Evans, 2; *OR* 30, Pt. I, 79.
16. Minty, *National Tribune*, January 2, 1893.
17. *OR* 30, Pt. II, 664, 667.
18. *OR* 30, Pt. I, 79-80.
19. McTeer, *National Tribune*, May 28, 1891.

1864: Through the Heart of the Confederacy

1. Wormser, 229.

I. Grant-Sheridan-Sherman-Thomas

2. Ibid., 237.
3. Evans, xvii.
5. Albert Castel. *Decision in the West: The Atlanta Campaign of 1864* (Lawrence: University Press of Kansas, 1992), 57.
6. Catton, *American Heritage*, 442. The "Army of Tennessee" was the name of the Confederate Army in the West. The "Army of *The* Tennessee" was the Union army in the West.
7. "Philip Sheridan: Small and Forceful Impact," http://www.anglefire.com/tn/AIB/sheridan.html. "A restless, irritable soldier, he forgave few mistakes, including his own. On his way [up the chain of command] he had marched with his troops, eaten with them, and rarely allowed himself the comforts of the warm tents and personal service that his own junior officers often insisted on for themselves."
8. Catton, *American Heritage*, 517-18.
9. Thomas B. Buell, *The Warrior Generals: Combat Leadership in the Civil War* (New York: Crown, 1997), 357.
10. Ibid.; Evans, xxviii.
11. Catton, *American Heritage*, 515.
12. Cleaves, 210; Buell, 357.
13. Catton, *American Heritage*, 517.

Major General George H. Thomas, USA

14. Buell, 387.
15. Ibid.
16. Ibid., 359.
17. Rhodes, "Cavalry Battles and Charges," 242.

18. Catton, *American Heritage*, 486.
19. Ibid., 487.
20. Cleaves, 202.
21. Johnson, R. W., 136.
22. Cleaves, 203-4.
23. Ibid., 209.
24. Ibid., 204. Sherman was "most embarrassed" by this General Order of the War Department. While he felt that it "doubtless secured the services . . . of veteran soldiers," it was like "disbanding an army in the very midst of battle." William T. Sherman, *Memoirs of General W. T. Sherman* (New York: Library Classics of the United States, 1990), 2: 424.
25. *OR* 32, Pt. II, 58.
26. Ibid., 290.
27. Larson, 215; Vale, 394.
28. *OR* 32, Pt. II, 40, 29; Wiswell Letters, "Huntsville, Alabama, January 17, 1864." It appears that Sgt. John M. Herberich, Co. I, may have been on leave during this time. Just days after Smith's expedition returned to Memphis on February 28, Herberich reenlisted at Huntsville, Alabama.
30. *OR* 32, Pt. I, 251-260.
31. Heitman, 235.
32. Wiswell Letters, January 17, 1864. This was apparently an issue Wiswell pursued even after the war. On the back of his discharge papers is the notation "Rejected 31 October '67. Soldiers enlisting in Regular Army prior to July 1, - 61, are entitled to no Bounty." Corporal James H. Wiswell, "An excellent Soldier," was discharged at Columbia, Tennessee, April 27, 1864. There is an additional notation on his discharge paper with the date, June 23, 1870: "Additional Bounty $100 paid . . ." "Additional bounty $100 paid . . . National Archives, Records of Veterans Administration. In his October 10, 1864, letter on the stationery of the "Acting Assistant Quartermaster's Office, Tennessee Troops, State Capitol, Nashville, Tennessee," James tells his family about his new, well paying position. In his later life he seems to have become an advocate for veterans benefits. James Wiswell, *National Tribune*, June 4 1903.
33. Bates Letters, "Huntsville, Ala January 24th 1864."
34. Larson, 215.

II. Sherman's Meridian Campaign

1. *OR* 32, Pt. I, 173.
2. Larson, 217, 224, 227, 235.

General Sooy Smith's Failed Expedition

3. *OR* 32, Pt. I, 35; *OR* 32, Pt. II, 40.
4. *OR* 32, Pt. II, 50.
5. *OR* 32, Pt. I, 255.
6. Ibid., 172. The Abstract from returns for February 29, 1864, shows "Aggregate present" of 450, "Aggregate present and absent," 876. The following companies were with the 4th US Cavalry: A, B, F, G, H, I, K, L, and M. "History of the 4th US Cavalry."
7. *OR* 32, Pt. I, 35; *OR* 32, Pt. II, 227.
8. *OR* 32, Pt. I, 37.
9. Ibid., 259.
10. Larson, 235.
11. Sherman, 2: 452. Correspondence to Brigadier-General W. S. Smith, January 27, 1864.
12. McTeer, "Smith's Raid."
13. Ibid.
14. Ibid.
15. Ibid.
16. Larson, 217.
17. Ibid., 221, 227.
18. Andrew Nelson Lytle, *Bedford Forrest and His Critter Company* (Southern Classic Series. Nashville: J. S. Sanders), 260; *OR* 32, 265.
19. McTeer.
20. *OR* 32, 265-70.
21. Ibid., 256.
22. Ibid., 256-57.
23. "Okolona." CWSAC Battle Summaries, The American Battlefield Protection Program. @ www.nps.gov/history/hps/abpp/battles/ms013.htm.
24. Lytle, 260; McTeer.
25. McTeer.
26. Vale, 258, quoting from a letter sent to him by brevet Major Joseph E. Hedges, February 19, 1886; McTeer.
27. Larson, 221-22.
28. McTeer.
29. Larson, 217.
30. Vale, 258-59.

Ellis Bridge

31. *OR* 32, Pt. I, 350.
32. Lytle, 261.
33. Henry, R., 225.
34. Ibid., 227. Quoted from *Whip and Spur*, by Colonel George E. Waring Jr. (Boston, 1875), 117.
35. *OR* 32, Pt. I, 238.
36. Henry, R., 226; *OR* 32, 350, 353.

The 4th United States Cavalry at Okolona, Mississippi

37. *OR* 32, Pt. I, 354.
38. Larson, 222.
39. Larson, 222; McTeer.
40. *OR* 32, Pt. I, 311-13; McTeer.
41. *OR* 32, Pt. I, 311-13.
42. Vale, 259; Larson, 223-24.
43. Larson, 222.
44. Hurst, 151; *OR* 32, Pt. I, 311-13, 353.
45. *OR* 32, Pt. I, 353.
46. McTeer.
47. Ibid.; *OR* 32, Pt. I, 311-13.
48. McTeer.
49. Larson, 223-24.
50. Ibid.
51. Larson, 223.

52. McTeer.
53. Ibid.
54. Ibid.
55. Ibid.
56. Larson, 224.
57. Ibid. According to Larson, the men were "J. Morgan, Sam Spangler and Parson." Larson writes of a premonition his friend John Morgan had the night before. Fearing he might fall the next day, he asked Larson to take his silver ring "and wear it until it is worn out." The ring became well known to Larson's family, but only his wife ever knew the story of how he acquired it and why he wore it.
58. Ibid. According to later reports, it was the Second New Jersey Cavalry along with the Second East Tennessee Cavalry that Larson saw. Those two regiments received most of the blame for the panic.
59. Ibid., 227.
60. Ibid.
61. McTeer.
62. Larson, 227-28.
63. OR 32, Pt. I, 353.
64. Larson, 228.
65. Ibid.
66. OR 32, Pt. I, 353.
67. Ibid., 283.
68. Larson, 229.
69. OR 32, Pt. I, 265; OR 32, Pt. I, 283.
70. OR 32, Pt. I, 274.
71. Ibid., 265.
72. McTeer.
73. Ibid.
74. OR 32, Pt. I, 305.
75. McTeer.
76. OR 32, Pt. I, 353.
77. Henry, R., 229; OR 32, Pt. I, 268.
78. OR 32, Pt. I, 268; Wills, 163.
79. OR 32, Pt. I, 354.
80. Larson, 231.
81. OR 32, Pt. I, 351.
82. Ibid., 349, 352.
83. Ibid., 355.
84. Ibid., 191-94.
85. Ibid.; Register of Enlistments. All five enlisted men were Regular Army, and their names appear on the West Point Monument.
86. OR 32, Pt. I, 353.
87. Ibid., 351.
88. Sherman, 2:423, 454-457. Sherman wrote: "General Smith never regained my confidence as a soldier . . . Since the close of the war he has appealed to me to relieve him of that censure, but I could not do it, because it would falsify history."
89. Larson, 232.
90. Ibid.
91. Ibid., 232-3.
92. Heitman, 235.
93. OR 32, Pt. I, 259.
94. Larson, 233, 240.

III. PREPARING FOR THE ATLANTA CAMPAIGN

1. Bowman, *Chronicles*, 138; Sipes, 98.
2. Larson, 240.

THE SPENCER CARBINE

3. Evans, 21.
4. Sipes, 114.
5. Bitter, 175. According to the report filed by Brig. Gen. James H. Wilson, Chief of Cavalry Bureau, April 4, 1864, the 4th Michigan received 700 Spencer carbines and the 4th U.S., 600. He also cites the 7th Pennsylvania "as one of the best regiments in the service." OR 32, Pt. III, 258.
6. Bates Letters, "Columbia Tenn April 24th /64."
7. Bitter, 175.
8. Ibid., 183.
9. Ibid., 188.
10. Vale, 259.
11. Wills, 179, 180.
12. Ibid., 180. As Wills points out, Forrest did not personally lead the attack, but watched from his "post four hundred yards away." Wills, 185.
13. Wills, 197.
14. Ibid., 200-212.

NASHVILLE, TENNESSEE

15. Sipes, 95-6.
16. OR 32, Pt. I, 258.
17. Sipes, 96.
18. Ibid.

THE COURT MARTIAL OF COLONEL ROBERT MINTY

19. Vale, 264.
20. Bitter, 173.
21. Ibid., 174.
22. Evans, xxix.
23. Ibid., xi-xiv. Evans provides the complete "Order of Battle, July 1 - September 2, 1864," for the Cavalry Corps, Army of the Cumberland.
24. OR 32, Pt. III, 238.
25. OR 32, Pt. I, 39.
26. Sipes, 96.
27. OR 32, Pt. I, 40.
28. Bitter, 176. This 1893 recollection differs somewhat from Minty's Official Report of September 13, 1864, in which he wrote, "marched from Columbia, Tenn., with over 2,200 men, 1,994 being included in the class mounted and equipped." OR 38, Pt. II, 811.
29. Evans, 4.
30. Bitter, 174.
31. Ibid., 176.
32. Ibid.
33. Bates Letters, "Camp in the field in front of the Enemy May 11th 1864."

The Secret Mission of the Horse Marines

34. Vale, 266.
35. *OR 32*, Pt. III, 255; Vale, 266. Vale incorrectly records the name of the boat as "Silver Lake."
36. Vale, 266.
37. *OR 32*, Pt. III, 243-244.
38. Bowman, *Chronicles*, 140.
39. *OR 32*, Pt. III, 244.
40. Ibid., 299.
41. *OR 32*, Pt. III, 276; Vale, 267.
42. Vale, 266-67.
43. Ibid.
44. Ibid., 270; Registers of Deaths.
45. Vale, 268.
46. *OR 32*, Pt. III, 275.
47. Ibid., 299; Vale, 268.
48. *OR 32*, Pt. III, 299.
49. Ibid.
50. Vale, 269.
51. Ibid.
52. Vale, 269.
53. Ibid., 269-70.
54. *OR 32*, Part III, 437.
55. Vale, 270.
56. Ibid., 271. This was not as novel an idea as might be supposed; Nathan Bedford Forrest used "horse marines" in his defense of the Tennessee River.

The Death of Major General "Jeb" Stuart, CSA

57. Brown, "War on Horseback," 311.
58. Catton, *American Heritage*, 444.
59. McClellan, 294.
60. Wormser, 226. The Confederacy never established an organized system providing horses for remounting, and by mid-1864 attrition won out. They could no longer remount an adequate cavalry force.

IV. The Atlanta Campaign - May 1864

1. Sipes, 108.
2. Evans, xxix.
3. Minty, *National Tribune*, November 16, 1893; *OR 38*, Pt. II, 811. Colonel Miller, 72nd Illinois, commanded the Third Brigade in place of the ill Col. John T. Wilder.
4. Minty, *National Tribune*, November 16, 1893. Vale also writes of this view, 278-80.
5. Vale, 278.
6. Sipes, 102.
7. Minty, *National Tribune*, November 16, 1893; Larson, 241.
8. Sipes, 102.
9. Minty, *National Tribune*, November 16, 1893.
10. Vale, 280.
11. *OR 38*, Pt. II, 811.
12. Vale, 280.

Rome, Georgia

13. Minty, *National Tribune*, November 16, 1893.
14. Larson, 242.
15. Minty, *National Tribune*, November 16, 1893.
16. Ibid.; Larson, 243; Bitter, 178.
17. Minty, *National Tribune*, November 16, 1893.
18. Ibid.
19. Ibid.
20. Larson, 242.
21. Minty, *National Tribune*, November 16, 1893.
22. Ibid., 178.
23. Ibid., 179.
24. Minty, *National Tribune*, December 21, 1893; *OR 38*, Pt. II, 811.
25. Vale, 284. Minty quoted this paragraph in his December 21, 1893, *National Tribune* article.
26. Larson, 243.
27. Ibid., 244.
28. Ibid. David Evans describes yet another way to destroy the rail lines: using board fence and whatever other wood was available, large fires would be set up and down the tracks at the rail joints. "As the fires burned hotter, the iron rails began to expand. Animated by the intense heat, they writhed like serpents, hurling spikes and crossties in every direction." Evans, 80.
29. Minty, *National Tribune*, December 21, 1893.
30. *OR 38*, Pt. II, 811; Minty, *National Tribune*, December 21, 1893, quoting Van Horne, *History of the Army of the Cumberland*, Vol. II, 74.
31. Minty, *National Tribune*, December 21, 1893.
32. Vale, 288.
33. Minty, *National Tribune*, December 21, 1893.
34. Vale, 292; *OR 38*, Pt. II, 812.
35. Minty, *National Tribune*, December 21, 1893.
36. Ibid., 183.
37. Vale, 295.
38. *OR 38*, Pt. II, 812; Vale, 297.
39. Vale, 298.
40. Ibid., 298.
41. Ibid., 301.
42. Ibid., 299. According to the "History of the 4th US Cavalry," Companies A, B, C, E, F, I, and M were involved in the fighting near Dallas, Georgia, on May 26 and 28.
43. Evans, 211.
44. Vale, 299.
45. Ibid., 300.
46. Ibid., 301.
47. Minty, *National Tribune*, March 1, 1894.
48. Vale, 301.

Infantry Duty

49. Larson, 245.
50. Ibid., 246.
51. Potter Letters No. 43, "In the field May 30 1864."

Sherman's Cavalry

52. Vale, 298.
53. Evans, 3.
54. Ibid., 477-78.
55. Ibid., 3.

56. Evans, 47; Heitman, 920.
57. Evans, 4-5.
58. Ibid., xxi-xxii, 10.
59. Bitter, 189-90.
60. Evans, 11 and 474. Stephen Z. Starr offers the same high opinion and includes Edward M. McCook of the 4th US Cavalry. Starr I, 19 and fn. 38.
61. Evans, 409.
62. Ibid., 474.
63. Bitter, 189.
64. Evans, 409.

Dallas, Georgia

65. *OR* 38, Pt. II, 812.
66. Larson, 246. Companies A, B, C, E, F, I, M, "History of the 4th US Cavalry."
67. Ibid., 247.
68. Bitter, 202. Burns was actually commenting on the Union hospitals in Big Shanty, GA, in 1864.
69. Sipes, 111.
70. Vale, 302.
71. *OR* 38, Pt. II, 812; Larson, 248.
72. *OR* 38, Pt. II, 812.
73. Larson, 248.
74. Potters Letters No. 44, "Camp on the Etowah River near Cartersville, Georgia, Sunday June 5th 1864."
75. Larson, 248; Minty, *National Tribune*, March 1, 1894.
76. Sipes, 111.
77. Larson, 248.
78. Sipes, 111; *OR* 38, 50.
79. Larson, 249. See also Vale, 304-5.

Big Shanty, Georgia

80. Bitter, 192.
81. Larson, 249.
82. Bitter, 193.
83. Larson, 249.
84. Ibid.
85. Larson, 250; Larson, *National Tribune*, August 9, 1894.
86. Vale, 308.
87. *OR* 38, Pt. II, 812; Sipes, 111.
88. Vale, 309. Vale estimates the Confederates numbered "forty-five hundred men pitted against [Minty'] fourteen hundred," 312.
89. Sipes, 111.
90. Vale, 310-11.
91. Sipes, 111; *OR* 38, Pt. II, 812.
92. Bates Letters, "Camped in the neighborhood of Big Shanty, June 20th."
93. Ibid, "June 20, 1864."

Brice's Crossroads, Mississippi, June 10, 1864

94. Catton, *American Heritage*, 520; McPherson, 748.
95. Catton, *American Heritage*, 520.
96. Bowman, *Almanac*, 208; Catton, 520.
97. Bowman, *Almanac*, 209; McPherson, 748. Sturgis would be promoted to colonel, 7th US Cavalry in May 1869 and continue to serve until his retirement in June 1886.
98. McPherson, 748-49.
99. Heitman, 934.

The Battle at Noonday Creek

100. Minty, *National Tribune*, March 14, 1895.
101. Ibid.
102. Vale, 313.
103. Minty, *National Tribune*, March 1, 1894.
104. Larson, *National Tribune*, August 9, 1894.
105. Minty, *National Tribune*, March 1, 1894.
106. Bitter, 201. As Minty recorded in his March 1, 1894 article, the Confederate troops consisted of "Kelly's Division - Anderson's Brigade - 1st, 2nd, 3rd, 5th, 8th, and 10th Confederate, and 5th Ga.; Hannon's Brigade, Martin's Division - Iverson's Brigade - 1st, 2nd, 3rd, 4th and 6th Ga.; Allen's Brigade - 1st, 34d, 4th, 7th, and 51st Ala. Independent Brigades - Dibrell - five Tennessee regiments; Williams - five Kentucky regiments." Bitter, 197-98.
107. Vale, 320; Larson, 255; Minty, *National Tribune*, March 1, 1894.
108. Minty, *National Tribune*, April 11, 1895; Larson, 254.
109. Minty, *National Tribune*, March 1, 1894, quoting General Jacob D. Cox, who later became a one-term governor of Ohio (1866-67), and Secretary of the Interior under President Grant. He was the author of numerous books and articles on the Civil War.
110. Minty, *National Tribune*, March 1, 1894.
111. Ibid.
112. Minty, *National Tribune*, March 1, 1894; Larson, *National Tribune*, August 9, 1894.
113. Minty, *National Tribune*, March 1, 1894.
114. Bitter, 201.
115. Minty, *National Tribune*, March 1, 1894.
116. Ibid.; Larson, 254.
117. Ibid. The 72nd Indiana, 17th Indiana, and the 123rd Illinois.
118. Larson, *National Tribune*, August 9, 1894; Larson, 254.
119. Bitter, 201.
120. Larson, *National Tribune*, August 9, 1894.
121. Minty, *National Tribune*, March 1, 1894.
122. Ibid.
123. Ibid.
124. Sipes, 112.
125. The 51st Alabama Cavalry was part of Allan's Division. One member of the 51st was Private Cicero C. Bain. He would become an in-law of 1st Sgt. Herberich when their children married in 1892. In the last years of their lives (they both died in 1904) the two old veterans would be next door neighbors in San Antonio, Texas, sitting on their porch having animated discussions about past battles.
126. Minty, *National Tribune*, March 1, 1894. In this article Minty writes, "The Marietta papers of June 22 placed

the Confederate loss at 94 killed and 361 wounded. . . . The loss sustained by the 7th [Pa.] was nine per-cent, and by the 4th [Mich.] nearly15 per-cent."
127. Bitter, 201.
128. Ibid., 202.
129. Larson, 249.
130. Bitter, 202.
131. Minty, *National Tribune*, March 1, 1894.
132. Ibid.
133. Bitter, 209. Letter from Major-General W. T. Sherman, Hdqrs. Military Division of the Mississippi. In the Field, near Marietta, July 25, 1864; *OR* 38, Pt. V, 251.

A Lonely End

134. Starr, 3: dedication page, quoting First Lieutenant Simeon M. Fox. 7th Kansas Volunteer Cavalry.
135. Larson, 257.
136. Register of Enlistments.
137. Bitter, 189.
138. Bates Letters, "Big Shanty, June 30, 1864."
139. Bitter, 218.
140. Ibid., 189.
141. Sipes, 107.
142. Bitter, 189.
143. Ibid.
144. Sipes, 100.
145. Bitter, 190.
146. Sipes, 103.
147. Larson, 250.
148. Evans, 4.
149. Sipes, 118-19.

Kennesaw Mountain

150. Sipes, 113. There seem to be two spellings of Kennesaw, the first contemporary, the second, Kenesaw, from earlier histories.
151. Vale, 320.
152. *OR* 38, Pt. II, 813; Bitter, 210.
153. Minty, *National Tribune*, May 31, 1894.
154. *OR* 38, Pt. II, 813; Larson, 258.
155. Larson, 258-59.
156. Evans, xxxiii.
157. Sipes, 113.
158. Minty, *National Tribune*, May 31, 1894; *OR* 38, Pt. II, 813.
159. Minty, *National Tribune*, May 31, 1894; Evans, xxxiii, 26.
160. Evans, xxxiii.
161. Evans, xxi; Potter Letters No. 47, "July 10/64, Camp 4th Mich on Chattahoochee."
162. Evans, xxi.
163. Ibid., xx-xxii.
164. *OR* 38, Pt. II, 813.
165. Evans, 10.
166. Ibid.
167. Ibid., 11.
168. Ibid.
169. Vale, 321.
170. Evans, 12.
171. Vale, 322-23.
172. Potter Letters No. 47.
173. *OR* 38, Pt. II, 813; Bitter, 212.
174. Evans, 26.

Roswell, Georgia

175. Evans, 11.
176. Ibid., 13, 18.
177. Potter Letters No. 47.
178. Ibid.
179. Evans, 13, 51. Hundreds of terrified female factory workers were forcibly relocated to Northern states by order of General Sherman. A book has been written by Deborah Petite, *The Women Will Howl*, that describes the Union Army capture of Roswell and New Manchester, Georgia, and the forced relocation of the mill workers, http://www.women-will-howl.com/book.html.
180. Vale, 231.
181. Evans, 71.
182. Ibid., 77.
183. *OR* 38, Pt. II, 813; Sipes, 115.
184. This report is strongly refuted by David Evans in personal correspondence with the author dated March 26, 2015. Hereafter referred to as Evans correspondence.
185. Evans, 79.
186. Ibid., 80.
187. Sipes, 115.
188. Minty, *National Tribune*, May 31, 1894.
189. Evans, 80.
190. Ibid., 87.
191. Ibid., 87.
192. Ibid.
193. Bates Letters, "Roswell Georgia July 19th 1864."

Garrard's Raid to Covington

194. Minty, *National Tribune*, May 31, 1894; *OR* 38, Pt. II, 813; Evans, 175.
195. Evans, 91.
196. Ibid., 175.
197. Ibid., 180.
198. Ibid., 181.
199. Ibid., 182.
200. Ibid., 186.
201. Ibid., 187.
202. Minty, *National Tribune*, May 31, 1894; Sipes, 115.
203. Bitter, 213.
204. According to Evans, Garrard suffered only five casualties during the raid to Covington. Evans correspondence.
205. Evans, 188.
206. Ibid., 187-88.
207. Ibid., 188.
208. Ibid., 188.
209. Ibid., 189.

210. Ibid., 193.
211. Ibid., 194.
212. Bitter, 213.
213. Ibid.
214. Ibid.
215. Sipes, 121-22.
216. Evans, 471-2.
217. Potter Letters No. 48, "Camp 5 miles from Atlanta, August 1st 1864."
218. Evans, 85.
219. Ibid., 86.
220. Ibid., 88.
221. Ibid., 96.
222. Konsam, 52.
223. David Evans, "The Battle of Brown's Mill." @ http://www.battleofbrownsmill.org.
224. Evans, 381.
225. Johnson, R.W., 4, 85-86.
226. Ibid., 4.
227. Ibid., 445.
228. Ibid., 398.
229. Catton, *American Heritage*, 445.

Stoneman's Raid - The Battle at Flat Rock (Shoals)

230. Evans, 199.
231. Ibid., 200, 203.
232. Ibid., 47, 50.
233. *OR* 38 Pt. V, 60-61.
234. Evans, 200.
235. Ibid., 202.
236. Ibid., 208.
237. Ibid., 204.
238. Minty, *National Tribune*, May 31, 1894; Evans, 202.
239. Evans, 208.
240. Ibid., 209.
241. Ibid.
242. Ibid.
243. Ibid.
244. Potter Letters No. 48.
245. Minty, *National Tribune*, May 31, 1894; *OR* 38, Pt. II, 813.
246. Bitter, 212.
247. Larson, 267.
248. Evans, 213.
249. Potter Letters No. 48.
250. Minty, *National Tribune*, May 31, 1894; *OR* 38, Pt. II, 813.
251. Evans, 213.
252. Ibid.
253. Bitter, 213-14.
254. Evans, 213.
255. Larson, 268.
256. Evans, 214.
257. Ibid.
258. Ibid., 215.
259. Ibid.
260. Ibid.
261. Ibid., 216.
262. Ibid.
263. Vale, 328; *OR* 38, Pt. II, 813.
264. Minty, *National Tribune*, May 31, 1894, quoting from Van Horn, *History of the Army of the Cumberland*, vol. 2:124.
265. Minty, *National Tribune*, May 31, 1894.
266. Heitman, 930.
267. Sipes, 115.
268. Vale, 326. David Evans gives a detailed reasoning for these failures which may have included gross overestimation of Confederate strength, fatigued troopers not having slept for days, or, most probably, failures of leadership. 472-74.
269. *OR* 38, Pt. II, 813.
270. Evans, 377.
271. "4th Regiment Michigan Cavalry."@ http://www.michiganinthewar.ord/cavalry/4thcav.htm.
272. Bitter, 219.
273. Evans, 472.
274. Henry 2:303.

A Well Deserved Leave

275. Larson, 269.
276. Ibid.
277. Ibid., 271.
278. Ibid., 274.
279. Register of Enlistments.

V. The Siege of Atlanta - August 1864

1. Catton, *Centennial History*, vol. 3:331; Konstam, 50.
2. Ibid.
3. Ibid.
4. Evans, 471; Konstam, 52.

Fighting in the Trenches

5. *OR* 38, Pt. II, 813.
6. Evans, 377.
7. Ibid.
8. Ibid., 377-78.
9. Ibid., 378.
10. Ibid.
11. Ibid.
12. Ibid.
13. Ibid.
14. Ibid., 379.
15. Ibid., 380.
16. Vale, 328.
17. Evans, 379; Vale, 328.
18. Vale, 328.
19. Bitter, 215; 218, quoting Burns.
20. Potter Letters No. 49, "On the left flank, in earthworks Friday Aug 5th 1864"
21. Ibid.
22. Evans, 380-81.
23. Ibid., 381.

24. Bitter, 218-19, quoting Burns.
25. Ibid.
26. Sipes, 116.
27. Vale, 329.
28. Vale, 331-32; Evans, 393.
29. Bitter, 215.
30. Minty, *National Tribune*, May 31, 1894; *OR* 38, Pt. II, 813.
31. Evans, 393.
32. Ibid., 396.
33. Ibid., 394.
34. Vale, 333.
35. Evans, 396.
36. Ibid., 396-97.
37. Ibid., 4.
38. Ibid., 401.
39. Ibid., 402.
40. Ibid., 398.
41. Ibid., 406. Albert Castel, in his book *Decision in the West*, is critical of Sherman's abilities as a commanding general and cites examples of Sherman placing blame for his failures on his subordinates. Castel, 539.
42. Ibid., 402.
43. David Nevin, *The Civil War: Sherman's March* (Alexandria, Virginia: Time Life Books, 1986), 50.
44. Evans, 383.
45. Nevin, 50.
46. Evans, 410.
47. Wilson, 2:13.

VI. KILPATRICK'S RAID

1. Evans, 406. The best researched, documented, and detailed description of the activities leading up to and including Kilpatrick's raid can be found in David Evans's 1996 book *Sherman's Horsemen: Union Cavalry Operations in the Atlanta Campaign*.
2. Evans, 407.
3. Minty, *National Tribune*, May 21, 1891.
4. Bitter, 288-89.
5. Evans, 398.
6. Bitter, 279.
7. Frank W. Mix (Major, 4th Michigan Cavalry) *National Tribune*, May 21, 1891. Contemporary Civil War historian Eric Wittenberg, who has written extensively on Union cavalry operations in the Eastern Theater, writes that Colonel Minty "was one of the very best Union cavalry brigade commanders but has been largely overlooked because of his service in the Western Theater. Had he fought in the Eastern Theater and accomplished the things he accomplished in the West, he would be in the pantheon of great cavalrymen of the Civil War. He deserves to be included in those exalted ranks." Eric Wittenberg, "Rantings of a Civil War Historian," http://www.civilwarcavalrylcom/?p=451>.
8. Bitter, 238-39.
9. Evans, 406.
10. Ibid., 407.
11. Ibid., 407-8, 411.
12. Ibid., 407.
13. Ibid. The seemingly small size of the regiments may be due to the fact, as reported by Sergeant Larson, that about 80 of the men of the 4th U.S. had taken advantage of the reenlistment furlough program. As he notes on page 269 of his biography, "This, of course, ended our service with Sherman's army as Atlanta fell before we returned and Sherman had started on his march to Savannah."
14. Ibid., 408.
15. Bitter, 221; Minty, *National Tribune*, July 10, 1890; Sipes, 125. Murray brought four guns of the 10th Wisconsin Battery.
16. Evans, 408; Bitter, 221.
17. Minty, *National Tribune*, July 10, 1890.
18. Evans, 409.
19. Bitter, 221.
20. Evans, 411.
21. Bitter, 221.
22. Ibid.
23. Evans, 411-12.
24. Sipes, 124. In his chapter on "The Fight at Lovejoy," Sipes quotes in full a letter that was written by Captain Robert Burns to his brother eight days after the raid. See also Bitter, 246.
25. Evans, 412.
26. Ibid., 431. One of the bands was the 92nd Illinois Band. While it was not uncommon for regiments to have bands, historian Albert Castel sarcastically comments, "Kilpatrick's band - something that no well-conducted cavalry expedition should be without, though Forrest somehow manages to get along without one . . ." *Decision in the West*, 472.
27. Potter Letters No. 53, "Head Quarters 'H' Camp near Atlanta Ga. Aug 24/64."; Evans 431.
28. Evans, 419.
29. William W. Webb, "Kilpatrick's Great Raid." *Frank Leslie's Popular Monthly*, December, 1889. Webb writes, "If any narrative of that terrible march, other than official reports, has appeared in print, I am not aware of it." Actually, Vale's history had been published three years earlier but was not as detailed nor did it provide as much information for future historians as did Webb's account. Webb originally joined the 3rd Battalion D. C. Volunteers on April 15, 1861. He was commissioned 2nd Lt., Co. K, 4th US Cavalry one month later. Heitman, 1012.
30. Evans, 419.
31. Minty, *National Tribune*, January 22, 1903.
32. Webb.
33. Ibid.
34. Webb; Sipes, 124.
35. Webb.
36. Minty, *National Tribune*, January 22, 1903; Sipes, 125.
37. Webb; *OR* 38, Pt. II, 813.

38. Webb.
39. Potter Letters No. 53.
40. Evans, 420.
41. Webb.
42. Sipes, 124; *OR* 38, Pt. II, 835-36.
43. Evans, 418.
44. Ibid., 450.
45. Sipes, 124, quoting Burns.
46. Evans, 424.
47. Sipes, 125.
48. Webb.
49. Minty, *National Tribune*, July 10, 1890; *OR* 38, Pt. II, 813.
50. *OR* 38, Pt. II, 813.
51. Potter Letters No. 53.
52. Minty, *National Tribune*, July 10, 1890; *OR* 38, Pt. II, 813.
53. Sipes, 125, quoting Burns.
54. Evans, 426; Sipes, 125.
55. Sipes, 125, quoting Burns; Minty, *National Tribune*, July 10, 1890; *OR* 38, Pt. II, 813.
56. Sipes, 125, quoting Burns.
57. Minty, *National Tribune*, July 10, 1890.
58. Evans, 426.
59. Ibid., 425.
60. Ibid., 426.
61. Minty, *National Tribune*, July 10, 1890; Vale, 341.
62. Vale, 341.
63. Minty, *National Tribune*, July 10, 1890; Evans, 426.
64. Vale, 341.
65. Evans, 426.

The Destruction of Jonesboro, Georgia

66. Bitter, 251.
67. Evans, 426.
68. Webb.
69. Evans, 427.
70. Vale, 341.
71. Webb.
72. Evans, 427.
73. "Battle Summary: Lovejoy's Station."
74. Evans, 429.
75. Webb.
76. Evans, 428.
77. Webb.
78. Evans, 428.
79. Webb.
80. Evans, 414, 430. The troopers also enjoyed the newly confiscated supplies of tobacco.
81. Ibid., 428.
82. Issac Sollars (Pvt., 4th US Cavalry), *National Tribune*, December 15, 1892.
83. Evans, 428.
84. Ibid., 429.
85. Ibid., 430.
86. Ibid.
87. Ibid., 431.
88. William L. Curry, "Raid Around Atlanta." *Four Years in the Saddle: History of the First Regiment Ohio Volunteer Cavalry: War of the Rebellion, 1861-1865* (Columbus: Champlin Printing, 1898, Reprint. Jonesboro, GA: Freedom Hill Press, Inc., 1984), 610-11; Curry, "Kilpatrick's Raid," *National Tribune*, June 23, 1910.
89. Evans, 431.
90. Ibid.
91. Potter Letters No. 53.
92. Evans, 431.
93. Potter Letters No. 53.
94. Bitter, 226.
95. Evans, 473.
96. Ibid., 432.
97. Ibid.
98. Ibid., 432-33.
99. Ibid.
100. Ibid., 434.
101. Johnson, Richard, 157.
102. Sipes, 126.

Lovejoy's Station - Nash Farm

103. Lucian B. Smith (Pvt., 4th Michigan Cavalry), *National Tribune*, July 21, 1891. Smith, who participated in the raid, quotes Kilpatrick who was giving a lecture at Dundee, Michigan in 1881 which Smith attended.
104. Minty, *National Tribune*, July 10, 1890.
105. Evans, 439.
106. Minty, *National Tribune*, July 10, 1890.
107. Ibid.
108. Ibid.
109. Evans, 440; Minty, *National Tribune*, July 10, 1890.
110. Minty, *National Tribune*, July 10, 1890; *OR* 38, Pt. II, 835-36. Evans, 440-41.
111. Minty, *National Tribune*, October 1, 1891.
112. Minty, *National Tribune*, July 10, 1890.
113. *OR* 38, Pt. II, 814.
114. *OR* 38, Pt. II, 835-36; Minty, *National Tribune*, October 1, 1891.
115. *OR*, 38, Pt. II, 835-36; *OR* 38, Pt. II, 814.
116. Evans, 440.
117. Ibid., 441.
118. Webb.
119. Ibid.
120. Evans, 442.
121. Ibid., 443.
122. Webb.
123. Potter Letters No. 53.
124. Minty, *National Tribune*, July 10, 1890.
125. Evans, 443.
126. *OR* 38, Pt. II, 814.
127. Minty, *National Tribune*, July 10, 1890; Evans, 446-49.
128. *OR* 38, Pt. II, 814.
129. Bitter, 252.
130. *OR* 38, Pt. II, 814.
131. Evans, 450.

132. Minty, *National Tribune*, July 10, 1890.
133. Bitter, 249.
134. Evans, 448.
135. Bitter, 252.
136. Minty, *National Tribune*, July 10, 1890.
137. Evans, 448; Bitter, 251-52.
138. Potter Letters No. 53.
139. Frank W. Mix (major, 4th Mich. Cavalry), *National Tribune*, May 21, 1891.
140. Minty, *National Tribune*, July 10, 1890.
141. Ibid.; Sipes, 130, quoting Burns.
142. Mix, *National Tribune*, May 21, 1891.
143. Minty, *National Tribune*, July 23, 1903.
144. *OR* 38, Pt. II, 814; Bitter, 239.
145. Mix, *National Tribune*, May 21, 1891.
146. Ibid.
147. Evans, 449.
148. *OR* 38, Pt. II, 814; Sipes, 130, quoting Burns.
149. Bitter, 251-52
150. Webb.
151. Sipes, 130, quoting Burns.
152. Minty, National Tribune, July 10, 1890.
153. Potter Letters No. 53.
154. Mix, *National Tribune*, May 21, 1891.
155. Sipes, 130, quoting Burns; Minty, *National Tribune*, July 10, 1890.
156. According to David Evans, there is no evidence for the number of guns Minty indicates. Evans correspondence.
157. Sipes, 130, quoting Burns.
158. Minty, *National Tribune*, July 10, 1890, quoting from the *Cincinnati Commercial*, August 31, 1864.
159. *OR* 38, Pt. II, 814.
160. Mix, *National Tribune*, May 21, 1891.
161. Sollars, *National Tribune*, December 15, 1892; Bitter, 251-52.
162. Minty, *National Tribune*, July 10, 1890, quoting from the *Cincinnati Commercial*, August 31, 1864.
163. Evans, 450.
164. *OR* 38, Pt. II, 835-36.
165. Sipes, 130-31, quoting Burns; Evans, 451. Thompson was captured and spent time recovering in a Confederate hospital. Heber S. Thompson, *Heber S. Thompson Papers, Aug.-Dec. 1864*, SCL Manuscripts Division, University Libraries, South Carolina Library.
166. Sipes, 131.
167. Evans, 450.
168. Potter Letters No. 53.
169. Minty, *National Tribune*, July 10, 1890, quoting from the *Cincinnati Commercial*, August 31, 1864.
170. Minty, *National Tribune*, January 22, 1903.
171. *OR* 38, Pt. II, 835-36.
172. Webb.
173. Evans, 450.
174. Webb.
175. Bitter, 252; Minty, *National Tribune*, January 22, 1903; Evans, 451.
176. Mix, *National Tribune*, May 21, 1891.
177. Evans, 452.
178. Ibid.
179. Ibid.
180. Ibid., 454.
181. Ibid.
182. Minty, *National Tribune*, May 31, 1894; Bitter, 252; Minty, *National Tribune*, January 22, 1903.
183. Bitter, 253; Evans, 454. Bailey, the Indian orderly, was at Minty's side when they were ambushed a year earlier near Sparta, Tennessee.
184. Potter Letters No. 53.
185. Evans, 453.
186. Bitter, 253.
187. Evans, 453.
188. Minty, *National Tribune*, January 22, 1903.
189. Evans, 451.
190. Ibid.
191. Ibid., 452.
192. Minty, *National Tribune*, July 2, 1891.
193. Ibid.
194. Minty, *National Tribune*, February 26, 1891.
195. Bitter, 253.
196. Evans, 456.
197. Minty, *National Tribune*, January 22, 1903.
198. Evans, 467.
199. Minty, *National Tribune*, January 22, 1903.
200. Joseph S. Hedges (major, 4th US Cavalry) "History of the Fourth United States Cavalry in the Battle of Nashville - Pursuit of Hood, &c.," reprinted by Vale, 392-94.
201. Evans, 478-79; *Thompson Papers*.
202. Evans, 467.
203. Ibid., 455.
204. Ibid.
205. *OR* 38, pt. II, 814-15; Evans, 455.
206. Evans, 457.
207. Ibid., 459.
208. Ibid., 461.
209. Webb.
210. Evans, 461.
211. *OR* 38, Pt. II, 815; Minty, *National Tribune*, July 10, 1890.
212. Evans, 463.
213. Minty, *National Tribune*, July 10, 1890.
214. Ibid.
215. Ibid.
216. Potter Letters No. 53.
217. Castel, 467; *OR* 38, Pt. II, 815.
218. Bitter, 254.
219. Ibid.
220. Minty, *National Tribune*, July 10, 1890, quoting *Memphis-Atlanta Appeal*, "published at Macon, Ga., early in September 1864." This is the newspaper article David Evans was unable to verify.
221. Smith, *National Tribune*, July 2, 1891.
222. Ibid.

223. Bitter, 279. Promotions are based on politics as well as merit. Sherman himself hinted at this when he noted that some of the colonels he recommended for promotion "seemed to have no special friends to aid them to advancement." Bitter, 288.
224. *OR* 38, Pt. II, 824; Minty, *National Tribune*, January 22, 1903.
225. Minty, *National Tribune*, May 31, 1894.
226. Minty, *National Tribune*, May 31, 1894; Minty, *National Tribune*, January 22, 1903; Heitman, 639.

A Question of Facts

227. In the 1890s and into the early 1900s, Minty wrote a series of newspaper articles in the *National Tribune* about his Saber Brigade and its activities during the war. He is rarely challenged in this public arena and vigorously supported. His two full-length accounts of Kilpatrick's Raid were published almost thirteen years apart. The first article in the *National Tribune-Washington, DC,* on July 10, 1890, generated a number of responses. In this article he reports the message interception of the telegraph operator and seems to imply that he received the information regarding Cleburne's and Martin's divisions from General Kilpatrick. He also quotes from Vale's unsubstantiated *Memphis-Atlanta Appeal* article on the presence of the two divisions. In a follow-up article written in the *National Tribune,* February 26, 1891, in reference to his July 1890 article, he states: "The absolute facts were given in detail." He again implies that it was Kilpatrick who told him "Pat Cleburne with 10,000 infantry is closing in on our right." In the same article he writes, "Cleburne followed us through the swamp." Minty refers to others who were present, "for the correctness of what I have stated": Gen. Eli Long, Gen. Eli Murray, Col. B. B. Eggleston, Major Frank Mix, and Captain George Robinson, Chicago Board of Trade Battery. Frank Mix, who was commanding Minty's 4th Michigan at Lovejoy's Station writes on May 21, 1891, in support of Minty and states flatly, "Every word of Minty's letter was true." Writing in the *National Tribune* on January 22, 1903, Minty once again comments on the presence of "Cleburne's Division of Infantry and Martin's Division of Cavalry." In the Federal pursuit of the routed Confederate forces, he reports that Col. Eggleston, 1st Ohio, who replaced the wounded Col. Long, "reported Cleburne's Infantry was endeavoring to turn both his flanks," until they were finally repulsed by the 4th Cavalry and 7th Pennsylvania "with heavy losses."

VII. The Fall of Atlanta

1. Minty, *National Tribune*, November 8, 1894.
2. Vale, 374.
3. Minty, *National Tribune*, November 8, 1894.
4. Ibid.
5. Ibid.
6. Vale, 376.
7. Minty, *National Tribune*, November 8, 1894.
8. Ibid; Vale, 376.
9. Vale, 377.
10. Ibid., 378.
11. Minty, *National Tribune*, November 8, 1894.

Chasing Hood - October 1864

12. Vale, 377.
13. Ibid., 378.
14. Minty, *National Tribune*, November 8, 1894, quoting from Major Robert Burns diary.
15. Ibid.
16. Ibid.
17. Vale, 378, quoting a letter from Major Burns, "Kalamazoo, Michigan, March 15th, 1883."
18. Minty, *National Tribune*, November 8, 1894.
19. Vale, 395-96.
20. Bitter, 296, quoting Burns.

Disbanding the Saber Brigade

21. Larson, 275.
22. Vale, 382-83.
23. Sipes, 138.
24. *OR* 45, Pt. I, 554; Vale, 383; Sipes, 139.
25. Registers of Deaths; Register of Enlistments.
26. Sipes, 151.
27. Larson, 275.

Major General James H. Wilson, USA

28. *OR* 45, Pt. I, 555.
29. Starr 3:535.
30. "Civil War Cavalry Battles and Charges."
31. Bitter, 307. Minty now found himself "the Junior Brigade Commander" in his own division. In a letter to the adjutant general of Michigan he writes: "When we returned we found that Colonel Long had been appointed a Brigadier. At Stones River he was a <u>Captain</u> and I a Brigade Commander. Since then he has repeatedly acted under my orders. Next time we go out together I will have to act under his." He ends his letter, "However it is the fortune of war." Bitter, 279.
32. "Civil War Cavalry Battles and Charges," 33; Bates Letters, "Camp Webster (near Nashville, Tenn.)."

VIII. The Franklin - Nashville Campaign
The Defeat of Hood's Army

1. Buell, 386.
2. Sipes, 143.
3. Bitter, 298; Bowman, *Chronicles*, 174.
4. Bitter, 310-11.
5. Ibid., 313. Captain Henry C. "Billy" Magruder was hanged in public on October 20, 1865, "for this and other murders." Vale, 419.
6. Bitter, 313.
7. Cleaves, 279.
8. Bitter, 319.

Defending Nashville

9. Buell, 383.
10. Buell, 380; Sipes, 143.
11. Catton, 546.
12. Vale, 378, quoting Burns; Sipes, 147.
13. Catton, *American Heritage*, 561.
14. Buell, 221.
15. Catton, *American Heritage*, 555.
16. Nevin, 119.
17. Buell, 395.
18. "Civil War Cavalry Battles and Charges."
19. James Harrison Wilson, *Under the Old Flag, Recollections of Military Operations in the War for the Union*, 2 vols. (New York and London: D. Appleton, 1912), vol. 2:52.
20. Nevin, 117.
21. Catton, *American Heritage*, 556.
22. Ibid., 559.
23. Ibid.
24. Nevin, 52; Wilson, 2:52. "By 1865 Wilson would have 13,000 troopers armed with the Spencers." Nevin, 87.
25. "Civil War Cavalry Battles and Charges."
26. *OR* 45, 95.

"The Little Regiment"

27. Bitter, 304; "History of the US Cavalry."
28. Larson, February 11, 1915, "Sketches and Echoes," *National Tribune*, February 11, 1915.
29. Ibid., 304.
30. United States. Army. 4th Cavalry Regiment, 1855-. "Fourth Cavalry United States Army, 1855-1930." Army Heritage Collection online, http://www.ahco.army.mil.
31. Heitman, 669; Captain McIntyre was in charge of the recruiting station in Baltimore, MD, on April 6, 1865. Post Returns, Carlisle Barracks, PA, April 1861-April 1865. Personal correspondence with Don Caughey, August 7, 2013.
32. Vale, 532-33; Heitman, 520.
33. Larson, 282.

The Election of 1864

34. Larson, 275.
35. Potter Letter No. 57, "Near Little River Ala ten miles below Gayleville Oct 26th 1864."
36. Bowman, *Chronicles*, 178.
37. Potter Letters No. 58, "Head Quarters 4th Mich Cav Chattanooga November 10th 1864."
38. Bates Letters, "Camp Webster (near Nashville, Tenn) November 15th 1864."
39. *OR* 45, Pt. I, 987.
40. Ibid., 1040.
41. *OR* 45, Pt. II, 465. By January 10, 1865 the number of enlisted increased slightly to 272; *OR* 45, Pt. II, 567.
42. Ibid., 1062.
43. Ibid., 988.
44. *OR* 45, Pt. I, 1041.
45. Ibid., 1062.
46. Ibid., 1117
47. Ibid., 1118.
48. *OR* 45, Pt. II, 6.
49. Ibid.
50. *OR* 45, Pt. I, 550-51.
51. Minty, *National Tribune*, February 21, 1865.
52. *OR* 45, Pt. II, 47.
53. Larson, 275-76.
54. Vale, 396-97.
55. *OR* 45, Pt. II, 106.
56. Potter Letters No. 60, "HdQrs 4th Mich Cav Dec 20th, 1864."

Under a New Command

57. Bitter, 318, quoting Dr. Fish.
58. Bitter, 318, quoting Major Burns.
59. Starr, 3:534.
60. Bitter, 316.
61. Ibid., 317.

The Battle of Nashville

62. Larson, 278; Kenner Garrard had been relieved of command of the 2nd Cavalry Division on October 29, 1864 and given command of the 2nd Infantry Division.
63. *OR* 45, Pt. I, 551.
64. Vale, 392.
65. Larson, 278.
66. Ibid.
67. Ibid.

Battle of Nashville - Day Two

68. Wilson II, 125.
69. Cleaves, 265.
70. Ibid.
71. Ibid., 266.
72. Ibid.
73. "Civil War Cavalry Battles and Charges," 7.
74. *OR* 45, Pt. I, 38.
75. Larson, 277-78.
76. Buell, 408; Wilson II, 129.
77. Wilson 2:126.
78. Cleaves, 267.
79. Wilson 2:112-113; Starr, 549.
80. Urwin, 130.
81. Buell, 405.
82. Starr, 551.
83. Larson, 281-82.
84. Wilson 2:124.
85. Larson, 281-82.
86. Larson, 282; *OR* 45, 564-5; Larson, 282.

The Battle at West Harpeth River

87. *OR* 45, Pt. I, 41.
88. Starr, 552.

89. Wilson 2:130; Cleaves, 270; Starr, 553.
90. *OR* 45, Pt. I, 565.
91. Ibid.
92. Wilson 2:131.
93. Hedges, "History of the Fourth United States Cavalry in the Battle of Nashville - Pursuit of Hood, &c."
94. W. F. Beyer and O. F. Keydel, eds. *Deeds of Valor: How America's Civil War Heroes Won the Congressional Medal of Honor* (New York: Smithmark Publishers, 2000), 469.
95. Larson, 283.
96. *OR* 45, 41; Larson, 283.
97. Hedges, as quoted in Vale, 393.
98. *OR* 45, 566.
99. Ibid.
100. Beyer, 469.
101. Wilson 2:131-32.
102. Hedges. Lt. Edward Fitzgerald died of his wounds on February 16, 1865. He enlisted in the 4th Cavalry in January 1858, and rose through the enlisted ranks to 1st sergeant. He was given field promotion to 2nd lieutenant February 19, 1863.
103. Beyer, 469.
104. Heitman, 520; Henry 2:286.
105. Allen Mikaelian, *Medal of Honor: Profiles of America's Military Heroes* (New York: Hyperion, 2002), xix. This was discontinued after Custer's disaster at Little Big Horn. A number of Civil War Medals of Honor were awarded during the 1890s through Congressional action. From 1890 on, requirements for recipients have been refined to the present day.
106. These two selections for the Medal of Honor came under the new criteria established in the late 1880s with the growing influence of Civil War veterans. They sought to clearly define the conditions under which the medal could be awarded in order to ennsure this honor be strictly given to individuals for "particular deeds of most distinguished gallantry in action." Criteria for recommendations were to "embrace a detailed recital of all the facts and circumstances." In 1916, the Medal of Honor Legion prevailed upon Congress to define the uniqueness of the award for "truly exceptional instances," and to review all past recipients. Over 900 names were removed and this review "validated the remaining Civil War recipients." For the period of the Civil War, a total of 1,522 Medal of Honor citations were awarded to army, navy, and marine personnel; 1,198 to the army. Source: Beyer, *Deeds of Valor*; Hardy, *Above and Beyond*; and Mikaelian, *Medal of Honor*.
107. Heitman, 217; Powell, 50.
108. Wilson 2:124.
109. *OR* 45, Pt. I, 553, 570; "Fourth Cavalry Regiment, 1855 - ."
110. Wilson 2:139.
111. *OR* 45, Pt. I, 567. Wilson writes, "The road from Pulaski to Bainbridge was as bad as it could possibly be, the country through which it runs almost entirely denuded of forage and army supplies. Both men and horses suffered greatly."
112. Larson, 283.
113. Starr, 553.
114. Johnson, R. W., 219.
115. *OR* 45, Pt. I, 567; Wilson 2:140-41.
116. Wilson 2:140-41; *OR* 45, 41-42; Larson, 284.
117. Larson, 284; Cleaves, 272.
118. Cleaves, 273.
119. Ibid., 272.
120. *OR* 45, Pt. I, 568. There was no information on casualties in the 4th US Cavalry.
121. *OR* 45, Pt. I, 568.
122. Starr, 3:549.
123. *OR* 45, Pt. I, 44.
124. Castel, 559.

1865: The Beginning of the End

I. The Last Campaign

1. Longacre, *Mounted Raids of the Civil War*, 337.
2. Wilson 2:55.
3. Catton, *American Heritage*, 563.
4. Rhodes, "Federal Raids and Expeditions in the West," 136.
5. Cleaves, 277-278.
6. *OR* 49, Pt. I, 343; Cleaves, 278.
7. Francis F. McKinney, *Education in Violence: The Life of George H. Thomas and the History of the Army of the Cumberland* (Detroit: Wayne State University Press, 1961), 433.
8. Johnson, R. W., 208.
9. McKinney, 434.
10. Wilson 2:137.
11. Larson, 289. On January 22, while at Gravelly Springs, Alabama, Sergeant John M. Herberich was promoted to 1st sergeant, Company I, Captain Napoleon B. McLaughlin's company. Captain McLaughlin was not with the regiment during the war, but First Sergeant Herberich would serve under him in Texas until his final discharge at Fort Concho, Texas, January 1, 1872.
12. Bates Letters, "Gravelly Springs, Alabama January 18th 1865."
13. Potter Letters No. 62: "Head Quarters 4th MVC Gravelly Spa, Ala, Feb 8 '65"
14. Minty, *National Tribune* February 21, 1895.
15. Bitter, 314.
16. Ibid.
17. Minty, *National Tribune*, February 21, 1895.
18. Bitter, 315.
19. Minty, *National Tribune*, February 21, 1895.
20. Ibid.
21. Longacre, 305.
22. Minty, *National Tribune*, February 21, 1895.

23. Bitter, 320.
24. Bowman, *Chronicles of the Civil War*, 189.
25. Ibid.
26. Ibid., 192.
27. Ibid., 192.
28. Ibid., 196.
29. Longacre, 311.
30. Ibid., 308.
31. Ibid., 310-11; Bitter, 321.
32. Bitter, 322.
33. Longacre, 310-11.
34. Ibid., 312.
35. Bitter, 322.
36. Vale, 424.
37. Larson, 289.
38. Bitter, 321.
39. Ibid., 323.
40. Ibid.
41. Longacre, 313.
42. Ibid., 312.
43. Bitter, 324.
44. Larson, 290.

II. Wilson's Selma - Macon Campaign

1. Bitter, 327.
2. Minty, *National Tribune*, October 1, 1891.
3. Wills, 305; Longacre, 313.
4. Ibid., 305.
5. Ibid., 306.
6. Ibid., 308.

Selma Alabama

7. Minty, *National Tribune*, October 1, 1891.
8. Larson, 293.
9. Longacre, 317. Abatis: A barricade of felled trees with branches facing the enemy. Palisade: Any one of a row of large pointed stakes set in the ground to form a fence used for fortification or defense.
10. Minty, *National Tribune*, October 1, 1891.
11. Longacre, 317.
12. Minty, *National Tribune*, October 1, 1891.
13. Longacre, 317.
14. Wills, 309.
15. Minty, *National Tribune*, October 1, 1891; Bitter, 333, quoting Fish.
16. *OR* 49, Pt. I, 359; Wills, 309-10; Longacre, 317.
17. Wills, 310.
18. *OR* 49, Pt. I, 359.

The Final Battle at Selma

19. Bitter, 333.
20. Minty, *National Tribune*, October 1, 1891.
21. Wills, 310.
22. Minty, *National Tribune*, October 1, 1891.
23. Wilson, 2:229.
24. Minty, *National Tribune*, October 1, 1891.
25. Wilson, 2:230.
26. Wills, 310.
27. Wilson, 2:231.
28. Bitter, 335.
29. Minty, *National Tribune*, October 1, 1891.
30. Wills, 310.
31. Bitter, 333.
32. Minty, *National Tribune*, October 1, 1891.
33. Ibid.
34. Bitter, 335-36.
35. Larson, 296-97.
36. "History of the 4th US Cavalry."
37. Bitter, 336.
38. William G. Rambo, Col., USA "The Selma Campaign, The Selma Charge," http://membersaol.com/wwhitby/campaign.html.
39. Bitter, 336.
40. Ibid.
41. Ibid.
42. Larson, 295.
43. Ibid., 298.
44. Ibid., 295.
45. Ibid., 299.
46. Wills, 310-11.
47. Ibid., 311.

The Massacre At Goodwin's Farm

48. Larson, 290-91.
49. Henry, R. S., 432-33. Several versions of this event indicate that Private Preas was captured, questioned, and then killed.
50. Ibid., 432-33.
51. Wills, 311.
52. Wilson 2:240; Wills, 311.
53. Larson, 299-300.
54. Bitter, 338.
55. Minty, *National Tribune*, October 1, 1891.
56. Bitter, 302.
57. Minty, *National Tribune*, October 1, 1891.
58. Ibid.
59. Starr 3:565.
60. United States, Army. 4th Cavalry Regiment, 1855-.

III. Up in Smoke

1. *OR* 49, Pt. I, 343.
2. Larson, 300-01.
3. Bitter, 340, quoting Burns.
4. Wilson 2:248; Bitter, 339, quoting Minty.
5. Bitter, 339, quoting Burns.
6. Wilson 2:248.
7. Bitter, 339-40.
8. Ibid., 341.

Montgomery, Alabama

9. Bitter, 340.
10. Wilson 2:251.
11. Ibid., 251-52
12. Bitter, 340.

13. Ibid., 341.
14. Ibid.
15. Wilson 2:255.

Columbus, Georgia

16. Larson, 301.
17. Ibid., 302.
18. Bitter, 343.
19. Ibid.

Macon, Georgia

20. Larson, 302.
21. Ibid.
22. Ibid.
23. Larson, 303.
24. Bitter, 343.
25. Ibid., 344.
26. Ibid.
27. Wilson 2:278.
28. Bitter, 345.
29. Ibid.
30. Ibid., 346.
31. Wilson 2:294-95.
32. Longacre, 327.
33. Urwin, 130-31.
34. Wilson 2:372.

IV. The Final Days

1. Wilson 2:365.
2. Larson, 303-04.
3. Ibid., 305.
4. Bitter, 347.
5. Ibid., 348.
6. Larson, 313.
7. Larson 313-14; Register of Enlistments. Even the spelling of her name remains a mystery. The most accurate appears to be on her marriage certificate: Zelina Roscincki. The handwriting of the clerk who filled out the document is difficult to read, but his last name, Smyth, helped clarify that the "Z" in Zelina was possibly correct. She may have "Americanized" the name by changing the first letter to an "S." Her maiden name could possibly be spelled Roscinski, as this is the common spelling for the name in Eastern Europe/Poland. That spelling also appears in Georgia and several eastern states.
8. Larson, 305.
9. OR 49, Pt. II, 681, 753
10. Potter Letters, No 63: "Head Quarters 4th Mich Cav Macon, Ga. May 14th 1865; No. 64:"Head Quarters, 4th Mich Cav. Near Macon Ga May 19 1865." Sherman had personally ordered Cobb's home and plantation to be destroyed during his march to the sea. Cobb was pardoned and for the remainder of his life vigorously opposed the Reconstruction policies of the federal government.
11. Larson, 306.
12. Ibid., 307.
13. Ibid., 306-07.
14. Bitter, 346, 349.
15. OR 49, Pt. II, 663.
16. OR 49, 401-02.
17. Bitter, 338; Wilson 365.
18. Wilson 2:365.
19. "The Civil War: The Cavalry."
20. United States. Army. 4th Cavalry Regiment, 1855-.
21. "History of the 4th US Cavalry."
22. Powell, 568; Heitman, 915.
23. Larson, 314.

V. The Casualties

1. Frederick H Dyer. *A Compendium of the War of the Rebellion*, 1908.(Reprint, National Historical Society, Dayton, OH: The Press of Morningside Bookshop, 1979), 46.
2. Ward, McMaster, Kerner, Simson, Stoll, Register of Enlistments; Heitman: Ward, 1001; McMaster, 677; Simson, 889; Stoll, 228; Colburn, 315; Henry II: Ward, 215; McMaster, 306; L'Hommedieu, 300, Xenia Sentinel (Xenia, Ohio) January 19, 1864.
3. Heitman: Sedgwick, 872; Bayard, 200; McMaster, 677; Simson 889.
4. Registers of Deaths; Regimental Returns; Register of Enlistments; West Point Monument.
5. Wilson 2:26-27.
6. The Goodwin Farm casualties were never officially recorded. The number here is estimated from figures provided by Larson, Wills, and the *Nashville Daily Union*, April 27, 1865.
7. Registers of Deaths; Norton Parker Chipman, Judge Advocate of the Military Court, *The Tragedy of Andersonville. Trial of Henry Wirz. The Prison Keeper* (Sacramento: Chipman, 1911), 290-291.
8. Registers of Deaths; Regimental Returns.
9. Ibid.

Epilogue

1. Stubbs, 11-12.
2. "History of the Fourth US Cavalry."

Bibliography

Archival Documents & Collections

Herberich, Blanche L. Personal Papers.
Michigan Historical Collection, Bentley Historical Library, University of Michigan, Ann Arbor.
The Letters of Henry Albert Potter, Captain: 4th Michigan Cavalry.
Edited by Michael Palmer Ruddy.
Army Records, National Archives and Records Administration, Washington, DC:
Combined Records of the Fourth United States Cavalry. RG 94:M-744 (40 & 41)
Records of the Veterans Administration, 1866-1869. RG 15.
Returns from Regular Army Cavalry Regiments, 1821-1916. RG 94
United States Army, Register of Enlistments, 1789-1914. RG 94.
United States Registers of Deaths in the Regular Army, 1860-1889. RG 94.
United States Returns from Regular Army Non-Infantry Regiments, 1812-1916. RG 94.
Special Collections Library, Duke University
James H. Wiswell Letters, 1861-1867.
University of Maryland
Papers of William Emory, May 1861-September 1862
University Libraries, South Carolina Library
Heber S. Thompson Papers, Aug.-Dec. 1864
Virginia Historical Society, Richmond, Virginia.
Civil War Letters of Charles E. Bates

Government Publications

The War of the Rebellion: A Compilation of the Official Records of the Union and Confederate Armies 1861 - 1865. 128 vols. In 3 series. Washington, DC: U. S. Government Printing Office, 1880-1901.

Published Sources

"The Story of a Cavalry Soldier: The Fourth Regular Cavalry at Murfreesboro." *Lancaster Daily Evening Press*, January 28, 1863.
Bates, Joseph Young. "A Sketch of the Service of Joseph Young Bates as a Confederate Soldier." *Washington County Historical Society (Fayetteville Arkansas), Flashback*, March 1862, 31-32.
Baumgartner, Richard A. *Blue Lightning: Wilder's Mounted Infantry Brigade in the Battle of Chickamauga*. Huntington, WV: Blue Acorn Press, 2007.
Beyer, W. F., and O. F. Keydel, eds. *Deeds of Valor: How America's Civil War Heroes Won the Congressional Medal of Honor.* New York: Smithmark, 2000.
Bitter, Rand K. *Minty and His Cavalry: A History of the Saber Brigade and Its Commander.* Michigan: Rand K. Bitter, 2006.
Boston Publishing Company, eds. *Above and Beyond: A History of the Medal of Honor from the Civil War to Vietnam.* Boston: Boston, 1985.
Bowman, John S., ed. *The Civil War Almanac.* Barns & Noble, Inc., 2005.
Bowman, John, gen. ed. *Chronicles of the Civil War.* Maryland: World Publications Group, 2005.
Brackett, Albert G., Major, USA. *History of the United States Cavalry, from the Formation of the Federal Government to the 1st of June, 1863.* 1865. New York: Argonaut Press, Ltd., 1965.
Bradford, Ned. *Battles and Leaders of the Civil War.* New York: Appleton-Century-Crofts, 1956.
Brown, Dee. "War on Horseback." *The Images of the War: 1861-1865,* vol. 4: *Fighting for Time.* William C. Davis and Bell I. Wiley, eds., the National Historical Society. Garden City, New York: Doubleday. 1983.
Buell, Thomas B. *The Warrior Generals: Combat Leadership in the Civil War.* New York: Crown 1997.
Castel, Albert. *Decision in the West: The Atlanta Campaign of 1864.* Lawrence: University Press of Kansas, 1992.
Catton, Bruce. *The American Heritage Picture History of the Civil War.* New York: American Heritage, 1960.
Catton, Bruce. *Centennial History of the Civil War: The Coming Fury.* Garden City, NY: Doubleday & Co., 1961.
Catton, Bruce. *Centennial History of the Civil War: Terrible Swift Sword.* Garden City, New York: Doubleday, 1963.
Chipman, Norton Parker, Judge Advocate of the Military Court. *The Tragedy of Andersonville. Trial of Henry Wirz. The Prison Keeper.* Sacramento: Chipman, 1911.

Cleaves, Freeman. *Rock of Chickamauga: The Life of General George H. Thomas*. Norman: University of Oklahoma Press, 1948.

Coates, Earl J. Coates John D. McAulay. *Civil War Sharpes Carbines and Rifles* (Gettysburg, Pennsylvania: Thomas, 1996)

Cox, Kurt Hamilton and John P. Langellier. *Longknives: The US Cavalry and other Mounted Forces, 1845-1942 - (The G.I. Series: The Illustrated Histories of the American Soldier, His Uniforms and His Equipment*; vol. 3). Pennsylvania: Stackpole Books, 1996.

Cozzens, Peter. *No Better Place to Die: The Battle of Stones River*. Urbana and Chicago: University of Illinois Press, 1990.

Cozzens, Peter. *This Terrible Sound: The Battle of Chickamauga*. Urbana: University of Illinois Press, 1991.

Curry, William L. "Kilpatrick's Raid." *National Tribune*, June 23, 1910.

Curry, William L. "Raid Around Atlanta." *Four Years in the Saddle: History of the First Regiment Ohio Volunteer Cavalry: War of the Rebellion, 1861-1865*, 1898. Reprint, Jonesboro, GA: Freedom Hill Press, 1984.

Custer, George A. "War Memoirs." *The Galaxy Magazine*, vol. 0021, Issue 5, May 1876.

Daniel, Larry J. *Shiloh: The Battle That Changed the Civil War*. New York: Simon & Schuster, 1997.

Dillahunty, Albert. *Shiloh National Military Park, Tennessee*. National Park Service. Washington: Historical Handbook Series No. 10, 1955.

Dougherty, Kevin J., Martin J. Dougherty, Parker Hills, Chris McNab, and Michael F Pavkovic. *Battles of the Civil War, 1861-1865*. New York: Metro Books, 2007.

Downey, Fairfax. *Cavalry Mount*. New York: Dodd, Meade, 1946.

Dyer, Frederick H. *A Compendium of the War of the Rebellion*, 1908. Reprint, National Historical Society, Dayton, OH: Press of Morningside Bookshop, 1979.

Esposito, Vincent J., chief ed. *West Point Atlas of War: The Civil War*. NY: Tess Press, 1995.

Evans, David. *Sherman's Horsemen: Union Cavalry in the Atlanta Campaign*. Bloomington and Indianapolis: Indiana University Press, 1996.

Freeman, Elsie, Wynell Burroughs Schamel, and Jean West. "The Fight for Equal Rights: A Recruiting Poster for Black Soldiers in the Civil War." *Social Education* 56, 2 (February 1992): 118-120. (Revised and updated in 1999 by Budge Weidman.)

Hagemann, E. R. *Fighting Rebels and Redskins: Experiences in the Army Life of Colonel George B. Sanford, 1861-1892*. Norman: University of Oklahoma Press, 1969.

Harpers Weekly, "The Battle of Dug Springs," August 24, 1861.

Heitman, Francis B. *Historical Register and Dictionary of the United States Army*, vol. 1. Washington: Government Printing Office, 1903.

Henry, Guy V. *Military Record of Civilian Appointments in the United States Army*, vols. 1 & 2. New York, D. Van Nostrand, Publisher, 1873.

Henry, Robert Selph. *"First with the Most" - Forrest*. Indianapolis: Bobbs-Merrill, 1944.

Herr, John K., Major General, USA (Retired) and Edward S. Wallace. *The Story of the US Cavalry 1775-1942*. Boston: Little, Brown, 1953.

Hurst, Jack. *Nathan Bedford Forrest: A Biography*. New York: Alfred A. Knoff, 1993.

Iowa City Citizen, "Iowa Old Press," November 3, 1917.

Johnson, Richard W. *Memoir of Maj. Gen. George H. Thomas*. Philadelphia: J. B. Lippincot, 1881.

Johnson, Robert U., C. C. Buell, eds. *Battles and Leaders of the Civil War*. New York: Century, 1887-88.

Johnson, Swafford. *History of the US Cavalry*. Greenwich, Conn: Crescent Books, 1985.

Jordan, Thomas, General, and J. P. Pryor. *The Campaigns of Nathan Bedford Forrest and of Forrest's Cavalry*, 1868.

Kenyon, W. Clark. "Skirmish at Dug Springs, Missouri, August 2, 1861." *The Trans-Mississippi News*, vol. 1. Fall, 1995.

Konstam, Angus. *The Civil War: A Visual Encyclopedia*. New York: Barnes and Noble, 2001.

Larned, Charles W. *History of the Battle Monument at West Point*. Battle Monument Association. New York: West Point, 1898.

Larson, James. *Sergeant Larson 4th Cav*. San Antonio, Texas: Southern Literary Institute, 1935.

Longacre, Edward G. *Lincoln's Cavalrymen: A History of the Mounted Forces of the Army of the Potomac, 1861-1865*. Mechanicsburg, Pennsylvania: Stockpole Books, 2000.

Longacre, Edward G. *Mounted Raids of the Civil War*. Lincoln: University of Nebraska Press, 1994.

Lossing, Benson J. *Mathew Brady's Illustrated History of the Civil War*. Avenel, NJ: Gramercy Books, Random House Value Publishing, 1994.

Lytle, Andrew. *Bedford Forrest and His Critter Company*, 1913. Reprint, Seminole, FL: Green Key Press, 1984.

McClellan, H. B. *The Life and Campaigns of Major General J. E. B. Stuart*. Boston, 1885 Reprint: Secaucus, NJ: The Blue and Grey Press, 1993.

McCracken, Harold. *The Frederic Remington Book: A Pictorial History of the West*. Garden City, NY: Doubleday, 1966.

McKinney, Francis F. *Education in Violence: The Life of George H. Thomas and the History of the Army of the Cumberland*. Detroit: Wayne State University Press, 1961.

McPherson, James M. ed., *The Atlas of the Civil War*. Philadelphia, PA: Running Press Book Publishers, 2005.

McPherson, James M. *Battle Cry of Freedom: The Civil War Era*. New York: Oxford University Press, 1988.

McReynolds, Edwin C. *Missouri - A History of the Crossroads State*. Norman: University of Oklahoma Press, 1962.

McTeer, William A., "Smith's Raid." *National Tribune*, May 28, 1892.

Merrill, James M. *Spurs to Glory*. Chicago: Rand McNally, 1966.

Mikaelian, Allen. *Medal of Honor: Profiles of America's Military Heroes from the Civil War to the Present*. New York: Bill Adler Books, 2002.

Miller, Francis Trevelyan, ed. *The Photographic History of the Civil War in Ten Volumes*. New York: The Review of Reviews, 1912.

Mix, Frank W., letter to the editor, *National Tribune*, May 21, 1891.

Ness, George T. Jr. *The Regular Army on the Eve of the Civil War*. Baltimore, Md: Toomy Press, 1990.

Nevin, David. *The Civil War: Sherman's March*. Alexandria, Virginia: Time Life Books, 1986.

Nevin, David. *The Old West: The Soldiers*. New York: Time Life Books, 1973.

Norris, David L., James C Milligan, and Odie B. Faulk. *William H. Emory: Soldier-Scientist*. The University of Arizona Press, 1998.

Obituary of Major Gen. Gordon Granger, *New York Times*, January 12, 1876.

O'Shea, Richard. *American Heritage: Battle Maps of the Civil War*. New York: Smithmark Publishers, 1992.

Piston, William Garrett, and Richard W. Hatcher III. *Wilson's Creek: The Second Battle of the Civil War and the Men Who Fought It*. Chapel Hill & London: The University of North Carolina Press, 2000.

Powell, David A. *The Maps of Chickamauga*. NY: Savas Beatie, 2009.

Powell, William H. *Powell's Records of Living Officers of the United States Army*. Philadelphia: L. R. Hamersly, 1890.

Rhodes, Charles D., Captain, General Staff, United States Army. "Cavalry Battles and Charges." *The Photographic History of the Civil War in Ten Volumes,* vol. IV: "The Calvary." New York: The Review of Reviews, 1912.

Rhodes, Charles D., Captain, General Staff, United States Army. "Federal Raids and Expeditions in the West." *The Photographic History of the Civil War in Ten Volumes,* vol. IV, "The Calvary." New York: The Review of Reviews, 1912.

Robertson, James I. Jr., and eds. *The Civil War: Tenting Tonight*. Alexandria, VA: Time-Life Books, 1984.

Robertson, William Glenn. "The Chickamauga Campaign: The Fall of Chattanooga." *Blue and Gray*, vol. XXIII, Issue 4, Fall, 2006.

Robertson, William Glenn. "The Chickamauga Campaign: McLemore's Cove." *Blue and Gray*, vol. XXIII, Issue 6, Spring 2007.

Robertson, William Glenn. "The Chickamauga Campaign: The Armies Collide." *Blue and Gray*, vol. XXIV, Issue 3, Fall 2007.

Robertson, William Glenn. "The Chickamauga Campaign: The Battle of Chickamauga." *Blue and Gray*, vol. XXV, Issue 2, Summer 2008.

Rodenbough, Theophilus Francis, Bvt. Brigadier General USA, William L. Haskin, Major, First Artillery, eds. *The Army of the United States, Historical Sketches of Staff and Line With Portraits of Generals-in Chief*. New York: Maynard, Merrill, 1896.

Rodenbough, Gen. Theophilus F., and William Haskin, eds. "The Fourth Regiment Cavalry." *The Army of the United States, 1789-1896*. New York: Maynard, Merrill, 1896.

Rodenbough, Theophilus F., Brigadier General, United States Army (Retired). "Cavalry of the Civil War - Its Evolution and Influence." *The Photographic History of the Civil War in Ten Volumes*. vol. 4, "The Cavalry." Francis Trevelyan Miller, editor-in-chief. New York: The Review of Reviews, 1912.

Roth, Dave, ed., "Editorial." *Blue & Gray*. vol. XXIV, Issue 3, Fall 2007.

Ruddy, Michael P., ed. "Captain Henry Albert Potter Diary and Captain Simmons' Book." http://freepages.genealogy.rootsweb.ancestry.com/~mruddy/Chicka.htm.

Sherman, William Tecumseh. *Memoirs of General William T. Sherman*. New York: Library of America, 1990.

Sipes, William B. *The Saber Regiment: The Seventh Pennsylvania Veteran Volunteer Cavalry*. 1906. Huntington, WV: Blue Acorn Press, 2000.

Smith, Lucian B. Letter to the editor, *National Tribune*, July 21, 1891.

Sollars, Issac, letter to the editor, *National Tribune*, December 15, 1892.

Stanley, David Sloan, *An American General: The memoirs of David Sloan Stanley*. Santa Barbara, CA: Narrative Press, 2003.

Starr, Stephen Z. *The Union Cavalry in the Civil War*, 3 vols. Baton Rouge: Louisiana State University Press, 1979-1985.

Steahlin, George F., letter to the editor, *National Tribune*, May 27, 1882.

Strayer, Larry M., Richard A. Baumgartner, *Echoes of Battle: The Atlanta Campaign*. West Virginia: Blue Acorn Press, 2004.

Stubbs, Mary Lee, and Stanley Russell Connor, Armor Lineage Series: *Armor-Cavalry Part 1: Regular Army and Army Reserve*. Washington, DC: Office of the Chief of Military History, United States Army, 1969.

Sword, Wiley. *Shiloh, Bloody April*. NY: William Morrow, 2001.

Tullos, Thomas R, "When Captain Freeman was Killed," *Confederate Veteran*, August 1913.

Urwin, Gregory J. W., *The United States Cavalry: An Illustrated History, 1776-1944*. Norman, Oklahoma: University of Oklahoma Press, 1983.

Uschan, Michael V., *The Cavalry During the Civil War*. San Diego, California: Lucent Books, 2003.

Vale, Joseph G, *Minty and The Cavalry: A History of Cavalry Campaigns in the Western Armies*, 1886. Reprint, Salem, Massachusetts: Higginson Book Company, 1998.

Van Horn, Thomas B., *History of the Army of the Cumberland*, 2 vols. Cincinnati: Robert Clark, 1875.

Wallace, Lew, Major General. "The Capture of Fort Donelson." *Battles and Leaders of the Civil War*, Ned Bradford, ed., NY: Appleton-Century-Crofts, Inc., 1956.

Webb, William W. "Kilpatrick's Great Raid." *Frank Leslie's Popular Monthly*, December 1889.

Wherry, William M. Brevet Brigadier-General, USV, 6th U.S. Infantry. "Wilson's Creek and the Death of Lyon." *Battles and Leaders of the Civil War*, edited by Robert U. Johnson & Clarence C. Buel, New York: Century, 1887.

Whitman, S. E., *The Troopers: An Informal History of the Plains Cavalry, 1865-1890*. New York: Hastings House Publishers, 1962.

Wills, Brian Steel. *The Confederacy's Greatest Cavalryman: Nathan Bedford Forrest*. Kansas: University Press of Kansas, 1998.

Wilson, James Harrison. *Under the Old Flag, Recollections of Military Operations in the War for the Union*, vols. 1 & 2. New York and London: D. Appleton and Company, 1912.

Witherspoon, J. G. "The Killing of Captain Freeman." *Confederate General*, vol. 21, 1913.

Wormser, Richard. *The Yellowlegs: The Story of the United States Cavalry*. Garden City, New York: Doubleday, 1966.

Wyeth, John A., MD. *That Devil Forrest: The Life of General Nathan Bedford Forrest*. New York: Harper & Brothers, 1899.

INTERNET SOURCES

1st Squadron, 4th United States Cavalry, "History of the 4th United States Cavalry." http://www.schweinfurt.army.mil/4th/History.htm.

"4th Regiment Michigan Cavalry," http://www.michiganinthewar.org.cavalry.4thcav.htm.

"American Civil War: Brigadier General William N. R. Beall," http://www.factasy.com/civil_war/southern_leaders/william_beall.shtml.

Bates, Alfred E., Major, USA "History of the 2nd US Cavalry," http://www.usregulars.com/UScavalry/2us_cav.html.

"The Battle of Shiloh," http://www.geocities.com/shiloh.html.

"Blind, Mad or Foolish: Nathaniel Lyon, Part ll." Suite 101.com, http://www.suite101.com/article.cfm/civil_war/103088.

"Brigadier General Nathaniel Lyon, Commander, Department of the West, Union Army," http://www.civilwarfamilyhistory.com/new_page_141.htm.

"Casualties for the Battles of Carthage and Dug Springs," http://www.chrisanddavid.com/wilsonscreek/rolls/CASUALTICAR.htm.

Caughey, Don. "Regular Cavalry in the Civil War." http://regularcavalryincivilwar.wordpress.com

"The Civil War: The Cavalry," http://pages.cthome.net/firecapt/TheCivilWar.html.

The Civil War Archive. Union Regimental Histories. United States Regular Army. 4th Regiment Cavalry, http://www.civilwararchive.com/Unreghst/unrgcav.htm.4th cav.

Civil War Battle Pages, http://members.fortunecity.com/thegunny1/index.htm.

"Description of the Battle of Shiloh," http://www.civilwarhome.com/shilohdescription.htm.

Evans, David. "The Battle of Brown's Mill," http://www.battleofbrownsmill.org.

"Fort Arbuckle," http://www.rootsweb.com/~okmurray/ft_arbuckle.htm.

"Fort Cobb," http://www.fortours.com/pages/ftcobb.asp.

"Fort Washita Official Records," http://civilwaralbum.com/washita/OR.htm.

"The Fourth Regiment of Cavalry," Compiled in the Office of the Military Service Institution. http://www.history.army.mil/books/R&H/R&H-4CV.htm.

Handbook of Texas Online. Texas State Historical Association:
    "Camp Verde," http://www.tsha.utexas.edu/handbook/online/article?CC/hrc.16.html.
    "Fourth United States Cavalry," http://www.tsha.utexas.edu/handbook/online/articles/viewFF/qlf2.html.
    "Indianola, Texas," http://www.tsha.utexas.edu/handbook/online/articles/II/hvi11.html.
    "Twiggs, David Emanuel," http://www.tshaonline.org/handbook/online/articles/TT/ftw3.html.
    "Emory, William Helmsley," http://www.tsha.utexas.edu/handbook/online/articles/EE/frm3_print.html.

History Central.com: Confederate Generals, s.v. "General James McQueen McIntosh, CSA," http://www.historycentral.com/bio/CWcGENS/CSAMcIntosh.html.

Keliher, John G., 25th Infantry Division Association. "The History of the 4th US Cavalry Regiment," http://www.25thida.com/4thcav.html.

Krautz, August V. "Krautz' Customs of Service (1864): Selections from the Customs of Service." Philadelphia: J. B. Lippincott & Co, 1864, http://www.usregulars.com/COShome.html.

Moore, John C., Colonel, CSA. "Missouri in the Civil War," vol. 9, Chapter IV, Confederate Military History. www.civilwarhome.com, s.v. "Missouri in the Civil War." http://civilwarhome.com/missouri7.htm.

Morton, Charles, Captain, 3rd U. S. Cavalry. "History of the 3rd US Cavalry," http://www.usregulars.com/UScavalry/3us_cav.html.

"Nathaniel Lyon," ehistory.osu.edu/World/PeopleView.cfm?PID=76.

National Park Service:
    "The Battle of Yellow Tavern, May 11, 1864" http://www.nps.gov/frsp/yellow.htm.
    Fort Donelson National Battlefield. "Fort Donelson United States of America Order of Battle," http://www.nps.gov/fodo/indepth/usaob.htm.
    "Fort Laramie," http://www.nps.gov/fola/units/htm.
    "Fort Smith National Historic Site," http://www.nps.gov/fosm/history/2ndfort.
    Midwest Archeological Center, Wilson's Creek National Battlefield, http://www.cr.nps.gov/mwac/wier_peri/wilsons_creek.htm.
    "Reading 1: The Soldiers and the Battle of Stones River," http://www.cr.nps.gov/NR/twhp/wwwlps/lessons/40stones/40facts1.htm.
    "Stones River – Reading," http://www.cr.nps.gov/NR/twhp/wwwlps/lessons/40stones/40facts1.htm.

National Park Service. CWSAC Battle Summaries:
    "Battle Summary: Boonville," http://nps.gov/history/hps/abpp/battles/mo001.htm.
    "Battle Summary: Franklin, TN," http://www.cr.nps.gov/hps/abpp/battles/tn016.htm.
    "Battle Summary: Lovejoy's Station," http://www.cr.nps.gov/hps/abpp/battles/ga021.htm.
    "Battle Summary: Nashville," http://www.cr.nps.gov/hps/abpp/battles/tn038.htm.
    "New Madrid/Island No. 10," http://www.nps.gov/history/hps/abpp/battles/mo012.htm.

National Park Service Historical Handbook: Chickamauga and Chattanooga Battlefields.

"New Bent's Fort," http//:www.stjohnks,net/santafetrail/spacpix/bent-new-fort-colorado.html.

"Official Records Related to Fort Washita," http.//www.civilwaralbum.com/washita/OR.htm.

"Old Fort Wise / Lyon Colorado." Santa Fe Trail Site, http://www.stjohnks.net/santafetrail/spacpix/oldftwise_lyon.html.

"Philip Sheridan: Small and Forceful Impact," http://www.anglefire.com/tn/AIB/sheridan.html.

"The Tullahoma Campaign," http://www.nps.gov/history/history/online_books/hh/25/hh25c.htm.

Phillips, Gervase. "Saber versus Revolver: Mounted Combat in the American Civil War," http://mmu.academia.edu/GervasePhillips/Papers/131153/Sabre_versus_Revolver_Mounted_Combat_in_the_American_Civil_War.

Potter, Henry Albert, Henry Albert Potter Diary - 1863. Archives of Michigan. Civil War Manuscripts, http://haldigitalcollections.cdmhost.com/seeking_michigan.

Rambo, William G., Colonel, USA, "The Selma Campaign," "The Selma Charge," http://membersaol.com/wwhitby/campaign.html.

Reiff, J. C., Adjutant, Fifteenth Pennsylvania (Anderson) Cavalry. "The 15th Pennsylvania Volunteer Cavalry, The Combatant's Story," http://www.swcivilwar.com/15CombatantsStonesRiver.html.

Ruddy, Michael P. "Captain Henry Albert Potter's Diary and Captain Simmons' Book," http://freepages.geneology.rootsweb.ancestry.com/~mruddy/chicka.htm.

Stubbs, Mary Lee and Stanley Russell Connor. Armor Lineage Series: Armor-Cavalry, Part 1: Regular Army and Army Reserve. Office of the Chief of Military History, United States Army, Washington, DC 1969, http://www.army.mil/cmh-pg/books/Lineage/arcav/arcav.htm.

"Thomas William Sweeny," http://www.virtualogy.com/thomaswilliamsweeny.

"U.S. Regulars at Wilson's Creek," http://www.chrisanddavid.com/wilsonscreek/roles/SOLDIERSUSREG.html.

United States. Army. 4th Cavalry Regiment, 1855-. "Fourth Cavalry United States Army, 1855-1930." Army Heritage Collection OnLine, http://www.ahco.army.mil.

United States. Army. "Medal of Honor," U.S. Army Center of Military History, http://www.history.army.mil/moh.html.

"War on Horseback," http://www.civilwarhome.com/horsebackwar.html.

Index

Aaron, John A.: captured, died at Andersonville prison, 178
Abates, 108-09; 238
Accidental deaths, 64, 253
Accouterments (see Cavalry, US)
Acoustic capacity, 290n56 Adams, Charles F., Jr.: characteristics of a cavalryman, 84
Adams, Daniel W., CSA, escapes from Selma, AL
Ahrus (Ahrens), Fred: wounded at Pittsburg Landing, 293n29
Aleshire, Charles: at Shelbyville, 109-10
Alexander, A. J.: Wilson's chief-of-staff, 222
Alexander, Thomas B., CSA: last 4th US Cavalry officer to defect, 64, 294n23
Alexander's Bridge, action at, 120-124
Allen, Alvey, 33, 43; wounded, 291n116; assigned to Co. C, 44; 97, 300n103
Allen, William Wirt, CSA, (Allen's Brigade), 176, 189,
Amory, Copley, 46, complains of General Pope's report, 47
Anderson, Robert, CSA, (Anderson's Brigade): at Noonday Creek, 176, 177
Andersonville (see Prisons)
Antietam Campaign, 62
Arkansas: votes for secession, 16
Armisted's Brigade, CSA, 216
Armstrong, Frank C., CSA, 133; Armstrong's Brigade, 204, 215
Army of the Cumberland, creation of Cavalry Division, 62-63 98, 101, 103, 105, 107, 108, 116, 119, 134; trapped at Chattanooga, 144; commanded by George Thomas, 153; size of, 163; most modern army in the war, 213
Army of the Mississippi, 59, 66, 153
Army of Northern Virginia, 103, 147
Army of the Ohio: Don Carlos Buell, 60
Army of Southwest Missouri, xv
Army of Tennessee (CSA), 61, 116 commanded by Joseph Johnston, 147; 188, 218, 229, 234
Army of the Tennessee (USA): at Pittsburg Landing, 55; commanded by Sherman, 147; 188
Army of the West, 37-38, 44
Arsenals (Federal): Liberty, Mo., 14, 35; Fayetteville, Ark., 14; Little Rock, Ark., 34; St. Louis, MO, 35
Artillery, US: 1st United States, 31; 5th United States, 31
Artillery, USV: 1st Ohio, 77, 85; Chicago Board of Trade Battery, 103;

Ashby, Henry M., CSA, 70
Athens, AL.: destruction of, 60, 218
Atlanta, GA, 147, 148, importance of, 193; siege of, 193 Atlanta Campaign, 147; Thomas prepares for, 148; 170 summary of, 216
Bailey, William: at Lovejoy's Station, 210; at Jonestown, 202
Bain, Cicero C., CSA, 177
Bands: Regimental, 3; 1st Cavalry, 8; 189, 195, 199; 92nd Illinois at Jonesboro, 203
Banks, Nathaniel P., 162; Red River Campaign, 162
Bardstown, Ky.: Companies F and H confront Morgan's cavalry, 100
Bars, Frank: killed in action at Okolona, 156
Bartlett, Jerome: captures 1st Alabama Cavalry standard, 98
Bates, Charles E., x, 29-30, 32, 33; on activities in Maryland and capturing deserters, 89; transferred to Western Theater, 89-90; comments on differences between the two armies, 89-90; appointed commissary sergeant, 90; expedition to Liberty and Snow Hill, 90; infested with "beggar lice", 90, 298n11; captures rebels, 90; attitude toward Negroes, 91; on size and spirit of 4th US Cavalry, 104; at Shelbyville, 111; captures rebels, 133, 135; on winter quarters at Huntsville, 140-41; on military strategy and McClellan's bid for presidency, 141; cited for gallantry, 144; expedition into western Tennessee after Forrest, 149; on spirit of Regiment after refitting, 160, 164, 174; appointed regimental ordinance sergeant, 174; praise for Sherman, 184; 218; writing from Gravelly Springs, AL 232
Baum, John: killed in action at Okolona, 156
Bayard, George D., 11; death of, 252
Bayard, William: cited for gallantry, 228; promoted and brevetted by Gen. Wilson, 251
Baxter, Nat., CSA: with Freeman's Battery, 92-93
Beal, William N. R., CSA, 11; at Corinth, 59
Beaumont, Eugene B., 28, 29; acting adjutant general, Cavalry Corps, 221; West Harpeth River, 228
Beauregard, Pierre G. T., CSA, 56
Bee, Bernard, CSA, 31
Beggar lice, 90, 298n11
Belknap, William, 10
Bellbuckle Gap: map, 65; 106, held by Confederates, 112
Bennett, Henry: Kilpatrick's Raid, 198, 201
Benton Barracks, St. Charles, Mo., 54,

Bent's Fort, Colorado Territory, 8
Bibb, Andrew J.: drowned in Mississippi River, 161
Big Shanty, GA, 172-173, 192
Biggs, Jonathan: at Flat Shoals, 190; wounded at Selma, AL, 240
Birch, Sgt. (4th Michigan): injured in ambush, 115
Bitter, Rand (Minty' biographer), xi, xiv
Black Beaver (Indian guide), 16
Blackwater Creek (Shawnee Mound), 45
Bloody Hill, Wilson's Creek, artillery duel, 40-41
Blue Book (Articles of War), 6
Boonville, Miss.: capture of, 59
Booth, Captain (McCrillis Staff): wounded at Okolona, 155; attempts to stop stampede, 155
Booth, John Wilkes, 249
Bowman, Charles S., 64, 294n22, 138; commanding 4th US Cavalry, 148; at Okolona, 150; 152, 155; leads cavalry charge, 156; brevetted major, 157;
Brackett, Albert G. (officer, historian), 11, 18, 23
Bradburn, John, 42
Bragg, Braxton, CSA, 1, 2, 10, 61, 64, 71, 73; failure at Stones River, 74; complains of Federal use of saber, 79; 106; evacuates Tullahoma, 112; retreats' to Chattanooga, 112; 113; consolidates forces, 117; at Chickamauga, 120; 123, 134, 139
Brandy Station (Beverly Ford), Va.: battle of, 66
Breckenridge, William C. P., CSA, 104
Brestworks, 193-94
Brevet rank, 26
Brice Crossroads, Miss., 159, 175
Bridgeport, AL, 116; bridge destroyed, 130, 148, 163
Brody, Dr., 47
Brown, John, 12
Brown, Joseph E. (Georgia governor): captured, 250; escorted by Lt. Bayard, 250
Brown, Thomas, 155
Brown's Mill, battle of, 188
Buchanan, James, 13
Buck Head, (Buckhead) Ga., 191, 192, 198, 213
Buckner, Simon B., CSA, 117, 119-20; Buckner's infantry, 120
Buell, Don Carlos: Nashville surrenders to, 54; commands Army of the Ohio, 55; contempt for undisciplined volunteers, 60; replaced by Rosecrans; 66
Buell, Thomas (historian): on George Thomas' cavalry tactics, 148; on Battle of Franklin (November 1864), 219
Buford, Abraham, CSA, 70; routed, 228; 236; escapes from Selma, 240
Buford, John, 18
Bull Run, battle of, 2, 29, 30

Burke, Bartholomew: killed at Bardstown, Ky., 101, 300n139; last words, 252
Burke, Joseph W., 70, 72
Burke, Walter: wounded at Wilson's Creek, discharged, 291n116
Burns, Robert L., xi; on functions of advanced guard, 69; on retreat to Nashville, 71-72; on foraging, 83; on movement of Minty's Brigade into Alabama, 113; on Emancipation Proclamation, 113; on marching in difficult conditions, 113; describes ambush involving Minty, 115; hardships of campaigns, 116; comments on refitting and spirit of brigade, 160; critical of brigade commander, 170; comments on Sherman, 170; gathering the dead, 177; on the difficult conditions of the Atlanta Campaign, 178-79; on Atlanta Campaign, 192; life in the trenches, 194-95; Kilpatrick's Raid, 198, 200, 201; Lovejoy's Station, 204, 208, 212-14; chasing Hood, 215-16, 218, 219; on Gen. Wilson, 223; Selma-Macon Campaign, 236; assault on Selma, AL, 230-41; at Macon, GA, 249
Burnside, Ambrose E., 28; commanding Department of Ohio, 100; 116, 117
Cairo, Ill.: Grant's headquarters, 44, 50, 161
Calfkiller Creek, TN, 114, 115
Callehan, James: at Shelbyville, 111; cited for gallantry, 144; promoted and brevetted, 228
Camp, Col., CSA (14th Texas): captured, 215
Camp Minty, 95
Camps, military (see Fourth United States Cavalry)
Canfield, Charles W., at Wilson's Creek, 38-40
Carbines (see Cavalry, US, weapons)
Carey, James, 8
Carlisle Barracks, Pa., 33, 36
Carmichael, John: killed in action at Okolona, 156
Carr, Eugene A., 2, 10, 11, 17; arrested by Lyon, 37; released from arrest, 38; at Wilson's Creek, 38-40; cited for conduct and promoted, 43; awarded Medal of Honor, 43
Carter, Lt. (4th Michigan Cavalry): on foraging detail, 83
Casey, Francis, 37
Cassell, George: killed in action at Lovejoy's Station (Nash Farm), 206
Castel, Albert (historian), 229
Casualties: Dug Springs, xvii, 282n25; Wilson's Creek, 43; Fort Donelson, 53-54; Pittsburg Landing (Shiloh), 56-57; Stones River, 74-75; Battle of Franklin (April 10, 1863), 94; (Nov. 30, 1864), 219; Shelbyville, 111; Reed's Bridge, 123; Kilpatrick's Raid, 211; Okolona, 156; Noonday Creek, 177
Catton, Bruce (historian), 17, 21, 30, 35; summarizes aftermath of Gettysburg and Vicksburg, 104

Caughey, Don (historian), xi, xiv,19
Cavalry, US Regulars (see also Fourth United States Cavalry): creation of, 1; pre-war status, 1, 19; organization of regiment, 3; company designations, 3; guidon (company flag), 3; recruiting stations, 4, 33; enlistment, 4; ethnic make-up, 4; uniforms, 4, 9, 11, 22; pre-war training, 5-6, 18, 33-34; Jefferson Barracks, Mo., 4-5; compared to Volunteers, 18; distain for Volunteers, 18, 37-38; strength of 20; sanitary standards, 34; discipline, 24, 36, 60, 62; horses, 21-22; accouterments, 22; reorganization, August 1861, 22; tactics, 23; Carlisle Barracks, 23; Cavalry Bureau, 24; remount depots, 24; weapons: Jaeger carbine, 6; Merrell and Perry, 3; Model 1852 Sharps breech loading carbine, 4; Model 1860 Colt Army revolver, 4; Navy Colt 36-caliber revolver, 1, 4; Sharps carbine, 4; Spencer rifle/carbine, 24, 79; Springfield rifle, 3; U.S. Model 1860 Light cavalry saber, 4, 22; independent operations, 49-50
Cavalry, US Regiments (as renumbered in August 1861): 1st (formerly 1st Dragoons), 1, 3 , 22; 2nd (formerly 2nd Dragoons), 1, 22; 3rd, (formerly Mounted Riflemen), 1, 22; 4th (see Fourth United States Cavalry); 5th (formerly 2nd Cavalry), 1, 13, 16, 22; in Eastern Theater, 89; 6th, 3, 17, 22; 7th, 175
Cavalry, US Volunteers: creation of, 20; 2nd Illinois, 47, 52; at Okolona, 155; 7th Illinois 58; 123rd Illinois: at Flat Shoals, 190; 2nd Indiana 117; 3rd Indiana, 92, 97, 104-05, 107-08, 113, 115, 117; 7th Indiana: at Okolona, 155; 72nd Indiana Mounted, 155; 1st Iowa, 46; 2nd Iowa, 58; 5th Iowa, 105, 107, 133 138; 5th Kentucky, 149; 2nd Michigan, 58; 3rd Michigan 58; 4th Michigan (see Fourth Michigan); 2nd Missouri, 45; 4th Missouri: at Okolona, 156; 2nd New Jersey: at Okolona, 155; charged with cowardice, 157; 1st Ohio, 181, 198, 201, 218, 233; 3rd Ohio, 71; 4th Ohio (Eli Long), 97; 7th Pennsylvania (see Seventh Pennsylvania);1st Middle Tennessee, 92, 107-08; at Shelbyville, 110; 2nd (East) Tennessee, 76, 149, 152, 154; charged with cowardice, 157; 3rd Tennessee, 149; 4th Tennessee, 149; 5th Tennessee: with 1st Brigade, 102, 104, 107
Cavalry Bureau: establishment of, 24
Cavalry Corps (Federal), 23
Cavalry Corps, Military Division of the Mississippi, 218, 245
Chalmers, James R., CSA, 152; in Battle of Nashville, 255-56; 236, 237; at Selma, AL, 238
Chattanooga Rebel (newspaper): reports on Minty ambush, 115
Chattahoochee River, 157, 172, 183, 198

Chattanooga, TN, 106; Bragg retreats to, 112; Confederates Evacuate, 117; Rosecrans' Army retreats to, 127-28; siege of, 130
Chattanooga, Battle of, 139
Chattanooga Campaign, 116
Chicago Board of Trade Battery (see also US Volunteers, Artillery): with 1st Brigade, 102; Rosecrans issues special orders for, 103; battery flag, 103; 113, 119; at Chickamauga, 121-23, 132; at Noonday Creek, 176; at Kennesaw Mountain, 180-83; 188; Kilpatrick's Raid, 198, 200-01, 204-05, 211, 234
Chickamauga, battle of, 29, 67, 116, 120-29
Chickamauga Creek, 119, 120
Chickamauga Station, 125
Chisholm Trail, 16
Church, John R., CSA, 11
Cincinnati Commercial (newspaper), 209, 213-14
Clark, John M.: drowned, 115
Clark, William H.: wounded at Wilson's Creek, 290n116
Cleaves, Freeman, 218
Cleburne, Patrick R., CSA, 203; Cleburne's Division, 213
Clifford, James A., 25
Coats, Albert, xvi; post war career, 254
Cobb, Howell, Jr., CSA, 247, 249, 250
Cody, John: at Lovejoy's Station, 204
Colburn, Albert V., 4, 14, 29; commanding Cos. A and E at Bull Run, 30-31; attached to Staff, Army of the Potomac, 32; death of, 32, 252
Colburn, John: captured, 86
Cole, Commodore P.: killed at Stones River, 75
Cole, Sgt. (4th Michigan): killed in action at Jonesboro, 200
Collins, Pvt., (see Burke, Bartholomew)
Columbia, S.C.: surrender of, 234
Columbia, TN, 215, 219, 221
Columbus Ga.: destruction at, 247
Companies, 4th United States Cavalry: A, B, C, D, E, I - at frontier outposts, 13; A & B at Fort Arbuckle, 10; A and E, 14, 25; assigned to Army of the Potomac, 29; at First Bull Run, 30-31, 32; Burnside's escort, 50, 64; ordered to join regiment, 67; B and C, protecting Springfield; B, C, D, I: with Army of Southwest Missouri, xv; at Fort Leavenworth, 14; results in Missouri, 25, 47; B, C, D: in Missouri, 28; to Freemont at St. Louis, 44; with Pope, 46, 50; ordered to Jefferson City, 50; at Island No. 10 and New Madrid, 54; released by Pope and transferred to Granger, 59; B, C, D, G, K: with Buell's Army of the Ohio, 60; rescuing McCook's ammunition train, 70; B, C, D, G, I, K: Buell's Escort, 84; 98, rescue McCook's ammunition train; B & I-Greenfield,

Mo.; C: at Dug Springs, xv-xvii; C and I at Fort Washita, 10, 14; C, D, E, I: with Army of Southwest Missouri, 35; D and E: at Fort Cobb, 10-11; at Fort Smith; D and I: at Wilson's Creek, 28; expedition to Middleton; F, G, H, K: building Fort Wise, 9-10; F, G, H, K, C: 11; at Fort Wise, 14; F and H: at Fort Wise, 14; at Fort Kearney, 28; at Fort Laramie, 64; rejoin regiment, 67; chasing Morgan, 100-01; G and K: Buell's escorts; Army of the Ohio, 50, 54-55; G, K, I: attached to Granger's command, 57; G, H, A, at Lovejoy's Station; H, guarding artillery; I: at Wilson's Creek, 39; sent to Grant at Cairo, 44,; duty around Paducah, Ky.; report to Grant, 50; at Pittsburgh Landing, 56; L & M: created near Murfreesboro, 50, 63, 75; L: Rosecrans' escort during Stones River Campaign, 68

Confederate Military Units: 1st Alabama Cavalry: standard captured, 98; 12th Alabama Cavalry: defeated at Oostenaula River, 165; 51st Alabama Cavalry, 177; 5th Georgia Infantry: at Noonday Creek, 176; 1st Tennessee Cavalry, 70; 4th Tennessee Cavalry, 81; 23rd Tennessee Infantry: at Reed's Bridge, 123; 8th Texas Cavalry, 112

Conway, Edwin J.: cited and brevetted by Gen. Wilson, 251

Cook, William R., 153

Cooke, Philip St. George, 17

Cooke, Flora (daughter): marries Jeb Stuart, 17

Corduroy roads, 59, 150, 173, 235

Corinth, Miss.: importance of, 54-55, 59; Union occupation of 59; 149

Corse, John M.: commanding Horse Marine expedition, 161-62

Costello, James: wounded at Wilson's Creek, discharged, 290n116

Cotton Indian Creek, Henry Co., GA: Kilpatrick crosses, 212

Cotton Port Ferry, TN, 130-131

Courier lines (see Cavalry, 4th US)

Covington, GA, 183, 185; results of Garrard's raid, 184, 186

Cowan, George, CSA: led attack at Goodwin's farm, 243

Cowerden, Charles: killed in action at Franklin, TN, 94

Cox, Jacob B., 196

Craig, James: comments on condition of Cos. F and H at Fort Laramie, 99

Craven, Patrick: accidentally killed, 106

Crittenden, Eugene W.: commanding Cos. B,C,D, 57; 59; post war career, 254

Crittenden, Thomas L., 68, 113, 117; at Chickamauga, 119-21; withdraws to Chattanooga, 126;

Crook, George, 71; commanding 2nd Cavalry Division, 117, 130; mentioned by Wiswell, 135, 139; 148, 149; criticized in Detroit Advertiser and Tribune, 160;

Croxton, John T., 236

Crump's Landing, TN, 55

Cumberland Mountains, 114, 115, 131, 162

Cummings, James, 33; assigned to Co. D, 44; to Co. C as sergeant, 64

Curry, Will: at Jonesboro, GA, 203

Custer, George A.: at Bull Run, 31, 175

Dallas, GA, 167; Union cavalry in the trenches, 168; Confederates evacuate, 171

Daugherty, David: killed at Boonville, Miss., 59-60

Davenport, Julius: survived massacre at Goodwin's farm, 244

Davidson's Brigade, CSA, 128

Davis, Charles C.: leads charge at Shelbyville, 110-111; awarded Medal of Honor, 110, 228

Davis, Jefferson, CSA 1, 16, 89; replaces Johnston, 187; captured by 4th Michigan Cavalry, 236, 250

Davis, Mrs. (wife), 16, 250; described by Captain Potter, 250

Davis, Jefferson C. (USA), 77

Davis, Wirt: at Guy's Gap, 108; at Shelbyville, 111; at Reed's Bridge, 122; cited for gallantry, 144; at Okolona, 155; cited for gallantry at Okolona, 157; at Noonday Creek, 176; gathering the dead, 176; praised by Minty, 214; cited by Minty, 245; escorting Henry Wirz, 250; promoted and brevetted by Wilson for actions at Selma, 251

Decatur, GA, 138, 183

Dennison, George (military historian): on Wilson's cavalry accomplishments, 249

Department of the Missouri, District of Nebraska, 90

Department of the West, 35

Desertion, 20, 193

Detroit Advertiser & Tribune (newspaper), 160; on Kilpatrick at Cotton Indian Creek, 212-13

Devlin Edward: killed in action at Dug Springs, 283n25

Dibrell, George C., CSA, 67, 116, 144;

Dibrell' Brigade, 113-15, 128, 177

Discipline: under Sturgis, 36; under Buell, 60; in Rosecrans, Army of the Cumberland, 62

Dixon, Samuel C., 194

Dobbs, George W.: killed in action at Selma, AL, 240

Dog tents, 140, 306n47

Dolan, John, 71; honorable mention, 143

Doolittle, Anson O., 64, 294n22

Douglas, Thomas: at Lovejoy's Station, 210

Dougherty, Edward: severely wounded at Dug Springs, discharged, 283n25

Dover, TN, 52, 77

Doyle, Thomas: missing in action, returned, 291n116
Dragoon Detachment of Recruits, 33, 39
Dragoons, 1, 162
Du Bois, John Van Duesen: escorting recruits, 288n15
Dubuque Herald (Iowa newspaper), xv
Duck River, Shelbyville, 110
Dug Springs, Mo., xv; casualties, xvii, 283n25;17, 28, 38
Duke, Basil, CSA, 105
Dyer, Frederick, 252
Eastport, Miss., 229, 231, 233
East Viniard Field (Chickamauga), 124
Egan, James: at Shelbyville, 111; cited for gallantry, 144
Elliott, Washington L.: at Boonville, Miss, 59; commanding cavalry under Thomas, 148; 160, 170, 188, 196
Elliott, William L., 138
Ellis Bridge, Miss., 152
Emancipation Proclamation, 113 Emory, William H., x, 2, 10, 14-16, 29; post war career, 254
Emory, Mrs.(wife), 16
Entrenchments, 178
Etowah River, GA, 165; scouting along, 167, 172; 215-16
Evans, David (historian), xi, 147; describes Spencer carbine, 158; evaluates Wheeler's cavalry, 168; evaluations of Long, Miller and Minty, 171; on Covington raid, 185; Kilpatrick's raid, 211, 214; 244
Evans, James (Negro cook), 92
Farrand, Charles E.: at Wilson's Creek, 38-39; 42, 51
Fay, James: at Lovejoy's Station, 204
Ferguson, Samuel W., CSA, 165, 166, 168, 174
Field hospital, description of, 171-72
Fish, George W. (surgeon, soldier), xi; praises Minty, 76, 170; attends to Pvt. Racine, 98; on pillaging of plantations, 102; on marching in difficult conditions, 113; comments on first day of battle at Chickamauga, 125; at Noonday Creek, 176; gathering the dead, 177; describes difficult terrain for cavalry, 178-79; describes desolation of Northern Georgia, 179; on Kilpatrick's raid, 211; on Gen. James Wilson, 222-23; on Selma-Macon campaign, 235; assault on Selma, AL, 240
Fish, Oliver H., CSA, 11
Fitzgerald, Edward E., 33; attack on Freeman's Battery, 92-94; honorable mention, 144; at Lovejoy's Station, 210; Battle of Nashville, 228; mortally wounded, 228, 252
Fitzhugh Lee, William H., CSA, 18
Flags: company guidon, 3; captured Confederate: 1st Alabama Cavalry, 98; at Shelbyville, 110; at Lovejoy's Station, 210-11; Buford's battle flag, 228

Flanagan, Patrick: wounded at Middleton, 98
Flat Rock (Shoals), GA, 188; skirmish at, 188-90
Fleas and pests: beggar lice, 90, 298n11; jigger, chickor (chiggers),112; Vale, 302n138; described by Burns, 178
Fletcher, Bird L.: attack on Freeman's Battery, 92-94; assigned to Co. H, 99-100; controversial order to Larson, 126-27; 140
Flint River, GA, skirmish at, 140
Foote, Andrew H., 53
Foraging (pillaging/pilfering), 36, 64, 83, 102; 136-37; foraging expedition, 84; around Atlanta, 194; 242; punishable by death, 247
Forrest, Nathan Bedford, CSA, 23; personality of, 50; at Fort Donelson, 52-53, escapes capture, 77; reacts to Federals use of saber, 79; leads attack on Franklin, TN, 92; at Columbia, 106; 109; wounded in brawl, 301n82; 111, 301n124; in Alabama,113; at Reed's Bridge, 123; 124, 128, 129; 147; at Okolona, 149-56; at Fort Pillow, 158; 174, 175; 219; Battle of Nashville, 226-27; 229; 236; defenses at Selma, AL, 237-38; Battle of Selma, 239-41; escapes from Selma, 242; surrenders, 248; mentioned: 24, 47, 66, 77, 102, 104, 111, 112, 114, 116, 119, 120, 125, 126, 134, 137, 221, 222, 232, 234
Forrest, Jeffrey E. (brother), 81, 149, 152; killed in action at Okolona, 156
Fort Donelson, TN, 47, 77; battle of, 52-53
Fort Henry, TN, capture of, 51
Forts: Atkinson, 11; Arbuckle: evacuation of, 14, 15; Bent's, Colorado Terr., 8-9; Cobb, 10-11, 14; evacuated, 15; Gibson: evacuated, 14; Kearney, Neb. Terr., 14; Laramie, Neb. Terr., 14, Cos. F and H, 99; Leavenworth, Kansas Terr., 7, 10, 12, 16, 28; Lyon, Colorado Terr., 9; Pillow, TN, 159; Riley, Kansas Terr., 7-8; Sam Houston, San Antonio, Tx., 252; Smith, Ark., 10, 11, 12, evacuated, 14, 15, 16; Sumter, 38; Washita, Ok. Indian Terr., 10, evacuated, 14, 15, 16; Wise (renamed Lyon), 8-10, regimental headquarters, 14
Fourteenth Army Corps (see Army of the Ohio)
Fourth Michigan Volunteer Cavalry, 74, at Franklin, 92; with 1st Brigade, 102; 104, 107-08; cavalry charge at Shelbyville, 109; 113, 115, 117, 119; at Chickamauga, 121-22; in entrenchments at Chattanooga, 130; posted as infantry, 136; refitted at Nashville with Spencer carbines, 159; in Garrard's 2nd Cavalry Division, 160; save bridge over Oostenaula River, 165; gallant attack near Dallas, GA, 168; overrun enemy breastworks, 173; at Noonday Creek, 176, 219, 233; capture of Jefferson Davis, 336; at Selma, AL, 240, 241

Fourth United States Cavalry: accouterments (see also Cavalry, U.S.), 22; advanced guard duty, 69; bounties, 2, 148; brevet rank, 26; camps, 55, 82; winter, 140-41; captured/surrendered, 101; Sullivan's squadron, 101; Stockton's squadron, 131; McCafferty's squadron, 151, exchanged, 156; McCormick: captured at Jonesboro, 204; exchanged, 211; cavalry charge, 109, 156, 174; casualties, 252-5; companies (see Companies, 4th U.S. Cavalry); courier duties, 68, 148, 157; creation of, 1; daily activities, 24; in the field, 178, 189, Gen. Wilson's escorts, 272; deprivations in the field, 81, 102, 113, 130, 132, 136, 145, 178, 184, 212, 225, 233; desertions, 20, 193; detached service, 2, 25; discharge, 147-48; duties of: pre-war, 1, 20; early war: 20, 24, 32, 63; Western Theater, 62, 66, 82, 84, 180; Eastern Theater, 89; enlisted field commissions, 25, 92, 144, 257-58, 259; enlisted roster, 259-81; enlistments: 4, 13, 33; in the field, 3, 63; entrenchments/earthworks/breastworks, 17, 32, 109, 168, 178-79, 193-94, 226; evacuating Texas and the frontier, 16; expeditions and skirmishes, 84; First Brigade, Second Cavalry Division, 26, 76; foraging, 83, 84; full compliment, 12 companies, 26; frontier duty, 12-14; functions of, 84, 131-32; health/hygiene, 18, 33, 174; horses/mounts (see also Horses), 21-22, gait (speed) of, 21; suffering of, 179-80; procurement, 222; fitting out (farriers), 233; horse marines, 161-62; in the field, 82-83, 178-79; Indians, 10-11, 13, 14, 15; infantry duty (trenches), 168, 193; light marching orders, 66, 76, 116, 145, 179, 235; The Little Regiment, 220, 228; marching, 21; forced, 113, 132, 163-64, 179, 199, 228; meals/rations, 128, 135, 181; Minty's Saber Brigade, 143; officers, 64, 255, 256, 257; civilian appointments, 19; Okolona, 152-156; organization of regiment, 3; pre-war duties/experience, 7, 11, 18, 19; prisoners: 101, 131, 211; at Andersonville, 178; provost guard duty, 32; raids, 24, 95; recruiting stations: St. Louis, Mo., 4; New York, 33; recruits, 19; at Wilson's Creek, 36, 39-40; reenlistment, 192; refitting, 160; regimental headquarters, 7, 8, 14, 28; resignations, 1, 11, 12, 13, 15, 17; roster of enlisted men, 259-81; scouting expeditions 132; retrograde movement, 154; sabers, 4, 6, 45, 78-80; Spencer carbine, 147, 153, 154, 157-58, 159; underwater, 182; strength of regiment: regulation, 3; average, 67; in the field: 97, 104, 118, 159, 161, 216, 221; sub-cooks (Negroes in service), 91-92; Gumbo: 102, 128, 129; Soap: 90-91; surrendering Texas and the frontier, 15-16; tactics, 23-25; training: pre-war, 5-6, 18-19, 25 in the field, 33-34, 50; training Volunteer cavalry, 2, 25, 64; tents/shelter: Sibley, 8; dog tent, 140, 306n47; uniforms/clothing: 4, 9, 22; in the field, 81, 179; use of: early war years, 20, 63; vedette duty, 20, 84, 131; West Point Battle Monument, 92, 282; weapons (see Cavalry, U.S.

Franklin, TN, battle of (April 10, 1863), 26, 67;

Franklin-Nashville Campaign, 218

Fredericksburg, Va., battle of, 64

Freeman, Samuel L., CSA, 81; killed by 1st Sgt. Strickland, 93;

Freeman's Battery: attacked, 92-93

Fremont, John C., 25, 28, praises Sturgis, 43; relieved of command, 50

Frey, John: severely wounded at Dug Springs, discharged, 283n25

Gaffney, Daniel: wounded at Middleton, 98

Galbraith, Robert: commanding 1st Middle Tennessee Cavalry, 107-08; at Shelbyville, 110

Garesché, Julius P.: killed at Stones River, 69

Garfield, James A., 122

Garrard, Kenner D.: commanding 2nd Cavalry Division, 160, 163; 165, 168; Sherman's opinion of; 173; at Noonday Creek, 175; 2nd Cavalry Division, 181, 183; surrounded at Flat Shoals, 189; 224; mentioned: 186, 196, 215, 216, 217

Georgia: ravaged by war, 179

Georgia Militia (CSA), 214

Gibbons, John Austin: killed at Dug Springs, xvii

Giesboro Depot, DC., remount depot for armies in the east, 24

Gilmore, Patrick: wounded at Wilson's Creek, 290n116

Gillem's Bridge (spanning Etowah River), 167

Glore, Capt. (5th Kentucky Cavalry), 153

Glynn, William H.: killed at Stones River, 75

Goddard, Calvin, 72

Goodwin's farm massacre, 243-45

Gordon, Henry, 46-47, 59

Grand Traverse Herald (Traverse City, Michigan newspaper), 44-45

Granger, Gordon, 33, 50; assigned to command of cavalry, 57; Brevet Colonel, 2nd Michigan Volunteer Cavalry, 75-76; reports on destruction of Freeman's Battery, 94; 106, 108, 111, 121

Granger's Reserve Corps, 112, 125

Grant, Ulysses S.: at Cairo, Ill., 44; at Fort Donelson, 52-53; at Pittsburgh Landing (Shiloh), 55; promoted to Brigadier General, 57-58; occupies Jackson, Miss., 103; siege of Vicksburg, 103; promoted to command of the West,131; promoted to Lieutenant General, 147, 231; mentioned, 62, 66, 104, 139, 188

Gravelly Springs, AL, winter quarters, 223; 232, 233, 235

Gray, Horace: commanding 4th Michigan Cavalry, 113; 131, 139

Gregg, David McM., 18
Griddle, John: drowned, 217
Grierson, Benjamin, 67; at Vicksburg, 103; on Meridian Expedition, 150,152, 155
Griffin, Charles (Griffin's Battery): at Bull Run, 31
Griffin, Trumbull D.: commanding section of Chicago Board of Trade Battery, 113; at Chickamauga, 121-22; at Noonday Creek, 176;
Griffin, William: drowned, 214
Grigsby House, 218, 233
Grundig, Augustus: wounded at Wilson's Creek, discharged, 290n116
Gum or Gumbo (Negro cook), 102, 128, 129
Guerrilla warfare: Morgan's guerillas, 90; Larson describes, 101; 113, 137, 218, 221, 233, 248
Gunther, Sebastian: cited and brevetted by Gen. Wilson, 251
Guidon (see Flags)
Gunboats, 54
Guy's Gap, TN: map, 65 ; Federal cavalry captures, 106-08
Haefling, Christian, 71; honorable mention, 143
Halleck, Henry W., 32, 46, 50, 51, 55, 62, 67, 70; denies Minty's promotion, 111; 234
Hamberg, TN: Granger's Division organized at, 57
Hampton, Wade, CSA, 234
Hannon, Moses W. (Hannon's Brigade), 177
Hardee, William J., CSA, 1, 69, 106
Harner, John: at Lovejoy's Station, 204
Harper's Weekly (magazine), xvi, xvii, 45
Harrison's Brigade, CSA, 216
Harrison Landing, Va., 33
Harpeth River, TN (see also West Harpeth), 92, 219
Harper's Ferry, 12
Harper's Weekly (magazine), 45
Hastings, Warren: wounded at Pittsburg Landing, 293n29
Hatch, Edward, 227
Hazen, William B., 117
Healy, Thomas: commanding Co. D in Mississippi, 57; 71, 92; mortally wounded at Franklin, 94; honorable mention, 143;
Hedges, Joseph B.: attack on Freeman's Battery, 92-94; brevetted, 144; at Jonestown, 202, 204; Lovejoy's Station, 206; replaces McIntyre, 220; 221, 222, 223, 224; West Harpeth River, 227-28; Medal of Honor, 228
Heintzelman, Samuel P., 28, 31
Heintzelman's Division, 28, 30
Henry, Robert Selph (historian), 243
Henshaw, Ambrose, 253
Hensinger, Frederick: killed in action at Franklin, 94
Hepburn, William P.: commanding Sooy Smith's 2nd Brigade, 150

Herberich, John M., x, xii, xiv, 4, 10; captured and exchanged, 44-45; wounded, 53, 292n29; 177; courting at Macon, GA; promoted to 1st sergeant at Gravelly Springs, 318n11; 250, 251; post war, 254
Herdkorn, John, 299n130
Herr, John K. (soldier, historian), describes N.B. Forrest, 23
Higgens, Daniel, stabbed to death at Macon, GA, 250
Hodge's Division, CSA, 133
Hood, John Bell, CSA, 186, 187, 211; passim, 215-221; 223, 225, 229, 232, 233, 234
Hooker, Joseph, 23, 29, 89, 139
Hoover's Gap, TN: map, 65; 106-07
Horses, 21-22: acquisition of, 138; deprivations of 165, 172, 179-80 suffering of, 112, 115, 136, 167, 170, 176, 179, 188, 217; shortages of, 115; loss of mount, 22, 167
Horse Marines, 161-62, 309n56
Howland, Horace N., 241
Hunter, David: at Bull Run, 30-31
Huntsville, AL: occupied by Buell, 60; Crook occupies, 140, 148
Huntt, George G.: at Fort Laramie with Cos. F and H; commands 4th US Cavalry at Macon, GA, 251-52; post war career, 254
Indian Tribes: Caddo, 10; Cheyenne, 7; Chickasaw, 10; Choctaw, 10, 13; Comanche, 10-11; Kiowa, 10-11; Seminole, 1; Wichita, 10; Yakama, 85
Infantry, US: 1st, 16; 2nd, xv, 36; 3rd: escapes Texas; 4th: Sheridan, 8th: captured in Texas, later exchanged, 14; 11th, 51; 16th, 31; 18th, 51; 138 US Colored, 25
Ingerton, William H.: attack on Freeman's battery, 92; at Shelbyville, 111; at Okolona, 144; cited for actions at Okolona, 154
Infantry, USV: 98th Illinois Mounted, 183, 184; 17th Indiana Mounted 181, 184; 72nd Indiana Mounted, 149; at Okolona, 155; at Dallas, GA, 168; 1st Iowa 46; 5th Iowa, 46; 10th Ohio, 70, 72, 90; 59th Ohio, 124; 1st Tennessee, 73; 23rd Tennessee, 123;
Ingraham, Edward, CSA, 11
Island No. 10, Miss., 54, 161
Ivey's Hill Farm: skirmish with Forrest, 156
Jackson, Andrew, Jr., 11
Jackson, Claiborne (Missouri governor), 35
Jackson, Thomas J. "Stonewall," CSA: mortally wounded, 103
Jackson, William H., CSA (Jackson's Division), 165
Jacobs, Charles: wounded at Dug Springs, discharged, 283n25
Jefferson Barracks, Mo., 1, 4, 6
Jennings, William H., 77, 198; commanding Saber Brigade, 215; 216

Johnson, Bushrod R., CSA (Johnson's Division), 70, at Chickamauga, 120-24

Johnson, John (Negro sub-cook), 9

Johnston, Albert Sidney, CSA: at Pittsburgh Landing (Shiloh), 56; killed in combat, 56

Johnston, Joseph E., C.S.A.: Lieutenant Colonel, 1st US Cavalry, 1; General, CSA, at Bull Run, 31; 166; at Dallas, GA, 168; 170; throwing up entrenchments, 178; at Kennesaw Mountain, 180; retreats through Marietta, GA, 181; relieved of command, 187

Jones, Presley, 184

Jonesboro, GA, 201; destruction of, 201-202

Kargé, Joseph, 155

Kauffman, Albert B.: at Pittsburgh Landing (Shiloh), 56; praised by Gen. Lew Wallace, 57, 293n32; declines appointment to 1st Colored Volunteers, 91, 298n22

Kelley, Jackson (Negro cook, soldier), 91-92, 298n26

Kelly, Michael J., xvi, 46, 57, 71; honorable mention,143; appointed chief of couriers 148;

Kennesaw Mountain., GA, 173, 174, 180

Kennett, John, 70, compliments Otis, 73

Kerner, Henry, 252

Kentucky Campaign: Bragg invades, 61

Ketron, Sam, 299n130

Kilpatrick, Hugh Judson, 196; replaces Lowe, 160; strikes at West Point railroad, 196; Kilpatrick's raid, 198, 313n13; 205-06, 210, 211-12; 214, praises Minty and recommends promotion, 214; 217

Kimble, Lorenzo A.: wounded at Franklin, TN, discharged, 299n58

Kingston, GA, 165, 167

Kline, Frederick: killed at Dug Springs, xvii

Kline, Robert, 105; commanding 3rd Indiana Cavalry, 113, 139;

Knipe, Joseph F.: at West Harpeth River, 227

Knox, Thomas (reporter, Herald), xv

La Fayette, GA: Bragg consolidates forces 117; 164

LaGrange, TN, 140, 150

Lambert, Michael H.: captured and exchanged, 44-45

Lamadue (French Lt.), 140

Larson, James, x, 2, 4, 9; passim, 5-10; 12; a defecting officer, 13, 285n7;14, 29; on light marching orders, 76; on sabers, 79-80; on continuous cavalry activities between Stones River and Chickamauga campaigns, 82-83; Cos. F and H journey from Ft. Laramie to Omaha and St. Louis, 99; injured by horse, 99-100; describes capture of Lt. Sullivan's patrol at Bardstown, Ky., 101; on Rosecrans, 102; marching in continuous rain, 113; 114; describes Rosecrans' advance across Tennessee River, 117; describes a breakfast in the field, 120; at Chickamuga, 121; Reed's Bridge, 121; cavalry support of reserve artillery, 125; orders from Lt. Fletcher at Chickamauga, 126; describes sounds of battle, 126; lost at Chickamauga, 127; Federal defeat at Chickamauga, 128; retreating to Chattanooga, 128-29; camp at Chattanooga, 129, 130; a daring escape, 131; chasing Wheeler, 132-34, at Maysville, AL, 136; foraging, 136-37; continual use of cavalry, 139; Love's Plantation, 140; Flint River, 140; marching from Maysville to Huntsville, 140; winter quarters in Huntsville, 140; on Sooy Smith's failed campaign, 149-50, 151; cavalry maneuvers at Okolona, 153-55; summarizes events at Okolona, 157; evaluates Spencer carbine, 157; describes action around Rome, GA, 166; destruction of railroads, 166; cavalry acting as infantry in the trenches, 168-69; occupation of Dallas, GA, 171; on medical treatment, 171-72; overrunning enemy breastworks, 173; at Noonday Creek, 175; on the dead at Noonday Creek, 177; on cavalry movements after Noonday Creek, 178; on starving horses, 179-80; guarding a battery, 180; 189; on re-enlistment policy, 192; taking leave, 192-93; returns from leave, 217; The *Little Regiment*, 220; bodyguards for Gen. Wilson, 220, 222; camp at Nashville, 223; *passim*: 224-229; winter camp at Gravelly Springs, 232; Selma-Macon campaign, 231, 236, 238; assault on Selma, AL, 239-41; aftermath of Selma, 242; massacre at Goodwin's farm, 243-44; on destruction at Selma, 245-46; war ends, 249; Macon, GA, 249-50; on bookkeeping, 251; leaving the theater of war, 252; post war, 254

Lauby, Otto: new recruit, 99, 300n130; captured, died at Andersonville prison, 178

La Vergne (Lavergne), TN, 68

Lawrenceville, GA, 185

Lawton, George W.: with the Horse Marines, 161

Lee, John, 72; honorable mention, 143; cited and brevetted by Gen. Wilson, 251

Lee, Robert E., CSA: appointed Colonel, 1st US Cavalry, 1; resigned commission, 15; 28, Antietam Campaign, 62; reports on Federal cavalry movements, 89; 103, 148, 231; surrender of, 247-48

Lee, Stephen D., CSA, 138, 151

Lemmon, John, 188; in the trenches, 193

Lewis, Philander B., 247

L'Hommedieu, Tillinghast, 68-69; death of, 71, 295n58, 252

Liberty, TN: expedition to, 90-91; results of, 90-91

Liberty Gap: map, 66; 106

Lightening Brigade, The, 88

Light marching orders (see Fourth United States Cavalry)

Lincoln, Abraham, 2, 14; appoints McClellan to build an army; 32; removes McClellan, 64, 104, 148, 218, 220, assassination, 249
Lithonia, GA, 188, 190, 191
Little Regiment, The, 220, 228
Lomax, Lunsford L. (CSA), 11
Long, Eli: promoted to colonel, USV, 71; brigadier general, USV, 71; wounded, 75; at Middleton, 97; commanding 2nd Brigade, 131-32, 133; promoted to colonel, commanding 4th Ohio Volunteer Cavalry, 142; commanding 2nd Cavalry Brigade, 160, 161; Starr and Evans evaluate, 170-71; 172, 188, 189, 196, 198; Lovejoy's Station, 204, 206, 208, 211, 212; chasing Hood, 216; commanding 2nd Division, 218, 233, 234
Longacre, Edward (historian), 66; on use of sabers, 78, 80; describes experiences of a cavalrymen, 84; describes cavalry raid, 95; 231, 238; writes on Wilson's cavalry expedition, 248
Longstreet, James, 29, 118; surges through Union lines at Chickamauga, 125, 134
Lookout Mountain, GA: map, 118; 122, 163
Louby, Otto (see Lauby),
Louisville, Ky.: occupied by Union army, 61; major federal supply center, 61, 217; procuring horses, 222
Lovejoy's Station, 204; battle of, 204-11
Love's Plantation, 140
Lowe, William W.: commands 1st Brigade in Minty's absence, 133, 148; on foraging, 136; 138; commanding 3rd Cavalry Division, 160
Lyon, Nathaniel, xv-xvi, 9, 12; commanding Army of the West, 37-38; recovers at McCulla's farm; withdraws to Springfield, 38, attacks at Wilson's Creek, 38-41; mortally wounded, 41

Macon, GA, capture of, 247
Magee, Ben, 190
Magruder, Henry C., CSA, 218
Manck, Clarence, 57; commanding Co. I, 71; brevetted captain, 71, 295n55; honorable mention, 143; wounded, 216
March, Randolph, 10
Marietta, GA, 173, 181, 215
Market, Valentine, 253
Marshall, Cato (Negro sub-cook), 92
Marshall, George C., Sr., 45, 291n137
Martin, Alexander, 37
Martin, William T., CSA (Martin's Division), 109, 133, 173, 174; at Noonday Creek, 177; 203, 214
Maysville, AL, 136, 140
McAfee's Bridge (over Chattahoochee River), 183
McAlpine, James, 71; honorable mention, 143

McArthur, John, 225
McCafferty, Neil J.: attack on Freeman's Battery, 92-94; cavalry charge at Shelbyville, 110-111; cited for gallantry, 144; on Meridian Expedition, 151; captured, 151, 156
McCann, Dick, CSA, 70; captured and escapes, 96
McClellan, George B., 1, 2, 10, 24, 28, 29; Lincoln appoints, 32; 33, 35, 43, 62, replaced by Burnside, 64; on use of sabers, 78; 103, 220, 221
McClellan saddle, 2
McClellan, Henry B., CSA (soldier, historian): comments on Federal Cavalry, 66, 162
McClernand, John A.: arranges prisoner exchange, 44; at Fort Donelson, 51; 52-53, 56, 58
McCook, Alexander McD., at Stones River, 68; ammunition train attacked, 70; McCook's Corps at Guy's Gap, 107; attacking Western & Atlantic Railroad, 116-117; Chattanooga Campaign, 117; withdraws to Chattanooga, 126; on starving horses, 188, 191, 212
McCook, Edward M., 50; praised by Buell, 57; commanding 2nd Indiana Cavalry, 117, 138; commanding 1st Cavalry Division, 138; defeated at Brown's Mill, 188
McCook's Division, 191; 192, 196, 199, 217
McCormick, Jacob: wounded at Franklin, TN, discharged, 299n58
McCormick, Thomas H., 30; attack on Freeman's Battery, 91-94; at McMinnville, 96; at Reed's Bridge, 122; at Cotton Port Ferry, 131; commanding 2nd Battalion at Okolona, 153; captured at Jonesboro, 204; prisoner exchange, 211
McCormick, Charles C.: wounded at Selma, AL, 240
McCormick, Robert: murdered by guerillas, 233
McCrillis, LaFayette: commanding Sooy Smith's 3rd Brigade, 152, 153, 155, 157
McCulloch, Ben, CSA, 12, 13, 38, 41; killed in action at Pea Ridge, Ark., 43
McCulloch's Brigade: at Okolona, 151
McDonell, Daniel, Co. D: killed at Stones River, 75
McDowell, Irvin, 30
McGorran Patrick: finds trooper hanging from tree, 102
McIlvanie, John: wounded at Dug Springs, 283n25
McIntosh, James McQueen., CSA: at Dug Springs, xvi; Captain, 1st US Cavalry, resigns 17, 40-41; killed at Pea Ridge, Ark., 43
McIntosh, John B. (brother), 17
McIntyre, James B., 10, 11, 30; provost guard duty, Washington, D.C., 32; 50, 67; escorts for Gen. Burnside, 89; assumes command of regiment, 90; 91, 92, attacks Freeman's Battery, 92-94; brevetted

major, 94; on leave, 96; at Middleton, 97; at Guy's Gap, 107-09; at Shelbyville, 110-111; 113, 114, 117; reports to Gen. Crittenden, 118; at Reed's Bridge, 122; at Rossville and Ringgold, 128; 127, 135, 139; cited by Rosecrans, 144; on leave, 148; commanding 4th US Cavalry, 160; 171; at Dallas, GA, 171; cited by McPherson for meritorious conduct, 174; 198; Kilpatrick's raid, 200, 202; Lovejoy's Station, 204, 205, 206, 209-10; praised by Minty, 214; takes leave of regiment, 220; untimely death, 220; 254

McLaughlin, Napoleon B., post war career, 254, 318n11

McLemore's Cove, 119-120

McMannus, John W.: wounded, at Wilson's Creek, discharged, 290n116

McMaster, Charles: commissioned 2nd Lieutenant, 71; at Shelbyville, 111; cited for gallantry, 144; mortally wounded at Battle of Front Royal, Va.

McMinnville, TN, 96, 114, 115; destruction at, 131-32

McNairy, Frank N., CSA, 221

McPherson, James B., 160, 165; marches into Kingston, GA, 167; praises Minty's Brigade, 168; 172, 173, 180, 181, 187, 196

McTeer, William H., on reaction to sharpened sabers, 80-81, 297n48; tribute to 4th US Cavalry, 145; on Smith's failed Meridian Expedition, 150, 152, 153

McWilliams, Joseph, wounded at Pittsburg Landing, 293n29

Meade, George: replaces Hooker, 104, 188

Medal of Honor, 111; Recipients: Charles C. Davis, 7th Pa. Cav., at Shelbyville, 111; Joseph B. Hedges, 4th US Cav., at West Harpeth River, 329; Eugene B. Beaumont, 4th US Cav., at West Harpeth River, 329; David S. Stanley, 4th US Cav., at Battle of Franklin (Nov. 30, 1864), 363

Medical care: at Fort Donelson, 54; at Dallas, GA, 171; Larson's observations, 171-72; described by Dr. Burns, 172

Memphis Appeal (newspaper): article on Battle at Noonday Creek, 177

Memphis-Atlanta Appeal (newspaper), 213

Memphis, TN, 158, 161

Meridian, Miss., 149, 150

Meridian Campaign, 149-50

Meridian Expedition (Gen. Sooy Smith), 150-57

Merrill, Lewis, (Merrill's Horse Cavalry), 44

Middle Tennessee: map, 65; 66, 104 Middle Tennessee Campaign (see Tullahoma Campaign).

Middleton, TN, 77; expedition to, 96-97; 107, 116

Military Division of the Mississippi, 217-18

Miller Abram O.: commanding 3rd Cavalry Brigade, 162; evaluated by David Evans, 171, 188, 190, 215; commanding Wilder's Brigade, 234; at Salem, AL, 239-40

Miller, Jacob: wounded at Dug Springs, 283n25

Miller, John: captures standard of 1st Alabama Cavalry, 98

Mills: Beards, 105-06; Bibbs Roller Mill, AL, destroyed, 236; Central Roller Mill, AL, destroyed, 139; Copper Rolling Mill, destroyed, 139; Gordon's, 119, 124; Hughes, 92; Ivy's, 182; Lebanon, 183; Lee and Gordon's, 120; McDonald's, 117; Mission, 129, 125; Peeler's, 119; Sperry's, 115; Walker's, 112; Walter's, 105; Red Mountain Ironworks, 236

Minty, Robert H. G., xi, 4, 26, 63; Rodenbough comments on, 66-67; 68; early years, 75-76; on use of saber, 79-80; orders sabers sharpened, 79; attitude on foraging, 83; commanding 2nd Michigan Calvary, 85; complimented by Sheridan, 87; evaluated by Starr, 87; praised by Rosecrans, 87; praised by Lt. Potter, 87; soldier's affection for, 88; recommended for promotion by Stanley and Rosecrans, 88; absent at Franklin due to illness, 94; at Middleton, 97; on capture of 1st Alabama Cavalry standard, 98; commands 1st Brigade in Turchin's Division, 104, 117; orders to scout on Middleton and Eaglesville Pike, 105; the cavalry charge at Shelbyville, 109-10; ambushed, 115; arrest of, 117, 133; court martial of, 106, 159; at Reed's Bridge, 119-123; at Rossville, 128; at Chickamauga, 119-129; ordered to cross Tennessee River, 130; evaluated by Starr and Evans, 170-71; 183, 184, 188; opinion of Stoneman, 191; 195; Kilpatrick's raid, 200-201; Lovejoy's Station, 205-06, 208, 210-12, 214; praised by Kilpatrick, 214, 316n223; praises McIntyre, 214; takes first leave, 215; commanding Wilson's 2nd Brigade, 218; finding horses, 222; on James Wilson, 223; at Gravelly Springs, 233; 235, 236; on fortifications at Selma, 238; assault on Selma, 239-41; evaluates Gen. Wilson, 245; at Macon, GA, 247-48; issuing paroles, 251

Minty's Brigade (see also Saber Brigade), 23, 73, 76; activities of, 95, designated Saber Brigade, 88; 131; 107-08, at Bellbuckle Gap, 112; marching into Alabama, 113; occupies Chattanooga, 130; at Reed's Bridge, 144; 145; march from Columbia, TN, to join Sherman's Army, 160, 163; saving Gilliam's Bridge, 167; praised by McPherson, 168, 172; evaluated by Evans, 171; 206; overrunning enemy breastworks, 173; at Noonday Creek, 175; 180, 181-82, 188; at Jonesboro, 203; Lovejoy's Station, 200-06, 212-13; chasing Hood, 216; heavy cost of Atlanta Campaign, 216; disbanding, 217; mentioned: 96, 114, 115, 116, 117, 120, 128, 138

Missouri, 28; importance of, 34-35

Missouri State Guard (Confederate), 36, 39

Missouri State Militia, xv
Mitchell, Robert B.: comments on Minty and his brigade, 111
Mitchell's Division, 111-112; 117
Mix, Frank, 105; commanding 4th Michigan Cavalry, 107; opinion of Minty, 198, on McIntyre, 198; on Regulars, 198; Kilpatrick's raid, 198, 208, 210
Montgomery, AL, 231; surrender of, 246
Morgan, John Hunt, CSA, 62, 96; raiding through Kentucky, 99; Cos. F and H at Bardstown, Kentucky 100-101; at Alexandria, 105; 114, 133; mentioned: 66, 70, 84, 105, 137, 168
Mounted Rifle Recruits, 39
Mounted Riflemen, 1
Mosby, John, CSA, 100
Murfreesboro, TN: Bragg's army at; 68
Murphy, Martin J., 71; killed in action, 119; honorable mention, 143
Murray, Douglas A., 64, 294n22
Murray, Eli H., 63; Kilpatrick's raid, 198
Mussel Shoals, AL, 131, 133
Nash Farm, GA (Lovejoy's Station), 206; cavalry charge, 208-210
Nashville, TN: Federal remount and supply center, 24; early importance of, 51; Grant moves toward, 54; Vale describes, 54; headquarters for Rosecrans' Army of the Cumberland, 61; 62, 68, 117, 158; 4th US Cavalry refitted, 159; Union center of operations, 219
Nashville Campaign, 223-228; summary of, 229
Nashville Daily Union (newspaper): report on massacre at Goodwin's farm, 244
Nashville, TN, 217, battle of, 223-228
Negroes: as contraband, 91, 297n16, 297n18; Emancipation Proclamation, 91, 113; treatment of, 91; Larson comments on, 91; recruitment of, 91; in service, 91-92, 102, 200; Minty's attitude toward, 91; in Alabama, 113, soldiers attitude toward, 185-86; as sub-cooks, 91-92;
New Madrid, Mo., 54
New York Herald (newspaper), xv
New York Times (newspaper), xv
Newby, Edward W. B., 8, 14; commanding Co. H at Fort Laramie, 99
Newell, Nathaniel M., 77, with 1st Ohio Artillery, 85, 105; commanding Battery D, 107
Newlin, Cyrus: at Noonday Creek, 176-77
Newton, John: division of infantry, 182
Nobel, Silas: at Fort Donelson, 52
Noonday Creek, GA, 173; battle of, 175-76, 180
North Carolina, 139
Oakes, James: commanding Buell's escorts, Cos. G and K, 55, 293n2; praised by Buell, 57; post war career, 254

O'Connell, William: commanding Cos. D and I at Middleton, 97; requests credit for capture of standard, 98; skirmish at Lebanon, 105; injured at Shelbyville, 111; cited by Stanley, 144; cited by Wilson, 228; leads cavalry charge at Selma, AL, 241; promoted and brevetted for actions at Selma, 251
Oglesby, Richard J.: at Fort Donelson, 51; 53
Oklahoma Indian Territory, 2, 10, 12, 15
Okolona, Miss, 110, 114, 149; battle of, 152-156
Oostenaula River, 165, 166, 216
Orange, James: killed in combat, 86
Orr, Archibald B.: killed in combat, 86
Otis, Elmer, 50; chief of couriers, 63; praised by Rosecrans, 67; 68; on performance of the 4th Cavalry, 69-70; praised by Stanley, 71; 72-74; destroyed mill, 76; sick leave, 90, 94; reports to Minty, 94; temporarily replaces McIntyre, 96; at Middleton, 97; praises Lt. O'Connell, 97; cited by Rosecrans, 143; recommended for promotion, 143; 144; post war career
Owens, Edward: captures artillery at Middleton, 97-98
Paducah, Ky., 44
Palmer, Innis, 30-31
Palmer, John M., 124
Park, Josiah B.: dislike of sabers, 80; honors Minty, 88
Parker, B., 300n30
Parkhurst, Henry C., 33
Parrott guns, 190
Patrick, Matthewson T.: commanding 5th Iowa Cavalry, 139
Pea Ridge, Ark., battle of, 43, 47
Pea Vine Creek, GA, 119, 121
Pea Vine Ridge, GA, 119; battle of, 121-22
Peachtree Creek, GA, 187, 193
Pegram, John, CSA, 119
Pegram's Division, 128
Peninsular Campaign, 32
Perciville, Richard J.: accidentally killed in horserace, 250
Perryville, Ky.: battle of, 61; summary of battle, 61-62
Pests (see Fleas)
Peters, William: at Wilson's Creek, 291n116; killed in action near Farmington, Miss., 59,
Pettitt, Levi: killed in action at Okolona, 156
Pierce, Franklin, 1
Pikeville, TN, 114, 115
Pillaging/pilfering (see Foraging)
Pillow, Gideon J., CSA, 44; at Fort Donelson, 53
Pinney, Oscar, 69
Pitt's Crossroads, 132
Pittsburg Landing (Shiloh), TN, 51; armies arrive at, 55; description of, 55
Pleasonton, Alfred, 18
Plummer, Joseph (Plummer's Battalion of Regulars),

38; at Wilson's Creek, 39; wounded, 39-41; driven from field, 41
Polk, Leonidas, 44; arranges prisoner exchange, 51; 106; at Chickamauga, 119-20; 149
Pope, John C., 46, 59; commands Army of Virginia, 66; 85
Port Tobacco, Md.: Cos. A and E, 89
Porter, Andrew: at Bull Run, 31; 32
Porthouse, Thomas: wounded at Wilson's Creek, discharged, 291n116
Potter, Henry Albert, xi, xiv; on foraging/pillaging, 83, 106, 136; praising Minty, 88; at Reed's Bridge, 121-22; 133; on chasing Wheeler, 136; expedition to Whitesburg and Decatur, 139; writes of eleven-mile march over Taylor's Ridge, 164; guarding Allatoona Pass, 172; in Marietta, GA, 181; on waterproof Spencer, 182; on Covington raid, 187; death of McPherson, 187; 189; in the trenches, 193; writing from Atlanta, 194; Kilpatrick's raid, 201-03, 205, 208-10, 212; 202; procuring horses, 222; 232-33; on Jefferson and Mrs. Davis, 250; on Howell Cobb, 250
Powell, James: promotion to 2nd lieutenant, 18th US Infantry, 51; commanding Co. I, Fort Donelson, 52; at Pittsburgh Landing (Shiloh), 56-57
Powell, James E., (1st US Infantry), 16
Preas, Henry J.: executed by Forrest's rebels, 243
Price, Sterling, CSA, 36, 39, 45
Prisons, Union: Camp Chase, Oh., 175; Johnson Island, Oh., 175; Confederate: Andersonville, GA, 178, 211, 247; Cahaba, AL, 211; Danville, Va., 211; Libby, Richmond, Va., 206
Pulaski, TN, 142, 228-29; 4th US Cavalry arrives by train, 168, 218, 229
Putman, Albert T.: wounded at Wilson's Creek, discharged, 291n116
Quartermaster Department (Federal): job of procuring horses, 22
Quartermaster Division: Wiswell assigned to, 134, 136
Racine, Edward: wounded, 98
Railroads: map, 58, 65; importance of, (supply lines), 23; destruction at McMinnville, TN. 96; at Rome, GA, 166; 183, 186; confederates rapid repair of, 188; at Jonesboro, 202; Atlanta and Augusta: destruction of, 183, 309n28; Atlanta and West Point: damaged, 200; Charleston and Memphis, 136, 186; Georgia: destruction of, 186; Georgia Central, 165; Louisville and Nashville, 61; Macon Rail Road: 187, 196; Kilpatrick attacks, 201-02; Memphis and Charleston, 58, 138; damaged, 59; 61; Mobile and Ohio, 150, 151; Montgomery and Atlanta: damaged, 200; Montgomery and Macon, 188; Nashville and Decatur, 92, 215, 219; Nashville and Northwestern, 221; at Selma, AL, 246; at Columbus, GA, 247; Rome and Kingston, 165; Virginia Central: attacked by Stoneman, 103; West Point RR: attacked by Kilpatrick, 196; Western and Atlantic: attacks on, 116; at Selma, AL, 246; at Columbus, GA, 247
Rains, James S., C.S.A, xv
Rankin, John: at Shelbyville, 111; cited for gallantry, 144
Ransom, Robert, Jr., 8
Ransom, Mrs. Robert (wife), 8
Ray, John (farmer), 39
Rea, John P., 201
Rebel yell: at Bull Run, 31; 79
Recruiting office, US Cavalry: St. Louis, Mo., 4; Albany, NY., 33
Red River Campaign, 162
Reed's Bridge, Chickamauga, TN, 119, 120 battle at, 26, 67, 120-23
Remount depots, 22; Giesboro, 24; St. Louis, 24; Nashville, 117
Rendlebock, Joseph: field commission, 68; at Stewart's Creek, 72-73; cited by Otis, 73; attack on Freeman's Battery, 81; 86; cited by Minty, 87; 91-94; at Middleton, 98; at Buy's Gap, 108; at Shelbyville, 111; at Chickamauga, 119-120; honorable mention, 143-44; brevetted, 144; cited by Stanley, 144; cited by Gen. Wilson, 228; at Selma, Ala, 239, 245; promoted and brevetted for Selma, 251
Reynolds, Daniel, H., CSA, 204
Reynolds, Joseph J., 95, 204
Rhodes, Charles, (historian), 67
Rhyman, Frederick, Co. I: mortally wounded at Pittsburg Landing, 57
Richmond, Va., 32, 148
Richmond, Joseph B, Co. K: killed in action at Stones River, 75
Ricketts, James B. (Ricketts' Battery): at Bull Run, 31
Riddick, Richard H., CSA, 11
Riggin, Sylvester: captures 1st Alabama Cavalry standard, 98
Riker, John: at Shelbyville, 111; cited for gallantry, 144
Ringgold, GA, 119, 125
Robertson, Felix H., 247
Robertson, Jerome B., CSA, 247-48
Robertson, William Glenn (historian): writing of Minty's Brigade at Chickamauga, 119
Robinson, Capt., CSA: captured, 138
Robinson, George I.: commanding Chicago Board of Trade Battery, 139; Kilpatrick's raid, 198-99
Roddey, Philip D., CSA: siege of Chattanooga, 130; 138, 236; at Selma, AL, 236
Rodenbough, Theophilus (historian), 66
Rolla, Mo., 42; Union forces retreat to, 44

Rome, GA, 165, 166; importance of, 215
Rose, John C.: at Lovejoy's Station, 209
Rosecrans, William S.: creates Cavalry Corps, Army of the Cumberland; 23; 29, 50; replaces Buell, 61; rebuilds army, 62; complains to Halleck, 73; praise for cavalry at Stones River, 75; on use of sabers, 78; writes to Halleck praising Minty, 87; bestows sobriquet *Saber Brigade*, 88; recommends Minty for promotion, 88; 105,106; orders attack on Guy's Gap, 108; comments on battle at Shelbyville, 110; on Tullahoma Campaign, 112; logistical challenges, 116, 117; 123; headquartered at Widow Glenn's house, 124; issues controversial order, 125; withdraws to Chattanooga, 126; occupies Chattanooga, 128, 129; after battle report, 129; replaced by Thomas, 131; on pursuing Wheeler's Cavalry, 134; 142; praises Stanley, 143; 252
Roscinski, Zelina (Selina), 250, 254
Ross, Lawrence Sullivan "Sul", CSA, 165, 168, 200-01, 203, 204, 208, 209-10
Rossmaier, Martin G., 150; cited for gallantry, 228
Roswell, GA, 158, 182; destruction of industries, 183
Rousseu, Lovel H., commanding Sherman's "expeditionary force", 160, 186
Rover, TN, 77, 85, 105
Roys, Elbridge G., xvii; 68; Rosecrans praise of, 74, 82, 85, 86; Minty praises, 87; attack on Freeman's Battery, 92-94; commands Co. H, 140; cited for gallantry, 143-44; with Horse Marines, 161; killed at Goodwin's farm, 243-45; cited for actions at Selma, AL, 245; 252
Rucker, Edmund W., CSA: captured, 226
Russell, Alfred A., CSA, 85
Rutgers, Major: defects with Carlisle Barracks payroll, 33
Saber, The (see also Cavalry, US, weapons), 4, 22, 67; use of, 78, effectiveness of, 158,180, 233
Saber Brigade, The (see also Minty's Brigade), 4, 23, Minty defines the honor, 88; 115, 144 145, 149; object of Wheeler's attack, 177, 178, 214, 215; disbanded, 217, 234
Sackett, Delos B., 2
Sale Creek, 116, 117, 130
Salem, TN, 112
Saller, Philip H.: killed in action near Washington, TN, 299n89
San Antonio, TX., 13; arsenal and barracks seized by rebels, 35;
Sandtown, GA, 198, 214
Sanford, George B., xvi
Savannah, TN, 148, 149, 229
Scavenging (see Foraging).

Schofield, John McA.: comments on Lyon's situation, 38; 40, 42; commanding Army of the Ohio, 147; under George Thomas, 160; 181, 187, 188, 193, 219; Battle of Nashville, 225
Scott, John, CSA: 125, 128
Scott, Winfield, 13, 15, 147
Sedgwick, John, 2, 7, 9, 28
Seibert, James J.: commanding 7th Pennsylvania Cavalry, 139
Selma, AL, 231, 234; battle of, 237-241; destruction at, 245-46
Selma-Macon Campaign, 236-242, Starr evaluates, 245
Selma-Montgomery Campaign, 231, 234-236
Senegan, William H.: killed in action at Franklin, TN, 94
Sequatchie Valley, TN, 114, 116, 117, 131, 133
Seven Days Campaign, 32
Seventh Pennsylvania Volunteer Cavalry, 73, 74, at Franklin, 92; with 1st Brigade, 102; 104, 107-08; cavalry charge at Shelbyville, 109-110; 113, 115, 117, 119; at Chickamauga, 121-22; entrenchments at Chattanooga, 130; posted as infantry, 136; in Garrard's 2nd Cavalry Division, 160; save bridge over Oostenaula River, 165; overrun enemy breastworks, 173; at Noonday Creek, 175, 233
Shafer, Frederick: killed by citizens, 297n60
Sharp, Joseph (farmer), 41
Sharps carbine (Cavalry, US weapons)
Shaw, Henry, Pvt., Co. C: wounded, at Wilson's Creek, 291n116
Shelby, Joseph (rebel leader), 46
Shelbyville, TN, 116; battle of, 67, 108-111; Cos. F and H meet regiment, 102, 106-07; aftermath of battle, 111
Shenandoah Valley Campaign, 147
Sheridan, Philip H., 20, 24, 62, 67, 71, 76, 85, 87, 139, 143; appointed chief of cavalry, Army of the Potomac, 147; at Yellow Tavern, 162; 231, 245
Sherman, William T., 85; commands all armies of the West, 147; Meridian Campaign, 149-57; assembles three veteran armies, 160; 161, 162; marches into Kingston, GA, 167, 170; headquarters at Big Shanty, 173, 175; cites Minty, Long and Miller, 177, 181; occupies Decatur, 183; upset with his officers, 196, 313n41; on Kilpatrick, 199; crosses Chattahoochee River, 216, 231; mentioned: 56, 139, 152, 162, 178, 179, 183, 184, 191, 192, 211, 215, 219, 229, 247, 251, 252, 253
Sherk, John L.: (doctor, soldier) murdered by guerillas, 233
Shiloh, TN (see also Pittsburgh Landing), 55-56
Sibley tent, 8

Siebert, James J., 139
Sigel, Franz: at Wilson's Creek, 38; passim 39-43
Simson, Thomas W.: orderly to Gen. Lew Wallace at Pittsburg Landing, 55; praised by Wallace, 57; attack on Freeman's Battery, 92-94; wounded, 94; death of, 252
Sipes, William B., xi, 26, 79; comments on continuous use of cavalry, 95; summarizes events of first-half of 1863, 104; describes a skirmish, 105; 106; commanding 7th Pennsylvania Cavalry, 107; the cavalry charge at Shelbyville, 109-10; 113, 114, 119; describes Confederate Army around Chattanooga, 130; chasing Wheeler's Cavalry, 132; siege of Chattanooga, 136; gathering horses and mules, 138; commands 1st Brigade, 139; provost guard at Huntsville, 140; crosses Chattahoochee River, 158, 159; overcoming rebel defenses, 162; the march to Snake Creek Gap, 164; 172, 174, 177; on light marching conditions, 179; stress on men and horses, 179-80; 186; in the trenches, 195; sums up history of Saber Brigade, 217
Skull Camp Bridge (Shelbyville), 110
Slade (Sledge), George (Negro cook), 92
Slaves (see Negroes)
Smith, Andrew J., 224
Smith, Charles E.: captures 1st Alabama Cavalry standard, 98; testifies at Wirz trial, 252
Smith, Charles F.: at Fort Donelson, 51, 55
Smith, George W. (surgeon, soldier): describes Spencer carbine, 158
Smith, Green Clay, 86
Smith, William Sooy, 114, 140, 148; Meridian Campaign, 149, 150-57; 161
Smith Rifle (see Cavalry, US, weapons)
Smith's Crossroads, 115, 130, 131, 132
Snake Creek Gap: Army of the Tennessee passes through, 164
Snow, Francis H.: orderly to Rosecrans, 74; honorable mention, 143
Snow Hill, TN: expedition to and results of, 90-91
Soap (Negro cook), captures rebels with Sgt. Bates, 90-91
Sokalski, George O.: escorting recruits, 289n15
Sollars, Issac, at Jonestown, 202; at Lovejoy's Station, 210, 213
Sommers, William: captures battle flag at Shelbyville, 110; cited for gallantry, 144
South Carolina, 234
Sparta, TN 113, 114
Spencer Carbine (see also Cavalry, US weapons): at Okolona, 24, 153, 154, 159; awarded to 4th US Cavalry, 157; description of, 158; used by rebels, 218
Spring Hill, TN, 86-87
Springfield Carbine (see Cavalry, US, weapons)

Springfield, Mo., xv-xvii, 28,
Stanley, David S., xv, 11, 285n98, 14, 26, 28, 37; commanding Cos. B and C, 38; 47, 50; on deprivations of Army life; Rosecrans petitions for, 62; commanding Cavalry Division, 63; Chief of Cavalry, 66; 73; at Stones River, 74; Rosecrans praise of, 74; on use of the saber, 79; leading foraging expedition, 84; on the importance of small expeditions, 84; recommends Minty for promotion, 88; battle at Franklin, TN, 92, 299n57; returns to Murfreesboro, 94; at Middleton 97; reports on destruction at Middleton, 97; comments on continual rains, 107; on defeat of Confederate cavalry at Shelbyville, illness, 137; praised by Rosecrans, 143; commanding occupying forces in Texas, 252; Medal of Honor, 252; mentioned, 15, 75, 83, 92, 104, 106, 108, 117, 142
Stanton, Edwin M., 148
Starnes, James W. (CSA): rescuing Freeman's Battery, 81; at Franklin, TN, 92-93; killed in action, 112
Starr, Stephen Z. (historian), 45; on Stanley and cavalry organization, 63; on Minty's actions at Shelbyville, 109, 111; on hazards of unfamiliar terrain,114; on Minty, McCook, Miller and Long, 171; praises Minty, 171, 178, 217 on James Wilson, 223, 229; summaries Selma-Macon Campaign, 245
Steahlin, George S.: at Shelbyville, 110-111
Steele, Frederick, xv-xvi, brevet Brigadier General, 44, 46
Stevenson, AL, 130, 137, 163
Stockton, Philip, CSA, 11
Stockton, Samuel W.: at Bull Run, 31, 288n33; captured, 131, 305n20
Stokes, James H.: commanding Chicago Board of Trade Battery, 117, 132
Stokes, Roger, Pvt., Co. C: mortally wounded at Dug Springs, 283n25
Stokes, William B., commanding 5th Tennessee Cavalry, 107
Stoll, Andrew: captured, died prisoner of war, 252
Stoneman, George: raid on Virginia Central Railroad, 104; relationship with Sherman, 170; 186; Raid to Flat Shoals, 188-89; defeat at Brown's Mill, 188; Minty's opinion of, 191; 192, 196, 199, 212
Stones River Campaign, 68-73
Stones River, battle of, 66; evaluation of, 74
Streight, Able D., 67
Strickland, Sherlock E.: kills Captain Freeman, CSA, 81, 93
Stuart, James E. B. (Jeb), CSA, 1, 19, 11, 12, 17, 24; at Bull Run, 31; Chambersburg raid, 62, 66; missing at Gettysburg, 104; mortally wounded at Yellow Tavern,162;
Stubbs, Mary (historian), 24

Sturgis, Samuel D., 10, 11, 12; commanding Fort Smith, 14; 17; evacuates Fort Smith, 15; 28, 29, 36-37; at Wilson's Creek, 38; passim, 39-43; praised by Gen. Fremont, 43; brevet Brigadier General, 44; 50, 57; defeat at Brice's Crossroads, 159, 175; post war career, 254, 310n97

Sub-cooks (Negroes), 91-92

Sullivan, Thomas W.: cited for gallantry at Dug Springs, xvi; assigned to Co. F, 99-100; surrender at Bardstown, Ky., 100-101; at Okolona, 155, 192; wounded at Lovejoy's Station, 204, 211

Sumner, Edwin Voss, 1, 13, 33

Sweeney, Edward, 127

Sweeny, Thomas W., 36-37

Sword, Wiley (historian), xi

Sylvan (see Sullivan, Thomas),Taylor, Richard, CSA, 234

Taylor, Thomas J., CSA, 236

Taylor, Zachary, 10

Telegraph: importance of, xv

Texas: Department of, 1; secedes, 13

Thielman's Dragoon Battalion (Illinois Independent Cavalry), 38

Thomas, George H., 59; at Stones River, 69; attack on Western and Atlantic Railroad, 116, 117; stand at Snodgrass Hill and Horseshoe Ridge, 126; withdraws to Rossville, 126-129; replaces Rosecrans, 131; chasing Wheeler's cavalry, 134; reorganizes Army of the Cumberland, 139; 144; cavalry tactics, 148; preparing for the Atlanta Campaign, 148; commanding under Sherman, 160; appoints James Wilson to command cavalry, 162; mentioned: 25, 26, 125, 130, 180, 181, 187, 188, 217

Thompson, John A., 14; commanding Co. F at Ft. Laramie, 99; commanding squadron 4th US under Gen. Thomas, 107; untimely death reported, 107

Thompson, Heber S., 178, 185, 194, Kilpatrick's raid, 209; captured, 211, 315n165

Thompson, Perry (Negro cook), 92

Thompson's Station, TN: Colonel John Colburn and infantry captured, 86;Thruston, Gates P., 70

Totten, James, 40; Totten's Battery, 41 brevet Brigadier General, 44

Toy, Alfred S.: killed by citizens, 297n60

Tracy, Patrick: mortally wounded, 46

Travellion, William: mortally wounded at Covington, Ga, 184

Trenches: Cavalries assigned to 193-195

Tudhope, William: at Shelbyville, 111; cited for gallantry, 146

Tullahoma, TN: evacuated by Bragg, 112

Tullahoma (Middle Tennessee) Campaign, 103, 106, 113

Tullos, Thomas, 299n54

Turchin, John B.: destruction of Athens, AL, 60, 97; Turchin's Division, 97; 105; commanding 2nd Division, 104; comments on miles covered by cavalry, 106, 117;

Twigs, David E., 13

Uniforms (see Cavalry, US, uniforms)

Unionville, TN, 77, 105

United States Volunteers (see Volunteers, US)

University of Alabama, 236

Upton, Emory: Battle of Selma, AL, 239-40, 242

Urwin, Gregory (historian), 283n2; evaluates Wilson's Cavalry Corps, 248-49

Vale, Joseph G., x; comments on officers who left army for Confederacy, 17; on the "rebellion," 28; on battle at Springfield and use of saber, 45; on activities in Missouri, 47; on early use of cavalry, 49-50, 63; on activities at Forts Henry and Donelson, 51; on occupation of Nashville, 54; on creation of Cavalry Division, 63; summary of 1861-62 Campaign in the West, 64; on Stones River, 69; describes cavalry attack, 77; on expedition against Wheeler, 77-78; on the use of sabers, 79-80; on Confederate reaction to the killing of Capt. Freeman, 81; describes the Federal camp at Murfreesboro, 82; on daily activities in camp, 83; no rest for the cavalry, 84, 85; effective use of sabers at Unionville, 86, 87; 95; capture and escape of Dick McCann, 96; reports on results of action at Middleton, 98; preparation to move on Shelbyville, 109; captures two artillery pieces, 110; injured in ambush, on pests, 112, 300n138; 115; comment on Longstreet's arrival at Chickamauga, 119; sums up results of Wheeler's raid, 133; summarizes events of 1863, 142; describes march from Memphis to Huntsville, 158; reports on Horse Marines, 161; describes journey from Columbia, TN, to Snake Creek Gap, 163-64; leads scout to Rome, GA, 165; comments on night maneuvers, 167; describes an attack by 4th Michigan Cavalry, 168; summarizes advance of Sherman's Army, 172; describes a cavalry charge against Ferguson's Division, 174; summarizes results of raid to Flat Shoals, 191; 177; in the trenches, 195; Kilpatrick's raid, 201; 214, 215; summarizes Atlanta Campaign, 216, 217

Van Cleve, Horatio P., (Van Cleve's Division): Minty assigned to, 113, 114

Van Dorn, Earl, CSA, 86, 92-93, 102

Van Horn, Thomas B. (historian): on Stoneman, 191

Versailles, TN, 76, 105

Vicksburg, Miss., 103; siege of, 103; surrender of, 104; 149, 161

Volunteers, US: early Volunteers, 32, 37; contempt for Regulars, 37; lack of discipline, xvi, 37; lack of sanitary standards, 18; disorganized, xvi, 37; poorly armed, xvi, 37
von Louby (see Lauby)
Wagner, George D., Wagner's Brigade, 76, 117
Walden's Ridge, TN, 116, 131
Walker, William S., CSA,
Wallace, Lew, 44, 47, at Fort Donelson, 51; 53, at Pittsburg Landing (Shiloh), 55-57; 292n29
Wallace, William H. L.: at Fort Donelson, 53; at Pittsburgh Landing, 55; mortally wounded, 56
Walsh, James: at Lovejoy's Station, 204
Waltz, Charles A., 25
Ward, Issac: killed in action, 252
Warring, George E., commanding Sooy Smith's 1st Brigade, 150, 152; attempts to stop stampede at Okolona, 155
Wartrace, TN, 133
Washington, TN, 116, 130
Washington, George, 147
Webb, Mr. (Confederate mill owner), 76
Webb, William W., Kilpatrick's raid, 199; destruction of Macon Railroad, 202; 204, 205, 208, 210, 213; captures Texas general, 215
Webster, John G., commissioned 2nd Lieutenant, 71; honorable mention, 143
West Harpeth River, battle of, 226-228
Wetzberger, Stephen: killed in action at Okolona, 156
Wharton, John A., CSA (Wharton's Brigade), 70, 84, 109
Wheaton, Frank: post war career, 254
Whelan, Michael, 11
Wheeler, Joseph, CSA, 67; escapes capture, 77; 104; at McMinnville, 106; 109; at Shelbyville, 110; siege of Chattanooga, 130; 116, 137; at Noonday Creek, 175-76; 215, 219
Wheeler's Cavalry, 70; at Guy's Gap, 107, 111, 131; Federal pursuit of, 132; crosses Tennessee River, 133; at Noonday Creek, 173, 188; at Flat Shoals, 189
White, Frank, 248
White, Moses, CSA, 100
Whitthorn, William, 70
Wilcox, John Andrew: post war career, 254
Wilder, John T.: 107, 117; at Chickamauga, 119-20; at Alexander's Bridge, 122, 123; withdraws to Gordon's Mill, 123; at East Viniard Field, 124; commanding 3rd Brigade of Mounted Infantry, 160; in the trenches, 168, capture of Dallas, GA, 171
Wilder's Brigade, 66, 69, 88, 143; issued Spencer carbines, 158
Wilkie, Franc (reporter), xv, xvii

Wilkins, John: mortally wounded at Dug Springs, 283n25
Williams, John S., CSA, 177
Williams, John: mortally wounded at Covington, 184
Wills, Brian Steele (historian), 159; the fortifications at Selma, AL, 238; the Battle of Selma, 239-44; Goodwin's farm massacre, 243-44
Wilson, James H., 24, 26, 147; at Yellow Tavern, 162, 217; arrival at Nashville, 218; at Battle of Franklin, 219; on use of cavalry, 219; 221-22; Battle of Nashville, 223-28; on Battle of Franklin, 231; begins Selma-Montgomery campaign, 231-33, 235, 237; assault on Selma, AL, 239-41; on Forrest, 244; evaluated by Minty, 245; 248; at Macon, GA, 249; disbursing his command, 251; 252, 253
Wilson's Creek, battle of, 28; Federal cavalry at, 37; 38; casualties, 43, 291n116
Wirz, Henry, 250
Wise, Henry, 9
Wiswell, James H., x; enlistment, 33; training, 33-34; on losing his mount, 22, 287n31; 28, 33, 36; at Wilson's Creek, 39; describes battle, 40, 290n62; describes the aftermath of battle, 43, 289n64; assigned to Co. C; 46, 51; at New Madrid, Mo, 54; 57; on the capture of Corinth, 59; on discipline under Buell, 60; describes Huntsville, AL, 60; comments of status of Federal army, 62; on Battle of Stones River, 74, on Otis, 74; on Volunteers, 74; 75; writes of experiences at Chickamauga and Chattanooga, 134; assigned to Quartermaster Division, 135; 136; on Union Army moving out of Chattanooga, 137; commenting on rivalry between the two Union Armies, 137; comments on Rosecrans and Thomas, 137, 139; writes from Huntsville, AL, 141-42; on reenlistments, 148, 307n32; takes his discharge, 149
Wood, Francis C.: at Middleton, TN, 97-98; mortally wounded, 97; cited by Stanley, 144; post war career, 253
Wood, Thomas J., 10, 11, 28, 29, 55, 117; Battle of Nashville, 226; 228, 254
Wormser, Richard (historian), 85; decline of Southern cavalry, 162
Writhe, Nathan: killed in action at Franklin, TN, 94
Wyatt, James, 25
Wyeth, John A., CSA (Confederate soldier, historian): describes Minty's attack on Shelbyville, 109
Wynkoop, George C., 63
Yellow Tavern, battle of, 13
Young, J. Morris: describes results of expedition, 138
Young, William H., CSA: captured, 215
Zagonyi, Charles, 45
Zham, Lewis, 68